The Coming of the New International

The Coming of

THE WORLD PUBLISHING COMPANY

the New International

A REVOLUTIONARY ANTHOLOGY
EDITED AND WITH AN OVERVIEW AND
INTRODUCTIONS BY

John Gerassi

NEW YORK AND CLEVELAND

Published by THE WORLD PUBLISHING COMPANY

Published simultaneously in Canada
by NELSON, FOSTER & SCOTT LTD.

First printing—1971

Copyright © 1971 by John Gerassi
All rights reserved

Library of Congress catalog card number: 73-124277

PRINTED IN THE UNITED STATES OF AMERICA

WORLD PUBLISHING
TIMES MIRROR

To Huey P. Newton and Charles Garry

If there is no struggle, there is no progress.
Those who profess to favor freedom, and yet
depreciate agitation, are men who want
crops without plowing up the ground. They want
rain without thunder and lightning. They
want the ocean without the awful roar of its
many waters. Power concedes nothing
without demand.

FREDERICK DOUGLASS

Revolution is the larva of civilization.

VICTOR HUGO

Acknowledgments

Though the idea for this work was born shortly after the first conference of the Tricontinental organization—the Organization of Solidarity of the Peoples of Africa, Asia, and Latin America—in January 1966, it did not really take shape until after three events that became crucial in my life: my trip to North Vietnam over Christmas–New Year's 1966–67, my attendance at the first conference of the Organization of Latin American Solidarity in Havana in the summer of 1967, and my friendship with Huey Newton, whom I used to visit regularly in the Alameda County jail in 1968. From the Vietnamese, I learned what peoples' solidarity is all about; from the OLAS delegates, many of whom had come directly from the guerrilla struggles of Latin America, I realized that only through such solidarity will man ever stop exploiting man; and from Huey Newton I understood that individual fulfillment is meaningful only when it is felt in and through such solidarity.

Both the Vietnamese and the Cubans and Latin American delegates to OLAS helped me obtain material for this book. Huey gave me invaluable insight into the Black Liberation Movement and dictated an article exclusively for this book. Many others, too, helped to track down needed documents, among them Bernardo García, Karen Wald, Torregian Sotere, the staff of the Hoover

Institute at Stanford, Beverly Axelrod and Anatole Anton in the Bay Area; Malcolm Caldwell, Farris Glubb, Russell Stetler, Antonio Cisneros, Peter Buckman, Ruth First, Basil Davidson, Jorge Montaña in London; staff members of the North American Congress on Latin America (NACLA), Liberation News Service (LNS), Elizabeth Sutherland Martínez, *The Guardian*, the Free School University in New York. Advice from and discussion and/or arguments with Irving Louis and Danielle Horowitz, Pat Bell, Reies Tijerina, David Horowitz, Herbert Marcuse, Carlos Romeo, Roberto Fernández Retamar, Ralph Miliband, William Pomeroy, Jerry Rubin, Jean-Pierre Vigier, Jean-Paul Sartre, Simone de Beauvoir, Sharon Krebs, Ricardo Romo, Danny Schechter, Ed Vickery, Sol Yurick, Carl Oglesby, Sean Gervasi, Steve Weissman, Julio Alvarez del Vayo, David and Barbara Stone, David Hilliard, Fred Groff, Mike Locker, John Levin, Margaret Leahy, Fred Gardner, Todd Gitlin, Carol Cina, Jane Alpert, Bobby Seale, Stokely Carmichael, Marcel Nidergang, Pito Colón, Chuck Bradley, D. F. Fleming, Bob Ockene, Keith Lampe, Jean Ripert, Jean Conilh, Fawwaz Trabulsi, Pamela Copp, Howard Senzel, Joe Berke, Jo Durden-Smith, Carol Brightman, Bruce and Judy Jacobs, Robin Palmer, James Petras, Robin Blackburn, Wilfred Burchett, Roger Pic, Alba Griñan Núnez, José Viera, Hernán Kesselman, Paul Dufeu, Diane Gerros, George Gourevitch, and especially Charles Garry and students at San Francisco State College helped me in my focus.

Besides the translators credited herein, I would like to thank the typists, proofreaders, and researchers who gave so much of their time to make this work possible, among them Lesley Churchill, Shirley Ward, Mara Sabinson, Sara Carter, Ruth Nelson, Camille Alonso, John Taylor, Johnny McGuigan, and Peter, Simon, and Collin. Helena Bradley in Berkeley, Sue LeGrand, Jenny James, and, especially, Heather Musgrove in London made up the real collective that got this book together.

Finally, I would like to thank all the unnamed revolutionaries in Asia, Africa, and America who took time out to answer my queries and requests. I can only hope that this collection will help make clear the reason and the cause for their actions and commitment.

Contents

Overview

EVERY now and then throughout history, lines harden, myths crumble, contradictions crystallize. From contradiction emerges confrontation, and from confrontation eventually surges progress. All over the world today, confrontation is developing into a way of life. The division between master and slave, exploiter and exploited, alienating and alienated, robot and rebel is becoming clearer. In the decades to come, familiar concepts will be discarded, systems will be smashed, empires will be destroyed. Once again, the future is Revolution.

Human progress, whether we like it or not, has always come about as a result of confrontation—and revolution. From gods to kings, from plutocracies to technocracies, change has been generated by people, men and women who drew the line, who shouted enough! and made their stand. No power has ever been strong enough, no class thorough enough, no elite shrewd enough, no army invulnerable enough, to suppress permanently the desire for redress by ordinary people.

Inevitably, at each stage, that general desire has been manipulated—channeled, sidetracked, misrouted, betrayed—by the few. And also inevitably, each step forward has been paid for in astronomical human costs. The line of progress is nowhere a straight vertical. Rather it is a jagged, broken line. But its overall path is firmly upward.

At each climactic confrontation, the slogans have varied. But not the cause, not the often unstated ideals. Whether the rebellions were against autocratic rulers who treated men as animals, or against dehumanized organizations which counted men as numbers, or simply against men whose privileges denied the necessities of other men, the goal of rebels has always been the same: freedom.

It is said that the word—freedom—means many things to many peo-

1

ple. Certainly it is often used to justify its opposite. To cite an obvious example, in Vietnam U.S. forces have destroyed innumerable freedoms that the people cherished, while claiming the right to do so in freedom's name ("I'll make you free even if I have to wreck your country to do it"). But the word is just as full of force and content today as it was when the Indians resisted the invading Puritans, when the French peasants of the middle ages revolted against their landlords, and when Spartacus rose against Rome.

Freedom is not the right to say or do anything you want that does not infringe on the freedom of others. Freedom means having the material and psychological *power* to say or do that thing. Freedom is the real possibility of being relevant, of being meaningful, of being total. Thus, clearly, no man who is poor when another is rich is free. No man who does not exert control, equal to all other men, over his courts, police, government, or army is free. No country which is financially, militarily, or geopolitically dependent on another is free. To talk about freedom of the press when only the rich control the media, to herald free enterprise when health (hospitals, doctors, medicine, etc.) costs money, to cherish free courts when lawyers, bail, appeals, etc., require wealth, in general to hail a society as free when money is the means by which one buys one's free choice is a travesty.

Obviously, no society is completely free—or probably ever will be. But some come closer to the great ideal than others. And in history, mankind has been approximating it bit by bit all along. That *is* history: man's struggle to be free. Most historians, of course, view it as the movement of forces, sometimes very abstract, and analyze events as if occurring somehow independently of people. Names, dates, places—that is the foodstuff of history books, while people tend to be merely cannon fodder. If one does scrutinize, say, a particular battle, it is perfectly true that the superiority of the fire-power of one army over the other, the quality of leadership, the economic resources of the opposing sides, etc., will explain the battle's outcome much more succinctly than, perhaps, the fact that the cannon fodder on one side believed itself to be fighting for something more meaningful than the other.

But in the long run and in the long view, what changes man's relationship to man (though perhaps not his countries' borders) is precisely that fodder. If today, you and I are relatively freer than were our grandparents it is not because Wilson was a better man than the Kaiser, or because Patton's tanks were faster than Rommel's, but because the gladiators refused to kill each other, because individual believers refused to buy through tithes their place in heaven, because the bourgeois of Paris wanted as much say in the affairs of France as the Bourbons, because farmers in New England did not want to be ruled by red-coated foreigners, because the workers of St. Petersburg went hungry once too often, because the Wobblies wanted to own their mines and factories.

Human progress is never initiated by governments. They merely reflect the will and desire of the ruling classes. Progress is won *from* governments as a result of struggle—strikes, demonstrations, rebellions, insurrections. If a particular government figure or bureaucracy enacts laws that do bring about some progress, it is only because the upsurge from below, the outcry of the fodder, has frightened the ruling class enough to allow concessions—for its own survival.

Depending on that strength from below, the ruling class either crushes dissent (reaction), gives in to some demands and incorporates reforms which do not change the fundamental structure (constitutionalism and/or liberalism), or is overthrown (revolution). When reforms are not enough to satisfy the discontent, the ruling class inevitably resorts to reaction. Inevitably, precisely because the reforms demanded require the ruling class to commit class suicide. It is as if we in the United States today demanded that all cars produced be indestructible, unpolluting, and cheap (all of which is technologically feasible). General Motors, Ford, the oil and the insurance companies would obviously object. They're in business to make profits, which they use to maintain their life style, buy politicians, control the television and radio media, etc. If people's demands are loud, they try a few reforms: more padding, better seat belts, a special carburetor which cuts down pollution and a policy of recalling cars to fix major defects at their expense (all of which they've done, or are doing). But suppose we still weren't satisfied, you and I and all the other fodder, and our discontent grew to the point that we were willing to seize General Motors, burn down the insurance companies (and the banks who finance the operations)? Then what? Well, Ford or General Motors bosses are certainly not going to give up their yachts and planes and villas in eight countries, nor the control they exercise through their wealth over every institution in the land. They'll tell their representatives (the government) to put an end to the dissent and the government will then try to jail or kill us. Our only alternative is revolution.

The first to try will fail. Revolution is a long process. Before every success lie scores of failures. Sometimes so many fail that the generation's spirit dies altogether. It doesn't start again until the next. But it succeeds eventually. Russia's Decembrists didn't get very far in the last century, but without them, there would have been no 1905 Revolution. That one failed too, but it set the stage for the success of 1917. Likewise in China, the revolutionaries almost got wiped out in 1927. The few who survived started literally from the bottom again—and didn't win until 1949. The Cuban Revolution of 1895 seized power in 1959. The Algerian "War" lasted only seven years, but the rebellions started more than a century before, and without them the FLN's victory would not have been possible. As Che Guevara once put it: "It does not matter what the results of today's struggles are. It does not matter, as far as the final result is concerned, whether one movement or another is momentarily defeated.

What is definitive is the determination to fight (which matures from day to day), the awareness of the need for revolutionary change, and the certainty that the latter is possible."[1]

The awareness of the need for revolutionary change certainly does exist throughout the world today. In varying degrees, to be sure, and against various "establishments" (ruling elites). The Czech youth, for example, considers the Soviet Establishment its main enemy, because the USSR controls the puppets who rule in Prague. The rebels of Angola, Mozambique, and Guiné-Bissau are fighting against Portugal, which occupies these lands as colonies. The leaders of the rebels are perfectly aware that behind Portugal is the United States, which furnishes it with the arms, planes, napalm, and money to wage the war. But the immediate enemy is nevertheless Portugal. In South Africa and Zimbabwe, the revolutionary forces know that without the connivance, support, trade and aid of international (mostly U.S.) capitalists, the apartheid regimes would have a harder time profiting from their vicious rule. But they cannot ignore, even if they do not talk about it, the fact that Russia and other so-called communist countries of Eastern Europe also trade with and benefit from these racist governments. In Guyana and Trinidad, in the Persian Gulf and Malayan Peninsula, the enemy is not only the United States, which owns most of the countries' resources, but also Great Britain, which constantly intervenes (inevitably prodded by the U.S.) into the countries' affairs in order to maintain the semifeudalistic capitalist structure. In Martinique, Guadeloupe, Réunion, and Chad, the villain is France.

Overwhelmingly, however, the center of reaction everywhere is the United States. In Asia, Africa, and America, through direct military intervention, indirect military blackmail, or neo-colonial domination, it is the U.S. which is master. And it is against the U.S. that the slaves are rebelling. The "U.S." is not necessarily you and me. It is our ruling class, those who profit most from our monopoly-capital system. It is that same system which fosters racism and exploits the black, brown, yellow, and red minorities at home. And it is that same system which has totally alienated a huge sector of our young.

In order to understand why people are rebelling at home and abroad and then go on to analyze the various forms of rebellion—the theory, strategy, and tactics of Revolution—it is necessary first to understand why the United States has become that world center of reaction. In other words, we must try to answer here four questions about the coming revolutions: Why? By whom? How? And, for doubting "liberal" readers, what then?

[1] "Guerrilla Warfare: A Method," in *Venceremos: The Speeches and Writings of Ernesto Che Guevara,* ed. John Gerassi (New York: Macmillan, and London: Weidenfeld and Nicolson, 1968), p. 279.

It is generally thought—and always said in Western institutions of learning—that the United States was once a humanizing, progressive country. Not so at all. The Puritans who invaded the east coast of what is today the U.S. not only considered themselves morally superior to whatever natives they encountered (now we would simply and correctly characterize them as racists), but they also viewed themselves as intellectually superior because they were technologically more advanced. The combination gave them the same justification to impose their way of life over the "savages" as U.S. "democrats" feel they have in forcing the "gooks" to live by U.S. standards in Southeast Asia today. And just as U.S. forces in Vietnam, Laos, Cambodia, etc., are wiping out a whole culture, so the early Americans unfortunately succeeded in exterminating Indian civilization, massacring 600,000 in the process. Because the expansion westward was accomplished without sacrificing too many of the basic civil rights of the whole settler population, its morality was rarely questioned. In fact, it was heralded, and early America took pride in its system.

Later, as New England entrepreneurs launched industrialization, the new immigrants—the working class—took the moral place of the Indians. It was all right to exploit them, overwork their children in the mills and mines, because the result was a strong America, and a strong America meant the victory of the Puritan spirit—hard-working, dedicated, law-abiding, God-fearing, morally superior. Then, as the U.S. did become strong and great, thus vindicating the ethics, the expansionism, and the brutality, it was only "natural" for the country to expand beyond its borders.

It did not matter that Jeffersonian Democracy, which liberal historians still praise as the moral backbone of America's current power, rested on the "haves" and excluded the "have-nots" (to the point of not allowing the propertyless to vote). Nor did it matter that later administrations ruthlessly sacrificed various sectors of the economy in order to consolidate the power of one of them (the monopoly trusts). The result —late nineteenth-century and twentieth-century America—was formidable. Therefore the system was perfect.

The system became known as "the American way of life," a way of life in which the successful were the ethical. The United States was founded from the beginning on the notion and religion that he who is poor deserves to be poor; he who is rich is entitled to the fruit of his wealth. The U.S. became the greatest country in the world precisely, and only, because it became the most successful. Since what is great is good, the American way of life became the epitome of morality.

From America's pride in its way of life followed its "right" to impose that way on non-Americans. Hence, Americans became superior, self-righteous, and arrogant. The result was that a new Jesuit company was

formed. It too carried the sword and the cross. America's sword was its
Marines, its cross was "American democracy." The cross justified U.S.
imperialism waged by the sword. The Puritan ethic developed into a
Social Darwinist philosophy of the domination of the fittest and into
a Protestant sense of duty to conquer.[2]

U.S. conquests, from Mexico and the Caribbean to the Philippines and
Guam, are known well enough.[3] What is perhaps not so well known or
is conveniently forgotten is the self-righteous rhetoric that accompanied
the massacres of Indians, Mexicans, Central Americans, Dominicans,
Cubans, Haitians, etc. Yet that rhetoric molds the intolerance of every
U.S. statesman, is part and parcel of the "explanations"—which border
on outright lies—issued by Adlai Stevenson and President Kennedy to
conceal U.S. designs in Cuba in 1961, by Johnson and Rusk to fool
Americans over the bombing of North Vietnam, by Nixon and Mitchell
to cover up their plots in Cambodia, their murder of Black Panther leader
Fred Hampton, their frame-up of the Conspiracy 8.

In his Farewell Address, Andrew Jackson told the world that it was
God himself who had chosen Americans to be "the guardians of freedom."[4]
A few years later, John L. O'Sullivan, editor of the influential *Democratic
Review*, spelled out the U.S.'s self-defined role as international gendarme.
"We have been placed in the forefront of the battle in the cause of Man
against the powers of evil," he said.[5] This was precisely what the U.S.
ruling class wanted. "The march of the Anglo-Saxon race is onward,"
boomed the *Washington Union*, ". . . and who shall say how far they
will prosecute the work?"[6] The *Democratic Review* claimed this march
to be divine: "The peculiar characteristics of our system,—the distinctive
evidence of its divine origin . . . is, that it may, if its theory is maintained
pure in practice, be extended, with equal safety and efficiency over any
indefinite number of millions of population and territory."[7] Stephen A.
Douglas, the Illinois politician later defeated by Abraham Lincoln, insisted that "Our federal system is admirably adapted to the whole continent."[8] Pennsylvania Senator (later Secretary of State, then President)

[2] See Alfred Thayer Mahan (a naval captain during the expansionist period), *The
Influence of Sea Power Upon History* (London: Methuen, 1965); and Kenneth M.
MacKenzie, *The Robe and the Sword: The Methodist Church and the Rise of Ameri-
can Imperialism* (Washington, D.C.: Public Affairs Press, 1961).

[3] For a rundown see Chapter 17 in my *The Great Fear in Latin America* (New York
and London: Collier-Macmillan, 1965).

[4] James D. Richardson, ed., *Messages and Papers of the Presidents* (Washington,
D.C.: Government Printing Office, 1896), III, p. 308.

[5] "The Progress of Society," *The United States Magazine and Democratic Review*,
July 1840, p. 87. See also Julius W. Pratt, "The Origins of Manifest Destiny,"
American Historical Review, July 1927, pp. 795–98.

[6] June 2, 1845.   [7] January 1838.

[8] *Congressional Globe*, 28th Cong., 2nd Sess., 1844, Appendix, p. 68.

James Buchanan agreed: "Providence has given to the American people a great and important mission, and that mission they were destined to fulfill—to spread the blessings of Christian liberty and laws from one end to the other of this immense continent."⁹ Michigan Congressman John S. Chipman shouted: "This continent will be our own."¹⁰ The *New York Herald* demanded that "the fact must be no longer disguised, that we, the people of the United States, must hold, and govern . . . the continent we inhabit."¹¹ And after he had launched the *New York Morning News*, O'Sullivan affirmed that it was "our manifest destiny to occupy and to possess the whole continent which Providence has given us."¹²

Manifest Destiny was not only crudely imperialist, it was also racist— and proud of it. "There seems to be something in our laws and institutions peculiarily adapted to our Anglo-Saxon-American race, under which they will thrive and prosper, but under which all others wilt and die," theorized Ohio Congressman Alexander Duncan in 1845. Why? Because others are unfit for "liberal and equal laws."¹³ In 1847, after the U.S. had invaded Mexico to rob it of the best sections of its territory, Congressman Lewis Cass complained that "we do not want the people of Mexico either as citizens or subjects. All we want is a portion of territory."¹⁴ Secretary of State James Buchanan wondered "how should we govern the mongrel race which inhabit" California?¹⁵ The *Democratic Review* complained that "the process which has been gone through at the North of driving back the Indians, or annihilating them as a race, has yet to be gone through at the South."¹⁶ But the *American Review* wasn't worried because Mexico would be swamped by "a superior population, insensibly oozing into her territories, changing her customs, and out-living, out-trading, exterminating her weaker blood."¹⁷

And so it went. After Mexico, it was Cuba, then Nicaragua, and the Caribbean. Always, the U.S. ruling class and its propagandists found "moral or "divine" reasons to justify aggression and racial reasons to put down the aggressed.¹⁸ Always the beneficiary were the ruling elites—in

⁹ *Congressional Globe*, 28th Cong., 1st Sess., 1844, p. 380.

¹⁰ *Congressional Globe*, 29th Cong., 1st Sess., 1846, p. 207.

¹¹ August 9, 1845.   ¹² December 27, 1845.

¹³ *Congressional Globe*, 28th Cong., 2nd Sess., 1845, Appendix, p. 178.

¹⁴ *Congressional Globe*, 29th Cong., 2nd Sess., 1847, Appendix, p. 215.

¹⁵ Buchanan to General James Shields, April 23, 1847, *Buchanan Papers*, Pennsylvania Historical Society.

¹⁶ March 1847.   ¹⁷ March 1847.

¹⁸ The *New York Evening Post* referred to Mexicans as "aboriginal Indians, and they must share the destiny of their race"; the *New York Sun* scoffed at their "prattle over their lost phantom of nationality," when they could "accept the ranks and rights of freemen"; the *Democratic Review* predicted that "once we are in possession" of Cuba, "an impartial and universal vote of the whites . . . would rush under the folds of our flag." See Norman Graebner, ed., *Manifest Destiny* (New York: Bobbs-Merrill, 1968).

land, minerals, strategic points for further expansion. In the process, the public was manipulated, hoodwinked, cajoled, or lied to. Inevitably it was convinced that U.S. aggression somehow was beneficial to the aggressed. Indeed, the propaganda was so pervasive that the average man remained proimperialist even when the government officially, but temporarily, was not. Nicaragua furnishes a case in point.

In 1854, the United States settled a minor argument with Nicaragua by sending a warship to bombard San Juan del Norte. Three years later, when one U.S. citizen was wounded there and President Buchanan levied a fine of $20,000 which Nicaragua could not pay, the U.S. repeated the bombardment, following it with Marines who proceeded to burn down whatever was still standing. The next year, the United States forced Nicaragua to sign the Cass-Irissari Treaty which gave the U.S. the right to intervene in its affairs for whatever purpose the U.S. saw fit. Then U.S. government policy "officially" switched and the U.S. insisted it was neutral. That was when William Walker came to trial.

A Nashville-born doctor, lawyer, and journalist who practiced none of these professions, Walker was a filibusterer, that is, a privateer who invaded countries for private U.S. corporations. He had once tried to conquer Baja California and failed, but in 1855, financed by a group of Boston corporations, he invaded Nicaragua, captured Granada, and declared himself "elected" president. He then sent a message to President Franklin Pierce asking that Nicaragua be admitted to the Union as a slave state, even though Nicaragua had long outlawed slavery. Before Pierce could act, however, Walker got into trouble. The companies financing him were rivals of Cornelius Vanderbilt's Accessory Transit Company, which had all the transportation "concessions" sewed up; so when "President" Walker canceled Vanderbilt's contracts, Vanderbilt, no lightweight capitalist, immediately financed and armed other forces, and they defeated Walker at Santa Rosa. Caught alive, he was handed to the U.S. Navy, which brought him back to New Orleans, where he was tried for violating U.S. neutrality laws. Walker was acquitted. In fact, reflecting its deep-rooted conviction that Nicaragua would be better off as a slave state in the Union than as a free country outside it, the jury cheered Walker enthusiastically.

Manifest Destiny was no aberration in U.S. history. In other periods it may have been called something else but the effect was the same. U.S. machinations in the Philippines illustrate the point. Although the Filipinos had long been waging a war of liberation against Spain prior to the phony Spanish-American War of 1898, the United States immediately annexed the Philippines once Spain was defeated. Even before the Treaty of Paris, by which Spain ceded the Philippines to the U.S., was ratified, President McKinley ordered total U.S. occupation. The Filipinos rebelled and General Arthur MacArthur, father of General Douglas MacArthur, was sent to suppress the insurrection. It didn't take him long to realize that the vast majority of Filipinos were for independence. "The towns, regardless of the fact of American occupation, and town organizations, are the actual bases for all insurgent military activities," he wrote. "The success of this unique system of war depends upon almost complete unity of action of the entire native population. That such unity is a fact is too obvious to admit of discussion."[19]

But popular sentiment had no effect on the United States. It launched a massive repressive war, employing 126,000 U.S. troops and 617 fortified enclaves. To subdue the Filipino population, thousands of villages were razed to the ground, hundreds of thousands of people were forced into strategic hamlets, and suspected Filipino rebels were tortured. By admission of General J. Franklin Bell, one-sixth or 600,000 persons of the population of Luzon died as a result of the war.

As in the Vietnam War, the American public was aware of how its government behaved in the Philippines. For one thing, the U.S. Senate investigated the war, much as did Senator Fulbright in 1967 and 1968. The following are some sample bits of information made public at the time:

SENATOR RAWLINS: If these shacks were of no consequence, what was the utility of their destruction?

GENERAL ROBERT P. HUGHES [Commander of Vasayas from June 3, 1899, to November 30, 1901]: The destruction was as a punishment. They permitted these people to come in there and conceal themselves and they gave no sign. It is always—

SENATOR RAWLINS: The punishment in that case would fall, not upon the men, who could go elsewhere, but mainly upon the women and little children.

GENERAL HUGHES: The women and children are part of the family, and where you wish to inflict a punishment you can punish the man probably worse in that way than in any other.

SENATOR RAWLINS: But is that within the ordinary rules of civilized warfare? Of course you could exterminate the family which would be still worse punishment.

GENERAL HUGHES: These people are not civilized.[20]

From the same hearings comes another document worth citing. Being questioned is Grover Flint, first lieutenant in the 35th Infantry Regiment occupying the Philippines:

[19] *Report of the War Department* (Washington, D.C.: Government Printing Office, 1900), I, Pt. 5, pp. 61–62.

[20] Senate Document No. 331, 57th Cong., 1st Sess., "Hearing Before the Committee on the Philippines in Relation to Affairs in the Philippine Islands " (Washington, D.C.: Government Printing Office, 1902), p. 559.

FLINT: . . . You want me to describe one individual case of a man being put through the water cure? . . . A man is thrown on his back and three or four men sit or stand on his arms and legs and hold him down, and . . . a wooden log or stone is put under his head—

SENATOR BEVERIDGE: Under his head or neck?

FLINT: Under his neck, so he can be held firmly.

SENATOR BURROWS: His jaws are forced open. . . . ?

FLINT: Yes, sir; as a gag. In the case of very old men I have seen their teeth fall out—I mean when it was done a little roughly. He is simply held down, and then water is poured onto his face, down his throat and nose from a jar, and that is kept up until the man gives some sign of giving in or becomes unconscious, and when he becomes unconscious he is simply rolled aside and he is allowed to come to. . . .[21]

Other testimony documenting the extensive use of torture included that of Lieutenant Ernest Hagedorn of the 16th Infantry Regiment, who proudly boasted that he had arrested "suspicious" civilians and "I then order them confined to the stocks with a diet of salt fish without water. The diet had excellent results. . . ." His commanding officer, Colonel Charles S. Hood, stated: "Lt. Hagedorn has been most energetic in the performance of his duties, and has rendered valuable services in the pacification of this district [Cabagan, Nuevo]."[22]

Colonel George S. Anderson of the 38th Volunteer Infantry then explained that "It is true that the word 'nigger' was very often used as applied to the natives, probably correctly," and that "many men were shot as they fled, but they probably all deserved it."[23] Cornelius Gardener, the U.S. governor of the province of Tayabas, reported: ". . . by reason of the conduct of the troops, such as the extensive burning of *barrios* in trying to lay waste the country so that the insurgents cannot occupy it, the torturing of natives by so-called 'water cure' and other methods to obtain information, the harsh treatment of natives generally . . . a deep hatred toward us engendered. . . . Almost without exception soldiers, and also many officers, refer to the natives in their presence as niggers, and the natives are beginning to understand what the word 'nigger' means."[24]

But none of this mattered to General Jacob H. Smith, commander of the Samar Island pacification campaign, whose directives affirmed that "neutrality must not be tolerated on the part of any native. . . . If not an active friend he is an open enemy."[25] And General Smith was no exception. In Batanyas, General J. Franklin Bell ordered all unoccupied

[21] *Ibid.*, pp. 1767–68.   [22] Senate Document No. 205, Pt. I, *ibid.*, pp. 19–20.

[23] *Ibid.*, p. 21.   [24] Senate Document No. 331, cited above, pp. 884–85.

[25] *Ibid.*, pp. 1571–73.

towns burned to the ground. "Any able-bodied male found by patrols or scouting detachments outside of protected zones without passes will be arrested and confined, or shot if he runs away," he said.[26] He concluded: "With very few exceptions, practically the entire population has been hostile to us at heart. In order to combat such a population, it is necessary to make the state of war as insupportable as possible, and there is no more efficacious way of accomplishing this than by keeping the minds of the people in such a state of anxiety and apprehension that living under such conditions will soon become intolerable."[27]

The war in the Philippines was "officially" terminated by President Theodore Roosevelt on July 4, 1902. From then on, the guerrillas were called bandits. But nothing much changed. The United States pursued the guerrillas relentlessly, eventually killing or imprisoning them all. One independence leader, Macario Sakay, who set up a Philippine Republic, was promised negotiations and total immunity if he surrendered. He did, then was swiftly tried and shot in 1906. Massacres were commonplace. Some finally did lead to heavy protests in the U.S., as did the Song My massacre in Vietnam. In March 1906, at Mount Dajo, more than 600 men, women, and children were slaughtered and the photographs of the heaped bodies were published in the U.S.[28] The June 1913 systematic extermination of the Moros of Mount Bagsak was reported by the U.S. Governor-General, W. Cameron Forbes, himself.[29] But to no avail. The Philippines remained a U.S. colony, ruled by U.S. guns, until after World War II. (Nominally a republic today, the islands are still ruled by the U.S., which owns most of their resources.) The U.S. protest movement against the occupation of the Philippines finally became every bit as vociferous (though always nonviolent) as the anti-Vietnam War movement. If anything, it proved that the U.S. ruling class which profited (and continues to profit) from its stranglehold of the Philippine economy, can totally ignore public opinion when it remains merely that—opinion.

In most cases, however, the U.S. public has no discernible opinion at all. U.S. intervention in Guatemala, for example, provoked nary a ripple. Before 1945, Guatemala was one of the most backward countries in Latin America. The rights of labor, whether in factories or in fields, including United Fruit Company plantations, were not recognized. Unions, civil liberties, freedom of speech and press were outlawed. Foreign interests were sacred and monopolistic. Counting each foreign corporation as a person, 98 percent of the cultivated land was owned by exactly 142 people (out of a population of 3 million). Only 10 percent of the school-age children attended school.

[26] *Ibid.*, p. 1619.   [27] *Ibid.*, p. 1628.

[28] Moorfield Storey, *The Democratic Party and Philippine Independence* (Boston: Ellis, 1913), p. 36.

[29] *The Philippine Islands*, II (New York: Houghton Mifflin, 1928), p. 36.

Then, in 1945, Juan José Arévalo became president, elected on a mildly reformist and nationalist platform. He and his successor, Colonel Jacobo Arbenz, elected by the greatest majority ever given a presidential candidate in Guatemala, tried to change these conditions. They enacted educational reforms, established free speech and press, legalized unions.[30] Finally, on June 17, 1952, Arbenz proclaimed Decree 900, a land reform which called for the expropriation and redistribution of large uncultivated estates, offering twenty-year bonds at 3 percent interest, assessed according to the owners' declared tax value.

U.S. agronomists and social scientists applauded Decree 900. As one wrote: "For all the furor it produced, Decree 900, which had its roots in the constitution of 1945, is a remarkably mild and fairly sound piece of legislation."[31] But since much of Guatemalan plantation land, including 400,000 acres not cultivated, belonged to the United Fruit Company, the U.S. government was horrified. And when Arbenz actually gave out the land to 180,000 destitute peasants, the U.S. condemned his regime as communist. The U.S. then convened the Organization of American States (the OAS, which is commonly known as the Organization of American Satellites) in Caracas to make the condemnation official, and found a right-wing colonel named Carlos Castillo Armas, a graduate of the U.S. Command and General Staff School at Fort Leavenworth, Kansas, to do its dirty work. It fed him arms and dollars to set up a rebel force in Honduras and Nicaragua and, furnishing the bombers flown by CIA pilots, helped him overthrow Arbenz. (Unlike Cuba during the Bay of Pigs in 1961, which was an identical operation, the Guatemala invasion worked because Arbenz was not a revolutionary and, unlike Fidel, had not armed the people.)

The fact is that no genuine Latin American reformer who tried to nationalize U.S. property has escaped direct or indirect U.S. intervention (except the current Peruvian military junta which, at the time of writing, was still surviving, thanks mainly to a combination of popular measures and pro-U.S. trade contracts). Yet no Latin American leader can enact meaningful reforms unless he does nationalize U.S. property, since without it no country can ever finance its development. Overall, the United States controls 85 percent of the continent's sources of raw materials. For every dollar invested in Latin America by U.S. corporations (mostly paper investments at that) three dollars are remitted home in profits. One company alone (United Fruit) controls over 50 percent of the foreign earnings (therefore the whole economic structure) of six Latin American countries. In Venezuela, the Standard Oil Company of New Jersey (Rockefeller) controls, through its subsidiaries, the Creole Oil

30 See *The Great Fear in Latin America*, cited above, pp. 167–72 and 180–86.
31 *Latin American Issues—Essays and Comments*, ed. Albert O. Hirschman (New York: The Twentieth Century Fund, 1961), p. 179.

Corporation and International Basic Economy Corporation,[32] all the sources and industrial base of the economy. The country is potentially the second richest in the world. Its $500 million-plus net annual revenue from oil could guarantee every family, counting it 6.5 persons, an annual income of almost $3,000. Instead, 40 percent of its population lives outside the money economy, 22 percent are unemployed, and the country uses over $100 million a year of its revenue to import foodstuffs, although it has enough land, under a proper agrarian reform, to be a food exporter.

In more recent times, in Latin America, the 1965 invasion of the Dominican Republic graphically illustrates the avarice of the U.S. ruling class. That was a case where the rebels, known as "Constitutionalists," were reformists who sought to re-establish the democratic regime of Juan Bosch, the popularly elected president who had been overthrown by a military coup. But the U.S. didn't like Juan Bosch: A mildly socialist nationalist, he was too independent of Washington. So it invaded the island with Marines, Special Forces, infantrymen, and military police. At first, the excuse was to save U.S. lives (as if Washington would tolerate an invasion of English troops to save Englishmen caught in a riot in New York). Then, the justification was to stop "spreading communism" and "the massacres."

Even at the time, there was overwhelming proof that the communist smear was fake.[33] As for the massacres, the only documented cases finger the anti-Bosch military, whom the U.S. helped.[34] The true reason for the intervention was that the U.S. ruling class was worried about its financial holdings—sugar, which is the island's main crop yet is owned by U.S. interests. It is revealing to identify some of the influential men in and near the government at this time:[35]

[32] IBEC is one of the largest holding corporations, with investments all over the world, but especially in the underdeveloped part.

[33] See Max Frankel, "Secret U.S. Report Details Policy in Dominican Crisis," *New York Times*, November 14, 1965; the articles by Tad Szulc in the *New York Times* from April 30 to June 30, 1965, and by Dan Kurzman in the *Washington Post* for the same period; Senator J. W. Fulbright, *The Arrogance of Power* (New York: Random House, 1966), Ch. 4; Theodore Draper, "The Dominican Crisis: A Case Study in American Policy," *Commentary*, December 1965, pp. 33–68; "The Roots of the Dominican Crisis," *The New Leader*, May 24, 1965; and "A Case of Defamation: U.S. Intelligence versus Juan Bosch," *The New Republic*, February 19 and 26, 1966. All of these sources are staunch supporters of "the American way of life" and vociferously anticommunist.

[34] Drew Pearson, "A Report of Imbert Atrocities," *Washington Post*, August 13, 1965; also articles in the *Washington Post* on June 10, 1965, and *New York Times* on June 10, 11, and 23, 1965.

[35] Research carried out by Fred Goff and Michael Locker of the North American Congress on Latin America and published in "The Violence of Domination: U.S. Power and the Dominican Republic," *Latin American Radicalism*, eds. I. L. Horowitz, Josué de Castro, and John Gerassi (New York: Random House, and London: Jonathan Cape, 1969), pp. 280–82.

Abe Fortas, one of President Johnson's top confidants at the time and later Supreme Court Justice, a twenty-year director of the Sucrest Corporation, third largest East Coast cane refiner, dependent on Dominican sugar for much of its profits.

Adolf A. Berle, Jr., long-time State Department expert and presidential adviser (Roosevelt, Kennedy, Johnson) on Latin America,[36] postwar board chairman and large stockholder of Sucrest. Berle's N.Y. law firm specializes in Latin American affairs for U.S. corporations.

Ellsworth Bunker, OAS ambassador and special envoy to the Dominican Republic, later ambassador to Saigon, past chairman, president and thirty-eight-year director of National Sugar Refining Co., the East Coast's second largest. Bunker, whose father was a founder of National Sugar, was described by *New York Post* columnist Joseph P. Lash as the "spokesman for the whole [sugar] industry vis-à-vis the government."[37] Bunker's previous directorships included American Hawaiian Steamship, Central Aguirre Associates, General Baking Co., Guantánamo Sugar Co., and Potrero Sugar Co., all of which have significant interests in Latin America. Bunker is a long-time trustee of the Atlantic Mutual Insurance Co., which uses as its legal counsel Senator George Smathers' Miami firm, Smathers and Thompson, whose board includes J. Peter Grace, president and director of W. R. Grace and Co., one of Latin America's most active U.S. corporations. Bunker's son, John B., is past president of the Great Western Sugar Co. and at the time of the Dominican occupation was president of the Holly Sugar Co. (a subsidiary of Houston Oil Field Material Co.). Bunker's brother, Arthur H., was a past partner and a long-time director of Lehman Brothers, one of whose subsidiaries was run by Edwin L. Weisl, a close Johnson adviser.

Averell Harriman, sent to Latin America by Johnson to explain the Dominican invasion, a partner of Brown Brothers, which owns part of National Sugar's stock. Harriman's brother, E. Roland Harriman, heads Brown Brothers and was with Bunker on the board of Atlantic Mutual. Another Brown Brothers partner, Knight Woolley, was on the board of Bunker's National Sugar.

Jacob M. Kaplan, who made part of his fortune from molasses in Batista's Cuba and Trujillo's Dominican Republic, used his Kaplan Fund to finance N.Y.'s Institute of International Labor Research, which in turn financed Costa Rica's International Institute for Political Education, a center for counterrevolutionary activity in Latin America.[38] The Kaplan Fund has since been accused of being a CIA conduit.

Joseph S. Farland, U.S. ambassador to the Dominican Republic (1957–

[36] Whose many machinations in Latin America led Brazil's conservative but independent (and therefore overthrown by a CIA-sponsored military coup) President Janio Quadros to accuse him of deliberately fomenting the coup. See *The Great Fear in Latin America*, p. 84; also pp. 197n., 244n., 263.
[37] January 27, 1957.   [38] See *The Great Fear in Latin America*, p. 209.

60) and Panama (1960–63), a director of South Puerto Rico Sugar Co.

Roswel Gilpatric, a former Deputy Secretary of Defense, managing executive partner of Cravath, Swaine, and Moore, the Wall Street legal counsel for National Sugar (as well as for Time, Inc., and General Dynamics).

Max Rabb, a secretary to Eisenhower's Cabinet and also a national committeeman for Johnson and Humphrey, was in the law firm Stroock, Stroock, and Lavan, which was Sucrest's legal counsel.

Is it surprising that U.S. intervention in the Dominican Republic was a formidable boon to U.S. business interests?[39] There has never been a significant difference between U.S. government policy and U.S. private enterprise policies. As Fred J. Borch, president of General Electric, put it: "Overriding both the common purposes and cross-purposes of business and government, there is a broader pattern—a 'consensus' if you will, where public and private interest come together, cooperate, interact and become the national interest."[40] And his treasurer, John D. Lockton, added: "Thus, our search for profits places us squarely in line with the national policy of stepping up international trade as a means of strengthening the free world in the Cold War confrontation with Communism."[41]

Just how are GE and the U.S. strengthening the "free world"? Economically, even if we take the figures of procapitalist social scientists, the gap between the poor countries and the rich is dramatically widening. From 1860 to 1960, the per-capita income of the U.S. rose from $420 to $1,900 while that of Latin America went from $100 to $330, of the Far East from $50 to $120, and of Southeast Asia from $48 to $70.[42] And just what does "strengthening" mean? The *New York Times* never had any illusions—no matter what it claimed in print later. "Indochina is a prize worth a large gamble," it said in 1950. "Even before World War II, Indochina brought an annual dividend estimated at 300 million dollars."[43] Nor did *U.S. News and World Report* in 1954: "One of the world's richest areas is open to the winner in Indochina. That's behind the growing U.S. concern. . . . Tin, rubber, rice, key strategic raw materials

---

[39] For a detailed rundown of U.S. investments and who really profited from the invasion and from U.S. government "aid" after the anti-Bosch coup and after the defeat of the Constitutionalists, see Goff and Locker in *Latin American Radicalism*, pp. 249–91.

[40] Speech before the Economic Club of New York, November 9, 1964, printed by General Electric Co., Schenectady, N.Y.

[41] Speech at Macalester College, St. Paul, Minn., April 22, 1964, printed by GE, Schenectady, N.Y.

[42] L. J. Zimmerman, *Poor Lands, Rich Lands: The Widening Gap* (New York: Random House, 1965), p. 61. The author is a professor of economics at The Hague Institute of Social Studies, and adviser to the U.N. and to the Organization for Economic Cooperation and Development.

[43] February 12, 1950.

are what the war is really about. The United States sees it as a place to hold—at any cost."[44]

Nor, indeed, did President Eisenhower himself in those days when the French were doing most of the fighting and dying for Western greed: "Let us assume we lose Indochina . . . the tin and tungsten that we so greatly value from that area would cease coming . . . so when the United States votes 400 million dollars to help that war, we are not voting a give-away program. We are voting for the cheapest way that we can to prevent the occurrence of something that would be of a most terrible significance to the United States of America, our security, our power and ability to get certain things we need from the riches of the Indo-Chinese territory and from Southeast Asia."[45] At that time Eisenhower didn't think of justifying U.S. lust with talk of freedom. Through the CIA his regime installed the ineffable Ngo Dinh Diem in Saigon, then had him cancel the 1956 elections, a cancellation in flagrant violation of the Geneva Agreements. Eisenhower explained in his memoirs, *Mandate for Change*, "I have never talked or corresponded with a person knowledgeable in Indo-Chinese affairs who did not agree that had elections been held, . . . possibly 80 percent of the people would have voted for the communist Ho Chi Minh."

Now that it is clear why the United States wanted (and wants) to "strengthen" the "free world," how is it doing it? In Vietnam, massacres have taken place all along. Long before the Song My murders, I carefully detailed a whole series of such massacres in my book *North Vietnam: A Documentary*.[46] But I was far from the only one to do so. The *New York Times* reported that "many of the 'enemy' dead reported by the government to have been shot were ordinary peasants shot down because they fled from villages as troops entered."[47] Ohio Senator Stephen Young said he had evidence that "The CIA has employed some South Vietnamese and they have been instructed to claim they are Viet Cong and to work accordingly. . . . Several of these executed two village leaders and raped some women."[48] Beverly Deepe told how "one of the most infamous methods of torture used by the government forces is partial electrocution—or 'frying,' as one U.S. adviser called it. . . . Other techniques, usually designed to force onlooking prisoners to talk, involve cutting off the fingers, ears, fingernails or sexual organs of another prisoner. Sometime a string of ears decorate the walls of a government military installation. One American installation has a Viet Cong ear preserved in alcohol."[49] William Tuohy added: "In more extreme cases, victims had

[44] April 4, 1954.

[45] Statement at State Governors' Conference, Seattle, Wash., August 4, 1953.

[46] (New York: Bobbs-Merrill, and London: Allen and Unwin, 1968.)

[47] July 25, 1965.   [48] *New York Herald Tribune*, November 21, 1965.

[49] *New York Herald Tribune*, April 25, 1965.

bamboo slivers run under their fingernails or wires from a field telephone connected to arms, nipples, or testicles."[50] The Associated Press witnessed a "Vietnamese woman who stared in hatred as the American infantry-men with shotguns blasted away at chickens and ducks. Others shot a water buffalo and the family dog. While her husband, father and young son were led away, the torch was put to the hut that still contained the family belongings. The flames consumed everything—including the shrine to the family ancestors."[51]

These horror tales are commonplace. They occurred (and still occur) every day—among America's Indians, in Mexico, Central America, and the Caribbean, in the Philippines, in Vietnam, Laos, and now Cambodia, in fact wherever the U.S. intervenes by force in order "to get certain things we need," as Eisenhower put it. Vietnam war correspondent Jack Langguth once reported a conversation that succinctly described U.S. policy. "I was greeted by an officer with one of the helicopter units. He was a jovial man, almost ready to return to the U.S. after a year in Vietnam. When he had talked with gathering gloom about problems in his province, I asked the question that usually ended a discussion.

" 'What's the answer?' I asked.

" 'Terror,' he said pleasantly."[52]

Today, as I write, that terror is being used in Cambodia, until recently a peaceful agricultural country which prided itself on its neutralism—a neutralism intolerable to the Nixon Administration, which as in the days of the U.S. occupation of the Philippines, sees anyone not actively friendly as a vicious enemy. Having spread the war to Laos and found its people strongly determined to resist,[53] the U.S. engineered a coup to overthrow the neutralist Cambodian regime. The U.S. then spurred vast massacres of Vietnamese residents in Cambodia, trying to generate a racial conflict there, and when both Vietnamese and loyal Cambodians rebelled, it announced its official intention to "help" the military coup-makers. The excuse? "A necessary and effective measure to save American and other free world lives."[54] The same phony excuse, the traditional prelude to massive terror.

To finance this terror the U.S. had spent $1,400,000,000,000 ($1.4 trillion) from World War II to the end of 1968,[55] enough to build 140 million fully equipped one-room schoolhouses or 140,000 modern hos-

[50] New York Times Magazine, November 28, 1965.

[51] New York World-Journal-Tribune, April 22, 1967.

[52] New York Times, September 19, 1965.

[53] I had personally witnessed and wrote about U.S. intervention in Laos in December 1966, but only in 1970 did Washington, which had denied it, finally admit its lies. See North Vietnam: A Documentary.

[54] Statement by Daniel Henkin, Assistant Secretary of Defense, London Times, April 30, 1970.

[55] United Press International, March 21, 1969.

pitals. Over half of every year's U.S. budget goes to maintain the military's power to wage this terror. That budget is paid for by people in taxes, but it goes to the ruling class in profits. In 1966, for example, such companies as General Dynamics, Textron, Inc., Grumman Aircraft Corporation, and RCA, all of which furnish the military with hardware, increased their profits by 22, 31, 30 and 29 percent, respectively.[56]

In general, the ruling class is made up of relatively few families who control the vast majority of the U.S. wealth. Precisely who they are, and how much they own, has long been debated. One list of ninety-nine individuals who are corporate directors and have personal holdings of $10 million or more in the corporations they direct (hence not including other corporations they rule through alliances, friends, etc.) does not even show J. Paul Getty, whom *Fortune*, in its yearly listing, classifies as the richest man in the world. This list of ninety-nine begins with Richard K. Mellon (worth $429,865,534 in companies he directs). Next come William du Pont, Jr. ($335,144,832), J. G. Ordway (Minnesota Mining & Manufacturing, $286,011,968), A. A. Houghton, Jr. (Corning Glass, U.S. Steel), etc.[57] Another study showed that in 1953, 1.6 percent of the adult population owned 32 percent of all private wealth, which amounted to 82.2 percent of all stock, 100 percent of state and local bonds (tax-exempt), 29.1 percent of all cash, 36.2 percent of mortgages and notes, 13.3 percent of life insurance reserves, 5.9 percent of pension and retirement funds, 18.2 percent of miscellaneous property, 16.1 percent of real estate, and 22.1 percent of all outstanding debts.[58] Back in 1937, Ferdinand Lundberg narrowed down the real base of power in America to just sixty families, and went on to prove in a classic study of internationally oriented capitalist structure, what most people assume intuitively: that capitalists profit from wars even if the people and the country as a whole suffer financially from it. Lundberg also showed how an increase in production does not, and did not in the U.S. from 1920 to 1930, lead to an increase in the average man's income; on the contrary, "as the nation multiplied in riches its people as a whole became poorer. And this was not the result of chance."[59]

Whether the really rich are sixty families, ninety-nine individuals, or 1.6 percent of the adult population does not matter. What matters is who makes financial policy. If I had $10 million in a savings account,

[56] *Business Week*, December 3, 1966 (preliminary figures).

[57] Don Vilarejo, "Stock Ownership and the Control of Corporations", Pt. III, Appx. 7, *New University Thought*, Winter 1962, pp. 63–65.

[58] Robert J. Lampman, *The Share of Top Wealth—Holders in National Wealth, 1922–56* (Princeton, N.J.: National Bureau of Economic Research, Princeton University, 1962), pp. 23, 192–93.

[59] *America's 60 Families* (New York: Vanguard Press, 1937), pp. 499–500, and the whole of Ch. II, Appx. B.

I would certainly be very rich, but I would not control the bank, nor exert meaningful pressure over its national and international policies. If, on the other hand, I owned $10 million worth of stock in a corporation worth $100 million, my 10 percent may still be worth only $10 million in assets, but I would most probably control the whole corporation. It is generally accepted by all economists that to own 5 percent of a big corporation's voting stock is tantamount to controlling the corporation itself (unless the majority is literally held by various members of the same family or group). In terms of political control over the corporation, my 10 percent would now be worth $100 million, not $10 million. What is significant, then, is not that 1.6 percent of the adult population in 1953 owned 32 percent of all private wealth—to use the figures of Lampman—but that 1.6 percent of the adults owned 82.2 percent of American's stock. That 1.6 percent hence determines policy, both nationally and internationally.[60]

Corporations own some two-thirds of America's wealth. Of those corporations less than 500 control two-thirds of the manufacturing economy. Even Adolf A. Berle, Jr., capitalism's super-apologist, is forced to cringe at such a situation. "This is, I think, the highest concentration of economic power in recorded history. Since the United States carries on not quite half of the manufacturing production of the entire world today, these 500 groupings—each with its own little dominating pyramid within it—represent a concentration of power over economics which makes the medieval feudal system look like a Sunday School party."[61] Since then, the concentration has increased. In 1962, Representative Wright Patman, chairman of the Select Committee on Small Business, concluded that "we are moving into a new phase of industrial and financial domination and control of American industry. Merger movements have fed this cancerous growth. The United States is rapidly becoming a nation of clerks and hired hands."[62]

[60] Lampman's figures are not universally accepted. Robert Heilbroner, for example, comes up with less than 1 percent of families owning over 80 percent of public industrial stock (*The Future as History* [New York: Harper, 1959], p. 125). Harvard economists Keith Butters, Lawrence E. Thompson, and Lynn L. Bollinger estimate that 0.2 percent own between 65 and 71 percent (*Effect of Taxation on Investments by Individuals* [Cambridge, Mass.: Riverside Press, 1953], p. 400). Whatever the accurate figures, we can certainly go along with C. Wright Mills who said that "at the very most, 0.2 or 0.3 percent of the adult population own the bulk, the pay-off shares, of the corporate world" (*The Power Elite* [New York: Oxford University Press, 1956], p. 122).

[61] *Economic Power and the Free Society* (New York: Fund for the Republic, 1957), p. 14.

[62] Staff Report of the Select Committee on Small Business, *Mergers and Superconcentration: Acquisitions of 500 Largest Industrial and 50 Largest Merchandising Firms* (Washington, D.C.: Government Printing Office, 1962), p. iii.

The men who run these corporations share the same life style. They know each other, attend the same schools, clubs, and resorts, and marry each other's sisters and daughters. They serve on each other's boards of directors. In fact, the interlocking of directors is so tight that it is absurd to imagine Big Business as competitive. Scores of studies prove the point, but here is one example in passing: All of the major steel companies, except Bethlehem, are interlocked with the Mellon group, which, through Consolidation Coal (among other companies) is tied to Hanna Mining, which controls Texaco, Gulf Oil, Phelps Dodge, etc., while Mellon is also linked to the du Ponts, especially through Remington Arms, one of whose owners (674,074 shares in 1962), M. H. Dodge, was married to Geraldine Rockefeller of the Rockefeller family which controls Chase Manhattan Bank (David Rockefeller) and First National City (J. Stillman Rockefeller), which . . . *ad infinitum*. Meanwhile Hanna controls most of Brazil's wealth, the Rockefellers most of Venezuela's, Colombia's, etc. As of December 1967, 52 percent of the assets of Standard Oil of New Jersey (just *one* of Rockefellers' vast oil holdings) were abroad, operating in 100 nations, worth more ($13.8 billion) than the U.S.'s gold supply.[63]

Such tycoons decide prices, development schemes, what infrastructure gets what aid, in fact the whole life style of the people—Bolivian, Jordanians, Laotians. Operating through fronts of various kinds (the Rockefellers have thirteen foundations, fifteen family trusts, and God knows—perhaps—how many financial mechanisms), the U.S. ruling class literally rules not only America but the underdeveloped world. And it keeps it underdeveloped. It must be accounted directly responsible for hunger, disease, poverty and death; it cannot have it both ways. As a class, the U.S. corporation directors must be collectively accounted guilty of murder —as well as political blunders.[64] And so are their representatives and

[63] *Time*, December 29, 1967.

[64] A. A. Berle, Jr., Gardner Means, David Bazelon, David Riesman, John Kenneth Galbraith, and others have tried to soften the blame on the directors through two arguments: (1) that since so many other people own stock (they talk of "people's capitalism") corporate policy in fact reflects the view of all of the U.S.; and (2) that it is the managers who actually run the corporations, not the owners. The first argument is sheer sophistry: "People's capitalism" does not exist (a few million have a few hundred shares each) and corporate policy is decided by directors, appointed by those who control the corporations through voting stocks, i.e., the owners. The second argument is based on the assumption that managers are not stockholders in general if they do not own stock in their own corporation, which is patently false: As a group, corporation officers are the biggest group of stock buyers, hence identify totally with the profit motive of the ruling class. Besides, most managers are also stock owners in their own corporations and no matter how small their stake, they see *their* fortunes solidly linked to the corporations'. Also, most corporation officers and executives today have stock options which are meaningful *only* if the worth of the stock rises, i.e., if they are successful in making the corporation grow. See G. William Domhoff, *Who Rules America?* (Englewood

spokesmen, especially corporation lawyers.[65] For all who oppose injustice, it is as much a moral right—indeed a moral imperative—to pull the teeth of this international U.S. ruling class as it is to destroy any enemy of freedom. And for all who suffer directly from this ruling class's greed, that is, for all the peasants, workers, intellectuals of the Third World, it is in their self-interest to do so. For the peoples of the world, revolution against the United States is inevitable, necessary, and just.

And for Americans? For those of us who suffer neither from want nor from napalm?

The majority of Americans seem to like their system. In fact, they seem to like it so much that they tolerate the power elites acting even more viciously and selfishly. According to a 1970 CBS poll, 76 percent of Americans answered No to this question: "As long as there appears to be no clear danger of violence, do you think any group, no matter how extreme, should be allowed to organize protests against the government?" A majority of Americans seemed to be willing to throw away the Bill of Rights: 58 percent wanted to junk the Constitution's no-double-jeopardy provisions, 58 percent were disposed to see their habeas corpus guarantees scrapped, 55 percent approved of government censorship of press and media, and 54 percent were opposed to free speech.[66] Perhaps the majority of Americans are still like the jurymen who freed and applauded William Walker—arrogant, totalitarian, chauvinistic, and immoral according to the

---

Cliffs, N.J.: Prentice-Hall, 1967); Gabriel Kolko, *Wealth and Power in America* (New York: Praeger, 1962); Ferdinand Lundberg, *The Rich and the Super-Rich* (New York: Lyle Stuart, 1968); C. Wright Mills, *The Power Elite*, cited above, and *Power, Politics, and People* (New York: Ballantine, 1963). On the psychology of managers, see Sumner H. Slichter, "The Power Holders in the American Economy," *Saturday Evening Post*, December 13, 1958.

[65] Because of the role played by U.S. universities in fomenting and maintaining these conditions, their presidents cannot escape the characterization of petty Eichmanns. In most cases, however, university presidents are as close to the U.S. ruling class as are the corporation managers. Sample: James R. Killian, chairman of the Massachusetts Institute of Technology who is also a director of General Motors, Polaroid, and the Cabot Corporation. In any case, most university structures—brain corporations instead of productive corporations, but corporations nonetheless—can be judged by their own boards. Columbia University, for example, is ruled by twenty-two men (eighteen trustees, four deans) whose participation in the ruling class is as follows: 8 are leading figures in major communications firms; 7 have primary ties to U.S. corporations or nonprofit organizations operating abroad, and 6 of the 7 are prominent functionaries in seemingly political organizations secretly funded by the CIA; 5 have primary relationships with leading national corporations and several have such secondary interests; 5 are representative of the military-industrial complex; 15 have primary interlocking relationships with major real estate and finance companies. Not one of Columbia's top twenty-two is simply a scholar or a scientist or a writer or an intellectual. Yet these twenty-two set policy. See *Who Rules Columbia* (New York: North American Congress on Latin America, 1968).

[66] *Time*, April 27, 1970.

ethical standards of any philosophy, religion, or humanitarianism sup-posedly recognized by America's self-professed ideals and taught in its schools. Perhaps polls are idiotic.

In any case, those who seek a revolution in the United States are a minority. Should that stop them? The fact is, every revolution—the French, the English, the American, the Russian—was launched and waged by a minority. In a speech to the Seventh All-Russia Conference of the RSDLP (Bolsheviks) on May 7, 1917, Lenin, aware that a poll of Russians would reveal statistics similar to those of the CBS poll, shouted, "Yes, we are a minority. Well, what of it? To be a Socialist while chauvinism is the craze means to be in the minority!"[67] And so in the United States. To be against racism is to be in the minority. To be against exploitation is to be in the minority. To be against rule by capitalists is to be in the minority. To be for world justice is to be in the minority. The point is, however, that the U.S. has such a minority. And it is increasing. It is made up of people, mostly young, who were first shocked by their social conditions and then became aware that only through revolution would such conditions be changed.

Consciousness builds on consciousness. For years, indeed centuries, America's blacks have been exploited, beaten, killed, yet by and large unrebellious. From 1882 to 1959, no less than 2,595 blacks were re-ported lynched without a single conviction, and thousands more met similar but unreported fates. Eventually, of course, a minority of blacks, organized to protest, convinced others that a life of slavery or bootlicking wasn't worth living. The consciousness of the fundamental racism of the U.S. system spread. As it did, so did repression. More blacks were beaten, tortured, killed. With each death, more awarenesses were molded, new rebels born, greater understanding created. Today, the blacks are the vanguard of the American Revolution. They are the most harassed, the most repressed. Almost every black man in the U.S. has understood that he cannot obtain justice from a white court, fairness from a white police-man, equality from a white government. If he has an education, if his old man managed to accumulate a bit of money, then he can kowtow to whites, mimic their manner, copy their style, join their institutions, and become "integrated." If he is poor and uneducated and lives in a ghetto, he can become a pimp, a hustler, a gangster, or a drug addict to escape his misery. Otherwise, the black man, rich or poor, has only one choice—to be proud, to defend his integrity, to herald his blackness, to fight the system, to be a revolutionary.

Very few stories of how blacks are mistreated by the white society ever get told, and when they do it is in books that few ever read. But

---

[67] V. I. Lenin, *Selected Works* (New York: International Publishers, 1967), II, p. 77. (Hereafter referred to simply as *Works*.)

some stories do become public. One that made headlines in San Francisco began like this:

"Michael O'Brien was returning with some friends from a Sunday outing at Lake Berryessa. The double date had not gone well: O'Brien had been drinking and was in an unpleasant mood. At one point, he made his date get out of the car with him and told her to 'be a little more affectionate' or walk home. She calmed him down a little, though, and they got back into the car.

"On the way across the San Francisco–Oakland Bay Bridge, he suddenly brandished a .38 revolver. After a minute he put the gun away, and a few minutes later they were at Brush Place.

"You'd have to be a pretty determined San Franciscan to know where Brush Place is. About two and a half blocks from the ugly new Hall of Justice, there's a little dead-end alley off Folsom Street called Hallam Street. Off that alley there's an even smaller alley, also a dead end. That's Brush Place. O'Brien kept his boat in one of the garages in Brush Place that are rented out for that purpose.

"Carl Hawkins, a mild-mannered black streetcar motorman, seems to have scraped O'Brien's boat trailer with his car. Hawkins immediately stopped and got out.

"This is how all the witnesses who were not police described what happened next:

"One thing quickly led to another. O'Brien yelled at Hawkins 'If you scrape my car, I'll shoot you!' People in the neighborhood, many of them black, came out or looked out their windows to see what was happening. Suddenly O'Brien pulled out his .38 and shouted, 'Get your heads back in, niggers, or I'll kill all of you. I'll blow your heads off.' Hawkins' wife went inside to phone the police; Mike's companion, Willis Garriott, went out toward Folsom Street on the same errand.

"As Garriott returned with Special Patrol Officer Raymond Adkins (a private policeman, but one with a uniform and a gun), there was the sound of a shot and confusion in the street; O'Brien had three black men at gunpoint, their hands against the wall at the end of the alley. O'Brien was getting nastier by the minute; according to witnesses, he said, 'I want to kill a nigger—I want to kill a nigger so goddamned bad I can taste it!'

"A black truck driver and neighbor of Hawkins, George Baskett, five inches shorter than O'Brien and 75 pounds lighter, picked up a slat out of a chair back, a thin piece of wood about 23 inches long and about an inch and a half wide, and tried to knock the gun away from O'Brien. Garriott and the special cop had their guns out by now and watched as O'Brien growled, 'Drop the stick, drop it, goddammit.' He counted in a rapid cadence, 'One . . . two . . . three. . . .' There was a sharp crack. The bullet ripped through Baskett's chest, severing a major artery. As

Baskett lay moaning and dying in the street, O'Brien approached him. 'Shut up, dammit,' he growled, 'shut up.' He kicked at Baskett's side, turning his victim over on his back. Baskett's pregnant wife ran out toward her husband. 'Get out of here, you black bitch," O'Brien shouted, forcing her down the street. Then he looked up at the black faces peering down from the windows above him. 'Get your heads back in, niggers,' he shouted, 'before I blow them off.' Within minutes, Baskett, twenty-eight years old and the father of five children, was dead. Michael O'Brien had killed his nigger.

"The police came, including San Francisco's head-cracking Tactical Squad. They immediately began questioning 'suspects.' They arrested Mr. and Mrs. Carl Hawkins, Mrs. Hawkins' son Richard Dickerson, and Otis Baskett, on charges of conspiracy, assault to commit murder, and assault with a deadly weapon. Then they helped the dazed O'Brien out of the alley and away from the angry crowd.

"O'Brien of course was white. And although he had never said so to anybody in Brush Place, that night or at any other time, Michael O'Brien was a cop. . . .

"Within four hours of the shooting of George Baskett in Brush Place, the official police investigation of the incident had been conducted and concluded. The two officers who submitted the report admitted in court that it had been rewritten three times on the orders of their superior, Lieutenant Daniel Mahoney, who had specifically ordered them not to mention any witnesses other than the policemen present. The report concluded that the killing of Baskett was 'justifiable homicide.' It was only *after* reaching this conclusion that the police questioned the arrested blacks, who for three hours had been kept handcuffed in the paddy wagon outside the Hall of Justice. Early Monday morning, Chief Thomas Cahill told reporters that the whole affair was a 'sad situation,' but 'a man has a right to defend himself.' He termed the shooting 'accidental' and informed them that his own private investigation was closed."

Eventually, because local protests were vociferous, O'Brien was brought to trial. All jurymen were white. The cop's lawyer, the famous Jake Ehrlich, hired by the Police Officers' Association, ranted like a slave trader. "These people," he told the jury, meaning all blacks, "would have killed . . . O'Brien, and they would have killed you, too, if you'd been there. They have absolutely no respect for an oath, the truth, or for common decency." To discredit a white witness, Ehrlich shouted: "I can realize our black brethren sticking together. . . . What I can't understand is Anderson coming apparently from a good home and selling his soul to prove his hatred for a policeman, what he calls a pig." (Anderson, who saw the murder, testified he never used the term "pig.") O'Brien was found not guilty.[68]

[68] *Ramparts,* July 1969.

Liberals' arguments that such miscarriages of justice are exceptions are valid only for those who will never take a long look at injustice in contemporary America. In Connecticut, four black juveniles were given sixteen years for supposedly raping a white girl who had no witnesses although all four youths swore they had refused to go to her apartment where she had tried to woo them, and one of the youths produced a letter written by the girl showing her amorous design. In Benson, North Carolina, five blacks were sentenced to twelve years in jail for burning the door of the Ku Klux Klan headquarters (damage: less than $100) on the day all of America was raging for the murder of Martin Luther King.[69] In San Jose, California, a Mexican-American youth was brought up on charges of having had intercourse with his sister. The boy denied it, but he was told that if he would plead guilty he'd avoid adult court and the judge agreed to release the boy in care of his grandmother. The judge, Gerald S. Chargin, kept to the deal, but only after he told the boy—and every other Mexican-American—what America thought of his race:

"THE COURT: There is some indication that you more or less didn't think that it was against the law or was improper. Haven't you had any moral training? Have you and your family gone to church?

"THE MINOR: Yes, sir.

"THE COURT: Don't you know that things like this are terribly wrong? This is one of the worst crimes that a person can commit. I just get so disgusted that I just figure what is the use? You are just an animal. You are lower than an animal. Even animals don't do that. You are pretty low.

"I don't know why your parents haven't been able to teach you anything or train you. Mexican people, after 13 years of age, it's perfectly all right to go out and act like an animal. It's not even right to do that to a stranger, let alone a member of your own family. I don't have much hope for you. You will probably end up in State's Prison before you are 25, and that's where you belong, anyhow. There is nothing much you can do.

"I think you haven't got any moral principles. You won't acquire anything. Your parents won't teach you what is right or wrong and won't watch out.

"The Country will have to take care of you. You are no particular good to anybody. We ought to send you out of the country—send you back to Mexico. You belong in prison for the rest of your life for doing things of this kind. You are lower than animals and haven't the right to live in organized society—just miserable, lousy, rotten people.

"There is nothing we can do with you. You expect the Country to take care of you. Maybe Hitler was right. The animals in our society

[69] *Time*, July 11, 1969.

probably ought to be destroyed because they have no right to live among human beings. If you refuse to act like a human being, then, you don't belong among the society of human beings. . . . When they are 10 or 12 years of age, going out and having intercourse with anybody without any moral training—they don't even understand the Ten Commandments. That's all. Apparently, they don't want to.

"So if you want to act like that, the Country has a system of taking care of them. They don't care about that. They have no personal self-respect. . . . What are we going to do with the mad dogs of our society? Either we have to kill them or send them to an institution or place them out of the hands of good people because that's the theory—one of the theories of punishment is if they get to the position that they want to act like mad dogs, then, we have to separate them from our society."[70]

There is no need to continue the file. Blacks, Chicanos, Puerto Ricans, every minority people living in the United States are revolutionaries or are becoming so. Because the U.S. is racist. It has been racist since its beginning. It will continue to be racist until the present system is broken. It is racist because the ruling class profits from racism; through racism it keeps the population divided, using the most exploited to threaten those a little less exploited and keep them insecure. By keeping the general population insecure, the ruling class can profit best. A united people can be very dangerous to exploiters. Thus the courts, the press, the media, the universities, every institution is directed so as to propagate this racism. It is hence necessary to smash those institutions.

Liberals insist that such a blanket condemnation of U.S. institutions is unfair. After all, they say, Oberlin College or Kenyon College is not racist. And we all know judges, cops, senators, or businessmen who are not racist. This is a typical liberal argument based on the theory that the United States is a pluralistic society. It combats class and system analyses with individualistic arguments. Of course, not all cops are racists. But the police structure is. So is the court system, no matter how many judges are nice guys. So is Congress as an institution representing the will and desire of the ruling class. Many congressmen are humanists. Many corporation executives too. There are probably quite a few corporation director-owners, members of the ruling class, who would allow, perhaps even hail, their daughters marrying a black man. But would that black man gain corporate power, that is, economic control over thousands of whites? Is it possible to conceive of the U.S. military-industrial complex being run by people who would rather help create good free schools throughout the Congo or Harlem or Watts or New Mexico instead of making money in Thailand? Is it conceivable that local communities control their own police? That each community elect its own judge, that the

[70] *Dock of the Bay*, October 21, 1969.

FBI be forced to investigate corporate mendacity and swindles, that universities be run by students and teachers, that Congress pass a bill making all who work on the land its owners, or that anyone who sells a defective car be prosecuted as strictly as anyone who pushes heroin?

Of course not. Liberals just will not understand, because they profit from the system. They have too much at stake to admit that the state, as Lenin said, "is an organ of class *rule*, an organ for the *oppression* of one class by another; it is the creation of 'order,' which legalizes and perpetuates this oppression by moderating the conflict between classes."[71] The consequence is clear: "The court is an organ of power. The liberals sometimes forget this, but it is a sin for a Marxist to do so."[72] And when one liberal—Yale University President Kingman Brewster—did not forget and said he did not believe that Black Panther Chairman Bobby Seale could get a fair trial in a U.S. court, it was to be expected that the ruling class—through one of its loudest representatives, Vice-President Spiro Agnew—would try to shut him up.[73]

Brewster got the headlines because he *is* a liberal, because he normally *does* represent the will of the ruling class on the Yale campus, and because he is a name. But the blacks and other minority groups have known the conditions of life in the U.S. for a long time. No court, no congressman, and no university president can delude them. That is why they are in the vanguard of the revolutionary movement. To them revolution is not only just but also necessary. And because of their growing consciousness, because of repressions, and because of their imposed social conditions which cannot be changed within the system, their revolutionary commitment is also inevitable.

The minorities make up only 20-odd percent of the population. Enough, perhaps, to bring about a dissolution of the state but not enough to win a class victory without white allies. What is making the situation critical is the fact that whites are becoming revolutionaries too.

At first, though they called themselves revolutionaries, these whites were mere middle-class rebels. Their parents, having suffered from the Great Depression, may not have overly feared losing their hard-won possessions, but deep inside them was a reluctance to "rock the boat." During the era of Senator Joe McCarthy, they hid, praying it would go away without putting into jeopardy their new way of life—not just the TV's and cars, vacations abroad, and pottery lessons, but also the liberal education they offered their children.

The new generation was not haunted by such apprehensions. For

[71] *The State and Revolution*, in *Works*, II, p. 271.

[72] Lenin, *Proletarskaya Revolutsia*, in *Works*, II, p. 165.

[73] *International Herald Tribune*, April 30, 1970. Agnew called for the Yale alumni organization to get rid of Brewster.

one thing, the Depression did not directly affect the kids; it was only a
historical fact to them with no particular relevance except in the abstract.
For another, they grew up in families that did not suffer privation, yet
seemed no happier or more generous than other families. Ask any of
them what life at home was like and you will hear a long catalogue of
nasty scenes, family quarrels, tensions, jealousies, infidelities, arrogance,
put-downs, and so on. Contrary to the liberals' contention, this does not
prove that man is selfish by nature; what it does prove is that our system
is such that it forces man to constantly compete with his fellowman.
That makes him want to get the better of everyone else, constantly. If
he has one thousand dollars, he wants two; if he has one million, he
seeks two; if the country dominates one continent, it lusts for two. In
the process men, women, and children become just as much commodities
as cars and TV's, as medicine and education. What parent really cares
if his child is truly happy? What parent does *not* care if that child doesn't
do well at school? Our society respects only achievements, and no one
is supposed to really feel sorry for the achiever even if the price of
achievement is anxiety attacks, ulcers, insomnia, and the rest.

Well, the young do care. To them it isn't worth it. Having rejected
(and rejecting more and more) the possession cult, their first impulse
was to drop out of society. Thousands did, living in communes very
cheaply, or working only for necessities and quitting when they had them,
borrowing clothes from each other, laughing at the rest of the people
who never found the time to look at flowers or the sea or each other.
Those who continued to go to schools and universities adapted a rejection
of their parents' values to that environment. Behavioristic psychology and
psychoanalysis became a joke; logical positivism and semantical philosophies, mental masturbation; political science, propaganda. Finally, it became clear that the whole educational process was geared to strengthening
the system. Why did every university have business schools, but none
feature labor schools? Why were there no courses on U.S. imperialism?
Why was Marxism taught only by non-Marxists? Why did "open campus"
mean letting the CIA and Dow Chemical and USIA come into recruit?

As fast as the questions were posed came answers. The university
system turned out to be a major accomplice in the wars, the war research, the industrial-military complex. No wonder, then, that the government had always allowed students to be deferred from the draft. Their
role in the industrial-military complex was much more important on
campus than in uniform. Thus, it became obvious that education in
America was violent. Its main function was to train young men to become
cogs in the grand design. Of course, the process was sophisticated. A
soldierlike automaton ordered to do or die just wouldn't fit in the genteel
atmosphere of academia. So, the myth of academic freedom—permission
to talk but not act according to one's conviction—was maintained. And to

safeguard against the possibility of anyone's challenging the whole academic system, there was always another great liberal myth: the importance of specialization. As long as a historian did not feel responsible for what went on in the chemistry lab, he could sign petitions against the war in Vietnam and defend the institution for allowing him that freedom. But as the kids began to challenge each part of the educational system, they realized that they had to confront the whole as well. If the university is meant to give *them* an education, why do they not have a voice in the curriculum, in university policy, in tenure committees, in administrative decisions? Why, they asked, did they never have a say in *any* decisions? Thus, they began to demand participation in the decision-making process.

This led them to the inevitable conclusion that the university was a microcosm of society at large: For who, in America, does take part in the decision-making process? Not the young, not the workers, not the middle class, not even the run-of-the-mill technocrats or bureaucrats. Only those who own the means of production and their managers—the regents, the boards, the chairmen, the advisers, the "Johnsons"—the power elite which either incorporates and includes the powerful, or crushes the dissidents or both. Where then were Galbraith's famous "countervailing forces"?[74]

America, concluded its young, is a closed society. It is an oppressive society—a form of dictatorship. It is a violent society. There is no pluralism in America—that's another liberal myth. The AFL-CIO works hand in hand with the CIA, the CIA with GM, GM with NASA, NASA with the University of California at Berkeley, Berkeley with the farm industry, the farm industry with the Department of Interior, Interior with the AFL-CIO. Everybody talks about free speech, free press, free assembly, but the American people are fed only that part of freedom which reinforces the myth and, at that, through media which are controlled by the boards, the chairmen, and the powerful.

The power elite was intelligent, however. Usually, except when the dissenters really became a threat (in which case, leaders were raided at home and pot was "found" in their rooms), they were incorporated into the system. They were either offered good jobs, or were bought by War on Poverty funds, or were allowed to hold their rallies, which was meant to convince everyone what a wonderfully free country America is. But never were the dissenters allowed to participate in the decision-making process. Except of course, every four years, at election time—for those old enough to vote.

To the young, that, too, became a farce. The American electoral process has never proven such a joke as in 1968. With the majority of Republicans favoring Rockefeller and the majority of Democrats supporting a

[74] See John Kenneth Galbraith, *American Capitalism: The Concept of Countervailing Power* (Boston: Houghton Mifflin, 1952).

McCarthy-Kennedy-McGovern type of candidate, they got Nixon and Humphrey, Tweedledee and Tweedledum. But even that election showed up only the most glaring aspect of American un-democracy. What difference would it have made had Kennedy or Rockefeller been the next president? Would either have worked for the destruction of the competitive society so as to replace it with a moral community? Even if either would have pulled the U.S. out of Vietnam, would he not have intervened in Thailand? in Venezuela? in Guatemala? in the Congo? Would either have ignored the cries of Creole Corporation (Rockefeller) when the Venezuelans nationalized the oil there? Would either have ignored the pleas of United Fruit or Sucrest in the Dominican Republic? Would GM stand for workers' control, decentralization, safe cars? Each of these questions and their obvious answers form part of the U.S. electoral system. As the kids understood, it had to be destroyed. And the only way to do that was by smashing it through counterviolence.

As much as counterviolence may be tactically necessary to stop official violence, so too is it psychologically crucial. For, as Fanon said about colonialized man, violence is a liberating force. After carefully observing the people of his native Martinique, of his adopted Algeria, and of black Africa, Fanon concluded that the process of colonialization is not just military, political, and/or economic domination by a foreign country, but is psychological and cultural oppression by that country as well. Thus, he insisted, if the Third World is to throw off the colonizer, it must free itself from the colonized spirit, characterized by defeatism, servility, inferiority, and Uncle Tomism. The only way for a colonized man to do so is to prove to himself that he *is* a man, that he can face the colonizer without fear, that he is fully capable of running his own life and his own society. In other words, the only way he can be free is to take his country and not accept it as a gift. He must reconquer that which is his.[75]

Likewise in the United States, it became clear that the only way the new generation could free itself from the bondage of its elders, their value system, their cultural oppression—their TV's and newspapers and publicity campaigns and educational consensus—was to seize the controls of the state cultural appparatus. The kids must then run it, must make the mistakes which will lead them to a better understanding of its functioning, doing with it whatever suits them, for it is theirs by right. To a certain extent the kids tried to fashion their new society through their own media, the underground press. They did so without violence, by working hard and putting together the *Berkeley Barb*, the New York *RAT*, the various "Free Presses," psychedelic papers, etc. Generally, however, these papers were owned by one "sugar daddy" who usually kept a tight control on editorial policy. What's more, they did not rep-

75 Frantz Fanon, *The Wretched of the Earth* (New York: Grove Press, 1966), pp. 40–94.

resent genuine free expression, but rebellion. Free expression remains impossible until the system itself allows and encourages it, and that will not be possible under profit-motivated and profit-oriented capitalism.

Besides, exposure through the underground press (as extensive as it may be in some places—viz., the *Los Angeles Free Press* with a circulation of 250,000)—is nowhere comparable to that achieved via television and the established press. So, while there is no denying the importance of America's current underground media, such acts as the forcible seizure of New York's Channel 13 by the Lower East Side anarchistic group known as "Up Against the Wall/Motherfuckers" were of primary necessity. Obviously, the ruling class could not tolerate such acts, and so repression grew.

The confrontations were important for breaking through those old values, the "hang-ups" the kids had from their elders. At Oakland's Stop-the-Draft Week and during the Chicago Democratic Convention battles, for example, a profound change of attitude took place among the street people. The struggle was, as Fanon predicted, liberating. Middle-class kids not only got over their "private-property bag" (as they smashed windows and slashed cop-car tires) but they also learned, without speeches, the meaning of solidarity. In such battles all rebels are equals. Leaders lead only by their acts, and only if those acts relate to the rebels' consciousness. The exhilaration that comes with street fighting is not, as Establishment (i.e., adaptation-oriented) psychiatrists insist, escapism, parental rejectionism, masochism, sadism, etc. On the contrary, it is achieving selfhood, independence, the feeling that one is a man, taking pride in oneself and one's comrades. It is, just as Fanon said, an act of growing up, not of adolescent nihilism.[76]

The struggle itself, then, not only freed the combatant from the "tie-ups" of his heritage, it also taught him new values. Solidarity, for example, is only a word until one relies on it. Then, it becomes part of one's life. When that happened in America, whites were ready to form alliances with blacks. Having become a minority themselves, the white rebels understood that only the victims of racism can define the racists, only the exploited can characterize exploitation. Having gone that far, they now could see why black nationalism was revolutionary while U.S. nationalism was chauvinistic. Lenin had explained it well in *The Right of Nations to Self-Determination*: "Just as in bourgeois society the defenders of privilege and corruption, on which bourgeois marriage rests, oppose freedom of divorce, so, in the capitalist state, repudiation of the right to self-determination, i.e., the right of nations to secede, means nothing more than defence of the privileges of the dominant nation and police methods of administration."[77] And in his *Political Testament* he insisted

[76] *Ibid*, p. 94.   [77] *Works*, II, p. 625.

that "a distinction must necessarily be made between the nationalism of an oppressor nation and that of an oppressed."[78] No longer were white kids fighting *for* somebody else. No longer were the white kids protesting against the Vietnam War out of altruism, no longer were they demonstrating against racism out of guilt. Now their own self-interest had led them to join the Viet Cong (symbolically) and the blacks (in practice) in a real struggle against those who oppress all three—the U.S. ruling class.

Karl Marx once wrote that "it is not the consciousness of men which determines their existence, but on the contrary it is their social existence which determines their consciousness."[79] In the U.S. context that means simply that, no matter how desperately the FBI, Governor Reagan, Mayors Daley and Alioto, and Agnew and Company search for "outside agitators" to explain the movement's increasingly militant activities, they won't find them until they look in the mirror. It is they and their ruling-class partners who are bringing about the Revolution. Since they will never relinquish power voluntarily, since the monopoly capitalists will not commit class suicide, and since the essence of that class is to make more and more money, that is, to attempt to increase their exploitation, revolution is inevitable.

Since the battle of Chicago (the 1968 convention), more kids have become revolutionaries in America than ever before. The reason is twofold. On the one hand, as a result of the piecemeal confrontations which failed to bring about substantive changes the kids began to confront the whole system as a class; in so doing they began to fight as a class themselves. On the other hand, the ruling class, which can tolerate individual dissent but not class war, felt itself threatened enough to resort to systematic class repression, which in turn increased the radicalization process. This twofold development is obvious enough when one looks at what has happened to the Black Panthers. As long as their militancy was directed against individual police forces, the struggle was relatively mild. Huey Newton was framed on a manslaughter rap and various other Panthers were arrested. But once the Panthers began to lead a class war by confronting the whole system (for example, the breakfast program which made two crucial points: white society cannot feed black children, the black revolution can), then harassment of the Panthers changed to attempted extermination: Cops raided Panther offices in San Francisco, Los Angeles, Seattle, Denver, Chicago, New York, and other cities, killed twenty-eight Panthers by the end of 1969, jailed hundreds, and are trying to wipe out the whole leadership.

The pattern is old. When feminists campaigned against U.S. sexual discrimination and their agitation gained strength, the ruling class gave

[78] *Works*, III, p. 749.

[79] Introduction to *Critique of Political Economy*, in *Capital and Other Writings*, ed. Max Eastman (New York: Modern Library, 1932), p. 11.

women the vote. Feminists fought for individual women's rights, not class rights. They didn't see themselves as an exploited class, only as not having the same possibilities as *their* men. The women's vote did not threaten the ruling class: There was no likelihood that women, as a class, would create their own party and, since they make up 52 percent of the population, elect 52 percent of the country's representatives. Why no likelihood? Because they do not share as a class the ownership of 52 percent of the wealth. In a capitalist society, only money leads to power.

Similarly, when workers began to agitate for better living conditions, union representation, collective bargaining, etc., the ruling class fought them for a long time. It used Pinkerton goons, jailed labor leaders, even killed a few. But it could and eventually did give in because labor's demand was merely for a fairer share of the economic pie. Labor did not question the capitalist structure as such. Since the ruling class controls prices as well as production, it could easily grant wage increases, recognize unions, etc., and still increase its profits by juggling the prices. Besides, the country's tax laws are all under its control. The U.S. takes pride in its graduated income tax, but who pays such a tax? Salaried people, not the ruling class, whose real wealth is from capital gains—on which tax is a flat 25 percent. A salaried employee has no escape from the tax law. A capitalist deducts his trips, his yachts, his cars, his liquor and entertainment expenses, even his tuxedo if he wants to. His lawyer is deductible. He can set up a foundation, name himself and friends trustees, deduct his gifts to the foundation, have it purchase thousands of shares of corporations, control those corporations through his foundation and thereby have real economic power, all without paying taxes. But the salaried employee cannot deduct even the cost of his transportation to go to work. Thus as long as workers demand just more money, the ruling class may oppose them viciously, but is prepared to give in—and change nothing.

When, however, workers struggle for meaningful changes, when they demand a voice in policy or partial control of their factories, when, in other words, the workers oppose the owners as class against class, then the rulers will resist to the bitter end. That, for example, is what happened to the Wobblies (IWW, Industrial Workers of the World). They were hunted, framed, ambushed by vigilantes paid by mine owners, constantly arrested and double-crossed at every stage by Samuel Gompers and the American Federation of Labor, which worked directly with the government and the bosses. Finally, in 1917, 166 IWW leaders were arrested and charged with conspiracy. Said U.S. Attorney General Thomas Gregory: "Our purpose being, as I understand it, very largely to put the I.W.W. out of business."[80]

[80] See Melvyn Dubofsky, *We Shall Be All: A History of the I.W.W.* (Chicago: Quadrangle Books, 1969).

Today, the white movement fighters are also operating as a class. They no longer confront just the university, no longer demand reforms, no longer agitate primarily for an end to the Vietnam War. They want to participate in the decision-making process, that is, they want to destroy the system, because this one will never allow them such participation—and they know it. Thus, they attack the capitalist enterprises (192 were bombed in 1969), the state machineries, the courts. What's more, they actually see themselves as a class. At the December 1968 SDS National Council meeting, a resolution called "Toward a Revolutionary Youth Movement" was passed; it stated in part: "To call youth or even the student movement a section of the bourgeoisie which must simply support any struggle fought by working people is economism. The struggle of youth is as much a part of the class struggle as a union strike." A few months later Jim Mellen, who went on to help form the Weathermen and is a member of the Weather Bureau (the Central Committee), wrote in *New Left Notes*, the SDS paper:

"The overwhelming majority of American youth (say 18–24) are students, soldiers and unemployed. Also, the overwhelming majority come from working class backgrounds—no matter how comfortable, mystified, or bourgeois an ideology they may have. The overwhelming majority, further, are destined for jobs and positions within society which are securely within the working class—no matter how conscious they are of the privileges their specific future positions offer. I would argue, however, that what gives specific class content to the struggles of youth—in the schools and in the army specifically—is the proletarianization of the roles youth play in those institutions.

"In the army, coerced though he may be to join and intangible though his product may be, the soldier provides a very necessary labor for capitalism—no different than any other service labor. In the schools, the training of labor which cannot be done by individual capitalists, is done by that agent of monopoly capital—the state. The student, by studying, creates value within himself in the form of skilled labor power and in so doing performs an exploited and alienated labor. The nature of the specific labor of the student gives his struggles to control or change the conditions of that labor a class content. The struggles of students to break out of their alienated labor and destroy the class institutions in which they exist are part of the class struggle.

"Some argue that students are intellectuals in the classic sense that Lenin and Mao conceived of revolutionary intellectuals imbuing the masses with the idea of socialism. It must be understood that Lenin and Mao were writing about societies more that 80 percent illiterate. Students then participated in more mass communications and were able to carry ideas from one sector to another. The student today is in a totally different role. All of society is literate and heavily saturated with mass communications. The student is merely a worker in training and is as mystified as the general population. Besides, anyone who has any experience in our organization knows that it is not an intellectual movement and does not pretend to be.

"Others argue that when students support working class struggles they are working class, and when they do not, they are not. This garbles the entire analysis; the class content of the students' struggle is determined by their objective class position. This does not mean there is never any false consciousness. Clearly the demand for student power is analogous to the skilled workers' struggle to protect privileges—say to constrict access to the skill in keeping out blacks. This kind of struggle for protection of privilege must be opposed. But neither the student seeking student power nor the skilled worker seeking exclusion is thereby outside the working class—he is struggling for a particular, rather than class, interest based on a false consciousness. To overcome this false consciousness it is necessary to continue to raise issues concerning the most oppressed sectors of the working class—especially the Vietnamese and the blacks—and to emphasize that their struggle is the same one."[81]

Finally in June 1969, what was to become the Weatherman faction of SDS issued its manifesto, "You Don't Need a Weatherman to Know Which Way the Wind Blows," and distributed it at the general SDS convention. It included this long passage:

"In general, young people have less stake in a society (no family, fewer debts, etc.), are more open to new ideas (they have not been brainwashed for so long or so well), and are therefore more able and willing to move in a revolutionary direction. Specifically in America, young people have grown up experiencing the crises in imperialism. They have grown up along with a developing black liberation movement, with the liberation of Cuba, the fights for independence in Africa, and the war in Vietnam. Older people grew up during the fight against Fascism, during the cold war, the smashing of the trade unions, McCarthy, and a period during which real wages consistently rose—since 1965 disposable real income has decreased slightly, particularly in urban areas where inflation and increased taxation have bitten heavily into wages. This crisis in imperialism affects all parts of the society. America has had to militarize to protect and expand its Empire; hence the high draft calls and the creation of a standing army of three and a half million, an army which still has been unable to win in Vietnam. Further, the huge defense expenditures—required for the defense of the Empire and at the same time a way of making increasing profits for the defense industries—have gone hand in hand with the urban crisis around welfare, the hospitals, the schools, housing, air, and water pollution. The State cannot provide

[81] "More on Youth Movement," *New Left Notes*, May 13, 1969.

the services it has been forced to assume responsibility for, and needs to increase taxes and to pay its growing debts while it cuts services and uses the pigs to repress protest. The private sector of the economy can't provide jobs, particularly unskilled jobs. The expansion of the defense and education industries by the State since World War II is in part an attempt to pick up the slack, though the inability to provide decent wages and working conditions for 'public' jobs is more and more a problem.

"As imperialism struggles to hold together this decaying social fabric, it inevitably resorts to brute force and authoritarian ideology. People, especially young people, more and more find themselves in the iron grip of authoritarian institutions. Reaction against the pigs or teachers in the schools, welfare pigs or the army is generalizable and extends beyond the particular repressive institution to the society and the State as a whole. The legitimacy of the State is called into question for the first time in at least 30 years, and the anti-authoritarianism which characterizes the youth rebellion turns into rejection of the State, a refusal to be socialized into American society. Kids used to try to beat the system from inside the army or from inside the schools; now they desert from the army and burn down the schools.

"The crisis in imperialism has brought about a breakdown in bourgeois social forms, culture and ideology. The family falls apart, kids leave home, women begin to break out of traditional 'female' and 'mother' roles. There develops a 'generation gap' and a 'youth problem.' Our heroes are no longer struggling businessmen, and we also begin to reject the ideal career of the professional and look to Mao, Che, the Panthers, the Third World, for our models, for motion. We reject the elitist, technocratic bullshit that tells us only experts can rule, and look instead to leadership from the people's war of the Vietnamese. Chuck Berry, Elvis, the Temptations brought us closer to the 'people's culture' of Black America. The racist response to the civil rights movement revealed the depth of racism in America, as well as the impossibility of real change through American institutions. And the war against Vietnam is not 'the heroic war against the Nazis'; it's the big lie, with napalm burning through everything we had heard this country stood for. Kids begin to ask questions: Where is the Free World? And who do the pigs protect at home?

"The breakdown in bourgeois culture and concomitant anti-authoritarianism is fed by the crisis in imperialism, but also in turn feeds that crisis, exacerbates it so that people no longer merely want the plastic '50s restored, but glimpse an alternative (like inside the Columbia buildings) and begin to fight for it. We don't want teachers to be more kindly cops; we want to smash cops; and build a new life.

"The contradictions of decaying imperialism fail hardest on youth in four distinct areas—the schools, jobs, the draft and the army, and the pigs and the courts. (A) In jail-like schools, kids are fed a mish-mash of racist, male chauvinist, anti-working class, anti-communist lies while being channelled into job and career paths set up according to the priorities of monopoly capital. At the same time, the State is becoming increasingly incapable of providing enough money to keep the schools going at all. (B) Youth unemployment is three times average unemployment. As more jobs are threatened by automation or the collapse of specific industries, unions act to secure jobs for those already employed. New people in the labor market can't find jobs, job stability is undermined (also because of increasing speed-up and more intolerable safety conditions) and people are less and less going to work in the same shop for 40 years. And, of course, when they do find jobs, young people get the worst ones and have the least seniority. (C) There are now two and a half million soldiers under thirty who are forced to police the world, kill and be killed in wars of imperialist domination. And (D) as a 'youth problem' develops out of all this, the pigs and courts enforce curfews, set up pot busts, keep people off the streets, and repress any youth movement at all.

"In all of this, it is not that life in America is toughest for youth or that they are the most oppressed. Rather, it is that young people are hurt directly—and severely—by imperialism. And, in being less tightly tied to the system, they are more 'pushed' to join the black liberation struggle against U.S. imperialism. Among young people there is less of a material base for racism—they have no seniority, have not spent 20 years securing a skilled job (the white monopoly of which is increasingly challenged by the black liberation movement), and aren't just about to pay off a 25-year mortgage on a house which is valuable because it's located in a white neighborhood.

"While these contradictions of imperialism fall hard on all youth, they fall hardest on the youth of the most oppressed (least privileged) sections of the working class. Clearly these youth have the greatest material base for struggle. They are the ones who most often get drafted, who get the worst jobs if they get any, who are most abused by the various institutions of social control from the army to decaying schools, to the pigs and the courts. And their day-to-day existence indicates a potential for militancy and toughness. They are the people whom we can reach who at this stage are most ready to engage in militant revolutionary struggle.

"The point of the revolutionary youth movement strategy is to move from a predominant student elite base to more oppressed (less privileged) working class youth as a way of deepening and expanding the revolutionary youth movement—not of giving up what we have gained, not giving up our old car for a new Dodge. This is part of a strategy to reach the entire working class to engage in struggle against imperialism;

moving from more privileged sections of white working class youth to more oppressed sections to the entire working class as a whole, including importantly what has classically been called the industrial proletariat. But this should not be taken to mean that there is a magic moment after we reach a certain percentage of the working class when all of a sudden we become a working class movement. We are already that if we put forward internationalist proletarian politics. We also don't have to wait to become a revolutionary force. We must be a self-conscious revolutionary force from the beginning, not be a movement which takes issues to some mystical group—'THE PEOPLE'—who will make the revolution. We must be a revolutionary movement of people understanding the necessity to reach more people, all working people, as we make the revolution"[82]

The Weatherman analysis has been severely criticized by many of the other New Left groups in the United States. Some of the criticism is based on differing class analysis. Other, such as that emanating from the pseudo-Maoist Progressive Labor Party, claims that all nationalism is reactionary and that therefore blacks as blacks can never be revolutionary vanguard. The Old Left, meanwhile, is down on the Weathermen for pushing terrorism, sabotage, and bombings. In general, most anti-Weathermen insist that the proletariat and only the proletariat can be the revolutionary force. Whatever the debate's ideological complexion, however, it centers fundamentally on the question of how the U.S. can be defeated rather than by whom. I think that in trying to answer "how" we can also find out "who."

In the modern era, only three types of revolution have successfully brought about a radical restructuring of society: insurrection; people's war; and *foco*-motor. The Russian Revolution of October 1917 best illustrates the insurrection model; so far it is also the only one. The Chinese Communist and the Viet Minh revolutions are examples of the second. So far Cuba furnishes the only example of a successful revolution triggered by a small group of guerrillas (a *foco*) acting as the motor to a general upheaval.

Other countries, to be sure, have undergone structure changes. And other countries, to be sure, have successfully made popular revolutions. Algeria and Yemen, for example, overturned their previous colonial regimes via long struggles involving aspects of people's war. The 1910–1917 Mexican Revolution included both insurrection and guerrilla warfare. The 1952 Bolivian uprising brought to power people who in no way previously participated in the ruling class. The military coups in Iran, Syria, Egypt, Sudan, and Libya also wiped out the previous ruling classes. So did the so-called revolutions in Eastern Europe and North

[82]*New Left Notes*, Convention Issue (June 1969). For complete documentation see "Debate Within SDS: RYM II vs. Weatherman," published by Radical Education Project, Detroit, Mich., 1969.

Korea, though their success, except for Yugoslavia, was due to the World War II liberating forces of the Soviet Red Army. Old colonialists and ruling classes have been thrown out of many other countries, such as Turkey (under Ataturk), the French Congo, Guinea, Ghana, Tanzania (including Zanzibar), Guyana, Indonesia, India, Ceylon, etc.

By our view, however, none of these countries has had a popular revolution. We should therefore define what we mean by a popular revolution. First of all, such a revolution means the participation of the people in its process to the end. That would automatically exclude most of the countries cited above, certainly the Middle Eastern countries and those former colonies where the colonialists decided, for one reason or another, to get out. To what extent this is important can be illustrated by the case of Kenya, where a vast number of Kikuyu tribesmen and some significant numbers of Luos fought the British for a long time (the Mau Mau rebellion, for example), but where the British left not as a result of being defeated militarily. Jomo Kenyatta was *allowed* to take power. That is, to a certain extent, he was picked by the British, not Kenyans. He would certainly have been put into power by Kenyans had they chased the British out, but the fact that he actually owed his place to England, not victorious revolutionaries (no matter how long and valiantly they had previously fought), made the change in rulers not a popular revolution. Frantz Fanon was perhaps one of the few to understand this. That is why he advised Kenyatta not to accept independence but to "seize it."[83] Jomo accepted it, and today Kenya is a neo-colonialized country run mostly by U.S. agents. In 1969, the majority of Kenyatta's own cabinet was made up of men who had opposed his release from a British concentration camp, while the vast majority of the forest fighters, who won his freedom, were dead or jailed, and the survivors landless and without a say in the running of the state.

The second criteria for a popular revolution is that it arm the people as they join the struggle, and *keep them armed* at least during the restructuring phase. This was certainly true in Russia where the proletariat kept their arms until the New Economic Policy (1921). It was true in China and Cuba, and still is. The people's militia in both those countries forms the backbone of the revolutionary governments (and of course in North Vietnam, which is at war). In every country where the government represents a class of exploiters, only the repressive forces are armed

---

[83] See his *Toward the African Revolution* (New York and London: Monthly Review Press, 1967); also *The Wretched of the Earth*, cited above. On Kenya see Josiah Mwangi Kariuki, '*Mau Mau*' *Detainee* (London: Penguin, 1964); Waruhiu Itote (General China), '*Mau Mau*' *General* (Nairobi: East African Publishing House, 1967); Oginga Odinga, *Not Yet Uhuru* (London: Heinemann, 1967); and especially the "Wananchi Declaration: The Programme of the Kenya People's Union," pamphlet, no date (1969).

(the police, armies, intelligence bureaus, etc.). In those where the government represents the popular classes, however, the people must be armed, at least during the transitional period to people's democracy. Otherwise a new class can easily install itself in the seat of government and become the new ruling class. This in fact is what happened in most Eastern European countries, and a case can be made that it happened in Russia itself after Lenin.

The third prerequisite for a popular *successful* revolution is that the winners totally junk the old machinery of state. To simply take it over and use it is to adapt the revolution to the old order's methodology. There can be no shortcuts to restructuring. Marx and Engels saw this when they analyzed the failure of France's Commune.[84] And Lenin stressed in *The State and Revolution*: "One thing especially was proved by the Commune, viz., that 'the working class cannot simply lay hold of the ready-made state machinery and wield it for its own purposes.' "[85] And again: "the working class must *break up, smash* the 'ready-made state machinery,' and not confine itself merely to laying hold of it."[86] The reason is simple enough: A popular revolution means a revolution by and for the popular classes. Its ultimate aim is to bring all classes into one, that is, destroy the class state. "Equality," said Engels in *Anti-Dühring*, "becomes a prejudice if it is not understood to mean the *abolition of classes*."[87] This can only be done by destroying the bourgeois bureaucracy, which in essence separates people into classes. The only way bureaucracy can be destroyed is by changing the administrative system altogether: Administrators must administer things, not people. "We can fight bureaucracy to the bitter end, to a complete victory, only when the whole population participates in the work of government," said Lenin in a speech to the Eighth Congress of the Russian Communist Party. "In the bourgeois republics not only is this impossible, *but the law itself prevents it*."[88] Certainly, participatory democracy—the war cry of the New Left—cannot be totally established until the whole country (perhaps the whole world) is socialist ("to each according to his ability") and moving to communism ("from each according to his ability, to each according to his need"). But the revolution can never be socialist as long as the apparatus created by bourgeois law (the bureaucratic state machinery) is not destroyed. And this is impossible unless the revolution smashes the old machinery and builds a new one from the base up. Russia under Lenin did so until 1921, China waged a cultural revolution to achieve it and Cuba continuously attempts it with various degrees of success. Nasser, the

[84] Last preface to the German edition of *The Communist Manifesto*, dated June 24, 1872, in *Works* (Moscow: 1962), I, p. 22.

[85] *Works*, II, p. 293.   [86] *Ibid.*, p. 294 (Lenin's emphasis).

[87] (Moscow: Foreign Languages Publishing House, 1962), p. 148 (Engels' emphasis).

[88] *Works*, III, p. 161 (Lenin's emphasis).

Ba'ath, the Bolivians, the Mexicans, Nkrumah, Sekou Touré, *et al.*, did not. Unless these three criteria—people's participation, arming the people, smashing the old machinery—mold the revolution, the total restructuring of society into a *popular* democracy cannot be achieved. The next question, then, is: How can one make sure these three criteria are fulfilled? Obviously, only by seizing power when conditions are so ripe for revolution that vast numbers of people are ready and willing to participate in it. Such conditions are called *objective*, because they have nothing to do with individuals' revolutionary acts and statements. Famine, war, racial conflict, flagrant exploitation, cruel repressions, depressions, etc.—these make up objective conditions for revolution.

But most countries in the world today endure such conditions, certainly the U.S.-dominated Third World. Yet revolutions are not exploding in each of them. The reason is that the masses have not been made conscious of their revolutionary potential. To make them thus conscious can be done only by revolutionary cadres. In other words, the *subjective* conditions must also be ripe: Leaders must be well trained, propaganda effective, analyses correct, etc. To Lenin, none of this was possible unless a solid revolutionary organization of full-time cadres knew exactly what to do and say in each circumstance, and no such organization could be welded unless its members were sure of their own aims, both in general and in particular. That is, the strategy (which is principled) must be clear before any tactic (which is not and can be varied) is devised. The revolutionary organization must hence be armed with revolutionary theory. "Without revolutionary theory," said Lenin in *What Is to Be Done?* "there can be no revolutionary movement."[89]

But the revolutionary is not born out of academia, ivory towers divorced from day-to-day reality. Indeed, Lenin himself wrote in *Pravda* in 1923: "Napoleon, I think, wrote: *'On s'engage et puis . . . on voit.'* Rendered freely this means: 'First engage in a serious battle and then see what happens.' "[90] This did not mean that Lenin favored spontaneous action. On the contrary, he often condemned spontaneity in revolution, especially in *What Is to Be Done?* But he also clearly stated that no popular revolution or rebellion can ever be wrong. Quoting Marx, he said: "Communists support every revolutionary movement."[91]

He did insist, however, that unless the spontaneous rebellions are quickly organized by the party, they would fail. "Absolutely hostile to all abstract formulas and to all doctrinaire recipes," he wrote in his essay on guerrilla warfare (see below, p. 84), Marxism "positively does not reject any form of struggle. . . . Marxism learns, if we may so express it, from mass practice, and makes no claim whatever to teach the masses forms of struggle invented by 'systematisers' in the seclusion of their

[89] *Works*, I, p. 117.   [90] *Works*, III, p. 768.   [91] *Works*, I, p. 166.

studies." What Marxism does demand is "an absolute historical examination of the question of the forms of struggle." In *The Right of Nations to Self-Determination*, he added, "The categorical requirement of Marxist theory in investigating any social question is that it be examined within *definite* historical limits, and, if it refers to a particular country (e.g., the national programme for a given country), that account be taken of the specific features distinguishing that country from others in the same historical epoch."[92]

To Lenin, then, there could be nothing dogmatic about revolutionary theory. It was to be born of the actual popular struggles. Each such struggle, analyzed historically and in its specific setting, would generate new ideas, used to elucidate trends, causes, reactions, etc. Building from one to the other, eventually the revolutionary cadre would become equipped with a theory rooted in experience, broadened by historical knowledge, tested by combat, and fortified by reflection. And, said Lenin, time is on the side of revolutionaries: "The revolution itself must not by any means be regarded as a single act . . . , but as a series of more or less powerful outbreaks rapidly alternating with periods of more or less complete calm."[93]

Why is it, then, that the Old Left today so severely condemns the tactics of the New Left? The criticism is based primarily on two major Lenin works—*What Is to Be Done?* (1902) in which he attacks spontaneity, and *"Left-Wing" Communism—An Infantile Disorder* (1920), in which he blasts the communist extremists in Germany and elsewhere who refuse to participate in legal struggles against the bourgeois regimes. In the latter, Lenin insists that communists must use both legal and illegal means of struggle, must work in the trade unions, must try to get elected to parliaments, etc. But, faithful to his dictum of analyzing within concrete situations, Lenin insists on this legal struggle precisely because it is possible. By his own approach to problems, it is most probable that Lenin would not consider running for elective office in the United States a correct tactic: The U.S. does not allow proportional representation, hence no communist candidate is "electable," and it does not give equal TV and radio time to "off-beat" candidates (as does France, for example). Thus, one of Lenin's primary considerations—namely, using the bourgeois system for communist propaganda—does not apply in the U.S.

But there is another aspect of Lenin's criticism which is very relevant to revolutionaries today. In *"Left-Wing" Communism*, Lenin insists on legal work because he has total faith in the incorruptibility of party cadre. By and large, he was right in his time. His own cadres were dedicated to the Party, to the working class, to the Revolution. In most cases, their total commitment dated from about 1900, and they seized power in 1917,

[92] *Ibid.*, p. 606.   [93] *Works*, I, p. 243.

a relatively short period; even in a man's own lifetime, two decades of struggle to victory is not too long to strain a man's incentive. Looking at Germany, where the success of the Revolution seemed nearer and nearer, even after the murders of Spartacist League leaders Rosa Luxemburg and Karl Liebknecht, Lenin could make his analyses without taking into account the *psychological* reality of men put into legal struggles for forty years without any sign of approaching victory. In the United States, for example, some of the old CP hacks have been used to comfortable houses, cars, travel, etc., for almost forty years. Is it feasible to assume that they will sacrifice it all at the drop of a hat when the crucial moment for revolution occurs? Is it wise to assume that such men, even if totally dedicated to revolution, will be able to judge correctly that crucial moment? And, more importantly, will those for whom the revolution is sought—the exploited and alienated—be able to have confidence in such men, who are obviously neither exploited nor alienated? These questions, to which we shall return when we consider the *foco* theory, are crucial today not only in the U.S. but all over the world.

The point remains: Lenin's criticisms, in fact all of his analyses, were based on historical data and specific conditions in time and space. Never did he mean to imply that his generalizations would apply to all cases in all times, only to those that have occurred in the past. "New forms of struggle, unknown to the participants of the given period, inevitably arise as the given social situation changes," he wrote in "Guerrilla Warfare." "The coming crisis will introduce new forms of struggle that we are now unable to foresee." Even terrorism, which he condemned because it tended to alienate people without building a revolutionary organization, he did so undogmatically.

In *What Is to Be Done?* Lenin did strongly attack both spontaneity and terrorism or adventuristic calls to action. "As for calling the masses to action, that will come of itself as soon as energetic political agitation, live and striking exposures come into play. . . . Calls for action, not in general, but in the concrete sense of the term can be made only at the place of action; only those who themselves go into action, and do so immediately, can sound such calls."[94] (Which is precisely the New Left's position: Agitate only for what you are prepared to do yourself.) But Lenin was condemning those who were trying to push the working class into militant street action by using their trade union demands. He opposed this for two reasons, both practical. On the one hand, he said, not to realize that the working class is perfectly capable of fighting for its own demands is to "*underestimate* the revolutionary activity of the masses," while to transform it into a force to shock, to use terrorism as a means of "exciting the working class movement," is to try to

94 *Works*, I, p. 156.

"substitute terror for agitation," which simply doesn't work.[95] On the other hand, not to use political agitation and propaganda to transform the working class into a revolutionary vanguard is to forget that "the history of all countries shows that the working class, exclusively by its own effort, is able to develop only trade union consciousness."[96] Finally Lenin found that spontaneity politics, i.e., agitational calls to action based around trade union demands, is the same as trade union politics (which he called economism), and both are bourgeois politics. But as far as terrorism in general was concerned, Lenin never discarded it *on principle.* "It was, of course, only on the grounds of expediency that we rejected individual terrorism," he said in *"Left Wing" Communism* (the very book which the Old Left cites most to put down the New).[97] It is a crucial distinction, first, because most revolutionaries, unfortunately, think it important to remain faithful to Lenin's teachings, and second, because it shows that Lenin was totally a pragmatist when analyzing tactics (but not when dealing with strategy), which is what all revolutionaries should be.

As a pragmatist, Lenin believed that the only way a revolution could come about in Europe in his time was by the creation of a revolutionary organization. That organization had to be tight, well trained, loyal to its central committee, dedicated—and narrow, not only for ideological reasons (hence purges and sectarian splits were to be encouraged during its formative years[98]) but also for security. "The more we *confine* the membership of such an organization to people who are professionally engaged in revolutionary activity and who have been professionally trained in the art of combating the political police, the more difficult will it be to unearth the organization."[99] And clearly, by training Lenin did not mean just study groups or trade union infiltration. He meant action. "Let the squads begin to train for immediate operations," he wrote after the 1905 massacre; "some can undertake to assassinate a spy or blow up a police station, others can attack a bank to expropriate funds for an insurrection. Let every squad learn, if only by beating up police."[100] (Which are precisely the tactics of black revolutionary movements and the Weathermen.)

Besides training and agitation (propaganda) among the masses, Lenin also strongly advocated infiltration and agitation in the state armies. In *The Proletarian Revolution and the Renegade Kautsky*, Lenin said: "Not

[95] *Works,* I, pp. 161–62.   [96] *Ibid.,* p. 122.   [97] *Works,* III, p. 348.

[98] And from 1902, when his vanguard organ, the paper *Iskra (Spark),* was barely functioning well, Lenin ruthlessly manipulated splits in order to weed out from the organization those he considered weak or unreliable.

[99] *Works,* I, p. 200.

[100] Letter to St. Petersburg Social Democrats, cited in "Lenin" by Brenda Jones, *The New York Times Magazine,* April 5, 1970.

a single great revolution has ever taken place, or ever can take place, without the 'disorganization' of the army. For the army is the most ossified instrument for supporting the old regime, the most hardened bulwark of bourgeois discipline, buttressing up the rule of capital, and preserving and fostering among the working people the servile spirit of submission and subjection to capital. Counter-revolution has never tolerated, and never could tolerate, armed workers side by side with the army."[101] Lenin's aim was to set up dual power before the revolution: the state above, and below, workers' power (what today would be called peoples' power, black power, brown power, etc. When the Black Panthers began establishing their breakfast program, they were in effect spreading this dual power—which is why they were so viciously repressed). But when all is said and done, Lenin's primary advice for revolutionaries was simple: *"de l'audace, de l'audace, encore de l'audace."*[102]

Audacity is precisely what characterized best Mao Tse-tung and the Chinese revolutionaries. But they also had an equal portion of tenacity. Thus when it appeared to all and sundry that they were beaten, they merely retreated, started anew, and gradually reassaulted their enemies, wiping them out more than twenty years later. The Chinese communists did not win through general insurrection as had the Russians. Nor did they focus their attention on the cities, as had the Bolsheviks. Instead, they fought in the countryside, establishing not dual power but separate power, that is, areas where they were in complete control, and then kept expanding those areas until they surrounded and strangled the cities. To do so, they had to fight a civil war. But then, so did the Bolsheviks, after they had seized power in central Russia.

Neither the Bolsheviks nor the Chinese communists shunned such conflagration. Both knew it was inevitable. As Lenin had said in 1906, more than a decade before, he was proved correct: "The enemies of our revolution among the people are few in number, but as the struggle grows more acute they become more and more organized and receive the support of the reactionary strata of the bourgeoisie. It is therefore absolutely natural and inevitable that in such a period, a period of nationwide political strikes, an uprising cannot assume the old form of individual acts restricted to a very short time and to a very small area. It is absolutely natural and inevitable that the uprising should assume the higher and more complex form of a prolonged civil war embracing the whole country, i.e., an armed struggle between two sections of the people."[103] In fact, civil war has always accompanied revolution, whatever its ideology. It

[101] *Works*, III, p. 91.

[102] *Works*, II, p. 427. Actually the slogan, often quoted by Engels, was transformed somewhat in the retranslation of Danton's original shout: *de l'audace, encore de l'audace, toujours l'audace.* (More or less: "audacity, more audacity, always audacity.")

[103] "Guerrilla Warfare"; see Introduction below, p. 84.

happened in France in 1789–93, for example, and also in the U.S. in 1776–80, where far more settlers, proportionally, left America in hatred of George Washington than from Cuba because of Fidel.

At first, the Chinese communist Revolution stuck faithfully to the Leninist program. The CP loyally cooperated with the bourgeois-military regime of Chiang Kai-shek (who had taken over as titular head of the Chinese Republic when Sun Yat-sen died in 1925), and focused most of its activities among the proletarians of the major cities. Receiving Russian aid, Chiang successfully defeated one warlord after another as he marched north on his "great unification" drive. But it was the workers, led by their dynamic and dashing leader, Chou En-lai, who seized Shanghai. Chou then agreed to turn over the city to Chiang and his Kuomintang (nationalist party), which the Russians viewed somewhat as the equivalent to their own provisional government. But Chiang was far worse than Kerensky. In April 1927, as Chiang's forces occupied Shanghai, they immediately set upon their allies, slaughtering thousands of workers and every communist they could find (Chou was tipped off by a friend at the last minute; Mao himself was captured but managed to dive into a long patch of high grass and escaped—only 200 yards away from the wall where he would have been shot).

After Chiang's double-cross, Mao, who was then not the top leader in the CP, led a peasant revolt. When it failed, he was repudiated as an adventurer by his Party comrades. Undaunted, he took his 1,000 weary, beaten, surviving peasants into the mountains of Chingkangshan along the border of Hunan and Kiangsi provinces and began to wage guerrilla warfare. In April 1928, he was joined by Chu Teh, a conscience-ridden Chiang general, and the 2,000 men he had managed to lead out of the Kuomintang army. Together, they established their first liberated area, where landlords were executed or exiled, land was given to peasants, corruption was totally eliminated, taxes lowered and collected fairly, etc. In his report to the Central Committee, Mao said: "China is the only country in the world today where one or more small areas under Red political power have emerged in the midst of a White regime which encircles them. We find on analysis that one reason for this phenomenon lies in the incessant splits and wars within China's comprador and landlord classes. So long as these splits and wars continue, it is possible for an armed independent regime of workers and peasants to survive and grow. In addition, its survival and growth require the following conditions: (1) a sound base, (2) a sound Party organization, (3) a fairly strong Red Army, (4) terrain favorable to military operations, and (5) economic resources sufficient for sustenance."[104]

Incredibly, however, Mao continued to honor the alliance with the

---

[104] November 25, 1928, in *Works* (Peking: Foreign Languages Press, 1965) I, p. 73.

Kuomintang as Russia demanded—except, of course, when attacked. In the same report, he explained his reasons: "We fully agree with the Communist International's resolution on China. There is no doubt that China is still at the stage of the bourgeois-democratic revolution. The programme for a thorough democratic revolution in China comprises, externally, the overthrow of imperialism so as to achieve complete national liberation,[105] and, internally, the elimination of the power and influence of the comprador class in the cities, the completion of the agrarian revolution in order to abolish feudal relations in the villages, and the overthrow of the government of the warlords. We must go through such a democratic revolution before we can lay a real foundation for the transition to socialism. In the past year we have fought in many places and are keenly aware that the revolutionary tide is on the ebb in the country as a whole. While Red political power has been established in a few small areas, in the country as a whole the people lack the ordinary democratic rights, the workers, the peasants and even the bourgeois democrats do not have freedom of speech or assembly, and the worst crime is to join the Communist Party. Wherever the Red Army goes, the masses are cold and aloof, and only after our propaganda do they slowly move into action. Whatever enemy units we face, there are hardly any cases of mutiny or desertion, to our side, and we have to fight it out. This holds even for the enemy's Sixth Army which recruited the greatest number of 'rebels' after the May 21st Incident.[106] We have an acute sense of our isolation which we keep hoping will end. Only by launching a political and economic struggle for democracy, which will also involve the urban petty bourgeoisie, can we turn the revolution into a seething tide that will surge through the country."[107]

Progress in the urban areas was much slower, however. Yet, despite the fact that every city uprising was crushed, the Chinese CP, obedient to the Russian experience, insisted that the Revolution must be waged by workers, not peasants, and refused to earmark any aid to the Mao-Chu enclave. Mao, whose solid peasant background gave him faith in his people, tried gently to persuade the Central Committee. In a letter to party cadre, entitled "A Single Spark Can Start a Prairie Fire," he wrote: "It would be wrong to abandon the struggle in the cities, but in our opinion

---

[105] China was still totally dominated economically by the great powers (England, France, Japan, the U.S.) and often militarily, politically, culturally and by the police as well. As late as 1905 a sign in a Shanghai park read: "Dogs and Chinese not allowed."

[106] On May 21, 1927, a counterrevolutionary coup in Changsha, in Hunan, led to vast peasant massacres. Many of the surviving peasants were then drafted into the Sixth Army. Changsha was Mao's home town; his first wife and her younger sister died in that massacre.

[107] *Works*, I, pp. 97–98.

it would also be wrong for any of our Party members to fear the growth of peasant strength lest it would outstrip the workers' strength and harm the revolution." It is then also that Mao issued his famous guerrilla warfare slogan: "the enemy advances, we retreat; the enemy camps, we harass; the enemy tires, we attack; the enemy retreats, we pursue."[108]

These tactics did not please the CP hierarchy. It ordered them changed in 1932, when it abandoned its Shanghai underground for the safety of Mao's liberated area, which was now in southern Kiangsi. Despite the fact that Mao and Chu were doing well—they had defeated sixteen out of the thirty-three divisions Chiang sent against them in his "annihilation campaign"—the CP theorists nevertheless insisted that Mao's policy of quick withdrawals was alienating the farmers left behind, and forced him to alter his tactics. With his mobility gone and Chiang attacking in strength (even when invading Japanese seized Manchuria and prepared to assault China proper) Mao, who still had the complete loyalty of the communist field commanders, decided to leave Kiangsi for northern Yenan— a forced march of 6,000 miles, a distance equivalent to that between the tip of South Africa and Glasgow. In the process, he took over complete control of the Political Bureau of the Party's Central Committee, and in December 1935 became top policy formation leader.

It is then that Mao called for a united front with his enemies, Chiang's Kuomintang, to fight the Japanese, who had invaded China proper. "If our government," said Mao, "has hitherto been based on the alliance of the workers, the peasants and the urban petty bourgeoisie, from now on it must be so transformed as to include also the members of all other classes who are willing to take part in the national revolution . . . it may include those who are interested only in the national revolution and not in the agrarian revolution, and even, if they so desire, those who may oppose Japanese imperialism and its running dogs, though they are not opposed to the European and U.S. imperialists because of their close ties with the latter. . . . In 1927, . . . the revolutionary united front had no mainstay, no strong revolutionary armed forces. . . . Today things are different. Now we have a strong Communist Party and a strong Red Army, and we also have the base areas of the Red Army. Not only are the Communist Party and the Red Army serving as the initiator of a national united front against Japan today, but in the future too they will inevitably become the powerful mainstay of China's anti-Japanese government and army, capable of preventing the Japanese imperialists and Chiang Kai-shek from carrying through their policy of disrupting this united front."[109]

The alliance was brittle. In 1936, Chiang was kidnapped by rebellious Kuomintang officers and *handed to the communists*. Under orders from

[108] *Works*, I, pp. 123, 124.   [109] *Works*, I, pp. 165–67.

Moscow, he was released—but only after promising to send his troops against the Japanese, not the Reds. Instead, Chiang held his troops back, letting the Red armies do most of the fighting. And they did it well. By 1937, Mao ruled 30,000 square miles and two million people. By 1939, the Eighth Route and the New Fourth armies, which had been welded into steel by Chu Teh, quadrupled the Red liberated areas. It was then that Mao wrote *The Chinese Revolution and the Chinese Communist Party* as a textbook for CP cadre-formation schools.[110] It is this text which elevated Mao's two-stage revolution from a tactic (means) to a strategy (principle). First, said Mao, organize a solid communist apparatus. Then, develop a Red army under the direction of the apparatus. Next, launch a patriotic or democratic war against foreign imperialists. Only when this has been brought to a successful conclusion, undertake the next stage—the socialist revolution. This means that the war will be very prolonged ("protracted," to use his word). It must be fought primarily in the rural areas: because the imperialists always control the cities; because guerrilla warfare needs the mobility possible only in an extensive territory; because the economy is always uneven, to the disfavor of the rural population; and because the counterrevolutionary camp is disunited outside its cities (in Vietnam later, for example, some U.S. militarists wanted only to hold the enclaves, others to constantly launch search-destroy-withdraw operations, and still others to occupy and pacify the whole country). But Mao also warned that unless the CP had strong links within the cities the rural apparatus would easily become isolated. Hence, city work was to remain important. But in the cities, the proletariat cannot win alone. It must, therefore, enter into alliances with every anti-imperialist force. The united front, then, must be prepared to join the legal struggle (elections, trade unions, etc.) and win over the national bourgeoisie. Thus, the first stage of revolution must be anti-imperialist (i.e., anti-foreign capital) but not anticapitalist (i.e., not anti-national capital).

Mao's strategy worked perfectly. Though Chiang's rested troops attacked Mao's war-worn armies immediately after Japan had been chased out of China, the country's moral support went solidly to the communists. Chiang was forced to use his troops to quell disorders in the cities, and could no longer control inflation. Within four years, despite massive U.S. aid, arms, and advisers, the Kuomintang was smashed. Mao and his men, their clothes in tatters but their spirits elated, entered Peking in March 1949, singing. Immediately, Mao went into stage two of the Revolution, and by 1951, China was communist.

To the Chinese, it was then clear that by following their model the people of any imperialized country could do as well. Marshal Lin Piao, Mao's heir-designate, saw in the Chinese experience a world-scale model;

[110] *Works*, II, pp. 305–34; included in this volume as "Revolution in Two Stages," p. 96 below.

in each underdeveloped country (especially in Asia), he said, communists should organize the peasants, lead a protracted people's war, surround and strangle the cities, the bastions of imperialism. In September 1965, Lin Piao wrote an article commemorating the twentieth anniversary of Japan's defeat. Published in *Renmin Ribae* (*People's Daily*), it soon became known the world over as the "Lin Piao theory" for people's war and revolution in the underdeveloped world through the "strangulation of the cities." Of fundamental importance to all Maoists, it not only explained how people's war was to be fought—stressing the need for united anti-imperialist fronts, that is, for alliances with the national bourgeoisies—but also emphasized the subordination of the military to the political. "During the anti-Japanese war our army staunchly performed three tasks, fighting, mass work, and production," he said. "It was at the same time a fighting force, a political work force and a production corps. Everywhere it went, it did propaganda work among the masses, organized and armed them and helped them set up revolutionary political power. . . . The essence of a people's army is that politics is the commander. Political work is the lifeline of our army."

Then, generalizing broadly, he added: "The countryside and the countryside alone can provide the revolutionary bases from which the revolutionaries can go forward to final victory. Taking the entire globe, if North America and Western Europe can be called 'the cities of the world' then Asia, Africa and Latin America constitute 'the rural areas of the world' . . . in this stage of revolution, imperialism and its lackeys are the principal enemy; it is necessary to rally all anti-imperialist patriotic forces, including the national bourgeoisie. . . . It is very harmful to confuse the two stages, that is, the national-democratic and the socialist revolutions."[111]

Just as the Russian model failed in the early days of the Chinese Revolution, so the Chinese model failed in other Asian countries afterwards. To be sure, the Chinese model was not adhered to strictly, and confirmed Maoists can point to these divergencies as reasons for their failure. And some of the divergencies were outstanding. In Indonesia, for example, the Indonesian Communist Party (PKI) on the one hand made an absolute fetish of its alliance with President Sukarno and his forces (the national bourgeoisie), while on the other, though PKI boss D. N. Aidit swore faithfully by Peking, it never developed liberated areas, never launched a Red army, never prepared its cadre for protracted struggle. It was thus caught totally off guard by the October 1965 military-CIA coup. The result: 700,000 communists dead.

In the Philippines, the Communist Party (PKP) was faithful to Moscow, not Peking, yet developed a formidable military guerrilla apparatus, the

111 See below, p. 122. The "Lin Piao theory" of revolution is still applied wherever the revolutionaries are Maoist.

Huks, first to fight against Japan, then against the U.S. neo-colonialized Philippine government. Today, the Huks are totally divorced from the PKP and their struggle has certainly been protracted. Yet, although they are growing, the Chinese pattern is not being repeated.

To understand why, we must briefly review the Huks' history. When first set up, the Huks, though commanded by PKP officials, were basically nationalistic. They were perfectly willing to cooperate with the allies, and always did when asked—despite the fact that the other Philippine wartime guerrilla group, the U.S.-led USAFFE force which General Douglas MacArthur left behind when he retreated in 1942, often attacked the Huks even when both were pursued by the Japanese. It was the Huks and not the U.S. or USAFFE which liberated most of Central Luzon, including Manila. Yet even before the Japanese had been driven off the islands, General MacArthur ordered the Huks disarmed, then rounded up and, at times, in some grisly chapters of U.S.-Philippine relations, massacred. The PKP reacted by ordering Huk partisans to regroup in the jungles—into the Huklong Mapagpagpalayang Bayan, the People's Liberation Army.

The postwar Huks' leader was Luis Taruc, a long-time peasant organizer, wartime Huk hero, and a member of the Central Committee of the PKP. Another Huk leader was the American communist William J. Pomeroy, who was also in charge of information, often wrote Huk or PKP position papers under various pseudonyms, and wrote Luis Taruc's autobiography.[112]

Continuously pursued by U.S. forces and the U.S.-trained Philippine Constabulary, constantly betrayed by starving peasants who were offered fat bribes by the government (yet were not self-defensively terrorized by the Huks), the guerrillas began to suffer heavy losses in the late forties and early fifties. By then, most of the PKP's leadership was already in jail. Early in 1952, Pomeroy was captured (jailed until 1961, he was finally released and went to England, where he still lives). Then Luis Taruc, the self-educated tenant peasant's son turned national hero, defected—and talked. Finally, in 1956, the PKP, whose armed-struggle policy seemed closely akin to China's, switched tactics, officially adopted Moscow's coexistence line, and ordered the Huks disbanded. The guerrilla menace was over—or so it was thought. The PKP got set to enter the legal (i.e., parliamentary) "road to power."

But under U.S. direction, the Philippines government remained unrelenting. In 1957, its "Anti-Subversion Act" not only outlawed the Party but also made membership a felony. The Constabulary continued to hound its leaders, and many are still in jail, including Dr. Jesus Lava, the PKP secretary-general who was caught in 1965. Nevertheless, presumably

[112] *Born of the People* (New York: International Publishers, 1953).

under Russian "guidance," the PKP stuck to its peaceful policy. It called for a "broad anti-imperialist united front."[113] Lava himself insisted that "we want to be independent and nationalistic, and then socialistic, these steps taking form under democratic process."[114] In England today, Pomeroy supports this view completely, insisting that the political struggle is primordial. In the Philippines, that struggle is limited mostly to organizational activity within the ranks of the National Youth Movement (Kabataan Makabayan—KM) and the Labour Party (Lapiang Manggagawa—LM). Though neither KM nor LM are PKP "fronts," the "nationalistic" tendencies of all three seem to coincide and they have waged joint campaigns against Philippine involvement in the Vietnam War.

But such political maneuvers remain quite irrelevant outside Manila union and intellectual circles, where peasants still live in miserable prewar conditions. "In Central Luzon," reported London's conservative *The Economist*, "seven out of every ten farmers are still tenants. The total of unemployed is estimated at over a million (out of 8,000,000). Corruption in government is rife. All over the country there is rampant crime and a pervading sense of helplessness among the poor. And while the good life eludes the masses, they see profligate ostentation among the irresponsible elite . . . and American aid has only maintained the status quo."[115]

To these poor, what—or who—can be relevant? The Huks—"Robin Hoods" who execute rustlers, crooked officials, and bandits;[116] who pay for services rendered, expropriate land, and carry out agrarian reforms;[117] and who operate an invisible government in the countryside, "seemingly immune from counterattack."[118]

No longer led by communists of the PKP (who sometimes refer to them as bandits) but by such populist-nationalist communists as Faustino del Mundo (Commander Sumulong) and Pedro Taruc (Luis' cousin), today's Huks are made up of old diehard partisans who refused to give up their arms and of "radical reformers" who abandoned all hope of substantive structural changes without revolution. Although the picture is occasionally confused by Mafia-type gangsters who call themselves Huks to obtain local help, the guerrillas, says *The Economist* "have wide mass support . . . and reportedly have been moving around in company strength where a year ago they moved in groups of 20 or 30."[119] According to *U.S. News and World Report*, "the Huks control 176 villages, roughly 1 out of 12, in the poorest areas of Central Luzon."[120] And *Time*

---

[113] *World Marxist Review*, November 1963.   [114] *Manila Chronicle*, June 6, 1964.

[115] February 4, 1967.   [116] *Ibid*.

[117] *Philippine Herald*, June 9, 1966, and *Solidarity*, April–June 1966.

[118] *Problems of Communism*, March–April 1967.

[119] *Op. cit.*   [120] November 13, 1967.

reluctantly admits that the Huks "are supported by thousands of sympathetic or frightened peasants."[121]

The tactical reasons why the Huks have not only survived but grown so spectacularly in the late 1960's is that they have combined self-defense terrorism to frighten would-be informers with genuine concern and aid for the impoverished countryside population. Also, all Huk leaders today are actual fighters in close, constant, personal contact with peasants. The analytic reasons why Huks fight, however, have not changed since the forties and fifties. Pomeroy himself explained those reasons quite clearly many times then. In *Ang Komunista*, which he edited clandestinely, he wrote (under the pseudonym Ernesto Diaz): "Unlike other countries, where the growth of capitalism fostered its own national bourgeois class, in the Philippines, capitalism failed to develop to a sufficient degree to end the feudal methods of production. The imperialists did not force our country 'to embrace bourgeois methods of production.' On the contrary, it set about to preserve the precapitalist social structure in order to realize excessive profits at little risk and with cheap labor, at the same time restricting the growth of the proletariat. In this way, feudalism formed the backbone of imperialism in this country. Feudal landowners and the comprador-bourgeoisie soon became the cohorts of the imperialists. . . . In solving the national question, we must therefore face the fact that we cannot gain national liberation in our struggle against American imperialism by embracing bourgeois democracy. Another course is required. This course is the one blazed by the Chinese revolution."[122]

The fundamental difference between China in the forties and the Philippines today is that the latter is not occupied by foreign imperialists. Mao and Chu could and did successfully wage a patriotic war because of the Japanese invaders. They could and did appeal to all nonimperialist sectors of the population, *inside* the cities as well as out, to rally to their cause. The Huks cannot. Hence, they are restricted to rural areas. Since the PKP now repudiates them and since they have no urban apparatus, their protracted war remains isolated. No matter how successful they are in the countryside, Manila and the other major cities can ignore them. Obviously, some *additional* tactic has to be devised, or else the Chinese model is deficient in neo-colonialized countries.

In Burma, the revolutionaries are totally committed to Mao's thought. There, too, they have been waging armed struggle—for some twenty-two years of the Communist Party's thirty years of existence. In 1945, the CPB was one of the leading parties. In 1948, the civil war began. By 1950, the communists controlled most of the rural areas and almost every town and city except Rangoon, the capital. Then the government—first U Nu, next Ne Win—launched a series of counterattacks. Well-planned and well-

[121] February 21, 1969. [122] *Ang Komunista*, August 1950.

armed (by the British and the U.S., which secretly gave the army modern weapons[123] and napalm[124]), the government offensive regained much of the ground. In 1965, however, the communists increased their activity in thirty-one of Burma's fifty-odd provinces. Then on September 24, 1968, Thakin Than Tun, the Party's chairman, was killed, and once again the CPB's fate seemed to ebb—despite considerable successes carried by Burma's minorities, the Kachins, Shang, Karens, and Kayas, who also oppose the government and are allied to the communists. A year later, the guerrillas, led by Thakin Ba Thein Tin, seemed to be gaining once again, though the minority armies appeared to be dormant.[125]

Subjectively the see-saw can probably be explained by Party errors, failed alliances, wrong tactics. Objectively, the explanation may again be that Burma is not under foreign invasion, and the "White Flag" Communist Party (as it is called, since the Red Flag CP refers to the smaller Trotskyist party) does not maintain an independent machinery in Rangoon proper. Or else, not enough propaganda had been carried out among the peasants to ensure the guerrillas of infallible intelligence and local support, which Mao and Chu always had before launching military operations. They obtained such support by immediately carrying out an agrarian reform in the areas they controlled. But in order to enforce such reforms, they had to hold the area first.

In China, the circle was breakable simply because of its size: the communists could seize a remote area—in Kiangsi or Yenan—and hold it long enough to restructure its social relations before any government invasion. Indeed, the necessity of holding liberated areas was always fundamental to Chinese communist tacticians; as early as 1935, they insisted on it as a matter of strategy (principle).[126] But in such a relatively small country as Burma, the military can easily attack the guerrillas long before they have established their administrative power. In fact, with helicopter warfare a normal aspect of counterinsurgency today, even space is no guarantee; government troops can descend into the remotest jungle backlands within hours. In such cases, perhaps the only remedy is to propagandize the peasants without reforms through social clubs, Party cell study groups, charity food programs, teachers, doctors, veterinarians, agronomists, lawyers, etc. But then, the two-stage revolution is out of the question as the general line of the revolution must be tied to local problems, and in the cases described, foreign troops are not present.

123 *Time*, March 10, 1969.

124 Thakin Ba Thein Tin, "Armed Struggle and Mao's Thought," *Peking Review*, August 25 and September 1, 1967. The author was then the CP's vice-chairman.

125 *Le Monde*, May 8, 1969.

126 See the article on "Liberated Areas," in *Communist International*, March 5, 1935, by a Chinese theoretician calling himself "Li."

In Vietnam, Laos, Cambodia, Puerto Rico, Panama, Palestine, the Arab Gulf, Eritrea, Chad, the Portuguese-colonized areas of Africa, the apartheid countries of Africa, a patriotic or national war against the foreigners— the United States, England, Israel, France, Portugal, or the white ruling minorities—can catch the enthusiasm of the population. But in technically unoccupied countries, places like Burma, India, Ghana, Congo-Kinshasa, most of Latin America, etc., where the domination by foreigners is in-direct—through control of the economy and the local repressive forces— people's war cannot operate in two stages. Even if the local army, police, and paramilitary goon squads are trained, financed, and directed by U.S. or British "advisers," the identifiable enemy is not the foreigners but the national profiteers—the oligarchy or comprador class. The revolutionaries' propaganda, hence, must be directly socialist. In fact, a case can be made that unless the revolution is socialistic from the start today, neo-colonial takeovers will generally follow stage one anyway, especially where the anti-imperialist liberation struggle is not very protracted or is mostly peaceful—viz., most of "independent" black Africa. But to prepare the revolution by preaching socialism usually means to create a tight party organization first, precisely the role played by most Moscow-oriented Communist Party structures. Otherwise, it means using the revolutionary intellectuals (i.e., petty bourgeoisie) as an advance guard, expecting them to commit class suicide before the revolution. A difficult task.

Yet Amilcar Cabral apparently succeeded in doing that in "Portuguese" Guinea. A brilliant agronomist, one of his country's four blacks with an advanced university degree, Cabral began his political work as an agricultural census-taker for the colonial administration (1952–54). In 1956, with five other "petty-bourgeois" intellectuals, as he calls himself, he launched the African Independence Party of Guiné and Cape Verde (PAIGC). For the next three years, their focus was internal Party development. Cabral himself led the group in serious analyses of the forces and classes of his country, concluding that neither the peasants nor the pro-letariat (virtually nonexistent) could act as the revolutionary vanguard.[127] That role was left up to his own class, the petty bourgeoisie. From 1959, Cabral and his petty-bourgeois comrades fanned out across their small country (15,500 square miles, roughly the size of Switzerland; 800,000 inhabitants) and intensively propagandized for reforms, changes, civil rights, equality. Whenever the Portuguese reacted with repression the PAIGC men then drove home the theme of counterviolence and war of liberation. Meanwhile, volunteers were being molded into the People's

[127] See Cabral's analysis below, p. 367; also Gérard Chaliand, *Armed Struggle in Africa* (New York and London: Monthly Review Press, 1969), and Basil Davidson, *The Liberation of Guiné: Aspects of an African Revolution* (London and Baltimore, Md.: Penguin, 1969).

Revolutionary Armed Forces (FARP) in the neighboring Republic of Guinea.

Repression hardened, massacres increased. Still, Cabral waited. He wanted the people to be ready, to be thirsting to fight. He wanted them so aware of the colonialist violence that, as Fanon said, they would be perfectly decided to "embody history" in each of their own persons in order to surge "into the forbidden quarters."[128] Cabral had to achieve what the Vietnam National Liberation Front's Nguyen Van Tien once said was primordial, "that people themselves discover the need for armed struggle. As for guns, those you can always find."[129] When his people were that ready, Cabral launched the offensive during the night of June 30–July 1, 1962. Today, as I write, the PAIGC has liberated two-thirds of the countryside—despite the 40,000 Portuguese troops armed with the most modern NATO (U.S.) weapons, planes, bombs, and napalm.

From the very first, Cabral characterized the armed struggle as much more than an anticolonial war. Chaliand reports that even in the bush, Cabral always plugged for socialism. For example, in a pep talk to illiterate guerrillas about to go into combat, he said: "If we wage this struggle just to chase out the Portuguese, the struggle is not worth it. We fight for that, yes, but also so no one may exploit anyone else, white or black. . . . We fight to build. Not the work of individuals, but of all, together. . . ."[130] In Havana, Milan, and Paris, but especially deep inside his own territory, Cabral repeatedly hammered away at the PAIGC's ultimate goals: African unity, socialism, a new society. Nevertheless, as original and astute a socialist thinker and leader as he is, the struggle he waged was first and foremost against the Portuguese invaders. In the minds of his people, the enemy was there—in the flesh, active, repressive. The PAIGC was hence fighting a two-stage revolution, eloquently displaying its merit in a war where the enemy, proportional to the population, had deployed more strength and fire-power even than in Vietnam.

Cabral's originality lies in the way he adapted the Chinese model to modern times, substituting a form of elitist indoctrination for the initial liberated zones, guiding his own class comrades to commit class suicide, and never forgetting that there is no such thing as a general class analysis, only particular analyses, anchored to specific times and places. Modification of the Chinese or PAIGC model seems to be working in Palestine, Angola, Mozambique, Eritrea (where the invaders are the Ethiopian troops of pro-U.S. Haile Selassie), Dhufar and the Persian Gulf, in the Sino-Tibetan regions of India where such dominated minorities as the Ahoms, Nagas, and Mizos fight Indian "pacification" troops who use

[128] Fanon, *The Wretched of the Earth*, p. 33.
[129] "Notre Stratégie de la guérilla," *Partisans* (Paris), January–February 1968.
[130] From the original French edition of Chaliand, *Little Armée en Afrique* (Paris: Maspero, 1967), p. 49 (my translation).

napalm and strategic hamlets. But where neo-colonialism is entrenched—in Kenya, Congo-Kinshasa, the Cameroons, Morocco—the wars of liberation are flagging.[131] Another model for revolution is needed.

Cuba has tried to furnish that model. It is called the *foco*. The word means a center or a nucleus of guerrilla operations rather than a base. Indeed, it is used precisely in contradistinction to base or liberated area, and refers to the unit of men fighting in a particular province or area rather than stationed in a specific place. The word first came into use in Cuba where the *Fidelistas* established a *foco* in the Sierra Maestra mountain range of Oriente Province, and from there directed the revolutionary war against the Cuban dictator, Fulgencio Batista. Régis Debray, in his *Revolution in the Revolution?*, thinks of *foco* as a force rather than center. The way to overthrow capitalist power in Latin America, he says, is "by means of the more or less slow building up, through guerrilla warfare carried out in suitably chosen rural zones, of a *mobile strategic force, nucleus of a people's army and of a future socialist state.*"[132] The *foco*, then, is thought of operationally rather than descriptively; it leads to the creation of a people's army. It is the *motor* to the revolution. Basically, this revolutionary theory claims that in most countries of the imperialized world, and certainly in Latin America, the objective conditions for revolution already exist. What is needed are subjective conditions—leadership, revolutionary fervor, faith, and hope. In such a situation, a few dedicated armed men, by establishing a *foco* in the countryside, can prove their tenacity and dedication through combat much faster and much more convincingly than through normal or usual propaganda-agitation means. After

[131] Eritrea, given as a trust to Emperor Haile Selassie after World War II, was totally annexed by him on November 13, 1962, and he then tried to "integrate" its mostly Moslem population (3,000,000 people) by imposing his language (Amharic) and religion (Coptic) with U.S. and Israeli guns, in exchange for naval (Massawa and Assab), airforce (Asmara), and tracking (Kagnew) bases (which Israel and the U.S. jointly control). The Eritrean Liberation Front (ELF) has been fighting Selassie through its Eritrean Liberation Army (ELA) since 1965. In northeastern India, the Ahoms, Nagas, and Mizos have been at war against India more or less since 1947; for years their arms came from Pakistan but today they are getting Chinese aid. The Cameroons, run by a pro-French neo-colonialist regime, are now the scene of some of black Africa's most bitter fighting but the National Liberation Army (ALNC) does not seem able to augment its liberated areas; on March 15, 1966, one of Africa's most notable economists and political scientists, Osendé Afana, who organized the Union of the Peoples of Cameroon (UPC) of which the ALNC is the fighting arm, was killed in battle. See his *L'Economie de l'Ouest-Africain* (Paris: Maspero, 1966). (Two other great African intellectuals who led the UPC and were murdered, apparently by the French, were Reuben Um Nyobe and Felix Moumié.) See also Ngouo Woungly Massaga (Commander of ALNC's second front), "Cameroon: A Watchword," *Tricontinental* (Havana), January–April 1968.

[132] Debray, *Revolution in the Revolution?* (New York: Grove Press, 1967), p. 24 (his emphasis).

the peasants become convinced that this *foco* is serious, they will join it and it will grow into a people's army.

Actually, the *foco* theory entails a deeper analysis, which has in fact been carried out by Debray, Guevara, Fidel, Armando Hart, Carlos Romeo, and others.[133] It goes like this. Because of the role played by Russia's Comintern and indeed because of half a century of habit, revolution has fallen into the domain of the official communist parties. These parties have always followed if not the dictates certainly the suggestions of the theorists inside the Kremlin.[134] Those theorists seem convinced today that capitalism's internal contradictions are so acute that it must crack by itself if brought into open, unrepressive world competition with socialist economies and if liberal bourgeois democracies allow free development of mass organizations. Because of the economic competition, hence the demand for an ever increasing labor force, and because the general awareness of peoples generates constant social demands, such a development is inevitable. Communists are therefore advised to concentrate their organizational efforts on the urban proletariat—which is in keeping with Leninist principles that communism can only be established by a dictatorship of the proletariat.

The *foco* theorists reject both the traditional CP's analysis and their methods. Capitalism is dynamic, not static, they say. It can constantly integrate workers into its structure at a high enough rate to perpetuate the myth of class mobility. What it cannot do, because that doesn't pay, is to develop the infrastructure in rural areas. Schools, roads, electricity, and housing in thinly populated places do not bring profits. Hence, the rural population is doomed to remain marginal or outside the money

---

[133] See Debray, *Essais sur l'Amérique Latine* (Paris: Maspero, 1967)—English edition, *Strategy for Revolution*, ed. Robin Blackburn (London: Jonathan Cape, 1970); Rubén Vásquez Díaz, *La Bolivie à l'Heure du Che* (Paris: Maspero, 1968); Che Guevara, *Guerrilla Warfare* (New York: Monthly Review Press, 1961) and *Venceremos, The Speeches and Writings of Ernesto Che Guevara*, cited earlier (especially Chs. 7, 9, 21, 35); Castro, *Aniversario del Triunfo de la Revolución Cubana* (Havana: Editora Política, 1967), "Criterios de Nuestra Revolución," in *Cuba Socialista*, September 1965, and the following speeches: February 4, 1962 ("Second Declaration of Havana"), January 15, 1966 (closing the Tricontinental Conference), March 13, 1967 (included below, p. 447), and August 10, 1967 (closing the First Conference of OLAS); Armando Hart, *Informe de la Delegación Cubana a la Primera Conferencia de las OLAS* (Havana, July–August 1967) (included below, p. 394); Carlos Romeo, "Revolutionary Practice and Theory in Latin America," in *Latin American Radicalism*, cited earlier; Miguel Arraes, *Le Brésil* (Paris: Maspero, 1969); Turcios Lima, untitled collection of writings (Havana: Instituto del Libro, 1968); Héctor Béjar Rivera, *Peru 1965: Apuntes Sobre una Experiencia Guerrillera* (Havana: Casa de las Américas, 1969); Carlos Marighella, *Pour la libération du Brésil* (Paris: Editions du Seuil, 1970).

[134] Fidel once referred to such parties as an "international mafia." See his OLAS speech, August 10, 1967.

economy altogether. Capitalist agrarian reform (buying and distributing the lands of owners who have become urban entrepreneurs anyway) cannot solve the problems of the rural peoples, because simply owning the land is not enough. Farmers must have access to markets (roads and transportation), modernity (refrigeration, hence electricity and training, hence schooling), and a certain economic flexibility (capital) to vary crops or survive disasters both natural (drought, storms, unseasonal cold, etc.) and commercial (sharp fluctuation in commodity prices). No capitalist system can solve these needs in the underdeveloped world, unless it totally mechanizes agriculture and forces the rural population into the urban centers—a plan once proposed by Lauchlin Currie, one of FDR's ex-brain trusters, in Colombia in 1962.[135] But if that were to happen, the huge demand for jobs and the massive development of workers' organizations would swamp the industrial bourgeoisie, forcing the government to intervene so extensively that socialism would take over by default—a fate that the bourgeoisie, which controls the government, wants to avoid at all cost. The contradiction between rural and urban areas is hence insoluble.

But capitalism, especially foreign (i.e., imperialism), is perfectly disposed never to solve that contradiction. It can pursue its goals without caring about the countryside at all. It can slowly increase production in the urban centers, turn them into high-consuming areas (such as Saigon, Caracas, Río de Janeiro, Lima, Buenos Aires, Casablanca, Nairobi, Manila, Rangoon, Singapore, etc.) where demand for its manufactured goods constantly rises. It can reinvest its capital, in fact import more capital, and see it grow. It can aid education, communication, and transportation via welfare imperialism. It can even help develop a so-called middle sector, which will be tied through holding companies to the capitalist-oligarchy partnership. And should labor agitation spread threateningly, it can always accede to union demands, catching back its profit margin through its control of prices, finances, export-import, and inflation.

Precisely because of this spiral, say the *foco* theorists, the CP is caught in an "economist" well. It must constantly agitate for trade union demands and, since it keeps winning them, must keep asking for more lest it lose its hold on the workers now accustomed to fighting for bread-and-butter issues only. As the CP develops into a Fabian Society, so does labor—and vice versa. The next step in the process is elections, positions of responsibility, an occasional judgeship, and finally a big, respectable party, as in France and Italy. In those countries, though they are thoroughly disciplined, the communists cannot even envision seizing power except through the ballot—when in fact they could take over with half their force. Thus an urbanized traditional communist party not

---

[135] See *The Great Fear in Latin America*, pp. 327–29, 443–46.

only abandons its revolutionarism, it actually becomes counterrevolutionary: its stake is identified with the game. It is part of the Establishment.

While playing the established game of elections and trade unionism in the cities,[136] some Latin American communist parties did send organizers into the countryside. This was especially true in Bolivia, where the miners of Camiri had a long tradition of militant action, and in Colombia, where the peasants of such almost totally isolated areas as Marquetalia, Riochiquito, El Pato, and Guayabero lived completely divorced from the civilization of Bogotá. In both countries, the communist policy was to solidify these workers into self-defense communities (so vast were the Colombian areas that they became known as "independent republics"). In Bolivia, where rapid progress was registered after the national bourgeois revolution of 1952, the communists were Trotskyists.[137] In Colombia, the CP was traditional and it formulated its self-defense policy as early as October 1949. Yet in 1964 and 1965, these self-defense communities were totally wiped out; many of the Colombian communists escaped, but only to become mobile guerrillas.[138] As a result, no revolutionary group today advocates self-defense warfare. Most communists insist on the legal struggle only. But even if they do practice armed struggle, their warriors are subservient to the Party. The guerrillas are under orders of city-based elites. Hence, say the *foco* theorists, they become tools in a political chess game waged by fat functionaries stretched out in carpeted offices amidst the hustle-bustle of asphalt alleys and acid addicts, high-rise hangars and highball hangovers.

A revolutionary, says Fidel, is not necessarily Marxist-Leninist. But he is necessarily someone who fights. To be in the vanguard, he must thus embody both political and military leadership. That means he has to

[136] Which, of course, was in accord with Lenin's teachings; see *What Is to Be Done?*, and above.

[137] In Peru's Convención Valley, Hugo Blanco, a Trotskyist official, rapidly and successfully organized peasant unions. His next goal was dual power. (See his "The Road of Our Revolution," *Arauco* [Santiago de Chile], February 1965.) The next stage was to be seizing power, at least in the valley. Presumably, after that, the area was to become a self-defense enclave—except that the military swooped down on the valley before he ever established dual power, and destroyed the Trotskyist apparatus. Blanco was condemned to twenty-five years, and is still in jail.

[138] The communist guerrillas are still fighting in Colombia, but not on a self-defense basis. They are now called the Armed Revolutionary Forces of Colombia (FARC). For a fascinating account of the 1964 government offensive and the description of day-to-day fighting from the communist side, see *Colombie: Guérillas du Peuple* (Paris: Editions Sociales, 1969) by Jacobo Arenas, member of the executive committee of the Colombia CP and current chief of staff of the FARC, who fought in Marquetalia and Riochiquito (he also lets Manuel Marulanda, known as *Tirofijo* or "Sure Shot," a member of the Central Committee of the CC and current FARC Commander-in-chief, talk extensively).

be in the field, where the action is. Communists who direct "revolutionary" operations from city offices cannot help losing contact with the masses, with the very people they supposedly fight for. Revolutionaries who practice what they preach learn in the process what they are truly fighting for. "The first law of guerrilla life," writes Debray,

> is that no one survives alone. The group's interest is the interest of each one, and vice versa. To live and conquer is to live and conquer all together. If a single combatant lags behind a marching column it affects the speed and security of the entire column. In the rear is the enemy: impossible to leave the comrade behind or send him home. It is up to everyone, then, to share the burden, lighten his knapsack or cartridge-case, and help him all the way. Under these conditions class egoism does not long endure. Petty bourgeois psychology melts like snow under the summer sun, undermining the ideology of the same stratum. Where else could such an encounter, such an alliance, take place? By the same token, the only conceivable line for a guerrilla group to adopt is the "mass line"; it can live only with their support, in daily contact with them. Bureaucratic faintheartedness becomes irrelevant. Is this not the best education for a future socialist leader or cadre? Revolutionaries make revolutionary civil wars; but to an even greater extent it is revolutionary civil war that makes revolutionaries.[139]

Everyone learns from revolutionary civil war. Fidel is no exception.

> Here [he wrote from the Sierra Maestra] the word 'people,' which is so often utilized in a vague and confused sense, becomes a living, wonderful and dazzling reality. *Now* I know who the people are: I see them in that invincible force that surrounds us everywhere, I see them in the bands of 30 or 40 men, lighting their way with lanterns, who descend the muddy slopes at two or three in the morning, with 30 kilos on their backs, in order to supply us with food. Who has organized them so wonderfully? Where did they acquire so much ability, astuteness, courage, self-sacrifice? No one knows! It is almost a mystery! They organize themselves all alone, spontaneously! When weary animals drop to the ground, unable to go further, men appear from all directions and carry the goods. Force cannot defeat them. It would be necessary to kill them all, to the last peasant, and that is impossible; this, the dictatorship cannot do; the people are aware of it and are daily more aware of their own growing strength.[140]

[139] *Revolution in the Revolution?*, pp. 110–11.

[140] Quoted in *ibid.*, p. 113. Debray comments: "From Fidel Castro's last letter to Frank País, written in the Sierra Maestra, July 21, 1957. The same wonderment is expressed today in the letters of Turcios, Douglas Bravo, Camilo Torres, and others. Of course this does not mean that it is easy to obtain peasant support immediately; but when it is obtained, it performs wonders. Fidel wrote the letter after eight months in the Sierra and after having escaped betrayal by several peasants" (written before the death of Turcios and Torres).

The *foco* theory, then, is much more than just a strategy for a new revolution. It is an ethical philosophy as well. Recognizing the fact that a man's life style gradually determines his activities, it demands of revolutionaries that they *act*, that is, fight. It also posits the corollary, namely, that people are impressed and convinced by what a man does, not what he says. As such, the *foco* philosophy combines Marxism and existentialism. Latin American peasants, long used to rabble rousers and agitators who quickly vanish when the Rangers descend or when the napalm begins to burn, may remain skeptical for extended periods. But when they see that the revolutionaries mean what they say because they continue to fight, the peasants will join the revolutionaries, becoming the "motor" of the revolution. In that motor, all men are equal—by necessity. They belong to the same class. As another heresy from Marxism, the *foco* theory thus defines class according to life style. From that life, in which political and military *engagements* become welded, the future of socialism is born—individuals become dedicated to the collective; the collective, a classless nucleus wrought in combat (hence efficiency), is dedicated to human harmony (hence morality). By fighting, the future leaders of socialism become tough, tenacious, and human. And they set that example by their behavior. "Guerrilla warfare," wrote Che in *Man and Socialism in Cuba,* "was carried out in two different environments: the people, an as yet unawakened mass that had to be mobilized, and its vanguard, the guerrilla, the thrusting engine of mobilization, the generator of revolutionary awareness and militant enthusiasm. This vanguard was the catalyst which created the subjective condition necessary for victory. The individual was also the basic factor in the guerrilla, in the framework of the gradual proletarianization of our thinking, in the revolution taking place in our habits and in our minds."[141]

As romantic as it sounded, liberals were shocked by the *foco* theory's conscious espousal of violence. They would be. But revolutionaries see their violence as counterviolence. "The Americans take their *rôle* of patron of international capitalism very seriously," Fanon wrote early in 1961, and their imperialism "is violence in its natural state, and it will only yield when confronted with greater violence. At the decisive moment, the colonialist bourgeoisie [or the liberals in the capitalist world], which up till then has remained inactive, comes into the field. It introduces that new idea which is in proper parlance a creation of the colonial situation: non-violence." He added: "At the level of individuals, violence is a cleansing force. It frees the native from his inferiority complex and from his despair and inaction; it makes him fearless and restores his self-respect."[142]

At his trial in Camiri, Debray tackled the problem of violence thus:

[141] *Venceremos,* pp. 387–88.   [142] *The Wretched of the Earth,* p. 62 and *passim.*

Each one has to decide which side he is on—on the side of military violence or guerrilla violence, on the side of the violence that represses or violence that liberates. Crimes in the face of crimes. Which ones do we choose to be jointly responsible for, accomplices, or accessories to? You chose certain ones, I chose others, that's all. . . .

Naturally the tragedy is that we do not kill objects, numbers, abstract or interchangeable instruments, but, precisely, on both sides, irreplaceable individuals, essentially innocent, unique for those who have loved, bred, esteemed them. This is the tragedy of history, of any history, of any revolution. It is not individuals that are placed face to face in these battles, but class interests and ideas; but those who fall in them, those who die, are persons, are men. We cannot avoid this contradiction, escape from this pain.[143]

A much more serious question—to revolutionaries anyway—is whether the *foco* theory works in practice. So far its record is bleak. In Peru, for example; its beginning was extraordinarily successful. Within very few months, the three *focos* established in 1965 by the Movement of the Revolutionary Left (MIR), led by Luis de la Puente Uceda and Guillermo Lobatón, two top-notch intellectuals and dedicated revolutionaries, gained wide local support and seemed invincible. From the *cordillera* of the Andes, "Lucho" de la Puente even wrote that he saw his MIR operation as the start of "the continental war of emancipation," though he warned that "American intervention in our country will come more quickly than in other nations, because the Pentagon is perfectly aware of the importance of a triumphant or developing insurrection in the very heart of Latin America."[144] But he himself underestimated his enemy. The MIR set up security zones and de la Puente boasted that "anybody daring to come near Illarec Ch'aska [his own area's security zone] will be wiped out!"[145] Preceded by raids of U.S. napalm and guided by U.S. Ranger and Special Forces "advisers," the Peruvian army then hit de la Puente precisely in that zone, turning what was meant to be the rear into the front line. "It was shown then that there is no spot inaccessible for an army having some knowledge of counter-guerrilla warfare," wrote Héctor Béjar, who led Peru's Army of National Liberation (ELN). "It was really only an excess of naiveté which could have led to the belief that the army cannot get to places that guerrillas can."[146]

In his book written from Peru's San Quintín prison, Béjar, a former member of the Central Committee of the Peruvian CP who was thrown out in 1958 for rejecting peaceful coexistence and in 1962 helped launch

[143] *Strategy for Revolution*, pp. 203, 205–06.
[144] *Monthly Review*, November 1965.
[145] *El Guerrillero* (underground organ of the MIR), September 5, 1965.
[146] *Peru 1965*, p. 102 (unpublished translation by Manolo González).

the ELN and was caught in 1966, explains some of the reasons why the ELN, too, failed:

"After many experiences which won us the sympathy of the locals, our overconfidence led us toward hard setbacks. One success after another made us overestimate our own forces. On the other hand, some desertions took place which decreased the number of guerrilleros, affecting their striking power.

"We were really a small group. In the most difficult moments there were hardly thirteen of us. Apart from that, the lack of communication with the urban centers prevented us from counting upon a permanent intake of men.

"We were surrounded. The siege did not not endanger the existence of the guerrilla, which moved under such conditions with quite a lot of comfort, but it prevented us from communicating with the outside world. At the end of 1965, our attempts in that direction had failed.

"It must be said that it had been our mistake not to give enough importance to this type of link and to have trusted to the recruiting of men within the area in which we were active. Our intention was to provide ourselves there with supplies and guerrilleros. The first aim was easy, especially for such a small group as ours. The second aim was feasible, but only as a slow process, because of the peasant's slowness in making decisions. The peasant finally decides to join the guerrilla, but he thinks it over and balances every possibility before joining. On the contrary, the guerrilla needs a numerous and quick intake to strengthen the group and improve its combat conditions.

"Our small numbers prevented us from undertaking large-scale actions against the army. However, we were confident in our knowledge of the terrain and in the many friends we had everywhere. We started to move by day, through known paths, trusting the information given to us by the population, and we neglected fundamental precautions. We based our confidence on the fruitless efforts made by the army to locate us and on their fear of crossing rivers, streams, and land features we were watching.

"But every guerrillero who feels master of the terrain and believes he knows it, tends, without realizing it, to become tied to to it. And in such a case he is lost, for not all the information he has corresponds to the facts and he does not have all the data about the enemy, as he normally should.

"At the end of 1965, unfavorable clashes came one after the other, until the 17th of September when the guerrilla was surprised by an army patrol in a spot known as Tincoj. In that clash three comrades died, one of them Edgardo Tello. The rest of the guerrilla was scattered and put out of combat.

"In such an uneven and dense jungle as the one in which we were operating, a regrouping was practically impossible. In spite of all our efforts, we were unable to get together again.

"Maybe a bigger group could have gone through those difficult moments, although damaged, but we were very few and the loss of a single man was a real blow.

"When the guerrilla was finally put out of combat and the fighters scatttered, everyone was left to himself and they gave their lives under the implacable fire of a real manhunt.

"The individual fate of comrades is not known. Some died fighting. Others were captured, put in jail, and later shot by the army's intelligence services. The rest are still being persecuted and searched for all over the country.

"In 1967, some ELN comrades also died, with Che, in the Nancahuazu action. Their names are: Juan Pablo Chang Navarro (El Chino), José Cabrera Flores (El Negro), and Lucio Galván (Eustaquio).

"Why did we fail? What were the reasons of the Ayacucho failure?

"The scattering and liquidation of the guerrilla was not due to the lack of peasant support. This existed in many forms, as we have seen earlier. The area, uneven and not known by the army, had been properly chosen. Then roots of the failure must be sought in the guerrilla itself and in its leadership.

"In this as in other cases, a group of men coming mainly from the cities, attempted to carry out military operations in an unknown medium.

"It is easy to get over lack of knowledge of the terrain in a short time, if the group is resourceful and active. The guerrilla was able to overcome this obstacle. But it did not always use its knowledge and many times preferred the easier but much more dangerous way of moving through well-known paths.

"By doing so, it was leaving behind a trail of information which many peasants could not keep secret when tortured or massacred. The guerrilla was not able to foresee, in fact, the extent to which repression would go.

"The guerrilla made a lot of friends but did not know how to look after them. Everyone knew who our collaborators were. When the army arrived on the scene, it only had to shoot them in order to terrorize the rest of the population.

"On the other hand, language was always the barrier separating the rebels from the natives. The peasant identifies the Spanish language with the master, especially in a spot such as Ayacucho, with a very high Quechuan percentage. If the guerrillero wants to inspire confidence he must speak Quechuan fluently, and not any type of Quechuan, but the one spoken in the area where he is operating, because, as is well-known, there are remarkable language differences from region to region in Peru.

"The habits are another barrier. Great discipline is needed if a group of men are to learn to respect, imitate, and *love* the very ancient habits of the peasants, if they are not to hurt his sensibility with awkward attitudes. Discipline, affection toward the peasant, and modesty are needed. And these are not always the characteristics of young students, or of politicians full of a kind of intellectual self-sufficiency which the ordinary man finds shocking. They behave daily in a way contradictory to the habits of the peasants.

"In spite of the sympathy it counted upon, the guerrilla showed a lack of identification with the habits of the natives. This would have allowed the group to know more accurately the turncoats and to get better and more opportune information on the enemy's movements.

"The tactics of guerrilla warfare, applied strictly with all their features of mobility, escape and hiding, quick attack and withdrawal, require the fighters to be in top physical shape and the best military ability from the leadership. And generally, iron discipline and operation in harmony by the whole group. The ELN guerrilla, in common with all those who operated that year, did not have the required conditions needed to overcome the difficulties and face a well-trained and numerous enemy.

"Under the present circumstances it is still possible for a small team of men to operate successfully in the peasant areas.

"To achieve this, it must strictly apply the principles of guerrilla warfare more or less rejected by the rebels in 1965. And it must tie its actions to those of the masses in the struggle for national and local demands.

"It must be a team with high political, organizing, and military qualities, setup not out of the liberalism of the urban Left, but out of the fire of battle. And it must promote, by means of resourceful conduct, new fighters native to the region.

"When the peasant sees the newly arrived guerrillero from the city in action and listens to him speaking in his defense, he feels sympathy and collaborates with him. But when he sees his own brother in the revolutionary army, speaking in his own language and with his accent, he follows him without much thought."[147]

In Venezuela, Colombia, and Guatemala the various *focos,* launched in the early sixties, have had their ups and downs (mostly due to internal disputes with the local communist parties), but have survived. In Venezuela and Colombia, they have spread slowly and seem solid. In Guatemala the two groups which once fought separately, then united, are now separate again—the MR-13 barely surviving deep in the jungles, fairly isolated from the rest of the country; the Revolutionary Armed Force (FAR) fighting mostly in the cities as urban guerrillas. In Nicaragua, after a dozen attempts to launch *focos* were thwarted by Somoza's forces, the Sandino National Liberation Front has finally managed to establish a viable column in the mountains of Jinotega and Matagalpa. In Argen-

147 *Ibid.,* pp. 132–38.

tina and Brazil, where *focos* led to disasters, all guerrilla forces now operate out of the cities. In the Congo, where Che and four other members of the Cuban Central Committee fought in 1965, rebellions occur constantly—but no particular *foco* seems active. In Mexico, a localized and very regional-minded *foco* in Guerrero led by Jenaro Vásquez Rojas is doing well, with much popular support, but the other *focos* have disappeared. The most famous, established in 1959 by Arturo Gámiz, a professor of Mexico City's Instituto Polytécnico, grew so considerably in the early sixties that it spread from its base in Chihuahua to neighboring Durango and Coahuila. Early in 1965, Gámiz was strong enough to stage various "conventions" in the mountains of his region and in July 1965 issued an ultimatum to Chihuahua's governor Práxedes Giner, telling him to "get out of the state which you serve so badly or we shall throw you out by force whatever the cost and whatever the blood."[148] But on September 23, 1965, in a massive attack on the province's Cuartel de Madera military encampment, Gámiz and thirty-two of his guerrillas were killed. Federal paratroopers then occupied the area, beat up, tortured, or shot whomever they suspected of being a *guerrillero* sympathizer, and crushed the movement.

The most dramatic failure of a *foco*, of course, was in Bolivia. In his diary Che blames Bolivian Communist Party boss Mario Monje for sabotaging the guerrillas' efforts, and Fidel, in his introduction, likewise refers to Monje as a sabotaging, chauvinistic "blockhead."[149] But the fact is that Che's *guerrilleros* were isolated in a forbidding part of Bolivia, and their communication with the outside world was hard and rare. Che did not have a functioning apparatus in La Paz, Cochabamba, Sucre, Santa Cruz, and the country's other major cities. Hence he had to rely on Monje, and thus the CP secretary-general's simple noncooperation (with the betrayal of Oscar Zamora, another city-based communist "coward"[150]) hampered Che's men seriously enough to lead to defeat.

The Left has leveled a great deal of criticism at the *foco* theory, specifically at Debray (a safer fall guy than Fidel), since Che's death.[151]

[148] Leaflet, "Ultimatum de los Guerrilleros a Giner," Sierra de Chihuahua, July 1965, signed by Arturo Gámiz and Solomón Gaytán. See also the pamphlets (mimeographed) issued by Ediciones Linea Revolucionaria (Chihuahua, 1965) after each "convention," entitled *Resoluciones: Encuentro en la Sierra.* In a special issue on students, *Participación de los Estudiantes en el Movimiento Revolucionario* (Chihuahua: Ediciones Linea Revolucionaria, 1965, mimeographed), Gámiz warned Mexico's youth that their protests, valiant as they are, will lead the bourgeoisie to massacre them (which, of course, is what happened in 1968 when at least 2,000 were gunned down in Mexico City). He asked them to join the armed struggle instead.

[149] Che Guevara, *Bolivian Diary*, Introduction by Fidel Castro (London: Jonathan Cape/Lorrimer, 1968).

[150] Fidel, in *ibid.*, p. 13.

[151] For example, see the whole July–August 1968 issue of *Monthly Review* (and Debray's reply in the February 1969 issue).

Some of it is absurd, as that which condemns Debray for not including a class analysis in *Revolution in the Revolution?* (Debray's answer: "This omission is so obvious as to leave no doubt that such an analysis was neither the purpose nor the subject of the work."[152]) Some of it is valid not just about the *foco* but any revolutionary grouping, as when William J. Pomeroy objects to the joining of the political and military on the grounds it might generate loyalty to a particular commander rather than the cause[153] (a fault of leadership, not structure). But the serious criticisms remain basically two: that the *foco* tends to operate in isolation; and that while it is young it is too much at the mercy of the enemy's vastly superior forces, now always very ably trained in counterinsurgency.

It is a misreading of both history and facts to assume that the Cuban Revolution was started by the *foco* established in the Sierra Maestra by Fidel, Che, Raúl, Almeida, Camilo Cienfuegos, *et al.* By the time the revolutionary yacht *Granma* discharged its eighty *guerrilleros* on the shores of Oriente Province, Cuba had long been well prepared for the invasion. Fidel himself had been known as a courageous "reformer" who became convinced that only revolution could bring about the changes needed. But he had tried peacefully first, by running for office in the Ortodoxo Party. Then, on July 26, 1953, he and his group attacked the Moncada barracks. They failed miserably but the defeat gave Fidel the opportunity to defend himself eloquently during his trial.[154] In that defense, Fidel did not frighten the liberal bourgeoisie; he demanded civil rights, justice, libertarian freedoms, a fair share for the masses, and a return to constitutionality. When he was released from jail and began organizing his guerrilla force, he also paid careful attention to his "July 26" organization inside Cuba. And when his plans were set, his organization was such that he could ask it to stage a general insurrection in Santiago. Frank País, who headed the organization in Oriente, had no major difficulty carrying out the order (though the insurrection failed). Finally, during all the time Fidel operated out of the Sierra, he never once lost

---

152 "Reply," *Monthly Review*, February 1969.

153 *Monthly Review*, July–August 1968, p. 42. In the very next paragraph Pomeroy says: "In the course of the prolonged armed struggle there were instances [among the Philippine Huks] in which armed units lost their links with party political guidance, or in which the more dedicated military cadres were killed, an attrition factor that is at work as soon as the struggle gets under way. As a result, a number of serious cases of banditry and of semi-banditry occurred. Wherever the party was not able to exercise its leadership and its control, the Huk armed forces tended to disintegrate or degenerate." Precisely! And what better way to eliminate this problem than by combining the military and political heads into one, and building up in combat all the cadre to think and operate likewise?

154 *History Will Absolve Me* (Havana: Ediciones Revolucionarias, 1967); available from various sources, including in *On Trial* (London: Lorrimer, 1968). Said Fidel: "I warn you: I have just begun!"

contact with the cities (including Havana, where the Directorio and other revolutionary organizations coordinated their activities with his). What's more, Fidel never alienated the bourgeoisie to the extent that it would turn against him, even if it did at times demand unacceptable conditions for its material aid. There is no doubt that Fidel's *foco* was the motor to the revolution in Cuba. But nor can there be any doubt that Fidel's organizational genius made sure that the *foco* remained at the center of a much bigger revolutionary movement, which it controlled or guided for its military and political advantage.

And that is the way it should be. Otherwise, isolation leads to disaster. "When a revolutionary organization has spent years fighting in town and countryside in the roughest conditions," said Héctor Béjar out of experience, "liaison through the urban centers is perfectly feasible. But when this experience is nonexistent and there is a tradition of liberalism and of negligence in the work, when there have been no real stages of hard underground life, to establish contacts through the town means to hand over militants to the enemy. In Latin America, many valuable guerrilla cadres have fallen prisoner or been murdered when trying fruitlessly to establish contact with the towns."[155]

By Cuba's experience, then, the *foco* may still well be the best tactic to mount the motor. But it needs a long period of preparation, intensive organizational work to set up an efficient, reliable machinery which will not only generate the atmosphere for armed struggle by *focos* but will also guarantee their logistic, communication, and propaganda network. The traditional communist parties of the world claim that they are doing just that—and have been, mostly peacefully, for forty years. That is not what Béjar had in mind when he said "real stages of hard underground life." Béjar, and New Left revolutionaries all over the world, know very well that a revolutionary life style is a warrior's life style. By stages he meant stages of combat, and that is precisely the way in which revolutionaries can be honed into the kind of organization capable of leading a people's war.

It is out of expediency—solid, revolutionary, necessary expediency (Leninists take note!)—that terrorism is being posited as the answer. Not indiscriminate terrorism. The kind of carefully thought-out operations carried out by the Tupamaros of Uruguay, for example. Blowing up imperialist centers, assassinating hated political and repressive-force personnel, kidnapping ambassadors, sabotaging imperialism's industrial-military complex, robbing banks and large companies, raiding police and military outposts to capture arms and ammunition, and the like. The object is manifold: (1) to threaten the Establishment, cause it to panic and make serious tactical mistakes, such as resorting to mass repressions which

[155] *Peru 1965*, pp. 99–100.

radicalize the population against them; (2) to establish the underground revolutionary apparatus, including both active participants and trusted but passive collaborators (who will later carry out the liaison, communication, logistic, and propaganda needs of the revolutionary armies in the hills); (3) to test new recruits in relative security, for, though police infiltrators are bound to creep in and stay in the organization for future need even if they have to kill their own to do so, the fact that for a long time urban groups will operate independently of each other keeps sweeping arrests of urban guerrillas down to a minimum; (4) to demoralize the rank and file and even the officers of the repressive forces, as they see themselves constantly but unexpectedly under attack (it is said that to kill policemen indiscriminately is to forget the working-class background of the cop on the beat; this is as absurd as trying to save the ordinary soldiers whom the Vietnamese must kill to survive); (5) to panic local capitalists to withdraw their funds from specific areas, thus hurting the local warlords and politicians who profit from these investments; (6) to frighten away foreign investors, which will affect the whole bureaucratic oligarchy; (7) to force the U.S. to constantly extend its intervention, which will tax its resources, hence increase discontent at home, and spread its imperialistic arms, rendering it more vulnerable abroad.

In Brazil today, urban guerrilla warfare is well entrenched. Some groups get caught, some leaders get killed—including on November 4, 1969, at fifty-eight, Carlos Marighella who fought, first in the CP Central Committee, then in a *foco* in the Belo Horizonte backlands, finally as a leader of the ALN (Action for National Liberation) urban guerrillas. But new recruits joined the groups. Recently one group explained how it began: "In 1968, we were just one little group of São Paulo militants, without any impact in the country. We had almost nothing. We had yet to engage ourselves in a single revolutionary act which might differentiate us from the numerous groups then engaged in endless discussions which led to nothing. Our first step was to go out, as an armed band, and expropriate arms. That revolutionary act determined us as a group with fire-power. It made us grow. We began with two weapons. We augmented our fire-power. Based on the principle 'the action makes the front,' we unleashed urban guerrilla warfare, without naming it. Our first actions caught the enemy by surprise; he thought we were just a bunch of hoods. He lost time pursuing false leads. When he understood, it was too late. The revolutionary war had begun."[156] The group? The ALN.

Today, the ALN operates in the three major cities of Brazil, kidnapping the U.S. ambassador, robbing banks, blowing up depots, harassing the police. It lives up well to the precepts laid down by Marighella who, in his

---

[156] The ALN (anonymously; i.e., collectively), "Du Rôle de l'Action Révolutionnaire dans la Constitution de l'Organization Révolutionnaire," *Les Temps Modernes*, November 1969 (my translation).

Minimanual of the Urban Guerrilla, explained what were the ALN's objectives:

"With his technique developed and established, the urban guerrilla bases himself on models of action leading to attack, and, in Brazil, with the following objectives:

"a. to threaten the triangle in which the Brazilian state system and North American domination are maintained in Brazil, a triangle whose points are Río, São Paulo, and Belo Horizonte and whose base is the axis Río–São Paulo, where the giant industrial-financial-economic-political-military-police complex that holds the entire decisive power of the country is located;

"b. to weaken the local guards or the security system of the dictatorship, given the fact that we are attacking and the *gorilas* defending, which means catching the government in a defensive position with its troops immobilized in defense of the entire complex of national maintenance, with its ever-present fears of an attack on its strategic nerve centers, and without ever knowing where, how, and when that attack will come;

"c. to attack on every side with many different armed groups, few in number, each self-contained and operating separately, to disperse the government forces in their pursuit of a thoroughly fragmented organization instead of offering the dictatorship the opportunity to concentrate its forces of repression on the destruction of one tightly organized system operating throughout the country;

"d. to give proof of its combativeness, decision, firmness, determination, and persistence in the attack on the military dictatorship in order to permit all malcontents to follow our example and fight with urban guerrilla tactics. Meanwhile, the government, with all its problems, incapable of halting guerrilla operations in the city, will lose time and suffer endless attrition and will finally be forced to pull back its repressive troops in order to mount guard over the banks, industries, armories, military barracks, prisons, public offices, radio and television stations, North American firms, gas storage tanks, oil refineries, ships, airplanes, ports, airports, hospitals, health centers, blood banks, stores, garages, embassies, residences of outstanding members of the regime such as ministers and generals, police stations, and official organizations, etc.

"e. to increase urban guerrilla disturbances gradually in an endless ascendancy of unforeseen actions such that the government troops cannot leave the urban areas to pursue the guerrillas in the interior without running the risk of abandoning the cities and permitting rebellion to increase on the coast as well as in the interior of the country;

"f. to oblige the army and the police, with the commanders and their assistants, to change the relative comforts and tranquillity of their barracks and their usual rest, for a state of alarm and growing tension in the expectation of attack or in search for tracks that vanish without a trace;

"g. to avoid open battle and decisive combat with the government, limiting the struggle to brief and rapid attacks with lightning results;

"h. to assure for the urban guerrilla a maximum freedom of maneuver and of action without ever relinquishing the use of armed violence, remaining firmly oriented toward helping the beginning of rural guerrilla warfare and supporting the construction of the revolutionary army for national liberation."[157]

The ALN sees itself as a cadre-formation group for the future rural guerrilla war. It is committed to the proposition that the best organizational tool is armed struggle. Having learned from the failures of previous *focos*, it does not want to become the actual motor to people's war until the country expects it to the point of awaiting it—which helps build the atmosphere of the *foco's* invincibility (which, in turn, guarantees support from the normally skeptical and overly cautious rural population). The ALN does not want to launch the *foco* until its urban apparatus is firm. But otherwise, it operates like a *foco*, refusing to split the political from the military. "In the Brazilian revolutionary war, there are no political commissars who guide the military cadre. *All the members of the organization are necessarily at the same time political and military cadres. They begin at both from the start.* Those who cannot fathom one and the other simultaneously do not meet our prerequisites. And we make no difference between the militants in charge of mass organization and those whose task it is to organize logistics."[158]

The most spectacularly successful of the new urban guerrillas are the Tupamaros, the name given to the fighters of Uruguay's National Liberation Movement in honor of Tupac Amaru, the great Inca chieftain who rebelled against Spanish rule in the eighteenth century. Brilliantly organized, they have burned down plants (including General Motors) without hurting a single worker, robbed impregnable fortresses (such as the Casino of Punta del Este), kidnapped hated officials and bankers, seized whole towns long enough to explain their purpose and revolutionary commitment, and assassinated key repressive agents, such as the chief of the police's Special Squad. In fact, by all accounts except the government's (but including those of foreign correspondents for the capitalist press), the Tupamaros are efficient enough to try to seize power. Yet they do not do so. The reason? They are waiting for the revolutionaries in neighboring Argentina and Brazil to develop forces strong enough to stop their military from invading Uruguay.[159] In other words, the Tupamaros are continental revolutionaries. They know that the real enemy is the

---

[157] *Tricontinental*, No. 16, 1970. Also published in Marighella's *Pour la libération du Brésil*, slightly cut, for no apparent political reason.

[158] ALN, *Les Temps Modernes* (ALN's emphasis).

[159] See the Tupamaros pamphlet *Thirty Answers to Thirty Questions*, printed below, p. 525.

United States, and that the U.S. will use its allies and resources to stop revolution anywhere in the world.

These resources are formidable. In the first place the United States controls the finances of every unliberated country in the Third World. Then it runs their armies, also through money. It gives them weapons, often free, but not ammunition which they have to buy (usually on credit) from the U.S.; and it invites most top officers (in Latin America, *every* officer from major up) to attend U.S. command or officer schools on U.S. scholarships (after which the trainees can import duty-free into their own countries the appliances and the car which they purchased on discounts at U.S. military PX stores). Next, the United States runs the unliberated Third World's intelligence agencies, and "advises" all branches of the military and police. But in addition to all this, the U.S. operates top-notch counterinsurgency schools throughout the Third World. These graduate elite corpsmen are given special consideration by their own brass and government, and the most modern antiguerrilla weapons available. Finally, U.S. "advisers" are usually on the spot to lead counterinsurgency campaigns (though the Pentagon and local defense ministries usually refer to these campaigns as "civic action" and list their cost among the U.S.'s altruistic "social progress" grants). And, of course, if anything goes wrong, the U.S. is always prepared to send thousands of Marines to intervene directly—as it did in Santo Domingo in 1965 and was set to do in Trinidad in 1970.

The United States was fooled by Fidel in 1959. It has no intention of ever being fooled again. The Cuban bourgeoisie was also fooled by Fidel. Since then U.S. corporations and their tax-free foundations have so tied the local bourgeoisies to U.S. interests that there is no such thing as a "national bourgeoisie" anymore. Hence, it is nearly impossible for revolutionaries either to obtain funds locally or to try to wage a two-stage revolution, even if U.S. troops are present.

But the U.S. cannot dispatch troops everywhere at the same time without very serious repercussions both at home and in the other developed countries' capitals. The U.S. ruling class has a hard enough time keeping forces in Vietnam. It has had to lie about its involvement in Thailand and Laos, which it did well enough for a while by pretending the troops were in Vietnam. But if it has to simultaneously intervene in Santo Domingo, it must do it fast—and get out. Suppose, however, that the ALN grew to such proportions that U.S. intervention was necessary to save the Brazilian dictatorship, and that at the same time the Tupamaros seized Montevideo while the Venezuelan Armed Forces of National Liberation (FALN) struck at oil-rich Maracaibo? And the Colombian Army of National Liberation (ELN) seized Bogotá? And the Eritrean ELN attacked Massawa? And the Dhufar Liberation Front dynamited the Persian Gulf's Texaco complex? And black power troops rebelled in

Trinidad? And Chile's MIR occupied Anaconda's Chuquicamata copper
mines? And the Huks assaulted the U.S. bases in the Philippines? And
Panama's Liberation Front blew up the Panama Canal? Could the U.S.
go to war with all these freedom fighters simultaneously? And if it could,
what would happen at home?

In the days immediately following the U.S. invasion of Cambodia, agitation at home spread so fast that in Ohio the local repressive forces—
the National Guard—panicked and killed four students. By the time this
analysis appears in print more Americans will have been killed. And
many, many more will have become revolutionaries. Obviously, then,
to coordinate the various liberation struggles is the correct tactic. That was
what Che meant by "create two, three . . . many Vietnams." He said, "we
must bear in mind that imperialism is a world system, the last stage of
capitalism—and it must be defeated in a world confrontation."[160]

The need for cooperation among revolutionaries of the Third World
was not discovered by Che in that 1967 "Message to the Tricontinental,"
nor did it die with his death in Bolivia or with the re-evaluation of the
foco theory that succeeded it. The need first expressed itself as solidarity,
and mostly by Third World statesmen who saw their newly won political
independence threatened by imperialism's financial domination via neo-
colonialism. In 1955, Asian heads of state met in New Delhi. A short
while later, they got together with their African counterparts in Bandung,
Indonesia. By 1958, a permanent Afro-Asian Solidarity organization was
set up in Cairo. Then, influenced by Fanon and Morocco's brilliant nationalist El Mehdi Ben Barka, the organization not only decided to include
representatives of popular movements from its two continents but also
from Latin America. In 1963, the organization accepted Fidel's offer to
hold the first Tricontinental Conference in Havana, and in 1965, at the
Winneba, Ghana, meeting, it set the date: January 1966. The Winneba
conference also proclaimed that "all wars, aggressions and interventions
of imperialism, its maintenance of military bases in foreign lands and its
support for cruel and corrupt dictatorships, spring from and are dictated
by economic exploitation."[161] Ben Barka, who was elected chairman of the
Tricontinental's preparatory committee, added: "We must achieve greater
coordination in the struggle of all the people, as the problems in Vietnam,
the Congo and the Dominican Republic stem from the same source: U.S.
imperialism."[162] Which is why shortly thereafter, Ben Barka was "arrested"
by French security policemen, taken to the villa of a double agent, and
murdered.

It may be true, as K. S. Karol reports, that Cuba is too pressed by the
economic problems created by the U.S. blockade and is too constricted

[160] *Venceremos*, p. 420.
[161] Proceedings, *The Tricontinental* (Havana: OSPAAAL, 1966).
[162] *Ibid.* See also *The Political Thought of Ben Barka*, Havana: Tricontinental, 1968.

by the blackmail politics of Russia's necessary economic aid to be very internationally minded these days.[163] My own view is that the failure of the first *foco* theory, the death of Che, the sectarian battles within remaining *focos* (Venezuela, Guatemala), as well as Cuba's excessive concern with a ten-million-ton sugar harvest for 1970 caused Cuba's temporary retrenchment.[164] In any case, the first Tricon Conference set into motion a new spirit which can only die at the top, not at the base of the world revolutionary movement. Indeed, the conference will probably go down in history as one of the most important of the second half of the twentieth century, for it gave formal birth to a new revolutionary international.

Not much was actually achieved at the Tricon to make the international operational, though OSPAAAL (Organization of Solidarity of the Peoples of Asia, Africa, and Latin America) bureaucracy continues to function in Havana. It keeps members informed of each other's activities, and publishes an important journal (*Tricontinental*, in French, Spanish, and English); moreover, through OSPAAAL the established revolutionary countries (Vietnam, North Korea, Cuba, Algeria) do actually aid and train revolutionary cadres of other countries. However, it has yet to become what Captain Osmany Cienfuegos, the boyish-looking former guerrilla who was elected OSPAAAL's secretary-general, said it would—"an organization of fighting peoples, with enough flexibility and capacity for action to assist the peoples of the three continents in the development of the national liberation movement and anti-imperialist struggle. We must give to the concept of solidarity an active, dynamic and militant content."[165]

Whether or not OSPAAAL can ever actually operate as the executive of the new international, the spirit generated at the Tricon was real. In Latin America, it led to OLAS (Organization of Latin American Solidarity) which in turn led to the final rupture between old-line Communist Party hacks and new-line revolutionary communists. It led to the Cuban position paper, prepared by Armando Hart, which commits the island's *Fidelistas* to continental revolution. It led to Che and other members of the Central Committee of Cuban Communist Party fighting in Bolivia. And if that led to the discard of the *foco* theory, it also brought about the new urban *foco* practice.

In Africa, the Tricon spirit helped ignite the need for alliances, one of

[163] K. S. Karol, *Les Guerrilleros au Pouvoir* (Paris: Laffont, 1970).

[164] Judging by the renewed international coverage in *Granma*, as well as by Fidel's speeches after April 1, the retrenchment seemed over by the end of May 1970. However, in an April 22, 1970, speech commemorating the one-hundredth anniversary of Lenin's birth, Fidel came out so strongly in support of Russia and its policies that Cuba's ideological independence at the top could seem questionable. See *Granma*, weekly English edition, May 3, 1970.

[165] Proceedings, in *The Tricontinental*.

which now includes Cabral's PAIGC, Angola's MPLA, Mozambique's FRELIMO, Zimbabwe's ZAPU, South Africa's ANC and South West Africa's SWAPO. Most of these liberation fronts are still too much influenced by Russia and local CP's, but the germ of the future is there. In Asia, the current coalition between North Vietnam, South Vietnam's NLF, Laos' Pathet Lao, and Cambodia's Sihanouk and Khmer Rouge forces represents the same commitment on the positive side, the same recognition of mutual self-interest on the side of survival.

On a global scale, the Tricon spirit brought the poor countries of the world closer to each other, crystallizing the nature of the class struggle which exists not only in each land but among nations as well. Today, North Korea's Kim Il Sung, trained by China and installed in power by Russia, is closer to Fidel than to Brezhnev. His brand of nationalistic communism at home and total revolutionary internationalism abroad has excited America's Black Panthers and Weathermen alike.[166] In general, the new Tricon spirit, born out of self-defense against international imperialism, wrought by long years of struggle and many defeats, and polished by a new understanding of man's need to participate in the decisions affecting his life, is both pragmatic and romantic. It reflects each man's need to make himself count and his awareness that no one ever does unless all do.

This spirit is today as much of a force inside the mother country of imperialism as out. It is part of the consciousness of the Black Panthers, who see themselves as one faltering battalion in the world people's army against the American ruling class. It is part of the consciousness of the New York bombers who wrote that the companies whose offices they had blown up—IBM, Socony Mobil, General Telephone and Electronics—"are enemies of all life. All three profit not only from death in Vietnam, but also from American imperialism in all of the Third World. They profit from racist oppression of black, Puerto Rican and other minority colonies inside America; from the suffering and death of men in the American army; from sexism; from the exploitation and degradation of employees forced into lives of anti-human work; from the pollution and destruction of our environment."[167] The Tricon is part of the Revolution in the U.S.

That revolution will be just as violent in the U.S. as out. It too will operate along new *foco* lines: bombings, sabotage, assassinations. These acts of terrorism will train the cadre for the revolutionary force of the future. It will also do its share to weaken imperialism's home base, to bring about panic, confusion, and the dissolution of the state. To traditional Marxists, such tactics are self-defeating: Terrorism never leads

166 See Kim's *Let Us Embody More Thoroughly the Revolutionary Spirit of Independence, Self-sustenance and Self-defence in All Fields of State Activity* (Pyongyang; Foreign Languages Publishing House, 1968).
167 *Guardian* (New York), March 21, 1970.

to revolution. That is perfectly true when the area to be restructured by revolution is self-contained. But imperialism is international. The Revolution is international. It is not the Weathermen who will bring down the ruling class. It is the Vietnamese, Congolese, Venezuelans, Brazilians, Koreans, Palestinians, Trinidadians—and the revolutionary blacks, browns, yellows and reds *and* revolutionary white youths of America. Not the organized, unionized, capitalized, skill-workerized, traditional "proletariat," which since the days of Samuel Gompers has stuck faithfully to its "economist" policies. But their sons, plus the unskilled, underemployed, ununionized, exploited, alienated, and self-conscious.

For this real proletariat to develop faith in its own strength will take a long time—many, many years. It will gain it slowly by seeing the mammoth monster rock from tiny bombs and constant but sporadic shooting. It will learn gradually to hate every policeman, every "law and order" agent, every hypocritical ruling class mouthpiece. "A people without hatred cannot vanquish a brutal enemy," Che said.[168] And the new American proletariat must hate if it is to win. Already, millions of youths hate a bit. Many hate totally. All will have to hate as much. But as the National Guard keeps shooting, as the Reagans and Agnews keep yelling, as the Tactical Police Forces keep torturing their captives, America's youth will hate enough to kill. No long-hair gets jailed overnight anymore without being beaten by the police. No long-hair comes out of jail anymore without hating. The Revolution has begun.

The beginning itself is slow. Years are spent demonstrating. With no result, some drop out, abandon the struggle, marry into suburbia, and try to forget, while the others escalate their activity, get beaten and jailed—and a few get killed. More drop out, though new recruits always join, and the cycle goes on, except now the radicals become rebels as they fight back, learn to become professionals, as Lenin said, "combating the political police." Once toughened up, they gain boldness and resort to sabotage. Then they disappear. Some drop out at this point too. Others perfect their skills. The war goes on. Those who continue to fight are revolutionaries. Who are they? You, me, clerks, students, bus drivers, teachers. This teacher, for example. His name is Jomo Raskin, and he was teaching at the State University of New York at Stony Brook when he was arrested at a demonstration on December 9, 1969, protesting the murder of Chicago Panther Chairman Fred Hampton. This is in part what he wrote about it:

"Four or five pigs pushed and pulled me to the sidewalk. There was broken glass everywhere. I remember one pig with blue splotched bell bottom trousers and a moustache, who kept yelling, 'He's mine, he's mine. Leave him to me.' Awfully possessive, these pigs. And he whacked

[168] *Venceremos*, p. 422.

me over the head with his nightstick, his identification mark. I put my hands over my head. Blood trickled down my face and my neck. It reminded me of my football days, of a big pile-up on the five-yard line. Then it was still. The noisy street was quiet. I was pulled to my feet and handcuffed to Bob Reilly, an actor, a teacher, the toughest battler I know. Arrested again. We were thrown into the pig car, taken to the 18th Precinct, driven down 5th Avenue, past all the expensive stores, past the stores filled with the loot of the world. At the 18th the pigs stood us in a corner, banged me in the head a few times. The pig with bell bottoms and a moustache was puffing away on a big cheap cigar. The blood kept flowing.

"Reilly and I walked upstairs, the pigs behind us, prodding us on. The pigs filled out cards, asked us questions. 'Where do you live?' 'Where do you work? When were you born?' They didn't like the fact that I teach at the State University at Stony Brook. 'This scum bag is a teacher at Stony Brook,' one pig kept repeating. If we didn't answer, or took our time answering questions, they clubbed us. We were put in a cell. One cop spat at me through the bars. His saliva oozed down the wall. He was safe with me behind bars. . . .

"From the 18th Precinct we were taken to Roosevelt Hospital. Reilly got twelve stitches in his head. I got five. We were cleaned up, X-rayed. A pig stood by, all the time, with his gun and nightstick. The nurses smiled cheerfully. The interns worked efficiently. Reilly rapped with them about the war, the murder of Fred Hampton. . . . A lawyer, Paul Chevigny, shows up, asks how we are, and is quickly hustled out of the Precinct. We're taken to the 17th.

"The 17th Precinct is a torturer's heaven. For an hour, Reilly and I were systematically and efficiently beaten by the pigs. We were taken into the squad room on the first floor. There were about twenty cops sitting and standing around. 'So here are the pig fighters,' they said. They put us in a corner. Our hands were handcuffed behind our backs. Our faces were to the wall. There was a metal coat rack and some pieces of wood with nails in them in the corner. We were thrown up against the metal coat rack and the lumber with the nails. Each pig had his special torture. One hit me with his nightstick in the calf. Another used a blackjack on my back. A third hit my elbow with a pair of pliers. A fourth took running jumps and kicked me in the back. Another jumped on my toes. Everyone took turns hitting, kicking, spitting, name-calling. I was called fuck face, douche bag, commie, scum bag, an afterbirth. At the start of the beating Bob Reilly had shouted out, 'Hey, lieutenant, how's about breaking up this caucus back here?' The lieutenant never did and the pigs only beat on him worse for yelling out. The brutality was calculated. They stopped, examined our bodies, figured out the best place to hit us, or poke us. They hated us, but they were in control of their emotions and acts. One pig at a desk in the 17th said he hated me because I was taking air from him, because I was breathing his air. They hated us because we're opposed to the war, because we support the NLF, because we defend the Panthers, because we're for armed struggle. They hated us because we're teachers. Their big joke was, 'Raskin teaches Riot I, and Reilly teaches Riot II.' They hated us because we're rioters, because we're fighters.

"The pigs who beat us tried to act tough, but they're wimps. They're puny. It doesn't take any courage for twenty pigs to beat on two guys who are handcuffed behind their backs. On 50th Street and 5th Avenue I saw a pig who was bleeding crying out for an ambulance, whimpering. The TPF (Tactical Police Force) are Hitler youth, New York's SS, and they're afraid, chicken.

"For about a half hour, we were beaten in the squad room. Another demonstrator witnessed much of the beating. Then we were taken downstairs into the basement. Everytime you go up or downstairs the pigs try to trip you. They push you up or down the stairs, stick out their feet and warn you, 'Watch it, you wouldn't want to hurt yourself.' They play petty games. The pig tells you your name is 'fuck face.' 'What's your name?' he asks. When you don't answer, he beats you. When you say, 'fuck face,' he stops. You play cat and mouse, see how much you can take.

"The room in the basement was dark. It had a cold cement floor and cold cement walls, a sink and a faucet. We were beaten for another half hour. Nightsticks were rammed into my stomach. The pigs asked us, 'Have you had enough?' 'You won't mess with us anymore, now, will you?' 'Going to fight pigs anymore?' One pig stuck pins in my back to see if I had any nerve sensations left. When I didn't feel anything he stopped beating on me.

"People have asked me how I stood the beating and what I was thinking about. I didn't do much thinking. . . . At one point between the beatings, Bob Reilly turned to me and said, with a smile, 'Chairman Bobby.' I was thinking about Bobby Seale, too. The pigs could never destroy that world, that connection, that feeling of comradeship in struggle.

" 'Bobby Seale, live like him.' 'Nguyen Van Trol, live like him.' Those words hadn't meant much before I was beaten. I had written them on walls. I had spoken them. But only in the 17th Precinct did they come to have meaning. The name Bobby Seale was like armor I put on to shield the pigs' blows. Nguyen Van Trol is a light inside the heart. They make you feel that you're a lot stronger than the pigs, that there are people all over the world fighting with you, that you're on their side. . . .

"From the 17th Precinct we were taken to the 4th Precinct. We spent the night on hard wooden benches. Going down to the 4th in the squad car there were three of us—Reilly, myself and a beautiful hippie. He was bandaged on the head. He had been beaten. Reilly and I were trying to catch our breath, leaning our heads back. This hippie rapped with the pigs and took the pressure off us. He cooled them, controlled them. This kid was up for anything and everything. He had been beat on bad but he was still going strong. He rapped with the cops about Tom Jefferson, communes, Senator Joseph McCarthy, *The Rat*, about communism. He wasn't afraid of anything. He would have taken on those pigs then and there if they had unhandcuffed him. My head was aching, my legs and arms were bruised, but inside, in my bones, this kid made me feel that the Revolution was coming. No mistake about it."[169]

I said at the beginning that I would try to answer the question: what then? What if the Revolution succeeds? It is symptomatic of the "liberals" to ask this question. They do not feel the repression, the exploitation, the hatred. Their concern is humanitarian, but their life style inegalitarian. They believe in individuals because they want to be separate from the masses. They talk of integrity, because they want to be pure. They have souls, complexes, and fetishes. They have bread, and so insist on "not by bread alone." They have personal ambitions, and so repeat that nature did not make all men equal. They cannot understand collectivism, because they never recognize classes. They proclaim their right to own works of art but demand that museums be free. They cherish individual morality but cheat on their spouses. They condemn the low wage scales but pay their maids standard rates. They deny the existence of a ruling class because they each know a businessman who is kind and generous. They think government makes policy, courts uphold the Constitution, and drug laws are for the people's good. They see no connection between the war in Vietnam and life in the ghetto, between *Newsweek* which opposes Reagan and the murder of James Rector at People's Park, between the assassinations of Malcolm X, Martin Luther King, and Fred Hampton, between Rockefeller's art collection and the fact that in northeastern Brazil men die of old age at thirty-two. They ask "What after the Revolution?" because they don't want a revolution.

My answer will be brief. When Spartacus rebelled against Rome he hadn't worked out just what kind of society he would replace it with if he won. He only knew that a society which ordered him to kill his fellow men for the entertainment of a few had to be destroyed. Today people all over the world are rebelling because they don't want to die or kill for the greed of a few.

No more ought to be said, but I'll risk a few more sentences. The world the new revolutionaries want to build will have no masters and no slaves. It will be administratively decentralized so everyone can participate in the decision-making process. It will recognize no "supernatural" talents: a man with an I.Q. of 60 is as much of a man as one with 160, and both have equal rights to have the collective respond to their needs.

[169] *Leviathan*, February 1970.

In the future, communities will run production, schools, technology. Administrators will administer things not people. All necessities will be free—housing, food, clothes, theaters, medicine, education, eyeglasses, television, transportation. Eventually there will be no need for money at all. But as long as international transactions use it, the best the revolutionary can do is pay people according to their need, and that need will be determined socially, in the collective. No problem will be considered personal. At the beginning the Revolution can only *try* to transform the personal into the social. It can abolish neither greed nor envy, except through years of education. So it will only control that greed by putting technology at the service of man, instead of against him. That control will be by the community whose representatives will always be recallable, whose police will always be reviewable, whose judges will always be removable. A collective society does not only establish collective rights, it demands collective responsibility as well. And it is through the exercise of that responsibility that the individual really learns to enjoy his collective rights.

But all this is a dream that is far, far away. The immediate task is to excise the cancer, stop the wars, arrest the violence. Unfortunately the only way to destroy the master-slave relationship is to kill the master, or at least take away his whip. But fortunately, as Fanon said, in the act of seizing the whip or killing the master, the slave surmounts himself. He stops being a slave. Huey Newton or George Jackson is in jail today, but he is not a slave. By rising against his masters, he became a man. In isolation, periodically beaten, constantly goaded and harassed, Huey or George is not alienated. He communicates all the time with hundreds of thousands of blacks and thousands of whites who are his comrades. In combat for all men, each man finds liberation.

The writers included in this volume are all comrades. They may not agree with each other on tactics or even strategy, but they have all put their lives at the service of man's liberation. Some died before I read their works. Others may die before you read them. Not one talks very much about future society; they were or are too busy fighting against this oppressive one to worry much about the next. Each continues to influence. Not many write well; they were or are men of action, not stylists (except for the introduction by Lenin and the conclusion by Huey Newton, each piece included here has been condensed, but accurately and only to eliminate repetitions). They are revolutionaries; men who always found audacity because they had faith—not in systems or causes or philosophies (though in them, too, sometimes) but faith in men.

May 1, 1970

Introduction

In the modern era, Russia's October Revolution was the first to establish a "people's democracy." It did so, basically, via general insurrection. The Eastern European revolutionaries who seized power after World War II relied mostly on the Soviet Red Army. As such theirs was not a revolution, even if it did lead to Soviet-style regimes (perhaps one reason why the people of Eastern Europe, nonparticipants in their "revolutionary" process, are far from satisfied with their imposed way of life). Since then, every successful restructuring socialist revolution has come about after some form of guerrilla warfare —as in China, Vietnam, Algeria, Cuba.

True, other governments claim to be carrying out social revolutions— in Syria, Iraq, Egypt, Sudan. But these "revolutionary" governments are in power as a result of a military coup; the people are not armed and do not participate in the decision-making process. As a possible conse-quence—some would insist a direct consequence—the restructuring of society inside these countries, whatever their government's foreign policies and ideological rhetoric, is not revolutionary. If that is so, it is another argument in the thesis that a direct relation exists between people's war and people's democracy, between arming the people and genuine socialism. Thus, many modern revolutionaries today claim that the main strategic weapon, as well as the ideological prerequisite, for a sweeping total revolution is guerrilla warfare—or people's war.

Old-style revolutionaries, however, often tend to disagree. Some insist that guerrilla war is only one, and not necessarily the most important, means of seizing revolutionary power. Soviet communists, for example, are convinced that capitalism's inherent contradictions must necessarily lead to its destruction if allowed to compete freely on an economic and propaganda level with totally planned communist societies (such as exists, they say, in the Soviet Union). Hence, they espouse and proselytize the *so-called peaceful coexistence line. Some of these "communists" who call themselves revolutionaries even believe that a revolution can be achieved by playing according to the rules imposed by their capitalist enemies. They point out that all revolutions which have succeeded since World War II have occurred in the occupied underdeveloped world, that part of the globe economically, politically, culturally, and militarily exploited and dominated by affluent capitalist nations. Since those poor lands are now relatively free of occupiers, guerrilla warfare, insurrection, even general political strikes tend to alienate rather than politicize the people, who have been fooled into believing that they are masters of their own political fates.*

Whatever the viewpoint, the fact is that only in those countries—of the underdeveloped world—where the people have taken up arms has the revolution been victorious (though the converse has not necessarily been true). Understandably then, guerrilla warfare remains the most discussed subject among revolutionaries. It seems appropriate, therefore, that this book begin with an analysis of guerrilla warfare by Lenin, who, after all, is recognized by all contemporary revolutionaries, whether they consider themselves Marxist-Leninists or not, as their greatest mentor.

Unlike most Marxist-Leninists of today, Lenin was rarely dogmatic. He was perfectly willing to admit, and does in the text that follows, that there are all sorts of forms of revolutionary struggle which neither he nor his comrades have yet imagined. Nor was he ever opposed to spontaneous revolutionary acts, as are those old leftists today who condemn the "New Left." He did insist, however, that a spontaneous act, say a local rebellion, that is not quickly organized is bound to fail. But those he would condemn for such a failure would not be the rebels but the trained party cadre who were incapable of recognizing the needs of those who rebelled. A popular rebellion can never be wrong, Lenin said, for it is conditions which cause people to say NO—*and mean it with guns or rocks. Likewise, the eruption of a guerrilla war is brought about by the conditions under which people live, and hence cannot be criticized, only aided and guided.*

The one fundamental truth—or dogma—that Lenin always upheld was that a revolutionary seizes power, he doesn't win it in a poker game, in an election, or by default. His task is to overturn a ruling class, not chase an individual out of a palace. And no ruling class ever willingly releases its grip on the machinery of a state in which and from which it profits. That is not to say that, tactically, a revolutionary cannot at times use peaceful means to advance his cause. But the actual revolution is the seizure, consolidation, and expansion of power—out of the hands of the "haves" (the bourgeoisie and up) and into the hands of the "have-nots" (the proletariat, peasants, petty-bourgeois intellectuals and down). That can only be done through force, which entails a civil war. Thus, "a

*Marxist cannot regard civil war, or guerrilla warfare, which is one of its
forms, as abnormal."*

*Many of Lenin's contemporary comrades criticized guerrilla warfare as
alienating, too polarizing and adventuristic, as apt to disorganize the
"movement," to get out of hand or be defeated, thus to set the revolution
back—arguments used by Soviet communists today to condemn Latin
American guerrilla fighters. Lenin's answer: "It is not guerrilla actions
which disorganize the movement, but the weakness of a party which is
incapable of taking such actions under its control"; and "every military
action in any war to a certain extent disorganizes the ranks of the fighters.
But this does not mean that one must not fight. It means that one must
learn to fight. That is all."*

V. I. LENIN: GUERRILLA WARFARE*

THE question of guerrilla action is one that greatly interests our Party
and the mass of the workers. We have dealt with this question in passing
several times, and now we propose to give the more complete statement of our views we have promised.

Let us begin from the beginning. What are the fundamental demands
which every Marxist should make of an examination of the question of
forms of struggle? In the first place, Marxism differs from all primitive
forms of socialism by not binding the movement to any one particular
form of struggle. It recognizes the most varied forms of struggle; and
it does not "concoct" them, but only generalizes, organizes, gives conscious expression to those forms of struggle of the revolutionary classes
which arise of themselves in the course of the movement. Absolutely
hostile to all abstract formulas and to all doctrinaire recipes, Marxism
demands an attentive attitude to the mass struggle in progress, which, as
the movement develops, as the class consciousness of the masses grows,
as economic and political crises become acute, continually gives rise to
new and more varied methods of defense and attack. Marxism, therefore,
positively does not reject any form of struggle. Under no circumstances
does Marxism confine itself to the forms of struggle possible and in
existence at the given moment only, recognizing as it does that new
forms of struggle, unknown to the participants of the given period, inevitably arise as the given social situation changes. In this respect Marxism

---

* Article, dated September 30, 1906, originally published in Lenin's newspaper *Pro-
letary*, No. 5 (October 13, 1906). English version in V. I. Lenin, *Collected Works*,
II (June 1906–January 1907), (Moscow: Foreign Languages Publishing House,
1962).

learns, if we may so express it, from mass practice, and makes no claim whatever to teach the masses forms of struggle invented by "systematizers" in the seclusion of their studies. We know—said Kautsky, for instance, when examining the forms of social revolution—that the coming crisis will introduce new forms of struggle that we are now unable to foresee.

In the second place, Marxism demands an absolutely historical examination of the question of the forms of struggle. To treat this question apart from the concrete historical situation betrays a failure to understand the rudiments of dialectical materialism. At different stages of economic evolution, depending on differences in political, national-cultural, living and other conditions, different forms of struggle come to the fore and become the principal forms of struggle; and in connection with this, the secondary, auxiliary forms of struggle undergo change in their turn. To attempt to answer yes or no to the question whether any particular means of struggle should be used, without making a detailed examination of the concrete situation of the given movement at the given stage of its development, means completely to abandon the Marxist position.

These are the two principal theoretical propositions by which we must be guided. The history of Marxism in Western Europe provides an infinite number of examples corroborating what has been said. European Social Democracy at the present time regards parliamentarism and the trade union movement as the principal forms of struggle; it recognized insurrection in the past, and is quite prepared to recognize it, should conditions change, in the future—despite the opinion of bourgeois liberals like the Russian Cadets and the Bezzaglavtsi.[1] Social Democracy in the seventies rejected the general strike as a social panacea, as a means of overthrowing the bourgeoisie at one stroke by nonpolitical means—but Social Democracy fully recognizes the mass political strike (especially after the experience of Russia in 1905) as one of the methods of struggle essential under certain conditions.[2] Social Democracy recognized street barricade fighting in the forties, rejected it for definite reasons at the end of the nineteenth century, and expressed complete readiness to revise the latter view and to admit the expediency of barricade fighting after the experience of Moscow, which, in the words of K. Kautsky, initiated new tactics of barricade fighting.

Having established the general Marxist propositions, let us turn to the Russian revolution. Let us recall the historical development of the forms of struggle it produced. First there were the economic strikes of workers

[1] Those affiliated with *Bes Zaglavia* (Without Title) magazine, published in 1906 by moderate socialists who sympathized with the left wing of the Constitutional Democrats (Cadets).—*Ed.*

[2] The general strike of August 1905 was absolute by October, forcing the government to issue the "October Manifesto" and pretend to form a semiconstitutional regime.—*Ed.*

(1896–1900), then the political demonstrations of workers and students (1901–02), peasant revolts (1902), the beginning of mass political strikes variously combined with demonstrations (Rostov, 1902, the strikes in the summer of 1903, January 9, 1905[3]), the all-Russian political strike accompanied by local cases of barricade fighting (October 1905), mass barricade fighting and armed uprising (1905, December), the peaceful parliamentary struggle (April–June 1906), partial military revolts (June 1905–July 1906), and partial peasant revolts (autumn 1905–autumn 1906).

Such is the state of affairs in the autumn of 1906 as concerns forms of struggle in general. The "retaliatory" form of struggle adopted by the autocracy is the Black Hundred pogrom, from Kishinev in the spring of 1903 to Sedlets in the autumn of 1906.[4] All through this period the organization of Black Hundred pogroms and the beating up of Jews, students, revolutionaries, and class-conscious workers continued to progress and perfect itself, combining the violence of the Black Hundred troops with the violence of hired ruffians, going as far as the use of artillery in villages and towns and merging with punitive expeditions, punitive trains, and so forth.

Such is the principal background of the picture. Against this background there stands out—unquestionably as something partial, secondary, and auxiliary—the phenomenon to the study and assessment of which the present article is devoted. What is this phenomenon? What are its forms? What are its causes? When did it arise and how far has it spread? What is its significance in the general course of the revolution? What is its relation to the struggle of the working class organized and led by Social Democracy? Such are the questions which we must now proceed to examine after having sketched the general background of the picture.

The phenomenon in which we are interested is the armed struggle. It is conducted by individuals and by small groups. Some belong to revolutionary organizations, while others (the majority in certain parts of Russia) do not belong to any revolutionary organization. Armed struggle pursues two different aims, which must be strictly distinguished: In the first place, this struggle aims at assassinating individuals, chiefs and subordinates in the army and police; in the second place, it aims at the confiscation of monetary funds both from the government and from private persons. The confiscated funds go partly into the treasury of the Party, partly for the special purpose of arming and preparing for an uprising, and partly for the maintenance of persons engaged in the strug-

---

[3] "Bloody Sunday," the trigger to the 1905 Revolution.—*Ed.*

[4] The Black Hundreds, right-wing terrorists organized by the secret police, were sent by the czarist regime against the Jews on the assumption that Russia's revolutionaries were all Jews and thus "retaliatory" pogroms would frighten the revolutionaries into abandoning their agitation.—*Ed.*

gle we are describing. The big expropriations (such as the Caucasian, involving over 200,000 rubles, and the Moscow, involving 875,000 rubles) went in fact first and foremost to revolutionary parties—small expropriations go mostly, and sometimes entirely, to the maintenance of the "expropriators." This form of struggle undoubtedly became widely developed and extensive only in 1906, i.e., after the December uprising. The intensification of the political crisis to the point of an armed struggle and, in particular, the intensification of poverty, hunger, and unemployment in town and country, was one of the important causes of the struggle we are describing. This form of struggle was adopted as the preferable and even exclusive form of social struggle by the vagabond elements of the population, the lumpenproletariat and anarchist groups. Declaration of martial law, mobilization of fresh troops, Black Hundred pogroms (Sedlets), and military courts must be regarded as the "retaliatory" form of struggle adopted by the autocracy.

The usual appraisal of the struggle we are describing is that it is anarchism, Blanquism, the old terrorism, the acts of individuals isolated from the masses, which demoralize the workers, repel wide strata of the population, disorganize the movement, and injure the revolution. Examples in support of this appraisal can easily be found in the events reported every day in the newspapers.

But are such examples convincing? In order to test this, let us take a locality where the form of struggle we are examining is most developed— the Lettish Territory. This is the way *Novoye Vremya*[5] (in its issues of September 9 and 12) complains of the activities of the Lettish Social Democrats. The Lettish Social Democratic Labor Party (a section of the Russian Social Democratic Labor Party) regularly issues its paper in 30,000 copies. The announcement columns publish lists of spies whom it is the duty of every decent person to exterminate. People who assist the police are proclaimed "enemies of the revolution," liable to execution and, moreover, to confiscation of property. The public is instructed to give money to the Social Democratic Party only against signed and stamped receipt. In the Party's latest report, showing a total income of 48,000 rubles for the year, there figures a sum of 5,600 rubles contributed by the Libau branch for arms which was obtained by expropriation. Naturally, *Novoye Vremya* rages and fumes against this "revolutionary law," against this "terror government."

Nobody will be so bold as to call these activities of the Lettish Social Democrats anarchism, Blanquism, or terrorism. But why? Because here we have a clear connection between the new form of struggle and the uprising which broke out in December and which is again brewing. This connection is not so perceptible in the case of Russia as a whole, but

[5] *Novoye Vremya* was a leading conservative newspaper of the day. The Lettish guerrillas, extremely well-organized, operated in the Baltic states.—*Ed.*

it exists. The fact that "guerrilla" warfare became widespread precisely after December, and its connection with the accentuation not only of the economic crisis but also of the political crisis is beyond dispute. The old Russian terrorism was an affair of the intellectual conspirator; today as a general rule guerrilla warfare is waged by the worker combatant, or simply by the unemployed worker. Blanquism and anarchism easily occur to the minds of people who have a weakness for stereotype; but under the circumstances of an uprising, which are so apparent in the Lettish Territory, the inappropriateness of such trite labels is only too obvious.

The example of the Letts clearly demonstrates how incorrect, unscientific, and unhistorical is the practice so very common among us of analyzing guerrilla warfare without reference to the circumstances of an uprising. These circumstances must be borne in mind, we must reflect on the peculiar features of an intermediate period between big acts of insurrection, we must realize what forms of struggle inevitably arise under such circumstances, and not try to shirk the issue by a collection of words learned by rote, such as are used equally by the Cadets and the *Novoye Vremya*-ites: anarchism, robbery, hooliganism!

It is said that guerrilla acts disorganize our work. Let us apply this argument to the situation that has existed since December 1905, to the period of Black Hundred pogroms and martial law. What disorganizes the movement more in such a period: the absence of resistance or organized guerrilla warfare? Compare the center of Russia with her western borders, with Poland and the Lettish Territory. It is unquestionable that guerrilla warfare is far more widespread and far more developed in the western border regions. And it is equally unquestionable that the revolutionary movement in general, and the Social Democratic movement in particular, are more disorganized in central Russia than in the western border regions. Of course, it would not enter our heads to conclude from this that the Polish and Lettish Social Democratic movements are less disorganized thanks to guerrilla warfare. No. The only conclusion that can be drawn is that guerrilla warfare is not to blame for the state of disorganization of the Social Democratic working class movement in Russia in 1906.

Allusion is often made in this respect to the peculiarities of national conditions. But this allusion very clearly betrays the weakness of the current argument. If it is a matter of national conditions then it is not a matter of anarchism, Blanquism, or terrorism—sins that are common to Russia as a whole and even to the Russians especially—but of something else. Analyze this something else concretely, gentlemen! You will then find that national oppression or antagonism explain nothing, because they have always existed in the western regions, whereas guerrilla warfare has been engendered only by the present historical period. There are many places where there are national oppression and antagonism, but no guerrilla struggle, which sometimes develops where there is no national oppression whatever. A concrete analysis of the question will show that it is not a matter of national oppression, but of conditions of insurrection. Guerrilla warfare is an inevitable form of struggle at a time when the mass movement has actually reached the point of an uprising and when fairly large intervals occur between the "big engagements" in the civil war.

It is not guerrilla actions which disorganize the movement, but the weakness of a party which is incapable of taking such actions under its control. That is why the anathemas which we Russians usually hurl against guerrilla actions go hand in hand with secret, casual, unorganized guerrilla actions which really do disorganize the Party. Being incapable of understanding what historical conditions give rise to this struggle, we are incapable of neutralizing its deleterious aspects. Yet the struggle is going on. It is engendered by powerful economic and political causes. It is not in our power to eliminate these causes or to eliminate this struggle. Our complaints against guerrilla warfare are complaints against our Party weakness in the matter of an uprising.

What we have said about disorganization also applies to demoralization. It is not guerrilla warfare which demoralizes, but unorganized, irregular, nonparty guerrilla acts. We shall not rid ourselves one least bit of this most unquestionable demoralization by condemning and cursing guerrilla actions, for condemnations and curses are absolutely incapable of putting a stop to a phenomenon which has been engendered by profound economic and political causes. It may be objected that if we are incapable of putting a stop to an abnormal and demoralizing phenomenon, this is no reason why the Party should adopt abnormal and demoralizing methods of struggle. But such an objection would be a purely bourgeois-liberal and not a Marxist objection, because a Marxist cannot regard civil war, or guerrilla warfare, which is one of its forms, as abnormal and demoralizing in general. A Marxist bases himself on the class struggle, and not social peace. In certain periods of acute economic and political crises the class struggle ripens into a direct civil war, i.e., into an armed struggle between two sections of the people. In such periods a Marxist is obliged to take the stand of civil war. Any moral condemnation of civil war would be absolutely impermissible from the standpoint of Marxism.

In a period of civil war the ideal party of the proletariat is a fighting party. This is absolutely incontrovertible. We are quite prepared to grant that it is possible to argue and prove the inexpediency from the standpoint of civil war of particular forms of civil war at any particular moment. We fully admit criticism of diverse forms of civil war from the standpoint of military expediency and absolutely agree that in this question it is the Social Democratic practical workers in each particular locality who must have the final say. But we absolutely demand in the name of the principles of Marxism that an analysis of the conditions of civil war should not be evaded by hackneyed and stereotyped talk about anarchism, Blanquism, and terrorism, and that senseless methods of guerrilla activity adopted by some organization or other of the Polish Socialist Party at some moment or other should not be used as a bogey when discussing the question of the participation of the Social Democratic Party as such in guerrilla warfare in general.

The argument that guerrilla warfare disorganizes the movement must be regarded critically. Every new form of struggle, accompanied as it is by new dangers and new sacrifices, inevitably "disorganizes" organizations which are unprepared for this new form of struggle. Our old propagandist circles were disorganized by recourse to methods of agitation. Our committees were subsequently disorganized by recourse to demonstrations. Every military action in any war to a certain extent disorganizes the ranks of the fighters. But this does not mean that one must not fight. It means that one must learn to fight. That is all.

When I see Social Democrats proudly and smugly declaring "we are not anarchists, thieves, robbers, we are superior to all this, we reject guerrilla warfare"—I ask myself: Do these people realize what they are saying? Armed clashes and conflicts between the Black Hundred government and the population are taking place all over the country. This is an absolutely inevitable phenomenon at the present stage of development of the revolution. The population is spontaneously and in an unorganized way—and for that very reason often in unfortunate and undesirable forms—reacting to this phenomenon also by armed conflicts and attacks. I can understand us refraining from Party leadership of this spontaneous struggle in a particular place or at a particular time because of the weakness and unpreparedness of our organization. I realize that this question must be settled by the local practical workers, and that the remolding of weak and unprepared organizations is no easy matter. But when I see a Social Democratic theoretician or publicist not displaying regret over this unpreparedness, but rather a proud smugness and a self-exalted tendency to repeat phrases learned by rote in early youth about anarchism, Blanquism, and terrorism, I am hurt by this degradation of the most revolutionary doctrine in the world.

It is said that guerrilla warfare brings the class-conscious proletarians into close association with degraded, drunken riff-raff. That is true. But it only means that the party of the proletariat can never regard guerrilla warfare as the only, or even as the chief, method of struggle; it means that this method must be subordinated to other methods, that it must be commensurate with the chief methods of warfare, and must be ennobled by the enlightening and organizing influence of socialism. And without this latter condition, all, positively all, methods of struggle in bourgeois society bring the proletariat into close association with the various nonproletarian strata above and below it and, if left to the spontaneous course of events, become frayed, corrupted, and prostituted. Strikes, if left to the spontaneous course of events, become corrupted into "alliances"—agreements between the workers and the masters against the consumers. Parliament becomes corrupted into a brothel, where a gang of bourgeois politicians barter wholesale and retail "national freedom," "liberalism," "democracy," republicanism, anticlericalism, socialism, and all other wares in demand. A newspaper becomes corrupted into a public pimp, into a means of corrupting the masses, of pandering to the low instincts of the mob, and so on and so forth. Social Democracy knows of no universal methods of struggle, such as would shut off the proletariat by a Chinese wall from the strata standing slightly above or slightly below it. At different periods, Social Democracy applies different methods, always qualifying the choice of them by strictly defined ideological and organizational conditions.[6]

The forms of struggle in the Russian revolution are distinguished by their colossal variety compared with the bourgeois revolutions in Europe. Kautsky partly foretold this in 1902 when he said that the future revolution (with the exception perhaps of Russia, he added) might be not so much a struggle of the people against the government as a struggle between two sections of the people. In Russia we undoubtedly see a wider development of this latter struggle than in the bourgeois revolutions in the West. The enemies of our revolution among the people are few in number, but as the struggle grows more acute they become more and more organized and receive the support of the reactionary strata of the bourgeoisie. It

[6] The Bolshevik Social Democrats are often accused of a frivolous passion for guerrilla actions. It would therefore not be amiss to recall that in the draft resolution on guerrilla actions (*Partiiniye Izvestia*, No. 2, and Lenin's report on the Congress), the section of the Bolsheviks who defend guerrilla actions suggested the following conditions for their recognition: "expropriations" of private property were not to be permitted under any circumstances; "expropriations" of government property were not to be recommended but only allowed, provided that they were controlled by the Party and their proceeds used for the needs of an uprising. Guerrilla acts in the form of terrorism were to be recommended against brutal government officials and active members of the Black Hundreds, but on conditions that (1) the sentiments of the masses be taken into account; (2) the conditions of the working class movement in the given locality be reckoned with; and (3) care be taken that the forces of the proletariat should not be frittered away. The practical difference between this draft and the resolution which was adopted at the Unity Congress lies exclusively in the fact that "expropriations" of government property are not allowed. (*Lenin's note.*)

The Unity Congress Lenin refers to here was the Fourth Congress of the Russian Social Democratic Workers Party held in Stockholm in April and May 1906. In September, the Moscow Bolshevik Party Committee came out in favor of "offensive tactics" and issued a general call for "partisan war." Lenin favored this militant line.—*Ed.*

is therefore absolutely natural and inevitable that in such a period, a period of nationwide political strikes, an uprising cannot assume the old form of individual acts restricted to a very short time and to a very small area. It is absolutely natural and inevitable that the uprising should assume the higher and more complex form of a prolonged civil war embracing the whole country, i.e., an armed struggle between two sections of the people. Such a war cannot be conceived otherwise than as a series of a few big engagements at comparatively long intervals and a large number of small encounters during these intervals. That being so—and it is undoubtedly so—the Social Democrats must absolutely make it their duty to create organizations best adapted to lead the masses in these big engagements and, as far as possible, in these small encounters as well. In a period when the class struggle has become accentuated to the point of civil war, Social Democrats must make it their duty not only to participate but also to play the leading role in this civil war. The Social Democrats must train and prepare their organizations to be really able to act as a belligerent side which does not miss a single opportunity of inflicting damage on the enemy's forces.

This is a difficult task, there is no denying. It cannot be accomplished at once. Just as the whole people are being retrained and are learning to fight in the course of the civil war, so our organizations must be trained, must be reconstructed in conformity with the lessons of experience to be equal to this task.

We have not the slightest intention of foisting on practical workers any artificial form of struggle, or even of deciding from our armchair what part any particular form of guerrilla warfare should play in the general course of the civil war in Russia. We are far from the thought of regarding a concrete assessment of particular guerrilla actions as indicative of a trend in Social Democracy. But we do regard it as our duty to help as far as possible to arrive at a correct theoretical assessment of the new forms of struggle engendered by practical life. We do regard it as our duty relentlessly to combat stereotypes and prejudices which hamper the class-conscious workers in correctly presenting a new and difficult problem and in correctly approaching its solution.

China

No contemporary revolutionaries have done more to popularize the concept of people's war than the Chinese communists. And with the most convincing reason possible: in China, it worked. It is too easy, however, to forget the price for such victory. In 1927, after years of hard struggle to help establish the Chinese Republic (1911) under the weak liberal patriarch Sun Yat-sen, and formidable sacrifices to help crush vicious regional warlords (especially in 1926 in the north), the communists were suddenly attacked by their long-time ally, Chiang Kai-shek, head of the Kuomintang (Nationalist) Party. Literally thousands, some say as many as 50,000, communists were arrested, tortured, and murdered as Chiang tried to consolidate his power over all of China. He almost succeeded. Surviving communists, having fled in all directions, had to reassemble and begin anew.

Inevitably, they were depressed, pessimistic, even defeatist. They challenged their theories, questioned their analyses, distrusted their own experiences. Most—but not all. One optimist was Mao Tse-tung, the self-educated peasant's son from Hunan who had attended the 1921 conspirators' meeting in the girls' school of the French Legation—where the Chinese Communist Party was born. Despite his antipathy for Sun Yat-sen, Mao had followed Leninist "principles" to work with the bourgeois government (in order to create a communist base) until Sun died in 1925, then, again despite his suspicion of Chiang as a glorified warlord, had stuck to dogma and doubled as a Kuomintang agent—even after Chiang's first purge of communists in 1926. Mao was caught in 1927 but managed to escape barely two hundred yards away from the wall where he would have been shot. On Party orders he then organized a peasant uprising, was defeated and repudiated by his Party bosses as a "military adventurer." Nevertheless, he led his thousand-odd raggle-taggle survivors to the southern mountains between Hunan and Kiangsi and

93

launched what would turn out to be the Red Army—without a single machine gun. By 1930, already, in effect, the true leader of the reorganized underground Communist Party, he wrote a letter to communist cadres exhorting them to action. Known today as "A Single Spark Can Start A Prairie Fire," the letter-article clearly explained that the Chinese revolution would have to proceed through "prolonged and tangled" guerrilla warfare, based on the use of peasants, establishing liberated areas first in remote townships, then in districts, then in counties. He explained how the many contradictions—between classes and among the imperialist powers controlling China's main cities—had to lead to eventual communist victory. "All China is littered with dry faggots which will soon be aflame," he wrote. He went on to list all the "objective" reasons why a peasant army fighting in its own territory (specifically in Kiangsi) could endure a massive enemy onslaught; spelled out the basis for the strangulation theory (later known as the Lin Piao theory); and detailed the way to form Red guards, Red militiamen and Red soldiers.

In this task he was helped by his faithful friend and comrade, Chu Teh, a former military-school-trained Chiang officer addicted to opium who had decided to reform himself (sailing back and forth on a British steamer where no drugs were available, he had often collapsed from insupportable cravings but came ashore cured), and joined the Communist Party. Strong but easygoing, Chu was a master military technician and did more than any other man, save perhaps Mao, to build the famous Eighth Route and New Fourth armies which eventually defeated the Japanese in China and then Chiang's Kuomintang Army in 1949. How to build such an army, a people's army, how to train it from the outset for the revolutionary seizure of power, and how to use it constructively for the consolidation of the revolution are the themes Chu Teh develops in the second article in this section.

All Mao's and Chu's talents, however, could not stop Chiang's endless supply of troops, money (from England), and advisers (mostly German) in the early thirties. Worse yet, Mao's Russian advisers insisted that flexibility and mobility demoralized the peasants when left alone to face the Kuomintang, and thus they deprived Mao's troops of their greatest asset. And so, in 1934, Mao and Chu, whose wives had been killed in actual combat, decided to abandon Kiangsi. Thus began the famous long march: 90,000 men, women and children, on foot, carrying not just guns and bullets, but printing presses, paper, scrap iron and farming machinery, marching 6,000 miles across China, the equivalent of marching from New York to San Francisco and back, all the while attacked by freshly rested troops, tanks, and planes. Mao never let up. Lin Piao, suffering from heart trouble, would often fall behind. Chou En-lai, bleeding from both feet for four months, never missed a battle. And so for the others. Yet on and on they went, crossing eighteen mountain ranges, twenty-four rivers, and ten different warlord armies. The battles they fought along the way could fill every page of this volume. And when at last they reached their destination, the northwest province of Shensi, near the Mongolian border, safe from Kuomintang attacks, they numbered barely 8,000—with new recruits picked up along the way counted in.

Yet, almost at once, they started again. They established a liberated area, carried out an agrarian reform, regrouped into two armies—the Eighth Route and New Fourth—and went on the offensive. Simultaneously, Mao issued his familiar call for a united China. Japan was menacing, he said; all Chinese should unite to fight as one. Incredibly, he was again willing to make an alliance with Chiang's Kuomintang. Once attacked by Japan, Chiang agreed, and Mao sent his troops against the invaders—while Chiang, predictably, attacked the communists. This time, Mao's troops were not caught by surprise; they either retreated from Chiang's forces or fought them off. But by and large, the communists stuck to the alliance, and Mao kept proclaiming his faith in a United Front and in the Patriotic War. In fact, he was following his old dictum: first consolidate the base, then destroy the enemy. In China from 1937 to 1945, that meant first fight the Japanese, organize more and more liberated areas, spread the agrarian reform, politicize the masses—all under the slogan of fighting the foreign aggressor. It was, as Mao explained in 1939, "Revolution in Two Stages," the first article in this section.

In actual combat, his tactics were also the same: "The enemy advances, we retreat; the enemy camps, we harass; the enemy tires, we attack; the enemy retreats, we pursue." And everywhere the Red armies went, they politicized. Where landlords were ousted for collaboration with the enemy, land was distributed to the peasants who worked it. Where the landlords remained loyal, rents were lowered. Revolutionary medical men treated the population. Teachers taught the children. Engineers or agronomists solved local agricultural problems. If a harvest was due, both soldiers and officers pitched in. If a region had been depleted, both soldiers and officers shared their rations. Never, in a Red army, was an officer better off than a soldier, and never were either better off than the people. It was inevitable that by 1945, the Chinese communists should control most of the northwest and 95 million people. The Red Army was now 500,000 strong, but weary from having borne all the major fighting against the Japanese. Chiang's forces, on the other hand, numbered 2,000,000 and they had been held back from the Sino-Japanese War in order to attack the communists. And so, despite a new Mao-Chiang pact signed in Chunking in 1945, Chiang immediately attacked Yenan.

But it was too late. Mao was ready. Once again he resorted to guerrilla warfare, then to surrounding the cities, then to strangling the cities one by one. Lin Piao, in his speech on "People's War" (the third article herein), explains why Chiang could not win—and in 1949 he and his Kuomintang were chased out of the Chinese mainland despite all the massive aid that they had received from both the United States and

Russia (which dealt with Chiang, not Mao, during World War II).

Out of the Chinese communists' revolutionary experience, their leaders —Mao, Lin Piao, Chou En-lai—have drawn iron-firm lessons. One is that without a people's war no revolution can succeed. Another is that a people's war must be divided into two stages, patriotic then socialist, national then class. That means that revolutionaries can and must work with the national bourgeoisie, at least during the first phase. After that, Mao has said in "Democratic Dictatorship" (June 30, 1949), "the people have a powerful state apparatus in their hands—there is no need to fear rebellion by the national bourgeoisie": a conclusion that a great many revolutionaries in Latin America, Africa, and even Asia will firmly challenge. Still another tenet which the Chinese uphold is that guerrilla warfare must be waged from the countryside until the cities are isolated: first because the imperialists control the cities; second, because the urban and rural economies are so uneven that the peasants feel little relationship to the cities; and third, because the counterrevolutionary camp is much more disunited in the countryside (but Mao insists that armed struggle cannot win unless it is coordinated with other forms of struggle, including legal ones, and he stresses the fact that unless the Party has strong ties in the cities, the guerrilla forces can be totally isolated).

On a world scale, says Lin Piao in "People's War," the cities are the capitalist strongholds of Europe and North America while the countryside is the underdeveloped world. Though he does not use the slogan "Create two, three . . . many Vietnams," made famous by Che Guevara, he spells out the same concept, convinced that the United States cannot sustain many people's wars all over the world, especially if they are waged simultaneously. And finally, as Chou En-lai succinctly states in his four-point "Imperialists Beware" (the fourth article in this section) the Chinese have learned that a dedicated, politicized, armed people—the result of a people's war—cannot be defeated. Hence, there is no reason to fear even such a technological titan as the United States. In the last analysis, say the Chinese, wars are won by people, not machines.

MAO TSE-TUNG: REVOLUTION IN TWO STAGES*

DEVELOPING along the same lines as many other nations of the world, the Chinese people (here we refer mainly to the Hans) went through many thousands of years of life in classless primitive communes. Some

---

* Textbook, originally entitled *The Chinese Revolution and the Chinese Communist Party*, written in Yenan in December 1939 (with help from other members of the Central Committee of the Chinese Communist Party) and used extensively in CP cadre-formation schools. English version in pamphlet published in Peking (Foreign Languages Press, 1966).

4,000 years have gone by since the collapse of these primitive communes and the transition to class society, which took the form first of slave and then of feudal society. Throughout the history of Chinese civilization its agriculture and handicrafts have been renowned for their high level of development; there have been many great thinkers, scientists, inventors, statesmen, soldiers, men of letters and artists, and we have a rich store of classical works. The compass was invented in China very long ago. The art of papermaking was discovered as early as 1,800 years ago. Block-printing was invented 1,300 years ago, and movable type 800 years ago. The use of gunpowder was known to the Chinese before the Europeans. Thus China has one of the oldest civilizations in the world; she has a recorded history of nearly 4,000 years.[1]

The Chinese nation is known throughout the world not only for its industriousness and stamina, but also for its ardent love of freedom and its rich revolutionary traditions. The history of the Han people, for instance, demonstrates that the Chinese never submit to tyrannical rule but invariably use revolutionary means to overthrow or change it. In the thousands of years of Han history, there have been hundreds of peasant uprisings, great and small, against the dark rule of the landlords and nobility. And most dynastic changes came about as a result of such peasant uprisings. All the nationalities of China have resisted foreign oppression and have invariably resorted to rebellion to shake it off. They favor a union on the basis of equality but are against the oppression of one nationality by another. During the thousands of years of recorded history, the Chinese nation has given birth to many national heroes and revolutionary leaders. Thus the Chinese nation has a glorious revolutionary tradition and a splendid historical heritage.

Although China is a great nation and although she is a vast country with an immense population, a long history, a rich revolutionary tradition, and a splendid historical heritage, her economic, political, and cultural development was sluggish for a long time after the transition from slave to feudal society. This feudal society, beginning with the Chou and Chin dynasties, lasted about 3,000 years.

The main features of the economic and political system of China's feudal era were as follows:

1. A self-sufficient natural economy predominated. The peasants produced for themselves not only agricultural products but most of the handicraft articles they needed. What the landlords and the nobility exacted from them in the form of land rent was also chiefly for private enjoyment and not for exchange. Although exchange developed as time went on, it did not play a decisive role in the economy as a whole.

[1] The compass was first invented in the third century B.C., used in the first century B.C., and all Chinese navigators seemed to rely on it by the twelfth century; gunpowder, invented in the ninth century, was used to fire cannon in the eleventh. —Ed.

2. The feudal ruling class, composed of landlords, the nobility, and the emperor, owned most of the land, while the peasants had very little or none at all. The peasants tilled the land of the landlords, the nobility, and the royal family with their own farm implements and had to turn over to them for their private enjoyment 40, 50, 60, 70, or even 80 percent or more of the crop. In effect the peasants were still serfs.

3. Not only did the landlords, the nobility, and the royal family live on rent extorted from the peasants, but the landlord state also exacted tribute, taxes, and corvée services from them to support a horde of government officials and an army which was used mainly for their repression.

4. The feudal landlord state was the organ of power protecting this system of feudal exploitation. While the feudal state was torn apart into rival principalities in the period before the Chin Dynasty, it became autocratic and centralized after the first Chin emperor unified China, though some feudal separatism remained. The emperor reigned supreme in the feudal state, appointing officials in charge of the armed forces, the law courts, the treasury, and state granaries in all parts of the country and relying on the landed gentry as the mainstay of the entire system of feudal rule.

It was under such feudal economic exploitation and political oppression that the Chinese peasants lived like slaves, in poverty and suffering, through the ages. Under the bondage of feudalism they had no freedom of person. The landlord had the right to beat, abuse, or even kill them at will, and they had no political rights whatsoever. The extreme poverty and backwardness of the peasants resulting from ruthless landlord exploitation and oppression is the basic reason why Chinese society remained at the same stage of socioeconomic development for several thousand years.

The principal contradiction in feudal society was between the peasantry and the landlord class.

The peasants and the handicraft workers were the basic classes which created the wealth and culture of this society.

The ruthless economic exploitation and political oppression of the Chinese peasants forced them into numerous uprisings against landlord rule. There were hundreds of uprisings, great and small, all of them peasant revolts or peasant revolutionary wars. The scale of peasant uprisings and peasant wars in Chinese history has no parallel anywhere else. The class struggles of the peasants, the peasant uprisings and peasant wars, constituted the real motive force to historical development in Chinese feudal society. For each of the major peasant uprisings and wars dealt a blow to the feudal regime of the time, and hence more or less furthered the growth of the social productive forces. However, since neither new productive forces, nor new relations of production, nor new class forces, nor any advanced political party existed in those days, the peasant uprisings and wars did not have correct leadership such as the proletariat and the Communist Party provide today; every peasant revolution failed, and the peasantry was invariably used by the landlords and the nobility, either during or after the revolution, as a lever for bringing about dynastic change. Therefore, although some social progress was made after each great peasant revolutionary struggle, the feudal economic relations and political system remained basically unchanged.

It is only in the last hundred years that a change of a different order has taken place. As China's feudal society had developed a commodity economy, and so carried within itself the seeds of capitalism, China would of herself have developed slowly into a capitalist society even without the impact of foreign capitalism. Penetration by foreign capitalism accelerated this process. Foreign capitalism played an important part in the disintegration of China's social economy; on the one hand, it undermined the foundations of her self-sufficient natural economy and wrecked the handicraft industry both in the cities and in the peasants' homes, and on the other, it hastened the growth of a commodity economy in town and country.

Apart from its disintegrating effects on the foundations of China's feudal economy, this state of affairs gave rise to certain objective conditions and possibilities for the development of capitalist production in China. For the destruction of the natural economy created a commodity market for capitalism, while the bankruptcy of large numbers of peasants and handicraftsmen provided it with a labor market.

In fact, some merchants, landlords, and bureaucrats began investing in modern industry as far back as sixty years ago, in the latter part of the nineteenth century, under the stimulus of foreign capitalism and because of certain cracks in the feudal economic structure. About forty years ago, at the turn of the century, China's national capitalism took its first steps forward. Then about twenty years ago, during the first imperialist world war, China's national industry expanded, chiefly in textiles and flour milling, because the imperialist countries in Europe and America were preoccupied with the war and temporarily relaxed their oppression of China.

The history of the emergence and development of national capitalism is at the same time the history of the emergence and development of the Chinese bourgeoisie and proletariat. Just as a section of the merchants, landlords, and bureaucrats were precursors of the Chinese bourgeoisie, so a section of the peasants and handicraft workers were the precursors of the Chinese proletariat. As distinct social classes, the Chinese bourgeoisie and proletariat are new-born and never existed before in Chinese history. They have evolved into new social classes from the womb of feudal society. They are twins born of China's old (feudal) society, at once linked to each other and antagonistic to each other. However, the Chinese proletariat emerged and grew simultaneously not only with the Chinese national bourgeoisie but also with the enterprises directly operated by the imperialists in China. Hence, a very large section of the Chinese proletariat is older and more experienced than the Chinese bourgeoisie, and is therefore a greater and more broadly based social force.

However, the emergence and development of capitalism is only one aspect of the change that has taken place since the imperialist penetration of China. There is another concomitant and obstructive aspect, namely, the collusion of imperialism with the Chinese feudal forces to arrest the development of Chinese capitalism.

It is certainly not the purpose of the imperialist powers invading China to transform feudal China into capitalist China. On the contrary, their purpose is to transform China into their own semicolony or colony. To this end the imperialist powers have used and continue to use military, political, economic and cultural means of oppression, as follows:

1. The imperialist powers have waged many wars of aggression against China, for instance, the Opium War launched by Britain in 1840, the war launched by the Anglo-French allied forces in 1857, the Sino-French War of 1884, the Sino-Japanese War of 1894, and the war launched by the allied forces of the eight powers in 1900. After defeating China in war, they not only occupied many neighboring countries formerly under her protection, but seized or "leased" parts of her territory. For instance, Japan occupied Taiwan and the Penghu Islands and "leased" the port of Lushun, Britain seized Hong Kong, and France "leased" Kwangchowwan. In addition to annexing territory, they exacted huge indemnities. Thus heavy blows were struck at China's huge feudal empire.[2]

2. The imperialist powers have forced China to sign numerous unequal treaties by which they have acquired the right to station land and sea

[2] From 1856 to 1860 Britain and France jointly waged war against China, with the United States and czarist Russia supporting them from the sidelines. The government of the Ching Dynasty was then devoting all its energies to suppressing peasant revolutions and adopted a policy of passive resistance toward the foreigners. The Anglo-French forces occupied such major cities as Canton, Tientsin, and Peking, plundered and burned down the Yuan Ming Yuan Palace in Peking, and forced the Ching government to conclude the treaties of Tientsin and Peking. Their main provisions included the opening of all major ports, and the granting to foreigners of special privileges for travel, missionary activities, and inland navigation of China's interior. In 1882–83, the French invaded the northern part of Indochina. In 1884–85 they extended their war to the Chinese provinces of Kwangsi, Taiwan, Fukien, and Chekiang. The Sino-Japanese War of 1894 was started by the Japanese bent on conquering Korea. In 1900 seven imperialist powers—Britain, the United States, France, czarist Russia, Japan, Italy, and Austria—sent a joint force to attack China to suppress a popular rebellion against the Ching Dynasty. The allied forces captured Taku and occupied Tientsin and Peking. In 1901 the Ching government concluded a treaty with the seven imperialist countries; its main provisions were that China had to pay those countries the huge sum of 450 million taels of silver as war reparations and grant them the special privilege of stationing troops in Peking and in the area from Peking to Tientsin and Shanhaikuan.—*Ed.*

forces and exercise consular jurisdiction in China, and they have carved up the whole country into imperialist spheres of influence.

3. The imperialist powers have gained control of all the important trading ports in China by these unequal treaties and have marked off areas in many of these ports as concessions under their direct administration. They have also gained control of China's customs, foreign trade, and communications (sea, land, inland water, and air). Thus they have been able to dump their goods in China, turn her into a market for their industrial products, and at the same time subordinate her agriculture to their imperialist needs.

4. The imperialist powers operate many enterprises in both light and heavy industry in China in order to utilize her raw materials and cheap labor on the spot, and they thereby directly exert economic pressure on China's national industry and obstruct the development of her productive forces.

5. The imperialist powers monopolize China's banking and finance by extending loans to the Chinese government and establishing banks in China. Thus they have not only overwhelmed China's national capitalism in commodity competition, they have also secured a stranglehold on her banking and finance.

6. The imperialist powers have established a network of comprador and merchant-usurer exploitation right across China, from the trading ports to the remote hinterland, and have created a comprador and merchant-usurer class in their service, so as to facilitate their exploitation of the masses of the Chinese peasantry and other sections of the people.

7. The imperialist powers have made the feudal landlord class as well as the comprador class the main props of their rule in China.

8. The imperialist powers supply the reactionary government with large quantities of munitions and a host of military advisers, in order to keep the warlords fighting among themselves and to suppress the Chinese people.

9. Furthermore, the imperialist powers have never slackened their efforts to poison the minds of the Chinese people. This is their policy of cultural aggression. And it is carried out through missionary work, through establishing hospitals and schools, publishing newspapers, and inducing Chinese students to study abroad. Their aim is to train intellectuals who will serve their interests and to dupe the people.

10. Since September 18, 1931, the large-scale invasion of Japanese imperialism has turned a big chunk of semicolonial China into a Japanese colony.

It is thus clear that in their aggression against China the imperialist powers have on the one hand hastened the disintegration of feudal society, and the growth of elements of capitalism, thereby transforming a feudal into a semifeudal society, and on the other imposed their ruthless rule on China, reducing an independent country to a semicolonial and colonial country.

Taking both these aspects together, we can see that China's colonial, semicolonial, and semifeudal society possesses the following characteristics:

1. The foundations of the self-sufficient natural economy of feudal times have been destroyed, but the exploitation of the peasantry by the landlord class, which is the basis of the system of feudal exploitation, not only remains intact but, linked as it is with exploitation by comprador and usurer capital, clearly dominates China's social and economic life.

2. National capitalism has developed to a certain extent and has played a considerable part in China's political and cultural life, but it has not become the principal pattern in China's social economy; it is flabby and is mostly associated with foreign imperialism and domestic feudalism in varying degrees.

3. The autocratic rule of the emperors and nobility has been over-thrown, and in its place there has arisen first the warlord-bureaucrat rule of the landlord class and then the joint dictatorship of the landlord class and the big bourgeoisie. In the occupied areas there is the rule of Japanese imperialism and its puppets.

4. Imperialism controls not only China's financial and economic arteries but also her political and military power. In the occupied areas everything is in the hands of the Japanese.

5. China's economic, political, and cultural development is very uneven, because she has been under the complete or partial domination of many imperialist powers, because she has actually been in a state of disunity for a long time, and because her territory is immense.

6. Under the twofold oppression of imperialism and feudalism, and especially as a result of the large-scale invasion of Japanese imperialism, the Chinese people, and particularly the peasants, have become more and more impoverished and have even been pauperized in large numbers, living in hunger and cold and without any political rights. The poverty and lack of freedom among the Chinese people are on a scale seldom found elsewhere.

The contradiction between imperialism and the Chinese nation and the contradiction between feudalism and the great masses of the people are the basic contradictions in modern Chinese society. Of course, there are others, such as the contradiction between the bourgeoisie and the pro-letariat and the contradictions within the reactionary ruling classes them-selves. But the contradiction between imperialism and the Chinese nation is the principal one. These contradictions and their intensification must inevitably result in the incessant growth of revolutionary movements.[3]

[3] Among them, the most important recent rebellions included the Revolution of 1911, led by Sun Yat-sen, which overthrew the Ching Dynasty and established the Chinese Republic; the May 30th Movement, a nationwide series of protests against British police massacres in Shanghai, which were also savagely put down by the

The great revolutions in modern and contemporary China have emerged and grown on the basis of the basic contradictions.

Only when we grasp the nature of Chinese society will we be able clearly to understand the targets, tasks, motive forces, and character of the Chinese Revolution and its perspective and future transition. A clear understanding of the nature of Chinese society, that is, of Chinese conditions, is therefore the key to a clear understanding of all the problems of the Revolution.

Since the nature of present-day Chinese society is colonial, semicolonial, and semifeudal, what are the chief targets or enemies at this stage of the Chinese Revolution?

They are imperialism and feudalism, the bourgeoisie of the imperialist countries and the landlord class of our country. For it is these two that are the chief oppressors, the chief obstacles to the progress of Chinese society at the present stage. The two collide with each other in oppressing the Chinese people, and imperialism is the foremost and most ferocious enemy of the Chinese people, because national oppression by imperialism is the more onerous.

The Chinese bourgeoisie, which is also a victim of imperialist oppression, once led or played a principal role in revolutionary struggles such as the Revolution of 1911, and has participated in revolutionary struggles such as the Northern Expedition and the present War of Resistance against Japan. In the long period from 1927 to 1937, however, its upper stratum, namely, the section represented by the reactionary clique within the Kuomintang, collaborated with imperialism, formed a reactionary alliance with the landlord class, betrayed the friends who had helped it—the Communist Party, the proletariat, the peasantry, and other sections of the petty bourgeoisie—betrayed the Chinese Revolution and brought about its defeat. At that time, therefore, the revolutionary people and the revolutionary political party (the Communist Party) could not but regard these bourgeois elements as one of the targets of the Revolution. In the War of Resistance a section of the big landlord class and the big bourgeoisie, represented by Wang Ching-wei, has turned traitor and deserted to the enemy. Consequently, the anti-Japanese people cannot but regard these big bourgeois elements who have betrayed our national interests as one of the targets of the Revolution.

It is evident, then, that the enemies of the Chinese Revolution are

---

British and thus made the Chinese consciously anti-imperialists; the 1926 "revolutionary army" expedition against brutal northern warlords which gained its communist leadership vast popular support but failed when CP's ally, Chiang Kai-shek, double-crossed the communists and slaughtered thousands of them; and the Agrarian Revolutionary War (1927–37) when the Red Army established power in many rural areas. Known as the Second Revolutionary Civil War, it was curtailed when the CP again entered into a pact with Chiang's Kuomintang (Nationalist) Party to fight the Japanese invaders.—*Ed.*

very powerful. They include not only powerful imperialists and powerful feudal forces, but also, at times, the bourgeois reactionaries who collaborate with the imperialist and feudal forces to oppose the people. Therefore, it is wrong to underestimate the strength of the enemies of the revolutionary Chinese people.

In the face of such enemies, the Chinese Revolution cannot be other than protracted and ruthless. With such powerful enemies, the revolutionary forces cannot be built up and tempered into a power capable of crushing them except over a long period of time. With enemies who so ruthlessly suppress the Chinese Revolution, the revolutionary forces cannot hold their own positions, let alone capture those of the enemy, unless they steel themselves and display their tenacity to the full.

In the face of such enemies, the principal means or form of the Chinese Revolution must be armed struggle, not peaceful struggle. For our enemies have made peaceful activity impossible for the Chinese people and have deprived them of all political freedom and democratic rights. In the face of such enemies, there arises the question of revolutionary base areas. Since China's key cities have long been occupied by the powerful imperialists and their reactionary Chinese allies, it is imperative for the revolutionary ranks to turn the backward villages into advanced, consolidated base areas, into great military, political, economic, and cultural bastions of the revolution from which to fight their vicious enemies who are using the cities for attacks on the rural districts, and in this way gradually to achieve the complete victory of the Revolution through protracted fighting; it is imperative for them to do so if they do not wish to compromise with imperialism and its lackeys but are determined to fight on, and if they intend to build up and temper their forces, and avoid decisive battles with a powerful enemy while their own strength is inadequate. Such being the case, victory in the Chinese Revolution can be won first in the rural areas, and this is possible because China's economic development is uneven (her economy not being a unified capitalist economy), because her territory is extensive (which gives the revolutionary forces room to maneuver), because the counterrevolutionary camp is disunited and full of contradictions, and because the struggle of the peasants who are the main force in the revolution is led by the Communist Party, the party of the proletariat; but on the other hand, these very circumstances make the revolution uneven and render the task of winning complete victory protracted and arduous. Clearly then, the protracted revolutionary struggle in the revolutionary base areas consists mainly in peasant guerrilla warfare led by the Chinese Communist Party. Therefore, it is wrong to ignore the necessity of using rural districts as revolutionary base areas, to neglect painstaking work among the peasants, and to neglect guerrilla warfare.

However, stressing armed struggle does not mean abandoning other forms of struggle; on the contrary, armed struggle cannot succeed unless coordinated with other forms of struggle. And stressing the work in the rural base areas does not mean abandoning our work in the cities and in the other vast rural areas which are still under the enemy's rule; on the contrary, without the work in the cities and in these other rural areas, our own rural base areas would be isolated and the Revolution would suffer defeat. Moreover, the final objective of the Revolution is the capture of the cities, the enemy's main bases, and this objective cannot be achieved without adequate work in the cities.

It is thus clear that the Revolution cannot triumph either in the rural areas or in the cities without the destruction of the enemy's army, his chief weapon against the people. Therefore, besides annihilating the enemy's troops in battle, there is the important task of disintegrating them.

It is also clear that the Communist Party must not be impetuous and adventurist in its propaganda and organizational work in the urban and rural areas which have been occupied by the enemy and dominated by the forces of reaction and darkness for a long time, but that it must have well-selected cadres working underground, must accumulate strength and bide its time there. In leading the people in struggle against the enemy, the Party must adopt the tactics of advancing step by step slowly and surely, keeping to the principle of waging struggles on just grounds, to our advantage, and with restraint, and making use of such open forms of activity as are permitted by law, decree, and social custom; empty clamor and reckless action can never lead to success.

Unless imperialist rule is overthrown, the rule of the feudal landlord class cannot be terminated, because imperialism is its main support. Conversely, unless help is given to the peasants in their struggle to overthrow the feudal landlord class, it will be impossible to build powerful revolutionary contingents to overthrow imperialist rule, because the feudal landlord class is the main social base of imperialist rule in China and the peasantry is the main force in the Chinese Revolution. Therefore the two fundamental tasks, the national revolution and the democratic revolution, are at once distinct and united.

In fact, the two revolutionary tasks are already linked, since the main immediate task of the national revolution is to resist the Japanese imperialist invaders and since the democratic revolution must be accomplished in order to win the war. It is wrong to regard the national revolution and the democratic revolution as two entirely different stages of the Revolution.

Since Chinese society is colonial, semicolonial, and semifeudal, since the targets of the Revolution are mainly foreign imperialist rule and domestic feudalism, and since its tasks are to overthrow these two oppressors, which of the various classes and strata in Chinese society constitute the forces capable of fighting them? This is the question of the motive forces of the Chinese Revolution at the present stage. A clear understanding of this question is indispensable to a correct solution of the problem of the basic tactics of the Chinese Revolution.

What classes are there in present-day Chinese society? There are the landlord class and the bourgeoisie, the landlord class and the upper stratum of the bourgeoisie constituting the ruling classes in Chinese society. And there are the proletariat, the peasantry, and the different sections of the petty bourgeoisie other than the peasantry, all of which are still the subject classes in vast areas of China.

1. The Landlord Class

The landlord class forms the main social base for imperialist rule in China; it is a class which uses the feudal system to exploit and oppress the peasants, obstructs China's political, economic, and cultural development, and plays no progressive role whatsoever. Therefore, the landlords, as a class, are a target and not a motive force of the Revolution.

In the present War of Resistance a section of the big landlords, along with one section of the big bourgeoisie (the capitulationists), has surrendered to the Japanese aggressors and turned traitor, while another section of the big landlords, along with another section of the big bourgeoisie (the diehards), is increasingly wavering even though it is still in the anti-Japanese camp. But a good many of the enlightened gentry who are middle and small landlords and who have some capitalist coloration display some enthusiasm for the war, and we should unite with them in the common fight against Japan.

2. The Bourgeoisie

There is a distinction between the comprador big bourgeoisie and the national bourgeoisie.

The comprador big bourgeoisie is a class which directly serves the capitalists of the imperialist countries and is nurtured by them; countless ties link it closely with the feudal forces in the countryside. Therefore, it is a target of the Chinese Revolution and never in the history of the Revolution has it been a motive force. However, different sections of the comprador big bourgeoisie owe allegiance to different imperialist powers, so that when the contradictions among the latter become very acute and the Revolution is directed mainly against one particular imperialist power, it becomes possible for the sections of the comprador class which serve other imperialist groupings to join the current anti-imperialist front to a certain extent and for a certain period. But they will turn against the Chinese Revolution the moment their masters do.

The national bourgeoisie is a class with a dual character. On the one hand, it is oppressed by imperialism and fettered by feudalism and consequently is in contradiction with both of them. In this respect it constitutes one of the revolutionary forces. In the course of the Chinese Revolution it has displayed a certain enthusiasm for fighting imperialism and the governments of bureaucrats and warlords.

But on the other hand, it lacks the courage to oppose imperialism and feudalism thoroughly because it is economically and politically flabby and still has economic ties with imperialism and feudalism. This emerges very clearly when the people's revolutionary forces grow powerful.

It follows from the dual character of the national bourgeoisie that, at certain times and to a certain extent, it can take part in the Revolution against imperialism and the governments of bureaucrats and warlords and can become a revolutionary force, but that at other times there is the danger of its following the comprador big bourgeoisie and acting as its accomplice in counterrevolution.

The national bourgeoisie in China, which is mainly the middle bourgeoisie, has never really held political power but has been restricted by the reactionary policies of the big landlord class and big bourgeoisie which are in power, although it followed them in opposing the Revolution in the period from 1927 to 1931. In the present war, it differs not only from the capitulationists of the big landlord class and big bourgeoisie but also from the big bourgeois diehards, and so far has been a fairly good ally of ours. Therefore, it is absolutely necessary to have a prudent policy toward the national bourgeoisie.

3. The Different Sections of the Petty Bourgeoisie Other Than the Peasantry

The petty bourgeoisie, other than the peasantry, consists of the vast numbers of intellectuals, small tradesmen, handicraftsmen, and professional people. Their status somewhat resembles that of the middle peasants, they all suffer under the oppression of imperialism, feudalism, and the big bourgeoisie, and they are being driven ever nearer to bankruptcy or destitution. Hence these sections of the petty bourgeoisie constitute one of the motive forces of the Revolution and are a reliable ally of the proletariat. Only under the leadership of the proletariat can they achieve their liberation.

The intellectuals and student youth do not constitute a separate class or stratum. In present-day China most of them may be placed in the petty-bourgeois category, judging by their family origin, their living conditions, and their political outlook. Their numbers have grown considerably during the past few decades. Apart from that section of the intellectuals which has associated itself with the imperialists and the big bourgeoisie and works for them against the people, most intellectuals and students are oppressed by imperialism, feudalism, and the big bourgeoisie, and live in fear of unemployment or of having to discontinue their studies. Therefore, they tend to be quite revolutionary. They are more or less equipped with bourgeois scientific knowledge, have a keen political sense, and often play a vanguard role or serve as a link with the masses in the present stage of the Revolution. In particular, the large numbers of more or less impoverished intellectuals can join hands with the workers and peasants in supporting or participating in the Revolution. In China, it was among the intellectuals and young students that Marxist-Leninist ideology was first widely disseminated and accepted. The revolutionary forces cannot be successfully organized and revolutionary work cannot be successfully conducted without the participation of revolutionary intellectuals. But the intellectuals often tend to be subjective and individualistic, impractical in their thinking and irresolute in action, until they have thrown themselves heart and soul into mass revolutionary struggles, or made up their minds to serve the interests of the masses and become one with them. Hence although the mass of revolutionary intellectuals in China can play a vanguard role or serve as a link with the masses, not all of them will remain revolutionaries to the end. Some will drop out of the revolutionary ranks at critical moments and become passive, while a few may even become enemies of the Revolution. The intellectuals can overcome their shortcomings only in mass struggles over a long period.

The small tradesmen, generally, run small shops and employ few or no assistants. They live under the threat of bankruptcy as a result of exploitation by imperialism, the big bourgeoisie, and the usurers. Handicraftsmen are very numerous. They possess their own means of production and hire no workers, or only one or two apprentices or helpers. Their position is similar to that of the middle peasants. Professional people, including doctors, do not exploit other people, or do so only to a slight degree. Their position is similar to that of the handicraftsmen. These sections of the petty bourgeoisie make up a vast multitude of people whom we must win over and whose interests we must protect because in general they can support or join the Revolution and are good allies. Their weakness is that some of them are easily influenced by the bourgeoisie; consequently, we must carry on revolutionary propaganda and organizational work among them.

4. The Peasantry

The peasantry constitutes approximately 80 percent of China's total population and is the main force in her national economy today. A sharp process of polarization is taking place among the peasantry.

First, the rich peasants. They form about 5 percent of the rural population (or about 10 percent together with the landlords) and constitute the rural bourgeoisie. Most of the rich peasants in China are semifeudal in character, since they let a part of their land, practice usury, and ruthlessly exploit the farm laborers. But they generally engage in labor themselves and in this sense are part of the peasantry. The rich-peasant form of production will remain useful for a definite period. Generally speaking, they might make some contribution to the anti-imperialist struggle of the peasant masses and stay neutral in the agrarian revolutionary struggle against the landlords. Therefore we should not regard the rich peasants as belonging to the same class as the landlords and should not prematurely adopt a policy of liquidating the rich peasantry.

Second, the middle peasants. They form about 20 percent of China's rural population. They are economically self-supporting (they may have something to lay aside when the crops are good, and occasionally hire some labor or lend small sums of money at interest); and generally they do not exploit others but are exploited by imperialism, the landlord class, and the bourgeoisie. They have no political rights. Some of them do not have enough land, and only a section (the well-to-do middle peasants) have some surplus land. Not only can the middle peasants join the anti-imperialist revolution and the agrarian revolution, but they can also accept socialism. Therefore the whole middle peasantry can be a reliable ally of the proletariat and is an important motive force of the Revolution. The positive or negative attitude of the middle peasants is one of the factors determining victory or defeat in the Revolution, and this will be especially true after the agrarian revolution when they become the majority of the rural population.

Third, the poor peasants. The poor peasants in China together with the farm laborers, form about 70 percent of the rural population. They are the broad peasant masses with no land or insufficient land, the semi-proletariat of the countryside, the biggest motive force of the Chinese Revolution, the natural and most reliable ally of the proletariat, and the main contingent of China's revolutionary forces. Only under the leadership of the proletariat can the poor and middle peasants achieve their liberation, and only by forming a firm alliance with the poor and middle peasants can the proletariat lead the Revolution to victory. Otherwise neither is possible. The term "peasantry" refers mainly to the poor and middle peasants.

5. The Proletariat

Among the Chinese proletariat, the modern industrial workers number from 2,500,000 to 3,000,000, the workers in small-scale industry and in handicrafts and the shop assistants in the cities total about 12,000,000, and in addition there are great numbers of rural proletarians (the farm laborers) and other propertyless people in the cities and the countryside.

In addition to the basic qualities it shares with the proletariat everywhere—its association with the most advanced form of economy, its strong sense of organization and discipline, and its lack of private means of production—the Chinese proletariat has many other outstanding qualities.

First, the Chinese proletariat is more resolute and thoroughgoing in revolutionary struggle than any other class because it is subjected to a threefold oppression (imperialist, bourgeois, and feudal) which is marked by a severity and cruelty seldom found in other countries. Since there is no economic basis for social reformism in colonial and semicolonial China as there is in Europe, the whole proletariat, with the exception of a few scabs, is most revolutionary.

Secondly, from the moment it appeared on the revolutionary scene, the Chinese proletariat came under the leadership of its own revolutionary party—the Communist Party of China—and became the most politically conscious class in Chinese society.

Thirdly, because the Chinese proletariat by origin is largely made up of bankrupted peasants, it has natural ties with the peasant masses, which facilitates its forming a close alliance with them.

Therefore, in spite of certain unavoidable weaknesses, for instance, its smallness (as compared with the peasantry), its youth (as compared with the proletariat in the capitalist countries), and its low educational level (as compared with the bourgeoisie), the Chinese proletariat is nonetheless the basic motive force of the Chinese Revolution. Unless it is led by the proletariat, the Chinese Revolution cannot possibly succeed. To take an example from the past, the Revolution of 1911 miscarried because the proletariat did not consciously participate in it and the Communist Party was not yet in existence. More recently, the Revolution of 1924–27 achieved great success for a time because the proletariat consciously participated and exercised leadership and the Communist Party was already in existence; it ended in defeat because the big bourgeoisie betrayed its alliance with the proletariat and abandoned the common revolutionary program, and also because the Chinese proletariat and its political party did not yet have enough revolutionary experience. Now take the present anti-Japanese war—because the proletariat and the Communist Party are exercising leadership in the Anti-Japanese National United Front, the whole nation has been united and the great War of Resistance has been launched and is being resolutely pursued.

The Chinese proletariat should understand that although it is the class with the highest political consciousness and sense of organization, it cannot win victory by its own strength alone. In order to win, it must unite, according to varying circumstances, with all classes and strata that can take part in the Revolution, and must organize a revolutionary united front. Among all the classes in Chinese society, the peasantry is a firm ally of the working class, the urban petty bourgeoisie is a reliable ally, and the national bourgeoisie is an ally in certain periods and to a certain extent. This is one of the fundamental laws established by China's modern revolutionary history.

6. The Vagrants

China's status as a colony and semicolony has given rise to a multitude of rural and urban unemployed. Denied proper means of making a living, many of them are forced to resort to illegitimate ones, hence the robbers, gangsters, beggars, and prostitutes, and the numerous people who live on superstitious practices. This social stratum is unstable; while some are apt to be bought over by the reactionary forces, others may join the Revolution. These people lack constructive qualities and are given to destruction rather than construction; after joining the Revolution, they become a source of roving-rebel and anarchist ideology in the revolutionary ranks. Therefore, we should know how to remold them and guard against their destructiveness.

We have now gained an understanding of the nature of Chinese society, i.e., of the specific conditions in China; this understanding is the essential prerequisite for solving all of China's revolutionary problems. We are also clear about the targets, the tasks, and the motive forces of the Chinese Revolution; these are basic issues at the present stage of the Revolution and arise from the special nature of Chinese society, i.e., from China's specific conditions. Understanding all this, we can now understand another basic issue of the Revolution at the present stage, i.e., the character of the Chinese Revolution.

Since Chinese society is colonial, semicolonial, and semifeudal, since the principal enemies of the Chinese Revolution are imperialism and feudalism, since the tasks of the Revolution are to overthrow these two enemies by means of a national and democratic revolution in which the bourgeoisie sometimes takes part, and since the edge of the Revolution is directed against imperialism and feudalism and not against capitalism and capitalist private property in general even if the big bourgeoisie betrays the Revolution and becomes its enemy—since all this is true, the character of the Chinese Revolution at the present stage is not proletarian-socialist but bourgeois-democratic.

However, in present-day China the bourgeois-democratic revolution is no longer of the old general type, which is now obsolete, but one of a new special type. We call this type the new-democratic revolution and it is developing in all other colonial and semicolonial countries as well as in China. The new-democratic revolution is part of the world proletarian-socialist revolution, for it resolutely opposes imperialism, i.e., international capitalism. Politically, it strives for the joint dictatorship of the revolutionary classes over the imperialists, traitors, and reactionaries, and opposes the transformation of Chinese society into a society under bourgeois dictatorship. Economically, it aims at the nationalization of all the big enterprises and capital of the imperialists, traitors, and reactionaries, and the distribution among the peasants of the land held by the landlords, while preserving private capitalist enterprise in general and not eliminating the rich-peasant economy. Thus, the new type of democratic revolution clears the way for capitalism on the one hand and creates the prerequisites for socialism on the other. The present stage of the Chinese Revolution is a stage of transition between the abolition of the colonial, semicolonial, and semifeudal society and the establishment of a socialist society, i.e., it is a process of new-democratic revolution. This process, begun only after the First World War and the Russian October Revolution, started in China with the May 4th Movement of 1919.[4] A new-democratic revolution is an anti-imperialist and antifeudal revolution of the broad masses of the people under the leadership of the proletariat. Chinese society can advance to socialism only through such a revolution; there is no other way.

The new-democratic revolution is vastly different from the democratic revolutions of Europe and America in that it results not in a dictatorship of the bourgeoisie but in a dictatorship of the united front of all the revolutionary classes under the leadership of the proletariat. In the present War of Resistance, the anti-Japanese democratic political power, established in the base areas which are under the leadership of the Communist Party, is the political power of the Anti-Japanese National United Front; this is neither a bourgeois nor a proletarian one-class dictatorship, but a joint dictatorship, of the revolutionary classes under the leadership of the proletariat. All who stand for resistance to Japan and for democracy are entitled to share in this political power, regardless of their party affiliations.

The new-democratic revolution also differs from a socialist revolution

[4] The May 4th Movement was an anti-imperialist and antifeudal revolutionary movement which began on May 4, 1919. In the first half of that year, the victors of World War I, i.e., Britain, France, the United States, Japan, Italy, and other imperialist countries, met in Paris to divide the spoils and decided that Japan should take over all the privileges previously enjoyed by Germany in Shantung Province, China. The students of Peking were the first to show determined opposition to this scheme, holding rallies and demonstrations on May 4. The northern warlord government arrested more than thirty students in an effort to suppress this opposition. In protest, the students of Peking went on strike and large numbers of students in other parts of the country responded. On June 3 the northern warlord government started arresting students in Peking en masse, and within two days about a thousand were taken into custody. This aroused still greater indignation throughout the country. From June 5 onwards, the workers of Shanghai and many other cities went on strike and the merchants in these places shut their shops. Thus, what was at first a patriotic movement consisting mainly of intellectuals rapidly developed into a national patriotic movement embracing the proletariat, the urban petty bourgeoisie, and the bourgeoisie. And along with the growth of this patriotic movement, the new cultural movement which had begun before May 4 as a movement against feudalism and for the promotion of science and democracy, grew into a vigorous and powerful revolutionary cultural movement whose main current was the propagation of Marxism-Leninism.—*Mao.*

in that it overthrows the rule of the imperialists, traitors, and reactionaries in China but does not destroy any section of capitalism which is capable of contributing to the anti-imperialist, antifeudal struggle.

There can be no doubt that the ultimate perspective of the Chinese Revolution is not capitalism but socialism and communism, since China's bourgeois-democratic revolution at the present stage is not of the old general type but is a democratic revolution of a new special type—a new-democratic revolution—and since it is taking place in the new international environment of the nineteen-thirties and -forties characterized by the rise of socialism and the decline of capitalism, in the period of the Second World War and the era of revolution.

However, it is not at all surprising but entirely to be expected that a capitalist economy will develop to a certain extent within Chinese society with the sweeping away of the obstacles to the development of capitalism after the victory of the Revolution, since the purpose of the Chinese revolution at the present stage is to change the existing colonial, semi-colonial, and semifeudal state of society, i.e., to strive for the completion of the new-democratic revolution. A certain degree of capitalist development will be an inevitable result of the victory of the democratic revolution in economically backward China. But that will be only one aspect of the outcome of the Chinese Revolution and not the whole picture. The whole picture will show the development of socialist as well as capitalist factors. What will the socialist factors be? The increasing relative importance of the proletariat and the Communist Party among the political forces in the country; leadership by the proletariat and the Communist Party which the peasantry, intelligentsia, and the urban petty bourgeoisie already accept or are likely to accept; and the state sector of the economy owned by the democratic republic, and the cooperative sector of the economy owned by the working people. All these will be socialist factors. With the addition of a favorable international environment, these factors render it highly probable that China's bourgeois-democratic revolution will ultimately avoid a capitalist future and enjoy a socialist future.

Some immature communists think that our task is confined to the present democratic revolution and does not include the future socialist revolution, or that the present revolution or the agrarian revolution is actually a socialist revolution. It must be emphatically pointed out that these views are wrong. Every communist ought to know that, taken as a whole, the Chinese revolutionary movement led by the Communist Party embraces the two stages, i.e., the democratic and the socialist revolutions, which are two essentially different revolutionary processes, and that the second process can be carried through only after the first has been completed. The democratic revolution is the necessary preparation for the socialist revolution, and the socialist revolution is the inevitable sequel to the democratic revolution.

CHU TEH: THE REVOLUTIONARY ARMY*

THERE are two kinds of armies, now as in the past. One kind organizes, arms, and trains the people to protect the interests of the people and serve the people. The other also organizes, arms, and trains the people; but it does so to protect the interests of the few—the big landlords, the big compradors, and big bankers—and to oppress, exploit, and enslave the people.

The people's army, for the very reason that it is closely united with the people, can effectively protect the country against foreign invasions, and, inside the country, can safeguard the people's rights to democracy and freedom. The army of the big landlords and bourgeoisie, for the reason that it is divorced from the people, is bound to be powerless to defend the country: it vacillates, becomes defeatist, and may even betray its trust (to the extent of becoming a puppet army). Moreover, it undermines and suppresses the democratic liberties of the people.

The people's army practices democracy within its own ranks. Officers and men are as one. It is democratic in relation to the people: people and army are as one. The army of the big landlords and bourgeoisie imposes within its own ranks a system of oppression and double-dealing. If that were not the case, it could not order its officers and men, the vast majority of whom come from the people, to act against the people. The recruiting system of an army of big landlords and bourgeoisie must necessarily be against the wishes of the people: without compulsion, nobody would join. Those who join our army come of their own free will because they want to resist Japanese aggression, save their country, and build up a China with a system of new democracy. Some of them are communists. The majority are not. The Eighth Route and New Fourth armies,[1] just because they have this close contact with the people, have an inexhaustible supply of manpower.

When in the future a coalition government and a joint supreme command are set up, a system of obligatory military service will possibly be adopted. But any such system will be radically different from the vicious

[1] The two main Red Army forces during World War II, which went on to defeat the forces of Chiang Kai-shek's Kuomintang (Nationalist) Party.—Ed.

---

* The military section of a report given on April 25, 1945 (before the end of World War II), to the Seventh Congress of the Chinese Communist Party, as reprinted in *The Battle Front of the Liberated Areas* (Peking: Foreign Languages Press, 1962). The thesis he develops here, though applied to the anti-Japanese struggle and post-World War II civil war, is still upheld as valid by the contemporary Chinese leadership, which still includes Chu Teh himself.

conscription system of the Kuomintang government, because it will be built on a voluntary basis, a basis of persuasion.

An army not based on, and in fact antagonistic to, the people maintains itself by exploitation of the people, and consequently by exploitation of the soldiers as well! But the method of a people's army is one based on love for the people, and consequently, love for the soldiers, too. The latter is the method practiced by the Eighth Route and the New Fourth armies.

Starting from the exploitation of the people and the soldiers, the reactionary clique in the Kuomintang employs various schemes to extort military funds from the people on the pretext that "the state should maintain the troops." Not satisfied with extorting money at home, it turns to foreign countries for loans in the name of the state. And when funds for military purposes are collected, the Kuomintang reactionaries pocket the money by "padding the payroll" and other devices. Embezzlement is rife among officers from top to bottom. The higher the officer's rank, the more he can appropriate for himself.

Our soldiers are armed peasants in uniform. Our army is a collection of ordinary people under arms and in uniform. They want to wear clothes, to eat, drink, rest, and work just like the common people. Their main material needs are clothing, food, housing, and transport. Their spiritual need is education.

The material upkeep of our army follows the principle that it shall not become too heavy a burden on the people, otherwise a conflict of interests will be created between army and people. If the people's life is made hard, army life will become hard, too. Its strength to fight the enemy will be sapped. When a situation develops requiring expansion of the army, it must be expanded without excessively increasing the burden on the people. When we run into difficult times, as we did in 1942, the principle we work on is to take into consideration the interests of both army and people: we reduce the number of troops, raise their quality, and simplify government administration in the enemy rear. Our treatment of the whole army is based on the principle of equal treatment for officers and men. The officers set an example by taking the rough with the smooth, along with their men. Only those who have the interests of their men at heart, who take into account what they have to put up with, and who do not stand aloof from the rank and file, can be considered good officers. We have in recent years introduced a completely new principle into the maintenance of the army, by enabling it, in intervals between periods of fighting and training, to engage in productive work, and, in so doing, help to meet the material needs of the army and lighten the burden on the people. For the army this new contribution is something extremely important. Experience gained in the border region from the army's participation in productive work shows that, in the absence of fighting, we can in the first year become partly self-supporting, in the second, half self-supporting, and in the third, wholly so. In areas where fighting is going on, the army may, by taking part in such work, become partly or half self-supporting. Personal participation of commanders in this productive work is an important means of drawing the army in, too. Whenever the army takes part in production, the people's burden is lightened, the ties between army and people become closer, army life becomes richer, the army becomes more close-knit, training is more effective, fighting spirit is enhanced; and an inexhaustible source of funds to maintain the army is tapped.

As regards special treatment for the families of fighting men and care of disabled or demobilized soldiers, we have taken a number of new measures in recent years. Besides getting their neighbors to plough the land of such families, giving them pensions and other assistance, we are helping soldiers' families to go in for production so that they can become economically independent. Indeed, many heroes of labor have emerged from among them, and they are not doing so badly. Every liberated area should endeavor to do this work well and see that they live comfortably.

The method used by an army not based on the people, one in fact antagonistic to them, is to treat soldiers as slaves, whereas the method used by a people's army is to treat them as politically conscious fighters. The big landlords and bourgeoisie organize and arm people so as to have an army to use against the people. That, of course, is no easy matter; and that is why an army of this kind resorts to all sorts of barbarities in leading its troops. The policy of the reactionaries is to keep soldiers in a state of ignorance, applying the maxim that "the most valuable quality in generals is wisdom, in soldiers ignorance."[2] For if soldiers were wise they would not act against the people. So the reactionaries devise a set of military codes, military orders, and discipline, on the basis of which they impose a ruthless system of dictatorship and absolute obedience. Those who fail to toe the line are punished, those who do, get promotion and grow rich! On the one hand the reactionaries use threats, on the other they dangle baits. What this means is that they do not regard their subordinates and soldiers as individual human beings, but bully and cow them, through this rotten system of absolute obedience, into allowing dictators to use the army just as they think fit.

We regard officers and men alike as individual human beings on an equal footing. The only difference between them is in matters of duty. No officers are allowed to oppress the men, no senior officers to oppress their juniors. Our soldiers join the army to serve the people, not the officers. We call for extremely strict discipline, both in military affairs and in relations with the people; but this kind of discipline is based on

[2] In my days as a drafted GI, the maxim we were told a million times was "Yours not to question why, yours is to do and die."—*Ed.*

political understanding, and observed by officers and men alike without exception.

The method employed in training an army not founded on the people but actually antagonistic to them is based on ignorance and compulsion; whereas the method used in training a people's army is based on political understanding and voluntary acceptance. The first thing in training an army is to train the mind of the soldier. There will be no spirit of initiative in an army whose political understanding is low, which does not know what it is fighting for. In that case no amount of training will get results. Courage without political understanding is brute bravery. Conscious courage resulting from political awareness is real courage. To heighten political understanding and military knowledge, a certain educational level is essential.

The political understanding of our army is high, and that is why it is unconquerable. As a result of our fight in recent years against tendencies to be dogmatic or formalistic, political training has become more practical and advanced. Both officers and men have systematically improved their military knowledge, and a considerable advance has been made in the study and application of strategy and tactics. With regard to all-round education, while we could show some results right from the start, we have done much better in recent years. As far as cultivation of mind goes, we have for the past year or so given our troops training for various productive occupations as well as political and general education.[3] Such training for production not only helps the campaign to secure greater output, but also fosters a sound attitude toward labor and prevents our men from becoming scoundrels in uniform or loafers. When the war is over they will still be useful members of society.

Fighting involves hand-to-hand combat, a matching of strength. Physical training, therefore, is important. Building physical strength demands, first of all, a full stomach and warm clothing. Next comes training in technique and tactics. In the past there was a tendency in our army to pooh-pooh the idea of physical strength and technique. It was regarded as enough for the army to have political awareness. This is quite wrong. During the last couple of winters we carried out training on a large scale. In some areas this developed into military training for the whole people. Our regular troops have improved enormously, and large numbers of the militia have now learned how to lay mines. To have done so much is pretty significant.

In recent years we have worked out a new method of training troops by replacing the "officer line," which gave officers and instructors sole control of conduct of training from above, with the "mass line" on a

[3] It should also be pointed out that we owe a great deal of the success of cultivation of mind in our army to the many intellectuals and young men of good education who have joined it.

basis of cooperation between officers and men. In our army we have introduced a new educational method, one of improving ourselves through
both teaching and learning. The officers teach the men and the men
teach the officers. The officers teach each other and the men teach each
other. Those who are intellectuals and those who are of worker or peasant
origin help and learn from each other. We place a high value on the
lectures on special technical skills given by our officers or military experts.
At the same time officers must not overlook the fact that every one of
the hundreds or thousands of men under their command has his own
strong points, that in our army there are highly skilled men from every
trade. Officers should not be too proud to learn from them. We have
changed the attitude of officers from one of conceit and superiority to one
of untiringly learning from others and teaching others. In short, the class-
rooms and drill grounds which the men used to fear have been turned into
places where military skill and knowledge are cultivated and tempered.
The whole atmosphere is different, interest has been heightened, and the
barracks have been turned into schools.

There are two different methods of carrying on a war. An army not
based on, and, in fact, hostile to the people, is necessarily limited to
cut-and-dried rules and formulas. But a people's army uses methods of
extreme flexibility and constantly adapts itself to the situation. Because
the army of the big landlords and bourgeoisie oppresses the people and
receives no help from them, because there is no community of interest
between officers and men, such an army cannot, when engaged in war,
rely on the initiative and morale of its junior officers and men. This
makes it very difficult to wage a war with such an army. The higher command issues orders based entirely on preconceived, cut-and-dried rules,
without weighing enemy strength against its own, and disregarding special
conditions of time and place. Consequently such orders are utterly impracticable. When a unit receives orders which cannot be carried out, it
makes a false report to the higher command. Both superiors and subordinates try to pull the wool over each other's eyes.

Whenever we are fighting we are helped everywhere by the people.
Since the organization of the militia and the starting of tunnel-digging
and mine-laying movements, the scale and importance of the help the
people have given us are incalculable. Within the army itself, because it
has a high degree of political understanding and because there is mutual
understanding and a feeling of solidarity between officers and men, everyone knows where he stands and can act on his own initiative. Having
a single aim, the fighters are mobile and swift; they can fight bravely.

Our policy in conducting the war may be summed up like this. Whether
we join battle depends on the weapons we possess, the kind of enemy
we have to cope with, and the time and place of the engagement. It means,
too, that battle has to be planned and fought on the basis of our own

equipment, the strength of the enemy, and taking into account the factors of time and place. This new method of conducting war is both practical and materialist. I use these words advisedly. Many a military expert, in China and abroad, both nowadays and formerly, failed disastrously in this respect. And some of our comrades who held "leftist" ideas in the past failed to understand just this point. Earlier on, when the only weapons at our disposal were rifles, spears, and big swords, we simply had to study conditions, make up our minds, and determine our tactics accordingly. We didn't talk in highfaluting terms about tactics of, a mechanized army. When we passed from the period of civil war to that of the anti-Japanese war, when the enemy we had to face was the Japanese army, we did not content ourselves with sticking to experience gained in the civil war period. On the basis of that experience we made the changes and improvements necessary. We made up our minds and determined our tactics through a thorough study of the situation of the enemy. And of course, on the battlefront of the liberated areas, we have to map out tactics applicable to the time and place of a battlefront of this kind. Alongside these general rules for conducting war goes a special feature—the unity between army and people. On the one hand, the fight waged by the army serves to help the various struggles in which the people are engaged; and on the other, the people's efforts—political, economic, cultural, and military, as well as disruption of the enemy lines of communication—serve to help the army wage war. This coordination in all spheres between army and people is thoroughly carried out on the battlefronts, in every campaign and in every battle. This is the new method of making war which we have worked out in the course of the people's war.

Officers, men, and people have one constant endeavor: to seek to attack the enemy in every possible way. Consequently, even if, once in a while, orders are impracticable or belated, no harm is done, because lower units are able to adapt themselves to circumstances, and judge and act independently. That is why we are winning all along the line.

Now a word on military theory. Whenever this subject is discussed, some people like to show off with a series of high-sounding military academy lectures, or quote at length from the military history of one country or another. What they say is all very profound, but unfortunately, their theories are not necessarily of practical value to the Chinese people. Undoubtedly we must absorb the military theories and experience of all countries. We ought to learn from them. It will be bad for us if we do not. What we must not do is to apply such theories and experience mechanically; we must not accept them as immutable dogmas. The Northern Expedition, the Agrarian Revolutionary War, and the eight years of the anti-Japanese war have given birth to a correct military science which, as events prove, best suits the needs of the Chinese people. It is a military science which combines theory with practice, and which has led to three basic principles: to avoid rashness in attack; to avoid conservatism in defense; and to resist any tendency to run in panic from the enemy when withdrawing from a point. These basic principles are bound up with the close fighting unity between army and people; and because of this unity they can be applied.

Our political work sets out: (1) to raise the political understanding of officers and men, to inspire them with love for their country and their people, and to fire them with a desire to re-educate themselves; (2) to bring about unity between friendly army units; (3) to cement the unity between army and people, so as to make the people more politically aware, to safeguard the country and democracy, and to help spread education and culture among the people; (4) to demoralize the Japanese and puppet troops by political and psychological means so as to sap their fighting strength; and (5) to consolidate and raise the fighting strength of our army, to guarantee the carrying out of orders, and to help the army itself make an intensive study of politics, military matters, general education, and production. These five aspects of our political work are interrelated and complementary to one another.

For several years the most difficult problem we have been up against on the battlefronts of the liberated areas is that of obtaining equipment and military supplies. We are solving it in several ways. First, we arm ourselves with weapons seized from the enemy. For several years now we have relied on this method of strengthening our forces and maintaining our fighting power. Secondly, we make use of materials obtainable locally. The abundance of coal and iron and metal obtained from dismantled railway tracks in northern China have greatly facilitated our manufacture of arms; and this is how the greater part of the militia forces have been able to extend the tactics of mine-laying. Thirdly, we have set up small-scale ordnance factories by assembling odds and ends of equipment captured from the Japanese and puppet troops. Fourthly, these factories, which often became the target of enemy "mopping-up" campaigns, must be dispersed and camouflaged. Greater armed protection must be provided for them so that ammunition can be uninterruptedly produced to supply the front. As far as medical supplies go, we have adopted the principle of using both Chinese herbal medicines and Western medicines. We manufacture only a small part of the medicines we use, the main source of supply being seizure from the enemy and purchase.

The armed forces in the liberated areas fall into three categories: the main forces, local forces, and self-defense militia forces. The main job of the militia and self-defense forces is to protect their own villages while carrying on with their regular work. By protecting homes and defending themselves they are, wherever they may be, fighting the war against Japan in conjunction with other districts and the whole of the liberated areas. Local and national tasks in this war go hand in hand. In the whole history of our armies there have never been militia forces on such a scale in the liberated areas, and the very fact that we have learned to organize such a militia speaks volumes. For once the militia is organized, it can fight either in coordination with the regular army or on its own. It has done a fine job in protecting the people so that they could push ahead and produce more; and the recovery of many positions behind the enemy lines owes a great deal to the success of the militia in tying down the enemy. For weapons, the militia use chiefly land mines. Besides these they have some rifles, hand grenades, and sundry primitive weapons, including improvised grenade throwers. To solve the problem of securing arms by their own efforts, in many places the militia reclaim plots of land and use the money raised by the sale of produce to buy arms. Moreover, the militia and local self-defense forces take an active part in production: they are both fighters and producers, both a military and a labor force. That is something that radically changes the former face of the countryside. The local forces occupy a place midway between the main forces and the militia. They are responsible for the defense of one or several counties. They are responsible not only for the comparatively important military task of launching counter-"mopping-up" campaigns, but for looking after the immediate interests of the people, for example, giving protection to the local people at the time of harvest or sowing, besides fighting flood, drought, and other hazards of nature. The men who form these local forces naturally love the locality where they were born, where they grew up, and where their forefathers are buried. That makes it possible for us to strengthen such forces so that they can act as local garrisons in the War of Resistance. Then, as each local force, in carrying out this task, becomes tempered and strong, it gets more like and more on the level of a main force. Sometimes the main forces are concentrated. At other times they are dispersed, and then it is necessary for them to join with local and militia forces to add to their strength and attack the enemy with greater weight. Working in unity with each other, the main, local, and militia forces become an organic whole. When circumstances are critical, we can act on the principle of dispersing the main forces and mingling them with the masses to our advantage. On the other hand, when the situation favors the expansion of our work, the militia and local forces can, in certain conditions, come together to cooperate with the main forces, or actually become part of the main forces themselves so as to fulfill the more important tasks called for by such expansion. By such measures our people's armies have created a militia of over two million men to serve as their support and reserve. That is one of the reasons why they can withstand protracted warfare. This is an enormous step forward in the process of building up our military forces in the liberated areas.

LIN PIAO: PEOPLE'S WAR*

IN the summer of 1937 Japanese imperialism unleashed its all-out war of aggression against China. The nationwide War of Resistance thus broke out. Could the War of Resistance be victorious? And how was victory to be won?

Japan was a powerful imperialist country. But Japanese imperialism was in its era of decline and doom. The war it had unleashed was a war of aggression, a war that was retrogressive and barbarous; it was deficient in manpower and material resources and could not stand a protracted war; it was engaged in an unjust cause and therefore had meager support internationally. China, on the other hand, was a weak semicolonial and semifeudal country. But she was in her era of progress. She was fighting a war against aggression, a war that was progressive and just; she had sufficient manpower and material resources to sustain a protracted war; internationally, China enjoyed extensive sympathy and support.

China's War of Resistance would be protracted, and prolonged efforts would be needed gradually to weaken the enemy's forces and expand our own, so that the enemy would change from being strong to being weak and we would change from being weak to being strong and accumulate sufficient strength finally to defeat him through three stages, namely, the strategic defensive, the strategic stalemate, and the strategic offensive. The protracted war was also a process of mobilizing, organizing, and arming the people. It was only by mobilizing the entire people to fight a people's war that the War of Resistance could be persevered in and the Japanese aggressors defeated.

In order to turn the anti-Japanese war into a genuine people's war, our Party firmly relied on the broadest masses of the people, united with all the anti-Japanese forces that could be united, and consolidated and expanded the Anti-Japanese National United Front. The basic line of our Party was: boldly to arouse the masses of the people and expand the people's forces so that, under the leadership of the Party, they could defeat the aggressors and build a new China.

---

* Originally the transcription of a speech published in *Renmin Ribae* (*People's Daily*), China, on September 3, 1965, the article was meant to commemorate the twentieth anniversary of Japan's defeat in China by the Red Army, but quickly became known as the "Lin Piao theory" of revolution in the underdeveloped world through "strangulation of the cities." The author, a veteran of the famous Long March and numerous guerrilla battles, was at the time of writing Vice-Chairman of the Central Committee of the Communist Party of China, Vice-Premier of the State Council, and Minister of Defense. At the Ninth Congress of the Communist Party, held in Peking in April 1969, Lin Piao was designated Mao's successor as Chairman.

In order to win a people's war, it is imperative to build the broadest possible united front and formulate a series of policies which will ensure the fullest mobilization of the basic masses as well as the unity of all the forces than can be united.

The Anti-Japanese National United Front embraced all the anti-Japanese classes and strata. These classes and strata shared a common interest in fighting Japan, an interest which formed the basis of their unity. But they differed in the degree of their firmness in resisting Japan, and there were class contradictions and conflicts of interest among them. Hence the inevitable class struggle within the united front.

The workers, the peasants, and the urban petty bourgeoisie firmly demanded that the War of Resistance should be carried through to the end; they were the main force in the fight against Japanese aggression and constituted the basic masses who demanded unity and progress.

The bourgeoisie was divided into the national and the comprador bourgeoisie. The national bourgeoisie formed the majority of the bourgeoisie; it was rather flabby, often vacillated, and had contradictions with the workers, but it also had a certain degree of readiness to oppose imperialism and was one of our allies in the War of Resistance. The comprador bourgeoisie was the bureaucrat-capitalist class, which was very small in number but occupied the ruling position in China. Its members attached themselves to different imperialist powers, some of them being pro-Japanese and others pro-British and pro-American. The pro-Japanese section of the comprador bourgeoisie were the capitulators, the overt and covert traitors. The pro-British and pro-American section of this class favored resistance to Japan to a certain extent, but they were not firm in their resistance and very much wished to compromise with Japan, and by their nature they were opposed to the Communist Party and the people.

The landlords fell into different categories; they were the big, the middle, and the small landlords. Some of the big landlords became traitors, while others favored resistance but vacillated a great deal. Many of the middle and small landlords had the desire to resist, but there were contradictions between them and the peasants.

In the face of these complicated class relationships, our Party's policy regarding work within the united front was one of both alliance and struggle. That is to say, its policy was to unite with all the anti-Japanese classes and strata, try to win over even those who could be only vacillating and temporary allies, and adopt appropriate policies to adjust the relations among these classes and strata so that they all served the general cause of resisting Japan. At the same time, we had to maintain our Party's principle of independence and initiative, make the bold arousing of the masses and expansion of the people's forces the center of gravity in our work, and wage the necessary struggles against all activities harmful to resistance, unity, and progress.

Our party made a series of adjustments in its policies in order to unite all the anti-Japanese parties and groups, including the Kuomintang, and all the anti-Japanese strata in a joint fight against the foe.

The government of the Shensi-Kansu-Ningsia revolutionary base area was renamed the Government of the Shensi-Kansu-Ningsia Special Region of the Republic of China. Our Workers' and Peasants' Red Army was redesignated the Eighth Route Army and the New Fourth Army of the National Revolutionary Army. Our land policy, the policy of confiscating the land of the landlords, was changed to one of reducing rent and interest. In our own base areas we shared power with noncommunists, drawing in those representatives of the petty bourgeoisie, the national bourgeoisie, and the enlightened gentry, and those members of the Kuomintang who stood for resistance to Japan and did not oppose the Communist Party. In accordance with the principles of the Anti-Japanese National United Front, we also made necessary and appropriate changes in our policies relating to the economy, taxation, labor and wages, anti-espionage, people's rights, culture and education, etc.

While making these policy adjustments, we maintained the independence of the Communist Party, the people's army, and the base areas. We also insisted that the Kuomintang should institute a general mobilization, reform the government apparatus, introduce democracy, improve the people's livelihood, arm the people, and carry out a total war of resistance. We waged a resolute struggle against the Kuomintang's passive resistance to Japan and active opposition to the Communist Party, against its suppression of the people's resistance movement and its treacherous activities for compromise and capitulation. The lessons learned at the cost of blood helped to sober many of our comrades and increase their ability to distinguish the correct line which included:

1. All people favoring resistance (that is, all the anti-Japanese workers, peasants, soldiers, students and intellectuals, and businessmen) were to unite and form the Anti-Japanese National United Front.

2. Within the united front, our policy was to be one of independence and initiative, i.e., both unity and independence were necessary.

3. As far as the military strategy was concerned, our policy was to be guerrilla warfare waged independently and with the initiative in our own hands, within the framework of a unified strategy; guerrilla warfare was to be basic, but no chance of waging mobile warfare was to be lost when the conditions were favorable.

4. In the struggle against the anticommunist diehards headed by Chiang Kai-shek, our policy was to make use of contradictions, win over the many, oppose the few, and destroy our enemies one by one, and to wage struggles on just grounds, to our advantage, and with restraint.

5. In the Japanese-occupied and Kuomintang areas our policy was, on the one hand, to develop the united front to the greatest possible extent and on the other, to have selected cadres working underground. With

regard to the forms of organization and struggle, our policy was to assign selected cadres to work under cover for a long period, so as to accumulate strength and bide our time.

6. As regards the alignment of the various classes within the country, our basic policy was to develop the progressive forces, win over the middle forces, and isolate the anticommunist diehard forces.

7. As for the anticommunist diehards, we followed a revolutionary dual policy of uniting with them, in so far as they were still capable of bringing themselves to resist Japan, and of struggling against and isolating them, in so far as they were determined to oppose the Communist Party.

8. With respect to the landlords and the bourgeoisie—even the big landlords and big bourgeoisie—it was necessary to analyze each case and draw distinctions. On the basis of these distinctions we were to formulate different policies so as to achieve our aim of uniting with all the forces that could be united.

History shows that when confronted by ruthless imperialist aggression, a Communist Party must hold aloft the national banner and, using the weapon of the united front, rally around itself the masses and the patriotic and anti-imperialist people who form more than 90 percent of a country's population, so as to mobilize all positive factors, unite with all the forces that can be united, and isolate to the maximum the common enemy of the whole nation. If we abandon the national banner, and thus isolate ourselves, it is out of the question to exercise leadership and develop the people's revolutionary cause, and this in reality amounts to helping the enemy and bringing defeat on ourselves.

History shows that within the united front the Communist Party must maintain its ideological, political, and organizational independence, adhere to the principle of independence and initiative, and insist on its leading role. Since there are class differences among the various classes in the united front, the Party must have a correct policy in order to develop the progressive forces, win over the middle forces, and oppose the diehard forces.

History shows that during the national-democratic revolution there must be two kinds of alliance within this united front, first, the worker-peasant alliance and, second, the alliance of the working people with the bourgeoisie and other nonworking people. The worker-peasant alliance is the foundation of the united front. Whether the working class can gain leadership of the national-democratic revolution depends on whether it can lead the broad masses of the peasants in struggle and rally them around itself. Only when the working class gains leadership of the peasants, and only on the basis of the worker-peasant alliance, is it possible to establish the second alliance, form a broad united front, and wage a people's war victoriously. Otherwise everything that is done is unreliable, like castles in the air or so much empty talk.

The peasantry constituted more than 80 percent of the entire population of semicolonial and semifeudal China. They were subjected to the three-fold oppression and exploitation of imperialism, feudalism, and bureau-crat-capitalism, and they were eager for resistance against Japan and for revolution. It was essential to rely mainly on the peasants if the people's war was to be won.

In the period of the War of Resistance against Japan, the peasants were the most reliable and the most numerous ally of the proletariat and constituted the main force of resistance. The peasants were the main source of manpower for China's armies. The funds and the supplies needed for a protracted war came chiefly from the peasants. The War of Resistance against Japan was in essence a peasant revolutionary war led by our Party. By arousing and organizing the peasant masses and integrating them with the proletariat, our Party created a powerful force capable of defeating the strongest enemy. To rely on the peasants, build rural base areas, and use the countryside to encircle and finally capture the cities—such was the way to victory in the Chinese Revolution.

During the War of Resistance against Japan, the Japanese imperialist forces occupied many of China's big cities and the main lines of com-munication, but owing to the shortage of troops they were unable to occupy the vast countryside, which remained the vulnerable sector of the enemy's rule. Consequently, the possibility of building rural base areas became even greater. Shortly after the beginning of the War of Resistance, when the Japanese forces surged into China's hinterland and the Kuomin-tang forces crumbled and fled in one defeat after another, the Eighth Route and New Fourth armies boldly drove into the areas behind the enemy lines in small contingents and established base areas throughout the countryside. During the eight years of the war, we established nineteen anti-Japanese base areas in northern, central, and southern China. With the exception of the big cities and the main lines of communication, the vast territory in the enemy's rear was in the hands of the people.

In the anti-Japanese base areas, we carried out democratic reforms, improved the livelihood of the people, and mobilized and organized the peasant masses. Organs of anti-Japanese democratic political power were established on an extensive scale and the masses of the people enjoyed the democratic right to run their own affairs; at the same time we carried out the policies of "a reasonable burden" and "the reduction of rent and interest," which weakened the feudal system of exploitation and improved the people's livelihood. As a result, the enthusiasm of the peasant masses was deeply aroused, while the various anti-Japanese strata were given due consideration and were thus united. In formulating our policies for the base areas, we also took care that these policies should facilitate our work in the enemy-occupied areas.

In the enemy-occupied cities and villages, we combined legal with illegal struggle, united the basic masses and all patriots, and divided and disintegrated the political power of the enemy and his puppets so as to prepare ourselves to attack the enemy from within in coordination with operations from without when conditions were ripe.

The base areas established by our Party became the center of gravity in the Chinese people's struggle to resist Japan and save the country. Relying on these bases, our Party expanded and strengthened the people's revolutionary forces, persevered in the protracted war, and eventually won the War of Resistance against Japan.

Naturally, it was impossible for the development of the revolutionary base areas to be plain sailing all the time. They constituted a tremendous threat to the enemy and were bound to be attacked. Therefore, their development was a tortuous process of expansion, contraction, and then renewed expansion. Between 1937 and 1940 the population in the anti-Japanese base areas grew to 100,000,000. But in 1941–42 the Japanese imperialists used the major part of their invading forces to launch frantic attacks on our base areas and wrought havoc. Meanwhile, the Kuomintang, too, encircled these base areas, blockaded them and went so far as to attack them. So by 1942, the anti-Japanese base areas had contracted and their population was down to less than 50,000,000. After this setback, the army and the people in the base areas were tempered and grew stronger. From 1943 onwards, our base areas were gradually restored and expanded, and by 1945 the population had grown to 160,000,000. Taking the entire course of the Chinese Revolution into account, our revolutionary base areas went through even more ups and downs, and they weathered a great many tests before the small, separate base areas, expanding in a series of waves, gradually developed into extensive and contiguous base areas. In these base areas, we built the Party, ran the organs of state power, built the people's armed forces, and set up mass organizations; we engaged in industry and agriculture and operated cultural, educational, and all other undertakings necessary for the independent existence of a separate region. Our base areas were in fact a state in miniature. And with the steady expansion of our work in the base areas, our Party established a powerful people's army, trained cadres for various kinds of work, accumulated experience in many fields, and built up both the material and the moral strength that provided favorable conditions for nationwide victory.

The revolutionary base areas established in the War of Resistance later became the springboards for the People's War of Liberation, in which the Chinese people defeated the Kuomintang reactionaries. In the War of Liberation we continued the policy of first encircling the cities from the countryside and then capturing the cities, and thus won the nationwide victory.

The special feature of the Chinese Revolution was armed revolution against armed counterrevolution. The main form of struggle was war and the main form of organization was the army which was under the absolute leadership of the Chinese Communist Party, while all the other forms of organization and struggle led by our Party were coordinated, directly or indirectly, with the war.

During the First Revolutionary Civil War, many fine Party comrades took an active part in the armed revolutionary struggle. But our Party was then still in its infancy and did not have a clear understanding of this special feature of the Chinese Revolution. It was only after the First Revolutionary Civil War, only after the Kuomintang had betrayed the Revolution, massacred large numbers of communists, and destroyed all the revolutionary mass organizations, that our Party reached a clearer understanding of the supreme importance of organizing revolutionary armed forces and of studying the strategy and tactics of revolutionary war, and created the Workers' and Peasants' Red Army, the first people's army under the leadership of the Communist Party in China.

At the start of the War of Resistance against Japan, the people's army led by the Chinese Communist Party had only a little over 40,000 men. The Kuomintang reactionaries attempted to restrict, weaken, and destroy this people's army in every conceivable way. Comrade Mao Tse-tung pointed out that, in these circumstances, in order to sustain the War of Resistance and defeat the Japanese aggressors, it was imperative greatly to expand and consolidate the Eighth Route and New Fourth armies and all the guerrilla units led by our Party. The whole Party should give close attention to war and study military affairs. Every Party member should be ready at all times to take up arms and go to the front.

Our people's army steadily expanded in the struggle, so that by the end of the war it was already a million strong, and there was also a militia of over two million. That was why we were able to engage nearly two-thirds of the Japanese forces of aggression and 95 percent of the puppet troops and to become the main force in the War of Resistance against Japan. While resisting the Japanese invading forces, we repulsed three large-scale anticommunist onslaughts launched by the Kuomintang reactionaries in 1939, 1941, and 1943, and smashed their countless "friction-mongering" activities.

During the anti-Japanese war our army staunchly performed three tasks, fighting, mass work, and production; it was at the same time a fighting force, a political work force, and a production corps. Everywhere it went, it did propaganda work among the masses, organized and armed them, and helped them set up revolutionary political power. Our army men strictly observed the Three Main Rules of Discipline and the Eight Points for Attention,[1] carried out campaigns to "support the government

---

[1] The Three Main Rules of Discipline and the Eight Points for Attention were drawn up by Comrade Mao Tse-tung for the Chinese Workers' and Peasants' Red Army during the Agrarian Revolutionary War and were later adopted as rules of

and cherish the people," and did good deeds for the people everywhere. They also made use of every possibility to engage in production themselves so as to overcome economic difficulties, better their own livelihood and lighten the people's burden.

The essence of building a people's army is that politics is the commander. Political work is the lifeline of our army. True, a people's army must pay attention to the constant improvement of its weapons and equipment and its military technique, but in its fighting it does not rely purely on weapons and technique, it relies mainly on politics, on the proletarian revolutionary consciousness and courage of the commanders and fighters, on the support and backing of the masses.

During the War of Resistance against Japan, Comrade Mao Tse-tung raised guerrilla warfare to the level of strategy, because guerrilla warfare is the only way to mobilize and apply the whole strength of the people against the enemy, the only way to expand our forces in the course of the war, deplete and weaken the enemy, gradually change the balance of forces between the enemy and ourselves, switch from guerrilla to mobile warfare, and finally defeat the enemy.

In the initial period of the Second Revolutionary Civil War, Comrade Mao Tse-tung enumerated the basic tactics of guerrilla warfare as follows: "The enemy advances, we retreat; the enemy camps, we harass; the enemy tires, we attack; the enemy retreats, we pursue."[2]

In the later period of the War of Resistance against Japan and during the Third Revolutionary Civil War, we switched our strategy from that of guerrilla warfare as the primary form of fighting to that of mobile warfare in the light of the changes in the balance of forces between the enemy and ourselves. By the middle, and especially the later, period of the

---

discipline by the Eighth Route Army and the New Fourth Army and the present People's Liberation Army. As these rules varied slightly in content in the army units of different areas, the General Headquarters of the Chinese People's Liberation Army in October 1947 issued a standard version as follows:

The Three Main Rules of Discipline:
1. Obey orders in all your actions.
2. Do not take a single needle or piece of thread from the masses.
3. Turn in everything captured.

The Eight Points for Attention:
1. Speak politely.
2. Pay fairly for what you buy.
3. Return everything you borrow.
4. Pay for everything you damage.
5. Do not hit or swear at people.
6. Do not damage crops.
7. Do not take liberties with women.
8. Do not ill-treat captives.—*Lin Piao*

[2] Mao Tse-tung, "A Single Spark Can Start A Prairie Fire," *Selected Works*, (Peking: Foreign Languages Press, 1965), I, p. 124.

Third Revolutionary Civil War, our operations had developed into large-scale mobile warfare, including the storming of big cities.

War of annihilation is the fundamental guiding principle of our military operations. This guiding principle should be put into effect regardless of whether mobile or guerrilla warfare is the primary form of fighting. It is true that in guerrilla warfare much should be done to disrupt and harass the enemy, but it is still necessary actively to advocate and fight battles of annihilation whenever conditions are favorable. In mobile warfare superior forces must be concentrated in every battle so that the enemy forces can be wiped out one by one. Comrade Mao Tse-tung has pointed out:

> A battle in which the enemy is routed is not basically decisive in a contest with a foe of great strength. A battle of annihilation, on the other hand, produces a great and immediate impact on any enemy. Injuring all of a man's ten fingers is not as effective as chopping off one, and routing ten enemy divisions is not as effective as annihilating one of them.[3]

In order to annihilate the enemy, we must adopt the policy of luring him in deep and abandon some cities and districts of our own accord in a planned way, so as to let him in. It is only after letting the enemy in that the people can take part in the war in various ways and that the power of a people's war can be fully exerted. It is only after letting the enemy in that he can be compelled to divide up his forces, take on heavy burdens, and commit mistakes. In other words, we must let the enemy become elated, stretch out all his ten fingers, and become hopelessly bogged down. Thus, we can concentrate superior forces to destroy the enemy forces one by one, to eat them up mouthful by mouthful. Only by wiping out the enemy's effective strength can cities and localities be finally held or seized. We are firmly against dividing up our forces to defend all positions and putting up resistance at every place for fear that our territory might be lost and our pots and pans smashed, since this can neither wipe out the enemy forces nor hold cities or localities. It is opportunism if one won't fight when one can win. It is adventurism if one insists on fighting when one can't win. Fighting is the pivot of all our strategy and tactics. It is because of the necessity of fighting that we admit the necessity of moving away. The sole purpose of moving away is to fight and bring about the final and complete destruction of the enemy. This strategy and these tactics can be applied only when one relies on the broad masses of the people, and such application brings the superiority of people's war into full play. However superior he may be in technical equipment and whatever tricks he may resort to, the enemy will find himself in the passive position of having to receive blows, and the initiative will always be in our hands.

[3] Mao Tse-tung, "Problems of Strategy in China's Revolutionary War," *ibid.*, p. 248.

During the War of Resistance against Japan, our Party maintained that China should rely mainly on her own strength while at the same time trying to get as much foreign assistance as possible. Our Party held that it was possible to exploit the contradictions between U.S.-British imperialism and Japanese imperialism, but that no reliance could be placed on the former. In fact, the U.S.-British imperialists repeatedly plotted to bring about a "Far Eastern Munich" in order to arrive at a compromise with Japanese imperialism at China's expense, and for a considerable period of time[4] they provided the Japanese aggressors with war *matériel*. In helping China during that period, the U.S. imperialists harbored the sinister design of turning China into a colony of their own.

The Kuomintang government gave the Eighth Route and New Fourth armies some small allowance in the initial stage of the anti-Japanese war, but gave them not a single penny later. The liberated areas faced great difficulties as a result of the Japanese imperialists' savage attacks and brutal "mopping-up" campaigns, of the Kuomintang's military encirclement and economic blockade, and of natural calamities. The difficulties were particularly great in the years 1941 and 1942, when we were very short of food and clothing.

Difficulties are not invincible monsters. If everyone cooperates and fights them, they will be overcome. The Kuomintang reactionaries thought that it could starve us to death by cutting off allowances and imposing an economic blockade, but in fact it helped us by stimulating us to rely on our own efforts to surmount our difficulties. While launching the great campaign for production, we applied the policy of "better troops and simpler administration" and economized in the use of manpower and material resources; thus we not only surmounted the severe material difficulties and successfully met the crisis, but lightened the people's burden, improved their livelihood, and laid the material foundations for victory in the anti-Japanese war.

The problem of military equipment was solved mainly by relying on the capture of arms from the enemy, though we did turn out some weapons too. Chiang Kai-shek, the Japanese imperialists, and the U.S. imperialists have all been our "chiefs of transportation corps." The arsenals of the imperialists always provide the oppressed peoples and nations with arms.

In order to make a revolution and to fight a people's war and be victorious, it is imperative to adhere to the policy of self-reliance, rely on the strength of the masses in one's own country and prepare to carry on the fight independently even when all material aid from outside is cut off. If one does not operate by one's own efforts, does not independently ponder and solve the problems of the revolution in one's own country and does not rely on the strength of the masses, but leans wholly on foreign aid—even though this be aid from socialist countries which

[4] Prior to December 7, 1941.—*Ed.*

persist in revolution—no victory can be won, or be consolidated even if it is won.

The Chinese Revolution is a continuation of the great October Revolution. The road of the October Revolution is the common road for all peoples' revolutions. The Chinese Revolution and the October Revolution have in common the following basic characteristics: (1) Both were led by the working class with a Marxist-Leninist party as its nucleus. (2) Both were based on the worker-peasant alliance. (3) In both cases state power was seized through violent revolution and the dictatorship of the proletariat was established. (4) In both cases the socialist system was built after victory in the revolution. (5) Both were component parts of the proletarian world revolution.

Naturally the Chinese Revolution had its own peculiar characteristics. The October Revolution took place in imperialist Russia, but the Chinese Revolution broke out in a semicolonial and semifeudal country. The former was a proletarian socialist revolution, while the latter developed into a socialist revolution after the complete victory of the new-democratic revolution. The October Revolution began with armed uprisings in the cities and then spread to the countryside, while the Chinese Revolution won nationwide victory through the encirclement of the cities from the rural areas and the final capture of the cities.

The people's war led by the Chinese Communist Party, comprising the War of Resistance and the Revolutionary Civil Wars, lasted for twenty-two years. It constitutes the most drawn-out[5] and most complex people's war led by the proletariat in modern history, and it has been the richest in experience.

In the last analysis, the Marxist-Leninist theory of proletarian revolution is the theory of the seizure of state power by revolutionary violence, the theory of countering war against the people by people's war. As Marx so aptly put it, "Force is the midwife of every old society pregnant with a new one." It was on the basis of the lessons derived from the people's wars in China that Comrade Mao Tse-tung, using the simplest and the most vivid language, advanced the famous thesis that "political power grows out of the barrel of a gun."

War is the product of imperialism and the system of exploitation of man by man. Lenin said that "war is always and everywhere begun by the exploiters themselves, by the ruling and oppressing classes."[6] So long as imperialism and the system of exploitation of man by man exist, the imperialists and reactionaries will invariably rely on armed force to

[5] By 1969, the Vietnamese Revolution, which began in 1945 (though the Vietnamese fought the Japanese during World War II as much as did the Chinese), had become the longest.—*Ed.*

[6] V. I. Lenin, "The Revolutionary Army and the Revolutionary Government," *Works* (Moscow: Foreign Languages Publishing House, 1962), VIII, p. 565.

maintain their reactionary rule and impose war on the oppressed nations and peoples. This is an objective law independent of man's will.[7]

In the world today, all the imperialists headed by the United States and their lackeys, without exception, are strengthening their state machinery, and especially their armed forces. U.S. imperialism, in particular, is carrying out armed aggression and suppression everywhere.

In the last analysis, whether one dares to wage a tit-for-tat struggle against armed aggression and suppression by the imperialists and their lackeys, whether one dares to fight a people's war against them, means whether one dares to embark on revolution. The history of people's war in China and other countries provides conclusive evidence that the growth of the people's revolutionary forces from weak and small beginnings into strong and large forces is a universal law of development of class struggle, a universal law of development of people's war. A people's war inevitably meets with many difficulties, with ups and downs and setbacks in the course of its development, but no force can alter its general trend toward inevitable triumph.

The establishment of rural revolutionary base areas and the encirclement of the cities from the countryside is of outstanding and universal practical importance for the present revolutionary struggles of all the oppressed nations and peoples in Asia, Africa, and Latin America against imperialism and its lackeys.

The basic political and economic conditions in many of these countries have many similarities to those that prevailed in old China. As in China, the peasant is extremely important in these regions. In committing aggression against these countries, the imperialists usually begin by seizing big cities and the main lines of communication, but they are unable to bring the vast countryside completely under their control. The countryside, and the countryside alone, can provide the broad areas in which the revolutionaries can maneuver freely. The countryside, and the countryside alone, can provide the revolutionary bases from which the revolutionaries can go forward to final victory.

Taking the entire globe, if North America and Western Europe can be called "the cities of the world," then Asia, Africa, and Latin America constitute "the rural areas of the world."[8] Since World War II, the proletarian revolutionary movement has for various reasons been temporarily held back in the North American and Western European capitalist countries, while the people's revolutionary movement in Asia, Africa, and

---

[7] Modern analysts would disagree, pointing to India as an example of a neo-colonialized (i.e., imperialist-dominated) country. Lin Piao would probably answer that the United States could not possibly control India's economy if U.S. military force was not implicitly behind India's capitalist structure.—*Ed.*

[8] Many revolutionary communists, today, would include Russia and Eastern Europe among the "cities."—*Ed.*

Latin America has been growing vigorously. In a sense, the contemporary world revolution also presents a picture of the encirclement of cities by the rural areas. In the final analysis, the whole cause of world revolution hinges on the revolutionary struggles of the Asian, African, and Latin American peoples who make up the overwhelming majority of the world's population. The socialist countries should regard it as their internationalist duty to support the people's revolutionary struggles in Asia, Africa, and Latin America.

The experience of the Chinese Revolution shows that the tasks of the national-democratic revolution can be fulfilled only through long and tortuous struggles. In this stage of revolution, imperialism and its lackeys are the principal enemy; it is necessary to rally all anti-imperialist patriotic forces, including the national bourgeoisie and all patriotic personages. All those patriotic personages from among the bourgeoisie and other exploiting classes who join the anti-imperialist struggle play a progressive historical role; they are not tolerated by imperialism but welcomed by the proletariat. It is very harmful to confuse the two stages, that is, the national-democratic and the socialist revolutions. The Chinese Revolution provides a successful lesson for making a thoroughgoing national-democratic revolution under the leadership of the proletariat; it likewise provides a successful lesson for the timely transition from the national-democratic revolution to the socialist revolution under the leadership of the proletariat.

Since World War II, U.S. imperialism has stepped into the shoes of German, Italian, and Japanese fascism and has been trying to build a great American empire by dominating and enslaving the whole world. It is the most rabid aggressor in human history and the most ferocious common enemy of the people of the world. Every people or country in the world that wants revolution, independence, and peace cannot but direct the spearheads of its struggle against U.S. imperialism.

Just as the Japanese imperialists' policy of subjugating China made it possible for the Chinese people to form the broadest possible united front against them, so the U.S. imperialists' policy of seeking world domination makes it possible for the people throughout the world to unite all the forces that can be united and form the broadest possible united front for a converging attack on U.S. imperialism.

At present, the main battlefield of the fierce struggle between the people of the world on the one side and U.S. imperialism and its lackeys on the other is the vast area of Asia, Africa, and Latin America. In the world as a whole, this is the area where the people suffer worst from imperialist oppression and where imperialist rule is most vulnerable. Since World War II, revolutionary storms have been rising in this area, and today they have become the most important force directly pounding U.S. imperialism. The contradiction between the revolutionary peoples of Asia, Africa, and Latin America and the imperialists headed by the United

States is the principal contradiction in the contemporary world. The development of this contradiction is promoting the struggle of the people of the whole world against U.S. imperialism and its lackeys.

Since World War II, people's war has increasingly demonstrated its power in Asia, Africa, and Latin America. The peoples of China, Korea, Vietnam, Laos, Cuba, Indonesia, Algeria, and other countries have waged people's wars against the imperialists and their lackeys and won great victories. The classes leading these people's wars may vary, and so may the breadth and depth of mass mobilization and the extent of victory, but the victories in these people's wars have very much weakened and pinned down the forces of imperialism. Today, the conditions are more favorable than ever before for the waging of people's wars by the revolutionary peoples of Asia, Africa, and Latin America against U.S. imperialism.

U.S. imperialism is stronger, but also more vulnerable, than any imperialism of the past. It sets itself against the people of the whole world, including the people of the United States. Its human, military, material, and financial resources are far from sufficient for the realization of its ambition of dominating the whole world. It has further weakened itself by occupying so many places in the world, overreaching itself, stretching its fingers out wide and dispersing its strength, with its rear so far away and its supply lines so long. When committing aggression in a foreign country, it can only employ part of its forces, which are sent to fight an unjust war far from their native land and therefore have a low morale. The people subjected to its aggression are having a trial of strength with U.S. imperialism neither in Washington nor New York, neither in Honolulu nor Florida, but are fighting for independence and freedom on their own soil. Once they are mobilized on a broad scale, they will have inexhaustible strength.

The struggles waged by the different peoples against U.S. imperialism reinforce each other and merge into a torrential worldwide tide of opposition to U.S. imperialism. The more successful the development of people's war in a given region, the larger the number of U.S. imperialist forces that can be pinned down and depleted there. When the U.S. aggressors are hard-pressed in one place, they have no alternative but to loosen their grip in another. Therefore, the conditions become more favorable for the people elsewhere to wage struggles against U.S. imperialism and its lackeys.

Everything is divisible. And so is the colossus of U.S. imperialism. It can be split up and defeated. The peoples of Asia, Africa, Latin America, and other regions can destroy it piece by piece, some striking at its head and others at its feet. That is why the greatest fear of U.S. imperialism is that people's wars will be launched in different parts of the world, and particularly in Asia, Africa, and Latin America, and why it regards people's war as a mortal danger.

Nuclear weapons cannot save U.S. imperialism from its doom. Nuclear weapons cannot be used lightly. U.S. imperialism has been condemned by the people of the whole world for its towering crime of dropping two atom bombs on Japan. If it uses nuclear weapons again, it will become isolated in the extreme. Moreover, the U.S. monopoly of nuclear weapons has long been broken; U.S. imperialism has these weapons, but others have them too. If it threatens other countries with nuclear weapons, U.S. imperialism will expose its own country to the same threat. For this reason, it will meet with strong opposition not only from the people elsewhere but also inevitably from the people in its own country.

However highly developed modern weapons and technical equipment may be and however complicated the methods of modern warfare, in the final analysis the outcome of a war will be decided by the sustained fighting of the ground forces, by the fighting at close quarters on battlefields, by the political consciousness of the men, by their courage and spirit of sacrifice. Here the weak points of U.S. imperialism will be completely laid bare, while the superiority of the revolutionary people will be brought into full play. The reactionary troops of U.S. imperialism cannot possibly be endowed with the courage and the spirit of sacrifice possessed by the revolutionary people. The spiritual atom bomb which the revolutionary people possess is a far more powerful and useful weapon than the physical atom bomb.

Vietnam is the most convincing current example of a victim of aggression defeating U.S. imperialism by a people's war. The United States has made South Vietnam a testing ground for the suppression of people's war. It has carried on this experiment for many years, and everybody can now see that the U.S. aggressors are unable to find a way of coping with people's war. They are deeply worried that their defeat in Vietnam will lead to a chain reaction. They are expanding the war in an attempt to save themselves from defeat. But the more they expand the war, the greater will be the chain reaction. The more they escalate the war, the heavier will be their fall and the more disastrous their defeat. The people in other parts of the world will see still more clearly that U.S. imperialism can be defeated, and that what the Vietnamese people do, they can do too.

The fundamental reason why the Khrushchev revisionists are opposed to people's war is that they have no faith in the masses and are afraid of U.S. imperialism, of war, and of revolution. Like all other opportunists, they are blind to the power of the masses and do not believe that the revolutionary people are capable of defeating imperialism. They submit to the nuclear blackmail of the U.S. imperialists and are afraid that, if the oppressed peoples and nations rise up to fight people's wars or the people of socialist countries repulse U.S. imperialist aggression, U.S. imperialism will become incensed, they themselves will become involved, and their fond dream of Soviet-U.S. cooperation to dominate the world will be spoiled.

Ever since Lenin led the great October Revolution to victory, the experience of innumerable revolutionary wars has borne out the truth that a revolutionary people who rise up with only their bare hands at the outset finally succeed in defeating the ruling classes who are armed to the teeth. The poorly armed have defeated the better armed. People's armed forces, beginning with only primitive swords, spears, rifles, and hand grenades, have in the end defeated the imperialist forces armed with modern airplanes, tanks, heavy artillery, and atom bombs. Guerrilla forces have ultimately defeated regular armies. "Amateurs" who were never trained in any military schools have eventually defeated "professionals" graduated from military academies.

The Khruschchev revisionists insist that a nation without nuclear weapons is incapable of defeating an enemy with nuclear weapons, whatever methods of fighting it may adopt. This is tantamount to saying that anyone without nuclear weapons is destined to come to grief, destined to be bullied and annihilated, and must either capitulate to the enemy when confronted with his nuclear weapons or come under the "protection" of some other nuclear power and submit to its beck and call. The Khrushchev revisionists assert that nuclear weapons and strategic rocket units are decisive while conventional forces are insignificant. They have staked the whole future of their country on nuclear weapons and are engaged in a nuclear gamble with U.S. imperialism, with which they are trying to strike a political deal. Their theory of military strategy is the theory that nuclear weapons decide everything. Their line in army-building is the bourgeois line which ignores the human factor and sees only the material factor and which regards technique as everything and politics as nothing.

The Khrushchev revisionaries maintain that a single spark in any part of the globe may touch off a world nuclear conflagration and bring destruction to mankind. If this were true, our planet would have been destroyed time and time again. There have been wars of national liberation throughout the twenty years since World War II. But has any single one of them developed into a world war? Isn't it true that the U.S. imperialists' plans for a world war have been upset precisely thanks to the wars of national liberation in Asia, Africa, and Latin America? By contrast, those who have done their utmost to stamp out the "sparks" of people's war have in fact encouraged U.S. imperialism in its aggressions and wars.

The Khrushchev revisionists claim that if their general line of "peaceful coexistence, peaceful transition, and peaceful competition" is followed, the oppressed will be liberated and "a world without weapons, without armed forces, and without wars" will come into being. But the inexorable fact is that imperialism and reaction headed by the United States are zealously priming their war machine and are daily engaged in sanguinary suppression of the revolutionary peoples and in the threat and use of armed force against independent countries. Our attitude toward imperialist wars of aggression has always been clear-cut. First, we are against them, and secondly, we are not afraid of them. We will destroy whoever attacks us. As for revolutionary wars waged by the oppressed nations and peoples, so far from opposing them, we invariably give them firm support and active aid. It has been so in the past, it remains so in the present and, when we grow in strength as time goes on, we will give them still more support and aid in the future. It is sheer daydreaming for anyone to think that, since our Revolution has been victorious, our national construction is forging ahead, our national wealth is increasing, and our living conditions are improving, we too will lose our revolutionary fighting will, abandon the cause of world revolution and discard Marxism-Leninism and proletarian internationalism. Of course, every revolution in a country stems from the demands of its own people. Only when the people in a country are awakened, mobilized, organized, and armed can they overthrow the reactionary rule of imperialism and its lackeys through struggle; their role cannot be replaced or taken over by any people from outside. In this sense, revolution cannot be imported. But this does not exclude mutual sympathy and support on the part of revolutionary peoples in their struggles against the imperialists and their lackeys. Our support and aid to other revolutionary peoples serves precisely to help their self-reliant struggle.

We are optimistic about the future of the world. We are confident that the people will bring to an end the epoch of wars in human history. All peoples suffering from U.S. imperialist aggression, oppression, and plunder, unite! Hold aloft the just banner of people's war and fight for the cause of world peace, national liberation, people's democracy, and socialism! Victory will certainly go to the people of the world!

Long live the victory of people's war!

CHOU EN-LAI: IMPERIALISTS BEWARE*

1. China will not take the initiative to provoke a war with the United States. China has not sent any troops to Hawaii; it is the United States that has occupied China's territory of Taiwan Province. Nevertheless, China has been making efforts in demanding, through negotiations, that

---

* The "Four-Point Statement on China's Policy Toward the United States" published in *Peking Review*, May 13, 1966. The author, currently Prime Minister of China, is an old communist organizer from Shanghai, a Long March veteran, and a former Foreign Minister.

the United States withdraw all its armed forces from Taiwan Province and the Taiwan Straits, and she has held talks with the United States for more than ten years, first in Geneva and then in Warsaw, on this question of principle, which admits of no concession whatsoever. All this serves as a very good proof.

2. The Chinese mean what they say. In other words, if any country in Asia, Africa, or elsewhere meets with aggression by the imperialists headed by the United States, the Chinese government and people definitely will give it support and help. Should such just action bring on U.S. aggression against China, we will unhesitatingly rise in resistance and fight to the end.

3. China is prepared. Should the United States impose a war on China, it can be said with certainty that, once in China, the United States will not be able to pull out, however many men it may send over and whatever weapons it may use, nuclear weapons included. Since the fourteen million people of South Vietnam can cope with over two hundred thousand U.S. troops, the six hundred and fifty million people of China can undoubtedly cope with ten million of them. No matter how many U.S. aggressor troops may come, they will certainly be annihilated in China.

4. Once the war breaks out, it will have no boundaries. Some U.S. strategists want to bombard China by relying on their air and naval superiority and avoid a ground war. This is wishful thinking. Once the war gets started with air or sea action, it will not be for the United States alone to decide how the war will continue. If you can come from the sky, why can't we fight back on the ground? That is why we say the war will have no boundaries once it breaks out.

India

No man has done more physical harm to the poor of the world than Mahatma Gandhi. He influenced millions to accept as "good" misery, suffering, disease, exploitation, and what is generally referred to as "unnatural" death. He refused to learn from anyone not "in touch" with nature, condemned all material progress, and told his people, over and over, that "Indian civilization is the best." He condemned sex except for procreation, and reinforced guilt among his Hindu followers for any "carnal desire." He told the Jews that if they had offered themselves to the butcher's knife of Nazi Germany the world would have been "aroused." He praised Marshal Pétain for surrendering to Hitler's storm troopers and appealed to the British to do the same: "If these gentlemen choose to occupy your homes, you will vacate them. If they do not give you free passage out, you will allow yourself, man, woman, and child, to be slaughtered." And to his own people, who listened and obeyed, he said that education enslaves, that children should learn not from books or schools but "from constant contact with the parents." He asked his followers to keep away from doctors, and medicine: "Hospitals are the instruments that the devil has been using for his own purpose, in order to keep his hold on his kingdom," he wrote; "they perpetuate vice, misery and degradation and real slavery." The net result has not been the "independence" of India (a cynical non-Gandhian elite having taken over the state from the British). Rather it has been that India's Hindu millions have accepted their oppressed existence more than any other people. Gandhi may have helped save their souls—no mortal can testify to that—but he certainly did strengthen their oppressors. In brute material terms, he was an accomplice—in fact, a conspirator—to the murder of millions of children whose parents, to this day, continue to believe that if they accept their "fate," that is, their place in the world, their own souls will be freed (for by what right can

140

*they say what's good or bad for the souls of their children?). And since
a revolutionary is he who knows that "one's place" is determined by man
and guns and not gods, it is little wonder that so few revolutionaries
exist among India's teeming millions.*

*The revolutionaries that have long been active in India are mostly
non-Indian—Nagas, Mizos, Ahoms, and other minorities in northeast
India. Among Indians proper, wars or violence are mostly limited to racial
or religious conflicts. But there are exceptions, and recently, some of these
exceptions have proven to be so serious that a people's war can no longer
be dismissed as an absurdity. In fact, the possible germ of such a war
exists now among the rebellious peasants of Terai, in the West Bengal
foothills of the Himalayas. There, in 1967, at a place called Naxalbari,
peasants actually seized arms, killed local representatives of government
authority and jotedars (rich landowners who do not cultivate their land
themselves) and retreated into the jungle hills to fight on.*

*At the time, both communist parties of India condemned the rebellion.
These two parties had originally split in 1964. The CPI-Right or pro-
Soviet party opposes all acts of violence. The CPI-Left or CPI-
M(arxist), which pretends to be Maoist, theoretically advocates armed
revolution. At least so states its program, adopted at its Seventh All-
India Party Congress in 1964 (both parties held "All-India" congresses that
year). But because the CPI-M, electorally strong in West Bengal, had
entered into a united front ministry, with bourgeois parties, the communist
leaders, specifically B. T. Ranadive and Promode Das Gupta, condemned
the Terai uprising. They couldn't do so on ideological grounds; instead
they criticized the timing, claiming that India is "not yet ripe" for revolution.*

*The article that follows was meant as a refutation of this "timing"
theory and explains the position of India's "revolutionary Marxists" who
condemn both the CPI-R and the Maoist CPI-M, although very pro-
Chinese themselves. The author's real name has been kept secret, perhaps
because members of this "revolutionary Marxist" group are actually involved in the Terai rebellion. Using traditional jargon as clearly
as he can, he tries to prove that the time for revolution in India is now.*

ASIT SEN: TIMING THE REVOLUTIONARY SITUATION*

IT is necessary to understand clearly the meaning of the term "revolution"
in order to ascertain whether the time for revolution has really come.
When we say that Darwin revolutionized the zoological science or that

---

* Originally published in Bengali in *Katha o Kalam* (Siliguri, Darjeeling) October
1967, then reproduced in English in *Liberation* (New Delhi), organ of India's
Marxist-Leninist communists (Maoists), in February 1968.

Marx ushered in a revolution in the interpretation of human history, the word "revolution" is used in a certain sense, and signifies that Darwin and Marx brought about fundamental qualitative changes in the realms of zoology and history, respectively. In both these subjects all existing theories sprang from an idealist or mechanical materialist world outlook and it was Darwin and Marx who substituted a scientific materialist outlook for the existing idealist and mechanical materialist outlook in their respective fields. Thus the word "revolution" denotes a fundamental, qualitative change. This, in general, is the meaning of revolution.

In politics we are concerned with social revolution—that is, a qualitative change in the existing social system. In nature everything changes. But it does not happen that a certain thing or phenomenon remains unchanged for a certain period of time and then all of a sudden undergoes a qualitative change. In reality, the changes in things or phenomena take place according to a law, which is that an unceasing process of quantitative changes brings about a qualitative change in them. The development of human society is also guided by this law. But the sphere of social development is a complex thing and so, the processes of change, both quantitative and qualitative, in this sphere are also complex. However, complex as they are, they are guided without exception by the basic law of change mentioned above. In other words, a particular social system undergoes a qualitative change only after and as a result of a long process of unceasing quantitative changes. Thus, social revolution is, like any other revolution, the end result of an unceasing process of changes. That is, the leap of a given social system to a qualitatively higher social system through a victorious social revolution takes place only as a result of a process of quantitative changes which goes on for an entire historical period.

The change in the social system does not, however, occur as a result of "divine" forces, nor by any directives of human thought. The causes of the change are inherent in the society itself. Every change is also the result of the conflict of two opposing forces. In human society, productive forces and production relations are the two opposing forces.

By productive forces are meant the human labor power and the material implements of labor, i.e., the things by which human labor power is applied profitably. Productive forces are the things that men use to exploit nature in order to satisfy their material and cultural needs.

In struggling against nature, which they must do to satisfy their needs, men inevitably enter into certain relations with one another—and these relations are called production relations, which do not depend on the likes or dislikes of men for their existence. Production relations constitute the real foundation of human society on which is erected a superstructure consisting of such things as politics, social justice, art and literature, philosophy, religion, law, etc. Although these things of the superstructure depend, in the final analysis, on the basis, i.e., production relations, and cannot have any existence independent of or separate from that of the basis—yet they can, within limits, act independently and sometimes exert some influence on the basis. Anyway, it is the basis that invariably determines the nature of the superstructure and never the other way round.

As stated before, men enter into certain production relations with one another, that is, live a social life. And these production relations in their turn go on developing the productive forces. But it so happens that a particular form of production relations can help develop the forces of production only up to a certain stage and the reverse process begins after this stage has been reached. In such cases production relations cease to develop the forces of production and gradually begin to impede the process of development of the productive forces. Once that stage is reached no further development of productive forces is possible without bringing about a fundamental change in the production relations, i.e., social structure. When the conflict between the production relations and productive forces in the old social system is thus aggravated, there begins an era of social revolution. In this way the old production relations gradually advance toward their own destruction over an entire period of time and after a certain stage is reached these old relations undergo a qualitative change giving birth to a new social system. Consequent to this revolutionary change in the basis, there begins a revolutionary change in the superstructure. But this change in the superstructure is effected over a much longer period.

It is this basic conflict inside a social system that caused the primitive human society to break up and laid the foundations for a higher social system, namely, the slave society. Later, the same process gave birth to the feudal society, the capitalist society, and the socialist society one after the other. While this basic conflict between the production relations and productive forces constitutes the real and root cause that brings about change in social systems, its developments do not always proceed freely and unobstructed.

When this conflict grew acute in primitive society, the existing social order began to break up but it so happened that no element of the superstructure exerted force from above to resist this breaking up. Therefore, there was no necessity for any force to be applied to free the forces of production. In all later forms of society, however, an additional conflict— the class conflict between the exploiters and the exploited—appeared. This happened because the means of production in such societies were owned and controlled by a handful of people. As a result, the unfettered development of the conflict between production relations and the forces of production was weighted down and influenced by the conflict between the classes. This class struggle intruded into the field of social development and got itself imposed upon the basic conflict. And so it became impossible for basic conflict in society to develop freely unless the contradictions between classes were resolved through class struggle. Marx and Engels were expressing this truth when they declared in the beginning of their *Communist Manifesto*: "The history of all hitherto existing society excepting the primitive communistic society is the history of class struggles."

But Marx and Engels did not restrict the real nature and intensity of class conflicts to the statement alone that human history is the history of class struggles. By concretely analyzing history they demonstrated how society gets differentiated into two parts—urban and rural, how the necessity of the exploiting classes to preserve the existing social order gives rise to the state power and how the state power is used to forcibly suppress class struggles. They discovered through an incisive analysis the real role of this state power in a class society and its relation to the entire society and exploded the myths and mystifications created by bourgeois historians around the question of the state. Marx announced this discovery during the lengthy debate at the Second Congress of the Communist League in 1847.

From what has been said above some conclusions can be drawn: (1) social revolution means a qualitative change in the social relations; (2) this qualitative change is nothing but a qualitative change in the relations between classes—that is, the exploiting class is overthrown and its domination is replaced by the domination of the exploited class, which aims ultimately at setting up a classless society; (3) no class can overthrow another class except through intense class struggle; (4) as the state is the organ of maintaining the old class relations by forcible suppression of the class struggle, no social revolution is possible without smashing the old state machinery in the final phase of the class struggle; (5) in order to protect and preserve the fruits of social revolution the exploited class must establish its own state power; (6) the class society determines the nature of state power and not vice versa; so, a new state power can be established only through class struggle. The conflicts between classes can never be abolished by capturing state power from above and by avoiding class struggle.

If we consider social revolution in this broad context, the question "has the time for revolution come?" will reveal two aspects. First, we shall be faced with the question whether the basic contradiction in social development, namely, the contradiction between the forces of production and production relations, has ripened to the stage of an antagonistic contradiction or not; in other words, whether the existing relations of production are still able to develop the forces of production. If the relations of production have already reached a stage when they act as an impediment instead of as a promoter of the productive forces, then it becomes clear beyond any shadow of doubt that we have arrived at the era of a social revolution. Secondly, the question arises as to whether the time has come to direct the class struggles with the object of quickening the pace of the social revolution, that is, of hastening to bring about a revolutionary change in class relations. If this be so, we shall have to try to turn the economic struggles into political class struggles as quickly as possible. In other words, the exploited classes must march forward quickly and resolutely to overthrow the exploiting classes by smashing all the legal and political trappings that protect the interests of the exploiters and establish their own political power. Again, as the law and order of the exploiting classes depend, in the final analysis, on the power of the armed forces for their preservation and protection, the exploited classes must, in their march toward establishment of political power through class struggle, build up their own armed forces step by step.

Now let us see if we, in India, have entered the phase of revolution. Lenin once remarked, in the course of his criticism of Kautsky, that broadly speaking, the era of competitive capitalism ended and the monopolist phase began by 1870. Lenin demonstrated through his analysis that this monopoly capital was the economic base of imperialism. That is, capitalism entered the era of imperialism after 1870, which transformed itself gradually into a world system. Lenin established further that imperialism is the highest stage of capitalism and is also the stage of the decay of capitalism, when no further sustained development of the forces of production is possible. Extending this argument further and taking the world as a whole, i.e., as a unit of social system, we may say that the whole world has entered the era of social revolution. This is not to say, however, that revolution will take place simultaneously at all places on the earth and a qualitatively new higher social system will be established in the world at once. Lenin pointed out that owing to the uneven development of capitalism, social revolution will take place in different countries at different times and in different ways. Judged from this point of view it becomes clear that India was already ripe for a social revolution even at the time when she was ruled by the British imperialists. This social revolution had as its objective—the overthrow of foreign imperialism and of native feudalism, which was preserved and protected by the former. But due to the lack of far-sightedness on the part of the exploited classes, that revolution could not succeed and a section of the native bourgeoisie managed, in active collaboration with the imperialists, to make certain changes in the political superstructure and trumpeted these changes as a great social revolution.

From what Lenin taught, every communist knows that the objective conditions for revolution and the necessity to carry it forward quickly to its full consummation are there when both the exploiting and the exploited classes are enmeshed in a nationwide crisis. At a time of such crisis the exploited classes deeply realize from their own living conditions that it is impossible to go on living in the old way. Similarly, the exploiting classes also realize the futility of maintaining their regime of oppression and exploitation in the old way and try to devise ever new methods to maintain the same. To these factors Lenin added one thing more—a revolutionary consciousness which favors the carrying forward of the revolution quickly to complete success. Does this mean, therefore, that the entire toiling people will realize the inevitability of revolution and will begin to act consciously to that end? To this, Lenin replied that what is necessary is that the majority of the working class, at least the majority of the class-conscious and politically active sections of the working class, must come to realize that a revolution is inevitable. When such a consciousness combines with the other objective factors of a revolutionary condition, it becomes necessary to orientate the class struggle quickly toward the objective of bringing about revolutionary changes.

It goes without saying that communists will continue to participate in bourgeois elections, if they are allowed to, till such a revolutionary situation matures. But then, they participate in it only to use it as a means of propagating the necessity of a revolution among the broad masses of the toiling people through their election campaigns, and certainly not to sing the glory of the bourgeois parliamentarism by sending in hundreds of choir-boys. In *"Left-Wing" Communism* Lenin clearly stated that communists never fight the elections to win more seats. Ranadive, who quotes so liberally from *"Left-Wing" Communism*, is, however, shrewd enough to skip over precisely those portions in the book which have a direct bearing on the discussion of the question of whether the time for revolu- has come or not. What else could he do? These are precisely the portions which clearly show the interconnection between the bourgeois elections on the one hand and the forces of revolution on the other, and clearly point out that the primary task before communists is to make the revolution a success and, if they have to participate in the bourgeois elections under special conditions, it is only to facilitate and quicken the achievement of their primary objective. In this alone lies the significance of their participation in bourgeois elections.

Let us now see how we can gauge the situation in our country according to the criteria set by Lenin regarding a revolutionary situation. First, that there is a nationwide crisis today requires no Marxism-Leninism to realize. The toiling people realize from their own experiences how cruel and deep is this crisis. The ruling classes are also sensing the depth of the crisis with their own class consciousness and as such are resorting to new methods to maintain their regime of exploitation. This is finding expression in such things as exploiting peasants through the new agrarian laws, retrenchment of workers in the name of automation and rationalization, and attempts to subdue the forces of revolution by opening the floodgates of rabid chauvinism.

To all this let us add the factor of revolutionary consciousness, and see what we have got. The class-conscious and politically active workers are the vanguard of the working class. Marx and Engels defined these advanced elements as communists. Lenin defined the Communist Party as the. highest class organization of the toiling people. Did not this vanguard and its highest class organization in this country openly admit in its Programme adopted at its well-attended Congress that the revolution is both inevitable and necessary?

The one thing more that, according to Lenin's *"Left-Wing" Communism*, is necessary is crisis in the government and the increasing participation by the backward sections of the people in political activities. Had there been no governmental crisis, no increased participation by the backward sections in political activities, how else can the fact be explained that eight of the existing state government were dislodged from power? In other words, the time for revolution has ripened to such an extent that not only the vanguard of the working class, but even the backward sections of the people also realize the necessity to break up the existing social order. And it was because of this that all through 1966 even the backward sections of the people repeatedly took part in death-defying struggles on various demands and the struggles for economic demands began to be quickly transformed into political battles. But the backward sections cannot realize on their own the real way in which they should advance in order to seize political power, and carry the social revolution through to the victorious end. It is the duty of the Communist Party, the highest class organization of the vanguard of the working class, to enlighten them on the way, the manner, in which they should advance to achieve their goal. The neo-revisionist leadership of the Communist Party (Maoist) precisely shirked this duty and for this purpose has artificially raised the bogey that the time for revolution has not yet come. Thus they have tried to push the question of revolution back to a position of secondary importance and to raise the question of elections to the position of primary importance. Instead of clarifying people's minds about the real connection that exists between the social order and the state machinery, they have shamelessly tried to capitalize on people's ignorance about it and have assiduously tried to raise false hopes in their minds, by sugarcoated talks and assurances that their living conditions can be bettered, even to a small degree, by replacing the Congress ministers by the so-called progressive ministers. In this way, this neo-revisionist leadership has been trying their utmost to reverse the process of revolutionary mass awakening. Why should they try to do this now? Precisely because a revolutionary situation exists in our country and the masses are waking up to the necessity of making a revolution, these neo-revisionist leaders are so keen on distracting people's attention from revolution and diverting it to the "blessings" of bourgeois parliamentarism and the game of cabinet-making.

There is further proof to show that these people are shouting "the time for revolution has not come" precisely for the purpose of hiding from the people the fact that the time for revolution is ripe. Let us remember that on many a previous occasion the people clashed with the police and many a precious life was sacrificed but never before were these people heard raising the bogey of untimeliness. On the contrary, they applauded those clashes in order to strengthen their own positions in the Party and the mass organizations. The reason for this is of course not far to seek. They are fully aware of the fact that in order to make the social revolution thoroughgoing, the basis of the social order must be smashed and that sporadic clashes with the state power, however valiant, can never achieve that. That is why these agents of the bourgeoisie found nothing to worry over struggles so long as these remained sporadic, and did not think of raising the bogey of untimeliness nor did they care to direct this fighting conciousness toward the main objective of social revolution.

But unfortunately for these men, history is created by the people themselves and not by leaders, however crafty and deceptive they may be. The true representatives of the people, taking lessons from the experience and consciousness of the struggling masses, have today revealed before millions of toiling people the path to be taken to make the social revolution completely successful. In the fields and forests of the Terai region they have ushered in a glorious peasant revolution which is the axis of the people's democratic revolution. They have refused to fritter away their revolutionary fighting strength by engaging in sporadic and futile clashes with the state power. Instead, they have started a peasant revolution on correct lines whose main objective is to overthrow the forces of feudalism in the countryside. Their struggle is thus a struggle for land, which, they realize well, can only be successful by using force and never through resort to the legalities or documents of the existing regime. The revolutionary peasants of Terai also realize that what they are up against is not merely the feudal landlords of the countryside, but also the armed might of the state, which protects the interests of the exploiting classes. For this reason, the revolutionary peasants there are getting prepared for an armed struggle and are developing their own armed might in the course of struggles. The essence of seizure of state power is to develop people's own armed power so as to provide an all-round protection for the rights of the people and to maintain decisive control over all matters involving such rights.

The main task of the Indian social revolution at the present stage has for the first time been undertaken at the foot of the Himalayas. It is happening at a time when the time is ripe for revolution in our country. That is why this spark kindled in Terai cannot remain and is not remaining confined to that region alone and is about to kindle a flame that will engulf the entire stretch of West Bengal.

Vietnam

In nonrevolutionary circles, academic debates, and the press, it is usual nowadays to talk and even to think of three different "loyalties" or inspirational source-centers—Moscow, Peking, Havana. Even revolutionaries tend to divide the communist world into these three "loyalty" areas. Basically, what is meant is that such-and-such a movement or individual is morally, materially, politically, and/or militarily supported by one of the three revolutionary countries. On an ideological level, the distinction is somewhat more meaningful: (1) the Moscowphile is said to believe that in the long run capitalism cannot sustain economic competition with the communist world and hence sees no reason to risk a world nuclear war for the momentary advantage that might result from some armed confrontation; (2) the Maoist is convinced that only through armed confrontation (though not necessarily conflagration) will capitalism ever be destroyed and that in order to be ready for such armed—people's—war, the masses have to be politically educated first; and (3) the Guevarists, agreeing with the Maoists that people's war is a prerequisite for the seizure of power, insist that fighting is the best politicization process. On a political-tactical level, the distinctions lead to Moscowphiles fostering alliances with liberals and establishing electoral united fronts, Maoists advocating national revolutions in which alliances are maintained with one sector of the exploiting capitalist class enemy known as the "national bourgeoisie," and Guevarists organizing openly socialist guerrilla groups operating in almost total isolation from the revolutionary or neo-revolutionary forces located in capitalist urban strongholds. In shorthand, these differences are trimmed to such an extent that the Moscowphile is seen as a "sell-out" or even as a counterrevolutionary, the Maoist as a dogmatic advocate of endless war, and the Guevarist as a subjectivist or elitist adventurer.

In reality, such distinctions and differences are much more fluid. While

149

it is true that Moscow-oriented communists constantly flee from confrontation (the missile crisis, 1962), refuse to seize power where there is the risk of a strong counterrevolution (France, 1968), actually give technical aid to oligarchies fighting other communists (Colombia), order "their" men to give up the armed struggle in exchange for legality and the possibility of joining the electoral process (Venezuela), and seem to prefer nonrevolutionary "nationalists" to committed fighters (in 1968, Egypt received twenty times more Russian aid than Vietnam), Moscow nevertheless does help guerrillas in Kurdistan, Palestine, Angola, Mozambique, and South Africa, and has continued to aid Vietnam (even if not as much as, and proportionally to its wealth much, much less than, China). And, more important for Vietnam, it is a fact that Russia's nuclear presence is the only deterrent that stopped John Foster Dulles and his "massive retaliation" policy from obliterating the Vietnamese with atomic bombs after Dien Bien Phu in 1954.

In its main development, the revolutionary struggle in Vietnam has followed the Chinese example, a protracted people's war against outside imperialist forces and, gradually more defined, their neo-colonialist local partners. It has been mainly a liberation or national revolution, led, as Mao would have it, by the Communist Party vanguard. And it has been a two-stage revolution: all patriots together until the French were driven out, then a socialist transformation in the north; all patriots together until the United States is driven out, then a socialist transformation in the south. The peasants in the countryside were and are the backbone of the Revolution, but the workers, petty bourgeoisie, and the "patriotic" elements of the national bourgeoisie are the fundamental partners without which the Revolution would risk isolation. All this is very clearly spelled out in all three articles in this section. Yet, the three authors disagree ideologically: Hoc Tap, *the theoretical organ of the Vietnamese CP, is Maoist;* Le Duan, *secretary-general of the CP, is Moscowphile; and General Giap, the brilliant military head of the Revolution against the French and of the war against the United States, is maintaining a Guevarist line—at least in this article.*

Actually, the three articles' variances are subtle. Hoc Tap *is perhaps the clearest: it completely rejects Russia's fear of atomic war ("nuclear blackmail"), scoffs at alliances with peaceful dissenters ("structural reformists"), and does not shrink from the risk of total civil war—on the contrary, following Lenin, sees it as the last stage in people's war. Its definition of violence pulls no punches: revolutionary violence is both necessary and beneficial, it is the only way to win and to end counterrevolutionary violence which always causes more suffering, ultimately, than a victorious though bloody civil war—a theme which will be expanded by Fanon and Che Guevara in later pages. But the editors of* Hoc Tap *are also quite careful to insist that revolutionaries must resort to violence only*

*when the people have been politicized, that is when the revolutionary
forces include vast sectors of the peasant and worker masses.*

*In the first part of his article, Le Duan says fundamentally the same
thing, but his emphasis is different. He opposes terrorism (assassination)
which, as we have seen, Lenin did not, and he is more concerned than
Hoc Tap about the cities, insisting that a revolution cannot be won without
the full participation of the urban workers. Today, all Moscow-oriented
communists stress this point, partly because traditionally, the communist
parties have had more success at organizing or seizing control of unions
than peasants and peasant leagues. After all, there isn't much one can
promise landless, exploited peasants besides land, which is a revolutionary
demand. Whereas a union leadership can gain a strong following simply
by promising, and obtaining, better working conditions, shorter hours,
higher wages—none of which is especially revolutionary. One way of
putting the difference, then, would be that one can fool city workers with
revolutionary rhetoric and reformist actions, but not peasants. Or, to
be cynical for a moment, that it is easier to co-opt or Fabianize workers
than peasants.*

*Proudhon said that private property was theft, and every social revolu-
tionary, Marxist or not, must agree, for unless private property is abolished, competition will remain the characteristic of how people relate
(the relation of productive forces, to use Marxist jargon, as Le Duan does
so extensively). It follows therefore that a true revolutionary must advocate and eventually fight for a collective society. But Le Duan does not.
He wants peasants to join cooperatives, a farming system whereby each
peasant owns his own land yet somehow helps both his fellow peasants
and the state. But if the peasant does own land, that "somehow" must
then entail some form of material benefit, which leads Le Duan to talk
of "market incentives with education and moral stimulation." The net
result is that the whole countryside must be highly centralized. Like
Russian communists, Le Duan ends up with a social structure in which
the "state" is more important than its people. He can then logically insist
that industrialization has priority over agriculture, the city over the
country, and the worker over the peasant. Without saying so, he is con-
demining the Debray-Guevara foco theory, China's Cultural Revolution,
and the whole New Left's concept of decentralization and participatory
democracy.*

*Not so for General Giap. Perhaps because of his years of day-to-day
relationship with guerrilla fighters, who must be decentralized to be
efficient (and survive), his class analysis, which at first glance seems quite
traditional and academically Marxist, betrays great empirical trust in
ordinary people. What's more, his experience with people's war makes
him conclude that warfare builds not only comradeship but also collectivism. It was he, after all, who had to coordinate the movement of thou-*

sands of peasants from hundreds of different localities and scores of distinct ethnic groups to attack the French at Dien Bien Phu. Since 1959, supposedly, he has been doing the same in the south against the United States. During the Têt offensive in 1968, literally thousands of guerrilla units were asked to launch correlated attacks. When one remembers that the National Liberation Front (or Viet Cong) operates through semi-autonomous units, each of which expects all its combatants to share in the decision-making process (down to actual discussion of attack plans), such coordination is no minor feat. It is perhaps this attitude toward war and peoples that has made it possible for the NLF to recruit noncommunists by the thousands—and for the "Alliance of National, Democratic and Peace Forces of Vietnam" to have joined the NLF in combat and in 1969 to have joined the Provisional Revolutionary Government of South Vietnam. That Alliance, set up after the Têt offensive by non-NLF anti-imperialist South Vietnamese, issued a manifesto on April 21, 1968, which insisted that after victory the political regime must be a republic that guarantees "freedom of speech, freedom of meeting, freedom of organization, freedom to go abroad. . . . All organs of state power are to be elected by the people through free and fair elections. All people's strata, men and women, all nationalities, all religious communities are to be represented in these organs. All Vietnamese citizens are to be equal in all respects."

Of course, the alliance could be just another "front" to corral non-communists into the "nationalist" struggle, as the Western press claimed. But the point remains that the south is decentralized, and that General Giap, who is commander-in-chief of the Vietnamese Army and Defense Minister of the Democratic Republic of Vietnam, has always worked through decentralization to guide his men to victory. Both nationally and internationally, he believes that each struggle waged, even if lost, ups the odds of quicker ultimate victory. Like Che Guevara, he is convinced that the United States cannot withstand many Vietnams simultaneously (Giap actually refers to the Dominican Republic almost as if he were saying "create two, three . . . many Santo Domingos"). Like Che Guevara, he believes that revolutionary practice is the best teacher of revolutionary theory—to the point of stating that "revolutionary practice will iron out divergencies among communists," e.g., Russia and China. And, like Che Guevara, finally, Giap is international in scope. He sees the Vietnamese Revolution as part of the world struggle against imperialism and hence believes that it is the duty of the Vietnamese to fight not only for a free and independent Vietnam but also "to actively contribute" to the struggle of all peoples, everywhere.

But then, on that score, every Vietnamese leader concurs. Ho Chi Minh, in his testament (written on May 10, 1969, and read by Le Duan on September 9, 1969, at Ho's funeral), said: "My ultimate wish is that

*our whole Party and people will be united in the struggle for peaceful
united independent democratic Vietnam and make a worthy contribution
to the world revolution." Le Duan himself led mourners in an oath to
carry on Ho's work, promising "to maintain the international orientation
of the Party, contribute to the unity of socialist peoples, and support all
revolutionary forces of other peoples struggling for independence, peace,
democracy, and socialism." When I was in North Vietnam during the
winter of 1966–67, I got the feeling that every Vietnamese was indeed an
internationalist. Wherever I went during my two-thousand-mile trip[1] I
noticed, first of all, that the north is quite decentralized and operates on
moral incentives much much more than one would gather from Le Duan's
article; secondly, that even isolated peasants were aware of the revolutionary struggles in the rest of Asia, Africa, and America; and thirdly,
that all felt, as Prime Minister Pham Van Dong told me: "Right now,
we happen to be in the front lines of the struggle against imperialism. But
it is a struggle of all exploited peoples everywhere and we consider ourselves just one part of that struggle. No one will really be totally free until
all are."*

FROM *Hoc Tap*: PEACE OR VIOLENCE*

HOW to get state power into the hands of the working class and how to
build the state power of the proletariat are the questions of primary concern to every true revolutionary. That is why the method of seizing state
power is one of the most important questions communists must study
and solve.

The state is the instrument of violence used by the ruling classes to
crush all resistance put up by the classes ruled by them. The rulers use
troops, policemen, spies, law courts, and prisons against the ruled. The
exploiting classes in power, on the one hand, are always employing
violence to keep down the exploited classes. On the other hand, they
use their "thinkers" to spread pacifism and the theory of "nonviolence"
in an effort to cause the exploited to be resigned to their destiny without
resorting to violence to resist the exploiting classes in power.

Those who have swallowed the poison of bourgeois pacifism and
humanitarianism oppose all kinds of violence. They make no distinction

---

[1] See John Gerassi, *North Vietnam: A Documentary* (New York: Bobbs-Merrill,
London: Allen and Unwin, 1968).

---

* Originally published in the September 1963 issue of *Hoc Tap (Study)*, the theoretical
organ of the Central Committee of the Vietnam Workers Party (CP) and issued in
English as a pamphlet by the Foreign Languages Press, Peking, 1964.

in the class character of the various kinds of violence. To them the violence used by the bourgeoisie to suppress the proletariat and the violence used by the proletariat to resist the bourgeoisie for its own emancipation are one and the same. To the pacifists, every kind of violence is evil. They can do nothing but moan and lament over the death caused by violence. They know nothing about the law of social development. They only see the ugly side of violence and do not understand that despite its ugliness it plays a revolutionary role in history. Marx once said that violence "is the midwife of every old society pregnant with a new one."[1]

Today, modern revisionists and right opportunists in the communist movement and the working-class movement keep wagging their tongues about "peace," and "humanitarianism"; they dare not mention the word "violence." For them violence is taboo. The fact is that they have negated Marxist-Leninist theory on the role of violence in history.

Communists are not Tolstoyists or the disciples of Gandhi preaching "nonviolence." Nor do they spread the idea of "violence for violence's sake." They are not "bellicose" and "bloodthirsty" as the reactionaries always slander them. They simply set forth a fact that violence is a social phenomenon, a result of the exploitation of man by man, a means used by the ruling, exploiting classes to maintain and extend their domination. Communists hold that the working class and other people—victims of exploitation and domination—must resort to revolutionary violence to crush counterrevolutionary violence, so that they can win their own emancipation and society can advance according to the law of historical development.

The revolutionary cause of the proletariat does not mean an ordinary reshuffle of government personnel or a mere cabinet change while the old political and economic order remains intact. The proletarian revolution must not preserve the state machinery (the existing police, gendarmes, armed forces, and bureaucratic structure), mainly used to oppress the people, but must crush it and replace it with an entirely new one. The bourgeois revolution does not smash the existing feudal state machinery but takes it over, preserves, and perfects it. On the contrary, the proletarian revolution smashes the existing state machinery of the capitalist system. It is a process of bitter struggle in which the bourgeoisie is overthrown, the bourgeois order is destroyed, the properties of the capitalists and landlords are confiscated, and the public ownership of the various chief means of production is realized. Smashing the existing state machinery is "the preliminary condition for every real people's revolution."[2]

[1] Quoted in Engels, *Anti-Dühring* (Moscow: Foreign Languages Publishing House, 1959), p. 254.

[2] Marx and Engels, "Marx to L. Kugelman," *Selected Works* (Moscow: Foreign Languages Publishing House, 1955), II, p. 463.

As the reformists see it, there is no difference between the nature of bourgeois democracy and proletarian democracy, there is no swift advance from the capitalist system to the socialist system, and capitalism can evolve gradually into socialism in accordance with the theory of evolution. Modern revisionism, like the revisionism of the early twentieth century, is reformism in essence. Revisionists, in the past, as at present, have made great efforts to sing the praises of the bourgeois parliamentary system. They have made a big fanfare about the entry into socialism through "parliamentary road." As a matter of fact, democratic rights under the bourgeois parliamentary system are, as Marx put it, nothing more than the rights to decide once every three or six years who of the ruling classes should "represent" the people in parliament and oppress them. Lenin said: "Take any parliamentary country, from America to Switzerland, from France to England, Norway and so forth—in these countries the real business of 'state' is performed behind the scenes and is carried on by the departments, chancelleries, and general staffs. Parliament itself is given up to talk for the special purpose of fooling the 'common people.' "[3] Lenin described bourgeois democracy as narrow, emasculated, false, and deceptive democracy, the paradise of the rich, but a trap and a deceptive fraud for the exploited and the poor.

The bourgeoisie in power has never voluntarily relinquished state power to the working class. In "Theses on the Fundamental Tasks of the Second Congress of the Communist International," Lenin pointed out that under the conditions of militarism and imperialism, "the very thought of peacefully subordinating the capitalists to the will of the majority of the exploited, of the peaceful, reformist transition to socialism is not only extreme philistine stupidity, but also downright deception of the workers, the embellishment of capitalist wage slavery, concealment of the truth. . . . Only the violent overthrow of the bourgeoisie, the confiscation of its property, the destruction of the whole of the bourgeois state apparatus from top to bottom—parliamentary, judicial, military, bureaucratic, administrative, municipal, etc., right up to the very wholesale deportation or internment of the most dangerous and stubborn exploiters—putting them under strict surveillance in order to combat inevitable attempts to resist and to restore capitalist slavery—only such measures can ensure the real subordination of the whole class of exploiters."[4]

The process of the proletarian revolutionary movement is, in the final analysis, one of making preparations for the dictatorship of the proletariat (before the seizure of state power) and putting such dictatorship into effect (after seizing state power). The proletariat must adopt all forms of struggle, legal and illegal, inside and outside parliament, ranging from strikes,

[3] Lenin, *Works* (Moscow: Foreign Languages Publishing House, 1951), II, Pt. 1, pp. 246–47.

[4] Lenin, *Selected Works* (London: Lawrence and Wishart, 1946), X, p. 164.

demonstrations, political general strikes up to armed uprisings, the highest form of struggle, so as to overthrow the bourgeois rule and establish the dictatorship of the proletariat. The more the revolutionary movement surges forward, the more frenzied will be the repressions by the ruling bourgeoisie and the more sharp and bitter will be the class struggle. "Revolution progresses by giving rise to a strong and united counterrevolution, i.e., it compels the enemy to resort to more and more extreme measures of defense and in this way devises ever more powerful means of attack."[5]

Marx said that "the weapon of criticism cannot, of course, take the place of criticism with weapons" and that material forces must be overthrown by material forces. Lenin pointed out that in the working-class struggle against the bourgeoisie, it was possible "at any time to substitute the criticism with weapons for the weapon of criticism." Lenin, therefore, pointed out the necessity of building up arms for the proletariat and disarming the bourgeoisie, for otherwise it would be impossible for socialism to win. In "The 'Disarmament' Slogan," Lenin wrote: "Our slogan must be: the arming of the proletariat for the purpose of vanquishing, expropriating, and disarming the bourgeoisie." "An oppressed class which does not strive to learn to use arms, to acquire arms, deserves to be treated like slaves."[6] Because in every class society the ruling classes possesses arms, and it is a fact that the bourgeoisie in power uses them to suppress the working class. Consequently, the working class has no alternative but to take up arms to overthrow its rulers and achieve its own liberation. Lenin also said: "Only after the proletariat has disarmed the bourgeoisie will it be able, without betraying its world-historical mission, to throw all armaments on the scrap heap; the proletariat will undoubtedly do this, but only when this condition has been fulfilled, certainly not before."[7]

Lenin also criticized Plekhanov's view that "they should not have taken up arms." In "Lessons of the Moscow Uprising" he said: "Nothing could be more short-sighted than Plekhanov's view, seized upon by all the opportunists, that the strike was untimely and should not have been started, and that 'they should not have taken up arms.' On the contrary, we should have taken to arms more resolutely, energetically, and aggressively; we should have explained to the masses that it was impossible to confine things to a peaceful strike and that a fearless and relentless armed fight was necessary."[8] Lenin taught us the need to spread the idea

[5] Lenin, *Collected Works* (Moscow: Foreign Languages Publishing House, 1962), II, p. 172.

[6] Lenin, *Collected Works* (New York: International Publishers, 1962), XIX, p. 354.

[7] *Ibid.*, p. 366.

[8] Lenin, *Collected Works* (Moscow: Foreign Languages Publishing House, 1962), II, p. 173.

of armed uprising to the broad masses, and he described armed uprising as a great mass struggle. He regarded recognition of armed uprising as a question of principle for the revolutionaries. "It is not enough to take sides on the question of political slogans; it is also necessary to take sides on the question of an armed uprising. Those who are opposed to it, those who do not prepare for it, must be ruthlessly dismissed from the ranks of the supporters of the revolution, sent packing to its enemies, to the traitors or cowards; for the day is approaching when the force of events and the conditions of the struggle will compel us to distinguish between enemies and friends according to this principle."[9]

Of course, communists are very cautious about armed uprising. They regard it as a peculiar form of political struggle with its own specific laws. Communists start an armed uprising only when the opportunity is ripe and when subjective and objective conditions are completely ready, and once it has started they intend to carry it through to the finish. Communists do not propose that arms be used at all times and under all circumstances. If there was a road which would involve less casualties and bloodshed, but which could lead to socialism, they would unhesitatingly take that road. Whether the working class adopts the form of armed struggle or the form of peaceful political struggle does not depend on the subjective desire of the working class but on the extent of resistance by the exploiting classes which first resort to arms to maintain their rule. Since the ruling classes will not surrender state power of their own accord, the working class must use arms to overthrow them.

In the final stage of World War II and for a time in the postwar years, because the Soviet Red Army had wiped out the Hitlerite fascists and smashed the fascist state machinery set up by Hitler in the various East European countries, the people's regimes led by the working class were established in those countries. With the help of the Soviet Red Army they switched to the tasks of the socialist revolution and the dictatorship of the proletariat after carrying out the work of the bourgeois democratic revolution, and so there was no need for an armed uprising. What happened in Czechoslovakia in February 1948 also belongs to the category of revolutionary change. By adopting administrative measures and combining these with mass demonstrations, the Czechoslovak people's regime smashed the plot of the bourgeoisie to foment a cabinet crisis and attempt to restore capitalism, and in this way led the country directly to the road of socialism. Some people are attempting to use the February 1948 event in Czechoslovakia as an example to support their argument for "peaceful transition." But this is falsifying history because they separate the February happenings from the liquidation of German fascism by the Soviet Red Army, from the armed uprising and guerrilla warfare of the people in Slovakia

[9] *Ibid.*, p. 176.

in 1944 and the people's general armed uprising in Prague in May 1945. Moreover, in the February 1948 event in Czechoslovakia, the role of revolutionary violence was also embodied in the determined suppression of the bourgeois rebellion by the people's regime, which was in essence a dictatorship of the proletariat, and in the armed demonstration of the Czechoslovak people supporting the administrative measures of the communist-led government.

Since the end of World War II, the colonial system of imperialism has been in the process of disintegration. Many nations under the yoke of imperialist enslavement have today achieved national independence. In their fight for national independence, some nations have adopted the form of armed struggle, others have gone through alternate periods of armed struggle and peaceful political struggle or have combined these two forms of struggle in the same period, while still others have attained political independence without armed struggle. Some nations have been able to achieve national independence peacefully because imperialism is steadily declining and a world socialist system has come into existence and is vigorously developing, thus bringing about a change in the balance of forces on a worldwide scale. Confronted with this situation, imperialism is forced to make its choice between two alternatives:

1. To stubbornly resist to the end and eventually be driven out of the colonies, with the result that the colonial nations which have gained complete independence will embark on the path of socialism;

2. To hand over political independence to the native bourgeoisie and in this way to retain its economic interests in the colonies and keep the former colonial nations within the orbit of capitalism.

Many imperialist countries "wisely" chose the second alternative, and this explains why some former colonial nations have been able to achieve political independence by peaceful means. However, the various nations have a long way to go from arriving at political independence to achieving complete independence and thence going over to socialism. So far, there is not yet a single "precedent" of peaceful transition to socialism in the world working-class history of revolutionary struggle. Speaking about this possibility, Stalin, in *The Foundations of Leninism*, said: "Of course, in the remote future, if the proletariat is victorious in the principal capitalist countries, and if the present capitalist encirclement is replaced by a socialist encirclement, a 'peaceful' path of development is quite possible for certain capitalist countries, whose capitalists, in view of the 'unfavorable' international situation, will consider it expedient 'voluntarily' to make substantial concessions to the proletariat. But this supposition applies only to a remote and possible future."[10]

Today two-thirds of the world population still live under capitalism.

[10] Stalin, *Works* (Moscow: Foreign Languages Publishing House, 1953), VI, p. 121.

Imperialism is in the process of an advanced development of militarism and bureaucracy. Every capitalist country possesses an enormous state machinery ever ready to suppress the people's revolutionary movement with violence. In these circumstances, the possibility for the prolefariat to seize power by peaceful means without launching an armed uprising remains extremely rare.

There are people who claim that as a result of the emergence of nuclear weapons the working class must not seize power by violence but by peaceful means, for revolution by violence will lead to civil war. Because one spark may spread into a conflagration, civil war may lead to a world war which in the present era is bound to develop into a destructive nuclear war. In the circumstances, the only way left for the working class in various countries is to attain state power by peaceful means. And the peaceful means they recommend is the theory of "structural reform."

For all their destructive power, nuclear weapons cannot change the law of development of human society. They can only cause certain changes in military strategy and tactics, but never in the strategy and tactics of the working class. Not at all times will a spark develop into a conflagration. This has been proved by the Chinese civil war, by the Korean war, and by the Algerian war. The revolutions of China, Vietnam, and Cuba were all revolutions by violence and were all won after the presence of nuclear weapons. It is therefore utterly groundless to assert that the working class should not seize power by violence following the existence of nuclear weapons.

In the face of enemies who are armed to the teeth and are prepared to stamp out revolution at any time by violence, the only way to seize state power is to resort to violence. The possibility of revolution developing peacefully can be realized only when the exploiting classes do not possess a dependable militarist-bureaucratic state machine or at a time when they have lost the will to use this machinery to suppress the revolution although it may still be in their hands. To translate the possibility of the peaceful development of revolution into reality, the working class must possess a mighty force which is equipped with closely knit organization and leadership. That force may be a mass political force, an armed force, or a combination of political and armed forces. Therefore, in striving to make revolution through a peaceful road—the road which involves the least suffering, the working class and its party must vigorously prepare for the seizure of state power by violence. It is only when the working class has organized into a mighty force and firmly taken up arms that it is possible to strive for the peaceful development of the revolution.

Ever since our Party was formed it has applied Marxist-Leninist principles on the strategy and tactics of revolution to the reality of our country. On the one hand, it has stood against the defeatist and capitulationist ideas and against the "theories" advocating nonrebellion and denouncing the use of arms. On the other hand, it has opposed the idea of organizing "secret societies" for conspiracies as well as such terrorist activities as assassination of individuals. During World War II, the Party particularly stressed the question of seizing state power by armed uprising. The resolution adopted at the seventh session of the Party's Central Committee (November 1940) provided: "The Party must be prepared to undertake the sacred missions of leading the oppressed nations in Indochina to launch armed rebellion and achieve independence and freedom." The eighth session of the Party's Central Committee (May 1941) also put forward the task for "preparing forces at all times," so that "when the favorable moment arrives, we can, by employing the power already at our disposal, victoriously lead area uprisings one by one in order to pave the way for a large-scale general uprising."

In August 1945, when Japanese fascism collapsed, our Party led the people throughout the country in starting a timely general armed uprising and seized state power. The August Revolution in Vietnam was a revolution by violence, by means of which the state apparatus was established. The August Revolution was the result of the prolonged revolutionary struggle and in which the peaceful political struggle of the masses was combined with the launching of local guerrilla war and the work of building bases in the rural areas. The August Revolution was the direct result of the armed struggle waged by all the people, mainly the result of combining the activities of professional armed forces with semiprofessional armed forces (liberation army, guerrilla forces, militia, and self-defense corps, etc.).

The August Revolution in Vietnam is different from the Russian October Revolution in that the latter was a general armed uprising, state power was first built in the cities and then in the countryside. The difference between Vietnam's August Revolution and the Chinese Revolution is that the Chinese Revolution was a prolonged armed struggle, state power was first seized in the countryside, which was used to encircle the cities and finally the cities were liberated.

In the course of decades of protracted and arduous revolutionary movement, our Party has skillfully combined the various kinds of struggles, economic and political, legal and illegal, struggle in the streets and in parliament, armed struggle and peaceful political struggle. During the period of the upsurge of the Revolution (1930–31), the Party led the masses in waging blow-for-blow struggles against the enemy. In places where the enemy's power had collapsed (Nghe An and Ha Tinh) the Party led the people in setting up the state power of the Soviets and training them in administering their own affairs. During the period of the ebbing of the Revolution (1932–35), the Party led the people in making a planned withdrawal, establishing secret organizations, and prepared for a new revolutionary upsurge. From 1936 to 1939, by taking advantage of the legitimate conditions brought on by the victory of the French People's Front, the Party launched a movement of open struggle, formed the Democratic Front, led the people in fighting for better living conditions and for democracy and freedom, and for participation in the election campaign and in carrying on a struggle inside parliament. At the end of 1939, the Party again went underground. Utilizing the latent and manifest contradictions existing between the two imperialist countries which then ruled our country, the Party launched guerrilla warfare and set up revolutionary bases. Simultaneously with peaceful political struggle, the form of armed struggle began to appear. This period ended with the general uprising in the August Revolution which was the peak of the movement and represented a skillful combination of the two forms of struggle, armed and political. In the more than one year following the August Revolution, our Party put emphasis on political struggle so as to consolidate the people's state power and build forces in various spheres, particularly the armed forces. At the same time it carried on armed struggle against the French colonialists staging a comeback and carrying out aggression against the southern part of our country, as well as against the Kuomintang-organized and -directed bandits harassing some provinces in the north. From the end of 1946, our Party led the people in waging a nationwide armed struggle against colonialist aggression.

Since 1954, revolution has gone over to the stage of socialism in the northern part of our country. Because state power already was in the hands of the working class during the stage of national-democratic revolution, "peaceful transition to socialism" has been realized in the north in the past few years. This does not mean that during the stage of the socialist revolution in the north, the role of revolutionary violence has ceased to exist. During the stage of the socialist revolution, the people's democratic state has carried out the task of the dictatorship of the proletariat which means using violence to crush counterrevolution.

The struggle being waged by our compatriots in the south at present still falls into the category of the national-democratic revolution. They are using revolutionary violence against the counterrevolutionary violence of the U.S. Of course, to make revolution by violence imposes the necessity of enduring hardship and sacrifices on the part of the broad masses of the people. But this can help shake off at an early date the long suffering and death caused by the brutal oppression and exploitation inflicted by the rulers on a countless number of people. During the general armed uprising in August 1945, only a few score of people were killed throughout the country. On the contrary, as a result of the rule of the Japanese and French fascists, some two million starved to death in the north from the end of 1944 to the first few months of 1945. History has proved that the extremely heavy losses suffered by the working people from the brutal rule of the exploiting classes cannot be matched by the losses of a revolution, however relentless it may be. The road involving the least suffering for the people is to go in for revolution to overthrow the enemy and win emancipation.

LE DUAN: REVOLUTIONARY MARXISM*

IN the history of the Vietnamese people's struggle against French colonialism, many patriotic movements followed one upon another, many armed insurrections broke out; some established resistance bases in hardly accessible mountain regions for a long-term struggle, as the uprising of Phan Dinh Phung which lasted ten years, or that of Hoang Hoa Tham stretching over nearly thirty years.[1] However, none of these movements brought the national-liberation cause to success. Their failure was due to many causes, but it clearly proves that revolution must be made by the broad masses, it must be a truly popular movement if it is to succeed.

Right after the founding of the Indochinese Communist Party, a mass revolutionary movement flared up throughout Vietnam, the apex of which being the Nghe An and Ha Tinh Soviets (1930–1931). Workers and peasants in these provinces[2] rose up to overthrow the colonial rule and the local administration of mandarins and despots, setting up worker-peasant power. Though suppressed, the uprising strongly awakened the revolutionary spirit of the entire people and pointed to the immense revolutionary capabilities of the workers and peasants.

From 1936 to 1939, in face of the fascist threat, the Party timely adopted a new orientation, shifting from underground to semiclandestine and semilegal activities, ingeniously combining these forms of struggle, even using "people's councils" and "colonial councils" to initiate throughout the country a powerful movement against the reactionary colonialists, feudalists, and aggressive fascists, for the conquest of democratic freedoms, the improvement of living standards, and the safeguard of world peace. This campaign involved millions of people and politically educated broad masses of the workers and peasants, greatly enhancing their patiotism and class consciousness.

After the outbreak of the Second World War and the occupation of

---

[1] Phan Dinh Phung led a rebellion against the French from 1885 until he died on January 31, 1896. Hoang Hoa Tham's peasant uprising in the north lasted from 1887 until he was murdered by a traitor on February 10, 1913.—*Ed.*

[2] In Central Vietnam.—*Ed.*

---

* One of two articles published in pamphlet form "on the occasion of the fiftieth anniversary of the October Revolution" entitled *Forward Under the Glorious Banner of the October Revolution* (Hanoi: Foreign Languages Publishing House, 1967). The author is secretary-general of the Vietnam Workers' Party (the Vietnamese CP).

Indochina by the Japanese fascists, the Party shifted its main activities to the countryside; while continuing to build up the political forces of the masses, it created armed forces, started a countrywide patriotic movement and local guerrilla activities against the Japanese and French fascists, and set up the Viet Bac[3] resistance zone and guerrilla bases.

The local insurrections and revolutionary tides started and led by our Party since 1930 were preludes to the August 1945 Revolution which creatively applied Lenin's principles of revolutionary violence and insurrection to conquer power. The August Revolution aptly combined political struggle with military struggle, local takeover in the countryside with insurrection in the towns, long-term preparation of political and military forces with rapid mobilization of the masses at the favorable moment to overthrow the imperialist and feudal power. It liquidated the colonialist and feudal power, and founded the Democratic Republic of Vietnam, the first worker-peasant state in Southeast Asia, ushering in a new era in the history of the country. But, protected by British troops, helped by the American imperialists, the French colonialists then came back and connived with the native reactionary forces to unleash a war of aggression in an attempt to re-establish the colonial and feudal rule.

Under the leadership of the Party, the entire Vietnamese people took to arms and resolutely waged an all-out and protracted war. Relying mainly on their own means, they set up a strong people's army, built up their forces while fighting, consolidated their rear while attacking at the front, waged an armed resistance while gradually implementing democratic reforms, then land reform, to improve the living conditions of the peasants and boost the potential of the patriotic war in every field. People's war vigorously developed in scope and strength, driving the French Expeditionary Corps to a stalemate, then defeat. The glorious victory of Dien Bien Phu brought the resistance war to a successful end, decided the fate of the French colonialists in Indochina, and compelled them to sign the Geneva Agreements recognizing Vietnam's independence, sovereignty, unity, and territorial integrity.

However, the national-liberation revolution of the Vietnamese people has not yet come to a close. While the completely liberated northern part has shifted to socialist revolution, the south has to fight on against the aggressions of the American imperialists. Indeed, for nearly a quarter of a century U.S. imperialism has been the enemy number one of the Vietnamese people. Having failed in helping the French colonialists to reconquer Vietnam, in prolonging and expanding the Indochina War, the Americans supplanted the French to continue the aggression against South Vietnam with a view to perpetuating the partition of our country, turning South Vietnam into a neo-colony and military base, preparing an offen-

[3] Mountain region north of the Red River.—*Ed.*

sive against North Vietnam and halting the revolution in South Vietnam and Southeast Asia. This is a component of the counterrevolutionary global strategy of U.S. imperialism to check the revolutionary wave storming the bulwark of U.S.-led international imperialism.

The process of the South Vietnamese revolution is one of uniting, organizing, and developing all revolutionary and patriotic forces to liberate the south, defend the north, reunify the motherland, safeguard the independence and peace in Vietnam, peace in Southeast Asia and the world. But the August Revolution, like people's revolutions in other countries, has taught the South Vietnamese revolutionaries that any revolution with a marked popular character must use both political and military forces to secure victory. Revolution being the uprising of the oppressed and exploited masses, one must adopt the revolutionary mass viewpoint to understand revolutionary violence which involves two forces—political and military forces—and two forms of struggle—political and armed struggle—and thereby to realize the offensive position of revolution when revolutionary situations are ripe. On the contrary, if one considers revolutionary violence merely from the point of view of armed struggle, and consequently takes into account only the military force of the two sides to appraise the balance of forces between revolution and counterrevolution, mistakes will be inevitable: either one will underestimate the strength of the revolution and dare not mobilize the masses for insurrection, or, once the insurrection has been launched, one will not dare step up the offensive to push ahead the revolution, or, when the armed struggle has been unleashed, one cannot avoid falling back to a defensive strategy.

In 1959–60, when the American imperialists and their henchmen used most barbarous fascist means to sow terror and carry out mass slaughter, the South Vietnamese revolutionaries held that the enemy had sustained a basic political defeat and could no longer rule as in the past, while the people had come to realize more and more clearly that they could no longer live under the enemy's yoke and had to rise up and wage a life-and-death struggle to liberate themselves. Under those circumstances the South Vietnamese people uprose, using mainly political struggle combined with armed struggle, broke the enemy's grip, controlled large rural areas, wrested back power, redistributed land, set up "self-management committees," made every effort to develop their forces in every field, and launched a widespread people's war to carry on their liberation struggle.

In South Vietnam, as the vast countryside has a natural economy not very dependent on the towns and an almost exclusively peasant population living on agriculture, the aggressors and their henchmen ruling in urban centers cannot establish a strict control over the rural areas. That is why, when conditions are ripe for revolution, the villages constitute the best areas for starting *local insurrections* and destroying the enemy's power apparatus. But victory cannot repose exclusively on the revolutionary forces in the countryside, it is dependent upon revolutionary forces in the towns as well. If the revolutionary upsurge in the countryside some years ago made its impact strongly felt upon the revolutionary movement in the towns, the seething struggle of the urban masses now has created highly favorable conditions for uprisings in the countryside and the extension of people's war. The recent fierce political struggle of the townsfolk has restrained, sometimes slowed down or seriously upset, the military activities of the enemy on the battlefields, thus efficaciously helping the offensive of the revolutionary armed forces; inversely, the military successes on the battlefields, like the repeated attacks by the liberation troops against the enemy's rear bases and his dens in the towns and cities, have accelerated the growth of the urban revolutionary movement. The south's final inevitable victory will be the result of both struggles, united into one mass movement.

In the north, meanwhile, the socialist revolution unfolding since 1954 represents revolutionary processes—revolution in the relations of production, technological revolution, cultural and ideological revolution— aiming at ceaselessly heightening the people's right as collective masters of the whole economy, down to each region and each production unit. *Revolution in the relations of production* was a necessary step of the socialist revolution, for we had first of all to transform the private capitalist industry and trade, and the small individual economy—peasant for the most part—in order to establish socialist relations of production. In the development of the modes of production it is the productive forces which assume the decisive role, but to promote these, appropriate relations of production are needed. The socialist relations of production set up in North Vietnam play a revolutionary part of great importance. They constitute the essential factor which makes it possible for the productive forces to develop and create social premises to consolidate the dictatorship of the proletariat and further the ideological and cultural revolution. In the initial period of socialist building in which the material and technical bases are still weak, if one knows how to repose on the superiority of the socialist relations of production in order to use properly the labor force brought into play by cooperativization, improve the organization and management of production, gradually ameliorate techniques while enhancing the sense of being collective masters among the people, then one can obtain a higher productivity, boost economic construction, and develop production.

In the revolution of relations of production, one must not only transform the relations of ownership of the means of production, but also pay attention to satisfactorily solving the problem of distribution so that in the process of distribution the laboring people realize that they are really masters of social economy. To this end, one must strictly apply the principle of distribution according to work done while ensuring the satisfaction of everybody's basic living requirements in accordance with the development of social production. One must also closely combine the method of material incentives with political education and moral stimulation to heighten the people's ardor in their work. The revolution in the relations of production does not come to an end with the establishment of new ones, but continues throughout the transition period; it must unceasingly consolidate, develop, and perfect those relations of production and at the same time proceed the building of the material and technical bases of socialism and the improvement of economic management.

For a country which advances toward socialism bypassing the stage of capitalist development, the transformation of relations of production is only a first step in the whole revolutionary process. To radically transform the Vietnamese society and firmly set up a socialist mode of production, the key problem is to promote the *technological revolution*. After the establishment of the dictatorship of the proletariat and new relations of production, the technological revolution constitutes the most important motive force to take North Vietnam to socialism. Only by accelerating the tempo of the technological revolution can one bring the productive forces to a high degree of development, create the material bases for the consolidation of the new relations of production and for the building of an advanced culture and science, thereby ensuring victory for socialism.

The advance from a small individual production to large-scale socialist production obviously requires *a new division of labor in the entire society* on modern material and technical bases. This new division of labor is closely related to the three above-mentioned revolutions, particularly to the technological revolution. To push ahead the technological revolution, to improve the instruments of production and provide a new technical equipment to all branches, is to create favorable conditions for a rational division of labor in each branch as well as in the whole economy, which in turn influences and stimulates the technological revolution. The key problem at present is to equip agriculture with a new technique in order to increase its productivity, and apply a rational division of labor in each branch as well as in the whole economy, which in turn influences and stimulates the technological revolution.

In the process of socialist revolution, the establishment of a new mode of production and the building of an economic basis constitute the decisive factor, but from a subjective point of view, the impact of man plays a very important role, for it is under the socialist regime that the laboring people make history consciously; moreover, the socialist system alone can liberate man from all social and natural fetters, and restore his genuine value. Indeed, there is a very great leap to make for a wage slave or an owner of a small plot of land to become a collective master of the means of production, of the society. This leap requires that the laboring people profoundly understand their role as collective masters and strive to acquire the capacities and virtues needed to be the true masters of the society, of nature, and of their own selves. All this shows that the *ideological and cultural revolution* acts also as an important motive force in socialist revolution.

From the ideological point of view, this revolution aims at educating and transforming the various strata of the laboring people in accordance with the requirements of the new social regime, at imbuing them with socialist ethics, with a Marxist-Leninist world outlook and a communist conception of life. From the cultural point of view, its objective is to liquidate illiteracy, raise the knowledge of the laboring people, transform backward customs and habits, and train an intelligentsia of the working class faithful to socialism. In short, the cultural and ideological revolution must on the one hand serve the revolution in the relations of production and the technological revolution, and on the other, form new men possessed of the best revolutionary virtues, the best qualifications for production, a high scientific and technical level, and a fine, rich, healthy cultural and moral life, men capable of continuing and promoting the precious national traditions while eliminating the negative aspects of the regime of small production and of the colonial and feudal society.

The socialist line of economic transformation and construction in North Vietnam is best reflected in two big movements: agricultural cooperativization and socialist industrialization. For lack of a large-scale industry, agricultural cooperativization has to go along with water conservancy and improvement of farming techniques in order to develop a diversified agriculture as *a basis for industrial development*. However, agriculture cannot advance vigorously unless it is impelled by large-scale industry. Therefore, the only way to transform the country's backward agriculture is to build a socialist industry, regarding this task as the central one of the transition period and to give priority to *heavy industry as the cornerstone of the national economy*. In the process of industrialization, one must have a correct orientation by developing both the centrally run industry and the regional industry, by serving first of all agricultural production and the consolidation of cooperatives, and by ensuring a harmonious development for industry and agriculture so as to make national economy progress vigorously and steadily.

The three above mentioned revolutions constitute the basic content of the socialist revolution in North Vietnam, the steps to be taken by a backward agricultural country in its advance toward socialism. To bring those three revolutions, agricultural cooperativization and social industrialization, to success one has to wage a fierce class struggle to solve the problem: Who will win between socialism and capitalism? If formerly the struggle for power was the basic content of class struggle, now that power has been conquered, *to carry out those three revolutions constitutes the basic content of class struggle throughout the transition period toward*

*socialism and communism. Those are also the essential tasks of the dicta-
torship of the proletariat.* To bring the dictatorship of the proletariat into
full play, the most important decisive problem is unceasingly to enhance
and strengthen the leadership of the working class, to build a Marxist-
Leninist party that is staunch, united, and closely linked to the masses,
to strive to consolidate the worker-peasant alliance, and to rely on the
workers and collective peasants as the main force to build socialism.

Socialist transformation of economy has been achieved in the main.
Cooperativized agriculture has overcome many trials and proved its
superiority over the former individual agriculture. After the first five-year
plan (1961–65), the initial bases of heavy industry have been established
together with many enterprises of light and regional industry. From 1955
to 1965 industrial production increased by 22 percent every year and
agricultural production by 4.5 percent, the part of industrial and handicraft production in the national economy rose from 17 to 53 percent.
Education, medical work, and culture also made outstanding progress:
illiteracy was wiped out, nearly one out of four people went to school,
the number of doctors was twenty-five times higher. These initial achievements have brought about a new strength and constitute a source of
enthusiasm which stimulates the North Vietnamese people to build a happy
life and resolutely defend the socialist regime.

VO NGUYEN GIAP: WAR OF LIBERATION*

WHEN U.S. capitalism reached the stage of imperialism, the Western
great powers had already divided among themselves almost all the important markets in the world. At the end of World War II, when the other
imperialist powers had been weakened, the United States became the most
powerful and the richest imperialist power. Meanwhile, the world situation
was no longer the same: The balance of forces between imperialism and
the socialist camp had fundamentally changed; imperialism no longer
ruled over the world, nor did it play a decisive role in the development
of the world situation. In the new historical conditions, U.S. imperialism,
which had a long tradition of expansion through trade, different from the
classical policy of aggression through missionaries and gunboats, is all the
more compelled to follow the path of neo-colonialism. The countries
under its domination enjoy nominal political independence, but in fact
are dependent on the United States in the economic, financial, national
defense, and foreign relations fields.

At the end of World War II U.S. imperialism already cast covetous eyes

---

* Published in *Vietnamese Studies* (Hanoi), No. 8 (January 1966).

on Vietnam and the other Indochinese countries. In the early fifties, as the situation of the French colonialists was becoming more and more desperate, the U.S. imperialists gradually increased their "aid" and intervention in the Indochina war. When the war ended with the defeat of the French Expeditionary Corps, they thought that the opportunity had come for them to take the place of the French colonialists. The images of former colonial rule now belonged to the past. The U.S. imperialists could not, even if they wanted to do it, restore to life the decaying corpse of old colonialism. In 1954, when the defeat of the French colonialists was imminent, the U.S. imperialists envisaged the use of "national forces," made up of reactionary forces in the country, in an attempt to give more "dynamism" to the war. And they began to prepare their "special war" against the South Vietnamese people.

U.S. neo-colonialism used its puppets in South Vietnam as its main tool to carry out its policy of aggression. Neo-colonialism derives its strength on the one hand from the economic and military potential of the metropolitan country, and on the other hand, from the social, economic, and political bases of the native reactionary forces. In the south of our country, the puppet regime was set up by the U.S. imperialists at the moment when our people had just won a brilliant victory against imperialism. That is why since it came into being, it has never shown any vitality, and has borne the seeds of internal contradictions, crisis, and war. Its social bases are extremely weak. The feudal landlord class and the comprador bourgeoisie, which had never been very strong under French rule, had become even weaker and more divided in the course of the Revolution and the Resistance. After peace was restored, they became still more divided, as a result of U.S.-French contradictions.

Under those circumstances, U.S. imperialism used every possible means to set up a relatively stable administration, camouflaged with the labels of "independence" and "democracy," in an attempt to rally the reactionary forces and at the same time win over and deceive other strata of the population. With this aim in view, they staged the farce of founding the "Republic of Vietnam" in order to perpetuate the partition of our country. Their puppets, claiming to have reconquered "independence" from the French colonialists, proclaimed a "constitution" with provisions on "freedom" and "democracy," and put forth slogans of anticommunism, ordered an "agrarian reform," and noisily publicized a program for the "elimination of vices" and the "protection of good tradition," etc.

However, the puppet regime could not remain in power if they did not cling to their masters and obey the latter's orders. Outwardly, the "Republic of Vietnam" has all the usual government organs of internal and external affairs, defense, economy, and culture, but all these organs, from the central to local level, are controlled by U.S. "advisers." The latter, who enjoy diplomatic privileges, are not under the jurisdiction of the puppet administration, whose civil and penal codes cannot be applied to them. They are directly under the U.S. ambassador's control. It is U.S. imperialism which determines the fundamental line and policies of the South Vietnam regime. Ngo Dinh Diem, fostered by U.S. imperialism, was "pulled out of Dulles' sleeve" after Dien Bien Phu. The Diem regime, far from springing, as it claimed, from a movement of "national revolution," was only the result of the replacement of French masters by U.S. masters.

Faced with a popular revolutionary upsurge, the puppet regime had to bluntly oppose the Geneva Agreements. It trampled on the people's most elementary rights and resorted to a most barbarous policy of terror and repression. For these reasons, despite the labels of "independence" and "democracy" and certain reforms of a demagogic character, the people immediately saw behind the puppet regime the hideous face of U.S. imperialism which hurriedly built up and trained an army of mercenaries to be used as a tool for the repression of the revolutionary movement, carrying out their perfidious policy of pitting Asians against Asians, Vietnamese against Vietnamese. Besides, U.S. experts have calculated that expenses for an Asian mercenary soldier are twenty-four times less than those required for an American soldier.

The South Vietnam "national army" is staffed by puppet officers from the rank of general downwards, but this is coupled with a system of military "advisers" controlling the puppet national defense ministry and extending down to battalion and company level, in the militia as well as the regular forces. U.S. advisers in the puppet army supervise organization, equipment, training, and operations. The U.S. imperialists try to camouflage under the labels of "mutual assistance" and "self-defense" the participation of their troops in fighting. With a view to turning South Vietnam into a U.S. military base, they have put under their effective control a large number of strategic points, all the main airfields and military ports.

Economic "aid" is used by the imperialists as a principal means to control South Vietnam's economy. This "aid" is essentially a way of exporting surplus goods and capital to serve their policy of expansion and war preparation. Three-fourths of the amount of yearly "aid" derives from the sale of imported goods. The U.S. aid organs completely ignore both the requests of the puppet regime and the needs of the country, and dump into South Vietnam market surplus farm products, luxury goods, and also consumer goods that could have been produced locally. Furthermore, this aid clearly has a military character. It turns South Vietnam's economy into a war economy, eight-tenths of the money being used to cover the military expenses of the puppet regime. This "aid" makes this regime totally dependent on the U.S. imperialists.

At first, the U.S. imperialists, thinking that they could rapidly consolidate the puppet regime and stabilize the political and economic situation in South Vietnam, had prepared the ground for the signing of unequal treaties to open the way to a large-scale penetration of U.S. finance capital. But the situation did not develop as they had expected, and so the money they invested in South Vietnam was insignificant, representing hardly 2 percent of the total investments in various branches of the economy. In general, U.S. money was invested in joint enterprises, in a very wily economic penetration. Although present conditions are not favorable to the development of the U.S. sector in the South Vietnam economy, U.S. "aid" and the creation of counterpart funds have ensured to USOM (United States Operations Mission) complete control over the budget, finances, and foreign trade, in fact over the whole economic structure of South Vietnam.

The comprador bourgeoisie in South Vietnam is economically entirely dependent on the imperialists—the French imperialists in former days and the U.S. imperialists in the present time. The comprador bourgeoisie and the feudal landlord class, bound together by many ties, are two reactionary social forces colluding with the imperialists whom they efficiently serve. The comprador bourgeoisie lives on U.S. aid, on trade with imperialist countries, and seeks joint investments with foreign capital. It includes elements from other social classes, such as the big landlords who seek refuge in the larger cities and become bourgeois. Speaking of the comprador bourgeoisie, we should first of all mention the bureaucratic comprador bourgeoisie essentially made up, in former days, of the Ngo Dinh Diem family, and at present, of high-ranking puppet officials and officers who use their power to get rich quick through pillage, extortion, graft, embezzlement, hoarding, and speculation, and to get hold of key positions in the economy and seize control over all the important branches.

In the new historical conditions, on account of their class character and their desperate situation in face of the victorious revolutionary movement, the pro-U.S. forces in South Vietnam are extremely reactionary and thirst for class revenge. They are also social parasites, divorced from national production and entirely dependent on U.S. dollars. This causes their ranks to shrink further and further, to become more and more heterogeneous and divided by conflicts of interests into rival groups and cliques tied up with different tendencies in U.S. political, military, and intelligence circles. Their position, already not very strong in face of the powerful revolutionary upsurge, has been further weakened and their ranks have become still more divided; consequently, coups d'état have succeeded one another and will continue to do so until their final collapse.

Despite its material power, U.S. imperialism has fundamental weaknesses.

a. Economically and militarily, the U.S.A. is the most powerful country in the imperialist camp. But faced with the socialist countries, the independent nationalist countries, and the revolutionary peoples of the world, its strength is declining further and further. Everywhere now, U.S. imperialism is reduced to the defensive; its forces, scattered all over the world, have proved incapable of saving it from disastrous defeats in continental China, Korea, and Cuba.

b. In its aggression against South Vietnam U.S. imperialism has revealed a fundamental weakness: It has been forced to resort to a neo-colonialist policy when important factors for the success of this policy are lacking.

Firstly, it has to try and deceive our people and pose as a "knight" defender of the independence, sovereignty, and freedom of the peoples. But the present conjuncture in the world as well as in South Vietnam is not favorable to such a maneuver. Our people, with their high revolutionary consciousness, have long since recognized in U.S. imperialism the enemy number one of the world's peoples. U.S. imperialism unmasked itself by supporting the French colonialists during the Indochina War, a war waged with French blood and U.S. dollars and weapons. It conceived a criminal plan in a vain attempt to save the French Expeditionary Corps from the Dien Bien Phu disaster. Our people did not wait until 1954 to see in U.S. imperialism an aggressor, and since that date, they have even more clearly recognized that it is the enemy number one of the Vietnamese revolution and people.

Secondly, U.S. imperialism cannot carry out its neo-colonialist policy without a strong support from local reactionary forces, without an outwardly "independent and democratic" native administration and a "national" army. But we can affirm that this extremely important, this crucial condition, which decides the fate of neo-colonialism, does not exist in South Vietnam. The reactionary forces, in the first place the most reactionary and pro-U.S. elements of the comprador bourgeoisie and the feudal landlord class, have become extremely weak socially and economically, and completely isolated in the political field. Billions of dollars and hundreds of thousands of tons of arms will not fill this political vacuum. U.S. imperialism will never be capable of creating a stable political regime with even an appearance of independence and democracy. U.S. imperialism is also incapable of building up an army with any fighting spirit; however modern its equipment, the South Vietnam puppet army will never be able to consolidate its sagging morale.

Thirdly, imperialism cannot carry out its neo-colonialist policy without revealing its aggressive nature. Repression of the revolutionary movement must be essentially the work of native reactionary forces, and the war of aggression must be waged mostly with native reactionary armed forces. But a problem arises: What if the puppet forces prove incapable of serving the aims of their masters? The only possible solution is to increase the number of U.S. "advisers," military personnel, and combat troops, and to take part more and more directly in the war of aggression.

The United States has been going further and further on this road full of insoluble contradictions.

The South Vietnamese working class, nearly one million strong, and concentrated in cities and plantations, constitutes the main production force in important economic enterprises. Having to bear the triple yoke of imperialism, the bourgeois class, and the feudal class, it is the most resolute, the most radically revolutionary of all social classes. In the past years the U.S. imperialists and their puppets, using terror and corruption, and through the setting up of reactionary trade union organizations, have been endeavoring to control and divide the ranks of the workers, and to weaken their class consciousness and national consciousness. However, the worker movement has been developing gradually and surely, with rich and varied forms of struggle and slogans and increasingly high organization and great solidarity. Fierce struggles regularly broke out in state enterprises under the South Vietnam puppet administration, and in enterprises under U.S. or joint U.S.-local comprador bourgeois management. The worker movement has been growing in intensity, going from small-scale actions to partial and general strikes, from economic claims in the interests of the workers to demands in favor of other sections of the population (such as distribution of land to the peasants, and pay increases for the soldiers) and to political slogans condemning the policy of terror and repression, denouncing the puppet administration and demanding the withdrawal of U.S. imperialism from South Vietnam.

In recent years, the growing strength of the worker movement has resulted in the weakening of the enemy's most vital positions. It has given a strong impulse to the struggle of the laboring masses, particularly the poorer sections of the urban population, and the students in the cities. Since the majority come from ruined peasant families, the workers, as a class, have many ties with the mass of peasants, and this has greatly facilitated the forming of the worker-peasant alliance-basis of the national democratic front—and political work among those of the puppet troops who evince some degree of patriotism, most of them being sprung from the laboring peasantry.

The South Vietnamese peasantry, more than ten million strong, is the largest revolutionary force, and with the working class constitutes the main forces of the revolution. Mostly made up of landless peasants working in hard conditions and living in misery, it has long since evinced a high revolutionary spirit, especially since it was placed under the leadership of the vanguard party of the working class. Together with the latter, it rose up to conquer power, and in the ensuing years, it has fought against the enemy to defend the people's power and the tillers' right to land ownership brought about by the Revolution. The peasantry has gained rich experience in political and armed struggle, guerrilla warfare, organization of armed forces, and the building of resistance villages.

When peace was restored, the U.S.-Diem clique, through a so-called "agrarian reform," heavy taxation, and "agricultural credit," robbed the South Vietnamese peasantry of two-thirds of the land it had been given during the resistance. The policies of "agricultural settlements," "prosperity zones" and "strategic hamlets," and the permanent terror directly and seriously threatened the peasants' lives and property. As a result, until 1959 in the South Vietnam countryside the peasantry was rapidly undergoing a process of differentiation which continues up to the present time in the zones still occupied by the enemy. For the majority of peasants, life has been seriously disrupted; working and living conditions have become unbearable, not only for land-poor and landless peasants, but also for middle peasants and even for the majority of rich peasants. The number of totally or partially unemployed persons in the country-side has been rising rapidly. A large number of peasants have been press-ganged into the puppet army, or herded into "agricultural settlements" for forced labor; others have had to leave for the towns looking for work.

Faced with the grave danger threatening his fatherland and his own family, the peasant has resolutely taken part in political actions against the enemy and, in recent years, has risen up in a fierce, large-scale revolutionary struggle which has shaken to its foundation and broken up the puppet administration in the countryside. This revolutionary upsurge is in essence an insurrectionary movement of the mass of peasants, in which they carry out successive uprisings, to take over power at the base and reconquer the right to land ownership. A guerrilla war has been started in the rural areas, which has gradually spread to every part of the country, in opposition to the counterrevolutionary war waged by the enemy.

The petty bourgeoisie comprises the mass of small merchants and manufacturers, handicraftsmen, members of the liberal professions, civil servants, intellectuals, college students, and school pupils. All these strata of the small bourgeoisie are oppressed and exploited by imperialism, the bureaucratic comprador bourgeoisie, and the feudal forces. Their living conditions have been worsening. Animated with fairly strong patriotism, they sympathize with the Revolution. They constitute the majority of the population of South Vietnam's towns and cities, which total nearly four million.

The small bourgeoisie's patriotism and political consciousness were heightened by the Revolution of August 1945 and the resistance against the French colonialists. With the northern half of the country completely liberated, the yoke imposed on the south by U.S. imperialism and its puppets only stimulates their patriotism and exacerbates their hatred of the invader. For this reason, the small bourgeoisie constitutes one of the motives forces of the Revolution and a sure ally of the working class which is the only leading force capable of helping them advance steadily on the road of the Revolution.

In the atmosphere of terror and demagogy created by the U.S. imperialists and their puppets in South Vietnam, a number of persons belonging to the small bourgeoisie, especially its upper strata, have fallen under the influence of reactionary forces and played into the hands of reactionary parties. Others are passive, indifferent, or vacillating. However, an increasingly large section of the small bourgeoisie in the cities has shown a growing revolutionary militancy. In many urban centers, the struggle movement of college students and school pupils, in coordination with that of the workers and the other poorer sections of the population, is growing in intensity, and on several occasions had a direct aggravating effect on the crisis suffered by the puppet regime in the cities. This movement will certainly play a more and more important role.

The intellectuals, college students, and school pupils, though belonging to different social strata, are in general animated with ardent patriotism; only a handful have become lackeys of the enemy, or fallen under their influence. They hate the U.S. imperialists, hate and despise the traitors. During the patriotic war against the French colonialists, they sympathized with the Resistance, supported it or joined it. At present, they approve of the political program of the National Front for Liberation, and large numbers of them are actively taking part in the struggle of the masses in the cities.

The national bourgeoisie, in the south as in the rest of the country, is economically weak, although economic enterprises in South Vietnam are generally more important than in other parts of the country. According to figures which have yet to be ascertained, in 1956, the national bourgeoisie comprised about 15,000 persons. Many have gone bankrupt since, and in 1963, only half of the above number were still in business, running a number of precarious enterprises. Oppressed by the imperialists and the feudal class, the national bourgeoisie to some degree evinces an anti-imperialist and antifeudal spirit.

Following the return of peace, the South Vietnamese national bourgeoisie had expected it would get something from the policy of "national economic rehabilitation" announced by the U.S.-Diem clique. But U.S. economic and military "aid" has only aggravated the situation of the South Vietnamese economy, and the national bourgeoisie has found it more and more difficult to engage in industry and commerce. A number of national bourgeoisie join the ranks of the compradors. As the U.S. imperialists expand their war of aggression in an attempt to enslave our country and impose their control over all branches of the economy, the contradictions between the national bourgeoisie on the one hand and the U.S. imperialists and their puppets on the other have become more acute. The national bourgeoisie is increasingly opposed to U.S. imperialism and its puppets, and more and more favorable to a policy of independence, peace, and neutrality. A number of national bourgeois even approve of a gradual advance toward national reunification according to the program of the NLF. However, on account of its economic and political weakness and the fact that it has not completely severed its ties with the imperialists and their puppets, the national bourgeoisie is not determined to take the road of the Revolution.

The national minorities in South Vietnam are more than twenty in number and total over a million persons living in strategically important mountainous regions which constitute two-thirds of the land. In these regions, imperialism pursues a "divide and rule" policy, pitting the national minorities against one another and against the Kinh.[1] But the national minorities of South Vietnam as in the rest of the country have long since become conscious of their interests and have foiled the perfidious maneuvers of the imperialists. Heirs to the national traditions of heroic struggle against foreign invaders, the minority people in South Vietnam greatly contributed to the triumph of the Revolution of August 1945 and actively took part in the Resistance against the French colonialists. At present, only a handful in the upper strata have been bought over by the enemy; the majority of the people believe in the victory of the Revolution and are resolutely fighting against the U.S. imperialists and their puppets.

The religions in South Vietnam comprise Buddhism, Christianity, Caodai, Hoahao, etc. Buddhism, practiced for many centuries, has no deep influence but has a relatively large number of believers. Christianity is practiced by about a million persons. The Caodai religion, a synthetic religion based on Buddhism, has over a million believers, mostly poor peasants. Hoahao, which is related to Buddhism, once had nearly a million believers. The religious sects were born and developed at a time when the people's revolutionary struggle was growing in intensity and scope. They have been used to some extent by the French colonialists, then by the U.S. imperialists to further their political aims. But these sects have also suffered from division, restrictions, coercion, and repression, and they are more or less opposed to imperialism and its puppets in matters of national, religious, and class interests. Under Ngo Dinh Diem's rule, even among the Catholics, there were, besides those who supported the puppet administration, those who were against it. The religious sects are in general heterogeneous in their political tendencies, but, as the majority of believers are laboring people, the progressive tendency has been gaining ground.

To build and enlarge the puppet army, the Saigon administration has had to institute compulsory military service and resort to press-ganging. Owing to the development of the revolutionary war and the repeated victories of the liberation forces, opposition to war is growing in the puppet army. U.S. imperialism is meeting with growing difficulties in the use of

[1] Majority people.—*Ed.*

this puppet army against the people. Political work among the soldiers of the army enjoys more and more favorable conditions for the eventual building of a united front of workers, peasants, and soldiers to fight against the U.S. imperialists and save the country.

The liberation war of our countrymen in the south will have to face still many difficulties and hardships, but our southern countrymen and the Liberation Army, with unequaled heroism, have won brilliant successes and created factors of strategic significance to bring about final victory. With the growth of the people's political power and that of the revolutionary armed forces, the liberated zones are continually expanding. The development of the situation in South Vietnam eloquently proves that in a revolutionary struggle, in a revolutionary war, the decisive factor remains the human factor, the political factor, and the decisive force, the force of the popular masses.

The South Vietnamese Revolution is an integral part of the world revolution. Each great event in the world has a bearing on our people's struggle; on the other hand the influence of this struggle on the revolutionary movement in other countries is by no means insignificant. Especially in the present time, the South Vietnamese Revolution in particular and the Vietnamese Revolution in general are more than ever closely bound to the world situation. All the fundamental contradictions in our time have appeared in Vietnam. The national liberation movement is seething on the Asian, African, and Latin American continents, dealing heavy blows to imperialism headed by U.S. imperialism, causing the old colonial system to collapse in big chunks. During the past twenty years, over fifty countries with a population of a billion have conquered political independence in different degrees. Many countries are in full revolution. National, regional, and international anti-imperialist fronts have come into being and are being consolidated, with extremely rich and varied forms of struggle.

Africa, only yesterday "the dark continent," has become the hotbed of anti-imperialist revolution, where many countries are actively struggling against colonialism and neo-colonialism, some of them carrying out an armed struggle. In the twenty countries of Latin America, this "backyard" of U.S. imperialism, the national liberation movement is developing powerfully. In Asia, the national liberation movement is mounting in a powerful upsurge, especially in Southeast Asia.

The revolutionary struggle for national liberation is directly altering the balance of forces between the socialist and the imperialist camps; it is shaking the rear of imperialism, is a great support for the construction of socialism in the socialist countries, and an active contribution to world peace. It forces imperialism headed by U.S. imperialism to scatter its forces, thus creating in the imperialist chain weak links where revolutionary situations appear which may lead the liberation struggle toward victory. This is an important aid and encouragement to the Revolution in the south of our country. To cope with an uprising of the Santo Domingo people alone, the U.S. imperialists had to send there tens of thousands of troops. What would they do when faced with other Santo Domingos?

In this third stage of the general crisis of imperialism, the contradictions among the imperialist countries are becoming ever more acute, as a result of their struggle for markets, which is conditioned by the law of unequal development of the imperialist countries and the narrowing down of territories under their control. The powerful economic growth of the capitalist countries of Western Europe and Japan in the past years more and more restricts the part of U.S. capitalism in the world's industrial production and exports. The West European countries now have more important gold reserves than the United States. A number of countries show a tendency to become independent, to free themselves from U.S. influence. In face of the impetuous development of the world revolutionary movement, the imperialist countries are forced to form alliances, but these alliances by no means exclude competition and contradictions. NATO is deeply divided. SEATO is dangerously cracked, due to opposition by France and Pakistan. CENTO now has only a symbolic character. With regard to a solution to the Vietnam question, conflicts of interests have caused the imperialist countries to hold different views, and the most visible contradiction is that opposing France to the United States.

In the West European countries and in Japan, the large working masses resolutely support the Vietnamese people's just struggle and severely condemn the U.S. imperialists' war of aggression. These great historical changes have created objective conditions which are extremely favorable to the world revolution and to the South Vietnamese Revolution. The world revolution follows a complex process of development, a zigzag course, but it continually forges ahead.

Recently, in the ranks of the international communist movement, which is the vanguard force in our time, differences have appeared, but they have only a temporary character and revolutionary practice will certainly iron them out. In face of imperialism, the common enemy, which more and more clearly reveals its aggressive and bellicose nature, the true communists in the world will close their ranks. The communist parties will come out stronger than ever in this struggle for the defense of Marxism-Leninism against modern revisionism, the principal threat to the international communist movement. The imperialists are seeking to exploit the differences in the socialist camp and the international communist movement. In the Vietnam question, the U.S. imperialists are also endeavoring to make full use of these differences. A front of the world's peoples against imperialism headed by U.S. imperialism has come into being, which comprises the socialist countries as the main force, and the oppressed peoples, the working class in capitalist countries, and the forces of peace and democracy. This front is developing and being consolidated continuously; it cannot be weakened by any reactionary force.

The position of U.S. imperialism in the world today is no longer what it was at the end of World War II. Not only has it not succeeded in achieving world hegemony, but even its supremacy in the capitalist world has been badly shaken. It no longer holds an atomic monopoly and can no longer blackmail the peoples of the world. Today, the Soviet Union has built up a powerful system of defense and holds a leading position in space researches. The People's Republic of China now has its atomic bomb. U.S. imperialism has been forced to change its military strategy, passing from "massive retaliation" aimed at attacking the socialist camp, to "flexible response" with the immediate aim of suppressing the national liberation movement, while frantically preparing for a new world war. Everywhere, it has been unmasked as an international gendarme, and this has greatly impaired its political prestige and aroused opposition by all the nations in whose affairs it intervenes. Never has U.S. imperialism found itself so isolated in the world. Lately, it has been forced to ask its allies to help it get out of the South Vietnam quagmire. But, besides some important satellites such as South Korea, Thailand, Taiwan, Australia, and New Zealand, most of its friends give only verbal support or stand aloof. The French government has publicly disapproved of U.S. armed aggression in Indochina and advocates the neutralization of all the countries of Southeast Asia. It has withdrawn its delegation from SEATO. French imperialism is the most important buyer of South Vietnamese goods, and French investments at times represent 50 percent of the total investments in South Vietnam; French property is valued at two billion francs; 90 percent of the rubber areas and a large number of light industrial enterprises belong to French capitalists. No wonder that such a situation has led to acute contradictions between France and the United States. The governments of Great Britain and Japan, though lately taken in tow by the United States in political matters, have expressed anxiety about U.S. policy of war expansion, which they fear may bring severe defeats to imperialism. Until 1965, the contributions by U.S. satellites in the war of aggression in South Vietnam represented hardly 3 percent of the total expenses. The contributions in manpower and equipment have somewhat increased but are still very small. Formerly, when the French Expeditionary Corps found itself in difficulties, it could expect assistance from the United States. Today, the U.S. imperialists, bogged down in South Vietnam, can expect aid from nobody. If in the Korean War, the U.S. imperialists managed to get the support of the majority of U.N. member countries, today they cannot even use the flag of this organization.

During the first years of the Resistance against the French colonialists, our country was surrounded by hostile neighbors. But the liberation war now being waged by the South Vietnamese people enjoys much more favorable conditions. The south is carrying out its struggle at a time when the other half of the country has been liberated, and the neighboring countries are friendly. Laos is heroically fighting against U.S. imperialism and its puppets, and the kingdom of Cambodia is resolutely defending its active neutrality. Furthermore, Vietnam as a whole is geographically linked with the mighty socialist camp; she is a close neighbor of China and lies in the heart of the zone of revolutionary tempest in Southeast Asia where large masses are rising up in revolutionary struggle and the Marxist-Leninist parties have gained a rich experience in revolutionary leadership. South Vietnam, regarded by U.S. imperialism as the main link in its Southeast Asia strategy, is now on the front line of the national liberation movement in this part of the world. And our country as a whole is regarded as the center of the peoples' revolutionary struggle against U.S. imperialism. Directed against a common enemy, the revolutionary movement now developing in Southeast Asia and other parts of the world constitutes an effective support and a great encouragement for the Vietnamese people. On the other hand, our people's *glorious international duty* is to fight resolutely against U.S. imperialism until final victory so as to actively contribute to the defense of peace in Indochina, Southeast Asia, and the world.

Korea

Among Asian revolutionaries, the
sharpest and, at times, loudest "Guevarist" is North Korea's Premier,
Kim Il Sung. Born Kim Sung Chu in the far north in 1912 and raised
in Manchuria, Kim fought with the Chinese Communist guerrillas until
1941, then went to Russia and returned to Korea with Russian troops in
1945 as a Soviet Army major. Immediately active in the pro-Russian
Korean CP, he was instrumental in convincing the pro-Chinese group,
known as the New Peoples' Party, to merge with his in 1948. The result
was the Korean Workers' Party and Kim was the head of it, becoming
also Premier of North Korea. Taking the name of one of Korea's legendary
anti-Japanese guerrilla fighters, Kim Il Sung consolidated his position in
1950, purged first the pro-Russian elements out of the Party, then the
pro-Chinese. In the 1960's Kim led his country to phenomenal economic
success and agricultural self-subsistency, and guided his party into a very
militant internationalist yet independent stance. On October 5, 1964, he
enthusiastically supported Fidel Castro's call for volunteers to Vietnam.
He has often criticized Russia's "modern revisionism" and its peaceful
coexistence line, as he does in the following article, but he has also told
China to stop deciding who's right and who's wrong according to pro-
Chinese allegiances. "It is impossible," Kim has said, "that any one
country become the 'center of world revolution.' "

In the article that follows—a 1965 speech rounded out with a 1966
article for Cuba's Tricontinental magazine—Kim not only gives a neat,
if somewhat pat, résumé of Korea's revolutionary experience but also
explains his (and his party's) view of revolutionary activity. That experience, of course, is primarily based on a Chinese-type protracted "liberation" or "patriotic" war against a foreign invader (Japan, which seized
Korea in 1910). Like Mao, Kim believed then that social revolution
proceeded in two stages, first against an outside enemy, then against inside

181

counterrevolutionaries (i.e., the class struggle). For the first, all "patriots"
are partners; during the second all class enemies as well as deviationists,
opportunists, revisionists, etc., have to be eliminated. And Kim did just
that—in the north. Because his country was divided, he insisted that
communists consolidate their power first, then move to the offensive,
in the south or elsewhere. In this sense, he was a strict old-time Leninist,
uncompromising in his addiction to rigid "democratic centralism," that
is, Party Central Committee leadership. "Fortify the Party, the general
staff of the Revolution," he says, "and rally the broad masses of the
people around it."

But to turn North Korea into an economic miracle, Kim felt obliged
to Koreanize its communism. First of all, he had to get his people to
work as never before, and so established the "Chollima" myth, the winged
horse meant to symbolize work and generate an almost supernatural
identification of national pride with individual production. Then he fostered
a form of national Marxism, which he called Juche, *heralding Korea's*
"national peculiarities." Fundamentally, Juche *means that Korea, though*
struggling to establish communism, has every right, in fact is obliged,
to do so not according to established Marxist precepts but within na-
tional traditions. In effect, then, Juche *is the opposite of dogmatism; as*
such, it was only a question of time before Kim lashed out, as he does
here, at the "worshipers of the great powers"—i.e., Russia and China.
Forced back onto themselves, Korean communists were then totally de-
pendent on their people, not only materially—North Korea has received
almost no aid from the socialist world since the Korean War ended—but
culturally as well. Hence direct continuous contact between the leaders
and the led became an absolute necessity. And so, Kim developed the ri
method, whereby each and every cadre, Kim himself included, had to go
live in the simplest of Korean communities—the ri—*at regular intervals.*
The ri *spirit became a form of renewing the lifeline or blood of the ruling*
elite. It certainly served to keep the leadership popular and accessible,
and, conversely, taught the leadership to trust the people. One tangible
revolutionary result has been that the Korean CP has not been afraid to
arm its people. Another has been the people's constantly growing revolu-
tionary consciousness, and, consequently, its feeling of solidarity with
other revolutionaries. Thus, North Korea has become more and more
militant, willing to help not only South Koreans but also any revolutionary
in Asia (or indeed in the world) to "overthrow" the U.S. Having begun
as a Chinese-trained, Moscow-educated "compromise" communist who
benefited very little from Soviet "internationalism" or Chinese "solidarity"
(after the Korean War), Kim Il Sung ended up a national communist,
totally committed to international revolutionary solidarity—a circuitous
though not really paradoxical route.

KIM IL SUNG: *Juche* AND REVOLUTIONARY SOLIDARITY*

THE nationwide March 1st Uprising in 1919 under the impact of the October Revolution demonstrated the militant patriotic spirit and the revolutionary vigor of the Korean people, but, on the other hand, in its failure, it revealed all the limitations and weaknesses of bourgeois nationalism. In the 1920's the working class grew in strength and took an active part in the struggle. Many workers', peasants', and youth organizations appeared and workers' strikes and other forms of mass struggles were unfolded. Then, in 1925, the founding of the Korean Communist Party tried to give new impetus to the development of the working-class, peasant, and national-liberation movements. Under its leadership the June 10th Independence Movement took place and mass struggles of the workers and peasants against the Japanese imperialists, landlords, and capitalists gained in scope. But in those days communists carried on their activities in difficult conditions in which Japanese imperialism was resorting to severe suppression and the Party itself was suffering from serious weaknesses. Most of the leading posts of the Party were held by the petty-bourgeois careerists; the Party organizations did not take root among the working class and the broad strata of the masses. Worse still, acute factional strife rendered it impossible for the Party to preserve the unity of its ranks. Consequently, it ceased to exist as an organized force three years after its foundation. This shows that the communist movement in Korea was then in the cradle and that the subjective and objective conditions were yet unripe for the movement.

From the late 1920's to the early 1930's the tyranny of Japanese imperialism grew unprecedentedly cruel, depriving the Koreans of every possibility of legal struggle. But such violent suppression was countered by the intensified violent struggle of the workers and peasants.[1] In this situation it was inevitable that our revolutionary workers and peasants organized and unfolded an armed struggle. Under the leadership of communists our revolutionary army then carried on sanguinary warfare for fifteen long years and, fighting battles shoulder to shoulder with the Chinese People's Army and the Soviet Army to wipe out the Japanese imperialists, won the historic victory of the country's liberation at last.

[1] Among the most violent were the general strike of the Wonsan dockers in 1929, of the workers of the Sinhung colliery and Pyongyang rubber goods factories in 1930, of the farmers of the Buri farm in Ryongchon in 1929, and of the peasants in Danchon in 1930 and Yonghung in 1931.—*Ed.*

* Speech celebrating the twentieth anniversary of the Workers' Party of Korea (CP), delivered in Pyongyang on October 10, 1965, and published in Kim Il Sung, *Selected Works* (Pyongyang: Foreign Languages Publishing House, 1965), II.

Thus, the communist movement in Korea grew in scope and strength in the course of the protracted anti-Japanese struggle for national liberation, and in the 1940's it was possible to found our Party on a solid basis even in the complicated circumstances after the country's liberation.

After the August 15, 1945, liberation, however, new, grave difficulties cropped up before the Korean Revolution.

The U.S. imperialists occupied South Korea; the reactionaries at home and from abroad flocked there; former lackeys of Japanese imperialism were turned into stooges of U.S. imperialism. We were confronted with the aggressive policy of the U.S. imperialists who were not only opposed to the Korean Revolution and the building of a unified independent state by the Korean people but were also seeking to extend their influence to North Korea. Therefore, for the time being, it was inevitable to carry on the Korean communist revolutionary movement in the north and the south separately, under different circumstances and in different forms.

In the north, under the leadership of the Party, our people's power successfully carried out democratic reforms including the land reform and the nationalization of industries with the support and participation of the broad masses of the people. On the basis of the implementation of the democratic reforms, construction in the economic and cultural fields made swift headway and the people's livelihood, too, became stable. At the same time, our Party, in order to defend the gains of the Revolution, founded the people's armed forces with the revolutionary cadres fostered and steeled in the course of the long-drawn anti-Japanese armed struggle as the backbone.

In this way the anti-imperialist, antifeudal democratic revolution was completed in the northern part of Korea in one or two short years following the liberation. As a result, the northern part began to develop as the reliable base of the Korean Revolution. It is the decisive guarantee for victory in the revolutionary struggle as well as the construction work to build up the revolutionary force, that is, to fortify the Party, the general staff of the Revolution, and rally the broad masses of the people around it. The merging of our Party and the New Democratic Party to form the Workers' Party, a united political party of the laboring masses, was an epochal event in reinforcing our revolutionary forces. As a result of the merger, our Party became a mass political party embracing in its ranks the advanced elements not only of the working class but also of the laboring peasants and the intellectuals serving the working people.[2]

The war imposed upon us by the U.S. imperialism and its stooges was the sternest trial for our Party and our people. The Korean people and the Korean People's Army, in concert with the Chinese People's Volun-

[2] What he calls here the New Democratic Party was the New People's Party, which was pro-Chinese. The regular party was Moscowphile.—*Ed.*

teers and enjoying the unanimous support of the peoples of all the socialist countries, waged a heroic struggle to repulse the armed invasion of the enemy and defended the independence of the country and the gains of the Revolution. And the U.S. imperialists suffered a miserable military defeat for the first time in the history of the United States. This meant the beginning of a downhill turn for U.S. imperialism. With the serious wound received in this war yet unhealed, the U.S. imperialists have been incessantly running the gauntlet of the revolutionary peoples of the world, and now they are sinking ever deeper into the morass of ruin.

In the postwar period, the social revolution and socialist construction became the mature requirements for the socioeconomic development in the northern part of Korea. They were urgently needed also for the political and economic reinforcement of our revolutionary base and for the acceleration of the country's unification and the victory of the Korean Revolution as a whole.

Following the armistice, therefore, our Party concentrated its efforts, first of all, on rehabilitating the war-ravaged national economy and on stabilizing and improving the livelihood of the people which had been deteriorated during the war, while vigorously pushing forward the socialist revolution. The Party put forward the line of giving priority to the growth of heavy industry and simultaneously developing light industry and agriculture to decisively reinforce the country's economic basis and ensure a stable livelihood for the people in a short time. Further, the Party's line of actively carrying out the socialist transformation of production relations in parallel with the reconstruction, made it possible to recover the productive forces at an early date and open up a broad avenue for their further growth. Industrial and agricultural production were not merely restored to their prewar levels but raised far above them.

Then the historic December 1956 plenum of the Party Central Committee gave rise to the unprecedented upsurge of the political and labor zeal of our working people, to a great upsurge in socialist construction and to the great Chollima movement.[3] Amid such revolutionary upsurge, in 1958 the cooperativization of agriculture and the socialist transformation of private trade and industry were completed. The basis of our own heavy industry with the machine-building industry as its backbone has been created; light industry has also made rapid progress. Our agriculture has been turned into a firm socialist rural economy and is being equipped with new techniques. The problems of food, clothing, and housing of the people have been solved in the main, and their material and cultural standards have been improved generally.

In the early post-armistice days the enemy used to prattle that North

[3] Chollima, the winged horse, symbolizing work, is like a national "totem" in North Korea, says Charles Meyer. "There is no other symbol in the whole world which is so dynamic and effective."—Ed.

Korea would be unable to rise to its feet again even in a hundred years. However, our people under the leadership of the Party, in ten years after the war, not only reconstructed the economy on the war debris but also eliminated the centuries-old backwardness and poverty, turned their country into a socialist industrial-agricultural state, and built up towns and villages more beautifully than ever.[4]

The postwar rehabilitation and construction in our country were carried on in the midst of the fierce struggle against the ceaseless subversive activities of the U.S. imperialists and their lackeys and against indescribable economic difficulties and privations. Particularly, as the socialist revolution was carried out on a full scale, class struggle grew very acute. Such struggle unfolding in our society could not but find its reflection within the Party; various opportunist trends raised their heads, against which the Party launched a vigorous struggle. The struggle against factionalism and for strengthening the Party's unity, the struggle against dogmatism and for establishing Juche,[5] and the struggle against modern revisionism and for safeguarding the purity of Marxism-Leninism, were the main struggles in the postwar years on the ideological front within the Party.

The composition of our Party was complex due to the fact that the Party itself was young, that it was organized by bringing together the communist groups which had been active separately in different parts of the country and that it developed rapidly into a mass political party after the merger with the New Democratic Party. This is why the Party has always paid the greatest attention to the strengthening of the unity and solidarity of its ranks. We have safeguarded the unity of the Party by

[4] Joan Robinson, the well-known English economist, visited Korea in October 1964, and reported that "Eleven years ago in Pyongyang there was not one stone standing upon another (they reckon that one bomb, of a ton or more, was dropped per head of population). Now a modern city of a million inhabitants stands on two sides of the wide river, with broad tree-lined streets of five-story blocks, public buildings, a stadium, theatres . . . a city without slums." She added that 70 percent of villages had electric light in each cottage, that North Korea was "a nation without poverty [or] illiteracy." Calling it the "Korean Miracle," she attributed its success to "enthusiasm rather than excessive toil." (Monthly Review, January 1965). —Ed.

[5] In another speech (to Party Propagandists and Agitators, December 28, 1955) Kim Il Sung defined Juche as "abiding by the principle of solving all problems of the Revolution and construction independently in accordance with the actual conditions of one's own country and primarily by one's own efforts. This implies a creative application of Marxism-Leninism and the experience of the international revolutionary movement in keeping with the historic conditions and national peculiarities of one's own country. It also signifies independent solution of one's problems in the revolutionary struggle and construction by displaying the spirit of self-reliance." Under this Juche form of independent Marxism-Leninism, Koreans concentrate intensely on national pride as well as national wrongs or errors.—Ed.

reinforcing the core of the Party and tirelessly educating and rallying all the Party members.

The struggle for the unity and cohesion of the Party was unthinkable without the work for establishing *Juche*. Our Party has always held fast to the general principles of Marxism-Leninism and at the same time adhered to the creative position of rejecting dogmatism and adopting Marxism-Leninism in conformity with our own historical conditions and national peculiarities. The Party has always maintained the independent position of opposing reliance on others, displaying the spirit of self-reliance and solving its own problems entirely by itself, while constantly strengthening the solidarity and cooperation with the international revolutionary forces. *Juche* in ideology, independence in politics, self-reliance in economy, and self-defense in national defense—these have been the Party's consistent position and line.[6]

But some obstinate dogmatists infected with flunkeyism toward the great powers continued to obstruct the implementation of the Party's correct lines and policies, doing harm to our work. All the factionalists who appeared in our Party were, without exception, dogmatists and the worshipers of the great powers. They even ignored the history, culture, and revolutionary traditions of their own country, not to speak of the actual conditions at home, and thus degenerated into national nihilists who looked down upon everything that was their own and looked up to everything that was from abroad. They did not have any faith in the strength of their own country, only willing to rely on others in everything.

As modern revisionism was getting rampant in the international communist movement, our fight against factionalism and dogmatism came to be combined with the struggle against the former. In our country revisionists were disseminating first of all illusions about U.S. imperialism, and they tried to divert out Party and people from resolutely fighting against it. They also opposed the socialist revolution in our country, prattling that it was as yet premature; they opposed our Party's line of socialist industrialization, the line of the construction of an independent national economy in particular; and they even brought economic pressure to bear upon us, inflicting tremendous losses upon our socialist construction. The aim of the modern revisionists was, in the final analysis, to make our Party betray Marxism-Leninism and revolution, give up the anti-U.S. struggle and take the road of right capitulationism, following them in their steps.

While the Patriotic War of Liberation was the grimmest struggle against the imperialist aggressive forces and the domestic reactionary forces in the twenty-year history of our Party, the antiopportunist struggle in the

---

[6] Soviet aid dwindled to insignificant amounts shortly after the Korean War. Joan Robinson reported (*op. cit.*) that North Korea was 93 percent self-sufficient in machine production by 1964.—*Ed.*

postwar period was the most serious struggle against the enemy within the communist movement. Through this struggle our Party was further steeled and strengthened and gained plenty of experiences and lessons. We fortified our revolutionary stronghold and opened up a broader highway for our Revolution and construction work.

To put the mass line into practice, it is necessary to constantly improve the system and method of Party work on the one hand and, on the other, steadily enhance the level of the political consciousness and ideology of the masses. We carried out a great deal of organizational and ideological work to establish a revolutionary system of work throughout the Party and to help the functionaries rid themselves of bureaucracy and acquire a revolutionary method of work of relying on the masses. The Chongsan-*ri* spirit and the Chongsan-*ri* method[7] signify an embodiment and development of the revolutionary mass line which is a tradition of our Party, in conformity to the new realities of socialist construction. The essentials of the Chongsan-*ri* method are that the higher organ helps the lower, the superior assists his inferiors and always goes down to work places to have a good grasp of the actual conditions there and to find correct solutions to problems, and gives priority to political work or work with people in all activities to give full play to the conscious enthusiasm and creative initiative of the masses so as to ensure the fulfillment of revolutionary tasks. This method is not only a powerful method of work enabling us to carry out the immediate revolutionary tasks successfully and substantially, but a powerful method of education that enhances the ideological and political levels and practical ability of the functionaries and revolutionizes the masses.

With the spread of the Chongsan-*ri* method, a change was brought about in the work of the Party, state, and economic organs, and the level of leadership of the functionaries in these organs was raised considerably. Since the Chongsan-*ri* method was accepted by the masses, the work of educating and remolding the masses became the work of the working people themselves, developing into their mass movement for remolding ideology. The implementation of the mass line and the generalization of the Chongsan-*ri* method tended to further enhance the leading role of the Party, expanded and reinforced our revolutionary ranks rapidly, and gave a powerful impetus to the upswing in socialist construction and the Chollima movement. The Party has done a tremendous work to reinforce the People's Army, arm the entire people and turn the whole country

---

[7] A *ri* is the lowest administrative unit in the countryside. The spirit and method Kim Il Sung is talking about is the now widespread tradition of leaders going to live in such *ris* periodically in order to learn from the base as well as to maintain contact with the people. Kim himself does so very frequently, in fact worked out Korea's agricultural reorganization plan after spending fifteen days in a remote *ri*.—*Ed.*

into a fortress, and has thus built up a strong self-defense capable of safeguarding the country and revolution against the encroachment of the enemy.

Our Party always deems the Revolution and construction in the northern part of Korea part of the Korean Revolution and regards North Korea as the revolutionary base for accomplishing the cause of national liberation throughout the whole of Korea. While steadily pushing forward the Revolution and fortifying the revolutionary base in the north, the Party has invariably striven to support the revolutionary struggle of the people in South Korea, liberate it from the yoke of U.S. imperialism, and achieve the country's unification. The American imperialists occupying South Korea, taking the place of the Japanese imperialists, have held sway over South Korea as new colonial rulers. Since the first day of their landing in South Korea, they have pursued the aim of reducing it to a colony as well as a military base for establishing their domination over the whole of Korea and for aggression in the Far East and Asia. From this aim have stemmed all the policies the U.S. imperialists have followed in South Korea over the past twenty years.

The U.S. imperialists' rule over South Korea has nothing essentially different from the rule of the Japanese imperialists in the past. The difference, if any, is that whereas Japanese imperialism ruled Korea through a governor-general, today the U.S. imperialists dominate South Korea by the more cunning neo-colonialist method of using the puppet regime as their instrument. The so-called government in South Korea serves as a screen for legalizing the military occupation of U.S. imperialism and covering up its colonial rule, and plays the role of a tool faithfully executing the aggressive policy of U.S. imperialism.

The Revolution in South Korea is an anti-imperialist, antifeudal democratic revolution resulting from the contradictions between the U.S. imperialist aggressive forces and landlords, comprador capitalists, and reactionary bureaucrats who are in alliance with them on the one hand, and the workers, peasants, intellectuals, youth and students, and people of other social strata in South Korea on the other, and this revolution is an integral part of the Korean Revolution as a whole.

Immediately after the surrender of Japanese imperialism, in South Korea, too, like in North Korea, revolutionary potentialities of the masses of the people erupted like a volcano and the patriotic democratic forces grew rapidly. Communists came out from the underground and the Communist Party was organized and began its activities, and the people's committees, the people's organs of political power, were formed all over South Korea. The successive national-salvation struggles included that waged by the miners of the Hwasun coal mine near Kwangju, the peasant riot on Haui Island in August 1946, the September general strike, the October popular resistance, the February 7, 1948, protest against the

May 10th separate elections, and the soldiers' mutiny in Ryosu in the same year.[8] The revolutionary struggle was frustrated temporarily, however, by the infiltration activities of the U.S. imperialists' agents and by factional elements who had wormed their way into the leading body of the Communist Party. By 1949 the Party organizations were completely destroyed. But the patriotic people in South Korea did not stop fighting. The heroic struggle waged by the Masan citizens against the fraudulent March 15 (1960) elections conducted by the Syngman Rhee regime was a signal indicating that the national salvation struggle of the South Korean people had entered a new stage. In the April Popular Uprising, the people in South Korea toppled the regime of Syngman Rhee, an old-time minion of the U.S. imperialists.

Frightened by this, the U.S. imperialists and their lackeys staged a military coup and tried to stifle the national salvation struggle of the South Korean people by resorting to fascist suppression. Nevertheless, the patriotic youth, students, and people in South Korea have fought heroically against the "South Korea-Japan talks" in defiance of the harsh repression by the traitorous Pak Jung Hi clique and are now carrying on their brave struggle for shattering the "South Korea-Japan agreements." The series of demonstrations staged in June 1964 and again in August 1965 were anti-imperialist, antifascist, and for the overthrow of the traitorous clique. The people have come to realize that, so long as the U.S. imperialist colonial domination continues, no solution can be found for any problem by the mere replacement of one U.S. puppet with another, and that the winning of genuine freedom and liberation and the achievement of the country's unification are possible only when the U.S. aggressors are driven out, U.S. imperialist colonial rule is eliminated root and branch, and the people seize the political power in their own hands.

The Revolution in South Korea has to deal with a strong enemy armed to the teeth, and it still has a tortuous way to go. However, the South Korean people have a tradition of valiant fight against foreign aggressors

[8] The Hwasun coal miners began by celebrating, on August 15, 1946, the first anniversary of Korea's liberation, went on to protest U.S. occupation, and were finally dispersed by U.S. troops and local police using tanks and killing scores of workers; a few days later, some 700 peasants of Haui attacked the local branch of the New Korea Company, a U.S.-military land exploitation agency, and were dispersed by gunfire; the September 1946 general strike, started by 40,000 railway workers demanding better living conditions, spread to 400,000 before the U.S. authorities gave in to some of the demands; the October riots mushroomed after the U.S. fired on 10,000 demonstrators in Taegu, eventually led to the U.S. declaring a state of siege and firing repeatedly into the up to two million protesters against occupation, killing literally thousands; the February 7, 1948, revolt, launched by students against separate (north-south) elections imposed by the United States through a U.N. commission, led to a nationwide protest and fairly successful boycott of the elections.—Ed.

and internal reaction. And they are not alone in their struggle. They have a powerful revolutionary base in North Korea and enjoy the active support of its people. Our Party and all the people in the north will do everything in their power to support the revolutionary struggle of the people in South Korea and will resolutely fight together with them for the complete liberation and independence of all Korea.

Our Party, always regarding it as the prime internationalist duty for Korean communists and the Korean people to carry out the Korean Revolution, makes every effort to promote the development of the international revolutionary movement as a whole.

It is the consistent policy of our Party in international affairs to safeguard the unity of the socialist camp and the solidarity of the international communist movement, to develop the relations of friendship and cooperation with the newly independent countries in Asia, Africa, and Latin America, to support the anti-imperialist national liberation movements of the peoples in these regions and the revolutionary movements of the peoples in all countries, to oppose the imperialist policy of aggression and war and to strive for world peace and the progress of mankind.[9]

In January 1966, the Tricontinental Peoples' Solidarity Organization was founded in Havana. It was an event of very great importance. The aims and ideals of this organization have aroused the sympathy of hundreds of millions of Asian, African, and Latin American people and are exerting profound influence on the course of the great changes taking place in the world today. Millions of people in the three continents are fighting for liberation and for the safeguarding of the achievements of the revolution they have already attained. The people who have achieved independence should crush the subversive activities of the foreign imperialists and domestic reactionary forces, tear down their economic footholds, strengthen the revolutionary forces, strive to set up a progressive social system, and build an independent national economy and national culture. Only by so doing can one safeguard the gains of the revolution, achieve the prosperity of the country and the nation and contribute to the common struggle of the peoples of the world over for burying imperialism.

Asia, Africa, and Latin America hold 71 percent of the land surface of the globe. These continents are inhabited by more than two-thirds of the world population and endowed with inexhaustible natural wealth. Im-

[9] The following insert is from an article written by Kim Il Sung for the first issue of *Tricontinental*, organ of the Organization of Solidarity of the Peoples of Asia, Africa, and Latin America (OSPAAAL), printed in Havana on August 12, 1967, and reprinted in *The People's Korea* (Tokyo), August 23, 1967. I have inserted it here because it follows naturally from Kim's 1965 speech while also developing his foreign policy views and commitment to the armed struggle line of the Third World.—*Ed.*

perialism grew and fattened by grinding down the peoples of those continents and robbing them of their riches. Still now imperialism is squeezing tens of billions of dollars of profit from these continents every year. The anti-imperialist, anticolonialist struggle of the peoples of Asia, Africa, and Latin America is a sacred liberation struggle of hundreds of millions of oppressed and humiliated people and, at the same time, a great struggle for cutting the life line of world imperialism in these areas. Together with the revolutionary struggle of the international working class for socialism, this struggle is a component of the two major revolutionary forces of our time. Those struggles are linked up together in one current which will carry imperialism to its grave.

The imperialists cannot make a gift of independence to colonial peoples. The oppressed peoples can liberate themselves only through their struggle. This is a simple and clear truth confirmed by history. It is necessary to expose the false propaganda of the imperialists and thoroughly dissipate the illusion that the imperialists will give away their position in the colonies and dependent countries with good grace. Where there is oppression, there is resistance. This is the rule. It remains as an inalienable right of the oppressed nations to rise in arms and fight against the aggressors.

It is wrong to try to avoid the struggle against imperialism under the pretext that though independence and revolution are important, peace is still more precious. Genuine peace will not come unless a struggle is waged against the breakers of peace, unless the slave's peace is rejected and the rule of the oppressors is overthrown. We are opposed to the line of compromise with imperialism. At the same time, we cannot tolerate either the practice of only talking big of opposing imperialism, but, indeed, being afraid of fighting against imperialism.

In order to fight against imperialism, it is important first of all to direct the spearhead of attack on U.S. imperialism. There is not a country on the globe whose sovereignty is not violated by U.S. imperialism or which is free from the menace of U.S. imperialist aggression. When Africa and Latin America are not free, Asia cannot enjoy freedom. On the other hand, victory on one front against U.S. imperialism will sap its strength that much, facilitating victory on other fronts. Therefore, it is necessary to form the broadest possible anti-U.S. united front to isolate U.S. imperialism thoroughly, and administer blows to it by united strength everywhere it is engaged in aggression. Only by so doing is it possible to disperse and weaken the force of U.S. imperialism to the last degree and lead the people on every front to beat U.S. imperialism with overwhelming power.

The U.S. imperialists are afraid of the united strength of the revolutionary peoples of the world more than anything else. That is why they are resorting to all kinds of tricks to obstruct the formation of an anti-U.S. united front and have adopted the stratagem of subduing weak and small countries one by one. This stratagem of U.S. imperialism must be thoroughly frustrated. The Asia, African, and Latin American countries have differing social systems, and many parties with differing political views exist in these countries. But all these countries and parties, except the stooges of imperialism, have common interests in opposing the imperialist forces of aggression headed by U.S. imperialism. The difference in social systems and political ideals can never be an obstacle to the joint struggle and concerted action against U.S. imperialism. No one must be allowed to split the anti-U.S. united front and refuse joint action, attaching the first importance to his own nation's or party's specific interests.

It is very important in the joint struggle against imperialism to defend the revolution which has already triumphed. It is an internationalist duty of all the revolutionary peoples to fight in defense of the gains of the Cuban Revolution. The revolutionary Cuba represents the future of Latin America and its very existence encourages the peoples of this continent in their liberation movement. It is for this very reason that the U.S. imperialists hate and are afraid so much of this small island country. Today the Vietnamese people's resistance war of national salvation against the U.S. invasion troops has become the focal point of the anti-imperialist struggle. The U.S. troops are sustaining one defeat after another by the heroic resistance of the Vietnamese people. The Vietnamese people's resistance war proves once again clearly that people who are determined to defend their independence and freedom at whatever sacrifice and who have the support of the peoples of the whole world, are invincible.

We must neither underestimate nor overestimate the strength of U.S. imperialism. U.S. imperialism can still commit lots more crimes. But U.S. imperialism is on the decline. The Korean War revealed that U.S. imperialism is by no means invulnerable, but can be beaten in fighting. The triumph of the Cuban Revolution has proved again this truth under circumstances different from ours. The Vietnamese people's resistance war of national salvation, too, clearly confirms this truth. By fighting in union against the U.S.-led imperialists, the peoples of Asia, Africa, and Latin America will make a great contribution to world peace and the liberation of mankind.[10]

. . . . To strengthen the international revolutionary forces and vigorously push forward the anti-imperialist struggle of the peoples, we must fight against modern revisionism. The biggest harm of modern revisionism lies in the fact that, scared by the nuclear blackmail of U.S. imperialism, it surrenders to the latter, gives up the struggle against imperialism and compromises with it, restrains and undermines the liberation struggle of the oppressed nations and the exploited peoples. Revisionism still remains the main danger in the international communist movement today.

---

[10] End of 1967 insert.—*Ed.*

We are communists fighting against imperialism and for revolution. The unity of the socialist camp and the solidarity of the international communist movement are unthinkable without the anti-imperialist struggle. Our Party will develop a common struggle together with the fraternal parties and countries in opposing imperialism headed by U.S. imperialism, and in supporting the revolutionary movement of the peoples, and will, through this struggle, endeavor to strengthen our unity. Our immediate supreme task at the moment is to liberate South Korea. The whole Party and the entire people must oppose all manifestations of indolence and weariness, sharpen vigilance, and maintain an unslackening attitude at all times. We should never become the prey of pacifistic feelings, and above all must wage a powerful ideological struggle to prevent the penetration into our ranks of the ideological trend of the modern revisionists who are afraid of war. We do not want war but do not fear it.

Indonesia

As a result of the October 1965 military coup which overthrew President Sukarno, the revolutionary theory and practice of the Indonesian Communist Party have been clearly exposed—and criticized. What emerges is that the CPI (or PKI, for Partai Kommunis Indonesia) was an incredibly dogmatic, elitist, and opportunist party obsessed with its own erroneous analysis of conditions, both objective (the class and economic structure) and subjective (the various forces' leaderships). These mistakes were due, in turn, mostly to the fact that the PKI was so Stalinist, and later Maoist, in orientation and allegiance that it stifled every independent or national outlook within its cadre. Incredibly, however, it persistently refused to prepare itself for armed struggle—on the grounds that the "United National Front" of anti-imperialist forces which it fostered was a growing reality. That "front" turned out to be totally illusory, and the consequences, over the years since 1948, have been the assassination of more than 1,000,000 communists.

The PKI was launched in 1920 and, almost from the start, its leader, Dipa Nusantara Aidit, repeated the slogans, but rarely the logic, of Russia's revolutionaries. Thus, though the PKI created armed guerrillas during World War II to fight the Japanese invaders, it fought only according to Stalin's "cooperative" wartime policy, that is, in Indonesia's case, under the direction of the Dutch colonialists—with the vague hope that the reward might be "an independent Indonesia within the Commonwealth of the Dutch Empire." Never did the PKI even contemplate an agrarian reform or the establishment of liberated areas during this period, and when the war of liberation began—launched by Sukarno's Nationalist Party—against the Dutch and British colonialists, the PKI again fought bravely but only for independence. Chairman Aidit's concept of two-stage revolution was so liberal that, although many sectors of the national bourgeoisie sided with the enemy, he would brand any Indo-

195

*nesian communist who opposed the alliance with the "middle sectors" as
a left deviationist. As late as 1964, Aidit was still insisting on such an
alliance. "The success and completeness of the leadership of the working
class in the revolution,"* he wrote in Be a Good and a Better Communist,
*"will be determined by the success of the alliance between the workers
and the national bourgeoisie."* To talk of socialism or Soviets was un-
*principled deviationism, he went on, adding as "proof" of his argument:
"In his speech to the students at the University of the Peoples of the East
on May 18, 1925, [Stalin] said that this left deviation contained within it
the danger of isolating the party from the masses."*

*After the "August 1945 Revolution" ended successfully in 1947 with
Indonesian independence, Aidit obeyed Stalin again and ordered his troops
to surrender their arms. At that time Indonesia didn't even have a regular
army, but the PKI leaders gave the reactionary government the time to
create one and in 1948 the "National Armed Forces," led by the same
Abdul Nasution who became co-leader and dictator of the 1965 coup,
launched an anticommunist terror campaign in which thousands of communist resistance fighters were massacred. Still, Aidit, his top aide M. H.
Lukman, and other members of the Central Committee refused to prepare
for armed struggle. By "emphasizing" that "we are going to make this
possibility" of a transition to socialism by peaceful means "a reality, we
can thereby show the people that if violence does occur, it was not started
by the communists,"* Lukman explained in About the Constitution *(1959).*

*The PKI's fallacious analysis was also grounded in Aidit's absurd reli-
ance on the urban workers as the main revolutionary force. In a country
where peasants comprise more than 60 percent of the population but
where the "proletariat" at most (by including agricultural workers) includes
less than 20 percent, Aidit dogmatically insisted that only the workers
could lead "the masses." This thinking was partly due to the fact that
the PKI leadership was city-based and had relatively little contact with
the countryside. More importantly, however, it was based on the proletariat's visible "politicization," a factor which, the Guevarists will say
later, has confused revolutionary parties almost everywhere in the underdeveloped world. For though it is true that urban workers join unions
and militate constantly for better conditions, it is equally true that they
feel more integrated into the capitalist economy than peasants and are
easier to buy off, frighten, or delude.*

*Altogether, the fiasco of the Indonesian "revolution" prior to 1965
shows that communists cannot and do not always control the "fronts"
that they create; that revolutionary principles and practice must never be
sacrificed for growth in numbers (from 1945 to 1965, the PKI's membership grew from 10,000 to 3,000,000); that the first stage of the two-
stage revolution is, as Mao himself said, inseparably linked to the second;
that the two-stage idea works only when a foreign invader generates a*

people's war and *the revolutionary party uses it to create liberated areas or bases; that no ruling elite ever willingly gives up power to its class enemy; and that the national bourgeoisie and any "proletarian element" that becomes incorporated into it (such as the armed forces) can never be trusted as an ally. Aidit and the whole PKI's Central Committee violated each and every one of these propositions. Manipulated by the national bourgeoisie, which was in power through President Sukarno, the PKI kept insisting that as long as "pro-people elements" were in the government and in the army, there was nothing to fear. Shortly before the coup, Aidit stated:* "We will not be provoked. If the army spits in our faces we will wipe it off and smile. We will not retaliate. Time is on our side. We shall win without a struggle."

On September 30–October 1, 1965, the army did not spit in Aidit's face. It cut it off. Lukman, too, was killed, as were seven other Central Committee men—and anywhere from 300,000 to 1,000,000 communists (700,000 is probably the most accurate figure; see L'Express, Paris, 23–29 May 1966). One member of the Central Committee who escaped, as he was in Peking at the time, was Jesuf Aditorop. He has since become head of the PKI—in exile. But all that he seems to have learned from the disaster was that the Party should have been ready for protracted armed struggle. The short passages by Aidit and Aditorop included below are meant simply to acquaint the reader with their thinking. The third article, by a young PKI member with Trotskyist connections, is more serious. It reflects the kind of analysis carried out in 1966 and 1967 in Indonesia proper where communists, having slowly reorganized in clandestinity, are now waging an armed struggle, apparently the beginning of a protracted people's war—without worrying very much about what the surviving PKI leadership is proclaiming from its Peking sanctuary.

D. N. AIDIT: FRAGMENTS*

—AS we give leadership to the bitter, difficult, and protracted struggle of the people, we must adopt tactics of taking the revolutionary struggle of the Indonesian people forward slowly and cautiously, but surely. In the course of carrying out this protracted struggle, we must unceasingly oppose two deviations, the deviations of surrenderism and of adventurism, both of which originate from petty bourgeois wavering. Since the enemies of the people make use of all forms of struggle, we too must be skillful at making use of all forms of struggle. We must be skillful at utilizing all forms of

---

* From *Indonesian Society and Indonesian Revolution* (Jakarta: Jajasan Pembaruan, 1957, and Demos, 1963).

open and legal struggle, the forms which are permitted according to law and the regulations, and according to habits and customs in society. The Fourth Plenum of the Central Committee of the CPI drew attention, among other things, to the fact that we "must be vigilant and must always hold ourselves in readiness and prepare the people in all respects so that the reactionaries will not be able to stand in the way of the people's desire to achieve fundamental social changes peacefully, by parliamentary means." Of course, the CPI's activities are not confined to parliamentary work alone but also and especially include activities among the masses, the masses of workers, the peasants, the intellectuals, and other masses of working people and democratic masses. All these activities, both within and outside Parliament, are aimed at changing the balance of forces between the imperialists, the landlord class, and the compradors on the one hand, and the forces of the people on the other. In order to attain the objectives of the Party, we must, in making use of these forms of struggle, base ourselves on the principles of justice, advantage, and a knowledge of how far we can go.

—The CPI Programme states that "the workers, the peasants, the petty bourgeoisie, and the national bourgeoisie must unite in one national front." The national front is the unification of the progressive and the middle-of-the-road forces. The middle-of-the-road forces are basically the forces of the national bourgeoisie. The CPI Programme also states that the way out of the semicolonial and semifeudal situation lies in "changing the balance of forces between the imperialists, the landlord class, and the comprador bourgeoisie on the one hand, and the forces of the people on the other. The way out lies in arousing, mobilizing and organizing the masses, especially the workers and the peasants." The Fourth Plenum of the CPI Central Committee (held at the end of July 1956) stated among other things that there are in Indonesian society three forces— the diehard forces, the middle-of-the-road forces, and the progressive forces. It further stated that at the present time, the forces of the people, that is, the combination between the progressive forces and the middle-of-the-road forces, are striving for the formation of an Indonesian state which is independent in the political and economic spheres.

Although the Indonesian proletariat contains within it certain unavoidable weaknesses, such as for example its smallness in number by comparison which the peasants, its young age by comparison with the proletariat in capitalist countries and the low level of its culture by comparison with the bourgeoisie, it is nevertheless the basic force pushing the Indonesian Revolution forward. The Indonesian Revolution will not succeed unless it is under the leadership of the Indonesian proletariat. As a recent example, the August Revolution was successful in the beginning because the proletariat more or less consciously took an important part in it, but later on, the Revolution suffered defeat because the role of the proletariat was pushed into the background and the upper strata of the bourgeoisie betrayed the alliance with the proletariat. Without the proletariat taking an active part, nothing will ever run properly in Indonesian society. This has already been proved and will continue to be proved by history and experience. It must be understood that although the Indonesian proletariat is the class which has the highest political consciousness and organizational understanding, the victory of the Revolution can never be achieved without the revolutionary unity under all circumstances with all other revolutionary classes and groups. The proletariat must build up a revolutionary front. Of the classes in society, the peasants are the firmest and most reliable ally of the working class, the urban petty bourgeoisie is a reliable ally, and the national bourgeoisie is an ally under certain circumstances and within certain limits: this is the fundamental law which has already been and is being proven by Indonesia's modern history.

—The workers, the peasants, the petty bourgeoisie, and the national bourgeoisie are the People, and make up the forces of the Revolution, the forces of the united national front.

—The CPI Programme has the following to say, among other things: "Bearing in mind the backwardness of the economy of our country, the CPI is of the opinion that this government (the People's Democratic government) is not a government of the dictatorship of the proletariat but a government of the dictatorship of the people. This government does not have to carry out socialist changes but democratic changes." In other words, the character of the Indonesian Revolution at the present stage is not a proletarian-socialist revolution but a bourgeois-democratic revolution. We can determine the character of our Revolution after we understand the specific conditions of Indonesian society which is still semicolonial and semifeudal, after knowing that the enemies of the Indonesian Revolution at the present time are imperialism and the feudal forces, that the tasks of the Indonesian Revolution are to complete the national revolution and the democratic revolution so as to overthrow the two basic enemies (imperialism and feudalism), that the national bourgeoisie can also take part in this Revolution, and that if the big bourgeoisie betray the Revolution and become an enemy of the Revolution, the direct blows of the Revolution must continue to be aimed more at imperialism and feudalism than at capitalism and private ownership of the national capitalists in general.

—Since the Indonesian Revolution at the present stage is marked by world socialist construction and the disintegration of world capitalism, there can be no doubt that the future of the Indonesian Revolution is not capitalism but socialism and communism. Whether we like it or not, whether we agree or not, whether we oppose it or not, this is the perspective for the Indonesian Revolution. But do not the perspectives of "socialism" and "communism" conflict with the objective of the Revolution at the present stage which "should not carry out socialist changes but democratic changes"? No, there is no conflict. It is indeed so that, seen from one angle, a capitalist economy will develop within certain bounds after the victory of the people's democratic revolution in view of the fact that the obstacles standing in the way of capitalism's growth will have been swept aside. But this is not surprising nor should it be cause for anxiety. The growth within certain bounds of national capitalism is only one aspect of the victory of the Indonesian Revolution. Another aspect is that the victory of the democratic revolution will mean the development of *socialist factors*, such as the growing political influence of the proletariat, the growing recognition by the peasants, the intellectuals, and other petty-bourgeois elements of the leadership of the proletariat, the growth of state enterprises as well as cooperatives among the peasants, the handicraftsmen, the fishermen, and other sections of the people. All these are socialist factors which provide the guarantee that the future of the Indonesian Revolution is socialism and not capitalism.

JESUF ADITOROP: OUR MISTAKE*

IN drawing lessons from the bitter experiences, it must be pointed out that one of the most important causes of the setback in the revolutionary struggle of our people is the mistake committed by the PKI in appraising the class nature of the state power in Indonesia. In reality, after 1949 when the reactionary Hatta government concluded the Round Table Conference Agreement with the Dutch imperialists, the state of the Republic of Indonesia has become an instrument in the hands of the Indonesian comprador bourgeoisie and landlords to protect the interests of imperialism and to maintain the remnants of feudalism, as well as to suppress the people, especially the workers and the peasants, who wage the struggle against imperialism and feudal vestiges. The revolutionary struggle of the Indonesian people since 1949 had achieved certain results which diminished the antidemocratic character of the bourgeois power. But this by no means altered fundamentally the class nature of this power. The exaggerated assessment of the gains of the revolutionary struggle in this period had given birth to the "theory" that the state power of the Republic of Indonesia was composed of two aspects, the "anti-people aspect" and the "pro-people aspect." According to this erroneous

---

* From a speech delivered at the Fifth Congress of the Party of Labor of Albania at Tirana, November 1966; English version in *Indonesian Tribune* (Tirana), December 1966.

"two-aspect theory," the state ceases to be the instrument of suppression in the hands of the ruling classes against other classes but can be made an instrument shared by both the oppressor and the oppressed classes. This "theory" had led to the illusion that the fundamental change in state power, that is to say the birth of a people's power, could be peacefully accomplished by developing the "pro-people aspect" and gradually liquidating the "anti-people aspect." In practice, this "theory" had deprived the proletariat of its independence in the united front with the national bourgeoisie, dissolved the interests of the proletariat in a position of tail-end of the national bourgeoisie.

To return the proletariat to the position of leadership in the struggle for emancipation of the Indonesian people, it is absolutely necessary for the PKI to rectify the error of the "two-aspect theory" and to establish the correct Marxist-Leninist principles on state and revolution. The PKI has stated that "the people will come to power only through an armed revolution under the leadership of the working class, to overthrow the power of the comprador bourgeoisie, the bureaucrat-capitalists, and the landlords who represent the interests of imperialism and the remnants of feudalism." At the same time our Party has also emphasized that "the armed struggle to defeat the armed counterrevolution must not be waged in the form of military adventurism, or in the form of a putsch, which is detached from the awakening of the popular masses," and that "it is the people who will liberate themselves."

The events in Indonesia have demonstrated the utter bankruptcy of the "peaceful-road theory" in whatever form, and the danger it has brought to the revolutionary movement. These events have shown with what great sacrifices the proletarian party has to pay when it harbors even the slightest illusion in the "peaceful road," and when it abandons the principles of People's War in solving the contradiction between the people and the domestic reactionary classes. This is the most important lesson from the bitter experiences of Indonesia.

T. SOEDARSO: LESSON FOR THE FUTURE*

REPORTS have appeared with increasing frequency recently, indicating that armed resistance is being mounted by the Indonesian revolutionary forces against the brutal suppressive measures of the Indonesian military-fascist regime. The armed struggle is occurring not only in Central Java,

---

* Article published in English by *World Outlook*, September 16, 1966; in three parts by *The Militant* (October 3, 10, 17, 1966); and in pamphlet form by Merit Publishers (New York: December 1966)—all three being publications of the Fourth International. The author is a young member of the PKI.

an area considered to be the stronghold of the revolutionary movement, but also in other islands of the Republic.

This armed struggle, however, is still uncoordinated. It is still sporadic and anarchistic in nature. It still lacks leadership, either political or military, capable of organizing an armed uprising. It seems that the Communist Party of Indonesia has not recovered from its defeat.

It is true, of course, that the future of the Indonesian revolutionary movement has not been destroyed—it cannot be. The movement will rise again in a mightier force that will finally end the system of exploitation of man by man in Indonesia. But it is a fact that it has suffered a serious defeat and setback.

Nevertheless there are some to be found who still do not regard it as a defeat but as a "blessing in disguise"; since now the line between friend and foe is very clear and the people really know that "it is not we who resort to violence but the reactionaries." Such people still maintain that the past policies of the Party were quite correct, the recent catastrophe being merely a "routine" incident in the revolutionary struggle. "Sacrifices always occur," they say. Thus these people do not consider it necessary to analyze the previous policies, strategy, and tactics of the Party; they even argue that it is "premature" to attempt this or "it is very dangerous because it can lead to a split in our movement." Their advice is to "just continue the struggle in line with the past policy, only with more caution and vigilance."

This stand is not correct. We must dare to uncover the mistakes of the past that led to this failure. And we must have the courage to make the necessary corrections so that we won't fall into the same fatal errors again. Criticism and self-criticism are necessities for a healthy revolutionary movement.

This was the most fundamental error: The PKI believed that socialism in Indonesia could be achieved by peaceful means. As stated in the constitution of the PKI: "To achieve its goal, the PKI follows peaceful and democratic ways. This is what is sought by the PKI and what will be consistently pursued."[1] And the second secretary of the Central Committee of the PKI, M. H. Lukman, explained:

"From the theoretical point of view, to affirm the possibility of a transition to socialism by peaceful means signifies affirming the truth that Marxism-Leninism does not point to absolutely the same road for socialism in all countries in different periods and in different international conditions. This also means that we Marxist-Leninists do not bind ourselves to certain forms, methods, and roads of completing the Revolution, because everything depends on the concrete balance of power among the existing classes, on the quality of the working-class organization and its enemy,

[1] *Constitution of the PKI* (Jakarta: Central Committee of the Partai Kommunis Indonesia, 1964), p. 16.

on the ability of the working class to attract its allies to its side, especially the peasants, and on taking into account the existence of democratic institutions in each country."

In the same speech, Lukman said further: "In accordance with the teachings of Marx and Lenin, namely by taking into account the objective conditions of the world balance of power between the socialist and democratic forces on the one hand, and the imperialist forces on the other, and considering the experiences in the East European countries where the transition to socialism did not occur through a civil war, Comrade Khrushchev at the Twentieth Congress of the CPSU stated the conclusion that in the present situation certain countries have a real possibility of reaching socialism in a peaceful way."[2]

It is therefore understandable why the PKI was unprepared for armed struggle when the crisis came last October 1. The PKI concentrated activity only on the "legal" or "parliamentary democratic" platform. It completely ignored preparations for armed struggle by the workers and peasants under the leadership of the working-class Party. This was well known to the reactionary forces: consequently they launched a quick brutal action to liquidate the revolutionary forces. The only hope for the revolutionary forces was to seek safe retreats, but it was already too late. The toll was very high.

Because of this belief in a peaceful way of achieving socialism, and perhaps especially because of the advice of "Comrade" Stalin and later "Comrade" Khrushchev, the leadership of the PKI willingly, if not even faithfully, followed Sukarno's personal leadership and teachings. Sukarno was considered by the party to be a "pro-people's element" and even the "great leader of the Revolution." The reactionary forces brutally massacred members of the PKI and other revolutionary forces in the name of Sukarno; yet Second Secretary Njoto still said, "The PKI recognizes only one head of the state, one supreme commander, one great leader of the Revolution—President Sukarno." Furthermore, "It is President Sukarno united with the forces of the people who will decide the destiny and future of Indonesia." In accordance with the October 10, 1965, instructions of the Political Bureau of the Central Committee of the PKI, Njoto continued, all Party members should "fully support the directives of President Sukarno and pledge themselves to implement these without reserve." (The October 10 instructions have not been withdrawn to this day.) The Party was still seeking to maintain the peaceful road. Njoto said, "Our Party is making every effort in its power to prevent a civil war."[3]

[2] M. H. Lukman: *About the Constitution* (Jakarta: Jajasan Pembaruan, 1959), pp. 26–27.

[3] These statements were made to a Japanese correspondent. See *Asahi Shimbun* (Tokyo), December 2, 1965.

As for the Indonesian Armed Forces, the PKI held that they constituted forces of the people, since the ranks were made up of the sons of workers and peasants. This viewpoint was maintained even after the "October 1 affair," Njoto saying: "We do not consider the Indonesian National Forces to be like the armies of imperialist countries or the army of India. When you appraise an army, you should study and take into account the history of its formation, its role in the struggle against imperialism and feudalism, its composition which is mainly made up of former poor peasants or workers. It is true that there are still anti-people's elements within the National Forces of Indonesia. This is also true concerning the republic as a whole." And he stated that "our Party has never had its own army."[4]

It was argued that it was necessary to follow a policy based on the possibility of a peaceful transition to socialism in order to counteract the propaganda of the reactionary forces, i.e., the propaganda that the communists are "terrorists," "monsters," etc. But what was the result? The repudiation of the use of armed struggle in achieving revolutionary goals only demonstrated the weakness of the revolutionary forces in the eyes of the reactionaries and created a feeling of insecurity among the masses.

The propaganda of the reactionaries can be counteracted by explanations and by action. The facts of history constitute the best sources to show the people the cruelty and brutality of the reactionaries. For example, the massacre committed by the reactionary Hatta government in 1948; the brutal "August Razzia" committed by the reactionary Sukiman government in 1951; the brutal armed suppression carried out by the reactionary generals against the peasantry in Sumatra, Java, Sulawesi, and other islands; the bombings carried out with planes furnished by the imperialist U.S., and the massacre committed by the reactionary rebels in 1958; etc., etc. Past experience provides the best lessons for teaching the people about the brutality of the reactionaries and the necessity to resist such brutality through armed struggle.

And the propaganda of action is still more important. The people will trust communists and have real confidence in the Party if communists genuinely defend their interests and show themselves prepared through sacrifice and armed struggle to safeguard the people from oppression and suppression by the exploiting classes. Communists must demonstrate that they are really cadres of working class and really on the side of the exploited masses; and are not merely pleaders with the "haves" nor collaborators with the "good people."

The Cuban *Granma* was quite correct when it said editorially: "We are not denying that in a given country, under certain very special conditions, an exception could occur in the future; nevertheless, not one case can be cited of a victorious revolution which has been able to avoid the use

[4] *Ibid.*

of violence, insurrection, or armed struggle as fundamental methods. This is a universal experience and the political position of the communist parties must be developed by taking into account what has been learned in the practical experience of revolution and by probing deeply into it."[5]

In the development of the Indonesian Revolution, many opportunities arose for the PKI to mobilize the workers and peasants into revolutionary armed forces and to counteract and liquidate the reactionary elements in the "National Armed Forces of Indonesia." These opportunities were ignored. For example, during the campaign for the liberation of West Irian from Dutch colonialism, the people were mobilized into voluntary units in anticipation of a clash with the Dutch imperialist forces. This should have been utilized by the Party to mobilize the workers and peasants and to set up bases for armed struggle. The Party did engage in this, but not with the objective of carrying out a socialist revolution. The movement was limited to liberating West Irian and it was disarmed after this aim was achieved.

Again during the campaign to crush the neo-colonialist regime of "Malaysia," the Party contributed greatly in mobilizing the masses, but without bringing in the idea of armed struggle for the socialist revolution. Thus the chance slipped by to set up bases for armed revolutionary struggle. Even worse, the Party left the leadership of the voluntary units in the hands of reactionary generals.

Another excellent opportunity came during the campaign for unilateral action to take over the land belonging to the big landowners. This action was led by the PKI. Day by day hundreds of thousands of peasants took part in the action. They faced armed suppression by the feudal forces backed by the reactionary generals. But the Party did not organize armed units of the peasants to counterattack. It left it up to the peasants to organize their own defense on the basis of their own courage and initiative. When this developed into a near-revolutionary crisis, with many clashes between the peasants and the reactionary forces, the campaign was stopped. The "great leader of the Revolution" Sukarno had given the order or "revolutionary command" to stop "any unilateral action." He gave the "command" that "every conflict or difference should be solved by consultation and agreement."

In accordance with the appeal from Sukarno in this situation, Aidit proposed the so-called "NASAKOM Code of Ethics."[6] Among other things this laid down the following: "Among all NASAKOM or MANIPOLIST groups there must be no confrontation. Only consultation to reach agreement."[7] Blood had been shed by the people, but the action was stopped. As the slogan put it, "We should have revolutionary patience."

[5] *Granma* (Havana), May 15, 1966 (English edition).

[6] NASAKOM is an abbreviation for Nationalism–Religion–Communism.—*Ed.*

[7] D. N. Aidit, *The Indonesian Revolution, Its Historical Background and Its Future* (Jakarta: Jajasan Pembaruan, 1964), p. 73.

During the struggle against the Japanese military occupation, the PKI was instructed or "advised," under Stalin's guidance, to cooperate with the Dutch imperialist government, to carry out "joint actions" against Japanese imperialism. (This also applied to all the other communist parties, who were told to cooperate with their respective bourgeois governments in fighting against the Axis.) Through such cooperation, the PKI hoped to "earn" independence for Indonesia at the end of the war. The program of the PKI as well as the CPN [Communist Party of the Netherlands] called for an "independent Indonesia within the Commonwealth of the Dutch Empire" as a step toward full independence. This remained a utopian dream. At the end of the war, the Dutch with the backing of the British and U.S. imperialists sent their armed divisions to reoccupy Indonesia. What attitude did the PKI take toward this?

A Republic had been proclaimed under the leadership of the bourgeois Sukarno. The masses as a whole were completely ready to defend their newly proclaimed Republic. But the PKI still clung to the old program of establishing Indonesia "within the Commonwealth of the Dutch Empire." Thus they followed the line of compromise in face of Dutch aggression. They supported the policy of the reactionary Sjahrir government in signing the Linggadjati Agreement, compromising with Dutch imperialism in 1947.

Then, still worse, the following government under Amir Sjarifuddin (a PKI leader at the time) signed the so-called "Renville Agreement." Under this catastrophic agreement, all pockets of the guerrilla forces were to withdraw from Dutch-occupied territory. The reactionary forces used this opportunity to send in reactionary armed units (under the command of Nasution, the present co-dictator) to dominate the liberated areas.

Realizing his mistake, Amir Sjarifuddin voluntarily surrendered his government back to Sukarno. This was followed by the formation of the most reactionary government, i.e., the Hatta regime. Under instructions from the U.S. and Dutch imperialists, this government introduced a program of "rationalizing" the Indonesian armed forces, which meant liquidating the people's armed units. The Hatta government wanted only "one type of army"; that is, the so-called "Indonesian National Armed Forces."

In 1948, Musso, who was one of the PKI leaders of the twenties and thirties, returned from abroad and called for a "New Road" for the PKI. Among other things this demanded renunciation of the old policy of compromise. The correction was accepted by the majority of the PKI leaders. But it was too late. Before the PKI could consolidate itself under the new program, the reactionary Hatta government launched a "white terror" in the so-called "Madium Affair." Thousands of Party members and most of the leaders were killed. This affair should have been a salutary lesson for the PKI not to abandon the method of armed struggle. Yet it was not.

When a federal Republic was established under the so-called "Round

Table Conference" Agreement, the PKI held it best to continue the struggle by "peaceful democratic" means. Aidit explained this as follows: "Against this RTC Agreement which was signed on November 2, 1949, by Hatta's government under instructions from U.S. imperialism, there were two opposing viewpoints in the party . . . the first group wanted to continue armed struggle against the federal Republic of the RTC . . . while the second, who based their position on revolutionary theory . . . wanted to maintain the Party's legality"; that is, continue the struggle by "parliamentary democratic" means.[8] Thus was a beginning provided for the repetition of the old errors.

On the question of the "Indonesian National Armed Forces," it is not correct to say that they are not "like the armies of imperialist countries or the army of India." At the beginning of the August 1945 Revolution there were no regular armed forces. Throughout the islands, the people formed their own armed units for defense against the imperialist aggression. There were many kinds of units. "The PKI built a Red Army, and had big influence on the Lasjkar Buruh [Workers' Army], Lasjkar Pesindo [Army of the Socialist Youth], Lasjkar Rakjat [People's Army], and Tentara Peladjar [Students' Corps]." Following the program of "rationalization" under Hatta, most of the irregular armies were liquidated. The most reactionary forces remained. After the RTC Agreement a new "National Armed Forces" was formed. This was an arithmetic combination of the previous Indonesian "National Armed Forces" plus the "Dutch East Indies Troops." These Dutch Troops (of Indonesian nationality) were much better trained. The remnants of the progressive units within the Indonesian National Armed Forces were subsequently liquidated. Of course, there were still some "pro-people's" elements within the Indonesian National Armed Forces, but as a whole they belonged to the same classification as the "armies of imperialist countries or the army of India."

The PKI followed the theory of two stages to the revolution; namely, a national democratic stage followed by a socialist stage.

"To confuse the two stages of the Indonesian Revolution and to say that we are already building socialism is demagogic, subjective, and reactionary. The national-democratic stage constitutes preparation for the socialist stage. The socialist stage cannot be achieved without first completing the national-democratic stage."[9] This was the stand of the PKI. It was said that this national-democratic stage constituted in essence a bourgeois-democratic stage, but of a new type; namely, one led by the working class.[10]

According to the Party's analysis, Indonesia at present still has a

---

[8] D. N. Aidit, *Forty Years of the PKI* (Jakarta: Jajasan Pembaruan, 1960), p. 59.
[9] D. N. Aidit, *The Indonesian Revolution, Its Historical Background and Its Future*.
[10] *Constitution of the PKI*, p. 7.

semicolonial and semifeudal system. And there are "three forces within Indonesian society; namely, first the diehards, i.e., the feudalists and compradors who collaborate with the imperialists. This is still a big force, but it is declining. Second, the progressive forces, i.e., the workers, peasants, petty bourgeoisie, and revolutionary intellectuals. This force is rather large and is increasing. Third, the middle-of-the-road forces, i.e., the national bourgeoisie and all other patriotic and other anticolonial forces, including the left group of landowners. This force is rather large. It stands between the reactionary and the progressive forces."[11]

About the alleged necessity to build a united front with the national bourgeoisie, Aidit said: ". . . I would like to emphasize once more that although an alliance with the national bourgeoisie is not as important as an alliance with the peasants, *the success and completeness of the leadership of the working class in the Revolution will be determined by the success of the alliance between the workers and the national bourgeoisie.* Therefore the communists must strive with all their power to preserve and further develop the alliance with the national bourgeoisie." (Emphasis added.)[12] And anyone in the Party who opposed the alliance with the national bourgeoisie was branded a "left deviationist."

In reality, following the policy of an alliance between the working class and the national bourgeoisie, the Party undermined the alliance between the working class and the peasants. The leadership of the "United National Front" was never in the hands of the working class or its Party, but always in the hands of the national or comprador bourgeoisie. In reality this line led to multiclass collaboration under the leadership of the national bourgeoisie, degenerating into compromises in ideology and in action under cover of the so-called "musjawarah for mufakat" (consulting to reach agreement).

Full acceptance of the so-called "Pantja-Sila philosophy"[13] (a product of the "genius-like thinking" of Sukarno) is an example of the open ideological compromise reflecting the "success" of multiclass collaboration. According to Aidit, "Pantja-Sila is a philosophy for unity. . . . In Indonesia one finds Catholic philosophy, Islamic philosophy, Buddhist philosophy, Protestant philosophy, Black Magic philosophy, Mystic philosophy . . . and Pantja-Sila unites what can be united."[14] In the same speech he said further: "The philosophy of Pantja-Sila cannot be separated from the philosophy of Empu Tantular 'Bhinneka Tuggal Ika' or 'Unity in Diversity.' This is very dialectical. 'Unity in Diversity'—differences, but in unity . . . I do not agree with liquidation of not only these various

---

[11] D. N. Aidit, *Forty Years of the PKI*, p. 83.

[12] D. N. Aidit, *Be a Good and a Better Communist* (Jakarta: Jajasan Pembaruan, 1964), p. 57.

[13] "Pantja-Sila" is "Five Principles": belief in a single god, national unity, humanitarianism, democracy, and social justice.

[14] D. N. Aidit, *In Defense of Pantja-Sila* (Jakarta: Jajasan Pembaruan, 1964).

kinds of philosophy but also political parties. In the second stage of the Revolution and the next stages, as differences remain among us, 'Unity in Diversity' and also Pantja-Sila will still be applicable. And in my opinion these differences *will exist forever* . . . thus in my opinion Pantja-Sila is also everlasting." (Emphasis added.) Is such a statement Marxist? Yet Aidit said, "I accept Pantja-Sila also from the Marxist-Leninist viewpoint." (In the same speech.)

Similar conclusions hold for the PKI's acceptance of the "genuine concept" of NASAKOM proposed by the demagogic bourgeois Sukarno. Aidit said, "Besides *uniting various kinds of classes and groups*, the National Front also unites various kinds of revolutionary ideas . . . namely: Islam, Nationalism, and Communism. . . . In the traditional struggle for national independence in Indonesia, we can find three political streams which were against Dutch colonialism; namely, nationalist, religious, and communist political thought. Thus it is natural to say that there will be national unity in Indonesia if these three political currents unite within the NASAKOM cooperation." And Aidit said, "This united national front has found its organization; namely, the 'National Front.' " At the top it is "headed by President Sukarno himself, who with his vice-presidents reflects the cooperation of NASAKOM . . . showing us how deeply rooted is the idea of the national united front among the masses. Now it is our duty to work hard to foster and consolidate it."[15]

During the struggle against the Dutch colonial power, it is true, there were many political groupings all of which were against the foreign imperialist rulers. But we could also see which were truly revolutionary, which were quasi-revolutionary, and which were opportunist. For example, the PNI [the Indonesian Nationalist Party founded by Sukarno] was clearly bourgeois. Then it degenerated into a vehicle of the national bourgeoisie, bureaucrats, compradors, and bribers. Thus during the struggle, it always swung opportunistically. And in times of revolutionary crisis, it was always on the side of the reactionary forces. A clear example was provided during the "Madium Affair" in 1948 when it served as the "vanguard" of the reactionary forces that murdered thousands of communist cadres and revolutionary rank-and-filers. Sukarno himself at the time issued the challenge: "Join Sukarno or Musso."

Again in the recent period (1964), during the campaign for unilateral action in taking over the land belonging to the big landowners, the members of this nationalist party joined in suppressing the peasant movement; and the "most progressive" leader of this party issued an order to "stop any unilateral action." Yet the PNI was considered by the PKI to be its true partner in the NASAKOM cooperation as the representative of the nationalist political stream.

Similarly with the Nadhatul Ulama, an Islamic scholars' party. The

[15] D. N. Aidit, *The Indonesian Revolution*, p. 72.

NU was very clearly the party of the feudalists and landowners. They used Islam as a cover for their reactionary activities in preserving their landownership and exploitation of the peasants. There is no instance in Indonesian history where this party has played a progressive or revolutionary role. Yet PKI sought to preserve unity with the NU within the so-called NASAKOM cooperation.

Besides the nationalist and religious parties in the so-called "National Front" led by Sukarno, there were other reactionary elements, including the generals. Thus the so-called "National Front" was not a revolutionary front led by the working class. It was not even the united front depicted theoretically in the documents of the PKI; namely, a united front of the working class, peasants, petty bourgeoisie, and national bourgeoisie led by the working class. It was clearly collaboration of all classes under the leadership of the demagogic bourgeois Sukarno.

Of course, the PKI cannot and must not struggle alone; the working class must not struggle alone. It needs allies. It should not isolate itself from the masses; but the masses are not the national bourgeoisie! In a country like Indonesia, in which poor peasants constitute more than 60 percent of the population, peasants are the real ally of the working class. The peasants should become the army of the revolutionary movement led by the working class. Poor city dwellers or the petty bourgeoisie are reserves to be drawn upon.

Toward the national bourgeoisie there should be a cautious and vigilant attitude. The revolutionary movement could and should support the progressive attitudes or actions of the national bourgeoisie, but there should be no class collaboration with the national bourgeoisie, since this can undermine the alliance between the working class and the peasants. The Communist Party should have its own policy based on the demands and experience of the most revolutionary class.

There is, naturally, the influence of Islamic teachings and nationalist thinking among the masses. This should be considered in propaganda work and in enlightening the masses. But it should never mask the class character of the struggle. The masses should be clear that this struggle is a class struggle and not a religious or racial struggle. The struggle is to overthrow the exploiters, to crush and abolish the system of exploitation of man by man. And the masses should even have a very concrete picture in their minds of the true character of the ruling class—the compradors, the bribers, the usurers, the feudalists, the ruling-class apparatus, the reactionary government apparatus, etc. They must be shown how and trained to overthrow these reactionary agencies. Only by such means can the united front among all the oppressed classes be tempered, strengthened, and made militant. Not through pleading with the "national bourgeoisie."

The PKI's program calls for making the Party "both a mass party and a cadre party." In 1952 the membership was only 10,000. In the national conference held that year, it was decided "to expand the membership from 10,000 to 100,000 *within six months*." (Emphasis added.)[16] And after the implementation of the first "Three-Year Plan" (1956–59), the membership increased to 1,500,000. At mid-year 1965 it was reported in the press to have reached 3,000,000. It is an amazing growth. A mass production of communist cadres! Perhaps no precedent exists for this in the history of communist parties. But is it guaranteed that all of these three million members were good revolutionists? Perhaps the CIA agents knew the answer to this better than the members themselves, so that the reactionary forces dared to launch a brutal and massive suppression of the PKI. Of course, the rapid recruitment by the PKI frightened the reactionary forces, but apparently they recognized the fatal weakness of the organization better than did the members of the PKI.

Obviously it is not easy to turn out good revolutionists with mass production methods. Aidit himself recognized the inherent weakness in this rapid growth and mass production of members. For example, he said, "In the beginning they become Party members because they seek protection from the rising revolutionary tide of the peasants. But their cultural level is higher than that of the agricultural workers and poor peasants, therefore within a short time they occupy the chair of leadership in the Party and for the time being the peasants grant them their trust. Besides there are cadres who joined the Party during the armed struggle in 1945 or even before then, thus in the days before the Party had an agrarian program. At the time they were good cadres; they implemented the Party's policy with high spirits against imperialism and took an active part in the campaign to crush the reactionary rebellion. But they are not agrarian cadres."[17]

Yet the slogan still remained, "Both mass party and cadre party." The fact is that the real cadres of the Party stood at a distance from the mass members of the Party. Thus the structure of the Party was more or less like a mass organization. The cadres did not completely trust the mass members and tended to form many tight, secret rings within the Party. The bureaucratic character of the Party was thus intensified. And in a time of crisis like last October, the Party could do nothing. Instead of issuing instructions on what to do to counteract the brutal massacre initiated by the reactionary forces, the top leadership scurried for safe spots (some of them going to President Sukarno's palace) which they knew about in advance, leaving the mass members in the lurch. Even two months after the disaster, there were still many in the rank and file who did not really know what was going on until they were massacred.

[16] D. N. Aidit, *Forty Years of the PKI*, p. 72.

[17] D. N. Aidit, *The Peasants Crush the Village Devils* (Jakarta: Jajasan Pembaruan, 1964), p. 55.

Experience shows that it is necessary to build a Party of real cadres who have a correct political line, who are actively engaged in political work among the workers and peasants, and who dare to conduct an armed struggle to achieve the goals of the Revolution. The Party must have a program "which reflects the thought and experience of an authentic revolutionary movement, aims at really aiding the highest possible revolutionary activity of the working class, while starting out from its most elementary demands." There can be no secrecy among the members, since all are cadres, while democratic centralism must rule. Everything is discussed by all members, but all act in unity!

Because of its policy of seeking to achieve socialism by means of a "parliamentary democratic" struggle and building a false "united national front," the Party concentrated its struggle at the top instead of the bottom. Collaboration at the top was considered to be the best way to inch toward socialism. Activities centered around the "coalition cabinet" beginning in 1955, then around the "cooperation cabinet" in 1959, the last one being the "NASAKOM cabinet" in 1963. The Party sought to gain power through "working together" with its enemies.

Considerable progress was registered throughout this period. The masses were moving toward a revolutionary crisis. But they were not armed—not armed with a correct political line and not armed with real weapons to crush the reactionary ruling class. The peasants were set in motion to take over the land, to smash the domination of the feudalists. But there was no clear political line. And even the land takeovers were stopped because of the "impending probable" formation of a "NASAKOM cabinet."

The Party did not protest the banning of strikes in industry because industry was considered to belong to the government, which was almost "a government of NASAKOM."

The Party did not issue instructions to counteract the military-fascist suppression through armed struggle because "Sukarno is still at the top," the "pro-people elements are still in the government."

The above criticism is not intended to undermine the role of the PKI nor to arouse distrust in Indonesian communism. But the revolutionary movement in Indonesia will be successful only if it learns from past experience, if it learns not to repeat the same mistakes. Only true revolutionists have the courage to correct errors. Criticism and self-criticism constitute the best method of reaching a more correct line. Mistakes are bad, but not to understand the mistakes is worse; and the worst is not to correct a mistake, having recognized it.

The situation is now quite favorable for a new line. People in arms are to be found everywhere. The line between friend and foe is very clear. The brutal character of the reactionary forces is very obvious. The opportunistic character of a bourgeois leader like Sukarno is very clear.

Whether the leadership of the Party likes it or not, the masses cannot wait out the increasing massacre against them any longer. What is needed now is a politically correct, class-conscious, and militant leadership, which will lead an armed struggle to abolish the whole system of exploitation of man by man in Indonesia and establish a workers' state!

Palestine

Because each side includes contradictory and opposing forces, the Israeli-Arab confrontations have long generated a series of myths which have tended to obscure the real revolutionary picture in the Middle East. In the West, for example, a great many radicals, who normally sympathize with the liberation movements of Asia, Latin America, and Black Africa but who, also, retain their sense of guilt for the liquidation of six million Jews by Nazi Germany, look upon the reactionary Arab regimes as proof that anti-Zionists are really anti-Semites. On the other hand, confirmed Jew-haters can oppose Israel on the safe issue that Zionists stole the Arabs' land. And, of course, both are right—as far as they go. For the majority of the Arab countries are indeed ruled by regimes much more antidemocratic that the Israeli government, and the Zionists did steal Arab lands. The only way, then, to look clearly at the situation, is to separate the two positions. Since Israel is a Zionist state, its ideology and activity should be laid bare without reference to what Hitler did in Europe or what Arab rulers do at home. And, likewise, the class conflict inside the Arab countries should be investigated on its own, without taking the statements of one or more of the rulers as representative of the masses.

The first point to remember is that Zionism was and is a colonialism. That is, settlers came to Palestine, seized or bought land, and decided to live there. Whether or not their ancestors had preceded them 2,000 years ago is immaterial to the form of society they established, the structure of the economy, how they treated the natives, etc. These settlers were a minority who imposed their ways on the majority. What were those ways? Usually, when foreign settlers colonize an area, they use the native population as a laboring class—for their benefit. But in Israel, this did not take place. The Jews or newcomers simply drove the Arabs or natives out. And that is exactly what the Zionist leaders wanted. In The Complete

Diaries of Theodor Herzl, *for example, that founder and leader of Zionism stated, long before the Jewish immigration began (in fact, Herzl was still thinking of Uganda, not Palestine, as the site for a Jewish state):*

When we occupy the land . . . we shall expropriate gently the private property on the estates assigned to us. We shall try to spirit out the penniless population across the border by procuring employment for it in the transit countries, and by denying it any employment in our country. . . . Both the process of expropriation and the removal of the poor must be carried out discreetly and circumspectly.

Zionism, then, was clearly meant to be territorial colonialism. And it still is. The following exchange is from the TV program Face the Nation *(CBS, June 11, 1967):*

SIDNEY GRUSON (of the *New York Times*): Is there any possible way that Israel could absorb the huge number of Arabs whose territory it has control of now?

MOSHE DAYAN (Israeli Defense Minister): Economically we can, but I think it is not in accord with our aims for the future. It would turn Israel into either a binational or a poly-Jewish-Arab state and we want to have a Jewish state. We can absorb them but it wouldn't be the same country.

GRUSON: Now is it necessary, in your opinion, to maintain this as a Jewish state and a purely Jewish state?

DAYAN: Absolutely, absolutely, we want a Jewish state like the French want a French state.

So Zionism is also territorial expansionism. From this policy alone, the Palestinian Arabs, who have been deprived of their land, their livelihood, and their country, are entitled to wage a patriotic war against the Israeli regime—and, by any analysis, revolutionaries and radicals should support them, at least until they have gained their right to self-determination.

Governments are not peoples. Even the Vietnamese, after massive bombings and invasion by half a million U.S. troops, still make a difference between the U.S. government (or, literally, Giac My, "U.S. imperialists") and the U.S. people. That distinction must be maintained by all revolutionaries, even if the Zionist state itself, by its essence, has deliberately confused—and fused—Zionism with the Jewish people. Thus, it is nonrevolutionary, in fact counterrevolutionary, to talk of "driving the Jews [or any people] into the sea."

The governments of Jordan, Saudi Arabia, Kuwait, and the Arab Gulf are feudal-fascist governments who are just as close to imperialism as is Israel. The Lebanese regime is run by a commercial and banking bourgeoisie in partnership with and dependent upon imperialism. The govern-

ments of Egypt, Syria, and Iraq are petty bourgeois—a class that, because it came to power without revolutionary struggle (via coups d'état), has no revolutionary consciousness (but lots of revolutionary-sounding rhetoric). In all those countries, the masses are agitated. They want or need a socialist revolution. To curtail their internal activities, these Arab regimes talk of "liberating" Palestine. Most don't really want to. And if some of the Ba'athi leaders in Syria and Iraq do, it is not in order to establish a new social structure for all of the Middle East, but as a way of generating a nationalist unity of the Arab countries. All these regimes, then, are either reactionary or opportunist, or both. All must be overthrown by people's revolution.

The above analysis, in brief, is detailed in the following articles. The first, by the Israeli Socialist Organization, a Marxist-Leninist group founded in 1962, explains best what Zionism is, why and how it has always been tied to imperialism (first British, then U.S.), why the Arab states' leaders play the revolutionary role, and what their links to imperialism are, and finally makes the class analysis needed by all genuine revolutionaries who are bent on launching people's war. The next article is the Seven-Point Platform of Al-Fatah, the Palestine Revolutionary Liberation Movement, which was one of the first Palestine organizations to engage in terrorist activity inside Israel (through its armed wing, Al Assifa). Though led by petty-bourgeois intellectuals, Al-Fatah did begin to make the kind of analyses described above and did condemn any other so-called movement which "did not spring from the masses themselves but was artificially imposed from above." It also stressed the fact that Al Assifa operations "are in no way aimed at the Jewish people as such with whom [Palestinians] have lived in harmony in the past for so many centuries" (pamphlet in English, January 1968).

The last two articles come from the same source, but technically have different authors—the Popular Front for the Liberation of Palestine (PFLP) and the Democratic Popular Front for the Liberation of Palestine or sometimes just the Democratic Front (DPFLP or just DPF). In August 1968, these two groups were still one, the PFLP. It had been formed shortly after the Six Day June 1967 defeat out of a merger between the Palestine branch of the Arab Nationalist Movement (ANM), which collapsed altogether as a consequence of the June fiasco, and a bunch of Palestine commandos known as the Jibril-Shruru group. Because strong Marxist-Leninist elements were included among the former, the PFLP as a whole came into conflict with the anticommunist Ba'ath Party of Syria (which arrested three PFLP leaders). The Jibril-Shruru group then swore allegiance to the Ba'athi regime and seceded from the PFLP. Thus, when PFLP met for its second annual conference in August 1968, it appeared solidly Marxist-Leninist. It was then that "The August Platform" (the third article below) was presented by the Left. The right wing, viewing itself outnumbered, voted for the platform—but only to gain time to regroup. When it did, the left wing quit the PFLP and set up the DPF. In 1969, all three liberation fronts represented here were coordinating their activities through the Palestine Armed Struggle Command; in 1970, however, the DPF, which disapproved of the command's "outside" (i.e., Egyptian and Ba'athi) influence, pulled out.

The DPF is by far the most revolutionary of the lot. It knows that a socialist Palestine can never be established until not only the Zionist but also the Arab reactionary and petty-bourgeois regimes are overthown. It also knows that another set of coups will accomplish nothing: genuine liberation, it says, . . . must come from the people—be they Arabs, Kurds, Armenians, or Jews—who must win their right to self-determination through long-protracted people's war.

ISRAELI SOCIALIST ORGANIZATION: THE OTHER ISRAEL*

OF all the problems bequeathed to the world by European imperialism, Palestine is among the most intractable. It is a peculiarly emotional issue, not only for those immediately involved. In the West the burden of guilt left by Hitler's crimes against the Jews has created a barrier which the injustices suffered by the Palestinian Arabs cannot penetrate. In many Arab countries hatred of the Jews is whipped up to divert the internal struggle against reactionary regimes into external channels. Western economic interests in the area, and the tendency of both East and West to exploit the situation for ideological or strategic advantage, further complicate the problem. To make matters worse, in both Israel and the Arab countries there is almost total ignorance of the other's history, people, and aspirations.

Emotions, however, whether rightly or wrongly based, cannot solve complex political problems. They are much more likely to lead to disaster. At the center of the emotional miasma surrounding Palestine lie two hard facts—the displaced Arab population who still live in refugee camps round Israel's border; and a new nation of Israel, with a complete class structure of its own, who by incessant propaganda and, to a certain extent, real achievement, is beginning to carve a place in the world. Neither can be forgotten, ignored, or annihilated. A political solution must sooner or later be found that is both realistic and just. The alternative

---

* Theses submitted for discussion to the Israeli Socialist Organization in August 1966 (later adopted) and published in English in pamphlet form by *Matzpen* (*Compass*), which is the ISO's Hebrew monthly journal (Tel Aviv), July 1968, followed by declaration by *Matzpen* from the same pamphlet.

is—eventually—war, which will at best only defer, not solve, the political problems.

In the first half of the twentieth century the population of Palestine was about 700,000, the overwhelming majority being Arabs. There were various minority communities, including some 70,000 Jews. Economically and politically these Jews were an integral part of the indigenous population, differing only by religion. They had nothing to do with colonization or Zionism.

The first step in the modern Jewish colonization of Palestine was taken in 1870 when Baron Edmund de Rothschild of France acquired some land near Jaffa and established an agricultural school (Mikveh Israel—"Gatherer of Israel"). This was followed by the building of some twenty villages, inhabited by some 5,000 Jews, mostly from Russia. Up to 1900 the Baron invested about £2 million in Palestine. The Rothschilds were (and still are) among the world's leading financiers, with the French and British branches of the family holding influential positions in the economy of these two countries. Baron Edmund combined his Jewish sentiments with his support for French interests in colonizing Palestine following the Algerian model. He wished to amalgamate the emigration of East European Jews with the colonial interests of French imperialism. He did not entertain the idea of an independent Jewish state in Palestine (he was no Zionist) but used his financial power in the Ottoman treasury in order to prepare a new sphere of influence for French interests, employing Jewish immigrants as settlers. His Palestine activities were thirty years old when Zionism was born.

Political Zionism was founded in 1897 at a congress held in Basle, Switzerland. It differed significantly from the Rothschild colonization in that it declared its intention of solving the Jewish problem by creating a national Jewish state. However, the Viennese journalist T. Herzl, the founder and first leader of the Zionist movement, did not consider Palestine as the indispensable location for such a state. On the contrary, he advocated Uganda as the most suitable place for Jewish colonization. But the majority of the Zionists rejected the Uganda scheme and insisted on fulfilling the Jewish religious sentiment toward Palestine.

From the very beginning, Zionism sought to achieve its aim by means of a deal with one imperialist power or another. The guiding principle of Zionist diplomacy was always to affiliate itself with that world power within whose sphere of influence Palestine happened to be. Herzl courted mainly the Turkish Sultan and the German Kaiser. After World War I Zionism was oriented toward British imperialism. Again after World War II Zionism switched its orientation to the U.S. and occasionally flirted with France.

When at the beginning of this century organized Zionist immigration started to pour into Palestine, the surprising fact that the country was already populated could no longer be ignored. Like every colonizing society, the Zionist settlers had to shape a definite policy toward the indigenous population. Here we come to the specific feature of Zionism which distinguishes it from all other colonizations of modern times. The European settlers in other colonies sought to exploit the riches of the country (including the labor potential of the "natives") and invariably turned the former population into a proletarian class in a new capitalist society. But Zionism wanted not simply the resources of Palestine (which were not very great in any case) but the country itself to serve for the creation of a new national state. The new nation was to have its own classes, including a working class. The Arabs were, therefore, not to be exploited, but totally replaced.

The Rothschild colonization clashed with the Palestine Arabs only over one issue—land ownership. The Baron bought land from feudal Effendis, sometimes by bribing the Ottoman administration, and drove the fellahin off the land. The expropriated fellahin were then employed as laborers in the Baron's settlements, following the usual colonial pattern. The Zionist colonization, however, raised the slogan "Jewish labor." Aspiring to create a Jewish working class as part of a new nation, it advocated a transition of people from middle-class occupations to manual labor, and it insisted that Jewish employers use Jewish labor only. The Zionists, therefore, clashed not only with the expropriated Arab peasants but also with the interests of the Baron's settlers who preferred to use the cheaper Arab labor. This issue was the main conflict within the settlers' community during the first three decades of the century. The main protagonists of the "Jewish labor" policy were the left-wing elements within Zionism. The bourgeois elements were always tempted to employ the cheaper Arab labor. Had the bourgeois attitude prevailed, Palestine might have developed along much the same lines as Algeria, South Africa, or Rhodesia. It was, however, the left wing of Zionism which prevailed. The funds of the Zionists' movement were often used to cover the difference between the cost of Arab labor and the more expensive Jewish labor.

The nascent Zionist society clashed with all the various classes of Palestine Arab society. It brought from Europe capital, modern technological know-how, and skills. Jewish capital (often backed by Zionist funds) gradually displaced the feudal elements simply by buying up their lands, and Zionist regulations forbade resale of land to Arabs. Possessing technological and financial advantages, the Zionist capitalist economy blocked the emergence of an Arab capitalist class. Having clashed with the Arab peasants by driving them off their land, Zionism also prevented them from becoming a proletariat in the Jewish sector of the economy. Since the Arab sector's capitalist development was retarded and hindered, the peasants (as well as the Arab intelligentsia) found it hard to get any employment at all—except in the British Mandate administration and public services.

This socioeconomic deformation was reflected in the political sphere.

Since the bourgeoisie, the proletariat, and the peasantry were denied a
normal path of development, they did not produce parties and leaders
of sufficient caliber. Political leadership of the Palestine Arabs inevitably
remained in the hands of the landowning class, who, although they liquidated themselves as a class by selling their land to the Zionists, made
enormous financial gains by these transactions. They retained the political
leadership of the Arabs by covert cooperation with the Zionists and the
British. In order not to be branded as traitors they assumed in public the
most extreme anti-Zionist stands, even declaring the sale of the land to
the Zionists to be treason.

But understanding existed between the Zionists and the Hashemite kings,
who were the main ally of British imperialism in the Middle East. In
1922 in London King Faisal (the son of Sherif Hussein of Mecca) signed
a joint political agreement with Weizmann, chairman of the Zionist movement. Article 3 of this agreement *endorsed* the Balfour Declaration. Article 4 states: "All necessary measures shall be taken to encourage and
stimulate immigration into Palestine on a large scale." This agreement
was the ancestor of the secret agreement between Ben Gurion and Abdullah in 1948, when they divided Palestine between them and virtually
arranged the result of the war.

Meanwhile, the anti-imperialist struggle throughout the Arab countries
reached an unprecedented scale. In Syria, a general strike was declared
in 1936 against French imperialism. This strike proved to be effective
and on the whole successful. It brought Syria substantially nearer political
independence. This made a great impression in Palestine, and there, too,
a long general strike was declared. Conditions in Palestine were, however,
very different because of the presence of Zionist economical infrastructure,
which did not, of course, take part in the strike. Moreover, the Zionists
exploited the fact that Arab workers in government administration and
services (e.g., railroads, ports, etc.) were on strike, and that Arab commerce was paralyzed to secure a grip on these large and important
sectors of the economy. The strike coincided with a great influx of Jewish
capital from Europe. Thus, while the Arab sector of the economy suffered a blow from which it never recovered, the Zionists secured a new
and decisive hold on the whole economy.

British imperialism, which ruled Palestine from 1918 to 1948, used the
familiar tactics of "divide and rule," exploiting to the utmost the possibilities which rivaling nationalistic movements offered. For the masses
it employed nationalist and religious incitement and provocation, which
proved to be effective. It employed Jewish policement against Arab population and vice versa. For the leaders it employed diplomacy, "white
papers," round-table conferences, giving contradictory promises to both
sides and acting as "mediators." It succeeded in diverting what threatened
to become an anti-imperialist struggle into the channels of nationalistic
strife.

The calculated ambiguities and "contradictions" in the British foreign policy increased the unrest and hostilities between Jews and Arabs, and involved considerable bloodshed. In the late thirties this factor turned from an asset into a liability. The religious, feudal, and bourgeois elements in Arab nationalism welcomed the rise of fascism in Germany and Italy, as fellow enemies of British imperialism. Contacts between these camps worried the British. The oil fields, pipelines, and Suez Canal seemed in danger. Zionist demands for more independence and increased immigration quotas for European Jews fleeing from persecution were other issues which had to be handled, too. But the Foreign Office, confident that the Nazis would never consider the Zionists as potential allies, produced another white paper in 1939, aimed at currying favor with the Arabs. It stated:

"His Majesty's Government now declare unequivocally that it is not part of their policy that Palestine should become a Jewish state. . . . It should be a state in which the two peoples in Palestine, Arabs and Jews, share authority in government in such a way that the essential interests of each are secured. . . ."

Before the war, the Palestine economy (especially the industrial and manufacturing sector) was dominated by the British metropolitan economy. The development of local light industry particularly was hampered by imports of consumer goods from Britain. Partly as a result of this, even in the Jewish community (numbering on the eve of war about 500,000 out of a total of 1,750,000), noticeable anti-British tendencies were beginning to form.

The war brought about an unprecedented boom in the Palestine economy. Palestine became a major base for the British garrison in the Middle East, which had to be housed, clothed, equipped, and fed. Supply lines from Britain were disrupted by the war, and the British economy was overstrained by the war effort. The British had to rely to a large extent on the local economy, and they encouraged its rapid development. In the Arab sector unemployment disappeared as thousand of workers were employed to build camps, roads, and airfields. But whereas Arab industry was not ready to benefit fully from the enormously increased demand, the Jewish sector was already organized along modern lines and had considerable reserves of manpower.

It therefore drew the maximum benefit from the increased demand and entered a period of great expansion, known as "The Prosperity." Whole industries grew from modest beginnings to formidable size within a period of four or five years. By 1942 there were 6,600 Jewish industrial enterprises, employing about 56,000 workers and producing at the rate of £20 million per year. The level of production in 1942 was more than double that of 1939 in the food, textile, metal, machinery, and chemical industries—treble in the electrical appliances industry. The Palestine diamond industry (exclusively in Jewish hands) grew at an even more spectacular rate as the European centers were cut off from their raw materials (in South Africa): from 1,000 carats (valued at £25,000) in 1940 to 58,000 carats (valued £2.6 million) in 1943 and to 138,000 carats (£6 million) in 1945.

When the war ended, industrial growth slowed abruptly, and imports from Britain again menaced local industry—but by now the wartime growth had made the Jewish sector of the economy a force to be reckoned with. It did not want to return to the prewar dominance by Britain, and by now a much larger section of the Jewish population had a stake in maintaining industrial expansion. This new situation provided the economic impetus for the postwar demands of the Jewish community for political independence. Unlike the Arabs, the Jewish community had made no such demands before World War II because it was clear that an independent Palestine would be a state with an Arab majority. The new Jewish dominance of the economy was one of the main factors that brought about a change of policy.

Even more significant were new political factors, which derived chiefly from the rise and defeat of fascism in Europe. During the thirties many right-wing Arab nationalists had regarded German and Italian fascism as allies in the struggle against British imperialism. Like other nationalists throughout the British empire, they maintained this attitude throughout the war. In 1945 this policy was shown to have been wrong in principle, and also to be a grave tactical and moral disadvantage. Few Arabs served in the British army and, as a result, the Arabs, unlike the Jews, failed to gain experience in modern organized warfare. Moreover, the right-wing nationalists, having supported the losing side, were demoralized by the allied victory and found it difficult to resume the momentum of the prewar struggle for political independence.

For the Jews the question of which side to support in the war hardly arose at all. A fascist Zionist party had existed during the thirties and had collaborated closely with Italian and Polish fascism. But the majority of Zionists maintained their pro-British orientation. By 1939 Nazi policy toward the Jews had forced even the fascist faction into the British camp. Of the 500,000 Palestine Jews, 50,000 volunteered for the British forces, encouraged and organized by the Zionist leadership. By the time the war ended 10 percent of the Jewish population had considerable military experience.

The Nazi crimes against the Jews also gave Zionists an entirely new status in the international arena. Previously, it had been a minority trend amongst the world's 18,000,000 Jews, with the majority either indifferent or hostile. After the extermination of 6,000,000 European Jews by Nazism, many more were attracted by the idea of an independent Jewish state. Zionism, which had always accepted anti-Semitism, became a major political tendency even among Jews who had no intention of personally emigrating to Palestine. The world powers began to regard Zionism as the representative of the whole Jewish people.

The war left large numbers of Jewish refugees in Europe, many of whom, encouraged by the Zionists, wanted to emigrate to Palestine. The Palestine Arabs had no wish to become a minority in their own country and pressed the British government to stop Jewish emigration. The Zionists thereupon began to organize clandestine emigration on a large scale. The British tried to prevent this not only because of Arab pressure but also because they were worried by the rising tendencies toward independence among the Palestine Jews. World opinion, especially in Europe and the U.S., was still reeling with the shock of discovering the enormity of the Nazi war crimes and inevitably sympathized with the refugees. The resulting political atmosphere was hostile both to the British government and to Arab nationalism. This atmosphere persists today and is one of the major assets of Zionism.

The emergence of the U.S. as a major world power after World War II and the decline of British imperialism brought about a gradual shift of Zionist orientation from Britain toward the U.S. A strong Zionist lobby was built up in Washington and at the same time the pro-American elements in world Zionism gained supremacy over the pro-British faction.

The combined effect of these economic and political factors precipitated the clash between the Zionists and the British government. The war had transformed the Jewish community in Palestine into a nation with its own economy, army, political organizations, language, and ideology. Its economic interests had become incompatible with direct colonial rule. It clashed with British policy on immigration, in a world atmosphere favorable to Zionism and hostile to Britain. Zionist reorientation toward the U.S. and the growing American interests in the Middle East hastened the collision.

In this new situation the Zionists demanded political independence in Palestine. The right wing demanded immediate independence for the whole of Palestine under Jewish minority rule; the centrists favored the partition of Palestine between Arabs and Jews; the left-wing Zionists (among them parts of the present-day "Mapam" Party) wanted to postpone independence until the Jews became a majority through increased immigration.

In essence there were three parties involved in the Palestine problem. British imperialism; the Jewish minority (about .6 million); and the Arab majority (about 1 million). Each of these had its own demands, in conflict with the other two. But—mainly owing to the deformation of Arab society by the process of Jewish colonization—the Palestine Arabs did not in fact constitute a major independent political force in the period 1945–1947. The struggle was waged mainly between the Zionists and the British.

During these years a series of conflicts, accompanied by armed violence, occurred between the Jewish community and the British administration. The Palestine Arabs, although they still outnumbered the Jews by about two to one, remained relatively passive—a complete reversal of the situation during the twenties and thirties, when Arab struggle for independence had a mass character and often used violent means. The British government, preoccupied with a fuel crisis and Indian independence, neared desperation.

In 1947 Britain referred the Palestine problem to the U.N., expecting disagreement in the U.N. to lead to a renewal of the mandate. This would lend a new lease of life to the precarious British authority in the area. In November 1947, the General Assembly adopted a resolution recommending the partition of Palestine into two independent, but economically linked, states. This solution was a victory for Zionism and was strongly opposed by the Arabs (who, of course, demanded an undivided independent Arab Palestine) and by British imperialism which struggled to retain its influence and power.

Both the U.S. and the USSR supported the resolution; the U.S. because they considered it a convenient way of gaining a foothold in the Middle East and replacing British imperialism; the USSR because it considered it the most practical way to drive British imperialism out of one of its strongholds. The USSR probably underestimated the strong links between Zionism and American imperialism. As for the Foreign Office, it was worried not only because the creation of a Zionist state meant loss of influence to the U.S. but also because the establishing of an independent Arab state in Palestine could have repercussions in the Arab world.

After the U.N. partition resolution, the British tried to provoke the Palestine Arabs against the Jewish population, to prove that a British presence was necessary to keep law and order. This attempt failed. Next, the British organized in Syria an irregular volunteer army (headed by Fawzi el Kaukji) which entered Palestine and attacked Jewish settlements. When this attempt failed too, the British finally decided to employ the regular armies of Trans-Jordan, Syria, Egypt, and Iraq in order to wage open war against the Zionist state, which (according to the U.N. resolution) was to come into existence on 15 May 1948. The political and military plans for this invasion were drawn up by General I. C. Clayton (one of the main British colonial agents in the Middle East) in a meeting of the Arab chiefs of staff held early in 1948 at Bludan, Syria.

The 1948 war became a military conflict between the Zionists and the Arab armies. These armies were not, however, playing an independent role for achieving Arab independence in Palestine, but rather serving British interests, through the puppet regimes of Farouk, Abdullah, and Nuri el-Said. The war was used by these regimes to divert the internal anti-imperialist struggle (especially in Egypt and Iraq) into an imperialist-sponsored Holy War. The conduct of the war exposed the utter corruption of these regimes and hastened their downfall.

The fate of Palestine was decided not only on the battlefield but also in secret talks between the Zionist leaders and Abdullah. These talks started immediately after the adoption of the partition resolution by the U.N. and went on until 1950. In these talks the two "friendly enemies," although ostensibly at war with each other, agreed to divide between them the territory which the U.N. resolution had allotted to the Palestinian Arabs, as well as Jerusalem which, according to the resolution, was to become a separate unit under the U.N. administration. The armistice agreement coincided, more or less, with the results of the political negotiations between the Zionist leaders and Abdullah.

A new set-up was thus established in Palestine: 20,000 square kilometers (instead of the 14,000 square kilometers allotted to it in the U.N. resolution) became Israel; and the remaining territory (except the Gaza Strip) was annexed by Abdullah, who renamed his kingdom "Jordan" (instead of Trans-Jordan). This new set-up expressed the new balance of influence among the Western powers. The area of the Zionist state was lost to British imperialism and came under U.S. influence; while the area annexed by Abdullah represented the remnants of British influence. This new division of spheres of influence received formal confirmation in the Tripartite (U.S., Britain, and France) Declaration of May 1950.

This state of affairs, established as a consequence of the 1948 war, persists today and is referred to as the "status quo" in the Middle East. It is an inherently unstable situation because the war was not terminated by a political solution of the Palestine problem but only by a temporary Armistice Agreement. Since Israel is interested in preserving the "status quo," it has become more and more dependent on the Western powers who guarantee its continuance. The same applies, of course, to the Jordanian regime, which because of its military weakness also depends indirectly on Israel. In spite of their seemingly hostile relations, these two regimes share a common interest—to preserve the "status quo." Thus, the sum total of the relations between imperialism, the Zionists, and the various Arab parties which was known up to 1948 as "The Palestine Problem" was transformed in 1948 into the "Israeli-Arab conflict," the latter being a direct continuation (albeit in a new form) of the former.

The losers and victims of the 1948 war were the Palestine Arabs, who hardly participated in the war. Their right to self-determination, which previously nobody—not even the Zionist leaders—had denied, was violated. Most of them became homeless refugees. The fate of those who remained in the area held by Israel was hardly better. They have lived ever since under military rule and are subject to constant and severe repression. The land remaining in Arab hands was gradually but systematically expropriated, often by administrative subterfuge, to make way for Zionist development. The Arabs are second-class citizens in their own country.

In the early fifties the anti-imperialist struggle intensified throughout the Arab world. In the Arab East this intensification was, in part, a result of the Palestine war. Britain, already too weak to defend its old positions, had to accept the fact that the U.S. was becoming dominant in this part of the world as in others. The global policy of the U.S. to surround the USSR by a chain of bases and military pacts was welded in the Middle East with the traditional British colonial policy into a single anti-Soviet and imperialist policy. Throughout the fifties these two powers tried to create a military alliance of Middle Eastern countries, to serve as a link in the chain of anti-Soviet alliances stretching from Scandinavia to Korea and to strengthen Western domination in the Middle East.

This policy encountered great difficulties, because the Arab masses were aware of its imperialist character and opposed it violently. On the government level, the consistent refusal of Egypt and Syria to participate in such pacts undermined the whole of Western policy in the region. The Israeli government, on the other hand, was always willing to participate actively in any such scheme, not only because of the traditional links between Zionism and imperialism, but also (and more specifically) because Israel's adherence to the "status quo" made it a natural ally of imperialism—an ally who identified his own national interests—indeed his very existence—with the imperialist presence in the Middle East.

The Israeli position was fully understood and utilized by the West. Whenever the governments of Egypt, Syria, or Jordan attacked the Anglo-American schemes, Israel was used as a threat against them. These threats often materialized in the form of armed raids by Israeli forces. Jordan, particularly, was raided during the period when the el Nabulsi government there conducted anti-Western policies. Usually, after such a raid, the Arab government concerned would turn to the West and ask for arms. The reply was always: "Join the Baghdad Pact, and you will get arms."

This Western policy was finally defeated when, after the big Israeli raid on Gaza on 28 April 1955, Nasser refused to submit to Western pressure and turned to Czechoslovakia for arms. This broke the arms monopoly of imperialism in the area, and considerably weakened its political influence. From this time onwards, the Soviet Union emerged as a protagonist in the Middle East scene. This development, followed by the nationalization of the Suez Canal, drove Britain and France to desperation. Employing an Israeli invasion of Egypt as a prearranged pretext, they launched a direct military attack on Egypt in order to regain possession of the Canal and to overthrow the neutralist and anti-imperialist governments in the Middle East. For Israel the failure of the Suez invasion meant that she was unable to force the Arab world to accept the "status quo." From that time the Palestine problem entered a period of stalemate.[1]

Israel is the most stable and reliable ally of imperialism in the area. In return, imperialism—which has an interest in preserving such an ally— grants Zionists its protection. Their hope is that the West will always be able to grant them this protection and will never let them down. Zionism has a powerful ally in Western public opinion. The 5,000,000 American Jews constitute a strong pressure group exerting considerable influence not only on U.S. official policy but also on American public opinion. Even that section of Western public opinion which opposes imperialism is reluctant to criticize Israel. This is a result of the deep feeling of guilt in the West after the massacre of 6,000,000 Jews by the Nazis. Even socialists in the West often mistakenly identify anti-Zionism with anti-Semitism. Zionist propaganda has another great advantage: It aims at consolidating an existing situation and therefore preaches peace. Arab policy wishes to change the situation, and cannot simply preach peace, but has the difficult task of explaining the injustices of the "status quo." Thus the Zionists appear as peace-seekers, the Arabs as aggressors.

The Zionists rely on military forces; knowing that eventually the balance of conventional forces will be against them, they have recently started to develop nuclear weapons. They hope that possession of such weapons will make it impossible for the Arabs to upset the "status quo." Alternatively, should the Great Powers force them to give up possession of nuclear weapons, the Zionists hope to get in exchange for this an East-West guarantee to maintain the "status quo."

In the long run, the Zionist policies cannot succeed. Even if they do manage to maintain the "status quo" for a relatively long period, Israeli will remain a small besieged fortress, economically unviable and dependent on outside economic aid for its very existence (about $400 million per year have been flowing into the country since 1950 to balance a constant deficit in the balance of payments). Its own natural resources are meager, and its markets extremely limited. It cannot compete with the advanced economies of the European countries, and Arab markets are closed to it. It is only the worldwide fund-raising activities of Zionist organizations such as the Jewish Agency, and the reparations paid by the Germans, which keep the standard of living in Israel at an artificially high level. If Israel's carefully cultivated image in the West—of a democratic, refugee-sheltering, peace-loving country — were seriously dented, the economic consequences could be very serious. The inevitable decline of imperialist influence, coupled with the progressive unification of the Arab world, will make Israel's position even more precarious.

Arab attitudes can be broadly divided into two: those of the feudal

[1] Until the Six Day War. This was written prior to the Israeli attack.—*Ed.*

regimes; and those of the bourgeois nationalist parties. Superficially similar, the attitudes of the two groups are backed by very different deeds and motivations. Neither proposes a political solution to the Palestine problem.

The Arab feudal regimes, like Zionism, had always been natural allies of Western imperialism. Today, as in the past, they share common political interests with Zionism as both depend for their existence on imperialist influence in the area. The feudal regimes cannot uphold such a policy publicly in the Arab world where the masses are anti-imperialist and clamor for political independence. To cover up their cooperation with imperialism they put out virulent anti-Zionist and anti-Jewish propaganda. A classic example occurred during King Faisal's visit to Washington in June 1966. While conferring with President Johnson on containing Nasser and his policies, and thereby running the risk of revealing his pro-imperialist policies to the Arab world, a press question gave him the opportunity to declare that "all the Jews in the world support Israel, and therefore are enemies of the Arabs." The mayor of New York City, which has more Jews than Israel itself, promptly canceled an official dinner with him. Faisal could only congratulate himself on this chance to consolidate his tarnished image in the Arab world.

Publicly, the feudal regimes advocate the annihilation of Israel: Privately—they cooperate with it. In some cases (Jordan particularly), they depend on it for their existence. Whenever the Palestinian Arabs in Jordan threaten the regime of King Hussein (grandson of Abdullah), the Israeli army moves to the armistice lines, ready to intervene if Hussein is overthrown. The rebellious masses are immediately "pacified" on the grounds that only Hussein's army can defend them from the aggressive Israelis. Although Hussein's throne has rocked violently more than once, it has withstood all attacks up to now, thanks to the intervention of Israel, which would regard the overthrow of Hussein as a violation of the "status quo"—a new regime in Jordan might refuse to recognize the Abdullah–Ben Gurion pact of 1948, and the Tripartite Declaration of 1950.

Thus, whereas on the surface the feudal regimes appear to be the most extreme enemies of Zionism, they are as concerned as Israel to consolidate and perpetuate imperialist influence and presence in the area. Zionism, and Arab feudalism, are, as always, "friendly enemies."

The bourgeois and petty-bourgeois parties throughout the Arab world approach the Palestine problem through the United Nations resolutions. This policy was first formulated by Nasser at the Bandung Conference (1955) and it was unanimously adopted. This policy meant essentially that Israel should repatriate the Arab refugees (according to a 1949 U.N. resolution); and that Israel should give up the territory annexed by it as a result of the secret pact with Abdullah. This policy would reduce the area of Israel but would not affect its Zionist character.

In fact, this conciliatory program (which represents a considerable concession to Zionism) would not provide a stable solution of the Palestine problem. It would probably be as dangerous as the "status quo." A smaller Zionist state would still be dependent on Western imperialism, and as such would continue to threaten Arab progress toward unity and socialism. This program was raised again by Bourguiba in order to embarrass Nasser, who dropped this formula after Suez, realizing that although the slogan of adhering to the U.N. resolutions had an attractive propaganda value, it did not provide for a stable solution. Moreover, since Nasser's approach to the problem of Arab unity is a basically bourgeois one, relegating class contradictions within Arab society to second place, he was led to seek an understanding with the reactionary regime in Jordan. But this regime is as much opposed to the U.N. partition resolution as the Zionists are, because Jordan too annexed part of Palestine territory. Nasser is now not so keen to raise the U.N. formula.

Today, the Nasserites and Ba'athists do not have any political solution. Instead, they talk in military terms and argue endlessly with each other whether to go to war with Israel ("liberate Palestine") in the near future (Syrian Ba'ath) or to postpone the war until a considerable progress is made toward Arab unity (Nasser). This military approach evades the main question. War can, at the very most, serve as a means to political solution; it can never replace one. Even if a war against Israel were to be won, the question of the political future of Palestine would remain unsolved. A military Arab victory would, at most, destroy the Zionist regime, but 2,000,000 Jews would remain, and probably constitute a problem similar to the Kurdish problem, unless a political solution is implemented. As is well known, the Nasserites and the Ba'athists do not have a political solution even to the Kurdish problem.

The slogan of "liberating Palestine," although emotionally satisfying, has even more serious political disadvantages. In the first place, it forces moderate Israelis and even anti-Zionist Israelis (there are some) to side with the Zionist government in sheer self-defense. The result is a rare degree of solidarity between public opinion and government. Internal dissension, which would inevitably arise in a normal situation, is muffled. In this atmosphere few Israelis dare question their country's reliance on imperialism, which at least protects their lives.

Moreover, this simple slogan damages the Arab case in the world arena. Apart from the unpopularity of military solutions, it also has the fault of identifying an entire population with the policies of the state, and requiring them to pay the prices for those policies. Such oversimplifications are no longer acceptable to progressive world opinion, especially anti-imperialist elements who demand political solutions to political problems. Even the North Vietnamese are careful to draw a distinction between the policies of Washington and the American people. As a result of these factors the Arab nationalists, in spite of the moral rightness of their case, have been consistently losing the propaganda war ever since 1948.

Any serious political solution to the Palestinian problem must take into consideration that, unlike the European settler communities in South Africa, Rhodesia, or Algeria, the Jews in Palestine constitute not an upper class but a whole nation, with a complete class structure of its own. The fact that this new nation was created artificially through Zionist immigration does not alter the fact that it exists. Whereas the political set-up of this community can be changed or destroyed, the nation itself cannot be eliminated. A stable solution must therefore fulfill two basic requirements: It must abolish the Zionist character of Israel; and it must establish the self-determination of this nation in a form which is in accordance with the interests of the Arab masses, with socialism and unification.

It is clear that the existence of an Israeli state (whatever the size of its territory) isolated from the Arab world is contrary to the interests of the Arab masses. It is also contrary to the interests of the Israeli masses. Such a state cannot exist without outside support and will always necessarily be dependent on imperialism. The inherent instability of such a situation will always be a threat over the heads of the Israelis. A stable solution must therefore provide for a non-Zionist form of self-determination for Israel within the framework of an Arab Socialist Union. The Palestine problem is, in fact, closely linked with the class struggle in the Arab world and with the problem of unification. This is the reason why those forces in the Arab world which are unable to solve the problem of Arab unity are also unable to solve the Palestine problem.

Another aspect of the Palestine problem is the self-determination of the Palestinian Arabs. Should they exercise this right and establish a state of their own? Naturally, both the Zionists and Hussein are hysterically opposed to any such suggestion. But progressive elements are also undecided on this issue, believing that the creation of a new small Arab state would have a harmful effect on the process of unification.

Here, too, any solution must be compatible with the interests of unification and socialism throughout the Middle East. If a political form of self-determination of the Palestine Arabs be established (because it is theirs by right) it must come about in a way that will conform with the interests of the masses throughout the Middle East. A unification based on the denial of the right to self-determination is morally, and politically, wrong, and whenever practiced in the past has introduced suspicion, mistrust, and instability into the union. If these are to be eliminated from the union of the Middle Eastern states, the fundamental national rights of the constituent members must be fulfilled. They should be given up by consent, not coercion.

The Palestine problem demonstrates the fact that nationalistic policies are unable to overcome the problem of unification of national states and unable to solve the problem of national oppression. They can only turn oppressed into oppressor. The underlying problems remain. Only those socialists who have gone beyond nationalistic ideology and policies hold the key to a stable solution to the joint problems of abolishing national oppression and unifying the national states.

*   *

The 1967 June War exposed and succinctly expressed fundamental contradictions and processes in the countries of the Middle East. In Israel, the Zionist character of this state and of its leadership was made more prominent; the propensity for annexation and expansion, half-dormant since the Suez War, has now reawakened. The bonds between Israel's Zionist regime and imperialism have also been manifested and strengthened sevenfold.

On the eve of the June War, Israel's rulers still disclaimed any desire for territorial expansion. But on the morrow all these declarations were forgotten. Appetite was whetted by eating. The truth is that the propensity for annexation and expansion had always been inherent in all the trends of political Zionism—not only in the Heruth Party, which openly declared it, but also in the more moderate trends that did not openly admit it, for political and propagandist reasons, when times did not seem opportune.

After the June War, Israel controlled the whole of the Palestine mandate territory as well as vast tracts of Egyptian territory and a region in the south of Syria. In the beginning, the leaders of Israel claimed that in this situation, where "Israel holds all the cards," they would be able to force a settlement to their liking upon the Arabs, who would have to accept Israel's terms. But these hopes proved to be false. Victory in the war, far from solving the Israeli-Arab problem, has actually intensified it.

The historical conflict between Zionism and Israel in its present form, on the one hand, and the Arab world, on the other, springs from the fact that the "Zionist endeavor" was from its very beginning a planned and deliberate process of colonization by outsiders who settled in this country, displacing its indigenous people; in this, Zionism was backed by imperialism and sided with imperialism against revolutionary developments in the Arab world.

The short-sighted attempt of Zionism to exploit this "opportune moment" for territorial gains and for forcing its own terms upon the Arabs will no doubt boomerang back in the long run on Israel itself. The belief that Israel's control over vast territories would improve her current security has also proven mistaken. Victory in the war has not put an end to guerrilla and sabotage actions. On the contrary, in this new situation they have assumed larger dimensions. But whereas world public opinion before the war largely took exception to such actions, they are now increasingly regarded as natural and legitimate means of resistance of a conquered and subjugated people.

The Palestinian Arab people, the chief and direct victim of Zionist colonization, a people whose greater part was reduced during and after 1948 to the state of pauperized refugees, and another part of which has lived for twenty years in Israel under severe conditions of discrimination and persecution—that people has now entirely become a conquered people. It has been robbed not only of the most elementary political rights, but also of the very prospect for national and human existence. Regarding the fate of that people, the various schemes suggested by Israeli government circles range from outright annexation to Israel (accompanied by pressures to emigrate from the annexed territory and even by measures intended to reduce the Arab birth rate, "to deal wisely with them lest they multiply"—as Pharaoh had once put it . . .) to the setting up of a Bantustan, a political "strategic hamlet" in the form of a protectorate camouflaged as a "federation" between Israeli overlord and Arab subject.

It is both the right and duty of every conquered and subjugated people to resist and to struggle for its freedom. The ways, means, and methods necessary and appropriate for such struggle must be determined by that people itself and it would be hypocritical for strangers—especially if they belong to the oppressing nation—to preach to it, saying "Thus shalt thou do, and thus shalt thou not do."

While recognizing the unconditional right of the conquered to resist against occupation, we can support only such organizations which, in addition to resisting against occupation, also recognize the right of the Israeli people for self-determination. On such a basis the struggle of the Palestinian people can become combined in a joint struggle of Arabs and Jews in the region for a common future.

One thing is obvious—tightening the yoke of repression, mass collective punishments, blowing up houses, large-scale massacre assaults (like that against Kerameh on 21 March)—all these are quite incapable of putting an end to resistance.

To those who express their abhorrence and indignation in view of the innocent Israeli victims of sabotage actions we say: your abhorrence and indignation are perfectly justified. This situation of horrible tragedy must be terminated at once; and the way to terminate it is immediate withdrawal from all the occupied territories. Only from that point will it be possible to advance toward a complete solution of the Israeli-Arab dispute and the Palestine problem.

The collapse of the Egyptian army in the June War exhibited before the world's eyes the grave social contradictions rending Egyptian society. These contradictions were only mirrored, and enlarged, in the army. The "Free Officers" coup, led by Gamal Abdel Nasser, established in Egypt a petty-bourgeois regime. It was a "halfway revolution." By its very nature, this regime is ever trying to balance between anti-imperialism and the tendency to compromise with imperialism; between Left and Right; between the pressure of the masses and the interests of the overprivileged bourgeoisie, bureaucracy, and officer caste.

That regime has carried through a series of important reforms, some of them quite far-reaching, it also served Egypt's exceeding dependence upon imperialism. But it has not fulfilled the hopes of the masses or realized their interests; it did not go over to a socialist revolution turning the toilers from subjects to masters of the state. The exploiting classes of the ancient regime were battered, not shattered. They have largely continued to exist side by side with a new bureaucratic-military stratum which is related to them by origin and outlook.

We hold that the solution of the main problems of the Middle East, including the Israeli-Arab problem, requires a radical transformation of the regimes throughout the region; a socialist revolution which will bring the working class to power, liberate the immense energies latent in the masses and channel them to actuate social and economic progress. Such a transformation is needed not only in countries now under feudal monarchy, but also in the relatively progressive Arab countries which are now under a petty-bourgeois, self-styled "socialist" regime.

As for Israel, here a socialist revolution is needed, radically to change the character of this state, transforming it from a Zionist state, an instrument for further Zionist colonization, a natural ally of imperialism—into a socialist state representing the true interests of the Israeli masses, a state oriented toward the surrounding region and both willing and capable to integrate itself in it.

We hold that the revolutionary socialist solution to the Israeli-Arab conflict remains valid—is, in fact, more valid than ever—in the new situation created after the war. De-Zionization of Israel and its integration in a socialist union with the Arab countries—this is the road for solution.

AL-FATAH: SEVEN-POINT PLATFORM*

1. The National Liberation Movement of Palestine (Al-Fatah) is the identity.

2. Al-Fatah is not fighting against the Jews as an ethnic and religious expression of the Palestinian people and of its determination to liberate its territory from Zionist colonization and to re-establish its national community. It is fighting against the Zionist and colonialist state of Israel with its racist, theocratic, and expansionist structure.

---

* Issued in all languages on January 14, 1969, by the Central Committee of Al-Fatah.

3. Al-Fatah rejects any solution to the Palestine problem which does not recognize the existence of the Palestinian people and its right to self-determination.

4. Al-Fatah categorically rejects the Security Council resolution of 22 November 1967 and the Jarring Mission resulting from it. This resolution disregards the existence of the Palestinian people and its national rights. Any so-called peaceful solution which disregards this basic fact is bound to fall. In any case, the acceptance by this or that party of the 22 November resolution is not binding, in any manner whatsoever, on the people of Palestine which is determined to pursue its resolute struggle against foreign occupation and Zionist colonization.

5. Al-Fatah solemnly declares that the final aim of its struggle is the restoration of the independent democratic Palestinian state where all citizens, whatever their creed, can enjoy equal rights.

6. Palestine forms part of the Arab homeland. Al-Fatah will work for the active participation of the Palestinian state in building a united and progressive Arab society.

7. The struggle of the Palestinian people, like that of the Vietnamese people and all other peoples of Asia, Africa, and Latin America, forms part of the historical process of liberating the oppressed people from colonialism and imperialism.

POPULAR FRONT FOR THE LIBERATION OF
PALESTINE: THE AUGUST PLATFORM*

IMMEDIATELY after the First World War, the imperialist countries took over the Arab east, and Britain issued the Balfour Declaration of 1917 which granted Zionists the right to a "national home" in Palestine. This pledge was not incidental but a logical outcome of the imperialist policies in the Middle East: to establish an armed, imperialist base to confront the rising tide of the Arab liberation movement whose victory would endanger the imperialist interests in this vital area of the world. This was why the Zionist colonizing ambitions found such favorable response from Britain.

The Arab feudal-bourgeois regimes had, from their inception, thrown in their lot with the imperialists, in a broad counterrevolutionary front against the Arab movements for national liberation. Their feudal-bourgeois composition made them unable to face the imperialist-Zionist designs with armed force and patriotic popular revolution: Reactionaries everywhere fear the people more than they do the imperialists. To oppose

---

* Pamphlet issued by the PFLP after August 1968. Translated by A. Shams.

these designs effectively required the mobilization and arming of the people—and it is this that the reactionary regimes, the enemies of national liberation, absolutely refuse to do since it would endanger their very existence which is linked to imperialism (in its old and new aspect) in the Arab lands.

For Palestine, from the beginning of the modern era, it was apparent that its fate would depend on the outcome of the national struggle—i.e., the class struggle between the forces of national liberation on one hand, and the imperialist-Zionist camp and its allies, the Arab reactionary regimes, on the other. The control, by the feudalists and compradors, of the state machine and its numerous instruments of repression and even of the leadership of parts of the nationalist movement up to 1948, made the fate of Palestine a foregone conclusion. The defeat of 1948, brought about by the feudalist-theocratic leadership of Haj Amin Husseini, the major bourgeois parties (Istiqlal, Difa'), and the Arab feudalist regimes, provides the concrete example for the dialectical relation between the Palestinian and the Arab situation, and between this situation and the international one.

The Palestinian resistance movement must pass judgment on the Arab regimes where the stand of these regimes on the problem of Palestine is concerned. Otherwise, the resistance movement would lose its identity, becoming a quantitative addition to the Arab regimes and institutions responsible for the abortion of the rebellion of 1936, the catastrophe of 1948, and the defeat of June 1967. The problem of Palestine could never be understood in isolation from a study of the Arab regimes responsible for the "historical impasse" facing the Palestine problem after the June defeat. The present Arab regimes, together with the Palestine resistance movement, now face a basic choice: either "liquidation" or the adoption of a program for a people's war. The choice that they will make is not divorced from the programs of action actually implemented by the Arab regimes and the Palestinian and Arab national liberation movements.

And just as the defeat of June was not merely military, so the catastrophe of 1948 was a defeat for all that the feudal-bourgeois regimes stood for. The formation of the state of Israel was the logical outcome for the backwardness of Palestine and the other Arab countries ruled by the feudal-bourgeois regimes, the allies of imperialism. The need arose clearly to view the catastrophe [of 1948] not by itself, but [as a function of] class rule, the economic and military [backwardness]; and to see that the liquidation of the state of Israel and the liberation of Palestine depend on the destruction of the feudal-bourgeois regimes—the liquidation of the real causes of the catastrophe. Nasser was correct when he told his comrades during the siege of Fallouja, "The defeat was not decided on the battlefield, but there, in Cairo." And, "The liberation of Cairo from the feudalist-bourgeois regime of Farouk, the ally of imperialism and Arab reaction, is the central concern in any program of action for the liberation of Palestine."

Thus, for Arab and Palestinian liberation movements, the central concern became the liquidation of the feudalist-bourgeois regimes responsible for the catastrophe of 1948, in order to open the way for the solution of the problems presented by the phase of national liberation which demand the construction of a modern national economy (industrialization and land reform), independent in its development of the world market. For without the construction of a solid economic base, it is impossible to build regular and popular armies capable of waging a protracted battle against the camp of counterrevolution on Palestine and the Arab lands (Israel and imperialism and Arab reaction).

After 1948, the bourgeoisie, leader of the Arab national liberation movement, produced a program of action, petty bourgeois in character, for the destruction of the feudalist-capitalist-imperialist alliance responsible for the defeat. Proclaiming the alliance of workers, poor peasants, soldiers and the petty bourgeoisie—the last providing the alliance with its ideology and leadership—it came to power then or shortly thereafter in the UAR, Syria, and Algeria (and in Iraq to some extent). Its petty-bourgeois program called for the construction of an economy based on light industry in the first instance, then for solving of the land question in the interests of poor peasants, and finally for the electrification of the country. The forces of counterrevolution, faced with the violence of the national class struggle, did not stay passive for long. In 1956, the tripartite aggression (British-French-Zionist) was organized with the objective of liquidating the patriotic anti-imperialist regime which was threatening the interests and positions of the counterrevolution in Palestine and elsewhere in the Arab world. After the aggression of 1956, neo-colonialism, represented by the U.S.A., attempted to contain the Arab liberation movements and the patriotic regimes "from the inside." But these regimes turned the approaches down, continuing, desultorily, in their indecisive petty-bourgeois fashion, to wage their patriotic fight against imperialism and neo-colonialism. The American neo-colonialism then recognized the failure of their "peaceful containment" policy for the subjection of the Arab national liberation movements. Hence, the objectives of the June War were not the reactionary regimes, but the patriotic regimes and all the sections of the Arab and Palestinian national liberation movements. Why, then, the defeat? And with what programs did the patriotic regimes and liberation movements face the June defeat?

Petty-bourgeois theoreticians have offered explanations for the defeat. In essence they all center around the question of technical, scientific, and cultural superiority of Israel and American imperialism supporting it. And as small, backward countries, they say, we could not confront American imperialism which has a war machine vastly superior to any in the underdeveloped world of Asia, Africa, and Latin America. These analysts then conclude that our victory over Israel requires overtaking it in science and technology.

Other petty-bourgeois theorizers explain the defeat by a series of military errors committed by this or that army—e.g., the unpreparedness of the UAR air force at the time of the sudden Israeli attack. These theorizers blithely disregard the facts of contemporary history when they discuss the Arab defeat in June. They purposely avert their eyes from the real causes of the defeat in six days despite such noisy sloganeering immediately before June 5 as "[Liberation] inch by inch!," "Scorched earth!," and "Peoples' war of Liberation!" And if the technical superiority of Israel and imperialism was the decisive factor in the defeat, how then could one account for the Vietnamese people's confronting half a million American soldiers in addition to half a million puppet regime troops? And if the defeat was merely the result of certain military errors, why then were they accepted?

In Vietnam and Cuba there are patriotic, revolutionary regimes which are proletarian and poor-peasant in composition. They place all the countries' resources, material and cultural, at the service of the struggle to overcome the problems of national liberation; the liquidation of all class privileges—material and cultural—and the construction of a solid base for economic and political independence by heavy industrialization, mechanization of agriculture, and electrification. The revolutionary classes in society stand at the head of the alliance of all class and political forces opposed to the capitalist-imperialist camp. Such a patriotic economic and political program is able to mobilize and arm all the classes struggling for the solutions of the problems of national independence against imperialism and colonialism. The slogan of "People's War!" takes a concrete expression: the vast toiling masses are mobilized in people's militia, partisan groups, and the ranks of the regular army for the defeat of imperialism and all its allies.

In our countries the situation is different. It is the petty bourgeoisie which assumes the leadership of the Palestinian and Arab movements for national liberation. This class had effected the social, economic, and military transformation of these countries—a transformation that remained within the ideological orientation of this class, and it was this ideology and the whole program that evolved from it that were defeated in June 1967. The economy could not withstand the Zionist-imperialist attack because it was mainly a "consumer economy" geared to light industry. In agriculture, division of land was at the expense of productivity. After the closure of the Suez Canal, an economy like this had to turn to the reactionary "oil regimes" for help.

In the field of ideology and politics the petty bourgeoisie remained at the top of the pyramid of power; the broad masses of the people remained at the base. The petty bourgeoisie, by nature, fear the masses as they fear the feudal-bourgeois alliance. They failed to build a national economy developing independently from the capitalist world market, and therefore could not sever all relations with the imperialist camp—especially the U.S.A.

After the defeat, the petty-bourgeois regimes were faced with a choice. They could choose the Vietnamese and Cuban way, which would mean a complete transformation of their programs of action: mobilizing all the material and human resources of society, arming the people for a revolutionary war against all imperialist, Zionist, and reactionary interests and positions, translating the slogan "Fighting Israel and those behind it" into a daily armed action on the widest possible front against all forces of counterrevolution. Only then would the balance of forces favor the Arab and Palestinian movements for national liberation. Or they could remain within the limits of the pre-June 1967 policies, which means that the Palestinian and Arab liberation movements would be doomed to continuous withdrawal in the face of Israel, imperialism, and Arab reaction. We note with bitterness that this choice was made by the Arab regimes. Their class composition and ideology could not allow them to implement a policy of "people's war," for this would have demanded of them the renouncing of their privileges, politically and materially.

A look at the U.N. resolution of November 1967 suffices to show that its acceptance and implementation herald the liquidation of the Palestine problem. The resolution itself is precisely such an imperialist attempt to liquidate the problem. It stipulates:

—The right of all states in the Middle East to live within "secure boundaries"

—Recognition of each state by all other states

—The right of "innocent" passage in the waterways of all states

—A "just" solution for the refugee problem.

The problem now for the Arab regimes and the Arab and Palestinian movements of liberation is not to weigh the pros and cons of the U.N. resolution. It is also not to argue whether the official stand regarding it is or is not merely a matter of tactical convenience. It is to see whether the economic, political, military, and ideological programs being adopted by the regimes and the liberation movements could lead to the liquidation of the effects of the June aggression, i.e., the liberation of Sinai, the western bank, and the Golan Heights, as a first step in the protracted war for the liberation of Palestine and the liquidation of the aggressive, racist Zionist structure.

The experiences of the national liberation movements in our countries (Palestine and the Arab world) and in the underdeveloped countries proves that the road to national salvation and liberation starts with the necessity of arming oneself with "revolutionary tools" capable of defeating the militarily and technically superior imperialist countries: revolutionary anti-imperialist, anti-Zionist ideology—a scientific ideology (the ideology of the proletariat). . . .

We must raise the patriotic, radical consciousness. Our people face a modern enemy supported by the largest imperialist power, the U.S.A. The relation between the people and the resistance movement should be based on a scientific outlook which implements "the concrete analysis of the concrete situation." The raising of the political level of consciousness starts by exposing the causes of the failures of the Palestinian and Arab liberation movements, whose glaring examples are the defeat of the rebellion of 1936 in Palestine at the hand of Palestinian and Arab reaction, the catastrophe of 1948, and the defeat of 1967. In those defeats are the lessons for our future victory.

We must reject all defeatist policies and the U.N. resolution and [insist] on a program for a popular war of liberation by arming and mobilizing the people in popular militias, so that the war can be fought on the widest possible front against Israel and those who are behind it (including the proimperialist Arab forces).

Protracted war waged by a mobilized, self-reliant people, armed with proletarian ideology, is the sole road for national salvation and for the defeat of the technically superior Israeli-imperialist enemy.

DEMOCRATIC POPULAR FRONT: WE ARE MARXIST-LENINISTS*

Question: What is the strength of the Democratic Front at the moment, compared with the PLFP?

Answer: The basis and resources of the Democratic Front are mainly and even exclusively the workers, peasants, and poor refugees of Palestine. On the other hand, the Popular Front represents in its leadership and in its ideology sizable sectors of the Jordanian and Palestinian bourgeoisie. Consequently the measure for the weight of each of the two should be not the numerical strength of each but rather the militancy of each. It is very unlikely that an organization representing the ideology and the class structure of the bourgeois class in Jordan could have the militancy and efficacy of an organization representing both the ideology and the class basis of the workers, peasants, and the poor masses in general. Even numerically the Democratic Front is stronger than the Popular Front at the present.

---

* Transcription of an unpublished taped interview by Bill Hillier of *Peace News* (London) with a top-ranking member of the DPFLP, London, May 16, 1969.

Question: What is the position of the DPF[LP] in relation to the regimes of Syria, Egypt, Iraq, and Algeria, and how does this compare with the attitudes of the Popular Front and the Al-Fatah as you see them?

Answer: That those regimes are the regimes of the petty-bourgeois ruling class and have amply illustrated and proved during the June War 1967 their incapacity of waging a long protracted popular war which would achieve victory. No victory is possible without an adoption of the revolutionary ideology of the working class and without a popular protracted war based on the Arab and Palestinian workers and peasants. The ruling petty-bourgeois class in Syria, Egypt, Iraq, and Algeria is incapable of organizing those classes because it is afraid of the revolutionary potential contained in the Arab workers and peasants which would obviously be directed against their regimes as such. The basic difference between the Democratic Front and the Popular Front is the refusal of the right-wing leadership of the Popular Front to analyze critically the reasons and causes that led to the military defeat of June '67, under the pretext of refusing to interfere in the internal affairs of the Arab states and the Arab regimes. In this sense the Popular Front has a position not dissimilar to the position of Fatah. The Democratic Front believes that the struggle for national liberation of the Palestinian people is intimately related to the struggle of the Arab masses against imperialism, reaction, and the petty-bourgeois regimes and as such it does not conceive of its own struggle except as part of this overall struggle in the whole of the Middle East.

Question: What is the ideological and organizational make-up of the Democratic Popular Front?

Answer: The Democratic Popular Front believes that all its members should actively participate in military activity, thus forging a well-built and strong military and militant detachment that will be capable of defeating imperialism, Arab reaction, and Zionism. This necessarily means that the Democratic Front is not divided into a political and military wing. All militants are equally political militants [and their politico-military activity is] based on the revolutionary ideology of the working-class Marxism-Leninism. This distinguishes the DPF from the other organizations of the Palestinian liberation movement. The DPF looks at the Palestinian people as one people without distinction of religion or creed. While refusing the concept of a binational state the DPF looks at the inhabitants of Palestine as one people. As the DPF puts the struggle in Palestine in its proper context, it aims at establishing in Palestine a Palestinian state under the leadership and hegemony of the working class. This Palestinian state would obviously grant *all* its inhabitants equal rights.

Question: Does this imply that the DPF would be happy to achieve a socialist Palestine in which, for a while, the Jews might be a majority, provided of course that the Zionist structure and the Zionist organizations abroad were dismantled?

Answer: Jewish numerical majority would be unlikely at present because the last census of population in Israel puts forward the figure of 2¼ million, among whom 350,000 are Arabs. On the other hand the Palestinian people now number about 2,000,000, which would mean that the situation would approach numerical equality between Arabs and Jews. Nevertheless the DPF accepts that Palestine is for all its inhabitants, Arabs and Jews, which have to have as a precondition the ending of *institutionalized* Jewish immigration to Palestine. Further immigration into Palestine would have to be decided by the new social order that is going to be instituted in Palestine. This means that any possible immigration would be discussed and decided upon its merits, and obviously that would not exclude anybody and needless to say it wouldn't exclude Jews from immigrating to Palestine.

Question: As I am sure you know, there is a small but growing left-wing revolutionary movement inside Israel. Do you foresee that at some time in the future the struggles of the Palestinian revolutionaries and the Israeli revolutionaries may be united?

Answer: The revolutionary Left you mention still emphasizes the need to preserve the national entity of the Jews in Palestine which negates what we have been emphasizing on the Palestinians as one people, one undivided people. As far as the second part of the question goes, inasmuch as this revolutionary Left proves itself in practice and proves by its activity the extent and militancy of its opposition to the Zionist regime presently controlling Palestine, cooperation and coordination with the revolutionary national liberation movement of the Palestinian people is possible. Only then could there be one broad class struggle in Palestine.

Question: What are the general military strategy and objectives of the Democratic Popular Front and how does this tie up with the political struggle inside the occupied territories?

Answer: The DPF seeks to move its bases from the eastern bank to the western bank so that the east bank bases would only be relay bases for the basic centers of its activities inside the occupied territories. At the same time the Democratic Popular Front prepares for mass action and mass participation of the workers of the east bank to offset any attempts at counterrevolution. This dual strategy in the view of the DPF is a specific implementation of the principles of popular protracted warfare in the context of Palestine, namely the activity and operations against Zionist occupation from within the occupied territories proper, and at the same time mass action and preparation inside the east bank against Hashemite and Arab reaction. The Democratic Front aims at building a wide popular front of all the forces that are opposed to Arab reaction, imperialism, and Zionism.

Question: Do you see a useful part as being played by the civilian struggle in the occupied territories and are you trying to develop this aspect as well as the military aspect?

Answer: The Democratic Popular Front considers that civilian resistance in the occupied territories is complementary to the military activity waged by the Palestinian liberation struggle. We would also like to emphasize that as far as the Democratic Front is concerned we do not distinguish between military and civilian activity. We believe that what popular warfare essentially means is that all the people carry out the most varied active participation in the struggle against occupation. What is a daily activity of the Democratic Front in the east bank is propaganda and action among Palestinian and Jordanian masses. This entails, for example, weekly visits of Democratic Front doctors to villages that are not regularly visited by the doctors of the Jordanian monarchy, political education, propaganda, etc. As for similar activities within the occupied territories it should be borne in mind that the recent emergence of the Democratic Front and the extreme difficulties that face its attempts to establish itself as an independent armed movement has not yet given it ample chance to develop its political organization inside the occupied territory. It should also be remembered in this context that in spite of those enormous difficulties the volume of activities of military operations carried on by the Democratic Front inside the occupied territories is quite considerable.

The Democratic Front has carried on a series of military activities inside the occupied territories which include the regular activities carried on by any liberation movement, namely, attacks on military Israeli occupation units, military targets, etc. Two or three operations of the Democratic Front are worthwhile commenting upon. These three operations have a clear propaganda value aimed especially at the Jewish community in Palestine and in this sense the Democratic Front is carrying on armed propaganda or propaganda by deeds. The first of those operations is the bomb in the cafeteria of the Hebrew University of Jerusalem. This operation carried out in March 1969 has been interpreted as follows in an official statement of the DPF: "The Hebrew University is responsible for producing the main cadres for the Israeli state, namely the administration, the police, and the army. It is also responsible for the inculcation of reactionary Zionist culture in the ranks of Jewish in-

243 DEMOCRATIC POPULAR FRONT

tellectuals. This is why the Democratic Front feels responsible to discourage Jewish intellectuals from criminally following the imperialist and Zionist policy." The meaning of this text is quite clear. The bomb in the cafeteria of the Hebrew University is a warning and at the same time an active propaganda act aimed at the Jewish intellectuals to open their eyes to Zionism and to turn them from it. The second operation of the Democratic Front was the demolition of the Labor Exchange at Nablus, carried on in the second half of April 1969. The DPF explained this activity in the following terms: "The Democratic Front aims at hitting the prominent Zionist military and political institutions in the occupied territories. This is why the demolition of the Israeli Labor Exchange in Nablus expresses the rejection by the Democratic Front and the masses of Nablus of the Zionist, political, and military policy of employing Arab labor in order that Israeli workers can be drafted into the occupation army. Moreover the establishment by the enemy of Labor Exchanges in occupied territories is designed to employ cheap labor, thus furthering the exploitation practiced by Zionist capitalism and increasing its wealth." The third operation was the demolition of a factory in the Golan Heights. The aim of this operation was the propaganda value directed at the Jewish workers in a similar manner as the Hebrew University operation was directed toward Jewish intellectuals.

Question: It is often said that the Zionist state thrives on the existence of war. Can it not be said that the carrying out of military operations against purely civilian targets as opposed to military or economic targets will make the task of the revolutionary Left inside Israel more difficult and tend to solidify the Israelis more and more behind Zionism?

Answer: Three points could be made in answering this question. First point: military operations against civilians form part and parcel of any struggle for national liberation. In this sense the national liberation struggle of Palestinian people is no different from any struggle, no different from the national liberation struggle waged by the Vietnamese people. Second point: the military operations carried by the armed struggle of the Palestinian people is designed to create as much disturbance and as much dislocation in the Zionist state occupying Palestine, to prove by deeds that the Zionist design is no longer comfortable, no longer profitable for anybody, and no longer viable even for the one people who initially believed in it. Third point is that those same military operations are designed to warn the Jewish community in occupied Palestine of the crimes committed in its name by Zionism against the whole people, i.e., against the Palestinian people.

The Palestine problem has uneven effects. Zionism is equally dangerous to both Arabs and Jews. One basic fact should be borne in mind: the principal victim of Zionism is the Palestinian people. The condition of the establishment of the Zionist state in Palestine has been the displacement of the Palestinian people. Consequently the principal contradiction at present is between the Palestine people in its majority—either under Israeli rule and the victim of racial persecution and oppression or displaced and in exile in the surrounding Arab countries on one side and the Zionist structure that binds the Jewish community together in Palestine on the other. The second point pertains to that concept of the Hebrew nation. This concept implies an inherent contradiction. If by asserting the existence of a Hebrew nation one implies from this the legitimate right of the Hebrew nation to possess and establish its own state then we sink back obviously into Zionism. Clearly this implication of the concepts goes against the whole interpretation and the whole rejection of Zionism. But if by the term Hebrew nation is meant that the Jewish community in Palestine possesses its peculiar cultural features and implies a code for respecting these cultural peculiarities, then clearly any revolutionary socialist platform in the Arab world respects and helps further the cultural development of all minorities in the Arab world. Not only Jews but Kurds, Armenians, etc. To clarify further, when we talk of minorities in this context, we refer to minorities in the context of a united socialist Arab republic in the Middle East.

Iraq

Except for traditional communists, politicians tend to be a violent lot in Iraq. For years, the youthful King Faisal and his perennial prime minister Nuri el-Said thought nothing of torturing and killing their critics. Then, on July 14, 1958, a batch of army officers, including Major General Abdul Karim Qassem ("Kassim" in the Western press), Colonel Abdel Salam Aref, and Major General Ahmed Hassan al-Bakr, overthrew the monarchy and established a republic; the king and his prime minister were promptly killed by a vengeful mob.

Qassem consolidated his power, "retired" Hassan al-Bakr, jailed Aref and condemned him to death, but forgot to kill him. On February 8, 1963, when a Ba'ath Party coup overthrew Qassem and installed Aref as a figurehead president, Aref did not forget to dispose of Qassem. He had him executed in front of television cameras. The Ba'athis then went on a rampage, slaughtering thousands of communists who had been Qassem's allies. Once that was taken care of, Aref tossed the Ba'athis out of power and ruled until April 1966, when he died in a helicopter crash. His brother, General Abdul Rahman Aref, took over next—until General Hassan al-Bakr made his comeback, and, with the Ba'ath right wing, seized power in July 1968.

With each coup, of course, hundreds of opponents were quietly liquidated and thousands tossed into jail. But one group, though constantly harassed, remained faithfully peaceful—members of the Communist Party of Iraq (ICP). This was not because they abhorred violence but because throughout Qassem's regime they were convinced that they "had the President's ear." In fact, the Central Committee of the ICP condemned as "leftist violationist extremist" every communist cadre who advocated peasant land seizures, defense committees, arming the people, even criticizing Qassem. As a result, when Qassem was overthrown, the ICP was totally unprepared for the ensuing repression—in which, among

245

thousands, Salam 'Adel (Hassan al-Radawi) and Jamal Haidat, respectively first and second secretaries of the ICP, were tortured to death.

Instead of challenging the whole ideological base and analysis of the Central Committee, the 1963 coups of February and October (Aref's ouster of the Ba'ath) brought about a hardening of the so-called "rightist tendency" within the ICP. The Central Committee's policies coincided totally with Soviet strategy: peaceful coexistence, non-anticapitalist road to socialism, full cooperation with the petty-bourgeois nationalist movements of the Arab world (Nasserism, then Ba'athism, which is a so-called Muslim-Arab form of socialism).

To support Aref or the Ba'ath just because they called themselves Arab nationalists and declaimed against Zionism was unacceptable to many communists, however, especially after so many of their comrades had been massacred by both. Thus many left the Party and, eventually, created two new groups: the Armed Detachment of the ICP, which began urban guerrilla activities, and the Group of Revolutionary Cadres, which undertook preparations for rural armed struggle. These two groups then forced a split in the ICP, with the revolutionary elements calling themselves the Central Command of the Iraqi Communist Party (ICP-CC). Headed by Aziz al-Hajj, a member of the old Central Committee, it issued the self-critical analysis below in September 1967 and called for a Party congress early in 1968.

By the time it convened in January, the urban guerrilla Armed Detachment had been uncovered by the police and liquidated. The Group of Revolutionary Cadres insisted that armed struggle be considered as "the decisive means" of attaining revolutionary power. The ICP-CC wanted the Plenum to consider it "one means of revolutionary struggle." A compromise was reached: The Front for Popular Armed Struggle (FPAS) would begin guerrilla operations in the south as an independent movement open to all revolutionaries, and Aziz al-Hajj's ICP-CC would officially and publicly support it. Meanwhile, it reported (pamphlet, dated January 5, 1968) that "the Plenum saw the need to subordinate diplomatic considerations to the principle of class struggle and to the requirements of internationalist solidarity, and the need to consolidate the fighting front against world imperialism led by the U.S." And it concluded that "the Plenum stressed that subjective conditions for achieving victory do not all ripen simultaneously, but crystallize through direct and resolute revolutionary struggle."

The FPAS began operations—successful attacks on a series of police observation posts near the marshlands of Al-Ahwar, where the guerrillas had their base. They were led by Khaled Ahmad Zaki, the ex-president of the Iraqi Students' Association in Britain and a former member of the secretariat of the Bertrand Russell Peace Foundation. Three days later, Zaki and twelve men were caught in an army encircle-

ment. For thirty-six hours, they fought, trying to retreat deep into the marsh, shooting down an army helicopter in the process. When the shooting stopped, five had made it, five were caught, and three guerrillas were dead—Zaki among them.

On June 11, the ICP-CC issued the following communiqué:

The sustenance and development of armed struggle in the Arab countryside; the passing over of the Kurdish revolution to the stage of revolutionary offensive; the role our Party can play in strengthening it and increasing its participation in it; the revolutionary operations in the cities and the crucial role that the popular revolution expects the revolutionary forces inside the army to play in order to tip the balance of power decisively to the side of the people—all these varied forces of revolutionary armed struggle are interlocked and interacting on one another; and they must all merge into one revolutionary drive in order to achieve final victory. Moreover, the mass struggles—both economic and political—play a concrete and necessary role in preparing for the armed struggles, for they help raise the general revolutionary mood, weaken the enemy forces and spread confusion in its ranks.

It was a mild statement of support—presumably because the FPAS had been wiped out. But it was a beginning.

CENTRAL COMMAND OF THE IRAQI COMMUNIST PARTY: SELF-CRITICISM*

IN both its sociopolitical content and participating forces, the July Revolution was a national-democratic revolution. It is impossible to understand the causes of its sudden eruption without a comprehensive knowledge of the preceding popular struggles of which our Party was the prime organizer. The national and social mass struggles in both city and countryside, the leading role played by our Party in those struggles, the deep national-democratic consciousness developed by the masses over decades, and the total isolation of the reactionary puppet regime—all are factors which account for the transformation of the military coup d'état of July 14 (in which military units occupied strategic positions in Baghdad) into the bridgehead of a genuine popular revolution in which millions of people participated. But the low level of class consciousness and the control of bourgeois and petty-bourgeois officers over the military operation which unleashed the Revolution led to the transfer of state power to the representatives of the national bourgeoisie and of certain sectors of

---

* Pamphlet issued in 1967. Translated from the Arabic by Fawwaz Trabulsi.

the petty bourgeoisie, to the exclusion of representatives of the working class and its Party. Despite the fact that our Party had taken the initiative in forming the "National Unity Front"[1] and in uniting the various groups of "free officers," it was the only party of this Front which had no representatives in the "Revolutionary Government."

The nature of any political regime can be defined on the basis of the ideology that guides it, its policies, and the interests it represents. The Revolution achieved political independence, dealt a mortal blow to the Baghdad Pact, initiated a progressive—though not radical—agrarian reform, established some basic democratic freedoms, and recognized certain national rights of the Kurdish people. Those national-democratic steps were implemented under constant pressure from the masses led by our Party. The ICP developed at a rapid rate after the Revolution and came to play a decisive role in organizing the masses of workers, peasants, students, youth, and women; led the mass campaign for arming the people; and was primarily instrumental in uncovering and defeating the successive reactionary plots.

Since the first days of the Revolution, a number of contradictions arose between the interests of the national bourgeoisie and some sectors of the petty bourgeoisie, on one hand, and those of the working class and its natural allies, on the other. So long as the national bourgeoisie was not in possession of state power, those contradictions were relegated to the background. But, once the Revolution put state power into the hands of the military representatives of the national bourgeoisie, the latter sought to contain the Revolution within prescribed limits, afraid lest its radicalization and progress lead to working-class control over the State. Those attempts soon clashed with the mounting revolutionary wave among the masses and their constant pressures—matters which the government had to take into account, especially since it was permanently subjected to reactionary plots.

It is true that Qassem was neither a "classic" representative of the national bourgeoisie, nor the leader of a bourgeois party in power. It is also true that he came from a petty-bourgeois background. Nevertheless, the spirit with which he conducted the country's policy shows that he was, from the beginning, a *conscious* representative of the national bourgeoisie. Or else, how can we explain his initial fears of the increasing influence of the ICP and the upsurge of working-class and peasant militancy, his reluctance to grant genuine popular freedoms, his leniency toward reaction, or his preservation of the reactionary state machine? All this occurred at a time when our Party was pursuing a policy of alliance with Qassem, lulled by the belief that the man was a revolutionary democrat who was bound to join the camp of the working class!

[1] Formed during the struggle against the monarchy and including the ICP, the Ba'ath, the National Democratic Party, and the Istiqlal Party, with the indirect participation of the Democratic Party of Kurdistan.—*Trans.*

At a time when we were foremost in propagating his cause and mystifying people about him.

Our first mistake did not lie in the lack of "diplomatic charm," but in our idealist, non-Marxist characterization of Qassem which put him over and above all classes and parties and considered him a member of the camp of the toiling masses and their revolutionary movement. This rightist view ultimately led to exaggerated support for Qassem and reluctance to criticize his wavering or provide the masses with a correct appreciation of the man and of the regime he led. Consequently, our calculations for the development of the Revolution were based on Qassem's own person, and his "good will." We lacked any revolutionary plan to radicalize the Revolution, free it of the straitjacket imposed by Qassem and the national bourgeoisie, and drive it forward toward fulfilling its essential tasks, namely a radical land reform and preparatory steps for its transformation into a socialist revolution.

Among the rightist, opportunist concepts deeply entrenched in our Party is the one which considers erroneous any attempt made, after July 14, 1958, to realize revolutionary democratic demands by relying on the masses, by starting "from below," "from the streets," etc. Such attempts, labeled "leftist," are considered liable to alienate our ally—the bourgeoisie —and even superfluous, since the same demand, more or less, can be realized by secret negotiations with the government or through diplomatic channels. In fact, this concept does not seek at educating the masses through practical revolutionary struggle, nor at deepening the Revolution or pushing it forward. It is a concept based on immediate, narrow interests which is alien to the Party's basic goals.

The Party opened offices for "Popular Resistance," started accepting recruits, and called upon the government to train and arm them. However, the immediate reaction of Qassem's government was to issue a military order to close down these offices. The question of acquiring arms by revolutionary means was then put on the agenda of an extraordinary meeting of the Central Committee, held in the last days of July 1958. The discussion ended by the victory of the rightist tendency which put forward a rare piece of wisdom: "Why this alarm about the new order? It has come to stay, and will know how to defend itself when the need arises!" "Reason" defeated "burning revolutionary passion" and the defense of the Revolution was entrusted to the bourgeoisie. Qassem's government, facing counterrevolution, was forced to establish and train Popular Resistance units, but kept the arms under lock and key in the police stations; the arms for the defense of the Revolution were put under the watchful eye of counterrevolution!! (For the security forces never changed under Nuri el-Said, Qassem's dictatorship, or the Ba'athi dictatorship of February 8, 1963[2]).

[2] Date of the Ba'athi coup d'état and the anticommunist witch hunt.—*Ed.*

Thus, the "Revolutionary Government" paralyzed the Popular Resistance even before it was born. Qassem did not even call it to arms when he was in danger just prior to February 8, 1963. What is even more surprising is that the rightist tendency, which opposed arming the people in July 1958, blamed the Party for calling the masses to armed resistance on February 8, 1963, without providing them with arms!

It is a well-known fact that our Party took the initiative in forming the National Unity Front composed of all Arab patriotic forces in Iraq and established a bilateral alliance with the Kurdish Democratic Party because the Front did not recognize the national rights of the Kurdish people. Our Party also took the initiative in uniting all the organizations of patriotic officers in the army and connected them with the Front. Despite all that, ours was the Party in this Front which was not represented in the "Revolutionary Government." At the enlarged Plenum of the Central Committee (on September 6, 1958), the slogan of "abolishing competition" was adopted to bridge the gap between the fact that our Party was not represented in the government composed of representatives of bourgeois and petty-bourgeois groups, and its active participation in the National Unity Front, whose emergence was the prime condition for the victory of the July 14 Revolution.

We never went beyond propaganda and agitation for the democratic demand that our Party be represented in the government in order to transform it into a genuine national coalition government. After the Shawwaf armed conspiracy in Mossul,[3] Qassem found himself in an embarrassing situation vis-à-vis his clique of officers because of his policy of conciliation between the nationalists and the democrats. This embarrassment ultimately led Qassem to seek to co-opt some communists into his Cabinet, but without formally recognizing this as a representation of our Party in government and refusing to relinquish his personal dictatorial powers to the Cabinet and, by so doing, transform it into a genuine national coalition government composed of representative of all the patriotic forces, including our Party. This embarrassment and Qassem's reaction led the rightist tendency in our Party to seek to abolish the difference between a genuine coalition government, which can only come through mass struggle, "from the streets," and a fake coalition government whose members are chosen according to the leader's personal whim.

Our Party lost about two months—from March 8 to the end of April 1959—in secret negotiations with Qassem on the participation of some comrades in the government. This phase was termed by reactionaries the period of the "Red Menace." At the end of these fifty days, the American commander of NATO forces in Turkey sounded the alarm and solemnly declared that the situation in Iraq had become hopeless. At a

[3] An abortive Nasserite coup led by Colonel Shawwaf in Mossul during the summer of 1959, which led to violent reprisals by Qassem and the ICP against the nationalists.—*Trans.*

time when the enemies of the Revolution were extremely vigilant, our Party passed through a unique revolutionary situation without even realizing it. The only means of those enemies of the Revolution was then to clamor and to slander, reflecting their deeply ingrained fear of victory of the revolutionary wave in Iraq. This fear soon found its way into our ranks through the infiltration of rightist conceptions and the existence of a strongly entrenched rightist tendency, and because of our constant fear of "leftist deviation." Our bourgeois enemy-allies scared us off by evoking the threat of a civil war, which is an ever present possibility. Yet, had one occurred then, it would have turned out in our favor. Whereas, when it did start effectively in February 1963, it took the form of an atrocious butchery against communists and revolutionary democrats. Reaction emerged victorious because it chose the appropriate time and place. As for our fear of civil war in 1959, it did not serve to avoid the catastrophe, but, on the contrary, helped render it inevitable.

During the revolutionary situation of the spring of 1959, there was no way out of the revolutionary crisis except by seizing power from Qassem, whose bargaining with the right wing had been evident before the [Shawwaf] conspiracy and who found himself in an embarrassing situation after it. Qassem knew how to retreat after the conspiracy and until the end of April 1959. As for us, we missed a historic opportunity and lost for the people a unique revolutionary situation.

The rightists claim that the main battle until mid-1959 was against imperialism and counterrevolution. Therefore, it was incorrect to press—even to press!—for developing the Revolution and the seizure of power by the revolutionary classes. The fact is that the national and the democratic contents of the Revolution are interlocked and therefore inseparable. We all know, for example, that the conflict with the nationalists and Cairo revolved essentially around the question of political democracy (in its popular, not bourgeois, sense); and that the fear of Iraq's development along the road to democracy and the fear of our Party's influence and that of the peasant movement are the only explanation why those parties were so keen on imposing their unionist policy (i.e., Arab unity devoid of any political democracy in which the communist parties be banned) on Iraq at any cost. Furthermore, the complete victory against imperialism (and its oil companies in particular) and the efficient resistance to the mounting wave of reactionary plots were only possible by relying on the broadest masses in an atmosphere of ample freedom, by winning over the great mass of peasants to the revolutionary camp and by organizing them on the basis of a radical agrarian reform in the implementation of which the peasant would have direct, structural participation. Therefore, the establishment of a revolutionary, national-democratic regime was required in order to sustain a resolute struggle against imperialism and to successfully defeat counterrevolution.

In the conditions of Iraq, this regime can only come about through an active and efficient, if not leading, role played by the working class and its Party in state power. As for us, we have idealized bourgeois nationalism and consolidated the bourgeois regime which was not even capable of preserving itself or its leader on February 8, 1963—all this in the name of fighting against imperialism and counterrevolution. The slogan of "defending the Revolution" exemplified this idealization of bourgeois nationalism. Whereas we should have raised, from the beginning, the slogan of a "revolutionary, national-democratic regime," educated the masses about the need for the participation of the ICP in state power, constantly exposing the ambivalence of the national bourgeoisie and its political organs, and organized the broadest masses to impose the implementation of a revolutionary democracy through the escalation of mass pressure, then moved to the overthrow of Qassem himself when he persisted in refusing to heed the will of the masses. Had we followed this strategy and adopted the appropriate revolutionary tactics, we would most probably have succeeded in seizing state power during the period of revolutionary upsurge in 1959, or at least initiated civil war in such a way as to make sure that we would have emerged from it victorious.

The principal factor which led to the defeat of armed resistance against the February 8 coup was a strategic and not a tactical factor: our adoption of an erroneous strategy based on negative defense. We resolved not to initiate armed struggle in defense of this regime when faced with a military coup. In other words, we decided not to initiate civil war, but avoid it at all costs—at a time when the other forces were preparing for it, sharpening their knives to butcher us. Indeed, we resigned initiative to the counterrevolution to choose the most appropriate moment to realize its dream of liquidating our Party and crushing the revolutionary movement.

The rightist ideas which have dominated our Party since 1959 were the cause of the defeat of armed resistance in 1963. But those ideas say the Party committed the mistake of calling the masses to arms on February 8 without providing them with a sufficient number of arms and ammunition. In fact, our Party had a following of thousands of officers and soldiers, and the great mass of soldiers at large was opposed to the coup. But four years of negative defense and leaving the initiative in the hands of the enemy paralyzed these effective "reserves" from launching armed resistance against the putschists (and the same applies to thousands of armed peasants).

In our plans for armed resistance, before February 8, we relied heavily on our peasant comrades-in-arms only to discover after the coup serious flaws in this vital sector. We lacked small armed bands composed of trained comrades devoted to armed struggle who could constitute the nucleus and the pole that attracts the mass of armed peasants. Those were serious tactical and technical flaws, but our basic mistake was a tactical one: we left the peasant masses in a vicious circle during the years 1958–59, did not encourage them to settle accounts with their class enemies—the big landowners and the feudalists—and refrained from training them to defend their acquisitions after Qassem's retreat which started in mid-1959. We left them "in reserve" to defend the Republic when the "decisive day" came, but without relating this to any of their vital interests. And when this "decisive day" finally came, only the vanguard of the peasantry moved.

Setting up revolutionary organizations inside the armed forces is a relatively easy task, but it is quite difficult to preserve such organizations for long in a country dominated by political reaction which deprives the people of its most elementary rights. The official, military command of the army, as distinct from its revolutionary command, controls military discipline which banks on a huge force—the force of habit. The military commander can move his troops by one order, whereas the revolutionary commander (i.e., the Party) requires the existence of a high revolutionary mood among his revolutionary forces, and needs strong levers in the form of special organizations (special armed detachments, shock troops, a vanguard, etc.).

One of the big flaws in our previous defense plan lay in the fact in that everything depended on winning or losing the battle in Baghdad. Our military and civilian organizations did not possess a plan to pursue armed struggle outside Baghdad. This was bound to lead to confusion or even sheer desperation. After the defeat of our first resistance, we should have operated a provisional, organized retreat, or at least withdrawn our cadres to a relatively safe area. Nothing of the sort happened. As usual, our organizations and cadres were put under strict emergency regulations; furthermore, they remained in the cities and did not take refuge as a whole in the countryside—a fact which facilitated their capture. Had there been a plan ready before the coup for withdrawal of some of our military and civilian comrades to the countryside, then we could have started the civil war in a relatively forceful manner, or, at least, our forces would not have been annihilated without fighting as was the case when some of our cadres defected.

Our military strategy was one of quick decision which resolves the conflict in one decisive blow ("all or nothing") and thus we lacked a long-term defensive plan. But this military flaw is a consequence of our political line which refrained from furthering the workers' and peasants' revolution but limited itself to "defending the Revolution" or ameliorating the situation in alliance with the bourgeois forces inside or outside government. It never occurred to us to organize the agrarian revolution or push it forward by encouraging the peasants to enforce the land reform law as a *fait accompli* by confiscating the lands of the feudalists or refusing to pay rent.

From the beginning of 1964, "the spirit of the age"—i.e., the age of transition to socialism on a world scale, the age of increasing might of the socialist camp and of its influence on the course of world events, the age of the disintegration of the colonialist system, etc.—was used to give priority to peaceful struggle (at a time when the country was plagued with a reactionary military dictatorship). Thus, giving priority to other means of struggle over the armed struggle was not conceived on the basis of the specific internal situation in Iraq (the enemy's strength, the strength of the democratic movement, the level of revolutionary consciousness among the masses, the Kurdish revolution, Iraq's strategic location, the oil economy, historical conditions, etc., etc.) but on a multitude of factors which contain not one single reference to internal conditions.

The rightist tendency further used the "spirit of the age" to prove that our Party and the democratic movement at large now play a secondary role not only in all the Arab countries, but also in all the newly independent states. Time and time again, our Party stressed the positive impact of the "spirit of the age" on Nasser, Ben Bella, and even Aref, to point out the possibilities of the development of the Arab Socialist Union in Iraq into an organization for all revolutionaries—only to discard the leading role of the working class in the Revolution, political democracy, and even the dictatorship of the proletariat.

How can communists exercise their political, intellectual, and educational influence and carry out their vanguard role without possessing their independent Party, with its developed ideology and organization? Is the dissolution of communist organizations in some independent Arab countries and the integration of communists into a formless organization which includes six million members[4]—full of reactionaries, characterized by ideological disunity and political apathy, and constituting an integral part of the existing regime—a solution in the interest of the revolutionary movement in this country? Were communists really able to exercise real and effective "political, intellectual, and educational influence"? Or have they been totally submerged in the dominant petty-bourgeois milieu? Was it not in the interest of the national-democratic—not to say socialist —revolution in [newly independent countries] that strong communist parties should have existed *at least* in order to face the threat of counter-revolutionary coups (e.g., the experiences of Ghana and Algeria)? Isn't the existence of such parties necessary *at least* to organize the masses for resisting those coups?

As for Cairo's Arab policy, it is a wavering opportunistic and short-sighted policy which is by no means governed by general revolutionary principles, despite its dominant anti-imperialist character. Although Nasser recognized, in 1962, the error of establishing a truce with Egyptian and

---

[4] Reference to the Arab Socialist Union (ASU), the ruling party in Egypt.—*Ed.*

Arab reaction, he nevertheless initiated the Arab summit conference [in 1964] in which he once more concluded peace with the ruling Arab oligarchies and bestowed upon them a false nationalist whitewash, only to launch a recent attack against summit conferences and so on, alternating between glorifying Bourguiba and Hussein and denouncing and attacking them.

As regards Iraq, Cairo's policy is to collaborate with any Iraqi government which is not openly hostile to it, whatever its nature may be and irrespective of the feeling of the Iraqi people toward it. Indeed Cairo wishes, and tries to get, its Iraqi friends in power. Yet it is well aware of their weakness and isolation. Therefore, it prefers to collaborate with any Iraqi government which is willing to be friendly with Egypt, however reactionary its internal policy might be. But Cairo would never accept a revolutionary, democratic solution to the government crisis in Iraq, i.e., a solution in which our Party would play a major role.

In view of Cairo's empiricist, opportunist policy, it is hardly surprising that it supported the February [1963] coup and concluded the April [1963] agreements with the putschists.[5] When Cairo failed to convince the Ba'athis to subordinate their rule to hers, she broke relations with them. In fact, Cairo did not break those relations because of the Ba'athis' bloody, fascist policy against the communists and democrats, nor for their aggressive chauvinism against Kurdish nationalism or their soft policy toward the feudalists and the oil companies; the conflict revolved around the refusal of the Ba'athis to bow down to Cairo orders. It is precisely for this same reason that Cairo then supported the October [1963] coup, collaborated with Aref and Taher Yahia, and concluded the "coordination agreement" with their regime. In practice, this agreement ran counter to all of Cairo's statements and platforms on "the unity of the Arab toilers" and to its "new" concept of Arab unity. For what has the "unity of the toilers" to do with concluding a "coordination agreement" with a reactionary military clique isolated from the vast majority of the Iraqi people? What kind of "progressive union" is it that does not care to collaborate with the revolutionary progressive forces in Iraq, but collaborates instead with a terrorist, chauvinist gang which is suppressing those forces? What is important is not the new unionist platforms, but their execution—i.e., the practical policy which Cairo is still following.

In Iraq, meanwhile, the communist leadership hailed the "coordinating agreement" as the first step toward the unity of all Arab toilers and a guiding light to all the future battles against imperialism in the area at large. The rightist tendency raised the slogan of the "identity of conditions in Egypt and Iraq," calling for the emulation of Egypt in all fields, "especially in internal policy and agrarian reform." Our position on the

[5] Which called for the establishment of a tripartite union between Egypt, Syria, and Iraq.—*Ed.*

"coordination agreement" should have been, instead, one of opposition because it was concluded with a reactionary dictatorship in Iraq and without any popular participation or control.

Repeating slogans of neutralism, peaceful coexistence, and of the need for closer relations with the socialist countries is not enough, presently, as a criterion to judge the anti-imperialism of a regime. One should be aware of the methods of neo-imperialism which is willing to accede to the raising of such slogans, provided the regime in question implements an anti-communist policy and preserves the economic interests of imperialism, especially oil. The real criterion for assessing the anti-imperialism of any regime is its position on the economic positions of imperialism, its acceptance of, or opposition to, the main imperialist policies concerning the major world issues.

The rightist line of our Party has simply forgotten that the question of political power is the central question in any revolution, and that progressive economic measures which are taken under various pressures cannot be implemented or consolidated if state power remains in the hands of reactionary groups which are hostile to the people. Even the "progressive" regimes in Syria, Egypt, and some African countries cannot last and push the Revolution forward without liberating the initiative of the masses and granting them freedom of organization and action, without effective and active participation of the masses in the running of the state. The struggle for political democracy (in its popular, revolutionary—and not bourgeois—sense) is a struggle for the right of the working class and the toiling peasants to organize themselves, have their independent class activity, and defend their vital interests.

Africa

No black man has more influenced African revolutionary thought and activity than Frantz Fanon. Born July 20, 1925, in Fort de France, in the impoverished French colony of Martinique, Fanon wrote his first enraged attack on colonialism when he was barely thirteen. Later, he journeyed to France and studied medicine at Lyons University, then enlisted in the French army and fought the Germans under General de Lattre de Tassigny. Reaching Algeria in 1952, in the midst of the Maghreb Rebellion, Fanon went to work in the psychiatric hospital of Blida, where, commented a friend, every day "he discovers in his patients the scars of colonialism—delirium, mental disturbances, fury, paranoia—all the evasions invented by the colonized in order to escape oppression. He finds a sort of refuge in madness: this—for lack of anything better—is his means of liberating himself." Fanon himself wrote at the time: "I want only one thing; for the exploitation of man by man to cease forever on this earth."

To help bring that end about, Fanon began to write furiously against French exploitation in Algeria. His voice gained listeners—and the wrath of the French occupiers. So, in 1956, he fled to Tunisia, where he joined the Algerian National Liberation Front, which appointed him editor of El Moujahid, the official organ of the Algerian revolutionaries. As the Algerian War progressed, Fanon changed—and showed it in his articles. "The challenging of the very principle of foreign domination," he wrote, "brings about essential mutations in the consciousness of the colonized, in the manner in which he perceives the colonizer, in his human status in the world."

Fanon went on to endorse Pan-Africanism and, as he traveled throughout Africa representing the Provisional Government of the Algerian Republic (GPRA), to proselytize for it. In fact, he became an African revolutionary, above and beyond his loyalty to Algeria. Finally, by 1961,

257

in his greatest and last book, The Wretched of the Earth *(for, as he knew, he was dying of leukemia), he broadened Pan-Africanism to Pan-Third Worldism—and advocated revolution by all peoples exploited by "the Americans [who] take their role of patron of international capitalism very seriously." Colonialism (by which he also meant imperialism) "is not a thinking machine, nor a body endowed with reasoning faculties. It is violence in its natural state, and it will only yield when confronted with greater violence. At the decisive moment, the colonialist bourgeoisie, which up till then has remained inactive, comes into the field. It introduces that new idea which is in proper parlance a creation of the colonial situation: nonviolence."*

The cry against violence is heard only when the victims are white, Fanon said. Who among America's liberal bourgeoisie talked about nonviolence when blacks were being beaten, lynched, slaughtered by whites in the South? Then, everyone insisted on nonviolence. "In 1945," Fanon wrote, "the 45,000 dead at Setif could pass unnoticed; in 1947, the 90,000 dead at Madagascar could be the subject of a simple paragraph in the papers; in 1952, the 200,000 victims of the repression in Kenya could meet with relative indifference." Had he lived until 1965, he would have pointed out that the murder of 1,000,000 Congolese elicited almost no outcry while the whole Western world wailed and shouted when the Congolese revolutionaries retaliated on a few hundred whites. Colonialism, concluded Fanon, must be racist to justify its violence. And then, once a man is racist, his violence eggs him on to be more of a colonialist.

Fanon was also one of the first Africans to understand that the United States and Russia basically see eye to eye; their entente, he said in 1961 (just before he died), eliminates progress, thus "peaceful coexistence between the two blocs provokes and feeds violence in the colonial countries." Against that violence—the violence of poverty, hunger, disease, ignorance, as well as modern warfare, and especially the violence caused by the privation of dignity—Fanon posited counterviolence, the violence of the revolutionary. "At the level of individuals," he said, "violence is a cleansing force. It frees the native from his inferiority complex and from his despair and inaction; it makes him fearless and restores his self-respect. Even if the armed struggle has been symbolic and the nation is demobilized through a rapid movement of decolonization, the people have the time to see that the liberation has been the business of each and all and that the leader has no special merit."

In the passages below, Fanon also concludes that in the struggle against imperialism, only the friendship "wrought in combat" is reliable. The passages are notes written after the summer of 1960, while the author traveled through Africa on diplomatic missions for the GPRA. In the first series, he is moved by the murder (by poison) of Felix Moumié, leader of the Union of Cameroon Population Party (UPC). Organized by

Moumié, Reuben Um Nyobe (who was also murdered, presumably also by French agents) and Osendé Afana, three of black Africa's greatest intellectuals, the UPC had tried to oppose the colonialism of France and Britain from the end of World War II to 1955, by legal means. That year, UPC launched an armed struggle which brought about official independence in 1960 and a partition of the Cameroons into a Federation in 1961. That Federation, totally submissive and directed by French-English neo-colonialists, provoked a new uprising and the UPC again launched guerrilla warfare operations. The first battles, in which Afana was killed, almost destroyed the National Liberation Army (ALN) of the UPC. But it regrouped, reorganized, and retrained. By mid-1969, the ALN had secured two fronts—despite the intervention of a French expeditionary force.

The second set of notes by Fanon was triggered by the murder of Patrice Lumumba (see Congo-Kinshasa, p. 307 below). What galled Fanon was the number of African leaders who were willing to betray their people for the pay of the imperialists—which, as he said, are led by the United States. He was convinced that part of the trouble was the absence of ideology. Had Africans been firmly imbued with a sense of unity, they would have had a better perspective on the Congo and the role there of Belgians, South Africans, and Americans, he said. Lumumba himself would have realized that the U.N. is nothing more than a "legal card" of the imperialists. His mistake, said Fanon, was "to believe in the friendly impartiality of the U.N." Grounded in a sound ideological base, other African leaders of independent countries would not have sent troops to serve under the U.N. command but directly to help Lumumba. Fanon concluded that Africans must learn to be self-reliant and build mutual cooperation through mutual commitment—"friendship wrought in combat"—to a united Africa.

Fanon himself cannot be pigeonholed into any of the world's prevalent revolutionary ideologies. He was a militant nationalist, Third Worldist (or Tricontinentalist), and anti-imperialist. He often did fall back on Marxist class analysis but was no communist—except in the most profound sense that he believed that all men should live and act and make decisions and rule themselves collectively. More than anything else, he was antiexploitation and he understood that man's exploitation of man will never end until the wretched of the earth have shaken off their inferiority complexes by grabbing arms and forcing their exploiters and all of their institutions, propaganda, aid programs, and cultural paternalisms out of their hands.

FRANTZ FANON: MISSIONS, MARTYRS, MOVEMENTS*

TO get Africa on the move, to work for its organizations, for its restructuring behind revolutionary principles; to participate in the ordered movement of a continent—that's what I really wanted to do. The take-off point, the first base, was represented by Guinea. Then Mali, ready for anything, fervent and brutal, coherent and singularly sharp, extended the bridgehead and opened precious perspectives. To the east, Lumumba was marking time. The Congo, which constituted the second beachhead for revolutionary ideas, found itself in a painful morass of sterile contradictions. It was not time yet to assault the colonialist citadels of Angola, Mozambique, Kenya, Rhodesia, the Union of South Africa. Yet everything was ready. And then the colonialist defense system was reviving old particularisms and undercutting the liberating lava. For the time being, then, it was necessary to hang on to the Congo and advance in the west.

For us, Algerians, the situation was clear. But the terrain remained difficult, very difficult. From the west, we had to prove that the continent was concrete. Behind the general options available to leaders, it was possible to determine the precise points where the peoples, the men and the women, could help, help each other, build in common. The specter of the West, the European tinges, was everywhere present and active. The French, English, Spanish, Portuguese areas remained in existence. Oxford opposed the Sorbonne, Lisbon was against Brussels, the British bosses against the Portuguese bosses, the pound against the franc, the Catholic Church against Protestantism or Islam. And on top of all this, the United States penetrated everywhere, dollars in the vanguard, also the black American diplomats, scholarships, broadcasts of the Voice of America. Difficult work. Fortunately, in every corner, arms signal us, voices answer us, hands grasp ours. Things move.

The rapid and reassuring noise of the liberated cities that smash their moorings and advance, grandiloquent but not at all grandiose, these veteran militants today having definitely passed their exams, who sit down and—remember. But the sun is still very high in the sky, and if one listens to it, with an ear glued to the red earth, one distinctly hears the sound of rusty chains, the groans of distress, and the shoulders droop from the bruised flesh in this stifling noonday. The Africa of everyday, oh not that of the poets, not the one that puts you to sleep, but the one that stops you from sleeping, for the people are impatient to do, to

---

* Series of notes written after the summer of 1960. The first set was published in *Révolution Africaine*, December 14, 1963; the second set, on the death of Lumumba, is from *Tricontinental*, July–August 1967. Translations from the French and Spanish by Juan Mechón.

play, to say. The people who say: I want to build myself as a people, I want to build, to love, to respect, to create. That people who cry when you tell them: I come from a country where women are without children and children without mothers and who chant: Algeria, brother country, country that calls, country that hopes.

That is the real Africa, the Africa we had to let loose in the continental furrow, in the continental direction; that Africa that we had to orient, mobilize, throw into the offensive. That Africa to come. The West. Conakry, Bamako. Two cities dead on the surface but below the temperature is unendurable for those who calculate, who maneuver, who profit. In Conakry and in Bamako, men strike Africa, forge it with love and enthusiasm.

Colonialism and its derivatives do not, as a matter of fact, constitute the present enemies of Africa. In a short time, the continent will be liberated. For my part, the deeper I penetrate into the cultural and political circles, the more I am convinced that the greatest danger menacing Africa is the absence of ideology. For nearly three years I have been trying to bring the misty idea of African Unity out of the subjectivist wells, to expose clearly the phantoms posited by the majority of its supporters. African Unity is at the same time a dream, a myth, a nightmare, a will power, and what not. African Unity is a principle from which we propose to establish the United States of Africa without going through the bourgeois-chauvinist phase, with its procession of wars and mournings. To initiate this unity all combinations are possible. Some, like Guinea, Ghana, Mali, and tomorrow maybe Algeria, put political action to the forefront. The UAR, on its side, puts a greater emphasis on cultural aspects. Everything is possible, and one and the other should avoid trying to discredit or denounce those who see that unity, that rapprochement among African states, differently from them.

Moumié. On September 30, we met at the Accra airport. He was going to Geneva for some very important meetings. In three months, he told me, we would see a massive decline of colonialism in the Cameroons. In Tripoli, the fog stopped all landings for three hours and the plane had to circle above. The pilot wanted to land anyway. The tower refused to give him permission but the courageous and heedless pilot decided to land his tens of thousands of tons. "These guys are gambling with people's lives," Felix said to me.

It was true. But were we not also gambling with ours? What was this intrepidity in comparison to our lives perpetually in suspense? Today, Felix is dead. In Rome, two weeks later, we were to meet again. He was not there. When I returned to Accra, his father saw me arrive alone at the airport and his face betrayed deep anguish. Two days later, I was informed that Felix had been hospitalized. It was suspected that he had been poisoned. Kigué, the vice-president of the UPC, and Marthe Moumié decided to go to Geneva. A few days later, we heard: Felix Moumié was dead.

We hardly felt his death. An assassination, but a bloodless one. Neither machine-gun volleys nor bombs; thallium poisoning. It made no sense. Thallium! How to understand such a cause? An abstract death striking the most concrete, the most alive, the most impetuous man. Felix's tone was constantly high, aggressive, violent, choleric, in love with his country, hating cowards and manipulators. Austere, hard, incorruptible. Of revolutionary essence packed into 60 kilos of muscle and bone.

In the evening we went to comfort the Cameroon comrades. The father, his face seamed, impassive, inexpressive, listened to me talk of his son. And gradually, the father made way for the militant. Yes, said he, the program is clear. We must stick to the program. Moumié's father, at that moment, reminded me of those Algerian parents who listen, stupefied, to the story of how their children died; who, from time to time, question, demand a detail, then relapse into that inertia of communion that seems to draw them to where they think their sons have gone.

Yet, that's where the action is. Tomorrow, in a moment, we'll have to take the war to the enemy, allow him no rest, no respite, no chance to breathe. Let's go.

We're now in Bamako, capital of Mali. Modibo Keita, always militant, understands rapidly. No need to make long speeches. Our work sessions are short. We're eight. One commando, the army, transmission, political commissars, the sanitary corps. Each of the pairs is to prospect according to his own discipline the possibilities of work. Our mission: to open the southern front. To transport arms and munitions from Bamako. Stir up the Saharan population. To infiltrate into the Algerian high plateaus. After having brought Algeria to the four corners of Africa, to come back with all of Africa toward Algerian Africa, toward the north, toward Algiers, the continental city.

What I want: great lines, great navigation canals through the Sahara. Subdue the desert, deny it, reassemble Africa, create the continent. That from Mali may descend on our territory Malians, Senegalese, Guineans, Ghanaians. And those from Nigeria, Togoland, the Ivory Coast. That all climb the slopes of the desert and flow over the bastion of colonialism. To turn the absurd and the impossible inside out and throw a continent into an assault against the last ramparts of colonial power.

We must hurry. Time presses. The enemy is still tenacious. In reality he does not believe in military defeat. But me, I have never felt victory so possible, so within reach. We need only to march, to charge. It's not even a matter of strategy. We have mobilized, and furious cohorts, loving our combat, are eager to work. We have Africa with us.

But who's preoccupied? A continent is set to explode and Europe is languishingly asleep. Fifteen years ago, it was Asia that stirred. Then,

Westerners were having fun. Today, Europe and the United States hunch their backs. The 650 million Chinese, calm possessors of an immense secret, are building a world by themselves. Are giving birth to a world.

*   *

Observers who happened to be in the capitals of Africa during the month of June 1960 could have been aware of a certain number of things. All sorts of strange people from the Congo, which had just made its appearance on the international scene, kept showing up. What did these Congolese have to say? It didn't matter.

But if one took aside one of these Congolese and interrogated him seriously, then one could have become aware that something very grave was being plotted against the independence of the Congo and against Africa.

Shortly after the independence celebration, Congolese senators and deputies left the Congo and went to the United States. Others installed themselves for a few weeks in Brazzaville. Trade unionists were invited to New York. Still in Africa, were one to buttonhole one of these deputies or senators, one would have learned that a whole very precise course of action was about to be put into motion.

From before July 1, 1960, had been launched the Katanga operation. To be sure, to safeguard the Union Minière. But it was Belgian interests that were being defended behind this operation. A unified Congo, with a central government, went counter to Belgian interests. To support the decentralization of the various provinces, to provoke such demands, to pour fuel over them, such was Belgian policy before independence. In their task, the Belgians were helped by the authorities of the Rhodesia-Nyasaland Federation. Today it is known—and Mr. Hammarskjöld knows it better than anyone—that, before June 30, 1960, a Salisbury-Elizabethville airlift supplied arms to Katanga. Lumumba had once proclaimed that the liberation of the Congo was the first phase in the complete liberation of central and southern Africa and had set his next objectives very precisely: support for the nationalist movements of Rhodesia, Angola, and South Africa.

A unified Congo with an anticolonialist at its head constituted a very real danger for that southern Africa, that very southern Africa before which the rest of the world veils its face. Or rather: before which the rest of the world is content to weep, as during Sharpeville, or to perform stylistic exercises on anticolonial day celebrations. Lumumba, as leader of the first country in that region to obtain independence and in concrete awareness of what colonialism was all about, had taken the responsibility, in the name of his people, to help physically bring about the death of that Africa. That the authorities in Katanga and Portugal had used everything at their disposal to sabotage the Congo's independence does not surprise us. That they reinforced the action of the Belgians and augmented the thrust of the centrifugal forces of the Congo is a fact. But this fact does not explain the coldly planned, coldly executed assassination of Lumumba. This colonialist collaboration is insufficient to explain why, in February 1961, Africa is about to experience its first great crisis over the Congo.

Its first great crisis because it will have to decide whether it wants to go forward or backward. It will have to understand that it is no longer possible to advance by regions; that, like a great body that fights off all mutilations, it will have to advance on all fronts; that there will not be one Africa which fights colonialism and another Africa that comes to terms with it. It will be necessary for Africa, that is to say Africans, to understand that there can never be greatness in procrastination and that there can never be dishonor in saying what one is and what one wants, and that in reality the advantage of the colonized, in the last analysis, can only be his courage, the lucid awareness of his objectives and of his alliances, and the tenacity that he brings to his liberation.

Lumumba believed in his mission. He had an exaggerated faith in his people. For him, the people not only could not deceive themselves but also could not be deceived. And in fact he seemed to be right. Each time, for example, that in some region or other the enemies of the Congo managed to undermine his policy, it was sufficient for him to appear, explain, denounce, for the situation to return to normal. But he would forget that he could not be everywhere at the same time and that the truth of his explanation was less than the truth of his person.

Lumumba had lost the battle for the presidency of the Republic. But, because he embodied from the beginning the confidence that the Congolese people had placed in him, because the African peoples confusedly understood that he alone was concerned with the dignity of his country, Lumumba continued to express the Congolese patriotism and the African nationalism which is most rigorous and noble.

As a result, other countries that are more important than Belgium or Portugal decided to take a direct interest in the matter. Lumumba was contacted, interrogated. After his trip to the United States, the decision was made: Lumumba must go.

Why? Because the enemies of Africa were not fooled. They realized perfectly that Lumumba had sold himself. Sold himself to Africa, of course. That meant that he was no longer up for sale.

The enemies of Africa realized with some horror that should Lumumba succeed in the very heart of the colonialist empire—with a French Africa being transformed into a renovated community, and Angola into a Portuguese "province," and finally eastern Africa—it was finished with "their" Africa, for which they had very precise plans.

The great success of the enemies of Africa is to have compromised the Africans themselves. It is true that these Africans were directly interested in the death of Lumumba. Chiefs of puppet governments, in the center of a puppet independence, confronted day after day by the massive opposition of their peoples, did not take long to convince themselves that the real independence of the Congo would put them personally in danger.

There were other Africans, a little less puppet, who became frightened of the idea of separating Africa from the West. One could say that these African chiefs of state always feared facing Africa. They too, although less actively but consciously, contributed to the deterioration of the situation in the Congo.

Little by little, the West agreed that it was necessary to intervene in the Congo, that one just couldn't let things evolve at such a rate. Little by little, the idea of intervention by the U.N. took shape. Then, as we can see now, two errors were committed by Africans. The first was by Lumumba, when he asked the U.N. to intervene. It was not necessary to appeal to the U.N. Never has the U.N. been capable of solving a single problem raised before the conscience of man by colonialism, and each time it has intervened, it has done so to give concrete help to the colonialist power of the oppressing country.

Look at the Cameroons. What peace do Ahidjo's subjects enjoy when they are held down by a French expeditionary force which, in large part, got its experience fighting in Algeria? Meanwhile, the U.N. has controlled the self-determination of the Cameroons and the French government has installed a "provisional executive."

Look at Vietnam. Look at Laos.

It is not true to say that the U.N. has failed because the cases are difficult. In reality, the U.N. is the legal card used by the imperialists when the card of brute force has failed.

The partitions, the joint control commissions, the trusteeships are all international legal means of torture, meant to crush the will to independence of the peoples, to cultivate anarchy, banditry, and misery.

For after all, there were no massacres in the Congo before the U.N. arrived. Despite the hallucinating rumors propagated to coincide with the departure of the Belgians, one could count only some ten dead. But since the U.N. arrived, we have become accustomed to learn every morning that the Congolese massacre each other by the hundreds.

Today, we are informed that repeated provocations were made by Belgian soldiers acting as soldiers of the United Nations. Today we learn that civilian functionaries of the U.N. had set up a new government already on the third day of Lumumba's investiture. So now we can understand much better what has been called Lumumba's violence, rigidity, and susceptibility.

In fact, everything shows that Lumumba was abnormally calm.

The chiefs of the U.N. mission made contact with Lumumba's enemies and with them decided to destroy the State of the Congo. In such a case, how should the head of government react? The aim sought and hoped for is the following: to manifest the absence of authority, prove the failing of the state.

And with that, then, motivate the sequestering of the Congo.

Lumumba's mistake, then, was, in the first place, to believe in the friendly impartiality of the U.N. He forgot that in the present state, the U.N. is nothing more than a reserve assembly, under the boot of the Great Ones, to carry on, between armed conflicts, the "peaceful struggle" for the partitioning of the world. If Ileo, in August 1960, was telling anyone who would listen to him that Lumumba had to be hanged, if the members of Lumumba's cabinet did not know what to do with all the dollars which at that time invaded Leopoldville, if, finally, Mobutu went to Brazzaville every evening to do and hear what we can now guess, why then turn with such sincerity, with such absence of reserve toward the U.N.?

Africans must remember this lesson. If outside help is needed, let us call upon our friends. Only they can really and totally help us to realize our objectives because the friendship which binds us has been wrought in combat.

But for their part, the African countries committed a grave error in sending their troops under the control of the U.N. By that fact, they let themselves be neutralized and, without suspecting it, allowed the others to do their work.

Surely, they should have sent troops to Lumumba—but not within the framework of the U.N. Directly. From friendly country to friendly country. The African troops in the Congo have suffered a historical moral defeat. With crossed feet, they watched without reacting (because they were U.N. troops) the disintegration of a state and nation which all of Africa had saluted and praised. A shame.

Our mistake, we Africans, comes from the fact that we forgot that the enemy never really means his withdrawals. He never understands. He may capitulate, but he is never converted.

Our mistake was to have believed that the enemy had lost his combativeness and his nefariousness. If Lumumba gets in the way, Lumumba gets put out of the way. Imperialism has never hesitated to murder.

Look at Ben M'Hidi, look at Moumié, look at Lumumba. Our mistake was to have been slightly confused in our action. Naturally, in the Africa of today, traitors exist. It is imperative to denounce them and combat them. That this is hard after the magnificent dream of an Africa bound together and subject to the same exigencies of true independence does not change the facts.

Africans have swallowed the imperialist policy in the Congo, have served as intermediaries, have swallowed the activities and the weird silences of the U.N. in the Congo.

Today they are afraid. They compete with one another in shedding hypocritical tears over the murdered Lumumba. Let us not be fooled any more: they fear their bosses. And the imperialists themselves are also afraid. And with reason, because many Africans, many Afro-Asians have understood. The imperialists are trying to mark time. They want to wait for the "legitimate emotion" to die down. We must take advantage of this short respite to abandon our fearful acts and to decide to save the Congo and Africa.

The imperialists decided to strike down Lumumba. They have done so. They decided to raise voluntary legions. Those are now in place.

The Katanga air force, under command of South Africans and Belgian pilots, began a few days ago to strafe the ground with machine guns. From Brazzaville, foreign planes come full of volunteers and paratroop officers destined to rescue a certain Congo.

No one knows the name of the next Lumumba. There is in Africa a certain tendency represented by certain men. It is this tendency, dangerous for imperialism, which is at stake. Let us be on guard never to forget it: that is our fate, the fate of all of us, that is at stake in the Congo.

Morocco

Though Che Guevara popularized the slogan, he was not the only early exponent of the "many Vietnams" theory. If he gets most of the credit for it today, if he is hailed as one of the all-time great revolutionaries by the thousands of liberation fighters engaged in actual combat in over sixty countries of the world, it is because Che himself lived and died as one of them. But the Moroccan nationalist, El Mehdi Ben Barka, ultimately played just as crucial a role in establishing solidarity among the liberation fighters of the Third World, and in developing what is known today as the Tricontinental spirit (of which the many-Vietnams theory is the military characteristic). That is why he, too, had to be killed.

The son of a Moroccan cop, Ben Barka grew up in Rabat as one of a hundred small-time rabble rousers against the French. At twenty-two, with a handful of Moroccan intellectuals, he organized the Istiqlal Party, which was strictly an independence movement, and hoped for a constitutional monarchy. (In fact, to earn his living, he gave math lessons to the royal prince who, later, as King Mohammed V, once appealed to him to stop his international intrigues by pleading, "I need my mathematics teacher here with me.")

Repeatedly jailed by the French, Ben Barka repeatedly escaped—and kept organizing. Small, mysterious, and self-effacing but with a disarming smile and a warm handshake, he remained in the background as much as possible, even after Morocco became an independent monarchy and he was elected president of its first National Council. Realizing, as he said, that true independence comes only when the wealth is owned by all the people, not just a small upper class in partnership with foreign capitalists, Ben Barka moved to the left, and organized another party, this time called the National Union of Popular Forces (UNFP). Its single motto was then "Land for the Peasants."

Early in 1963, Ben Barka and twenty-eight of his comrades were elected to the National Assembly. But a few weeks later, the UNFP was accused of plotting to overthrow the monarchy, and Ben Barka was condemned to death. Escaping once again, he first tried to organize internal resistance, then went into exile to stir things up outside.

Hounded by the Moroccan secret police, which acted under the direct supervision of Morocco's Minister of Interior, General Mohammed Oufkir, a Foreign Legion veteran of Vietnam and long-time CIA operative, Ben Barka dodged assassin's bullets as he hopscotched from Cairo to Geneva, Algiers to Hanoi, Paris to Havana. As he did so, his vision expanded: No longer did he work for the liberation of Morocco alone; he now sought the liberation of all of Africa, and eventually of the whole Third World. Indefatigable, persuasive, coldly thorough, it was he who did most to convince the Afro-Asian representatives attending the 1965 conference at Winneba that their common enemy was capitalism. That Afro-Asian Solidarity meeting proclaimed that "all the wars, aggressions, and interventions of imperialism, its maintenance of military bases in foreign lands, and its support for cruel and corrupt dictatorship, spring from and are dictated by economic exploitation." Ben Barka then drew the logical consequence: "We must achieve greater coordination in the struggle of all the peoples, as the problems in Vietnam, the Congo, and the Dominican Republic stem from the same source: U.S. imperialism."

That coordination was to be the Organization of Solidarity of the Peoples of Africa, Asia, and Latin America (OSPAAAL), known today as the Tricon. And as Ben Barka had done more than anyone to weld it together, he was elected chairman of its preparatory committee. But he never actually attended the Tricon. For, one fall day in 1965, he was "arrested" by French policemen as he chatted with friends in a Paris café, taken to the villa of a French mafioso and murdered, apparently in the presence of Minister Oufkir (who was indicted for the crime but released when Ben Barka's body was not found). Dumped in the Essonnes River near Corbeil, the body was presumably recovered and discreetly disposed of by France's Gaullist Police parallèle, a parapolitical organization of Marseilles underworld figures who carry out "delicate missions in the interests of the State"—anything Gaullism dislikes—from the kidnapping of right-wing rebellious generals after the Franco-Algerian entente to the liquidation of potential revolutionaries (e.g., Felix Moumié and Reuben Um Nyobe of the Cameroons).

Ben Barka's greatest contribution to Third World revolutionary theory was his insightful analyses of neo-colonialism. In the first part of the article below, a report written in January 1960, he clearly foretells how imperialism will adapt itself to ruling the underdeveloped world from afar —through neo-colonial institutions. Pushing their so-called concept of so-called liberal democracy, he says, the imperialists will try to convince the newly independent nations of Africa that pluralism, religious freedom, open unions, market-oriented economics, and the use of the old intellectual bureaucracies are all fundamental ingredients for the creation of a viable new country. In fact, and the imperialists know it full well, each of these ingredients confuses and debilitates the new state. Pluralism leads to the creation of new parties, the richest of which will represent the interests of the old profiteers (the imperialists themselves and the reactionary classes); religious freedom is merely a way to justify the existence and political activity of extreme right-wing sects; open unions lead to the influx of CIO-AFL agents who are more committed to capitalist structures than proletarian welfare; market-oriented economics is nothing less than the laissez-faire system by which the trading bourgeoisie links up with international capitalists (imperialism); and reliance on the old intellectual bureaucracy is the way by which imperialists propagate their value system, socially and psychologically. A newly independent country which seeks an independent economy—without which, Ben Barka said, there can be no real independence—cannot afford any of these "ingredients." It must stick firmly to its objective: the nationalization of the whole country. The basic task of national liberation, he said in 1963 (second passage below), is "the effective and total transfer of power to the genuine representatives of national revolution, even if this causes a resumption of armed struggle."

EL MEHDI BEN BARKA: NATIONAL LIBERATION AND AFRICAN SOLIDARITY*

WHEN the representatives of the various countries of Western Europe gathered around the Berlin conference table to divide Africa into zones of influence, that action in itself demonstrated that behind their quarrels and disagreements lay unity, a solidarity of colonizers. For through them, through their national diversity, the rising capitalism of the nineteenth century was continuing its march toward unification and its irrepressible tendency to create a world market and secure the sources of raw materials and energy for itself.

The impact of Western capitalism was everywhere the same for African societies, too, which differed in their traditions and the pattern of their civilizations but whose productive forces were at similar stages of de-

* Report presented at the Second African Peoples Conference, Tunis, January 25–29, 1960, in the name of Morocco's National Union of Popular Forces (UNFP); followed by Ben Barka's concluding remarks at the Afro-Asian Peoples Solidarity Conference, Moshi, Tanganyika (Tanzania), February 1963. Translations by Judith Landry.

velopment. The way in which these societies were disorganized, in which a new structure has, gradually, taken the place of the traditional one, was essentially the same. The liberation movements too, which are a necessary and inevitable reaction against the colonial presence, have consequently also had a common origin, a common makeup and a common aim.

Because of its geographical position, Morocco was the first and last to receive the blows of Western imperialism. It was on the soil of the Maghreb that Portugal, the first modern colonizing people, first tried its strength, closely followed by Spain.

In 1912, after the first negotiations between the European powers on the subject of the division of Africa (Entente Cordiale of 1904 and Franco-German Agreement of 1911), Morocco fell under French rule. But resistance did not falter and, after half a century of various types of struggle, military (in particular the 1925 Riff revolt under the leadership of Abdel Krim al Khettabi), then political ("pacification"), and finally in the form of popular armed resistance during 1952–56, Morocco gained its independence.

Here a whole people was involved. It was not just the action of a bourgeois or intellectual minority. In Morocco the liberation movement is the conjunction of three basic forces: the peasantry, the middle-class townspeople, and the proletariat.

The rural masses constituted one of its basic elements. They were the first to suffer from the military operations and then from eviction from the land that was their livelihood. The French colonists settled, in less than twenty-five years, over more than one million hectares [2.47 million acres] of agricultural land, one-third by means of direct seizure made possible by the complicity of a Moroccan feudal system.

The townspeople were very soon to benefit from the means of communication, information, and education, which settlement inevitably brought with it, thus engendering the agents of its own destruction. It was then that nationalist political organizations emerged.

Finally, the industrial revolution achieved by French capitalism created a working class that was significant numerically and aware of its rights. The struggle which brought it into conflict with the foreign ruling class, safeguarded by the administration of the Protectorate, was as much political as economic.

This is why the whole of Moroccan society remained united in the face of imperialism. The only elements excluded from this nationwide union were those cliques who, vestiges of a dead past, saw only the colonial presence as a guarantee of their outdated privileges. These were the administrative overlords or the religious auxiliaries of the Protectorate and part of the big trading bourgeoisie which grew up as an intermediary during the establishment of the colonial structures and which could not continue except through the continuance of these structures.

This is the explanation for the profoundly popular, progressive, and broadly national character of the Moroccan liberation movement. The same is true of the liberation movements of all African countries where the organized laboring masses are increasingly in the fore.

The work of this movement, which has been growing particularly during the last few years, is already producing results. The year 1960 will welcome the independence of several African states. But other peoples must continue the struggle against entrenched colonialism. Their cause is ours as well. Here we must examine their situation and the conditions in which they are carrying on their just fight, with the greatest attention.

The path of progress toward political independence is imposed upon each people by the machinery the relevant colonial powers put into action. It is they who force liberation movements to have recourse to violence and armed struggle. Negotiation is never rejected the moment it appears possible in conditions that could conceivably hasten the achievement of national aspiration.

Those African countries which are approaching independence possess considerable reserves of energy and enthusiasm, thanks to their national forces of liberation. The problem is therefore to safeguard this potential. What measures should be taken to avoid the disillusion which has followed independence almost everywhere in Asia and which is already appearing in a number of independent African countries? In other words, our problem is to know how to prevent the persistence of neo-colonialism, which is a new form of foreign presence in our country.

It is quite clear that the declaration of independence which is a purely political achievement, indeed even a legal one, cannot change the fundamental structures of a country that was originally colonized. Independence is the condition, the promise of a liberation, not liberation in itself.

During the first three years of its independence Morocco has seen the features of its economic dependence and backwardness on the administrative and technical level perpetuated and even intensified. Its foreign trade has remained centered on the French market. Its currency has remained a camouflaged French currency. Most of its dynamic industrial sectors are still controlled by French capitalism which had free transfer between Morocco and the franc zone in its power. The growing of export produce, which is modern agriculture par excellence, is dominated by the powerful French settlers.

No policy of independence can be truly followed if the country's economy is not first of all freed from a crushing dependence. By the creation of a national currency, breaking away from the French franc; by the setting up of an Economic Development Bank to encourage and direct investments in the vital sectors; by a Foreign Trade Bank to supervise the diversification of Morocco's trading patterns with other countries of the world; and lastly, by a general control of the transfer of capital.

Any independence which is satisfied with representing the features of colonial domination under new names can only be a snare and a delusion.

The former colonial powers use their economic superiority to keep important military forces in our countries. Capital investment, the presence of a settler colony, constitute both a reason and an excuse for their military presence, which also fits into the world strategy of the cold war.

The foreign military forces of occupation, far from being a stabilizing factor, constitute a constant threat to the very existence of the young sovereign states. Furthermore, they utilize the liberated territories as bases for aggression to carry on the colonial war with neighboring peoples. Suffice it to cite here the example of the dissidence of the Moroccan governor (Addi ou Bihi) whose revolt, organized in the first year of our independence by reactionary and antinationalist elements, was armed by the French forces stationed on our territory and was to make possible the reinforcement of the Algerian War via the south of Morocco.

But it is not only a question of the liquidation of the aftereffects of colonial occupation. Our chief concern is to get our country working to build itself up economically, politically, and socially. Such a long-term task demands that we establish a lasting peace and keep our country out of all military alliances and block quarrels alien to us.

Our efforts in this context have just culminated in our declaration that the American bases are to be evacuated.[1] We shall continue to work for the evacuation of other foreign forces, the French and Spanish, so as to guarantee complete success to our foreign policy of nondependence.

This policy of nondependence is all the more vital since new ideas in neo-colonialist milieus in Europe regard Africa as a stake and trump in the politics of world equilibrium.

In this context, Africa is still considered in these milieus as an endless source of the minerals and energy necessary to the economy of the industrialized countries of the West. All the projects aiming to associate Africa with the European Common Market to build a Eurafrica or to found bodies of shared investments, may well move in a direction which gives primacy to foreign capitalist interests and can only slow down the smooth and rapid development of the African economy.

We must not forget that for a quarter of a century, as the prices of manufactured products imported from Europe increased, the price of raw materials sent out of our continent has been falling continuously. The economic progress and expansion of the industrial countries of Europe have therefore taken place at the expense of the underdeveloped sources of raw materials.

Faced with the growing liberation movement in Africa, these same imperialist interests try to perpetuate the relations of economic exploita-

[1] By October 1969, those bases were still in U.S. hands.—*Ed.*

tion in the deceptive guise of cooperation. Our countries are finding themselves faced ever more clearly by positive blocs whose aim is to dictate a new colonial pact.

The duties of our African countries, like other developing countries in Asia and Latin America, are to organize themselves so as to produce and proclaim a common attitude, to seek out effective formulae of cooperation, and to arm themselves against every dangerous form of exploitation.

Our analysis of the evidence for neo-colonialist manifestations in Africa would be incomplete if we did not stress the dangers constituted by the national forces of reaction. Imperialism would stand no chance of survival in Africa if it could not camouflage itself behind the interests of certain retrograde elements. With the conquest of political power, certain positions have changed their meaning and certain sectors of the population which, during the period of struggle, remained neutral or supported the liberation movement, have taken quite another attitude after independence. The rural or pseudoreligious feudal system, or what remains of it, is intensified by independence and is striving to take the place of the weakened colonial power. Escaping the purge, it makes use of the new power given it by the democratic and parliamentary organization to ground its privileges in new legal bases.

The forms of political organizations of a European type, whose pluralism no longer expresses the same economic or ideological realities for us, act as havens for those antinationalist elements aiming to corrupt political mores. The pointless polemics, the demagogic campaigns, sow doubt and skepticism which prepare the people to undergo any disguised form of colonial exploitation.

These reactionary elements, instruments of neo-colonialism, are now tackling even the working classes whose unity was forged during the period of national struggle. The vain attempts to create an artificial union movement are simply another form of neo-colonialism.

Side by side with these antinational and reactionary elements, imperialism finds a second ally. The big trading bourgeoisie which derives all its power from liberal economic policy, suddenly finds itself allied with the colonial presence the moment it is no longer experiencing the misdeeds of the political preponderance of imperialism. Then it sets itself up ferociously against all attempts to guide economic and commercial policy toward a real independence, which forces it either to enter the production cycle or else to disappear.

Lastly, habitual servitude has left a large part of the intellectual and administrative cadres, inherited from the colonial period and which took scarcely any part in the liberation movement, with a lack of imagination, enthusiasm, and honesty that makes them unfit to work effectively for popular aspirations, and they soon find themselves enslaved by the holders of power.

The danger dogging the newly independent countries is that the conjunction of these forces of evil may perpetuate an economic dependence, underdevelopment, which makes political independence pointless. The alliance of a powerful and reactionary feudality, a servile and craven bourgeoisie, and an ineffective and rotten administrative mandarinate threatens to constitute a regression even in comparison with certain forms of imperialism.

A popular and progressive political force is absolutely vital to ward off this danger, to fight this alliance. In Morocco this was done by the creation of the National Union of Popular Forces. In our manifesto of September 6, 1959, we noted the bankruptcy of the parties with bourgeois structures which frequently resort to manipulating the popular masses for specific ends, the failure likewise of three years of hesitation and indecision which have blunted popular enthusiasm. We have succeeded in drawing all the basically popular forces into the Union in our desire to build up a true independence and real democracy, so as to be able to tackle the real problems.

Faced with local reactionary forces—which inevitably come together sooner or later and rally to imperialism to defend their interests, which sow division in the ranks of the people and try to interest them in secondary problems like those of formal democracy and thus leave the field free to the real dangers of an economy based on neo-colonialism, which try to involve us in quarrels which have nothing to do with us—it is vital that in each African country the popular patriotic forces should unite and form the structured and united political organization which will be the instrument of genuine African liberation.

If we consider the lessons to be learned from the experiences of India and China, the countries of central Europe, the Middle East, and Latin America, we come to the conception of a model of economic growth which is of scientific inevitability. In this realm, we have gone beyond the stage of sectarian discussion.

We know now that in no case can the way of liberal capitalism be followed in our countries. This is why liberalism with us is nothing more than the excuse of reactionary forces.

We know now that the conditions necessary for us to emerge from underdevelopment are, internally, a rapid reform of the agrarian structure, rapid and genuine industrialization, an effective and logical investments policy and, externally, the furtherance of foreign and technical cooperation.

In the economic and social building up of the new Africa, we must stress the predominant role of the working class and organized peasantry. These forces are the only guarantees and permanent upholders of this policy—because it is bound to be attacked both by external imperialism and by its agents within the country itself. We know now that progress toward independence is a difficult and obstacle-strewn path. Imperialism knows it too. That is why in Africa it no longer puts up as savage a resistance as hitherto to political independence, hoping to safeguard its economic domination with time.

We must take care that political independence, when it has been granted and not fought for, does not become a weapon in the hands of imperialists to get others to defend its main economic privileges. To fight this alliance of imperialism and the national forces of reaction we must work for alliance with the liberal and progressive forces of other former colonies and the union of the national patriotic forces of all African countries.

It is in this context that the various unification movements in Africa will have their full meaning. These unions will be founded on economic and political necessity: They will be a defensive reaction against the union of imperialist interests in Africa.

Based on an independent economic policy founded on cooperation and mutual aid, on a peace policy tending to give a new direction to the competition between East and West, and on a reaction against the alliance of the imperialist forces and those of national reaction, tendencies toward unification in Africa constitute the main element of the successful development of our continent.

If political independence is not an end in itself, if it is not sufficient in itself, it is nonetheless the necessary condition for all the changes which can undermine a colonial structure. The union of Africa, the building up of Africa's future, demand the liberation of all Africa.

We are thinking in particular of the atrocious struggle which for five years has been bloodying a territory bordering our own, which is dear to us and which is faced with a blind and stubborn colonialism.

We must not forget that it was Algeria, though it is still struggling for its independence, that gave the signal for the liberation of French Africa. When French imperialism was bleeding itself white in an inconclusive war in Indochina, there was no shortage of pundits to launch the slogan: "Quit Asia and hang on to Africa." They thought that they had fat years of peace and exploitation ahead of them. It was the revolt of All Saints Day of 1954 that tolled the knell of these hopes for Africa. Everything happened as though these same pundits were applying the following policy: "Abandon everything in Africa and hang on to Algeria." Whatever the obstinacy of the French government, whatever the skill of French diplomacy (which consists of recognizing the right to self-determination for the Algerian people without agreeing to guarantees elementary for free choice, after five years of struggle and suffering), we ourselves know that French colonialism will ultimately loosen its grip on Algeria as it has loosened its grip on its Asian and other African possessions. But we must do all we can to hasten the end of this conflict whose horror we are constantly presented with through every possible variety of evidence, and indeed even by Red Cross reports.

This same blind colonialist obstinacy emerges from the decision of the French government to explode its atomic bomb in the middle of the African continent, defying world opinion and taking no account of the repeated protests of the African peoples and the condemnation of the U.N. General Assembly.

And to hasten the liberation of these territories, still under colonial domination, as well as to consolidate already acquired independence, the deeply felt desire for unity that has emerged almost all over Africa must be made concrete.

Firstly, within each country, all the forces of progress, unionist, political, and intellectual, must unite to formulate and apply a policy worthy of our aims. The long and difficult struggle now beginning, to make up for a time lag of a century and to give our countries a modern and prosperous economy, requires the union of all relevant forces and the abandoning of every form of selfish and sterile partisan sectarianism.

This movement for the concentration of forces must be extended to all Africa.

To counter colonial solidarity, we must promote a solidarity of the African peoples to intensify our struggle, both internally against the reactionary forces and externally against imperialist maneuvers.

To counter the economic bloc of the imperialist powers, we must consider every form of aid and economic and commercial cooperation capable of withdrawing our economic relations from the domination of imperialist monopoly.

To study our problems and experiences, our successes and sometimes our failures, deeply and seriously, we must encourage all forms of cultural cooperation, the only way to educate consciences in the mystique of African union.

Lastly, this solidarity must extend even further to all the liberation movements throughout the world, particularly to genuinely progressive movements in the West which have the same basic aims as ourselves: the material well-being and the dignity of man.

*   *

It is certain that the colonizer's desire is that the political power that he holds should be transferred to an heir (individual or group of interests) able to ensure him the running, by remote control, of the affairs of the new state and above all the continuity of economic power to the benefit of the original mother country.

But matters do not always work as the colonizer would like, particularly where the popular will in the country concerned is expressed through a movement of national liberation. Which leads to the variety of solutions offered us by current experience.

We know the extreme cases of People's China, Vietnam, and Cuba, for instance, where the struggle which began as national liberation moved gradually toward economic and social revolution with the seizure of power by the People's Army after total victory over the colonial or reactionary forces.

At the other end of the scale we have the purely neo-colonial solutions.

Between these two extremes the problem of power finds intermediate solutions after negotiations, compromises which are dependent on the relation between the forces of the two factors involved. But experience shows that a single path leading to independence may arrive at different solutions to the problem of power.

In the case of Algeria, for example, the compromise reached at Evian is a revolutionary compromise, i.e., it makes possible a definite achievement, the recognition of Algeria's independence, and does not shut off any of the vistas of Revolution, in so far as the latter's instrument is safeguarded, i.e., the armed forces of the FLN, the vanguard of the fighting people of Algeria. But for months we have been watching the unmistakable neo-colonialist maneuvers working toward an unwavering goal: to destroy the solution of the problem of power from the start, and to act in such a way that the Evian solution shall be harmful to the basic interests of the Algerian people's Revolution.

In Guinea, even if the operation has taken place without any bloodshed, it is nonetheless true that power has been gained for the people thanks to the activity and vigilance of the Guinea Democratic Party.

In the case of Morocco, the power held by the French, Spanish, and international protectorates was transferred—under the pressure of the liberation movement—not to the king alone, though he is theoretically the sovereign, but to a coalition including the popular forces. It took more than six years for the heirs recognized by colonialist interests to succeed in seizing power and getting themselves set up in 1962 with a prefabricated constitution, and going from corruption and falsification to violence and repression.

The pseudoconstitutional method was also used at the same time by neo-colonialism to consolidate the fascist regime in South Korea.

Similarly in Kenya we find stubborn attempts to impose a prefabricated coalition to prepare for the subsequent transfer of exclusive power to the heir presumptive of British authority.

What must we conclude after this brief survey?

That the basic problem in our national liberation movement is that of political power: Every care must be taken for independence to be immediately expressed by the effective and total transfer of power to the genuine representatives of national Revolution in the country concerned, even if this causes a resumption of armed struggle.

The prime role of a national revolution is to gain hold of the machinery of the colonial state to put it at the service of the people.

The condition for independence not resulting in the creation of a neo-colonialist state is naturally the existence of a popular organization whose leadership must be fiercely convinced that everything except political and economic power is mere idle dreaming. It must be armed against the risks of gradual degeneration after the seizure of power, be constantly alert to the maneuvers of imperialism and its internal allies and ready at all times to counter the aggressor, whoever he may be.

Our duty is to talk openly and frankly to our masses so as to protect them from the disappointment a false security can give. It is important to promote and develop a sense of vigilance which will make them permanently aware of the maneuvers of imperialism without closing our eyes to our own weaknesses and mistakes.

On the national level of each country, as an Afro-Asian People's Solidarity movement, we must draw particular attention to the daily struggle, help with the improvement, however partial, of the lot of the laboring masses, educate and organize the people, sharpen their awareness, and build up their revolutionary potential so that they can come to power when the time is ripe. We must not relax our bonds of solidarity, but help it to confront all foreign or counterrevolutionary intervention.

On the inter-African, inter-Asian, Afro-Asian level, too, we must welcome any attempt at rapprochement, regrouping, or unity as positive, provided it is the genuine expression of national wills, even if there are temporary divergencies or contradictions of interests. The principles on which these meetings will be based will remain those of each country's complete equality of rights, mutual cooperation, and independence.

The success of this double action, on a national scale and internationally, lies in the feeling of innate fraternity and solidarity among all these people, and in their ever deepening awareness of our common destiny.

It is in the common struggle of our popular organizations against all forms of colonial, capitalist, and feudal exploitation, and through the success of this struggle, that we shall develop this awareness of our common destiny, and that new international relations whose aim is to serve mankind will develop.

Algeria

If the Algerian Revolution has indeed failed—as its left-wing opponents claim—the cause is not to be found in its leaders. For they, like the whole country, were products—deformations—of the most brutal colonialism. For 132 years, the French ruled Algeria with the kind of insidious racism that does not establish apartheid separation but permeates so deeply into the minds and hearts of men that the victims end up colonizing themselves. It was such destruction of spirit that convinced Frantz Fanon that the colonized man would never be free until he drowned the last colonizer-exploiter in his own blood—in self-expressive violence of liberating epuration.

This war of national liberation was violent all right, but not cleansing. During the more than seven years of struggle, the French devastated the country, razed 8,000 Algerian hamlets, and killed more than 1,000,000 people—one-tenth of Algeria's population. Thousands of acres of forest land, which served to stop soil erosion, were burned. Four out of the seven million head of cattle, the Algerian fellah's main food, were slaughtered. Three million Algerians were rendered homeless; 400,000 were interned in concentration camps; 409,000 went into exile; and 300,000 fought with the National Liberation Army (ALN) of the National Liberation Front (FLN).

The Algerian war divided the population into three basic elements—the veterans; the collaborators; and the émigrés. Many of these latter were in French jails (like Ben Bella), but many more joined the Algerian army which was formed in Morocco and Tunisia. Among these was Colonel Houari Boumedienne. This army was well trained, well equipped and well fed, and by the war's end, with the guerrilla movement basically collapsing, it moved into Algeria, quashed those elements of the guerrilla ALN trying to seize power, and established order.

Ben Bella and Boumedienne were friends (the former had enlisted the latter into the FLN in 1954 when Boumedienne was an Arabic teacher in Cairo). Released from jail only a few months before the Evian agreement, Ben Bella was alone. He had no aides, no strong ALN allies, not even any bodyguards, and certainly no loyal party with which to contest the power of the Provisional Government of the Algerian Republic (GPRA), then headed by elements of the national bourgeoisie. Ben Bella despised these professional old-style politicians who, he correctly thought, would end up establishing a neo-colonial regime in Algiers. Nor could Ben Bella turn to the ALN guerrillas who either were in disarray or else wanted to seize power themselves. So Ben Bella called on his old friend with his efficient army—Boumedienne.

Boumedienne was equally opposed to the old politicians. In fact, he disliked all civilians, especially in government; they were all corrupt or corruptible demagogues, he thought. To the colonel (highest rank in the FLN army), Ben Bella was a veteran fighter, a long-time militant with army-like discipline. Thus he gave him full support, installed him in power, and put the army at his disposal—within limits. And Ben Bella, who defended Boumedienne before the Party, felt those limits. He made Colonel Tahar Zbiri, a veteran ALN commander, the People's Army chief of staff, and kept a wary eye on Boumedienne. He once even introduced him to an Egyptian journalist as "that man who is preparing a plot against me" and asked the colonel, "How is the intrigue progressing?"

Boumedienne, who answered, "Very well, thank you," kept an even firmer watch on Ben Bella. But for three years the men seemed to get along. They appeared almost everywhere together—Ben Bella in front, quick, sharp, at ease in all situations; Boumedienne in back, shadowy and silent. Ben Bella was no petty-bourgeois reformer; he tried to move Algeria toward a socialist revolution. He pushed the agrarian reform, stimulated the youth movement, generated a strong labor movement which advocated workers' control (called "self-management" by Algerians), wiped out the landowner class, and fought his tradition-minded colleagues' view of women ("Now the men will again shut us up in our homes," women complained when Ben Bella was overthrown). But totally lacking a noncolonialist bureaucracy, Ben Bella was too hamstrung to move faster. Besides, as a residue of the war and his own colonized spirit, he trusted no one, jailed too many critics, justified himself with too many speeches. He was too much of a politician and too little of an army man to satisfy Boumedienne, too much of a dictator to please Colonel Zbiri, too secretive to elicit mass support. On June 12, 1965, he told the Political Bureau (half filled with Boumedienne's men) that he would present a plan for changing the army command and crushing its opposition to him at the next week's session. At 2 A.M. on June 19, a few hours before that *session was to begin, Colonel Zbiri arrested Ben Bella. A few moments later Colonel Boumedienne was in full control.*

Boumedienne did not drastically change Algeria's foreign policy, nor the rhetoric of its domestic policy. But he stopped the socialist revolution. The land reform was no longer carried out. Workers' control stopped, then was reversed as government-appointed functionaries displaced the workers' councils. French economic interests grew and labor militancy was forcibly curtailed. Even the New York Times concluded (April 26, 1968) that industrial planning in Algeria should be described not as socialism but as state capitalism.

Meanwhile, a left-wing opposition sprang up through the Organization of Popular Resistance (ORP), headed by militant FLN veterans Hocine Zahouane and Mohamed Harbi and one of the secretaries of the Algerian Communist Party, Bachir Hadj Ali. These three were quickly arrested, however, and the ORP enlarged itself into a militant popular revolutionary front called the Socialist Vanguard Party (PAGS, though generally still known as the FLN-ORP). Then, in November 1967, Chief-of-Staff Colonel Zbiri demanded a meeting of the Revolutionary Council (the FLN's supreme body, which neither Ben Bella nor Boumedienne listened to very much); Zbiri wanted an end to Boumedienne's arbitrary rule and the establishment of collective leadership. Instead, Boumedienne rigidified the FLN party machinery under Kaid Ahmed, his former Minister of Finance and a close personal friend. On December 14, Colonel Zbiri rebelled. But he was defeated and condemned to death (in absentia, as he escaped).

Where the Algerian Revolution will go from here is hard to say. The FLN-ORP is still active, though in 1969 it began to give limited support to some of Boumedienne's policies (and ORP leaders were transferred from jail to house detention). The labor unions are still agitating for workers' control and Boumedienne has not succeeded in smashing their militancy. Many FLN guerrilla veterans have regrouped and are demanding a return to the revolutionary march. The Kabylie mountain Berbers are in open defiance (their leader, Ait Ahmed, who rebelled against France, Ben Bella, and Boumedienne, escaped from jail in 1966). And Boumedienne himself is reverting to more socialistic measures. What is still missing is the commitment, in practice, to the Algerian Charter, that magnificently idealistic program adopted by the FLN after the French were driven out of Algeria.

The Algerian Charter was actually based on the program written and adopted by the National Revolutionary Council of the FLN in exile, at Tripoli, Libya, in June 1962. Known as the Tripoli Program, it is an eloquent statement of a people's struggle, what it means, how it can be perverted, and what Algerian revolutionaries' hopes were then. Since those who wrote it and survived are now within the ORP, the following program is still alive in Algeria today.

THE NATIONAL LIBERATION FRONT:
THE TRIPOLI PROGRAM*

THE Evian agreement of March 18, 1962, ending the long war of extermination conducted by French colonial imperialism against the Algerian people, constitutes an irreversible political victory ending the colonial regime and longstanding foreign domination. However, this victory of principles should not let us forget that victory was obtained above all by the continuous revolutionary processes and political and social factors of historical significance created by the armed struggle of the Algerian people.

It was these factors, brought into play in the course of the war of liberation, that secured the only durable victory. It has been through direct action against colonialism that the Algerian people have achieved and consolidated their national unity. In the course of this action, they have ejected from their ranks the sectarianism of the old parties and cliques, and have overcome the many divisions that the French occupation instituted as a political system.

It is in the unity of its action against colonial oppression that the nation has regenerated itself and has achieved the full measure of its dynamism. Through this action, in which the Algerian nation has revived the tradition of struggle, the task of achieving independence and national sovereignty has been brought to a successful conclusion.

It was the participation of the masses that has shaken the foundations of colonialism and has exposed definitively the old reactionary institutions, accelerating the destruction of the many taboos and social structures of feudal origin which acted as obstacles to the further development of Algerian society.

The participation of the Algerian masses has created a new collective awareness of the tasks required for the reconstruction of our society on new bases. The Algerian people, by taking the situation into their hands, and by persistently affirming their will to struggle, consciously or unconsciously have tied this will to struggle to the historical necessity to conquer and untiringly promote every aspect of progress in its most efficient revolutionary form.

The colonial war conducted by France against the Algerian people took the form of a campaign of extermination. It necessitated sending to

* Program of the National Liberation Front of Algeria, adopted by the National Revolutionary Council of the FLN in exile, at Tripoli, Libya, in June 1962. Published as a pamphlet in French by the FLN's Foreign Policy Department, and in English by the Workers'Vanguard, Toronto, Canada, in February 1963.

Algeria the strongest army of all times. Equipped with the most modern weapons, backed by a strong colonial administration, and helped in this campaign of repression, terror, and collective massacre by the French population in Algeria, this army concentrated its attacks on the defenseless civilian population, and harassed the ALN (Algerian Liberation Army) in vain. In this way, more than a million Algerians were annihilated and a million more either deported, imprisoned, or forced into exile. This war of colonial domination could not have lasted as long as it did without the support of NATO, or the military and diplomatic support of the U.S.A. The extreme degree of cruelty with which this war was waged can only be explained by the very nature of the French policy of colonialization, and the acquiescence of the French people, who have long been deceived by the myth of a "French Algeria." The nationalistic and chauvinistic character of this colonial war was well illustrated by the constant participation of the different classes of the French society, including the working class. The French political Left, which has always played a role in the anticolonial struggle on a theoretical level, revealed itself powerless in face of the unforeseen implacable development of the war. Their political action remained timid and ineffective because of their old assimilationist conceptions, and their erroneous idea of the evolutionary nature of the colonial regime, and its ability to reform itself peacefully. The obstinate struggle of the Algerian people forced French colonialism to show its true nature as a totalitarian system, producing in turn militarism and fascism. This truth, demonstrated by events, escaped the attention of the French democrats for a long time.

Despite the colossal tactical and material reinforcement of the French forces in Algeria, of which the Challe Plan has been one of the most significant contributions, their failure became obvious. The Gaullist government was pressed to change the classical colonial regime into a neocolonialist regime, aiming to maintain under a different form the essential financial and strategic interests of France in Algeria. The Constantine Plan, conceived during the worst period of the war in order to create the economic basis of a "third force in Algeria," was the first outline of this pseudoliberal policy.

Under the many pressures of the liberation struggle and the international situation, France finally admitted to the necessity of a peaceful solution to the Algerian situation by agreeing to negotiate with the GPRA. The conferences of Melun in June 1960, Evian in 1961, and Lugrin in July of the same year, successively failed due to the obstinacy of the French government, which asked for a camouflaged surrender, and insisted on the division of the Algerian territory, claiming that section in the Sahara. However, the resurgence of the peoples' struggle, progressing during the historic days of December 1960, and the insistence of the GPRA on the basic positions of the Revolution, forced the French government to begin serious negotiations.

The Evian agreement of March 18, 1962, guarantees the recognition of national sovereignty to Algeria and the integrity of its territory. However, this agreement includes a policy of cooperation between Algeria and France as a counterpart to independence. This cooperation as outlined in the agreement implies a maintenance of ties of dependence in the economic and cultural fields. It also gives, among other things, precious guarantees to the Algerian French of an advantageous place in our country. It is evident that such a concept of cooperation constitutes a typical feature of the neo-colonial policies of France. This is the phenomena of neo-colonialism substituting itself for classical colonialism.

The immediate task of the FLN is to liquidate, by all means, colonialism as it still manifests itself after the cease-fire in the virulent form of the criminal actions of the OAS.[1] But it must also elaborate at this time an effective strategy to deal with neo-colonialist maneuvers, which constitute a grave danger for the Revolution as they appear under the seductive features of liberalism and apparently disinterested economic and financial cooperation.

The present antagonism between the old and the new colonialism must not deceive us. At any rate, there is no question of preference between one or the other: both must be opposed. The hesitations of the Gaullist power in its fight against the OAS is due to the natural affinity that exists between the French colonialists of both sides of the Mediterranean, and this hesitation expresses a tactical collusion aiming to force the Algerians into a choice in favor of neo-colonialism. This attitude of the French government leads in fact to an opposite reaction. The refusal to effectively repress the activities of the OAS proves without a doubt the complicity of the French government with the ultra-colonialists of Algeria, dealing a hard blow against cooperation.

In this regard, French propaganda aims to perpetuate the myth that the French are indispensable to the economic and administrative life of this country. But for over a century, more than three-quarters of Algeria, the agricultural regions in particular, have been abandoned to their fate without any serious planning or proper equipment. Except for their technical skills, the great majority of the French of Algeria, because of their colonialist mentality and their racism, cannot be useful to the Algerian state.

Even if the traditional colonialists are forced to realize that Algeria is lost to them, they do not look upon themselves as being definitively defeated. The OAS aims to institute fascism in France and to begin the colonial war in Algeria again. In practicing terror, the colonialists hope to arouse brutal reaction from the Algerian people, and by so doing to annul the cease-fire agreement. It is evident that this plan consists in

[1] Organisation de l'Armeé Secrète, the ultra-right-wing Organization of the Secret Army, which tried to stop Algerian independence by terrorizing the liberal and reformist community, both in France and in Algeria.—*Ed.*

making Algeria a springboard for a coming fascist coup d'état supported by the French army and directed against the governmental power in France. It is important however not to underestimate the colonialist threat directed toward Algeria. One of their methods, in fact, is the systematic sabotage of the Algerian economy. This tactic is not new. It was used previously in Vietnam, more particularly during the colonialist debacle.

By the Evian agreement, the French of Algeria will not be considered entirely as foreigners. They will enjoy for a three-year period all rights as Algerian citizens, after which time they will have to make a definite choice as to their nationality. This presence of the French in Algeria gives rise to a complex problem, in fact one of the most serious the Algerian state has to solve. The predominant influence of the French of Algeria remains in the economic, administrative, and cultural spheres, and contradicts the fundamental perspectives of the Revolution. It must be noted that the abolition of privileges, the "acquired rights" of colonization, is an inseparable part of the struggle against neo-colonialism in general. A correct solution of the French minority problem will be found in a consistent policy of anti-imperialism.

According to the terms of the Evian agreement, the French government has the right to maintain its troops in Algeria for a certain period and use the naval airport of Mers-El-Kebir, and military airports and atomic installations in the south of the country. This military occupation, which is the result of a neo-colonialist strategy directed toward North Africa in general and Algeria in particular, will be lessened at the end of the first year of self-determination. The contingent of the French army will then be reduced to 80,000 men, the evacuation being scheduled for the end of a second two-year period. As long as Algerian territory is occupied by foreign forces, the freedom of the state is limited and its national sovereignty endangered. The first months of independence will be particularly difficult.

The Provisional Executive has not succeeded two months after taking power in imposing its authority or in controlling the colonial administration, most of the members of which actively support the OAS. It is a vital necessity to regenerate and completely reorganize the administration. This task will prove to be a very delicate one considering the vast territory, the acute daily problems, and the lack of qualified Algerians, many of whom were killed in the war.

The national and moral consequences of the practice of genocide carried on for so many years against the Algerian people will be felt more and more. Hundreds of thousands of orphans, tens of thousands of invalids, and thousands of families of only women and children abandoned to their fate, are waiting for adequate measures to be taken by the national power. The wounds of the nation are deep and will not disappear before many decades. Some of them are extremely serious, and could paralyze our society in its forward march. Two million Algerians, most of them women and children, are leaving the camps to which they had been driven. The hundreds of thousands of refugees from Morocco and Tunisia must be repatriated soon.

The problems resulting from this situation are economic and social, but their solution is a matter of politics and organization. To launch national and international campaigns to obtain aid for housing, nutritional, and hygienic problems will not be sufficient. These problems, the most serious, brought to us by the war, show tragically the immense chaos our country finds itself in. Not partial and immediate measures, but a basic solution and decisions of a strong social bearing and in accord with an overall plan are required. The economic and social revolution will deal first with these problems or it will fail to even make a beginning. The Revolution will be judged by this test which will determine its future development.

The future government of Algeria inherits an anaemic and exhausted country. Large rural zones, once throbbing with life, are now only desolate areas. In the large and middle-sized cities, crushing misery consumes the population, who are crowded in the old sections and in the *bidonvilles* (villages built of used oil drums). We have to see immediately about removing this intolerable condition by procuring work for the adults, providing schools for the children, fighting against famine and sickness, bringing back a zest for life by means of the collective reconstruction of the country.

Sovereignty has been won, but now we must face the task of giving substance to the national liberation. After having opposed our independence, the French government is trying to interfere according to its imperialist interests. The Evian agreement constitutes a neo-colonialist platform which France is ready to use to propagate its new form of domination.

The French government will not only use its armed forces and its French minority to divert the evolution of Algeria. It will exploit above all the political and social contradictions of the FLN and will attempt to find in this movement of allied currents some which might be detached from the Revolution and turned against it. This imperialist tactic can be summarized as follows: to develop a "third force" in the ranks of the FLN composed of moderate nationalists dedicated to independence but hostile to any consequent revolutionary action, and to oppose the elements of this "third force" to the militants and cadres who remain faithful to popular aspirations by continuing the anti-imperialist struggle. The obvious intention of the French government is to see a "moderate" tendency gain control over the revolutionary forces of the FLN, making possible a French-FLN agreement in the framework of neo-colonialism.

The FLN, which at the beginning of the insurrectional action of November 1, 1954, had decided upon an armed struggle for the sole purpose of

national liberation, could not have foreseen all the implications an
different developments resulting from the war in the popular consciousnes
and in Algerian society in general. The FLN was not aware of the pro
found revolutionary potential of the rural people. The little they knev
about the situation was confined to a superficial evaluation which was th
traditional outlook of the old nationalist parties.

We can say in fact that the FLN, a vanguard tendency at its ver
beginning, broke with the practices, methods, and conceptions of the ol
parties as it became a movement. But this break could not have bee
beneficial and definitive without being accompanied at the start by
vigorous effort of ideological demarcation, and a far-reaching program t
cope with the coming events that the struggle was to provoke in Algeria
society.

The FLN did not intend to surpass the one objective inscribed on th
traditional program of nationalism, that is, independence. On the othe
hand, the FLN neglected to foresee the eventuality of two major fact
that classical nationalism had never been able to conceive: (a) the ver
character of the colonial war in a country where the foreign populatio
plays the role of agent and auxiliary of French imperialism; and (b) tha
the armed struggle involving massive participation by the colonial popula
tion, rejecting domination, never develops according to a simple scheme
a guidebook, resulting in national liberation without difficulty.

The inevitable consequence of the totalitarian colonialist oppression o
a nation newly freed is a thorough criticism and revision of the struc
tures of the oppressed country. This revision in question completes itsel
spontaneously, simultaneously, and in an infallible manner by the searc
[for] and the discovery of new structures, of new modes of thought an
action, in a word by a process of continual transformation which con
stitutes the direction of the Revolution.

Paradoxical as it may appear, the national revolutionary struggle i
perceived and felt in its newness and its originality by the popular masse
more than by the leadership and the directorates. The latter are incline
to underestimate or overestimate certain new facts, to artificially com
pare their own revolutionary movement to other revolutionary move
ments and to copy other ideologies, which often gives their conception
an irrelevant and unrealistic character. The view of the world is con
fused and unformulated in a country at war. The people will expres
themselves in a very incomplete and empirical way as long as the struggl
lasts and facts cannot be analyzed with the help of precedent, example
and analogy.

This original thinking, the result of a real evaluation by the people o
their Revolution and of their collective experiences, has not been take
sufficiently into consideration by the Revolution as one of its treasures.

Instead of the Revolution taking this thinking into consideration, w
have witnessed and are still witnessing a very serious lack of contac

between, on the one hand, the collective consciousness tested in reality, and on the other hand, the practice and authority of the FLN at all levels. Very often, in a paternalistic manner, this authority has purely and simply substituted itself for political responsibility which is inseparable from the search for an ideology. This authority, which was most of the time on the level of technicalities and removed from an ideological research, produced concepts which could be termed as antirevolutionary.

The FLN, sworn enemy of feudalism, even though it has fought feudalism throughout our old social institutions, has done nothing in return to preserve itself from feudalistic concepts at certain levels of its own organization. It has forgotten in this regard that naïve conceptions of authority, the absence of rigorous criteria, and political ignorance, favor the development of a feudal mentality.

This feudal mentality does not only develop within the traditionally preponderant class, that class which possesses the land and exploits the people. It continues to survive under various forms as a relic of a past epoch, in African and Asian countries, even under popular revolutions when the latter lack ideological vigilance.

Just as there is feudalism in land—material feudalism—there can also exist political feudalism of the bosses and their cliques, whose coming to power was made possible by the absence of all democratic education on the part of the militants and the citizens.

In addition to the feudal mentality which has impregnated all the life of the Maghreb since the end of the Middle Ages in the economic, social, cultural, and religious spheres, and which the FLN has been unable to completely eradicate, we must note also one of its most surreptitious effects—*paternalism*.

Paternalism constitutes a real hindrance to political development and to the conscious and creative initiative of the militant and of the citizen. It conveys a deceptively mild, antipopular, and secret type of archaic authority, and, inevitably, an infantile conception of responsibility.

This distortion of revolutionary values has also resulted in substituting deficient political maturity with superficial attitudes, resulting in *formalism*. It is in this way that patriotism and revolutionary spirit are interpreted in terms of being only frantic gestures. This artificial romanticism and shameless taste for heroic bombast is contrary to the reserved temperament of our people. Formalism serves as an alibi for those who seek to escape from their day-to-day revolutionary duties.

Next we must denounce another state of mind, one never denounced enough because it has caused numerous catastrophes and has done as much harm to the Revolution as the feudalistic inheritance—the *petty-bourgeois* attitude. The lack of ideological firmness within the FLN has allowed this attitude to infiltrate the ranks of a great part of the rank-and-file and the youth.

The easy ways inherited from the old parties with an urban base, the

escape from reality due to a lack of revolutionary education, the individualistic longing for stability, for the seeking of profits and ostentation,
the prejudice that many have toward the peasants and obscure militants,
all this constitutes the salient characteristics of the petty-bourgeois attitude. This attitude becomes easily impregnated with pseudointellectualism
—empty of any knowledge—with the most outmoded and harmful concepts of Western mentality. In addition, this attitude tends toward a new
bureaucratic class, demarked from the majority of the people.

The ideological poverty of the FLN, and the feudal mentality and
petty-bourgeois attitudes which are the indirect result of this poverty,
could reduce the future Algerian state to a mediocre and antipopular
bureaucracy in fact, if not in principle.

One of the essential causes that slowed the development of the FLN
on the ideological plane, aggravating its weaknesses and worsening the
general situation of the war in Algeria, arises out of this chasm between
the leadership and the popular masses. The installation of the headquarters
of the FLN outside of Algeria at the end of the third year of war, even if
it was necessary at the moment, nevertheless isolated the FLN from the
national situation.

This isolation could have been fatal to the liberation movement as a
whole. One of the most obvious consequences of this state of affairs has
been the progressive depoliticization of those organs which remained in
Algeria as well as those groups created or taken outside of Algeria by
the Directorate. It must be understood here that by the depoliticization
is meant the absence of all general ideological direction constituting a
firm tie between the Algerian people and their leaders on both sides of
the frontiers. By depoliticization is also meant the toleration during the
armed struggle of disparate and contradictory political currents, and individualistic actions escaping all control, and allowing some people to
become dignitaries without precise functions.

Besides, the GPRA, which merged at its beginning with the leadership
of the FLN, has contributed to the weakening of the two concepts of
state and party.

The amalgamation of the state institutions and the organs of the FLN
has reduced the latter to a merely administrative apparatus. In the interior, this amalgamation resulted in depriving the FLN of its responsibilities to the advantage of the ALN, and, with the help of the war,
practically annihilated it.

The experience of the seven and a half years of war proves that without
an elaborate ideology developed in contact with the national reality and
the popular masses, there cannot be a revolutionary party. The *raison
d'être* for a party is its ideology. It ceases to exist should its ideology fail.

The war of liberation victoriously conducted by the Algerian people
has re-established national sovereignty and independence. However, the

struggle has not ended with this victory. On the contrary, it must continue with the construction of a revolutionary state in order that the conquests of the armed struggle may be extended and consolidated.

If we look into the general situation, we see that Algeria is only starting to emerge from colonial domination and a semifeudal status. These two characteristic features of Algeria will not automatically disappear with the coming of independence. They will persist as long as a radical transformation of society has not been achieved.

Algeria, as with most of the countries of Africa and Asia, has known feudalism as an economic and social system. This system has continued to exist until today after having undergone a series of retreats and transformations since 1830.

At the time of colonial conquest, the Algerian feudal proprietors, who were already unpopular, immediately joined with the enemy, not hesitating to participate in their war of looting and continued repression. Emir Abdelkader, chief of the Algerian state and artisan of the resistance, undertook an implacable fight against them. He succeeded in destroying their coalition at the battles of Mahares and Mina in 1834. In its traditional politics, colonialism has constantly leaned on the support of these Algerian feudal proprietors in order to defeat nationalist aspirations. To save them from destruction and popular vengeance, colonialism organized them officially in 1838 as a permanent corps.

From the military and landholding caste that it was, the Algerian feudal gentry gradually became an administrative caste. This role permitted them to pursue their exploitation of the people and to enlarge their landholding wealth. Thus, this corps of *caids* has been perpetuated until today and is the most typical expression of this feudalism.

Parallel to this agrarian and administrative feudalism, we must note the existence of another type of feudalism—that of the great congregations of the marabouts.[2] The marabouts, who played a positive role in the national struggle before 1830 and at various times up until 1871, have been converted partially into this administrative feudalism. In the obscurantist context of colonialism they have exploited the religious sentiment of the people by superstition and other ignorant practices.

In the course of the liberation struggle the Algerian people shook the colonial structure and dealt a death blow to feudalism as an administrative and patriarchal power. However, even if the institutions of feudalism have disappeared, its ideological relics and social vestiges remain. These relics and vestiges have contributed the alteration of the Islamic spirit and have carried along with them the immobility of Moslem society.

Feudalism, product of the decadence of the Maghreb at a certain moment of its history, could only be perpetuated in the context of de-

[2] A Moslem hermit or holy man.—*Ed.*

clining social, cultural and religious values. Based upon the principle of patriarchal and paternalistic authority, a source of arbitrariness, it represents as well an acute form of parasitism.

It is from these two aspects that it encourages the persistence of structures and concepts of another age: tribal attitudes, regionalism, discrimination against and segregation of women, obscurantism, and taboos of all kinds. All these conceptions and reactionary practices which still exist in the rural life of Algeria constitute an obstacle to progress and the liberation of man. The Algerian peasantry, which has always fought against oppression and the immobility inherent in the feudal system, could not alone triumph. It is the role of the Revolution to liquidate definitively the antinational, antisocial, and antipopular relics of feudalism.

Since November 1, 1954, a new dimension appeared in Algerian society which had remained static until then. This new dimension was the collective participation of the people in the national struggle. This movement of the masses, by its depth and continuity, has put into question all the values of the old society and posed the problems of the new society.

An analysis of the social content of the liberation struggle makes it clear that it is the peasants and the working people generally who have been the active base of the movement and have given it its essentially popular character. The massive participation of the workers swept the other social layers of the nation into the struggle along with them. More particularly, it has created the important phenomena of the total participation of Algerian youth regardless of their social background. We must note in this regard that it is largely the youth who come from the bourgeoisie who have determined the support of the bourgeoisie themselves to the cause of independence.

This popular movement resulted in the armed struggle being impelled beyond the objective of national liberation toward a further perspective—that of the Revolution itself. By its continuity, its untiring effort, and its immense sacrifices, it has given the fragmentary national consciousness a more homogeneous form. Furthermore, it has resulted in a collective consciousness oriented toward the revolutionary transformation of society. This fact, which we can not overemphasize, has given to the liberation movement its essential character in contrast to the other nationalist movements in the Maghreb.

This implies necessarily an effort of analyses, of adequate arrangement, a firm and correct orientation, and clear decisions. Two main criteria should inspire our action: (1) we should proceed from Algerian reality in the direction of the objective conditions and the aspirations of the people; (2) we should express this reality taking into account the requirements of modern progress, the achievements of science, the experiences of other revolutionary movements, and the anti-imperialist struggle across the globe.

The word "revolution" has long been thrown about carelessly without any precise content. However, it has never failed to galvanize the popular masses, who instinctively give to the word a meaning beyond the objectives of the war of liberation. What was lacking in the meaning of "revolution" and what is still lacking to reveal its full significance, is an essential ideological basis. During the war of liberation, the momentum of the struggle was sufficient to propel and carry forward the revolutionary aspirations of the masses. Today, when the struggles have stopped with the end of the war and the re-establishment of national independence, it is important that this momentum now be carried over onto the ideological plane without delay. After the armed struggle must come the ideological struggle, after the struggle for national independence must come the Popular Democratic Revolution.

The Popular Democratic Revolution is the conscious construction of a country according to socialist principles with the power in the hands of the people. In order that the development of Algeria be rapid and harmonious, and in order that the primary economic needs of the people be satisfied, it must be conceived within a socialist perspective, within the framework of the collectivization of the basic means of production and within the framework of a rational plan.

An important task of the Revolution is to consolidate the newly independent nation, and restore all the values stifled and destroyed by colonialism, by restoring a sovereign state, a national economy, and a national culture. These values must be conceived and organized within a modern perspective. This means the abolition of the social and economic structures of feudalism and its hangovers, and the establishment of new structures and institutions favoring and guaranteeing the emancipation of man and the full and entire enjoyment of his liberties.

The sense of responsibility, the greatest emanation of the democratic spirit, must everywhere replace the principle of authority which is the essence of the feudal or paternalistic character. The democratic spirit must not be a matter of purely theoretical speculation. It must be concretized in clearly defined state institutions in all sectors of social life of the country. The economic conditions of the country determine in a large measure its social, cultural, and political character.

Since the fate of the individual is tied to the fate of society as a whole, democracy for us should not only mean the expansion of individual liberties, but above all the collective expression of popular responsibilities.

The building of a modern state on a democratic antifeudal basis will be possible only through the initiative, the vigilance, and the direct control of the people. Only such a state will be able to find an effective solution to the problem of health, housing, and the improvement of the living conditions of the families.

In this framework, the Algerian woman, emancipated by the revolutionary struggle, will be able to assume the full responsibility to which she is entitled.

The tasks of the democratic revolution in Algeria are immense. They cannot be realized by one class alone in society, as enlightened as it might be; only the people can carry these tasks to their completion—the peasants, the workers, the youth, and the revolutionary intellectuals.

The experience of certain countries which have recently gained their independence teaches us that a privileged social layer can take power to its exclusive benefit. In so doing it robs the people of the fruits of their struggle and isolates itself from them in order to ally itself with imperialism. In the name of national unity, which it exploits for opportunistic purposes, the bourgeoisie pretends to act in the interests of the people, asking for their support.

The seizure of power in Algeria must be clearly understood. National unity is not unity based upon the bourgeoisie. It affirms the unity of the people on the basis of the principles of the Popular Democratic Revolution to which the bourgeoisie must subordinate its interests. The logic of history and the basic interests of the nation make this an imperative. The patriotism of the bourgeoisie will be demonstrated to us by their acceptance of this imperative, by their support of the revolutionary cause, and by their renunciation of the aim of directing the destiny of the country.

The bourgeoisie is the purveyor of an opportunist ideology of which the main characteristics are defeatism, demagogy, an alarmist spirit, a contempt of principles, and a lack of revolutionary conviction—all the characteristics favoring the establishment of neo-colonialism.

The Revolution is not a series of formulas to be applied in a routine and bureaucratic fashion. There is no finished ideology; there is only constant and creative ideological striving.

The construction of a modern state cannot take place without the complete rejection of all forms of subjectivism: improvisation, approximation, intellectual laziness, a tendency to idealize reality and to emphasize only those aspects which are spectacular and romantic. Furthermore, we must be on guard against moralizing, an idealistic and infantile tendency which consists in wishing to transform society and to resolve its problems on the basis of moral values alone. That is a concept which leads to errors and confuses revolutionary action in its constructive phase. Moralizing, often professed by a few, is an easy excuse for an inability to act on social reality and to organize constructively. Revolutionary endeavor cannot be narrowed down to good intentions alone, as sincere as they might be; it requires above all actions based on objective conditions. Individual moral values, even if they are respectable and necessary, cannot be the determinant factors in the construction of society. In a sound society the conditions will be created for their collective flourishing.

Algerian culture will be national, revolutionary, and scientific. Its role as a national culture will consist, first of all, in restoring to the Arab language, the living expression of the cultural values of our country, its dignity and its effectiveness as a language of civilization. To this end, it will work to reconstitute, revitalize, and promote our national inheritance and its dual classic and modern humanism in order to reintroduce it into the intellectual life and the education of the people. In so doing, it will combat cultural cosmopolitanism and the overwhelming Western influence which have contributed to the contempt which many Algerians have held toward their language and national values.

As a new revolutionary culture it will contribute to the emancipation of the people. It will neither be a caste culture, closed to progress, nor a luxury of the mind. Popular and militant, it will enlighten the masses and assist them in their political and social struggle in all its forms. Being a dynamic culture dedicated to the service of the people, it will enhance the development of the revolutionary consciousness, always reflecting the aspirations of the people, their real situation, their new conquests, and thus all forms of their artistic traditions.

This necessity is imposed upon us because the Arab language has not been used as an instrument of modern scientific culture and therefore has to be developed for its future role by rigorously concrete and perfected methods. Algerian culture developed in this way must constitute the indispensable living link between the ideological effort of the Popular Democratic Revolution and the concrete everyday tasks of building the country. In this light, the indispensable raising of the cultural standards of the militants, the cadres, those holding administrative responsibilities, and of the masses, becomes of the utmost importance.

The revolutionary vanguard of the people must provide an example by adopting the objective of raising its own cultural level, and making this objective its motto. We must vigorously denounce the tendency to underestimate intellectual effort and to profess, as sometimes happens, uncalled-for anti-intellectualism. To this attitude another extreme— close to petty-bourgeois moralism—often responds. This flows from a tendency to exploit Islamic values for demagogic purposes in order to evade the real problems. No doubt, we belong to Moslem civilization, which had a lasting and profound impact on the history of humanity, but it would be doing an injustice to this civilization to believe that its revival could take place by repeating simple subjective formulas relating to general behavior and religious practice.

We cannot ignore the fact that Moslem civilization, in order to become a concrete reality, had to begin and develop through positive effort on the level both of work and thought, of economy and culture. Moreover, the spirit of discovery which animated it, its orientation toward science, foreign cultures, and the universal character of the epoch, brought a creative exchange between Moslem civilization and other civilizations. These criteria—of creativity, of efficient systematization of values and contributions of Moslem culture—contributed greatly to human progress in the past. In a genuine cultural renascence this heritage must be taken into account. A nostalgic attitude toward the past, however, will certainly result in impotence and confusion; we must use the past as a source of inspiration for building on the basis of concrete realities according to rigorous methods. Once Islam is freed from all its excrescences and super- stitions, which have strangled and distorted it, it will be certain to con- tribute more than as a religion, but as a vehicle of two essential factors— culture and national identity.

The Algerian economy has been a colonial economy, dominated by France and entirely in the hands of foreigners. Algeria has been primarily a source of raw materials and a market for manufactured products. Its dependent status is demonstrated by the high proportion of foreign trade in relation to national production, and by the preponderance of France in this foreign trade—Algeria has always been the major customer and supplier of France—by the extent of foreign investment and of foreign control of Algeria's balance of accounts, and by the lack of important industrialization.

Two economic sectors united by a fragile commercial link coexist in Algeria: (a) The modern and dynamic sector is the capitalist sector. It constitutes a real outpost of the French economy and involves European agriculture geared to urban markets and export trade, diverse industrial branches, transportation, big commerce, and goods and services. Algerian contribution to this sector is mainly in manpower. And (b) the tradi- tional sector, in which the essential part of the Algerian population (5,225,000 persons) makes a living, still retains the structures inherited from the past. A subsistence economy and precapitalist production re- lationships are dominant. Financial and technical means are almost nil.

The social consequences of this dependent, disjointed, and dominated economy are severely felt by the majority of the Algerian population as is shown by the great disparity in income. The average income of the French Algerian is more than 340,000 francs annually, whereas the average income of Algerians is less than 50,000 francs annually, which means less than 20,000 francs annually for the masses living in the old sector.

The social consequences can be seen equally in the failure to integrate into the economy 2,500,000 Algerians (990,000 of whom are partially or totally unemployed in the cities, and 1,500,000 of whom are unem- ployed in the countryside), the rural exodus, the emigration of 400,000 to France, the illiteracy of more than four-fifths of all those over six years of age, in housing shortages, in the lack of sanitation, which has resulted in many slums and *bidonvilles*, and the very poor sanitation in the countryside.

In countries newly freed from foreign domination, the methods of classical liberal economics do not permit a real transformation of society. This method of economic development creates anarchy of the market, reinforces dependence upon imperialist countries, establishes the state as an apparatus for transferring the wealth of the country into the hands of the possessing classes, and contributes to the maintenance of parasitic social layers tied to the imperialist world.

The native bourgeoisie gradually replaces the foreign bourgeoisie in the deteriorating sectors of production, and enriches itself while the people remain in misery and ignorance.

The limited national revenue and private capital in our country, the export of most of the profits, the use of local capital for speculation purposes, commercial profits, and high-interest loans, the waste encountered from unemployment of our powerful working force, are all factors which exclude the capitalist method of developing our economy.

Our Party cannot leave the very important work of solving the fundamental problems of our country in the hands of an embryonic bourgeoisie tied by the nature of their activities to imperialism. In 1954, out of 4.5 billions of private investments in our country, 8 percent of this amount was local capital. We cannot allow foreign capital to dominate our economy and expect that they will modernize our industry.

Foreign capital is reluctant to invest in low-profit industries and will not therefore take an interest in certain fields which are the most urgent. The fields to which foreign investments are attracted relegate it to a secondary role in the development of our economy.

Planning and nationalization of the industries involving the participation of the workers are essential measures in order to achieve three main aims: to eliminate the power of the monopolies as basic changes are made in economic relations with foreign powers, mainly France; to eliminate internal obstacles to planning by a radical change in the structures of rural life; to industrialize our country in order that we might supply our people with the necessities of life.

Only planning allows the necessary accumulation of capital required for productive industrialization within a relatively short period; only planning allows the centralization of the most important investments and eliminates unnecessary spending caused by competition between industries.

Workers' participation in the management of the economy will permit the control and execution of the plan and its continual adaption to the possibilities inherent in the situation.

The creation of an internal market and the laying of the basis of industrialization can only be achieved with a revolution in the rural mode of life. From an economic point of view, due to the present conditions in the farming areas—due to the nature of production on the farms of the big French *colons* and big Algerian proprietors and the degree of mechanization on these farms—our Party advocates collective forms, a policy of the land being distributed without fragmentation. This solution should be applied with the consent of the peasants themselves in order to avoid the disastrous consequences of forced collectivization.

The agrarian reform must be accomplished according to the slogan "The Land to Those Who Work It" and according to the following rules: (1) immediate ban on transactions in land and in means of agricultural production; (2) restrictions on landholding according to the kind of crop and the size of the crop; (3) expropriation of properties larger than the maximum allowed; (4) distribution of the expropriated land to the poor peasants; (5) democratic organization of the peasants into cooperative forms of production; (6) creation of state farms on the expropriated land and participation of the agrarian workers in the administration and the sharing of benefits—these farms will facilitate contact with the market and will constitute a training ground for the formation of better qualified agrarian cadres; (7) a ban on sales or rental of land in order to avoid the reconstitution of the big properties; (8) the annulling of the debts of peasants and workers owed to landholders, moneylenders, or to public services; (9) material and financial aid from the state.

The overpopulation of rural areas will allow the rapid mobilization of the work force to reconquer the land. This is of the utmost importance. The democratic organization of rural work yards will eliminate unemployment, will help recuperate large areas, and will liberate all our productive forces.

This transformation of the agricultural structure must be the point of departure for the development of the foundation, the nationalization of credit and foreign trade, in a first stage, and the nationalization of natural resources and energy in a second stage. These measures will accelerate the tempo of the industrialization of our country.

The rail and road systems of our country were built according to the economic and strategic requirements of the period of colonization. During the war, numerous new rail lines and side roads were built to facilitate the mobility of French troops. These can now be used as a basis for the development of a suitable foundation to facilitate the progress of trade and to eliminate all obstacles to the broadening of the internal market and to the exchange of agricultural produce. The policy of the Party must be in the direction of the nationalization of the means of transportation and of the establishment of connecting communication lines between the main routes and the rural markets.

The nationalization of banks has to be completed within the next period. The banks are so numerous that they are not easily brought under national control. They have been recently converted into "societies for development," but this change must not obscure the fact that their essential character is to be an instrument of financial blackmail.

Algerian commercial policies must be inspired by the following principles:

—to drastically eliminate at an appropriate rate the preferential status that France has long had with Algeria.

—to assure trade based on equality and reciprocal advantage with other countries. To increase trade with countries offering stable prices and long-term agreements where we may buy our supply of equipment at the lowest possible prices.

—to nationalize on a scale of priorities the essential branches of foreign trade and of wholesale commerce, and to create state societies for each different product or group of products—such an organization allows a real state control on imports and exports, facilitates efficient action toward the fulfillment and procuring of commercial benefits for investments in the productive branches.

—to control prices and create state stores in the rural centers in order to combat speculation and usury.

Unless there is an economic and technical base provided by industrial development, the development of the agrarian sector of our economy and the mobilization of the masses cannot meet the problems confronting our country. A sector of our industry is already nationalized. The state has to extend this sector to mines, quarries, and cement factories.

The long-term development of the country is conditional upon the development of basic industries necessary to modern agriculture. In this respect Algeria presents tremendous possibilities for the petroleum and uranium industries. In this domain it is the responsibility of the state to provide the necessary conditions for the development of a heavy industry.

During the period when it will be necessary to allow a private sector to exist it will be necessary to have a correct orientation. On no account should the state contribute in any way to the creation as has happened in certain countries of an industrial basis for the benefit of the native bourgeoisie, whose development it must check by appropriate means. Foreign private capital is desirable within the confines of certain conditions—as a complementary factor within the framework of mixed enterprises. The rate of profit must be controlled and a certain percentage of profits must be reinvested within our country.

The enthusiasm of the masses and their social mobilization must become a constant factor in the life of the country. In order to make this possible, extravagant spending, waste of public funds, extreme luxury, and very high incomes must be severely condemned. These abuses contribute to the conviction of the masses that they alone carry the burden of building the country. Moreover, the administration by the state of certain enterprises must under no circumstances justify a deterioration in the living conditions of the workers, who must keep the right to go on strike.

Previous to November 1, 1954, Algerian people expressed their attachmen to national values elaborated in the framework of the Arab-Moslem civilization by creating and maintaining the *medersas libres* (free cultural organizations) in spite of the opposition of the colonial authorities. And, in the course of the struggle for independence, some of the leaders of the *willayas* (military zones) strove to make Algerian culture accessible to the masses. In our country, the cultural revolution involves many tasks:

a. The restoration of a national culture with a progressive introduction on a scientific basis of the Arab language and culture into the schools. Of all the tasks confronting the Revolution this is the most delicate one, requiring modern cultural media, and cannot be accomplished rapidly without great danger of disorientating and confusing whole generations.

b. The preservation of the popular national culture.

c. The broadening of the school system to ensure all levels of education for everyone.

d. Adaption of educational programs to Algerian reality.

e. Extension of the methods of mass education and the mobilization of all national organizations to fight against illiteracy and to teach all the citizens how to read and write in the shortest possible period.

The economic and social stagnation in rural society, the hasty resettlement of the population after the conquest, has resulted in a proliferation of slum areas in the country around the big cities and urban centers. The war aggravated this phenomenon by "regrouping" two million peasants. The Party must take immediate measures to give decent housing to citizens harassed by the long war and initiate a plan of building projects to locate them close to points of production.

Medical care and clinical facilities must be rapidly nationalized so that everyone can get free medical attention with the least possible delay. This should be done by developing a National Health Service in charge of hospitals and medical installations. This National Health Service will employ full-time physicians who will enjoy the best working conditions and opportunities for research. Only these doctors will be admitted to university or hospital careers. This National Health Service will gradually replace the old classical liberal sector.

The contribution of the Algerian women to the struggle for freedom brought favorable conditions for their liberation from their traditional yoke. They should take part fully in the administration of public affairs and in the general development of our country. The Party must remove all obstacles to the liberation and development of women, and support and promote women's organizations. In the past we have had a negative attitude regarding the role of women in society. In many ways the idea of feminine inferiority still permeates our society, and women themselves are imbued with these traditional prejudices.

The Party cannot go forward without a persistent struggle against reactionary beliefs and social prejudices. In this field, the Party must not only denounce antifeminine prejudices, but must make absolutely irreversible an aim that it has inscribed in its declaration, by allocating responsible posts in the Party to women.

A foreign policy with a correct orientation can be an important instrument in consolidating our independence and in constructing a national economy. Algeria has gained its independence at a time when the world relationship of forces continues to unfold in favor of the masses and against imperialism. The struggle of the liberation movements in Africa, Asia, and Latin America, the consolidation of independence in countries which had long been colonies, the action of democratic forces in the imperialist countries, and the gains accomplished by socialist forces—this struggle has accelerated the disintegration of imperialism. In the last few years, this struggle has claimed many victories.

This new situation has brought numerous changes in imperialist policies. The imperialists have become more and more flexible, trying to associate with small groups of the native bourgeoisie or bureaucracy in the interest of exploiting the people. They are attempting to demobilize the forces of liberation in order to maintain their economic and strategic interests in the colonized countries.

The alliance of imperialist countries with the governments of some African, Asian, and American nations has temporarily delayed the ebb tide of imperialism. But the general trend of our epoch is the reduction of imperialism's capacity to maneuver, not the enlargement of it.

The foreign policy of Algeria, in view of the constant dangers threatening our country, must be directed toward fighting colonialism and imperialism, toward helping the movements of unification of the Maghreb, of the Arab world and of Africa, and toward supporting liberation forces and the fight for peace.

The great lesson we draw from our own struggle for independence is that the imperialist countries, confronted by the rising tide of the masses, are seeking solidarity in spite of their minor differences. Our struggle has raised an echo from the masses in these countries, but it has also met with hostility from certain groups. In its drive to maintain its domination over Algeria, France received material and moral support from all the Western countries, especially from the U.S.A. Our revolutionary struggle will still meet many more obstacles. This must not keep us from making the maximum effort to persist in our anti-imperialist fight.

The struggle against imperialism has produced political and social forces which have been oriented in the same direction toward attainment of the unity of the Maghreb, the Arab world, and Africa.

The achievement of unity among different countries is a gigantic task which must be considered in the framework of the ideological, political, and economic paths common to all their people. In the Maghreb, and in the Arab world as in Africa, the divide-and-rule policies of imperialism, the conflicting and particular interests of the ruling classes, are the main obstacles to realizing unity, which they often reduce to a mere demagogic slogan.

The main task of our Party is to help the Maghreb, the Arab world, and Africa to reach a correct evaluation of the formidable challenge of such an accomplishment as unification. Meeting this challenge must be done through the vanguard organizations and mass organizations so that we can see concretely what obstacles must be overcome.

At the level of the governments, the development of trade, the realization of common economic projects, a concerted foreign policy, and a total solidarity in the fight against imperialism are objectives which, being in the interest of the peoples, impel us toward unification.

The Algerian war of liberation, because of its power and intensity, increased the tempo of the struggle for freedom in all African countries. Independent Algeria must give complete support to the masses who are constantly struggling to liberate their countries. We must pay close attention to Angola, South Africa, and the nations of East Africa. Our solidarity against colonialism will broaden our line of defense against imperialism and reinforce the movement for unification.

International cooperation is needed to utilize all human and material resources for progress in a climate of peace, and can only be won by a permanent mobilization of the masses against imperialism.

The Congo
(Kinshasa)

In recent African history, few countries have suffered more than the old Belgian Congo. Second only to the Sudan in size, second only to South Africa in wealth (and potentially richer), it has been ravaged by slave-hunters and mercenaries, U.N. troops and U.S. guns, Cuban exiles and CIA agents. And though the fate of its many revolutionaries has been bleak, it is the source and inspiration of people's armed struggle for all of black Africa.

Lying just south of the continental center, the Congo was first conquered by the Portuguese, then by Arab merchants of Zanzibar and finally by the Belgians, whose King Leopold "owned" it as his personal property until 1908 when it was annexed to Belgium. The first colonial administration was not established until 1930, and by 1959, the country was ruled by 9,600 Belgian colonists and 7,000 missionaries—besides civil servants and the army (reinforced repeatedly since 1895, date of the first of many Congolese rebellions). The Belgians never attempted to develop the country's infrastructure, and by 1959, there was not a single Congolese secondary school teacher and only thirty university graduates. More than 75 percent of the colony's 14 million people lived below subsistence level, engaged in primitive agriculture, hunting, and fishing. Meanwhile, the Congo was turning out three-fourths of the world's industrial diamonds, 69 percent of its cobalt, and a large share of its copper, zinc, gold, tin, silver, cadmium, manganese, tungsten, bismuth, and germanium, plus of course high-grade uranium (from which the Hiroshima bomb was made).

But the Congolese got none of the profits. These went to the Belgians, British, French, and, through stock ownership in Britain's Tanganyika Concessions (TANKS) and the Oppenheimer combine, to America's Rockefeller group. In 1960 alone, for example, net mining profits from Katanga reached $407 million. From 1950 to 1959, Union Minière

303

(mostly Belgian but also some English and American interests) derived 31 billion Belgian francs from its Congolese investments.[1]

At a mass rally in Leopoldville *(now Kinshasa)* on January 3, 1959, the head of the Congolese National Movement *(MNC)*, Patrice Lumumba, said that such conditions could not go on. He demanded immediate and total independence. The next day, 30,000 Congolese demonstrated in the streets—and were savagely put down by the Belgian army. But as the movement grew, Belgium agreed finally to pull out in 1960. General elections were held before independence, and Lumumba's MNC won most of the elective posts, with Joseph Kasavubu's ABAKO party second. Independence came on June 29, 1960. Two weeks later, egged on by the Belgians, the Congo's richest province announced its secession and on July 12, 1960, Lumumba, who was then Prime Minister, appealed for help from the United Nations.

That act was to be his undoing. Guided by members of the U.N.'s "Congo Club" *(one Englishman, two Indians, and three Americans)*, the U.N. forces immediately stepped in to prevent Lumumba from consolidating his power. Under the direction of the Congo Clubman Andrew W. Cordier, later president of Columbia University but then executive assistant to U.N. Secretary-General Dag Hammarskjöld (and, through his membership in the Century Association and the Council on Foreign Relations,[2] a close associate of Dean Rusk, Allen Dulles, McGeorge Bundy, David and Nelson Rockefeller, et al.), the U.N. occupied the Leopoldville airport, stopping aid to Lumumba, and seized the radio station, prohibiting Lumumba from speaking to his people. The U.N. force, however, did not stop the rebellious and pro-American troops of Sergeant *(later "General" and now "President")* Joseph Mobutu from kidnapping Lumumba and taking him to Camp Hardy near Thysville, beating him all the way. Once there, Katanga secessionist *(and later Congo "Prime Minister")* Moise Tshombe had him killed—in his presence. Shortly before his death, Lumumba then thirty-six, wrote to his home:

My dear wife,

I am writing these words not knowing whether they will reach you, and whether I shall still be alive when you read them. All through my struggle for the independence of my country, I have never doubted for a single instant the final triumph of the sacred cause to which my companions

[1] See the various articles in Association of the Bar of New York City, *Legal Aspects of the U.N. Action in the Congo* (New York: 1962).

[2] In 1960, the Council received $112,200 from American Metal Climax, Inc., IBM World Trade Corp., Mobil International Oil Co. (whose director, Grayson Kirk, was Cordier's predecessor at Columbia University), the *New York Times*, the Rand Corp., Standard Oil Co.—in exchange for "free consultation with members of the Council's staff on problems of foreign policy."

and I have devoted all our lives. But what we wished for our country, its right to an honorable life, to unstained dignity, to independence without restrictions, was never desired by the Belgian imperialists and the Western Allies, *who found direct and indirect support*, both deliberate and unintentional, *amongst certain high officials of the United Nations*, that organization in which we placed all our trust when we called on its assistance.

They have corrupted some of our compatriots and bribed others. They have helped to distort the truth and bring our independence into dishonor. How could I speak otherwise? Dead or alive, free or in prison by order of the imperialists, it is not myself who counts. It is the Congo, it is our poor people for whom independence has been transformed into a cage from whose confines the outside world looks on us, sometimes with kindly sympathy, but at other times with joy and pleasure.

But my faith will remain unshakable. I know and I feel in my heart that sooner or later my people will rid themselves of all their enemies, both internal and external, and that they will rise as one man to say No to the degradation and shame of colonialism, and regain their dignity in the clear light of the sun.

We are not alone. Africa, Asia, and the free liberated people from all corners of the world will always be found at the side of the millions of Congolese who will not abandon the struggle until the day when there are no longer any colonialists and their mercenaries in our country. As to my children, whom I leave and whom I may never see again, I should like them to be told that it is for them, as it is for every Congolese, to accomplish the sacred task of reconstructing our independence and our sovereignty: for without justice there is no dignity, and without independence there are no free men.

Neither brutality, nor cruelty, nor torture will ever bring me to ask for mercy, for I prefer to die with my head unbowed, my faith unshakable, and with profound trust in the destiny of my country, rather than live under subjection and disregarding sacred principles. History will one day have its say, but it will not be the history that is taught in Brussels, but the history which will be taught in the countries freed from Imperialism and its puppets. Africa will write her own history, and to the north and south of the Sahara it will be a glorious and dignified history.

Do not weep for me, my dear wife. I know that my country, which is suffering so much, will know how to defend its independence and its liberty.

Long live the Congo! Long live Africa!

Patrice

Following Lumumba's murder, on February 14, 1961, and the violent repressions unleashed by Mobutu, Lumumba's forces rallied. First Antoine Gizenga set up a rebel regime in Stanleyville (now Kisangani) and held out until 1962 when he was crushed by Mobutu's forces assisted by the U.N. Then, Bocheley Davidson and Pierre Mulele, who had been Lumum-

ba's Minister of Education, created the National Council of Liberation (CNL). Mulele journeyed to China for training and, in November 1963, opened the first guerrilla center in the southwestern province of Kwilu. Next Gaston Soumaliot and Christophe Gbenye led a rebellion in Kivu which swept down into Stanleyville and again established a rebel regime, this time called the Revolutionary Congolese Government, with Gbenye as president.

But toward the end of 1964 a few hundred Belgian paratroopers and mercenaries from Rhodesia, South Africa, and West Germany, and some 200 Cuban exiles commanded by CIA operatives, were dropped from U.S.-piloted U.S. C-130 planes, and a massacre began that cost 30,000 Congolese lives before Gbenye was beaten. Soumaliot fled into the jungles and, like Mulele, adopted guerrilla warfare tactics. The war spread. More mercenaries came. U.S. bombers, U.S. military aid, and U.S. "advisers" were dispatched to the area in increasingly heavier quantities—on the justification, as U.S. Under Secretary of State Harriman said, of "the dangers of Chinese Communist influence in the Congo" although London's Guardian reported that there was "no proof of Chinese intervention while the presence of U.S. bombers and military personnel was public knowledge."

The Kivu rebellion failed. Only Mulele's CNL kept fighting, joined now by the forces of Soumaliot and Gaston M'Galo. Meanwhile, General Mobutu deposed Tshombe, who had maneuvered himself into the Congo's premiership. In 1967, Mobutu ordered the assassination of Lumumba's wife and four children. That same year, in June, the Patrice Lumumba Battalion, headed by Thomas Mukwidi, went into battle, opening up a new rebel front. Che Guevara and other Cuban guerrilla fighters had helped organize it, and had even fought with it for a while. It was Che's theory (as it had been that of Frantz Fanon) that the Congo was the key to all of black Africa. But Mulele was no longer interested; he had stopped fighting. In September 1968, he was publicly offered a pardon and a cabinet post by Mobutu's Foreign Minister Justin-Marie Bomboko (who had worked first for Lumumba, then Kasavubu, then Tshombe, and now Mobutu). Mulele accepted. Bomboko went to escort him home from Brazzaville. The next day, Mulele was arrested, tried for war crimes— and executed two days later.

The articles which follow are from Mulele's forces. They are extracts from two of six notebooks found near Lake Leopold II after an assault in June 1965 on Nioki by his CNL forces. The notebooks were all of the same type: school-size, of 100 pages each. Other documents found with them indicated that the rebels had been trained in Boende and Gambona just across the Congo River into Congo-Brazzaville, and that it was at these camp sites that the lectures recorded in these notebooks were given. All six notebooks, written in longhand by various people, give accounts of lectures which were obviously delivered by professional revolutionaries.

NOTEBOOKS OF WAR 307

of Maoist conviction (though the only non-Congolese name to appear is that of the Cameroon scholar-revolutionary, Osendé Afana, who died in the first 1961 guerrilla assault on the neo-colonial Cameroon regime). The lectures were in French and were transcribed, with photostatic longhand samples, by Belgium's Centre de Recherche et d'Information Socio-Politique (CRISP). In his introduction, Benoît Verhaegen, CRISP's scientific consultant, explained that the lectures' changing tone was caused by the fact that there were various instructors giving the lectures.

Basically these lectures explain Mao's united front theory of revolution, complete with class analyses and a definition of "democratic centralism" which is the apparatus of leadership crucial to all Marxist-Leninists. The lectures are interesting, however, because they are aimed at political unsophisticates. They also show how Maoists are perfectly willing to adapt themselves to local conditions—in the case of the Congo, even to the point of defining a three-stage revolution: the national (armed struggle), which is anti-imperialist; the democratic (nationalization), which is anti-reactionary; and the socialist, to be put into effect much later when a consciousness for socialism exists. But once again, as with all Maoists, one point remains a firm dogma: that the national bourgeoisie is a revolutionary force during the national revolution phase. In the Congo, General Mobutu, who had killed most of the rebels and who was president in 1969, is the perfect representative of that proimperialist so-called national bourgeoisie.

NOTEBOOKS OF WAR*

FIRST NOTEBOOK: POLITICS

*Lecture One: The Enemies of the Congolese
Revolution and What It Has to Do (12-28-64)*

WHEREVER there is revolution you will find its friends on one side and its enemies on the other. Like every other revolution the Congolese one has its friends and its enemies; and every revolution has its duties which it must undertake so that it can achieve its ends.

In this lecture we are going to study the enemies of the Congolese Revolution at the present moment and consider what it has to do.

---

* Lectures, in French, reproduced, with sample longhand photostats, by the Centre de Recherche et d'Information Socio-Politique (CRISP) of Brussels in their *Travaux Africains du CRISP*, Dossier documentaire No. 3, November 1965, in a booklet entitled *Les Cahiers de Gambona: Instructions Politiques et Militaires des Partisans Congolais (1964–1965)*. Translation by Martin Rossdale.

What is the Congolese Revolution against? It is against the enemies of the Congolese. And who are these enemies? They are: (1) Neo-colonialists and Imperialists (Belgians, Americans, the British, the Italians, and the French). (2) The Congolese bureaucratic or comprador bourgeoisie. (3) Reactionary feudal elements in the Congo (traditional or *de facto* tribal chiefs), the agents of Imperialism and Neo-colonialism.

The main enemies of the Congolese Revolution are the Neo-colonialists and the Imperialists. These are the foreigners whose military presence tramples the people of the Congo day in and day out. They have military bases in the Congo and military specialists, etc., here as well. They use them to oppress the Congolese.

Of the enemies of the Congolese, the American and Belgian imperialists are the most important, followed by British and Italian imperialists and then by the French and Japanese. Remember that the number one enemies of the Congolese are the American and Belgian imperialists. Collaborating in their dirty work—exploiting and enslaving the people of the Congo, murdering hundreds them—there are:

The Congolese bureaucratic or comprador bourgeoisie; tools of imperialism such as these hold managerial positions in government offices, in the gendarmerie, in the police, throughout the administration, as magistrates, as teachers, in short in every branch of the public services including deputies of the puppet Assembly and members of the foreign House in the Congo. This class of Congolese have united their interests to those of imperialism.

Then there are the natural allies of imperialism. When we attack them we attack imperialism and vice versa. The class interests of these elements are also unshakably bound to those of imperialism; thus, for example, this is so of traditional and *de facto* chiefs such Kiamvou in Kwango province and Mpaneline in Kwilu province. If imperialism is to be eradicated in the Congo these class enemies must be fought and crushed:

1. Imperialists.
2. Congolese bourgeois bureaucrats and compradors.
3. Feudal reactionaries.

The struggles against the bureaucratic or comprador bourgeoisie and against the reactionary feudal minority which oppresses the people is part of the democratic revolution. But if these two struggles are carried out together, that is, if they are combined, then this is *National* Democratic Revolution. These struggles must be waged together, because imperialism in the Congo will never be eradicated if its local agents are not fought, nor can the agents of imperialism in the Congo be eradicated alone.

These two struggles, then, are intimately bound together, although they are, to some extent, separate.

Remember that the struggle against imperialism is the basic duty, the core of the Revolution, but remember too that the democratic revolution should not be neglected although it is of secondary importance. They

ust be taken together while the priority of the national revolution is
nderstood. Our task is a National Democratic Revolution.

The duties of the democratic revolution

1. To overthrow the regime of the reactionary classes, that is, the
minority which governs the interior; the agents of imperialism, the bureau-
ratic or comprador bourgeoisie, and the Congolese feudal reactionaries.
2. To achieve agrarian reform.
3. To establish and to honor the democratic and trade union rights
f all the national anti-imperialist forces.
4. To give the country political institutions popularly elected and under
emocratic control: A National Assembly and a government which is
nswerable to it, etc.

The duties of the national revolution

1. To overthrow the neo-colonialist regime.
2. To get rid of all foreign military bases, to abrogate all the unjust
reaties which were forced on the country by the imperialists.
3. To reorganize the army, the gendarmerie, the police, the administra-
ion, justice, and teaching, etc., so that their primary object is the service
f the whole people.
4. To put patriots in all positions of authority, to set up an independent
urrency.
5. To nationalize the national resources (mines, forests, etc.), agri-
ulture, ranching, commerce, banking, and industry which have been
rabbed or controlled by foreign capitalists, to establish an independent
ational economy.
6. To give a national scientific and popular content to the courses of
nstruction at all levels, primary, secondary, and higher. To ensure that
he teaching program from the primary grades through the secondary
tages to the higher levels is organized inside the country and that the
ame applies to technology as well. To nationalize all teaching and wel-
are institutions (hospitals—dispensaries), all the organs of the press, in-
ormation, and propaganda which are instruments of neo-colonialism, and
o prevent the establishment or opening of further channels for them.
    If the National Democratic Revolution carries out its duties, it will
chieve its ends, otherwise it will have to continue its struggle.

Lecture Three: Leadership and Guidance of the Revolution (no date, 1965)

    Our text is taken from the book by Comrade Osendé Afana,[1] Doctor of
cience in economics, politics and philosophy, and a barrister. The book
s called *Economic Growth and Monoculture in West Africa.*
    What is the leadership? It has the role of guiding a social class during

Cameroon sociologist, political scientist, nationalist, and revolutionary killed in
ombat as a guerrilla against the neo-colonial regime in 1961.—*Ed.*

the Revolution. According to the teaching of the greatest revolutionarie
and from daily experience, leadership has nothing to do with shoutin
commands all day long nor with making others agree to one's point o
view by brutality or arrogance.

Guidance consists of persuading and showing others by setting a jus
example, by giving them the example of work well done and getting then
to do likewise and to accept our precepts willingly. To be a successfu
leader, three essential conditions have to be satisfied:

a. A policy, a program has to be designed which is just and adequate
and which corresponds to the interests and needs of everybody.

b. A good example must be set by working well, so that the program
can be realized.

c. All the revolutionary forces inside the country have to be thoroughl
organized and mobilized so that the program can be realized.

Who satisfies these conditions best, members of the peasantry, the petty
bourgeoisie, or the proletariat?

Leadership by the peasantry has no consistent or unequivocal quality
since there is no single class of peasants. There are numerous socia
classes, all more or less different, from the richest to the poorest. Over
all the peasantry is full of contradictions which are more or less shar
and even opposed. Consequently the only scientific approach to the
problem is to study whether a group of the peasantry can exercise leader
ship.

The most progressive groups of the peasantry, poor peasants and the
intermediate strata of the middle peasants, are necessarily called upon
to play a very important part in the national democratic revolution o
the African people. As has been the case in China and Cuba, to quote
only two examples, the main body of revolutionary soldiers can onl
come from the peasants in underdeveloped countries which are basically
agrarian. But can the peasants be thought of as the vanguard at the hea
of the Revolution, can they exercise the kind of leadership we have jus
described, especially in view of the fact that they are not homogeneous
This question can only be answered by studying the leadership potentia
of each rural group. All the evidence shows that feudal elements, land
owners, whose character is essentially feudal, the bureaucratic or com
prador bourgeoisie, cannot lead the revolution on to victory.

The middle bourgeoisie is weak in Black Africa, but it is revolutionar
to some extent, insofar as it struggles against the domination of foreig
capital and for the establishment of a society whose politics are unde
its control, and for the development of a national capitalism which i
independent. Once that is achieved though, the political program of the
middle bourgeoisie becomes illusory and leads to a neo-colonial or neo
feudal regime under the bureaucratic or comprador bourgeoisie. Further
more, to achieve even that, the middle bourgeoisie has to struggle no

nly against imperialism, bureaucratic capitalism, and reactionary feudalsm, but also against the workers who cannot allow themselves to be xploited. This is why the actions of the middle bourgeoisie are as much lirected against progressive forces led by the proletariat as they are against eactionary forces led by imperialism. The middle bourgeoisie's economic mbiguity makes it incapable of mobilizing the revolutionary forces.

The petty bourgeoisie also has two aspects, particularly in Black Africa. t too, consequently, suffers the same problems regarding leadership as loes the middle bourgeoisie. Despite this, the revolutionary qualities of he African petty bourgeoisie are worth a special study. Its characteristics re very pronounced and will endure, because the petty bourgeoisie of Africa is of very limited power, and because it has had to struggle long nd hard against imperialism to reach the stage it has. On the other and, the African proletariat, which has come into being in foreign businesses, is relatively more mature and more combative than the African etty bourgeoisie. The former has been under greater threat from members of its own class in the West and even in Asia and Latin America.

When his enemy is strong and ruthless, when it crushes him as it did luring the classical colonial regime, the bourgeoisie makes an alliance vith the popular masses to fight him. Once, however, a revolutionary onsciousness develops among the working masses, the bourgeoisie allies tself with the enemy to defeat them.

Because of its strong tendency to subjectivism and individualism, by eason of its sectarianism and its economic shakiness, Africa's new petty ourgeoisie falls an easy victim to neo-colonialism in the Kennedy style. Iistory will show that despite its indubitable worthiness at the present tage of our struggle, this class cannot lead the African Revolution to its iltimate and final victory.

Only *the proletariat* is capable of this historic task. Why? In the first lace because all the other social classes are unable to do so. But furthermore, and more importantly, because the proletariat is far and away the nost revolutionary class. The proletariat knows better than any other lass how to bring this just program to fruition. In fact this class knows etter than any other how it is exploited.

There are those who claim that in Africa the peasants are more exloited. In monetary terms this may be so, but in terms of real value, nd especially if a comparison is made between the pay of each in conrast to the amount they add to the national wealth, then there can be o doubt that the proletariat is subject to greater exploitation. Obviously hey produce more than the peasants but their real wealth and purchasing ower is usually the same if not lower. In fact, despite all his means of roduction the African proletarian resembles the grossly underpaid peasant vith this further disadvantage, that he has to buy goods at prices which re often too high, whereas the peasant consumes a proportion of what he produces and thereby avoids the exploitation of imperialism and i allies to some extent. This is especially so where peasants are neithe serfs nor slaves, which is true of the majority of peasants in Black Afric.

Anyway the proletariat are more aware that they are being exploite. This higher level of consciousness arises in the great difference betwee their own permanent wretchedness and the effrontery with which the cla enemy, personified in the employer, gets rich quick.

But the enemy of the landowning peasants of Black Africa is almo disembodied. His enemy helps himself to public money, he is the money lender and the merchant. As far as the peasant is concerned it is immateri. whether they are imperialists or not. Consequently the peasants' resen ment is vague. So far as organization is concerned the proletariat is fa more significant than the peasantry and can easily organize itself int an independent political force. This, together with its association wit the more advanced forms of the economy, means that it is more ac customed to discipline.

All these advantages contribute to the superiority of the proletari. which everyone can see in the social life of the African people. Worker unions are invariably set up before peasant organizations and they ge erally exhibit a higher degree of aggressiveness. The proletariat also show its superiority when it comes to organizing and mobilizing the shattere remnants of other classes, especially those of peasant origin. This is pa ticularly true of Africa where there are such large numbers of sem proletarians. Furthermore there is a natural affinity between the pr letariat and their most trustworthy ally, the peasant.

In international relations the proletariat can also count on the tot. solidarity of the international working-class movement. Foreign capitalist however, only support the African bourgeoisie insofar as the latter offe them no competition. It is true that the proletariat is a smaller class tha the peasantry and that it has a lower cultural level than the bourgeoisi but all the evidence shows that no other class in society unites in itse so many leadership qualities as it does. The only reason why it has nc exercised its role of leadership in Africa yet is because the objective an subjective conditions have not yet occurred in sufficient degree. Th countries of Africa are still far from achieving the objective and subjectiv conditions necessary for the setting up of a socialist government.

When we state that the people of Africa have obviously got an intere. in choosing socialism we are taking the long-term view and not speakin of an immediate transition to socialism.

But [Lecture Four (no title, no date)] in the stage in which the Cor golese Revolution is at present, if it is to provide a satisfactory answe for the interests and aspirations of the whole people, it cannot—mu. not—be a bourgeois revolution. Yet it cannot be a socialist revolutio either.

At present the Congolese Revolution must be a new democratic revolution.

a. Politically the new democracy is typified by an alliance between all the national revolutionary classes under the leadership of the proletariat. All these classes take an effective share of political power but it is accepted that the proletariat is at the helm.

b. The economy of the new democracy is characterized by the nationalization of business enterprises which belong to foreign capital, and to the bureaucratic or comprador bourgeoisie. Priority is given to the development of the public sector, to agricultural reform, and to the formation of cooperatives of independent agricultural workers, artisans, traders, etc., etc.

Priority will be given to existing establishments and to the development of socialized public property. The speedy development of the country will be kept up. In passing we should stress the main similarities and differences between the national democracy and the new democracy. Both regimes are based on the alliance of all revolutionary classes, as such they are against the imperialists, their aggressive military blocs, and against feudalism. Both regimes insist that all revolutionary forces and the government should respect democratic liberties. By contrast with the reactionaries they are anxious to protect all aspects of political independence and to strengthen them by achieving ever increasing economic independence. The people must choose between these two transitional regimes, between the capitalist and the socialist paths of development.

The main differences between the regimes are as follows: a national democracy can only be found in a country where the social classes are not yet sharply distinguishable from one another and where, in consequence, the proletariat can hardly exercise its leadership uncontested (e.g., Guinea, Mali, Indonesia). Once the social classes are sufficiently differentiated and once the leadership of the proletariat is more markedly imposed, the regime becomes a new democracy. It is the more progressive of the two. The new democracy turns into a popular democracy, essentially, when the political and economic power of the bourgeoisie shifts over to the proletariat allied to the poor peasantry.

Could a new democratic regime win through in the Congo? Yes. Why? Because every day the requisite conditions come together in a way which is almost ideal. What are these basic conditions which favor the new democratic revolution?

a. The determination of the vast majority of the people to overthrow the neo-colonialist regime by any means and to set up a new democratic regime. This determination expresses itself by the development of mass movements despite the conditions of virtual fascism. The Congolese proletariat has an increasingly important vanguard role. It is the most numerous, the most conscious, and the most combative of all Black Africa.

b. The discrediting of intermediary forces and semirevolutionary solutions (e.g., the petty bourgeoisie and the middle bourgeoisie) which have suppressed all democratic liberties and even attacked moderate nationalists. They are allied to the neo-colonialists whose regime has shown the people that the only way of satisfying the just aspirations of the population was that of total revolution as advocated by the CNL [National Council of Liberation].

c. The developing contradictions within the counterrevolutionary camp first between the various imperialists. The English, Italian, and American imperialists are attempting to supplant their Belgian colleagues. One may expect contradictions, though only infrequently, between the imperialists and their puppets, and finally between the puppets themselves. Thus Tshombe and his group refused to join Kasavubu's ABAKO[2] and there is already open competition between these two for the next presidential elections. There will be contradictions between the new bureaucratic bourgeoisie, which is somewhat favorable to agrarian reform, and the feudal elements who are opposed to it, etc. It is true that there are also contradictions among the revolutionaries, but our differences can and will soon find peaceful solutions, while the contradictions between our enemies should, by and large, exacerbate as time goes on.

Lecture Five: The Weapons of the Congolese New Democratic Revolution (no date)

As usual we should ask ourselves today what are the long-term objectives of the Congolese Revolution. Will it be a capitalist regime, guaranteeing political power and cultural and material comforts to a small minority of the bourgeoisie and the feudal elements, or will it be a socialist regime which will enable the country to achieve complete independence and the speedy development of all its potentialities, so that all social classes which are anti-imperialist and anticolonialist can benefit?

First of all, however, we must tackle the major problem which confronts us today. Once the Congo has its natural independence the burning question for the Congolese Revolution will be whether it can continue to go forward or whether it will be blocked in a prolonged or complete checkmate. The victory of the Revolution depends on critical weapons which are:

1. A vanguard revolutionary party.
2. A fine liberation army.
3. A powerful peasant movement.
4. A united front of all these.

[2] Neo-colonialist but verbally anti-imperialist movement which held power in 1964-65.—Ed.

The Party is the most important of these. This is why we will go over the basic question of the Party again and again and why we will do no more than simply outline the basic needs of the other principal weapons of the Revolution.

A political party is the means by which a class or a part of a class wields its dictatorship. Parties are political organizations by means of which classes or parts of classes take power, hold it, reinforce it, broaden its base, and thus look after their interests and aspirations.

Political parties, therefore, have a well-defined class content, even if some parts of their programs serve the interests of many classes. Their primary objective is the promotion and consolidation of the interests of a given class.

This is the esssential difference between a political party and a political movement: a movement chooses generalized objectives which satisfy the needs of numerous classes at any given time rather than the particular interests of one class or part of a class. In practice, however, the dominant class always leads the movement according to its class interests, e.g., the peace movement, the movement for national integrity and independence, for African Unity, etc. These movements meet everybody's objectives, but every class interprets their meanings differently and attempts to achieve them according to their own interests.

If a party is to enable a class to gain and reinforce its hold on power it must fulfill four functions:

1. Mobilize the masses, give them a sense of direction and educate the class and all the people according to the class interests which it wishes to protect.

2. Mobilization of the masses means pushing them in this kind of action.

3. Organize actual struggles against whatever stands in its way so as to achieve the Party's objectives.

4. Keep a tight grip on the way the Party's orders are carried out.

The CNL must have theory—if it is to lead the Congolese Revolution to final victory. It must satisfy certain criteria, of which the following are the four most important:

A. It must comprise a unified body of the Congolese revolutionary class. In the interests of unity all CNL militants must be one in the intention and unshakable determination to serve the interests of the Congolese revolutionaries, i.e., they must be willing to translate their unity of intention into unity of action. Their every act must be directed to the same class interests and directives. Unity has no place for intraparty rivalries. Our experiences in recent years stress that the CNL cannot defend or consolidate its unity if it does not fulfill the three following conditions satisfactorily.

B.1. It must be a vanguard body of the most revolutionary classes in

the Congo, which entails three consequences: the CNL must be guided
by revolutionary theory. Without that no party can distinguish the enemies
of the Revolution from the forces which are driving it forward, no party
can pick out what has to be done and how that relates with other needs,
and, therefore, no party can succeed in closely uniting revolutionary forces
so as to isolate the reactionaries and pick them off one by one. For
example, we have had many illusions about the United Nations: they
prevented us from making serious preparations for armed struggle. In
the Congo we have often overestimated the revolutionary capacity of
the Congolese bourgeoisie. We must avoid the sin of sectarianism, we
must not write off all except a tiny minority of Congolese as revolutionary.
We must not exclude militants and those from certain clans and tribes.
If we do so we will be failing to mobilize important revolutionary elements
and may even provoke violent attacks against them. All this shows that
there can be no revolutionary movement without a revolutionary theory,
that without it we cannot lead the revolution to final victory.

B.2. If the CNL is to be a vanguard body, it must recruit its militants
and especially its leading cadres from the best elements of the national
middle and petty bourgeoisie, from among the intellectual revolutionaries,
and especially from the peasants and working class. There are certain class
characteristics of organizations which do not primarily depend on the
class origin of the constituent members but on the class interests which
it serves, on its ideology, and on the actual political struggles in which
it engages. Thus working-class parties are not proletarian parties even
if the majority of their members are workers. Man's consciousness is
determined by his social conditions. That is why the militants and leading
cadres of a vanguard revolutionary party should primarily be recruited
from the vanguard revolutionary classes.

B.3. To be an vanguard body means that the CNL must set up, and
then maintain and extend, close links with the masses. If the CNL is not
well rooted in the masses everybody will not be able to support it, and
it will not be able to lead the Revolution to victory.

C. All the evidence shows that the CNL cannot be united, and cannot
be a vanguard body of the revolutionary classes, if it is not also a well-
organized body. What does that mean? The experiences of other revolutions in recent years show us that in the main good, revolutionary organizations mean three factors:

1. All CNL members must be active members of the grass-root CNL
organizations.

2. All CNL institutions, especially those of the leadership, must follow
normal CNL procedure, i.e., our Revolution must not suffer because the
executive committee or less important institutions such as the financial
control commission are not carrying out their duties properly so that

the executive committee is consequently paralyzed. Again it is most important that the upper echelons of the CNL carry out their duties in continuity.

3. All CNL organizations must work according to the principles laid down in the Statutes of the Congolese National Revolution. These are the most important rules:

a. Democratic centralism.

b. There must be criticism and self-criticism at all levels of the CNL.

c. The leadership must follow the mass line closely and avoid becoming separated from the people.

d. The CNL must have a better structure and a better organization than the other revolutionary parties. This will ensure that its leadership of the most revolutionary class organizations is effective. It must be the cutting edge of these organizations, the pattern which all other revolutionary classes will imitate.

The CNL is not the only means by which the members of the revolutionary classes defend their interests and aspirations. There are numerous other organizations which serve this purpose, unions, cooperatives, bodies of women, young people, students, and peasants. There are cultural, sporting, religious associations, etc. Why should all these organizations have a single leadership? Because they are all defending the same class interests, they share a common purpose.

The CNL can lead all these organizations by becoming an even more closely united body, a vanguard, a highly organized, revolutionary, and class organization. The CNL must continuously develop its fundamental leadership qualities. Because it employs a theory of revolution it will be able to tailor its programs to everybody's class interests. By constituting itself from the finest elements of the most revolutionary classes, its cadres will receive the best schooling. As the most experienced organization it will enjoy the greatest prestige among the masses. In short, by becoming a new kind of revolutionary party the CNL will be best able to lead all the other revolutionary organizations. The CNL should lead through its militants within these organizations. This means: CNL militants should play an active part in all existing organizations and in any which may be formed; CNL militants should lead by example. Those who do not agree with their Party's line should be persuaded by the example of the militants' conscientiousness and selflessness within their respective organizations. To act otherwise is a violation of the letter and spirit of the Revolution.

Why does the CNL need its own army? The army is the main instrument of class dictatorship. Reactionaries are always the first to resort to violence, e.g., South Vietnam, Cuba, Algeria, Angola, South Africa, and our own country, the Congo. If oppressed nations and classes do not learn how to handle weapons, if they only try to liberate themselves by using peaceful means, they will never be free. In the Congo, especially, armed struggle is essential because:

1. The armed forces of the counterrevolution oppress our people and butcher them daily.

2. The people have no democratic liberties or political rights.

3. The imperialists and their stooges invariably rebuff all peaceful attempts of liberating the Congo whether we attempt to negotiate for it or win it electorally.

The imperialist and people's armies recruit from different strata of society. But there are other extremely important differences. The army of the CNL is the blade of a vanguard revolutionary party, a new kind of people's army, because there are only Congolese patriots in it and no foreign mercenaries. It takes orders only from Congolese, not from foreigners. It is closely tied to the people and the Party by the same revolutionary theory and the same just cause as that of the CNL; by the CNL leadership, the Party having set up organizations within the army; by democratic methods of organization and control, notably the practice of political, economic, and military democracy within the ranks; and by its productive labor, as it works to mobilize and organize the masses.

THIRD NOTEBOOK: THE REVOLUTION (NO DATE, 1965)

The Revolution is the expression of the revolt of the masses. Once they have tried every peaceful means of implementing their demands and have been thwarted by the brutality and the violence of their enemies, they resort to violence themselves as the only and necessary means of getting what they want.

Wherever there is a revolution you will find the objective causes of it. Take the struggle against neo-colonialism in the Congo or in the Cameroons. Rightfully the Congo should be held to belong to the people of the Congo, first, last, and always. Its political, economic, and military administration should be in Congolese hands alone. All inhabitants of the Congo, natives and foreigners alike, should be subject to Congolese law.

Such would be the case if men treated one another honestly, with justice and equaliy. But in fact this is not the case. Hence the Congolese, who never stopped hearing how rich the Congo was, saw only how wretched they were, and they looked for the cause of their misfortunes. The work of whose fruits they were cheated cleared their eyes and led them to ask, and peacefully, for the complete independence of their country. But their enemies answered their peaceful demands with violence and denied them their legitimate requests (e.g., the arrest of Patrice Lumumba before the Brussels round table meeting).

As we all know, the Congo was declared independent by the Belgian imperialists in 1960, but we also know that the Belgians interpreted the meaning of independence differently from the Congolese patriots. The proof of this is the death of Patrice Lumumba and his friends and what is happening in the Congo today.

The people of the Congo repeated their demand that their country should have genuine independence and peacefully asked the Belgian neo-colonialists to discontinue all meddling in Congolese affairs. Instead the Americans, the Belgians, the French, and the English have sent bombers, weapons of all kinds, mercenaries, and paratroops to slaughter the peaceful and unfortunate people of the Congo. But the Congolese had determined to win full independence and they made up their minds to answer the violence of the imperialists and their stooges with popular violence.

The people can rely, essentially, only on themselves. They must wage their own war and win it by relying on their own forces. But they are not alone in their struggle. They can depend on the stalwart support of all revolutionary men and women the world over, led by the mighty socialist camp. As for the supply of weapons, the people of the Congo have already learned that they must be taken from the enemy. The cause is just, we are determined to defeat our enemies at any cost.

But if we want to win, if we want to build a united, democratic, vigorous Party, a Party with room in it for everyone, tribalism must be eradicated. We must denounce this scourge, and expose it in whatever form it takes. We must fight it, drive it out of politics. This is the only way we will be able to pursue policies which will promise us victory against the enemies of liberty and progress in our country.

Tribalism is an undesirable form of thought and action in which priority is given to the selfish interests of one's own tribe or clan. More or less overtly a tribalist believes that the men and women of his own tribe or clan are better than other people who should wait on them and obey them. The tribalist tries to impose the sovereignty and preeminence of his clan or tribe on others. Usually tribalist ideas and sentiments are exploited so as to form a following which will serve their interests and selfish ambitions.

Tribalism takes different forms. These are the main ones:

1. The tribalist is always exaggerating and boasting of the fine qualities and deeds of the people of his clan or tribe. He ignores or tries to minimize their faults, but he behaves in quite the opposite way when it comes to people of another clan or tribe.

2. The tribalist practices favoritism toward the members of his own tribe or clan. They are usually allowed to do what they like, even if it is against the law, or the rules and regulations of the Party. He trusts them and will tell them his secrets, even those which are critical to the

Party and the state. But in his dealings with members of other clans or tribes, the tribalist is sectarian. He has no confidence in their efforts or their honesty and sometimes he will not even pass their orders on to them.

3. A tribalist will try to offer privileges and responsible jobs to members of his own tribe or clan, e.g., study grants, and responsible posts which are not appointed by open election are usually picked out by tribalists for the members of their own tribe or clan.

4. Again he will try to let these same people out of their duties and obligations, especially if hard work or danger is involved, or if the assignments are tough or humiliating.

5. The tribalist also hands out drugs, clothing, food, and party, army, and governmental funds to his cronies. He hurriedly compiles reports for them and keeps the best beds in hospital for them. All his zeal and devotion vanishes the moment he has to work for members of another clan or tribe.

6. Occasionally a tribalist will even decide that a member of another clan or tribe is too wealthy or fortunate to deserve any help from him. He may even refuse them help when they are really in difficulties. Sometimes he will go so far as to say that they should not have the little they have and that they should hand it over to the members of his tribe or clan. The next step is an easy one, which has, alas, been taken by many tribalists who see nothing wrong in stealing from or exploiting the members of other tribes and clans.

7. There are even those who take tribalism so far that instead of contemplating marriage with a member of another tribe they would rather see marriage between Blacks and Whites. The Kasavubu government, for example, could have given competent personnel, who had come from the south, posts in the north, but it preferred simply to hand over that part of our country to colonialists who were well known to have committed atrocities in the south or in Indochina or Algeria.

8. Politically, tribalism finds its highest expression in attempts to set up so-called independent republics which are actually tribal enclaves. If this device does not succeed they campaign for "a federation with regional autonomy" by which, of course, they mean the parceling up of political and administrative power in little tribal lots. We have all met cases of such "federalism" and of such tribal "autonomy." The most glaring examples are Congo-Leopoldville and the federalist fancies of the Kenya African Democratic Union (KADU).

History has shown that imperialists and all reactionaries are constantly trying to stimulate tribalist feelings among the people so as to divide them among themselves, so that their exploitation can be more effective and grinding. Even when tribalism is not met in its worst forms, it is a factor which causes splitting and weakness so that the masses are less able to struggle against foreign domination and underdevelopment. History also shows that every tribalist is primarily interested in satisfying the selfish interests of his own tribe at the expense of other tribes, that within the tribe itself he is promoting the interests of his own clan and that within the clan itself he is looking after his own family. In the last analysis tribalism is a feudally engendered kind of selfishness. This is the reason why tribalist associations always end by splitting and going under, usually in very sharp internecine struggles.

All the evidence indicates that the primary cause for the survival and development of tribalism is backwardness in the formation of the nation. The concrete evidence of this backwardness is the host of tribes found in the body of the state. Thus there are 140 in the Cameroons and 300 in Nigeria, etc. But this is not such a serious problem, for these tribe-families all belong to the same racial stock, either because of natural parenthood, or because of the way they have been geographically mingled together, or because they have shared a common history for a fairly long time. What's more, prolonged colonialist and imperialist domination has done much to unite the different tribes. It is true that no country in Tropical Africa has made itself a nation yet, that is, established a stable community, set up historical institutions, and integrated its tongue, land, economic life, and physical characteristics into the culture of the community. But small racial groups and the fact that the nation has not yet constituted itself in an ideal way is not a major bar to the campaign against tribalism. Already a national consciousness has developed in the course of the struggle against foreign domination.

The main obstacle to the campaign against tribalism are underdevelopment and imperialism. Imperialism, neo-colonialism, and colonialism intend to govern; that is why they are continually stirring up hatred and rivalry between tribes. They say to the members of this tribe or that: There are more of you and you are the wealthiest. You should govern the Congo. Then they say to some others: You are the clever ones, you should lead the country. And even while they are saying this other imperialists' agents or neo-colonialist stooges are saying the very same words to other tribes or clans.

The most important fact to grasp is that the Congolese Revolution will never win if the majority of the Congolese cannot take part without discrimination. History shows this clearly. Consider the Iraqis who are obviously in a majority position in their own country and who receive substantial support from abroad. Despite this they cannot overcome and defeat the Kurds, nor can they build a genuinely independent, democratic, and prosperous country. In the Congo itself there have been extraordinary developments in the Revolution which have been, unfortunately, confined to one or two regions, not to say tribes. Sananga-Maritime is a well-known recent example. Despite exceptional feats of heroism and self-sacrifice in these districts, despite even the antitribalist policy of the

CNL, we have not been able to overthrow the colonialist or neo-colonialist government. The liberation of the Congo will naturally begin in one or a few regions, but the Revolution will not win if it is not actively supported by the great popular masses throughout the length and the breadth of the land.

Every man must be equal before the law which imposes duties upon us but also accords us rights. The campaign for democracy and equality of rights should encompass the struggle against tribalism and here the best weapon is education, which must have a national, popular, and scientific character at one and the same time. Educationalists should never cease putting the evils of tribalism in the limelight and emphasizing the necessity of uniting the people of the Congo against the enemies which they all have, imperialism, neo-colonialism, and underdevelopment. People must be taught that every individual and all men have good and bad qualities and that everybody should be judged according to what he says and does, not according to whether he is a member of this family or that tribe. Education should also be scientific insomuch as it should encompass technical knowledge and practical skills, and progressively eradicate subjectivist and irrational concepts. Schooling and education should be available to all, so that everyone can exploit his abilities, develop his personality, and win the regard and respect of others no matter what tribe he belongs to.

The struggle against tribalism is an integral part of the struggle within the Party. It is consequently absolutely essential. This is particularly so because every Party militant or leader in the CNL has come from one tribe or another and has been and still is under the influence of tribalism. Others will have to campaign continually, tenaciously, for many years. The struggle is at once the condition and the reward of our victory over imperialism, neo-colonialism, misery, ignorance, and disease.

Tribalism and nepotism are the essence of factionalism. Nepotism is family spirit translated into the field of politics. A man who has this fault consciously or unconsciously regards the Party, the army, the state, and the Revolution as family businesses. With all his heart, the nepotist wants to give all the advantages he or she can to his or her parents, children, spouse, brothers, and sisters. Like the puppet Ngo Dinh Diem he reckons that power and all the advantages which can be derived from it should be given to the members of his own family in the first place.

Should it happen in our ranks, it will be used by the imperialists and all other reactionaries to attack and denigrate the whole Party and its revolutionary policies. The inevitable consequence is the paralysis or even the death of the organizations which are afflicted by tribalism and nepotism and their resulting power struggle. The pity of it is that good elements allow themselves to be drawn into these fratricidal struggles unleashed by a handful of individualists pursuing their personal ambitions. A house divided against itself cannot stand. If we want to survive and win, we must remove this cancer from our midst.

Everything shows that the main source of the power struggle lies in individualism, pride, and selfishness. One thinks oneself superior to everyone else, and as such worthy of power and all that normally goes with it: honors, glory, and material benefits. In addition, the absence of strong traditions about the birth and development of political power and the way personal relations are more important than indispensable programs or theories, together with many other social factors, can make the leaders dizzy, tempting them to build up their personal power to the point of making themselves into chieftains each with their own clients and vassals.

Naturally imperialists, neo-colonialists, right-wing nationalists, and all the other enemies of our Party's revolutionary line try to exploit to the full all the factors mentioned above in order to split our leadership, weaken and smash our Revolution, and finally force puppets in their pay upon us as our leaders.

Even in truly independent countries that are economically and technically advanced and well organized, political consciousness is invariably unevenly spread. Society renews itself continually, and after it has done so, the militants of the Party, the army, and the state must do so. Now militants and young cadres need to struggle for a fairly long period in order to familiarize themselves with the Party's principles and just methods of leadership. During this period many rapid and often profound social upheavals occur. The leaders do not always quickly succeed in finding the just principles and methods that should govern the new relationships among the leaders, between the leadership and the rest of the Party, between the Party and the masses, between fraternal parties and so on. Even in the most advanced societies it can be said that, to various extents of course, the power struggle had its origin in ignorance and violation of just principles, or even pure and simple betrayal of the Revolution.

The campaign against the power struggle is hence an integral part of struggle within the Party. To fight the power struggle we must therefore show through education and personal example that the exercise of power is a heavy burden and an inexhaustible source of sacrifices, not of personal satisfaction. To take on a responsible post means above all to accept serving others, not oneself or one's own. It means putting myself at the disposal of the body that gives me responsibility at all times. And the higher the responsibility the more heavy and dangerous the burden. First because peaks attract lightning. It is against the leaders and those in responsible positions that our enemies are dead set. They murder them without pity at the very first opportunity.

Those who see in positions of responsibility a way of helping themselves and those close to them should realize that their selfishness and their pride are bound to bring them many personal enemies in addition to imperialists and all other reactionaries, the sworn enemies of the Revolution.

How is one to avoid the blows of so many enemies? There is only one solution: giving up one's ambitions and selfish interests and putting oneself wholeheartedly at the service of others. But how is one to serve somebody else without knowing his specific needs and difficulties? How is one to know them without their help? The inevitable conclusion is that to fulfill his task a leader must put himself disinterestedly at the service of others and learn from them. He also needs everyone's support and must surround himself with many capable, dynamic, and disinterested elements like himself.

In a country like the Congo, engaged in a struggle as difficult as the one against imperialism, neo-colonialism, and underdevelopment, a country in which everything has to be done, it is not responsible positions which are in short supply but dignified cadres able to fill them usefully. One of the safest criteria for telling whether somebody is a true revolutionary, capable of giving good leadership, consists in seeing if he wants to unite without discrimination all elements capable of taking part in the Revolution and if he establishes effective links with the masses, that is, follows the mass line.

If the Revolution is to triumph there must be fidelity to a correct political line, one in the interests of the whole people. A general truth should be stated clearly: it is necessary to satisfy everyone's legitimate needs, including spiritual ones such as the need for prestige, if we are to struggle effectively against the power struggle. The vital and fundamental principle is that everyone's needs should be satisfied according to his work and merit alone. Once this principle is accepted we should apply ourselves to the correct definition of the relations between leaders and led. All societies need leadership. Effective and correct leadership must exist in its organization as a fish lives in water, in close unity with the led. The leader has the right to more private goods and funds than those under him but only so far as they are absolutely necessary to permit him to carry out his duties. For example, a leader needs a car for his work but there is no need for it to be a luxurious one. Generally speaking, one must ensure that the honors and material benefits of leadership do not separate him from the masses and don't encourage him to think of himself as a god or demigod.

All these measures and others analogous to them have the same end in view: to combat the causes of and pretexts for the power struggle, to check the tendency toward personal power and the establishment of privileged castes, but, at the same time, to promote the development of a democratic and socialist society in which all will thrive free from any exploitation. Thus you can see that the problems of everyday life are closely linked to the problems of organization.

The Conference of Cadres, convened in Accra in December 1960, stipulated that the greatest care must be taken to see that responsible comrades are:

1. The most faithful to the mass line.
2. The most capable of taking decisions rapidly.
3. The most devoted to the Party and the most disciplined.
4. The most dynamic.

The CNL must add another criterion which is not mentioned here, class background. Revolutionary theory and history show that the classes are not equally revolutionary. The proletariat lead, followed by the semi-proletariat, the poor peasants, and the small peasants. In those of our countries which are economically little developed, the petty bourgeoisie has, so to speak, a higher revolutionary potential than it has in the economically developed countries. In short, experience shows that the best cadres are those who follow the most revolutionary class line.

It is unusual for a single person to fulfill all these conditions to a very high degree. We should at least make sure that the organization and leadership teams are well balanced and that they form a perfect blend of all these qualities. Leadership organizations at all levels must above all be relatively stable. Every time there's a replacement, an important part of the outgoing organization should be included in the new. This allows continuity of action and experience to be maintained by the leadership.

It is neither enough to elect good leaders nor to make up the organization of the leadership sensibly. Cadres must also be correctly formed, chosen, and treated. The great importance of these questions is due to the fact that once a political line has been adopted, everything depends on the cadres. Under every unexpected condition and situation, their application may be good or bad, their adaptation correct and revolutionary or incorrect and even counterrevolutionary. The only way of handling cadres correctly is to give them proper working conditions while placing obstacles to the foolish ambitions which lurk in all of us, and of arousing in them unlimited devotion and enthusiastic dynamism for the service of the whole people. Such a policy cannot be achieved without respect for democratic centralism.

Democratic centralism simultaneously unites discipline and democracy while ensuring that democracy is subordinate to discipline. Discipline means that every individual Party member obeys his committee and the organization in which he is active. It also means that the minority obeys the majority, that junior organizations obey senior organizations, and that the whole Party obeys the congress of the executive committee in between congresses. Discipline should be the same for everyone. Everyone should obey the law, the statutes, and other key Party texts. Thus the principle of respecting the hierarchy applies not only to the led but also to the leaders. If discipline is to be really tight it must be freely agreed to. This means that democracy and free discussion should occur at all levels.

Comradeliness must be found throughout the leadership organization, that is, the collective leadership must be combined with individual responsibility. All important decisions concerning policy and organization must be talked over, collectively adopted and then applied to everyone. Similarly, the administration of their execution is a joint responsibility but the execution itself is entrusted to one or a few members of the leadership. All decisions concerning the jurisdiction of general assemblies which meet regularly should be taken by vote following discussion at which every Party member has the same opportunity to express his opinions freely without having any pressure brought to bear on him or needing to fear any reprisals. Once decisions have been adopted in these circumstances, the kind of discipline discussed above applies to all.

Democratic centralism also means that organizations and junior leaders are forbidden to give opinions on questions not yet treated by their superiors. They must learn to submit suggestions, and their superiors must not shirk their responsibility to solve difficult problems. These demands lead directly to the keystone of democratic centralism: the mass line.

The *mass line* is attained only when those who hold responsible positions at all levels of the army and the Party gather opinions and criticisms from militants and people in general; consider these opinions together in the light of the Party's policy and objective, as well as in the experience of revolutions of other lands; consequently, make a just decision and convince militants and the people that the position is a just one; make sure that orders are carried out and then go on to repeat the process. This definition of the mass line literally allows leaders and those with responsibility to live with the people as the fish lives in water. In this way they can quickly spot where their policy is lacking and how they can put matters right. However little they are able to make scientific analyses and undertake self-criticism, as long as they are naturally honest, revolutionary leaders can find in the mass line the best conditions in which to know and to serve the people and their wishes, and especially the effective way to wage the struggle for power.

South Africa

Toward the end of the 1960's, every nationalist, would-be nationalist, revolutionary, and pseudorevolutionary party or movement throughout southern Africa tried to define itself as the most militant. What's more, each group spent a great deal of time and effort denouncing the others. For example, in South Africa or "Azania," as nationalists call it, the two main liberation "fronts"—the African National Congress (ANC) and the Pan-Africanist Congress (PAC)—were engaged in such savage verbal warfare that their true achievements often passed unnoticed. And those achievements were considerable, especially since both groups were declared illegal after years of open political activity which had made their leaders perfectly known to the repressive forces.

The South African government is surely one of the most totalitarian in the world today. With widespread collusion from all imperialist countries (whatever their "official" policy toward apartheid), the white regime has brought the 3,000,000 whites the highest standard of living in the world, but only at the expense of the total subjugation and enslavement of the country's 15,000,000 blacks, who furnish the South African whites and foreign interests an unlimited supply of cheap labor.

That investment totals more than $4 billion from the U.S., West Germany, France, and Japan alone. The country accounts for 43 percent of the mineral output of the entire African continent and more than two-thirds of the world's gold production. It also exports capital: $600 million by 1963, of which almost $400 million was invested in the Rhodesias. Inside the country, the whites own 87 percent of the land. Their per-capita yearly income in 1959 was $1,200, compared to $109 for Africans (blacks) and $151 for other nonwhites (Asians, West Indians, etc.). Today infant mortality for whites (27 per thousand) is among the lowest in the world, while for the blacks (400 per thousand) it is the highest. In addition, of course, the blacks have no rights whatsoever: They cannot vote, join unions,

327

organize parties, stage protests, refuse to obey whites, go for a walk after 11 P.M., and so on. Many are compelled to live in "reserves"—concentration camps. Families are split for the convenience of whites and, most symbolically degrading of all, every nonwhite is forced to carry a "passbook," which can be demanded by any policeman or white person (of any profession) at any time.

What is even more incredible, however, is that most of these conditions have existed for centuries—with few rebellions. Partly, this is due to Mahatma Gandhi, the same dogmatic pacifist and nationalist who led India's millions of wretched to accept their exploited fates. For it was Gandhi who set the tone for the peaceful form of protest that permeated South Africa when, in 1894, he founded the Natal Indian Congress (which later became part of the South African Indian Congress). When the ANC was formed a few years later, it took its inspiration from Gandhi, and for the next half-century, it consistently advocated nonviolent, legal opposition to white rule. So firm was ANC's reformist line that in 1960, its President-General, Chief Albert John Luthuli, was awarded the Nobel Peace Prize. Though he was arrested for high treason in 1956 and banished to his village under the Suppression of Communist Activities Act in 1959, and though he recognized in 1966 that the "fruits of moderation" have resulted only in "new laws . . . issued during the past thirty years which restrict our rights and our progress to the extent that today we practically have no rights at all," the ANC remained basically reformist until past his death in July 1967. As late as January 1966, with the whole Third World volatile with revolutionary fervor, ANC was still hoping to find a peaceful way to crush South African fascism; at the Tricon meeting in Havana, ANC's delegate said he expected international pressure and U.N. sanctions.

But by then, as ANC leader Nelson Mandela explained at his trial for sedition, ANC had created an armed wing—the Umkonto We Sizwe (MK) or "Spear of the Nation." How that decision came about in 1961 (partly as a result of the 1960 Sharpeville massacre and the banning of ANC), is well detailed in Mandela's statement before the court during the "Rivonia Trial"—in which he was condemned to life imprisonment (he is now incarcerated at Robben Island). But in that statement (see the first article below), Mandela shows that ANC was still working for a nonviolent solution, using the MK's sabotage tactics as a bargaining force to gain political points.

Mandela was clearly no communist. But so many of ANC's cadre were, that the policy and strategy of ANC was indistinguishable from those of the South African Communist Party (SACP). Indeed, by 1961, the SACP had also come out in favor of armed struggle. In the program adopted by its Fifth National Conference in 1962 (second article below), it stated categorically that "the slogan of 'nonviolence' is harmful to the cause of the democratic national revolution in the new phase of the struggle." But its reformism remained undaunted. Once people are armed, the SACP concluded, "the crisis in the country, and the contradictions in the ranks of the ruling class, will deepen. The possibility would be opened of a peaceful and negotiated transfer of power to the representatives of the oppressed majority of the people."

Such statements are not communist naïveté but communist policy. During his trial for sabotage at Pretoria in March 1966, Abram ("Bram") Fischer (who was also condemned to life imprisonment) said: "I believed when I joined the illegal Communist Party that South Africa had set out on a course which could lead only to civil war of the most vicious kind whether in ten or fifteen or twenty years. Algeria provided the perfect historical example of that. I believed moreover, and still believe, that such a civil war can never be won by the whites of this country. They might win some initial rounds. In the long run the balance of forces is against them, both inside and outside the country. In Algeria, a close historical parallel, a French army of half a million soldiers backed by one of the world's great industrial powers could not succeed. But win or lose, the consequences of civil war would be horrifying and permanent. Clearly it is imperative that an alternative 'solution' be found, for in truth civil war is no 'solution' at all."

Bram Fischer was a courageous man who lived by his conviction. But what kind of revolutionary "ideology" could lead such a man to consider the Algerian Revolution, which did win, as no solution at all? It was inevitable, then, either that ANC and SACP would drop their reformism or else that new revolutionary groups seize the vanguard role. And it is the Pan-Africanist Congress which has tried hardest to do just that. Strongly influenced by Maoism, at least in rhetoric, it has blasted both the ANC and the CP. Shortly after Fischer was convicted, for example, PAC leader K. A. Jordaan wrote of his statement to the court: "He who wants to change the old society, but recoils from the only effective method of doing so [armed struggle], ends up by accommodating himself to that society." Writing in the September 1966 issue of Azania News *(a PAC publication), Jordaan defined the CP as counterrevolutionary and concluded: "It is only by changing their environment in the furnace of a revolution that Azanians can also change themselves and be fit to master their own affairs"—a view already made famous by Fanon (see above). And in a pamphlet published about the same time, Cardiff Marney, who had been an ANC ally but now joined the PAC, wrote that ANC's "warning the world that unless a peaceful solution was imposed from the outside, preferably by U.N. intervention, South Africa would be engulfed in a bloodbath and reduced to 'chaos' and 'lawlessness' . . . means nothing less than saying that the independent armed struggle of the people is undesirable. The training of ANC saboteurs and guerrillas was therefore not seriously intended: it was merely to serve as a threat to extract sanctions from the imperialist powers [who rule the U.N.] and secure their intervention. Freedom, in other words, would be brought to the people on the point of imperialist bayonets! This peaceful approach of the ANC is in line with the policy of peaceful coexistence of the Soviet Union who is giving the ANC considerable financial backing."*

On its side, PAC got financial backing from China. It formed an alliance with the Zimbabwe (Rhodesia) African National Union (ZANU) and proclaimed it was unleashing guerrilla wars in both Rhodesia and South Africa. ANC, which made an alliance with the Zimbabwe African Peoples Union (ZAPU), then announced it would do the same. And each group has been claiming a better fighting score ever since.

Both ANC-ZAPU and PAC-ZANU are indeed engaged in actual combat in Rhodesia and South Africa today. After some serious mistakes which almost wiped out its forces, the former is now slowly establishing a firm revolutionary base. PAC, however, has been wracked with informers, agents, and militant speechmakers who spend their time hopscotching from one friendly country to another. By October 1969, PAC had not yet even elaborated a clear ideological-military position.

That, ANC did. At a conference in Morogoro, Tanzania, in April 1969, it worked out its strategy (see the third article below) which turned out to be the strongest condemnation yet of the Guevarist line. Justifying its half-century of reformism as consciousness-building, ANC clearly still saw armed struggle as only one weapon in the arsenal of a political party's march toward power. Liberation was seen as the overthrow of the regime. As for the future, that was to remain in the hands of the Party. Totally missing was the concept of armed struggle as a way of liberating the men who fight from the decades in which they have internalized their own oppression. That the foundation of the future society is laid during the course of the Revolution itself seemed to remain an alien concept to the ANC and its traditional communist ideologues.

NELSON MANDELA: I AM PREPARED TO DIE*

SOME of the things so far told to the Court are true and some are untrue. I do not, however, deny that I planned sabotage. I did not plan it in a spirit of recklessness, nor because I have any love of violence. I planned it as a result of a calm and sober assessment of the political situation that had arisen after many years of tyranny, exploitation, and oppression of my people by the Whites.

---

* Statement made by the author during the "Rivonia Trial" for sedition and sabotage, which ended, in June 1964, with his conviction, issued as a pamphlet by ANC, 1964.

I admit immediately that I was one of the persons who helped to form Umkonto We Sizwe,[1] and that I played a prominent role in its affairs until I was arrested in August 1962. I, and the others who started the organization, did so for two reasons. Firstly, we believed that as a result of government policy, violence by the African people had become inevitable, and that unless responsible leadership was given to canalize and control the feelings of our people, there would be outbreaks of terrorism which would produce an intensity of bitterness and hostility between the various races of this country which is not produced even by war. Secondly, we felt that without violence there would be no way open to the African people to succeed in their struggle against the principle of White supremacy. All lawful modes of expressing opposition to this principle had been closed by legislation, and we were placed in a position in which we had either to accept a permanent state of inferiority, or to defy the government. We chose to defy the law. We first broke the law in a way which avoided any recourse to violence; when this form was legislated against, and then the government resorted to a show of force to crush opposition to its policies, only then did we decide to answer violence with violence.

But the violence which we chose to adopt was not terrorism. We who formed Umkonto were all members of the African National Congress, and had behind us the ANC tradition of nonviolence and negotiation as a means of solving political disputes. We believed that South Africa belonged to all the people who lived in it, and not to one group, be it Black or White. We did not want an interracial war, and tried to avoid it to the last minute.

The African National Congress was formed in 1912 to defend the rights of the African people which had been seriously curtailed by the South Africa Act, and which were then being threatened by the Native Land Act. For thirty-seven years—that is, until 1949—it adhered strictly to a constitutional struggle. It put forward demands and resolutions; it sent delegations to the government in the belief that African grievances could be settled through peaceful discussion and that Africans could advance gradually to full political rights. But White governments remained unmoved, and the rights of Africans became less instead of becoming greater. In the words of my leader, Chief Luthuli, who became president of the ANC in 1952, and who was later awarded the Nobel Peace Prize:

> . . . who will deny that thirty years of my life have been spent knocking in vain, patiently, moderately, and modestly at a closed and barred door? What have been the fruits of moderation? The past thirty years have seen the greatest number of laws restricting our rights and progress, until today we have reached a stage where we have almost no rights at all.

[1] "Spear of the Nation," the military wing of the ANC. It is sometimes referred to as MK as well.—*Ed.*

Even after 1949, the ANC remained determined to avoid violence. At this time, however, there was a change from the strictly constitutional means of protest which had been employed in the past. The change was embodied in a decision which was taken to protest against apartheid legislation by peaceful, but unlawful, demonstrations against certain laws. Pursuant to this policy the ANC launched the Defiance Campaign, in which I was placed in charge of volunteers. This campaign was based on the principles of passive resistance. More than 8,500 people defied apartheid laws and went to jail. Yet there was not a single instance of violence in the course of this campaign on the part of any defier. I and nineteen colleagues were convicted for the role which we played in organizing the campaign, but our sentences were suspended mainly because the judge found that discipline and nonviolence had been stressed throughout.

During the Defiance Campaign, the Public Safety Act and the Criminal Law Amendment Act were passed. These statutes provided harsher penalties for offenses committed by way of protests against laws. Despite this, the protests continued and the ANC adhered to its policy of nonviolence. In 1956, one hundred and fifty-six leading members of the Congress Alliance, including myself, were arrested on a charge of high treason and charges under the Suppression of Communism Act. The nonviolent policy of the ANC was put in issue by the state, but when the Court gave judgment some five years later, it found that the ANC did not have a policy of violence. We were acquitted on all counts, which included a count that the ANC sought to set up a communist state in place of the existing regime. The government has always sought to label all its opponents as communists.

In 1960, there was the shooting at Sharpeville, which resulted in the proclamations of a State of Emergency and the declaration of the ANC as an unlawful organization. My colleagues and I, after careful consideration, decided that we would not obey this decree. The African people were not part of the government and did not make the laws by which they were governed. We believed in the words of the Universal Declaration of Human Rights, that "the will of the people shall be the basis of authority of the government," and for us to accept the banning was equivalent to accepting the silencing of the Africans for all time. The ANC refused to dissolve, but instead went underground. We believed it was our duty to preserve this organization which had been built up with almost fifty years of unremitting toil. I have no doubt that no self-respecting White political organization would disband itself if declared illegal by a government in which it had no say.

In 1960 the government held a referendum which led to the establishment of the Republic. Africans, who constituted approximately 70 percent of the population of South Africa, were not entitled to vote, and were not even consulted about the proposed constitutional change. All of us were apprehensive of our future under the proposed White Republic, and a resolution was taken to hold an All-In African Conference to call for a National Convention, and to organize mass demonstrations on the eve of the unwanted Republic, if the government failed to call the Convention. The Conference was attended by Africans of various political persuasions. I was the secretary of the Conference and undertook to be responsible for organizing the national stay-at-home which was subsequently called to coincide with the declaration of the Republic. As all strikes by Africans are illegal, the person organizing such a strike must avoid arrest. I was chosen to be this person, and consequently I had to leave my home and family and my practice and go into hiding to avoid arrest.

The stay-at-home, in accordance with ANC policy, was to be a peaceful demonstration. Careful instructions were given to organizers and members to avoid any recourse to violence. The government's answer was to introduce new and harsher laws, to mobilize its armed forces, and to send saracens, armed vehicles, and soldiers into the townships in a massive show of force designed to intimidate the people. This was an indication that the government had decided to rule by force alone, and this decision was a milestone on the road to Umkonto.

It was only when all else had failed, when all channels of peaceful protest had been barred to us, that the decision was made to embark on violent forms of political struggle, and to form Umkonto We Sizwe. We did so not because we desired such a course, but solely because the government had left us with no other choice. In the Manifesto of Umkonto published on the 16th of December, 1961, which is Exhibit "AD," we said:

> The time comes in the life of any nation when there remain only two choices—submit or fight. That time has now come to South Africa. We shall not submit and we have no choice but to hit back by all means in our power in defense of our people, our future and our freedom.

This was our feeling in June of 1961 when we decided to press for a change in the policy of the National Liberation Movement. I can only say that I felt morally obliged to do what I did.

As far as the ANC was concerned, it formed a clear view which can be summarized as follows:

a. It was a mass political organization with a political function to fulfill. Its members had joined on the express policy of nonviolence.

b. Because of all this, it could not and would not undertake violence. This must be stressed. One cannot turn such a body into the small closely knit organization required for sabotage. Nor would this be politically correct, because it would result in members ceasing to carry out this essential activity: political propaganda and organization. Nor was it permissible to change the whole nature of the organization.

c. On the other hand, in view of this situation I have described, the ANC was prepared to depart from its fifty-year-old policy of nonviolence to this extent, that it would no longer disapprove of properly controlled violence. Hence members who undertook such activity would not be subject to disciplinary action by the ANC.

I say "properly controlled violence" because I made it clear that if I formed the organization I would at all times subject it to the political guidance of the ANC and would not undertake any different form of activity from that contemplated without the consent of the ANC.

As a result of this decision, Umkonto was formed in November 1961. When we took this decision, and subsequently formulated our plans, the ANC heritage of nonviolence and racial harmony was very much with us. We felt that the country was drifting toward a civil war in which Blacks and Whites would fight each other. We viewed the situation with alarm. Civil war could mean the destruction of what the ANC stood for; with civil war racial peace would be more difficult than ever to achieve. We already have examples in South African history of the results of war. It has taken more than fifty years for the scars of the South African War to disappear. How much longer would it take to eradicate the scars of interracial civil war, which could not be fought without a great loss of life on both sides?

The avoidance of civil war had dominated our thinking for many years, but when we decided to adopt violence as part of our policy, we realized that we might one day have to face the prospect of such a war. This had to be taken into account in formulating our plans. We required a plan which was flexible and which permitted us to act in accordance with the needs of the times; above all, the plan had to be one which recognized civil war as the last resort, and left the decision on this question to the future. We did not want to be committed to civil war, but we wanted to be ready if it became inevitable.

Four forms of violence were possible. There is sabotage, there is guerrilla warfare, there is terrorism, and there is open revolution. We chose to adopt the first method and to exhaust it before taking any other decision.

In the light of our political background the choice was a logical one. Sabotage did not involve loss of life, and it offered the best hope for future race relations. Bitterness would be kept to a minimum and, if the policy bore fruit, democratic government could become a reality. This is what we felt at the time, and this is what we said in our Manifesto (Exhibit AD):

> We of Umkonto We Sizwe have always sought to achieve liberation without bloodshed and civil clash. We hope, even at this late hour, that our first actions will awaken everyone to a realization of the disastrous situa-

tion to which the Nationalist policy is leading. We hope that we will bring the government and its supporters to their senses before it is too late, so that both the government and its policies can be changed before matters reach the desperate stage of civil war.

The initial plan was based on a careful analysis of the political and economic situation of our country. We believed that South Africa depended to a large extent on foreign capital and foreign trade. We felt that planned destruction of power plants, and interference with rail and telephone communications would tend to scare away capital from the country, make it more difficult for goods from the industrial areas to reach the seaports on schedule, and would in the long run be a heavy drain on the economic life of the country, thus compelling the voters of the country to reconsider their position.

Attacks on the economic life lines of the country were to be linked with sabotage on government buildings and other symbols of apartheid. These attacks would serve as a source of inspiration to our people. In addition, they would provide an outlet for those people who were urging the adoption of violent methods and would enable us to give concrete proof to our followers that we had adopted a stronger line and were fighting back against government violence.

In addition, if mass action were successfully organized, and mass reprisals taken, we felt that sympathy for our cause would be roused in other countries, and that greater pressure would be brought to bear on the South African government.

The affairs of the Umkonto were controlled and directed by a National High Command, which had powers of co-option and which could, and did, appoint Regional Commands. The High Command was the body which determined tactics and targets and was in charge of training and finance. Under the High Command there were Regional Commands which were responsible for the direction of the local sabotage groups. Within the framework of the policy laid down by the National High Command, the Regional Commands had authority to select the targets to be attacked. They had no authority to go beyond the prescribed framework, and thus had no authority to embark upon acts which endangered life, or which did not fit into the overall plan of sabotage. For instance, MK members were forbidden ever to go armed into operation.

Umkonto had its first operation on the 16th December, 1961, when government buildings in Johannesburg, Port Elizabeth, and Durban were attacked. The selection of targets is proof of the policy to which I have referred. Had we intended to attack life we would have selected targets where people congregated and not empty buildings and power stations. The sabotage which was committed before the 16th December, 1961, was the work of isolated groups and had no connection whatever with Umkonto. In fact, some of these and a number of later acts were claimed by other organizations.

The Manifesto of Umkonto was issued on the day that operations commenced. The response to our actions and Manifesto among the White population was characteristically violent. The government threatened to take strong action, and called upon its supporters to stand firm and to ignore the demands of the Africans. The Whites failed to respond by suggesting change; they responded to our call by suggesting the laager.

In contrast, the response of the Africans was one of encouragement. Suddenly there was hope again. Things were happening. People in the townships became eager for policial news. A great deal of enthusiasm was generated by the initial successes, and people began to speculate on how soon freedom would be obtained.

But we in Umkonto weighed up the White response with anxiety. The lines were being drawn. The Whites and Blacks were moving into separate camps, and the prospects of avoiding a civil war were made less. The White newspapers carried reports that sabotage would be punished by death. If this was so how could we continue to keep Africans away from terrorism?

Already scores of Africans had died as a result of racial friction. In 1920 when the famous leader, Masabala, was held in Port Elizabeth jail, twenty-four of a group of Africans who had gathered to demand his release were killed by the police and White civilians. In 1921, more than one hundred Africans died in the Bulhoek affair. In 1924 over two hundred Africans were killed when the Administrator of South West Africa led a force against a group which had rebelled against the imposition of a dog tax. On the 1st May, 1950, eighteen Africans died as a result of police shootings during the strike. On the 21st March, 1960, sixty-nine unarmed Africans died at Sharpeville.

How many more Sharpevilles would there be in the history of our country? And how many more Sharpevilles could the country stand without violence and terror becoming the order of the day? And what would happen to our people when that stage was reached? In the long run we felt certain we must succeed, but at what cost to ourselves and the rest of the country? And if this happened, how could Black and White ever live together again in peace and harmony? These were the problems that faced us, and these were our decisions.

Experience convinced us that rebellion would offer the government limitless opportunities for the indiscriminate slaughter of our people. But it was precisely because the soil of South Africa is already drenched with the blood of innocent Africans that we felt it our duty to make preparations as a long-term undertaking to use force in order to defend ourselves against force. If war were inevitable, we wanted the fight to be conducted on terms most favorable to our people. The fight which held out prospects best for us and the least risk of life to both sides was guerrilla warfare. We decided, therefore, in our preparations for the future, to make provision for the possibility of guerrilla warfare.

All Whites undergo compulsory military training, but no such training was given to Africans. It was in our view essential to build up a nucleus of trained men who would be able to provide the leadership which would be required if guerrilla warfare started. We had to prepare for such a situation before it became too late to make proper preparations. It was also necessary to build up a nucleus of men trained in civil administration and other professions, so that Africans would be equipped to participate in the government of this country as soon as they were allowed to do so.

At this stage it was decided that I should attend the Conference of the Pan-Africa Freedom Movement for Central, East, and Southern Africa, which was to be held early in 1962 in Addis Ababa and, because of our need for preparation, it was also decided that, after the Conference, I would undertake a tour of the African states with a view to obtaining facilities for the training of soldiers, and that I would also solicit scholarships for the higher education of matriculated Africans. Training in both fields would be necessary, even if changes came about by peaceful means. Administrators would be necessary who would be willing and able to administer a nonracial state and so would men be necessary to control the army and police force of such a state.

I started to make a study of the art of war and revolution and, whilst abroad, underwent a course in military training. If there was to be guerrilla warfare, I wanted to be able to stand and fight with my people and to share the hazards of war with them. I also made arrangements for our recruits to undergo military training. But here it was impossible to organize any scheme without the cooperation of the ANC offices in Africa. I consequently obtained the permission of the ANC in South Africa to do this. To this extent, then, there was a departure from the original decision of the ANC, but it applied outside South Africa only. The first batch of recruits actually arrived in Tanganyika when I was passing through that country on my way back to South Africa.

I returned to South Africa and reported to my colleagues on the results of my trip. On my return I found that there had been little alteration in the political scene save that the threat of a death penalty for sabotage had now become a fact. The attitude of my colleagues in Umkonto was much the same as it had been before I left. They were feeling their way cautiously and felt that it would be a long time before the possibilities of sabotage were exhausted. In fact, the view was expressed by some that the training of recruits was premature. This is recorded by me in the document which is Exhibit R. 14. After a full discussion, however, it was decided to go ahead with the plans for military training because of the fact that it would take many years to build up a sufficient nucleus of trained soldiers to start a guerrilla campaign, and whatever happened the training would be of value.

The ideological creed of the ANC is, and always has been, the creed of African Nationalism. It is not the concept of African Nationalism expressed in the cry, "Drive the White man into the sea." The African Nationalism for which the ANC stands is the concept of freedom and fulfillment for the African people in their own land. The most important political document ever adopted by the ANC is the "Freedom Charter." It is by no means a blueprint for a socialist state. It calls for redistribution, but not nationalization, of land; it provides for nationalization of mines, banks, and monopoly industry, because big monopolies are owned by one race only, and without such nationalization racial domination would be perpetuated despite the spread of political power. It would be a hollow gesture to repeal the Gold Law prohibitions against Africans when all gold mines are owned by European companies. In this respect the ANC's policy corresponds with the old policy of the present Nationalist Party which, for many years, had as part of its program the nationalization of the gold mines which, at that time, were controlled by foreign capital. Under the Freedom Charter nationalization would take place in an economy based on private enterprise. The realization of the Freedom Charter would open up fresh fields for a prosperous African population of all classes, including the middle class. The ANC has never at any period in its history advocated a revolutionary change in the economic structure of the country, nor has it, to the best of my recollection, ever condemned capitalist society.

As far as the Communist Party is concerned, and if I understand its policy correctly, it stands for the establishment of a state based on the principles of Marxism. Although it is prepared to work for the Freedom Charter, as a short-term solution to the problems created by White supremacy, it regards the Freedom Charter as the beginning, and not the end, of its program.

The ANC, unlike the Communist Party, admitted only Africans as members. Its chief goal was, and is, for the African people to win unity and full political rights. The Communist Party's main aim, on the other hand, was to remove the capitalists and to replace them with a working-class government. The Communist Party sought to emphasize class distinctions whilst the ANC seeks to harmonize them. This is a vital distinction.

It is true that there has often been close cooperation between the ANC and the Communist Party. But cooperation is merely proof of a common goal—in this case the removal of White supremacy—and it is not proof of a complete community of interests.

The history of the world is full of similar examples. Perhaps the most striking illustration is to be found in the cooperation between Great

Britain, the United States of America, and the Soviet Union in the fight against Hitler. Nobody but Hitler would have dared to suggest that such cooperation turned Churchill or Roosevelt into communists or communist tools, or that Britain and America were working to bring about a communist world.

South Africa is the richest country in Africa, and could be one of the richest in the world. But it is a land of extremes and remarkable contrasts. The Whites enjoy what may well be the highest standard of living in the world, whilst Africans live in poverty and misery. Forty percent of the Africans live in hopelessly overcrowded and, in some cases, drought-stricken reserves, where soil erosion and the overworking of the soil makes it impossible for them to live properly off the land. Thirty percent are laborers, labor tenants, and squatters on White farms and work and live under conditions similar to those of the serfs in the Middle Ages. The other 30 percent live in towns where they have developed economic and social habits which bring them closer in many respects to White standards. Yet most Africans, even in this group, are impoverished by low incomes and high cost of living.

The highest-paid and the most prosperous section of urban African life is in Johannesburg. Yet their actual position is desperate. The latest figures were given on the 25th March, 1964, by Mr. Carr, manager of the Johannesburg Non-European Affairs Department. The poverty datum line for the average African family in Johannesburg (according to Mr. Carr's department) is R42.84 per month.[2] He showed that the average monthly wage is R32.24 and that 46 percent of all African families in Johannesburg do not earn enough to keep them going.

Poverty goes hand in hand with malnutrition and disease. The incidence of malnutrition and deficiency diseases is very high amongst Africans. Tuberculosis, pellagra, kwashiorkor, gastroenteritis, and scurvy bring death and destruction of health. The incidence of infant mortality is one of the highest in the world. According to the Medical Officer of Health for Pretoria, tuberculosis kills forty people a day (almost all Africans), and in 1961 there were 58,491 new cases reported. These diseases not only destroy the vital organs of the body, but they result in retarded mental conditions and lack of initiative, and reduce powers of concentration. The secondary results of such conditions affect the whole community and the standard of work performed by African laborers.

The complaint of Africans, however, is not only that they are poor and the Whites are rich, but that the laws which are made by the Whites are designed to preserve this situation. There are two ways to break out of poverty. The first is by formal education, and the second is by the worker acquiring a greater skill at his work and thus higher wages. As

[2] One South African rand is worth ten shillings or $1.20.—*Ed.*

far as Africans are concerned, both these avenues of advancement are deliberately curtailed by legislation.

The present government has always sought to hamper Africans in their search for education. One of their early acts, after coming into power, was to stop subsidies for African school feeding. Many African children, who attended schools, depended on this supplement to their diet. This was a cruel act.

There is compulsory education for all White children at virtually no cost to their parents, be they rich or poor. Similar facilities are not provided for the African children though there are some who receive such assistance. African children, however, generally have to pay more for their schooling than Whites. According to figures quoted by the South African Institute of Race Relations in its 1963 journal, approximately 40 percent of African children in the age group between 7 to 14 do not attend school. For those who do attend school, the standards are vastly different from those afforded to White children. In 1960–61 the per-capita government spending on African students at state-aided schools was estimated at R12.46. In the same years, the per-capita spending on White children in the Cape Province (which are the only figures available to me), was R144.57. Although there are no figures available to me, it can be stated, without doubt, that the White children on whom R144.57 per head was being spent all came from wealthier homes than African children on whom R12.46 per head was being spent.

The other main obstacles to the economic advancement of the African is the industrial color bar under which all the better jobs of industry are reserved for Whites only. Moreover, Africans who do obtain employment in the unskilled and semiskilled occupations which are open to them, are not allowed to form trade unions which have recognition under the Industrial Conciliation Act. This means that strikes of African workers are illegal, and that they are denied the right of collective bargaining which is permitted to the better-paid White workers. The discrimination in the policy of successive South African governments toward African workers is demonstrated by the so-called "civilized labor policy" under which sheltered unskilled government jobs are found for those White workers who cannot make the grade in industry, at wages which far exceed the earnings of the average African employee in industry.

The government often answers its critics by saying that Africans in South Africa are economically better off than the inhabitants of the other countries in Africa. I do not know whether this statement is true and doubt whether any comparison can be made without having regard to the cost-of-living index in such countries. But even if it is true, as far as the African people are concerned it is irrelevant. Our complaint is not that we are poor by comparison with people in other countries, but that we are poor by comparison with the White people in our own country, and that we are prevented by legislation from altering this imbalance.

The lack of human dignity experienced by Africans is the direct result of the policy of White supremacy. White supremacy implies Black inferiority. Legislation designed to preserve White supremacy entrenches this notion. Menial tasks in South Africa are invariably performed by Africans. When anything has to be carried or cleaned the White man will look around for an African to do it for him, whether the African is employed by him or not. Because of this sort of attitude, Whites tend to regard Africans as a separate breed. They do not look upon them as people with families of their own; they do not realize that they have emotions—that they fall in love like White people do; that they want to be with their wives and children like White people want to be with theirs; that they want to earn enough money to support their families properly, to feed and clothe them and send them to school. And what "house-boy" or "garden-boy" or laborer can ever hope to do this?

Pass laws, which to Africans are among the most hated bits of legislation in South Africa, render any African liable to police surveillance at any time. I doubt whether there is a single African male in South Africa who has not at some stage had a brush with the police over his pass. Hundreds and thousands of Africans are thrown into jail each year under pass laws. Even worse than this is the fact that pass laws keep husband and wife apart and lead to the breakdown of the family life.

Poverty and the breakdown of family life have secondary effects. Children wander about the streets of the townships because they have no schools to go to, or no money to enable them to go to school, or no parents at home to see that they go to school, because both parents (if there be two) have to work to keep the family alive. This leads to a breakdown in moral standards, to an alarming rise in illegitimacy, and to growing violence which erupts, not only politically, but everywhere. Life in the townships is dangerous. There is not a day that goes by without somebody being stabbed or assaulted. And violence is carried out of the townships in the White living areas. People are afraid to walk alone in the streets after dark. Housebreakings and robberies are increasing, despite the fact that the death sentence can now be imposed for such offenses. Death sentences cannot cure the festering sore.

Africans want to be paid a living wage. Africans want to perform work which they are capable of doing, and not work which the government declares them to be capable of. Africans want to be allowed to live where they obtain work, and not be ejected from an area because they were not born there. Africans want to be allowed to own land in places where they work, and not to be obliged to live in rented houses which they can never call their own. Africans want to be part of the general population, and not confined to living in their own ghettos. African men want to have their wives and children live with them where they work, and not be forced into an unnatural existence in men's hostels. African women want to be with their menfolk and not be left permanently widowed in the

reserves. Africans want to be allowed out after 11 o'clock at night an
not be confined to their rooms like little children. Africans want to b
allowed to travel in their own country and to seek work where they wa
to and not where the Labor Bureau tells them to. Africans want a ju
share in the whole of South Africa; they want security and a stake i
society.

Above all, we want equal political rights, because without them o
disabilities will be permanent. I know this sounds revolutionary to th
Whites in this country, because the majority of voters will be African
This makes the White man fear democracy.

But this fear cannot be allowed to stand in the way of the only solu
tion which will guarantee racial harmony and freedom for all. It is n
true that the enfranchisement of all will result in racial domination. Pol
tical division, based on color, is entirely artificial and, when it disappear
so will the domination of one color group by another. The ANC has spe
half a century fighting against racialism. When it triumphs it will n
change that policy.

This then is what the ANC is fighting. Their struggle is a truly n
tional one. It is a struggle of the African people, inspired by their ow
suffering and their own experience. It is a struggle for the right to live

During my lifetime I have dedicated myself to this struggle of th
African people. I have fought against White domination, and I have fougl
against Black domination. I have cherished the ideal of a democratic an
free society in which all persons live together in harmony and with equ
opportunities. It is an ideal which I hope to live for and to achieve. Bu
if needs be, it is an ideal for which I am prepared to die.

SOUTH AFRICAN COMMUNIST PARTY: NATIONA
DEMOCRATIC REVOLUTION

THE conceding of independence to South Africa by Britain, in 1910, wa
not a victory over the forces of colonialism and imperialism. It was de
signed in the interests of imperialism. A new type of colonialism wa
developed, in which the oppressing White nation occupied the same ter
ritory as the oppressed people themselves and lived side by side with them

A rapid process of industrialization was set in train, especially durin
the two world wars. South African heavy industry and secondary in

---

* Program of the South African CP adopted by its Fifth National Conference in 196
as published by *The African Communist*, an official quarterly of the South Africa
CP, in a pamphlet entitled *The Road to South African Freedom* (no date, bu
early 1963).

ustry grew to occupy first place on the continent. This process had pro-
ound effects on the country's social structure. It concentrated great wealth
nd profits in the hands of the upper strata of the White population. It
evolutionized the economy, transforming it from a predominantly agri-
ultural into an industrial-agricultural economy, with an urban working
lass, mainly non-White, which is the largest in Africa.

On one level, that of "White South Africa," there are all the features
f an advanced capitalist state in its final stage of imperialism. There are
ighly developed industrial monopolies, and the merging of industrial and
nance capital. The land is farmed along capitalist lines, employing wage
abor, and producing cash crops for the local and export markets. The
outh African monopoly capitalists, who are closely linked with British,
Jnited States, and other foreign imperialist interests, export capital abroad,
specially in Africa. Greedy for expansion, South African imperialism
eaches out to incorporate the territories—South-West Africa and the
Protectorates.

But on another level, that of "Non-White South Africa," there are all
he features of a colony. The indigenous population is subjected to ex-
reme national oppression, poverty and exploitation, lack of all democratic
ights, and political domination by a group which does everything it can to
emphasize and perpetuate its alien "European" character. The African
Reserves show the complete lack of industry, communications, transport,
nd power resources which are characteristic of African territories under
olonial rule throughout the continent. Typical, too, of imperialist rule
s the reliance by the state upon brute force and terror, and upon the
most backward tribal elements and institutions which are deliberately
nd artificially preserved. Non-White South Africa is the colony of White
outh Africa itself.

All Whites enjoy privileges in South Africa. This gives the impression
hat the ruling class is composed of the entire White population. In
act, however, real power is in the hands of the monopolists who own and
ontrol the mines, the banks and finance houses, and most of the farms
nd major industries. The gold and diamond mines are owned by seven
mining-financial corporations and controlled by a handful of powerful
inanciers. These seven corporations are closely linked with British and
American imperialist interests. They control capital investment in mining
alone of R490 million, and employ almost 500,000 workers. In addition,
hey dominate large sections of manufacturing industries. They are linked
with the main banks, two of which control assets of over R2,000 million,
mainly in the forms of loans to industry, commerce, and the state. They
own vast tracts of arable land and mining rights in almost every part of
the country. In agriculture, too, monopoly dominates. Four percent of
the farms make up an area amounting to almost four-tenths of the total
White-owned farmland. Thus, in mining, industry, commerce, and farming,

monopolists dominate the country's economy. They are also closely linked with *state monopoly capital* ventures, such as Iscor (Iron and Steel), Escon (Electricity), and Sasol (Petrol).

These monopolists are the real power in South Africa. The special type of colonialism in South Africa serves, in the first place, their interests. Low non-White wages; the reserves of poverty; the compound labor system and the importation of hundreds and thousands of contract laborers from beyond our borders; the pass laws and poll tax and rigid police control of labor and of movement—all are designed to keep their profits high. In 1961 these seven mining corporations and their subsidiaries made a working profit of nearly R212 million and paid out dividends of R101 million to shareholders.

One-quarter of the capital of the seven mining-financial groups is owned abroad, mainly by British and American investors. In 1958, dividends of R43 million were paid out abroad. The two biggest banks are largely controlled from Britain, and in recent years United States capital investment in South Africa has grown rapidly, exceeding all other American investments in the rest of Africa put together.

Effective economic domination in South Africa is thus exercised by an alliance of local White monopoly interests in mining, industry, and agriculture, together with foreign imperialists and representatives of state monopoly capitalism. These interests have conflicts among themselves, which are reflected in the main White political parties and groupings. But they find common ground in the perpetuation of the colonial-type subjugation of the non-White population.

On the whole, the White workers represent an "aristocracy of labor." The monopolists have extended numerous concessions to them. They receive relatively high wages. Non-White miners receive an average of R144 a year plus food and compound housing: White miners R2470. African male farm workers average R68 a year; Whites R1050. Whites have a monopoly of the best-paid jobs, and of entry into skilled trades. They are invariably given positions of authority over non-Whites. The relatively high standards of life and wages enjoyed by White workers represent, in reality, a share in the super profits made by the capitalists out of the gross exploitation of the non-Whites. Systematically indoctrinated with the creed of White superiority, the White worker imagines himself to be a part of the ruling class and willingly acts as a tool and an accomplice in the maintenance of colonialism and capitalism. However, in reality, the White worker, like the non-White worker at his side, is subjected to exploitation by the same capitalist owners of the means of production. White workers' wages in general are high in comparison with those of non-Whites. But many categories of White workers are paid little more than non-Whites, and also struggle to support their families. The White worker is subjected to the insecurity of the capitalist system, with its constant threats of depression, short time, and unemployment. The division of trade unions on racial lines weakens all sections of workers in their constant struggle with the bosses for better pay and conditions and shorter hours of work. The fundamental interests of all South African workers, like those of workers everywhere, lie in unity: unity in the struggle for the day-to-day interests of the working class, for the ending of race discrimination and division, for a free, democratic South Africa as the only possible basis for the winning of socialism, the overthrow of the capitalist class and the ending of human exploitation.

There are no acute or antagonistic class divisions at present among the African people. Most of them are wage workers in industry or agriculture. There are no large-scale African employers of labor. The professional groups, mainly teachers, do not, as a rule, earn salaries or live differently from their fellow Africans. Even the people of the Reserves, especially the menfolk, spend much of their lives as migrant wage laborers in the mines, in agriculture or industry.

One-third of the African people live on the Reserves. The largest of these are the Transkei and Ciskei, in the Cape Province, but there are also other scattered areas widely separated in the other three provinces. The government speaks of the Reserves as the "homelands" of the African people, but so far from being able to sustain additional population, they are grossly overcrowded already and far too small to maintain their present population of 3½ million. Most Africans on the Reserves are not independent peasants and have no land or insufficient to make a living. To support their families and avert starvation, most of the men in the prime of life are usually away working for White employers and leaving the farming to old people and womenfolk. The smallness and the overcrowding of the Reserves leads to soil exhaustion. There is no opportunity for intensive farming, crop rotation, or scientific cattle pasturing, because there is not enough land. The Reserves are the most backward and underdeveloped areas in the country, typical of colonial Africa. They lack industries, communications, and power resources. There is no capital for improvements or mechanization.

The government is attempting, through the "Bantu Authorities" system to enforce a return to tribalism, using chiefs who are prepared to collaborate, and deposing and deporting those who refuse. The effect is actually to hasten the breakdown of tribal institutions. Those chiefs who collaborate with the government have become the most hated group in the countryside, relying on dictatorship and terror, contrary to African traditions, to enforce the laws of the White authorities on the unwilling people. The people of the Reserves are boldly calling the government's "Bantustan" bluff. They are fighting bitter struggles, including armed struggles, against the Bantu authorities. The peasant in the countryside today is not the unsophisticated tribesman of the previous century. Millions have at some time or other come to work in the towns. They have come into contact with the challenging outlook and the advanced methods of organization of the trade unions, the Congress movement, and the Communist Party. These "new peasants" have awakened the countryside, transforming the African peasantry from a reserve of conservatism into a powerful ally of the urban working class in the struggle against White colonialism, and for freedom, land, equality, and democracy.

Millions of agricultural laborers and labor tenants are employed on White-owned farms throughout the country. These are the most exploited workers in South Africa. They work without any protection from labor laws, from dawn to sunset, at hard and exhausting labor, for wretchedly low wages. The food they are given is too little, it is always the same, and it is an unhealthy diet. On most farms the housing for them is worse than what is provided for the farm animals. The use of convict labor and compound labor, and other forms of forced labor, is common on farms in many parts of South Africa. Farmers and their foremen frequently employ physical violence against African farm laborers, beating them with sjamboks, often to death. Wages for farm labor are the lowest in the country. Agricultural laborers are not really free workers. They are tied, often for life, to a particular farmer because of the operation of the labor tenancy system, the pass laws, and in particular the so-called "trek-pass," the Native Service Contract, and the Masters and Servants Acts. Organization of agriculture workers' unions and other bodies for farm workers is also made exceptionally difficult because of the close supervision maintained over them by the farmers.

The 400,000 African laborers working in the gold and coal mines have to do the most backbreaking, dangerous, and unhealthy work, for wages which are a scandal and a disgrace in an industry which distributes millions of rands annually to its shareholders. They are separated, for long periods, from their wives and families. A large proportion of them are "imported" from territories outside the Republic, the Protectorates, South-West Africa, the Portuguese colonies, Nyasaland, Tanganyika, and elsewhere, although conferences of African states have decided to work toward ending this practice. The migratory labor system leads to a continual turnover of personnel, making the organization of mine workers a difficult task, and the mine owners go to great lengths to stamp out the development of trade unionism among them. Especially since the great strike led by the African Mineworkers' Union in 1946, they are subject to constant surveillance by police, spies, and informers.

The workers of the towns, the Africans employed in factories and in transport, in steel works and power stations, in shops and offices, comprise the most dynamic and revolutionary force in South Africa. The wages of urban African workers, in relation to their high living costs, are scandalously low. They are forced to live far from their places of work, involving exhausting and expensive journeys by bus or train. In shops and factories they are relegated to the most arduous and least rewarding work. Pass laws and urban areas legislation make the tenure of their jobs and their residences precarious, and they are subjected to never ending raids and surveillance by the police. It is illegal for African workers to strike and their trade unions are unrecognized and vigorously discouraged by the state. Even when employers are prepared to enter into collective bargaining with African workers, the state intervenes to stop it. Despite these and many other disabilities, and the daily struggle for existence, this class, the most numerous and experienced working class on the African continent, has time and again shown that it is the vanguard of the African people. It has built up a number of stable and effective trade unions, devoted to the cause of African liberation and of workers' unity on our continent and throughout the world. African workers constitute the core of the African National Congress and the Communist Party. They have repeatedly come out on nationwide political general strikes and have been the leading force in every major struggle of the liberation movement. Disciplined and taught the lessons of organization and unity in the harsh school of capitalist production, driven by their conditions of life into united struggle for survival, this class alone is capable, in alliance with the masses of rural people, of leading a victorious struggle to end White domination and exploitation.

The Colored and Malay people, a population of 1½ million living mainly in the Western Cape Province, are a national group comprising workers, farm laborers, professional people, and small businessmen. Like all non-Whites, the Colored people are subjected to many forms of racial discrimination, reflected in low standards of living, education, housing, nutrition, and health. Colored workers, despite a tradition of craftsmanship which is the oldest in the country, find access to senior posts is withheld from them and given to Whites; Colored farm laborers work and live under wretched conditions. Their pay is scandalously low, and on the wine farms is partly made up by a liquor ration—the "tot" system, which undermines their health. Colored teachers and other state employees are paid much less than their White counterparts for doing the same work. Nevertheless, for many years, this community occupied a privileged position in relation to the Africans. The White ruling group extended various concessions—such as a qualified franchise, trade union rights, property rights—in order to prevent the emergence of a Colored national consciousness, and the formation of a united front of oppressed non-White peoples for equality and the ending of White colonialism. This policy was not without success. But, with the deliberate removal by the government, one after another, of all the privileges extended to the Colored people in the past—the abolition of the common roll franchise, the introduction of apartheid and job reservation, White baaskap in the trade

unions and separate university educations—working-class and democratic leaders have come to the fore. The Colored people are rejecting
apartheid and moving toward the path of struggle, side by side with
African and other freedom fighters.

The Indian community, of half a million, are mainly the descendants
of indentured laborers who came to work in the Natal sugar fields a
century ago. From the earliest times all sorts of degrading and discriminatory restrictions have been placed on South African Indians, restrictions which they have resisted in many historic struggles. Today there
is a substantial class of Indian industrial and agricultural workers, especially in Natal, but also, increasingly in the Transvaal. There is also a
considerable class of Indian merchants, factory owners and small shop-
keepers. The Indian workers face appalling problems of unemployment
and overcrowding in slum conditions. Indians do not enjoy voting and
other democratic rights. Indian businessmen, and all sections of the community, are subjected to innumerable disabilities, especially relating to
land and property ownership and economic and educational opportunities.
They are not allowed to move from one province to another without
special permits, and are completely debarred from the Orange Free State.
The Nationalist government has applied the Group Areas Act with particular ferocity against the Indian communities in the cities and small
towns, uprooting them from their homes and livelihood and threatening
to "resettle" them in isolated areas where they face complete ruination.
The Indian people have turned their backs on the reformist bourgeois
leadership which counseled paths of compromise with oppression and the
seeking of sectional privileges regardless of democratic principles and the
fate of the masses. They have unreservedly joined in the many united
struggles of the African and other oppressed peoples over the past two
decades.

The Nationalist Party, which has governed South Africa since 1948,
has brought this country to the verge of revolution. The Afrikaner Nationalist movement, which was always corrupted by White chauvinism,
has today lost all trace of the anti-imperialist element it once had, during
the period of its struggle against British rule. Dominated by the Afrikaner
capitalist class and large-scale farmers, the Nationalist Party is controlled by the fascist "Broederbond" secret society. Deeply influenced by
the Nazi movement in Germany, it adopted many of Hitler's ideas and
worked for a fascist victory in the Second World War. The Nationalist
Party has become the instrument of the most racialistic and imperialistic
sections of the capitalist class. The declaration of a Republic in May
1961 in no way lessened the dependence of the South African economy on
British and American finance capital. The Republic left the British Commonwealth not by choice of the Nationalist government but because the
unpopularity of its racial policy among African and Asian member coun-

ries faced it with expulsion. In all major questions of international policy the Nationalist government identifies itself with the most aggressive elements of international imperialism in the United States, Britain, France, West Germany, and Japan. It is dependent on financial armaments aid from these countries to maintain its rule in South Africa.

The other White parliamentary parties can offer no way out of this crisis. The United Party, traditionally the instrument of the gold-mining interests and the English-speaking capitalists, laid the basis for all the excesses of the Nationalists during the many years in which it governed South Africa prior to 1948. As the main "opposition" group in Parliament it has steadily retreated before Nationalist reaction. It is compromised by its own antidemocratic class character and afraid lest genuine opposition to the government might result in disturbances which would adversely affect business and the confidence of foreign investors. It vies with the Nationalists in appealing to the racial prejudices of the White voters. It has actively or passively assisted the Nationalist Party at every stage of its march to fascism.

Disgusted with the surrender of the United Party and alarmed at the dangers to the country's stability and future presented by Nationalist policy, a number of former United Party MPs and members broke away in 1959 to form the Progressive Party. Backed by influential business interests, such as the Oppenheimer mining group, and supported by a section of urban, middle-class Whites, the Progressive Party seeks to avert the coming democratic revolution in South Africa by offering a "qualified" franchise to middle-class non-Whites and concessions to ease the intolerable burden of apartheid.

A more radical tendency among progressive middle-class and intellectual circles is represented by the Liberal Party. This Party proposes a universal franchise, but since it expressly confines itself to "parliamentary and constitutional methods," it suggests no realistic or convincing method to obtain this. Its insistence on anticommunist and antisocialist policies and its failure to attack the roots of race oppression in the economy of the country seriously lessen the Liberal Party's usefulness and effectiveness. Its adherence to the "West" in the cold war continually conflicts with its opposition to the National government, and makes the liberation movement doubt its reliability as an ally in the struggle.

The deep-rooted crisis in South Africa can only be resolved by a revolutionary change in the social system which will overcome these conflicts by putting an end to the colonial oppression of the African and other non-White people. The immediate and imperative interests of all sections of the South African people demand the carrying out of such a change, a national democratic revolution which will overthrow the colonialist state of White supremacy and establish an independent state of National Democracy in South Africa.

The Communist Party considers that the slogan of "nonviolence" is harmful to the cause of the democratic national revolution in the new phase of the struggle, disarming the people in the face of the savage assaults of the oppressor, dampening their militancy, undermining their confidence in their leaders. At the same time, the Party opposes undisciplined acts of individual terror. It rejects theories that all nonviolent methods of struggle are useless or impossible, and will continue to advocate and work for the use of all forms of struggle by the people including noncollaboration, strikes, boycotts, and demonstrations.

The Party does not dismiss all prospects of nonviolent transition to the democratic revolution. This prospect will be enhanced by the development of revolutionary and militant people's forces. The illusion that the White minority can rule forever over a disarmed majority will crumble before the reality of an armed and determined people. The crisis in the country, and the contradictions in the ranks of the ruling class, will deepen. The possibility would be opened of a peaceful and negotiated transfer of power to the representatives of the oppressed majority of the people.

AFRICAN NATIONAL CONGRESS: STRATEGY AND TACTICS*

TO ignore the real situation and to play about with imaginary forces, concepts and ideals is to invite failure. The art of revolutionary leadership consists in providing leadership to the masses and not just to its most advanced elements; it consists of setting a pace which accords with objective conditions and the real possibilities at hand. The revolutionary sounding phrase does not always reflect revolutionary policy, and revolutionary-sounding policy is not always the springboard for revolutionary advance. Indeed, what appears to be "militant" and "revolutionary" can often be counterrevolutionary. It is surely a question of whether, in the given concrete situation, the course of policy advocated will aid or impede the prospects of the conquest of power. In this—the only test, the advocacy of armed struggle can, in some situations, be as counterrevolutionary as the advocacy of its opposite in other situations. Untimely, ill-planned, or premature manifestations of violence impede and do not advance the prospect for revolutionary change and are clearly counterrevolutionary. It is obvious therefore that policy and organizational structures must grow out of the real situation if they are not to become meaningless clichés.

---

* Report, adopted by the Consultative Conference of the ANC held in Morogoro, Tanzania, April 25–May 1, 1969, and published in *Sechaba* (July 1969), the official organ of the ANC.

Future historians may well be able to pause at some moments during the evolution of our struggle and examine critically both its pace and emphasis. But, in general, without the so-called reformist activities of the previous half-century, the prospect of advancing into the new phase would have been extremely small. This is so because even in the typical colonial-type situation armed struggle becomes feasible only if:

—there is disillusionment with the prospect of achieving liberation by traditional peaceful processes because the objective conditions blatantly bar the way to change;

—there is readiness to respond to the strategy of armed struggle with all the enormous sacrifices which this involves;

—there is in existence a political leadership capable of gaining the organized allegiance of the people for armed struggle and which has both the experience and the ability to carry out the painstaking process of planning, preparation, and overall conduct of the operations; and

—there exist favorable objective conditions for such plans.

In one sense these conditions are connected and interdependent. They are not created by subjective and ideological activity only, and many are the mistakes committed by heroic revolutionaries who give a monopoly to the subjective factor and who confuse their own readiness with the readiness of others.

These conditions are brought about not only by developing political, economic, and social conditions but also by the long hard grind of revolutionary work. They depend on such factors as the response of the enemy, the extent to which he unmasks himself and the experience gained by the people themselves not in academic seminars but in actual political struggle.

We reject the approach which sees as the catalyst for revolutionary transformation only the shortcut of isolated confrontations and the creation of armed resistance centers. Does this mean that before an actual beginning can be made to the armed challenge we have to wait for the evolvement of some sort of deep crisis in the enemy camp which is serious enough to hold out the possibility of an immediate all-round insurrection? Certainly not! We believe that given certain basic factors, both international and local, the actual beginning of armed struggle or guerrilla warfare can be made and having begun can steadily develop conditions for the future all-out war which will eventually lead to the conquest of power. Under the modern highly sophisticated police state (which South Africa is) it is questionable whether a movement can succeed in a program of mass political organization beyond a certain point without starting a new type of action. Also, it is not easy to determine the point at which sufficient concrete political and organizational preparations have been carried out to give our armed detachments the maximum chances for survival and growth within any given area. There is no instrument for measuring this. But we must not overdo the importance of the subjective factor and before embarking upon a path which is in one sense tragic, although historically inevitable and necessary, certain of the basic minimum conditions already mentioned must be present and certain minimum preparations must have been made.

The opening steps in 1961—organized sabotage mainly in the urban areas—served a special purpose and was never advanced as a technique which would, on its own, either lead to the destruction of the state or even do it great material damage (although guerrilla activity in the urban areas of a special type is always important as an auxiliary). At the same time there was a threefold need to be met in order to lay the foundations for more developed and meaningful armed activity of the guerrilla type.

The first was the need to create a military apparatus and, more particularly, to recruit large numbers of professional cadres who were to be trained and who would form the core of future guerrilla bands.

The second was the need to demonstrate effectively to all that we were making a sharp and open break with the processes of the previous period which had correctly given emphasis to militant struggle short of armed confrontation.

The third was the need to present an effective method for the overthrow of White supremacy through planned rather than spontaneous activity. The sabotage campaign was an earnest indication of our seriousness in the pursuit of this new strategy. All three needs were served by this convincing evidence that our liberation movement had correctly adjusted itself to the new situation and was creating an apparatus actually capable of clandestinely hitting the enemy and making preparation for a more advanced phase. The situation was such that without activity of this nature our whole political leadership may have been at stake both inside and outside the country and the steps which were simultaneously taken for the recruitment and preparation of military cadres would have met with less response.

When we talk of revolutionary armed struggle, we are talking of political struggle by means which include the use of military force even though once force as a tactic is introduced it has most far-reaching consequences on every aspect of our activities. It is important to emphasize this because our movement must reject all manifestations of militarism which separates armed people's struggle from its political context.

Reference has already been made to the danger of the thesis which regards the creation of military areas as the generator of mass resistance. But even more is involved in this concept. One of the vital problems connected with this bears on the important question of the relationship between the political and military. From the very beginning our movement has brooked no ambiguity concerning this. The primacy of the political leadership is unchallenged and supreme and all revolutionary formations and levels (whether armed or not) are subordinate to this leadership. To say this, is not just to invoke tradition. This approach is rooted in the very nature of this type of revolutionary struggle and is borne out by the experience of the overwhelming majority of revolutionary movements which have engaged in such struggles. Except in very rare instances, the people's armed challenge against a foe with formidable material strength does not achieve dramatic and swift success. The path is filled with obstacles and we harbor no illusions on this score in the case of South Africa. In the long run it can only succeed if it attracts the active support of the mass of the people. Without this life-blood it is doomed. Even in our country with the historical background and traditions of armed resistance still within the memory of many people, and the special developments of the immediate past, the involvement of the masses is unlikely to be the result of a sudden natural and automatic consequence of military clashes. It has to be won in all-round political mobilization which must accompany the military activities. This includes educational and agitational work throughout the country to cope with the sophisticated torrent of misleading propaganda and "information" of the enemy which will become more intense as the struggle sharpens. When armed clashes begin they seldom involve more than a comparative handful of combatants whose very conditions of fighting existence make them incapable of exercising the functions of all-round political leadership. The masses of the peasants, workers, and youth, beleaguered for a long time by the enemy's military occupation, have to be activated in a multitude of ways not only to ensure a growing stream of recruits for the fighting units but to harass the enemy politically so that his forces are dispersed and therefore weakened. This calls for the exercise of all-round political leadership.

Guerrilla warfare, the special, and in our case the only, form in which the armed liberation struggle can be launched, is neither static nor does it take place in a vacuum. The tempo, the overall strategy to be employed, the opening of new fronts, the progression from lower to higher forms and thence to mobile warfare; these and other vital questions cannot be solved by the military leadership alone, they require overall political judgments intimately involved with the people both inside and outside the actual areas of armed combat. If more awareness of oppression combined with heroic examples by armed bands were enough, the struggle would indeed be simple. There would be no collaborators and it would be hard to find neutrals. But to believe this is to believe that the course of struggle is determined solely by what we do in the fighting units and further involves the fallacious assumption that the masses are rocklike and incorruptible. The enemy is as aware as we are that the side that wins the allegiance of the people, wins the struggle. It is naïve to believe that oppressed and beleaguered people cannot temporarily, even in large numbers, be won over by fear, terror, lies, indoctrination, and provocation to treat liberators as enemies. In fact history proves that without the most intensive all-round political activity this is the more likely result. I is therefore all the more vital that the revolutionary leadership is nation wide and has its roots both inside and outside the actual areas of combat Above all, when victory comes, it must not be a hollow one. To ensure this we must also ensure that what is brought to power is not an army but the masses as a whole at the head of which stands its organized po litical leadership. This is the perspective which is rooted at all levels o our liberation movements whether within or outside the army. Ou confidence in final victory rests not on the wish or the dream but on ou understanding of our own conditions and the historical processes. Thi understanding must be deepened and must spread to every level of ou movement. We must have a clear grasp not only of ourselves and of ou own forces but also of the enemy—of his power and vulnerability.

On the face of it the enemy is in stable command of a rich and varied economy which, even at this stage when it is not required to extend itself, can afford an enormous military budget. He has a relatively well trained and efficient army and police force. He can draw on fairly large manpower resources. In addition, the major imperialist powers such a Britain, West Germany, France, the United States, and Japan who have an enormous stake in the economy of our country constitute a formidable support for the apartheid regime. Already now before the crisis deepens the imperialist partners of South Africa have done much to develop the economy and armament program of South Africa. In a situation of crisi they may pass over from support to active intervention to save the racist regime.

If there is one lesson that the history of guerrilla struggle has taugh us, it is that the material strength and resources of the enemy is by no means a decisive factor. Guerrilla warfare almost by definition present a situation in which there is a vast imbalance of material and military resources between the opposing sides. It is designed to cope with the situation in which the enemy is infinitely superior in relation to every conventional factor of warfare. It is par excellence the weapon of the materially weak against the materially strong. Given its popular characte and given a population which increasingly sides with and shields the guerrilla whilst at the same time opposing and exposing the enemy, the survival and growth of a people's army is assured by the skillful exercise of tactics. Surprise, mobility, and tactical retreat should make it difficul for the enemy to bring into play its superior fire-power in any decisive battles. No individual battle is fought in circumstances favorable to the enemy. Superior forces can thus be harassed, weakened, and, in the end destroyed. The absence of an orthodox front, of fighting lines; the need of the enemy to attenuate his resources and lines of communication ove ast areas; the need to protect the widely scattered installations on which his economy is dependent; these are among the factors which serve in the long run to compensate in favor of the guerrilla for the disparity in the starting strength of the adversaries. The words "in the long run" must be stressed because it would be idle to dispute the considerable military advantages to the enemy of his high-level industrialization, his ready-to-hand reserves of White manpower and his excellent roads, railways, and air transport which facilitate swift maneuvers and speedy concentration of personnel. But we must not overlook the fact that over a period of time many of these unfavorable factors will begin to operate in favor of the liberation forces:

—The ready-to-hand resources including food production depend overwhelmingly on non-White labor which, with the growing intensity of the struggle, will not remain docile and cooperative.

—The White manpower resources may seem adequate initially but must become dangerously stretched as guerrilla warfare develops. Already extremely short of skilled labor—the monopoly of the Whites—the mobilization of a large force for a protracted struggle will place a further burden on the workings of the economy.

—In contrast to many other major guerrilla struggles, the enemy's economic and manpower resources are all situated within the theater of war and there is no secure external pool (other than direct intervention by a foreign state) safe from sabotage, mass action, and guerrilla action on which the enemy can draw.

—The very sophistication of the economy with its well-developed system of communications makes it a much more vulnerable target. In an undeveloped country the interruption of supplies to any given region may be no more than a local setback. In a highly sensitive modern structure of the South African type, the successful harassment of transport to any major industrial complex inevitably inflicts immense damage to the economy as a whole and to the morale of the enemy.

In the vast expanse that is South Africa, a people's force will find a multitude of variations in topography, deserts, mountains, forests, veld, and swamps. There might not appear to be a single impregnable mountain or impenetrable jungle but the country abounds in terrain which in general is certainly no less favorable for guerrilla operations than some of the terrain in which other guerrilla movements operated successfully. Also the issue must be looked at in the context of guerrillas, who are armed and operate in the terrain. The combination makes an area impregnable for the guerrilla. South Africa's tremendous size will make it extremely difficult, if not impossible, for the White regime to keep the whole of it under armed surveillance in strength and in depth. Hence, an early development of a relatively safe (though shifting) rear is not beyond the realm of practicality.

The main content of the present stage of the South African Revolution is the national liberation of the largest and most oppressed group—the African people. This strategic aim must govern every aspect of the conduct of our struggle whether it be the formulation of policy or the creation of structures. Amongst other things, it demands in the first place the maximum mobilization of the African people as a dispossessed and racially oppressed nation. This is the mainspring and it must not be weakened. It involves a stimulation and a deepening of national confidence, national pride, and national assertiveness. Properly channeled and properly led, these qualities do not stand in conflict with the principles of internationalism. Indeed, they become the basis for more lasting and more meaningful cooperation; a cooperation which is self-imposed, equal, and one which is neither based on dependence nor gives the appearance of being so.

But none of this detracts from the basically national context of our liberation drive. In the last resort it is only the success of the national democratic revolution which—by destroying the existing social and economic relationships—will bring with it a correction of the historical injustices perpetrated against the indigenous majority and thus lay the basis for a new—and deeper internationalist—approach. Until then, the national sense of grievance is the most potent revolutionary force which must be harnessed. To blunt it in the interests of abstract concepts of internationalism is, in the long run, doing a service neither to revolution nor to internationalism.

"Portuguese" Africa

In the so-called developed world, the poorest and most backward country is Portugal, where the 9,000,000 people have lived under dictatorship since 1926. In all those years, the dictators (Gomes da Costa behind the scenes for a few years, Oliveira de Salazar for forty, and now Marcello Caetano) have taken most pride in giving their people peace and stability. Actually, they achieved neither: rebellions occurred in 1931, 1936, 1946, 1947, 1952, 1959, 1961, and 1962, and some form of political agitation and unrest has continued ever since. But at home, the dictators have so far managed to keep a tight hold on their people, whose rate of income, education, health, housing, and mobility is the lowest in Europe.

Outside Portugal, however, the dictatorship has not nearly been as successful. To the Lisbon regime, Portugal's foreign colonies are "overseas territories"—Goa, for example, which was seized by Nehru, is still referred to as "our possession in India under temporary foreign occupation." Though the government correctly interprets the policy of its NATO allies (especially the United States, England, and France, who claim to oppose Portuguese colonialism) as nothing more than a maneuver to replace it with their own neo-colonial rule, Lisbon has learned very little from the wave of African liberation movements. It keeps its colonies, specifically in Africa, under very rigid control, giving local populations no political rights, no education (95 percent illiteracy), no modern training of any kind. As Peter Ritner put it (in The Death of Africa*): "Portuguese Africa is one of the worst governed areas of the world." On the other hand, whatever the area produces of worth (iron, diamonds, copper, bauxite, uranium, oil, cotton, tea, coffee, sugar, nuts, rice) is owned and exported by foreign companies—Portuguese, American, Belgian, Rhodesian, South Africa, Italian, British, and German (Krupp). As a result of the Portugal-Rhodesia-South Africa alliance, more than 10,000 blacks from*

Portuguese Africa are sent to work in mines in the other two countries—
as forced labor.

"Portuguese" Africa is composed mainly of three separate countries:
Mozambique on the Indian Ocean, with Tanzania to the north, South
Africa to the south and Zambia and Rhodesia to the west, has 7,000,000
blacks, 200,000 whites; Angola (and its Cabinda enclave just above the
Congo River), framed by the Atlantic, the Congo-Kinshasa on top, Zambia
on the east, and South Africa's colony, South-West Africa, on the bottom,
is the sixth biggest country in the continent and is populated by 6,000,000
blacks, 300,000 whites; Guinea-Bissau, a tiny (36,000 square kilometers)
bush lowland squeezed on Africa's western hump, has only a few thousand
whites and 600,000 blacks. Each of these countries is now in revolt,
with armed liberation movements occupying considerable portions of the
countryside. To fight them, the Portuguese have brought in 150,000 troops
(the military eats up 42 percent of Portugal's budget) and are constantly
bombing the countryside with napalm. They also use Vietnam-like strategic hamlet tactics to try to pacify the rural population.

Each country has various guerrilla operations. In Angola, where the
rebellion was launched in 1961, and in Mozambique, where it began in
1967, the most successful liberation movements are those whose ideology
is closest to that of traditional Communists: the Popular Movement for
the Liberation of Angola (MPLA) and the Mozambique Liberation Front
(FRELIMO). After initial successes, both have had major difficulties,
mainly because of internal squabbling and rivalries with other guerrilla
fronts. In Angola, for example, MPLA fighters are often ambushed by the
"guerrillas" of Holden Roberto's GRAF (Republican Government of
Angola in Exile) which is aided by the Congo-Kinshasa's General Mobutu
and the CIA. FRELIMO has also suffered from the infiltration of agents
working for Portugal's secret police (PIDE), and by the CIA. It is generally believed, for example, that the assassination of its president,
Eduardo Mondlane, in Dar es Salaam in February 1969, was the operation of such agents.

Since then, however, both the MPLA and FRELIMO have increased
their revolutionary activities. FRELIMO now fields some 12,000 guerrillas (against 60,000 Portuguese troops), controls 20 percent of the countryside (where it is carrying out agrarian reforms), and is entering a
new phase of trying to coordinate its actions with the forces of ANC-
ZAPU. The MPLA, which is also linking up with this alliance, controls
an even larger proportion of its area.

Ideologically, none of the liberation movements of Angola or Mozambique, neither the MPLA or FRELIMO, nor the Chinese-oriented movements which are also active, has offered new insights into guerrilla
warfare. At FRELIMO's second congress, which was held inside the
liberated area from July 20 to 25, 1968, the resolution on armed struggle

stated: "Our war is essentially a political one, and its duration is defined by the Party. The people's army is part and parcel of the Party, and its strategic plans are made by the top leadership of the Party." On the other hand, it went on to state: "In order to conduct correctly the struggle, all the leaders should be involved in the armed struggle. Only in this way, following the struggle step by step, can the leaders be able to solve all the complex problems arising daily. The people's army performs its task in accordance with the policy defined by FRELIMO." As late as 1966, in a speech in London, Uriah Simango, the priest who became FRELIMO's vice-president, then one of three council presidents succeeding Mondlane, and finally a renegade thrown out of the front, maintained the hope that boycotts, sanctions, and perhaps British intervention were what was needed to bring down the racist Rhodesia government. "The people of the Portuguese colonies," he concluded, "will not lay down their arms until Portugal has agreed to enter negotiations and to grant independence. This is the only condition for peaceful coexistence with Portugal."

Mondlane himself seems to have been less of a reformist. In The Struggle for Mozambique *(Penguin Books, 1969), which was finished just a few weeks before he was killed, he wrote: "Whatever happens [to the war], whether we have to go on for ten or twenty years, fighting our way inch by inch down to Lourenço Marques [the capital], or whether the Portuguese give up and move out within the next few years, our problems will not end with independence. If the war has been long, however, these may be less acute. For the achievement of independence in itself does not change overnight the attitudes of the people. . . . People are beginning to realize that their future is now in their own hands. This is why we can view the long war ahead of us with reasonable calm."*

Agostinho Neto, MPLA's president, expressed somewhat the same thoughts when, in an interview in Algeria (Révolution Africaine, May 1–7, 1967), he said: "The aims of the MPLA are not only political independence for the country, but also a basic transformation of the people. . . . The common struggle against Portuguese colonialism is already an important element in the formation of the national consciousness of our people." In practical terms, what that consciousness achieves is perhaps best explained by Spartacus Monimambu, the military commander of the MPLA's eastern region, in the 1968 interview below.

But by far the sharpest fighting ideologue in Portuguese Africa—and indeed in the whole continent—is Amilcar Cabral, head of the African Independence Party of Guinea and the Cape Verde Islands (PAIGC). Formed in September 1956 by Cabral and other "petty-bourgeois intellectuals," as he says, the PAIGC focused on internal organization until 1959, then on political and propagandistic preparation for armed struggle until 1962. The first attack was launched during the night of June 30–July 1 of that year. By October 1969, despite 40,000 Portuguese troops using bombers, napalm, helicopters, and brutal pacification, the PAIGC had liberated two-thirds of the countryside, forcing the enemy to communicate between fortified towns through the air.

In the three passages below, Cabral demonstrates one reason why the PAIGC has been so successful—his own power of analysis (he explains some of the other reasons). That analysis, of the objective conditions of his country, led him to junk most of the formal descriptions and prescriptions for revolution. For one thing, he discarded the notion of the peasantry as a revolutionary force. For another, he found that as there was no working class, to talk of the revolution led by the proletariat was absurd. He did accept the notion of a two-stage revolution, but only because the first would politicize the masses for the second. To Cabral, there was only one revolutionary "motor"—the petty bourgeoisie. It alone could form the military vanguard and it alone was the political vanguard. As a nucleus (a political foco, to use a Guevarist term), the petty bourgeoisie could mount an effective armed offensive against Portuguese colonialism. But unless that offensive was transformed into a genuine war against domination and exploitation, that is, against neo-colonialism (and, therefore, capitalism), it would not be a "national liberation."

Yet Cabral understood that such a liberation must end up demanding that the petty bourgeoisie commit class suicide—when it could hope to rule and profit after political independence. Objectively, the petty bourgeoisie cannot so rule and profit unless it ties itself to neo-colonialism, which, in turn, would push it out of the foreground to make room for that bourgeoisie with the assets—not the petty (servicing, intellectual, and bureaucratic) bourgeoisie, but the national bourgeoisie. Hence the winning motor force, the petty bourgeoisie, will have only this choice: class suicide, to die in order to be reborn with a proletariat mentality, or selling out.

The choice, says Cabral, is not dialectical. It is moral. It can and must be brought about by the petty bourgeoisie itself as it wages and leads the patriotic war—in which it finds the roots for the class struggle to follow. Cabral believes in man, in men, and that is surely one fundamental reason for the "petty-bourgeois" PAIGC's revolutionary ("Proletarian") success.

SPARTACUS MONIMAMBU: IN MPLA LIBERATED AREAS*

Question: On January 3, the MPLA announced that it was going to shift its headquarters from Brazzaville to Angola. How do you think this will affect the course of the struggle?

---

* Interview with Don Barnett in Dar es Salaam on March 21, 1968, shortly before Monimambu, who had been wounded, returned to his command post. Published in *The Guardian* (New York), April 27, May 4, and May 11, 1968.

Answer: This is very important for us. As you know, every revolutionary struggle must be carried out inside the country. And this cannot be done very well if the leaders themselves are not among the people. We are a mass organization, a popular movement, so we must be among the people. They must see that the leaders themselves are inside to direct and orient the struggle. This will give more courage to the people, and even to the guerrilla fighters. All of our political leaders, except for two or three, have now been trained militarily. So they can go inside and lead and help train the local leaders. What we need, what we want is for local leaders to become conscious enough to lead their own people in the villages. The top leaders must bring these people to a high level of political consciousness and understanding.

Question: Maybe you could now comment generally on the relationship within Angola between the military and political leadership.

Answer: Our principal aim is to combine the military and the political. Everyone must be both, political and military together. We know that our basic problem is a political one, but it cannot be solved without violence. So, while the military aspect is secondary to the political, there is an interdependence between the two. The military and political actions must complement each other and develop parallel to one another. That is why we have both political and military leaders in the central committee. Here, both military and political people come together and lead the struggle together. But the people inside the country understand the necessity of representation outside, because without this there would be little chance of getting supplies or carrying out diplomatic activities.

Question: Is the head of each zone a military leader, a political leader, or a combination of both?

Answer: In each of the five zones there is a military command, headed by a first commander who is himself both a military and political leader. Then in the whole of the Eastern Region, made up of these five zones, we have a regional command comprised of six or seven officers. Four of these, including myself, are on the Eastern Region Steering Committee. So we are both political and military officers. There is no difference between political and military leaders inside now. Every person holding a leadership position participates in both the military and political aspects of the struggle.

Question: How does the popular militia function in relation to the MPLA's guerrilla forces?

Answer: Without the militias the semiregular forces of MPLA couldn't control this area. Moxico itself, you know, is four times larger than Portugal. So, to control this area, we need the help of the militia. This is why we are working hard to organize and train them. Their leaders have been trained by us inside, politically and militarily. And despite some difficulties with supplies they are able to patrol their area and help protect their people. You know there are people going to fish, to their gardens to cultivate, to the bush to collect honey from trees—they are still going everywhere. But each one has an important mission: to look after the place, to see who is coming in and who is going out.

Question: How many people would you say are living in an average village in the semiliberated area?

Answer: It depends on the number of people who belong to such and such a chief. Sometimes there are 50, sometimes 80; and we have decided that no more than 100 can remain together in one place—with their houses close together but still a little separated. It depends on the bush. If it is not heavy, then not too many people will stay together. If it is heavy then they will be safe. All the houses will be well camouflaged and can't be seen from planes.

Question: Perhaps you could discuss the scale of MPLA's operations in the Eastern Region. How much territory and how many people are involved?

Answer: The Eastern Front is about 500 miles long and some 310 miles deep. But these figures were calculated last year. Our people are still moving ahead. They are now in Bic and to the north we have already sent organizers and a guerrilla group into the Lunda district. So I can't tell you at this time exactly how far our zone of operation extends inside the country. As for the territories controlled or semicontrolled by us, they are Moxico and most of Cuando Cubango districts—with many enemy posts in between.

You can't find a single place in this area where people have remained in their traditional villages. They have already abandoned them. Or the Portuguese have caught them and brought them near their posts to live in concentration camp villages. Most have run away. But it is up to them to choose. They can either go to the Portuguese for help or to the freedom fighters. Most people come to the bush and live with us, some go with the Portuguese. But those who go with the Portuguese don't stay more than two or three months. After that they will die of hunger because they can't go into the bush to look after their crops. They are allowed to go there just one day a week, followed by Portuguese guards. But it is not enough for them; they feel they are in a prison, that they are not free there. So many of them run away and come to join us. Or when the freedom fighters go there they ask us to take them away from the place. There is not a very large population in these areas. Now we can say that there are more than 30,000 living with us in the semiliberated areas. But not all of these have been politicized. We have sent organizers to many places to politicize the people, to mobilize them, organize them. We have found that those who quickly take our ideas to heart are the young chaps. The older ones, they must want to be safe, to avoid being killed, and they just continue doing their ordinary activities, that's all. It is very difficult. But we know that you find people like that everywhere. They still need much help—with medicine, clothes, salt, and soap. These are the most important needs of the people inside, because now many live without these things. They understand what our difficulties are in getting these things. We have already tried to do something about this. The problem is not completely solved but a part has been solved and we have given some satisfaction to the people.

Question: Last June, at a meeting held in the Eastern Region, a number of new programs were put forward. Perhaps you could comment generally on the progress that has been made. Let's take them one at a time, beginning with your efforts in the sphere of agricultural production.

Answer: Agricultural production in the semiliberated areas is increasing. In every zone the people are organized, in sectors; a zone may have five or six sectors. In each sector there is a Revolutionary Committee of Action, a people's organization which concerns itself with the people's problems. They have a chairman, a secretary, a treasurer, etc. Committee members are elected by the people. There are about 300 of them in an average sector. The people in each sector collectively cultivate what we call a people's plantation. All of them work together in one field. The products which come from their collective work are then used for the benefit of the people themselves. These people's plantations don't develop quickly in all zones. Where we have made the greatest progress in agriculture is in zones C and D. We already have thirty-five collectives in these zones. The important crops grown are rice, cassava, potatoes, manioc, and maize. Apart from the collective each person has his own traditional garden where he can work. But on certain days everyone must work on the people's plantation, because on those days we use the militia to surround and protect the place. If they see a plane coming from very far away they will go into their trenches and camouflage themselves. They are safe there.

Question: How many days a week do they work on the people's plantation?

Answer: They work two days on the collective, then two days in their own gardens. The other days are for meetings, literacy classes, political education, etc. So they have two days of agricultural work on the collective, two days of personal work, and two days of education; and then on Sundays they sing, dance, etc., because national culture is important also. We want to develop it, too.

Question: In the area of education and cadre training you have set up Centers for Revolutionary Instruction (CIR). How have these progressed?

Answer: These Centers are very important to us. Before the end of 1967 we had already trained more than 2,000 cadres outside, in many countries. But we find that it is more important to train them inside the country. We lack materials and have to do without many things—but these CIRs are very helpful to us now. Between August and February the first course was held and it was very successful. And many people's cadres, people trained educationally, militarily, and politically, are now able to go and organize people, be active among the people. They also learned how to maintain themselves—to keep chickens, cultivate, sow, and so on. They were taught many things there. On March 14 we started the second course, the second part of the program. Angola, you know, is a country with many illiterate, uninformed people who don't know how to read and write—probably worse than any other African country. The Portuguese have done it deliberately. Now it is up to us. We can't wait until we're free, but must begin now to educate our people, to teach them how to read and learn. The most important language is Luvale. But when one speaks Luvale, the Mbunda tribe can't understand it, the Chokwe tribe can't understand it. Now we have two languages: Luvale and Portuguese. But we also have people who translate from Portuguese to other local languages.

Question: What is the basic content of the political education program? Is it essentially nationalist in character or is it socialist and internationalist?

Answer: Political education is, first of all, nationalist. The people must understand that we are all Angolans. But we know that tomorrow there will be many problems in Angola and that to solve them requires that we educate people in the ideological sphere. For us ideology is most important within the Party because today we are a mass movement, a popular movement, and not yet a party with the structure of a party. But tomorrow there will be a party with its philosophy, its determined ideology, and its structure. And to reach that level we must begin to prepare the way from today. That is why the MPLA is very interested in giving ideological education to our militants. For the people in general, at least for now, they need only nationalist education.

Question: You mentioned national culture. What are you doing to make people aware of their Angolan national culture?

Answer: Apart from Angolan traditional songs and dances, in our Centers for Revolutionary Instruction we are trying to give people a consciousness of themselves as Angolans. We put on theatrical performances showing the people what it was like before the Portuguese came in, and how our people resisted the Portuguese. Then, after that, how the struggle for our liberation began, and how it is progressing. This is what we're trying to organize, so that tomorrow we will have cultural unity throughout Angola. This is for the people to enjoy, but it is also very important educationally. If the people see what it was like before the Portuguese, after they came, during the early resistance, and the present liberation struggle, it will be easier for them to see themselves as Angolans. We have some intellectuals in Angola, our own intellectuals within the Revolution. And they are helping us with national culture. Some of these young chaps just coming from school are poets, like Dr. Neto, and we are trying to use their poems to build our theater, trying to execute them in theatrical form. That is another part of the effort we are making. In addition, there are now many revolutionary songs which we are teaching the people.

Question: How do the people participate in decision-making at different levels? How do you engage them in the process of making new kinds of decisions?

Answer: The action committees are related to MPLA's central committee. The instructions come from the central committee and are passed through the military command to the action committees. But it is not possible for the central committee to control everything directly. That is why we have created three regional steering committees whose members also serve on the central committee. They meet in various places, make their decisions, and if these decisions pertain to the people inside the country, they are sent through the military command (for security reasons) to the action committees at the zone level. These action committees will then meet and transmit the information to the people through the committees at the sector and group levels. We have four levels, then: group, sector, zone, and region. Within a sector there are many groups, which are residential units. There is only one chief in a sector, but he has responsibility for a large area within which there are smaller villages—which we now call groups—and these groups have their own organization. They, the people in each group, elect members to serve on their action committee.

Question: Do you find that people in the groups and sectors tend to elect traditional leaders to the action committees? Or do they elect people with more progressive ideas?

Answer: Today the traditional leaders are still respected. But if a traditional leader is not very interested in the struggle, he will not have power, he will not be elected by the people. Someone else will be on top. The chief will remain chief but he will be without power. But if he is a good chief, a revolutionary one, it is better for him to lead his people.

Question: So at the group level people elect their own action committee which sends representatives to the sector action committee?

Answer: Yes. And then from the sector level they send their representatives to the zone action committee. In each zone there are some who are very intelligent and they represent their people on the regional committees. The central committee selects one or two from each zone who are militants, who are already politically educated, and they represent their zones on the regional committee. With the help of the military command these action committees keep registers of all marriages, births, deaths, and so on. They also administer justice. Those traditional chiefs are well versed in local laws and customs, but we must take care with the traditional laws and habits which are not good, which are not adapted to the revolutionary conditions of today. So we must help them to settle some cases. In addition, they have their own police, recruited from the militia. The militia is paramilitary, but within a militia group they choose some to be police. They keep order in the villages, or groups, and in the sector.

Question: You mentioned women's organizations. Perhaps you could discuss this question of the role of women in a little greater detail.

Answer: For us the role of women in the struggle is very important. Because in Angola, as everywhere in Africa, it is the women who have suffered most under colonial rule. Our Organization of Angolan Women (OMA) is now fighting for the emancipation of the women of Angola. This organization is a part of the MPLA and shares our orientation. But inside the country they've got their own structures, programs, etc., and represent the interests of the women through their organization. We find it is better if they have their own women leaders, who can lead them inside the country. They are now participating in the struggle without discrimination. When the OMA was formed, MPLA was located only in the northern region of Angola; now we are in the east and south, so we must train their leaders—women leaders—both politically and militarily. We already have a number of women guerrillas and nurses, and we are training others to carry out political work among the women. In the guerrilla forces the women are not separated from the men; they serve right along with the men, under the same conditions.

Question: Do women also serve on the action committees?

Answer: They have their own OMA groups at every level, with their own elected officers and their women's militia, too. Then in each zone the women have one representative who represents them on the zone action committee.

Question: Have you also introduced democratic procedures within the military structure?

Answer: Our movement is a democratic one and so our structures, both military and political, must also operate according to democratic principles. We have ranks within the military, but these ranks only separate the different areas of responsibility. There are no privileges which go with higher ranks. We all eat the same food and other rations are distributed equally.

Question: Are there possibilities for the lower-ranking freedom fighters to express their views or criticize the actions or decisions of the leadership at the various levels?

Answer: Yes, of course. All militants have the right to criticize others, and also themselves, as in the Party. In our political life we follow this principle of criticism and self-criticism. If someone or something is not going right in the Party, politically, militarily, in production, etc., one has the right to say, "This is not good for such and such reasons." Anyone, whatever his rank—he may be a political or military leader, he may be in the central committee or the military commission, or a guerrilla or a member of the women's organization—if he is in the party he has a right to speak freely, to say whatever he wants. At all levels and for all ranks there exists criticism and self-criticism.

AMILCAR CABRAL: THE POLITICS OF STRUGGLE*

I. LIBERATION AND THE PETTY BOURGEOISIE

IN the rural areas we have found it necessary to distinguish between two distinct groups: on the one hand, the group which we consider semifeudal, represented by the Foulas, and, on the other hand, the group which we consider, so to speak, without any defined form of state organization, represented by the Balantes. There are a number of intermediary positions between these two extreme ethnic groups (as regards the social situation). I should like to point out straight away that although in general the semifeudal groups were Muslim and the groups without any form of

---

* From a series of speeches delivered at a seminar in Treviglio, Italy, May 1–3, 1964, convened by the Centro Frantz Fanon of Milan, and published in *International Socialist Journal*, August 1964.

state organization were animist, there is one ethnic group among the animists, the Mandjaks, which had forms of social relations which could be considered feudal at the time when the Portuguese came to Guinea.

I should now like to give you a rapid idea of the social stratification among the Foulas. We consider that the chiefs, the nobles, and the religious figures form one group; after them come the artisans and the Dyulas, who are itinerant traders, and then after that come the peasants properly speaking. Although certain traditions concerning collective owner-ship of the land have been preserved, the chiefs and their entourages have retained considerable privileges as regards ownership of land and the utilization of other people's labor; this means that the peasants who depend on the chiefs are obliged to work for these chiefs for a certain period of the year. The artisans, whether blacksmiths (which is the lowest occupation) or leatherworkers or whatnot, play an extremely important role in the socioeconomic life of the Foulas and represent what you might call the embryo of industry. In general the peasants have no rights and they are the really exploited group in Foula society. Women take part in production but they do not own what they produce. Besides, polygamy is a highly respected institution and women are to a certain extent con-sidered the property of their husbands.

Among the Balantes, which are at the opposite extreme, we find a society without any social stratification: there is just a council of old men in each village or group of villages who decide on the day-to-day problems. In the Balante group property and land are considered to belong to the village but each family receives the amount of land needed to ensure subsistence for itself. The means of production, or the instruments of production, are not collective but are owned by families or individuals. The Balantes still retain certain tendencies toward polygamy, although it is mostly a monogamous society. Balantes women participate in production, but they produce and this gives them a position which we consider privileged as they are fairly free; the only point on which they are not free is that children belong to the head of the family, and the head of the family, the husband, always claims any children his wife may have; this is obvi-ously to be explained by the actual economy of the group where a family's strength is ultimately represented by the number of arms there are to cultivate the earth.

In the rural areas I should mention the small African farm owners; this is a numerically small group but all the same it has a certain im-portance and has proved to be highly active in the national liberation struggle. In the towns (I shall not talk about the presence of Europeans in the rural areas as there are none in Guinea) we must first distinguish between the Europeans and the Africans. The Europeans can easily be classified as they retain in Guinea the social stratification of Portugal (obvi-ously depending on the function they exercise in Guinea). In the first place, there are the high officials and the managers of enterprises who form a stratum with practically no contact with the other European strata. After that there are the middle officials, the small European traders, the people employed in commerce, and the members of the liberal professions. After that come the workers, who are mainly skilled workers.

Among the Africans we find the higher officials, the middle officials, and the members of the liberal professions forming a group; then come the petty officials, those employed in commerce with a contract, who are to be distinguished from those employed in commerce without a contract, who can be fired any moment. The small farm owners also fall into this group; by assimilation we call all these the African petty bourgeoisie (obviously, if we were to make a more thorough analysis the higher African officials as well as the middle officials and the members of the liberal professions should also be included in the petty bourgeoisie). Next come the wage earners (whom we define as those employed in commerce without any contract); among these are certain important subgroups such as the dockworkers, the people employed on the boats carrying goods and agricultural produce; there are also the servants, who are mostly men in Guinea; there are the people working in repair shops and small factories; also there are the people who work in shops as porters and suchlike—these all come under the heading of wage earners. You will notice that we are careful not to call these groups the proletariat or the working class.

There is another group of people whom we call the déclassés, in which there are two subgroups to be distinguished. The first subgroup is easy to identify, what would be called the lumpenproletariat if there was a real proletariat: beggars, prostitutes, and so. The other group, not really déclassé, to which we have paid a lot of attention, has proved to be extremely important in the national liberation struggle: it is mostly made up of young people, connected to petty-bourgeois or workers' families, who have recently arrived from the rural areas and generally do not work; they thus have close relations with the rural areas, as well as with the towns (and even the Europeans). They sometimes live off one kind of work or another but they generally live at the expense of their families. Here I should just like to point out a difference between Europe and Africa; in Africa there is a tradition which requires that, for example, if I have an uncle living in the town, I can come in and live in his house without working and he will feed me and house me. This creates a certain stratum of people who experience urban life and who can, as we shall see, play a very important role.

Schematically, the methodological approach we have used has been as follows: first, the position of each group must be defined—to what extent and in what way does each group depend on the colonial regime? Next we have to see what position they adopt toward the national liberation struggle. Then we have to study their *nationalist* capacity and lastly, envisaging the post-independence period, their *revolutionary* capacity.

Among the Foulas, the chiefs and their entourages are tied to colonialism; particularly as in Guinea the Foulas were once conquerors (the Portuguese allied themselves with them in order to dominate Guinea at the beginning of the conquest). Thus the chiefs (and their authority as chiefs) are very closely tied to the Portuguese authorities. The artisans are extremely dependent on the chiefs; they live off what they make for the chiefs who are the only ones who can acquire their products so that there are some artisans who are simply content to follow the chiefs. The main point about the Dyula is that their permanent preoccupation is to protect their own personal interests; at least in Guinea, the Dyula are not settled in any one place, they are itinerant traders without any real roots anywhere and their fundamental aim is to get bigger and bigger profits. It is precisely the fact that they are almost permanently on the move which provided us with a most valuable element in the struggle. It goes without saying that there are some Dyula who have not supported our struggle, and there are some who have been used as agents against us by the Portuguese, but there are some whom we have been able to use to mobilize people, at least as far as spreading the initial ideas of the struggle was concerned—all we had to do was give them some reward, as they usually would not do anything without being paid.

Obviously, the group with the greatest interest in the struggle is the peasantry, given the nature of the various different societies in Guinea (feudal, semifeudal, etc.) and the various degrees of exploitation to which they were subjected; but the question is not simply one of objective interest.

Foula peasants have a strong tendency to follow their chiefs. Thorough and intensive work was therefore needed to mobilize them. The Balantes and the groups without any defined form of state organization put up much more resistance against the Portuguese than the others and they have maintained their tradition of resistance to colonial penetration intact. This is the group that we found most ready to accept the idea of national liberation.

Does the peasantry represent the main revolutionary force, then? In Guinea, it must be said at once that *the peasantry is not a revolutionary force*—which may seem strange, particularly as we have based the whole of our armed struggle for liberation on the peasantry. A distinction must be drawn between a physical force and a revolutionary force; *physically*, the peasantry is a great force in Guinea: it is almost the whole of the population, it controls the nation's wealth; it is the peasantry which produces. But we know from experience what trouble we had convincing the peasantry to fight. It was not possible for our Party militants and propaganda workers to find the same kind of welcome among the peasantry in Guinea for the idea of national liberation as the idea found in China.

The Europeans are, in general, hostile to the idea of national liberation; they are the human instruments of the colonial state in our country and they therefore reject *a priori* any idea of national liberation there. It has to be said that the Europeans most bitterly opposed to the idea of national liberation are the workers, while we have sometimes found considerably sympathy for our struggle among certain members of the European petty bourgeoisie.

As for the Africans, the petty bourgeoisie can be divided into three subgroups as regards the national liberation struggle. First, there is the petty bourgeoisie which is heavily committed, and compromised with colonialism; this includes most of the higher officials and some members of the liberal professions. Second, there is the group which we perhaps incorrectly call the revolutionary petty bourgeoisie; this is the part of the petty bourgeoisie which is nationalist and which was the source of the idea of the national liberation struggle in Guinea. In the middle lies the part of the petty bourgeoisie which has never been able to make up its mind between the national liberation struggle and the Portuguese. Next come the wage earners, which you can compare roughly with the proletariat in European societies, although they are not exactly the same thing; here, too, there is a majority committed to the struggle, but, again, many members of this group—wage earners who had an extremely petty-bourgeois mentality and whose only aim was to defend the little they had already acquired—were not easy to mobilize.

Next come the déclassés. The really déclassé people, the permanent layabouts, the prostitutes, and so on, have been a great help to the Portuguese police for giving them information; this group has been outrightly against our struggle, perhaps unconsciously so, but nonetheless against our struggle. On the other hand, the group of mainly young people recently arrived from the rural areas with contacts in both the urban and the rural milieus has proved extremely dynamic in the struggle. Many of these people joined the struggle right from the beginning and it is among this group that we found many of the cadres whom we have since trained.

The importance of this urban experience lies in the fact that it allows *comparison*: this is the key stimulant required for a *prise de conscience*. It is interesting to note that Algerian nationalism largely sprang up among the émigré workers in France. As far as Guinea is concerned, the idea of the national liberation struggle was born not abroad but in our own country, in a milieu where people were subjected to close and incessant exploitation. Many people say that it is the peasants who carry the major burden of exploitation; this may be true, but so far as the struggle is concerned it must be realized that it is not the degree of suffering and hardship involved as such that matters: even extreme suffering in itself does not necessarily produce the *prise de conscience* required for the national liberation struggle. In Guinea the peasants are subjected to a kind of exploitation equivalent to slavery; but even if you try and explain to them that they are being exploited and robbed, it is difficult to convince them by means of an unlived explanation of a technico-economic kind that they are the most exploited people; whereas it is easier to convince the workers and the people employed in the towns who earn, say, 10 escudos a day for a job in which a European earns between 30 and 50, that they are being subjected to massive exploitation and injustice *because they can see it.* To take my own case as a member of the petty-bourgeois group which launched the struggle in Guinea, I was an agronomist working under a European whom everybody knew was one of the biggest idiots in Guinea; I could have taught him his job with my eyes shut but he was the boss: this is the *confrontation* which really matters.

It is our opinion that if we get rid of colonialism in Guinea, the main contradiction remaining, the one which will then become the principal contradiction, is that between the ruling classes, the semifeudal groups, and the members of the groups without any defined form of organization. The first thing to note is that the conquest carried out first by the Mandingues and then by the Foulas was a struggle between two opposite poles which was blocked by the very strong structure of the animist groups. There are other contradictions, such as that between the various feudal groups and those between the upper group and the lower. All this is extremely important for the future, and even while the struggle is still going on we must begin to exploit the contradiction between the Foula people and their chiefs, who are very close to the Portuguese. There is a further contradiction, particularly among the animists, between the collective ownership of the land and the private ownership of the means of production in agriculture. I am not trying to stretch alien concepts here; this is an observation that can be made on the spot: the land belongs to the village, but what is produced belongs to whoever produces it—usually the family or the head of the family.

There are other contradictions which we consider secondary. You may be surprised to know that we consider the contradictions between the tribes a secondary one; our struggle for national liberation and the work done by our Party have shown that this contradiction is really not so important. The Portuguese counted on it, but as soon as we organized the liberation struggle properly the contradiction between the tribes proved to a feeble, secondary contradiction. This does not mean that we do not need to pay attention to this contradiction; we reject both the positions which are to be found in Africa—one which says: there are no tribes, we are all the same, we are all one people in one territorial unity, our party comprises everybody; the other saying: tribes exist, we must base parties on tribes. Our position lies between the two; all structural, organizational, and other measures must be taken to ensure that this contradiction does not explode and become a more important contradiction.

This has led us to the following conclusion: we must try and unite everybody in the national liberation struggle against the Portuguese colonialists. It is imperative to organize things so that we always have an instrument available which can solve all the other contradictions. This is what convinced us of the absolute necessity of creating a party during the national liberation struggle. There are some people who interpret our Party as a front; perhaps our Party is a front at the moment, but within the framework of this front there is our Party which is directing the front, and there are no other parties in the front. For the circumstances of the struggle we maintain a general aspect, but within the framework of the struggle we know what our Party is, we know where the Party finishes and where the people who just rallied for the liberation struggle begin.

When we had made our analysis, we had some knowledge of other experiences and we knew that a struggle of the kind we hoped to lead—and win—has to be led by the working class. We looked for the working class in Guinea and did not find it. What then were we to do? We were just a group of petty bourgeois who were driven by the reality of life in Guinea, by the sufferings we had to endure, and also by the influence events in Africa and elsewhere had on us, in particular the experiences some of us acquired in Portugal and other countries in Europe.

And so this little group began. We first thought of a general movement of national liberation, but this immediately proved unfeasible. We decided to extend our activity to the workers in the towns, and we had some success with this; we launched moves for higher wages, better working conditions, and so on. But we obviously did not have a proletariat. We quite clearly lacked revolutionary intellectuals, so we had to start searching, given that we—rightly—did not believe in the revolutionary capacity of the peasantry.

One important group in the towns were the dockworkers; another important group were the people working in the boats carrying merchandise, who mostly live in Bissau itself and travel up and down the rivers. These people proved highly conscious of their position and of their economic importance and they took the initiative to launch strikes without any trade union leadership at all. We therefore decided to concentrate all our work on this group. This gave excellent results and this group soon came to form a kind of nucleus which influenced the attitudes of other wage-earning groups in the towns.

We also looked for intellectuals, but there were none, because the Portuguese did not educate people. In any case, what is an intellectual in our country? It would probably be someone who knew the general situation very well, who had some knowledge, not profound theoretical knowledge, but concrete knowledge of the country itself and of its life, as well as of our enemy. We, the people I have talked about, the engineers, doctors, bank clerks and so on, joined together to form a group.

There was also this other group of people in the towns, which we have been unable to classify precisely, which was still closely connected to the rural areas and contained people who spoke almost all the languages that are used in Guinea. They knew all the customs of the rural areas while at the same time possessing a solid knowledge of the European urban milieus. They also had a certain degree of self-confidence, they knew how to read and write (which makes a person an intellectual in our country) and so we concentrated our work on these people and immediately started giving them some preparatory training.

We were faced with another difficult problem: we realized that we needed to have people with a mentality which could transcend the context of the national liberation struggle, and so we prepared a number of cadres from the group I have just mentioned, some from the people employed in trade and other wage earners, and even some peasants, so that they could acquire what you might call a working-class mentality. You may think this is absurd, that in order for there to be a working-class mentality the material conditions of the working class should exist, a working class should exist. In fact we managed to inculcate these ideas into a large number of people—the kind of ideas, that is, there would be if there were a working class. We have trained about 1,000 cadres at our Party school in Conakry; in fact for about two years this was about all we did outside the country. When these cadres returned to the rural areas they inculcated a certain mentality into the peasants and it is among these cadres that we chose the people who are now leading the struggle. We are not a communist party or a Marxist-Leninist party but the people now leading the peasants in the struggle in Guinea are mostly from the urban milieus and connected with the urban wage-earning group. When I hear that only the peasantry can lead the struggle, am I supposed to think we have made a mistake? All I can say is that at the moment our struggle is going well.

The concept of a party and the creation of parties did not occur spontaneously in Europe, they resulted from a long process of class struggle. When we in Africa think of creating a party now we find ourselves in very different conditions from those in which parties appeared as historico-social phenomena in Europe. This has a number of consequences, so that when you think "party," "single party," etc., you must connect all these things up with conditions in Africa, and with the history of the different societies.

A rigorous historical approach is similarly needed when examining another problem related to this—how can the underdeveloped countries evolve toward revolution, toward socialism? There is a preconception held by many people, even on the Left, that imperialism made us enter history at the moment when it began its adventure in our countries: this preconception must be denounced. For somebody on the Left, and for Marxist n particular, history obviously means the class struggle; our opinion is exactly the contrary. We consider that when imperialism arrived in Guinea t made us leave history—our history. We agree that history in our country s the result of class struggle, but we have our own struggles in our own country. The moment imperialism arrived, colonialism arrived. Obviously, we agree that the class struggle has continued, but it has continued in a very different way: our whole people is struggling against the ruling class of the imperialist countries, and this gives a completely different aspect to the historical evolution of our country. As we see it, in colonial conditions no one stratum can succeed in the struggle for national liberation on its own, and therefore it is all the strata of society which are the agents of history. This brings us to what should be a void—but in fact it is not. What commands history in colonial conditions is not the class struggle; do not mean that the class struggle in Guinea stopped completely during the colonial period, it continued, but in a muted way. In the colonial period it is the colonial state which commands history.

Our problem is to see who are capable of taking control of the state apparatus when the colonial power is destroyed. In Guinea the peasants cannot read or write, they have almost no relations with the colonial forces during the colonial period except for paying taxes, which is done indirectly. The working class hardly exists as a defined class, it is just in embryo. There is no economically viable bourgeoisie because imperialism prevented it being created. What there is is a stratum of people in the service of imperialism who have learnt how to manipulate the apparatus of the state—the African petty bourgeoisie. This is the only stratum capable of controlling or even utilizing the instruments which the colonial state used against our people. So that we come to the conclusion that in colonial conditions it is the petty bourgeoisie which is the inheritor of state power (though I wish we could be wrong). The moment national liberation comes and the petty bourgeoisie takes power we enter, or rather we return to history, and thus the internal contradictions of our social and economic conditions will break out again.

When this happens, and particularly as things are now, there will be powerful external contradictions conditioning the internal situation, and not just internal contradictions as before. What attitude can the petty bourgeoisie adopt? Obviously people on the Left will call for the Revolution; the Right will call for the "nonrevolution," i.e., a capitalist road or something like that. The petty bourgeoisie can either ally itself with imperialism and the reactionary strata in its own country to try and preserve itself as a petty bourgeoisie or ally itself with the workers and peasants, who must themselves take power or control power to make the Revolution. We must be very clear exactly what we are asking the petty bourgeoisie to do. Are we asking it to commit suicide? Because if there is a revolution, then the petty bourgeoisie will have to abandon power

to the workers and the peasants and cease to exist *qua* petty bourgeoisie
For a revolution to take place depends on the nature of the party (and
its size), the character of the struggle which led up to liberation, if there
was an armed struggle, what the nature of this armed struggle was, and
how it developed.

This connects with the problem of the real nature of the national libera
tion struggle. In Guinea, as in other countries, the implantation of
imperialism by force and the presence of the colonial system considerably
altered the historical conditions and aroused a response—the national
liberation struggle—which is generally considered a revolutionary trend
but this is something which I think needs further examination. I should
like to formulate this question: is the national liberation movement some
thing which has simply emerged from within our country, is it a result
of the internal contradictions created by the presence of colonialism, or
are there external factors which have determined it? In fact I would
even go so far as to ask whether, given the advance of socialism in the
world, the national liberation movement is not an imperialist initiative
Is the jurisdical institution which serves as a reference for the right of
all peoples to struggle to free themselves a product of the peoples who
are trying to liberate themselves? Was it created by the socialist countries
who are our historical associates? Let us not forget that it was the im
perialist countries who recognized the right of all people to national
independence. Even Portugal, who is using napalm bombs against our
people in Guinea, signed the declaration of the right of all peoples to
independence. One may well ask oneself why they were so mad as to do
something which goes against their own interests and whether or not it
was partly forced on them. The real point is that they signed it. This
is where we think there is something wrong with the simple interpretation
of the national liberation movement as a revolutionary trend. The objective
of the imperialist countries was to prevent the enlargement of the socialist
camp, to liberate the reactionary forces in our countries which were being
stifled by colonialism, and to enable these forces to ally themselves with
the international bourgeoisie. The fundamental objective was to create a
bourgeoisie where one did not exist, in order specifically to strengthen
the imperialist and the capitalist camp. The rise of the bourgeoisie in
the new countries, far from being anything surprising, should be considered
absolutely normal. It is something that has to be faced by all those
struggling against imperialism. We are therefore faced with the problem
of deciding whether to engage in an out-and-out struggle against the bourgeoisie right from the start or whether to try and make an alliance with
the national bourgeoisie, to try to deepen the absolutely necessary contradiction between the national bourgeoisie and the international bourgeoisie which has promoted the national bourgeoisie to the position it
holds.

What really interests us here is neo-colonialism. After the Second World War imperialism entered on a new phase: on the one hand, it worked out the new policy of aid, i.e., granted independence to the occupied countries plus "aid," and, on the other hand, concentrated on preferential investment in the European countries. This was, above all, an attempt at rationalizing imperialism. Even if it has not yet provoked reactions of a nationalist kind in the European countries, we are convinced that it will do so soon. As we see it, neo-colonialism (which we may call rationalized imperialism) is more a defeat for the international working class than for the colonized peoples. Neo-colonialism is at work on two fronts—in Europe as well as in the underdeveloped countries. Its current framework in the underdeveloped countries is the policy of aid, and one of the essential aims of this policy is to create a false bourgeoisie to put a brake on the Revolution and to enlarge the possibilities of the petty bourgeoisie as a neutralizer of the Revolution. At the same time it invests capital in France, Italy, England, and so on. In our opinion the aim of this is to stimulate the growth of the workers' aristocracy, to enlarge the field of action of the petty bourgeoisie so as to block the Revolution. In our opinion it is under this aspect that neo-colonialism and the relations between the international working-class movement and our movements must be analyzed. *En passant,* I might point out that imperialism is quite prepared to change both its men and its tactics in order to perpetuate itself; it will make and destroy states and, as we have already seen, it will kill its own puppets when they no longer serve its purposes. If need be, it will even create a kind of socialism, which people may soon start calling "neo-socialism."

If there have been any doubts about the close relations between our struggle and the struggle of the international working-class movement, neo-colonialism has proved that there need not be any. Obviously I don't think it is possible to forge closer relations between the peasantry in Guinea and the working-class movement in Europe. What we must do first is try and forge closer links between the peasant movement and the wage-earners' movement in our country.

I. DIRECTIVES *

—In the liberated regions do everything possible to normalize the political life of the people. Section committees of the Party (*tabanca* committees), zonal committees, regional committees, must be consolidated

---

* Series of directives issued by Cabral in 1965. Translated by Basil Davidson and published in his *The Liberation of Guiné: Aspects of an African Revolution* (Baltimore, Md.: Penguin, 1969).

and function normally. Frequent meetings must be held to explain to the population what is happening with the struggle, what the Party is endeavoring to do at any given moment, and what the criminal intentions of the enemy may be. In regions still occupied by the enemy reinforce clandestine work, the mobilization and organization of the populations, and the preparation of militants for action and support of our fighters.

—Develop political work in our armed forces, whether regular or guerrilla, wherever they may be. Hold frequent meetings. Demand serious political work from political commissars. Start political committees, formed by the political commissars and commander of each unit, in the regular army. Oppose tendencies to *militarism* and make each fighter an exemplary militant of our Party.

—Educate ourselves, educate other people, the population in general to fight fear and ignorance, to eliminate little by little the subjection to nature and natural forces which our economy has not yet mastered. Fight without useless violence against all the negative aspects, prejudicial to mankind, which are still part of our beliefs and traditions. Convince little by little, and in particular the militants of the Party, that we shall end by conquering the fear of nature, and that man is the strongest force in nature.

—Demand from responsible Party members that they dedicate themselves seriously to study, that they interest themselves in the things and problems of our daily life and struggle in their fundamental and essential aspect, and not simply in their appearance. Learn from life, learn from our people, learn from books, learn from the experience of others. Never stop learning.

—Responsible members must take life seriously, conscious of their responsibilities, thoughtful about carrying them out, and with a comradeship based on work and duty done. Nothing of this is incompatible with the joy of life, or with love for life and its amusements, or with confidence in the future and in our work.

—Reinforce political work and propaganda within the enemy's armed forces. Write posters, pamphlets, letters. Draw slogans on the roads. Establish cautious links with enemy personnel who want to contact us. Act audaciously and with great initiative in this way. Do everything possible to help enemy soldiers to desert. Assure them of security so as to encourage their desertion. Carry out political work among Africans who are still in enemy service, whether civilian or military. Persuade these brothers to change direction so as to serve the Party within the enemy ranks or desert with arms and ammunition to our units.

—We must practice revolutionary democracy in every aspect of our Party life. Every responsible member must have the courage of his responsibilities, exacting from others a proper respect for his work and properly respecting the work of others. Hide nothing from the masses of our people. Tell no lies. Expose lies whenever they are told. Mask no difficulties, mistakes, failures. Claim no easy victories.

III. IDEOLOGY AND ARMED STRUGGLE *

It is often said that national liberation is based on the right of all peoples freely to decide about their destinies and that the aim of this liberation is to obtain national independence. Although we do not disagree with this vague and subjective manner of expressing a complex reality, we prefer to be objective since, for us, the basis of national liberation, whatever the formula adopted by international law, lies in the inalienable right of each people to have its own history; and the aim of national liberation is the reconquest of this right usurped by imperialism, i.e., the freeing of the process of development of the national productive forces. For this reason, in our opinion, any national liberation movement which does not give due weight to this base and this aim, may indeed fight against imperialism, but it will certainly not be fighting for national liberation.

This implies that, bearing in mind the essential features of the world economy of our time as well as of experiences already gained in the realm of anti-imperialist struggle, the main aspect of the struggle for national liberation is the struggle against neo-colonialism. Furthermore, if we consider that national liberation demands that a deep change should take place in the process of development of the productive forces, we see that the phenomenon of *national liberation* necessarily corresponds to a *revolution*. What matters is being aware of the objective and subjective conditions in which this revolution takes place and knowing the forms or form of struggle best suited to its realization.

We shall not here repeat that these conditions are frankly favorable at the present stage of the history of humanity; it is sufficient to recall that there also exist unfavorable factors, both on the international level and within each nation struggling for its liberation.

On the international plane, it seems to us that the following factors are at the very least unfavorable to the movement of national liberation: the neo-colonial situation of a large number of states achieving political independence being added to others having already achieved it; the progress made by neo-colonialism, particularly in Europe, where imperialism has recourse to preferential investment, encouraging the development of a privileged proletariat with the subsequent lowering of the revolutionary

* Speech delivered at the First Conference of the Organization of Solidarity of the Peoples of Asia, Africa, and Latin America (OSPAAAL or Tricontinental Conference), held in Havana, January 3–12, 1966. Translation by Judith Landry.

level of the laboring classes; the neo-colonial situation, whether overt or disguised, of some European states which, like Portugal, still possess colonies; the policy known as "aid to the underdeveloped countries," practiced by imperialism with the hope of creating or strengthening the autochthonous pseudobourgeoisies, necessarily enfeoffed to the international bourgeoisie, and thus blocking the path to revolution; the claustrophobic revolutionary timidity, which led several newly independent states with internal economic and political conditions favorable to revolution to accept compromise with the enemy or its agents; the growing contradictions between anti-imperialist states; and, lastly, the threats, by imperialism, to world peace with atomic warfare. These factors contribute to reinforcing imperialism against the movements of national liberation.

Internally, we believe that the most important weaknesses or unfavorable factors lie in the socioeconomic structure and in their evolutionary tendencies under imperial pressure or, to be more exact, in the little, or complete lack of, attention paid to the characteristics of this structure and these tendencies, by the national liberation movements in the working out of the strategies of struggle.

This point of view does not claim to diminish the importance of other internal factors unfavorable to national liberation, such as economic underdevelopment, the social backwardness of the popular masses resulting from it, and other less important discrepancies. But it should be pointed out that the existence of tribes does not emerge as an important anomaly except in terms of opportunistic attitudes, generally coming from detribalized individuals or groups within the national liberation movement. Contradictions between classes, even embryonic ones, are far more important than contradictions between tribes.

Although the colonial and neo-colonial situations are identical in essence, and though the main aspect of the struggle against imperialism is the neo-colonial aspect, we believe that it is vital to distinguish these two situations in practice. Indeed, the horizontal structure of autochthonous society, though more or less differentiated, and the absence of a political power composed of national elements, make possible the creation of a broad front of unity and struggle in the colonial situation, indispensable moreover to the success of the national liberation movement. But this possibility does not exempt us from rigorous analysis of the indigenous social structure, of the trends of its development, and of the adoption in practice of appropriate measures to guarantee a real national liberation. Among these measures, we regard as indispensable the growth of a solidly united vanguard, aware of the true meaning and aim of the national liberation struggle it must lead. This need is all the more pressing since we know that, with a few rare exceptions, the colonial situation does not allow or demand the significant existence of vanguard classes (self-aware working classes and rural proletariat) which could ensure the vigilance of the popular masses with regard to the development of the liberation movement. Inversely, the generally embryonic character of the working classes and the economic, social, and cultural situation of the most important physical force in the struggle for national liberation—the peasantry—do not enable the two main forces of the struggle to distinguish, on their own, true national independence from factitious political independence. Only a revolutionary vanguard, generally an active minority, can be aware, from the start, of this difference and bring it, through struggle, to the notice of the popular masses. This explains the basically political character of the struggle for national independence and, to some degree, the importance of the form of struggle in the final result of the phenomenon of national liberation.

In the neo-colonial situation, the more or less accentuated vertical structure of the indigenous society and the existence of a political power composed of autochthonous elements—national state—actually intensifies the contradictions within this society, and makes the creation of a front as broad as in the colonial case difficult, if not impossible. On the one hand, the material effects (mainly nationalization of the state bureaucracy and the increase of the economic initiative of the indigenous element, particularly on the commercial level) and psychological effects (pride of believing oneself led by one's own compatriots, exploitation of a religious or tribal solidarity between a few rulers and part of the popular masses) help to demobilize a considerable part of the nationalist forces. But the necessarily repressive character of the neo-colonial state vis-à-vis the forces of national liberation, the worsening of class discrepancies, the objective permanence of agents and signs of foreign domination (settlers who retain their privileges, armed forces, racial discrimination), the increasing pauperization of the peasantry and the more or less obvious influence of external interests, help to keep the flame of nationalism burning, progressively to sharpen the awareness of vast sectors of the people, and to rally the majority of the population to the ideal of national liberation as a way out of its neo-colonial frustration.

Furthermore, while the autochthonous ruling class is becoming progressively more bourgeois, the development of a working class composed of town workers and agricultural proletariat, all exploited by the indirect domination of imperialism, opens new vistas to the growth of national liberation. This working class, whatever its degree of political awareness (beyond a minimum limit, which is *awareness of its needs*) seems, in the case of neo-colonialism, to constitute the real popular vanguard in the struggle for national liberation. But it will never be able completely to achieve its mission within the framework of this struggle (which does not end with the gaining of independence) if it does not join solidly with the other exploited classes, the peasants in general (farm workers, sharecroppers, agricultural laborers, small farm owners), and the nationalist petty bourgeoisie. The realization of this alliance demands the mobilization and organization of nationalist forces within the framework (or through the agency) of a strong and well-structured political organization.

Another important distinction between the colonial and neo-colonial situation is to be found in the perspectives of the struggle. The colonial case (where the *nation-class* is fighting against the repressive forces of the bourgeoisie of the colonizing country) may lead, at least apparently, to a nationalist solution (national revolution); the nation wins its independence and hypothetically adopts the economic structure which most suits it. The neo-colonial case (where the laboring classes and their allies are fighting simultaneously against the imperialist bourgeoisie and the autochthonous ruling class) is not resolved by a nationalist solution; it requires the destruction of the capitalist structure implanted by imperialism on the national territory, and postulates, precisely, a socialist solution. This distinction results mainly from the difference in level of the productive forces in the two cases and from the subsequent intensification of the class struggle.

It would not be difficult to show that, in the past, this distinction is barely apparent. One need only remember that in our present historical conditions—liquidation of imperialism which perpetuates its domination over our peoples by all possible means, and consolidation of socialism over a considerable part of the world—there are only two possible paths for an independent nation: to go back to imperial domination (neo-colonialism, capitalism, state capitalism) or the path of socialism. This option on which compensation for the efforts and sacrifices of the popular masses during the struggle depends, is strongly influenced by the form of the fight and the degree of revolutionary awareness of those leading it.

Facts spare us from proving that the essential element of imperialism is violence. If we accept the principle *according to which the struggle for liberation is a revolution*, and that this ends only when the flag is hoisted and the national anthem sung, we shall see that there is not and cannot be national liberation without the use of liberating violence on the part of the nationalist forces, to counter the criminal violence of the agents of imperialism. No one doubts that, whatever may be the local characteristics, imperialism implies a state of permanent violence against the nationalist forces. No people on this earth having been subjected to the imperialist yoke (colonial or neo-colonial) has conquered its independence (nominal or actual) without victims. What matters is to determine what forms of violence may be used by the forces of national liberation not only to counter the violence of imperialism, but also to guarantee, through struggle, the final victory of its cause: real national independence.

Past and present experiences of certain peoples, the current situation of the struggle for national liberation throughout the world (particularly in Vietnam, the Congo, and Zimbabwe) as well as the situation of permanent violence, or at least of discrepancies and uncertainties, of certain countries which have gained their independence by so-called pacific means, show us that not only are compromises with imperialism inoperative but also that the normal path of national liberation, imposed upon the peoples by imperialist repression, is *armed struggle*.

It is evident, too, that both the effectiveness of this path and the stability of the situation to which it will lead after liberation, depend not only on the characteristics of the organization of the struggle but also on the political and moral awareness of those who, for historical reasons, are in position to be the immediate heirs of the colonial or neo-colonial state. For the facts have shown that the only social sector capable of awareness of the reality of imperialist domination, and of running the state machinery inherited from this domination, is the autochthonous petty bourgeoisie. If we bear in mind the unpredictability, the complexity of the national tendencies inherent in the economic situation of this social structure or class, we shall see that this specific inevitability of our situation constitutes one of the weaknesses of the national liberation movement.

The colonial situation, which does not admit of the development of an autochthonous pseudobourgeoisie and in which the popular masses do not as a whole reach the necessary level of political awareness before the unleashing of the phenomenon of national liberation, offers the petty bourgeoisie the historical opportunity of running the struggle against foreign domination. Because of its objective and subjective situation— higher level of life than that of the masses, more frequent contacts with the agents of colonialism and hence more opportunities for humiliation, higher level of education and political culture, etc.—it is the stratum which most rapidly becomes aware of the need to free itself from foreign domination. This historical responsibility is taken on by the sector of the petty bourgeoisie that can, in the colonial context, be called revolutionary, while the other sectors ally themselves with colonialism to defend their social situation, however deludedly.

The neo-colonial situation, which demands the liquidation of the autochthonous pseudobourgeoisie for the achievement of national liberation, also gives the petty bourgeoisie the opportunity of fulfilling a front-rank, indeed decisive, role in the struggle for the liquidation of foreign domination. But, in this case, in virtue of the progress achieved in the social structure, the function of direction of the struggle is shared (to a greater or lesser degree) by the more educated of the laboring classes and even with elements of the national pseudobourgeoisie, imbued with patriotic feeling. The role of the sector of the petty bourgeoisie which takes part in leading the struggle is even more important, particularly since in the neo-colonial situation itself it is more apt to take over these functions, either because the working masses have economic and cultural limitations, or because of the complexes and limitations of an ideological nature which characterize the sector of the national pseudo-bourgeoisie which is involved in the struggle. In this case, it is important to note that the mission entrusted to it demands from this sector of the petty bourgeoisie a greater revolutionary conscience, the ability to interpret the aims of the masses faithfully at each phase of the struggle and to identify with them more and more.

But, however great the degree of revolutionary awareness of the sector of the petty bourgeoisie called upon to fulfill this historical function, it cannot free itself from this objective reality: the petty bourgeoisie, as a service class (i.e., which is not directly involved in the process of production), does not have at its disposal the economic bases which would guarantee it the assumption of power. Indeed, history shows us that, whatever the role—sometimes important—played by individuals of the petty bourgeoisie in the course of a revolution, this class has never been in possession of political power. And it could not be, because political power (state) is based on the economic capacity of the ruling class and in the conditions of colonial and neo-colonial society. This capacity is held by only two entities: imperialist capitalist capital and the national laboring classes.

To retain the power that national liberation puts into its hands, the petty bourgeoisie has only one path: to give free rein to its national tendencies of embourgeoisement, allow the development of a bureaucratic bourgeoisie—and of intermediaries—in the goods cycle, in order to become a national pseudobourgeoisie, i.e., to betray the revolution and rally necessarily to imperialist capital. Now all this corresponds to the neo-colonial situation, i.e., to the betrayal of the objectives of national liberation. So as not to betray these aims, the petty bourgeoisie has only one path: to strengthen its revolutionary conscience, repudiate the temptations of embourgeoisement and the national pressures of its class mentality, identify with the laboring classes, not set itself up against the normal development of the process of revolution. This means that the revolutionary petty bourgeoisie must be capable of class suicide, to come to life again as revolutionary workers. This shows us that though national liberation is essentially a political problem, the conditions of its development lend it certain characteristics which belong to the moral sphere.

Cuba

In the ideological world of Marxist-Leninists, three "models" of successful revolutions are carefully studied and, often, imitated—the Russian, the Chinese, and the Cuban. The Russian because of its success through general insurrection; the Chinese because of its drawn-out ("protracted") people's war; the Cuban because an invincible guerrilla nucleus (later to be called foco) brought about the collapse of the bourgeois state. So far no other model has emerged, although many other countries have established revolutionary regimes, some as a result of tactics and strategy also used in the basic three. The Algerians, for example, fought a guerrilla war against an outside power —France—much like the "patriotic" first stage of the two-stage Chinese Revolution. The Vietnamese, not yet totally victorious by the end of 1970, also waged a national war against foreign domination, first the French, then the United States. As for Eastern European revolutionaries, they came to power with the Russian Red Army, while the North Koreans profited both from people's war against the Japanese and the Red Army. The Middle East "socialist" countries, revolutionary mainly only in rhetoric, are the consequences of coups d'état.

Of the three "models," China's way seems most appropriate where imperialists are intervening with full force (Vietnam, Laos, Thailand, Eritrea, Palestine, Chad). Russia's example appears as the best guide for revolutionaries in developed capitalist countries where an organized proletariat is politically conscious of the class struggle. And Cuba, which fought foreigners only indirectly (U.S. agents, infiltrators, bribed counterrevolutionaries, etc.) until the Bay of Pigs invasion (which, though using Cuban exiles, must be considered U.S.). remains fascinating for the rest of the underdeveloped world not occupied by imperialist military forces.

And yet, most revolutionary theorists, whether Marxist-Leninist or not, insist that Cuba is an "exception." The reasons: (1) until he fully

385

controlled the machinery of state, Fidel fooled the United States by pretending to be just another bourgeois reformist; (2) now that it has lost Cuba and just about lost Vietnam, now that revolutionary fervor is widespread throughout the world it dominates economically, the United States will never take a chance again; the next time it suspects that some ferment may lead to a revolution it will intervene directly, as in the Dominican Republic. As Lyndon Johnson said when he was president, the United States will never tolerate "another Cuba."

Che Guevara, who began to work out the "many Vietnams" theory as early as 1960 and 1961 (see the first article below), did not consider Cuba an exception. Long before the U.S. invasion of the Dominican Republic, in fact even before the Bay of Pigs, he concluded that the United States would indeed try to stop another Cuba by massive attack if necessary. But he still did not think that Cuba's experience was worthless for the rest of the neo-colonized world. On the contrary, he decided that the nucleus guerrilla operation that worked in Cuba was the best solution for all predominantly agrarian Third World countries (the vast majority).

A few well-trained men setting up a foco in the jungles and mountains of almost any country in Latin America would not elicit massive U.S. attack. And if the guerrillas were swift and mobile, even such an assault would not be necessarily deadly. And it would arouse the opposition of both the invaded population and the rest of the world. And if the foco was able to survive and show its seriousness to the local population, eventually it would pick up peasant support and grow. Then, if the United States attacked, the foco would become simply the vanguard of a peasant army—people's war. And if such focos sprang up all over the Latin American continent, U.S. intervention would be impossible—or so costly and diffuse as to be easily defeated.

Refined with touches of French rationalism and strengthened with various practical examples, Che's ideas ended up being known as "the Debray theory." Revolution in the Revolution?, *the booklet that became a best-seller, was not meant by its author Régis Debray to be any more than the schema for a much longer and fuller study based on Che's views. As such it contained many mistakes of fact, omission, and interpretation. But it has also been severely but unfairly attacked because it has been identified with Che's Bolivian venture—as if the foco theory led directly to Che's death. In fact, Debray's foco theory is, as the author has consistently maintained, only part of a theory of revolution in America carried on over the years since 1961 by a whole collective of Cuban and Latin American revolutionaries. A much better analysis can be found in Armando Hart's* Informe, *the Cuban position paper prepared for the OLAS conference held in Havana in August 1967 (see the second article below).*

A long-time student revolutionary against dictator Batista, Armando

Hart Davalos was jailed in 1957, made a dramatic courtroom escape while on trial, and joined Fidel in the Sierra Maestra. Appointed Minister of Education after the 1959 victory, he soon showed extraordinary talents as both a Party organizer and a theorist. Fidel hence put him to work building Cuba's new Communist Party and working out its ideological basis as well. A member of all top-echelon committees, he is considered today—with President Osvaldo Dorticós Torrado—to be the most important Cuban leader below Fidel.

In his Informe, Hart carefully analyzes the history, economy, classes, and prospects of the Latin American continent before describing the so-called foco theory (he never uses the term) of revolution. The most important point he makes is that the foco is not the Revolution but a revolutionary vanguard, a catalyst, a way of preparing the ground, the strategy, and the politics for people's war. As such, the guerrilla unit is a "political vanguard." Like Maoists, he believes in the two stages but never dogmatically and never hypercritically. "A revolution cannot triumph by hiding its aims," he says. As a realist, he knows full well that any individual foco can be defeated by the United States—the Informe was written before Che's defeat—but, says Hart, the United States cannot eliminate many focos operating simultaneously. That, he insists, should be American revolutionaries' goal—continual revolution.

Like Che, Fidel, Debray, and most Marxist analysts, however, Hart makes a few conclusions which some sympathetic Latin American observers would contest:

1. According to Hart, the peasant is basically petty-bourgeois because his main concern is obtaining land for himself. The worker, on the other hand, is not tied to factory or place, and hence can be genuinely proletarian in his way of thinking (his class—and class-struggle consciousness). Thus, although the guerrilla is based on the peasant and hence guerrilla warfare takes on the aspect of a peasant war, it must have a proletarian ideology, lest it become another agrarian petty-bourgeois movement which will corrupt the Revolution. Critics might point out, however, that though the city worker is indeed not tied to factory or place, his drive for possessions —TV's, cars, etc.—is equally petty-bourgeois. Besides, modern capitalism is dynamic, not static, and it creates enough mobility (even in the underdeveloped world) to generate the myth of overall mobility. By constantly giving in to demands for better wages and working conditions (the cost of which the capitalist recoups in higher prices, added efficiency, etc.), the capitalist can and often does reinforce the reformist, Fabian aspect of the labor movement, thus co-opting the proletarian consciousness of the worker. The peasant's demand for land, meanwhile, can only be satisfied by such total restructuring of the economy that it necessitates a full social revolution.

2. Like most Marxist analysts, Hart assumes that the local military

forces, dictated to and manipulated by the ruling bourgeois-oligarchy-imperialist alliance, have no moral raison d'être *and hence cannot match, ultimately, the revolutionaries' commitment. And, says Hart, since they are badly paid and distrusted by the brass, the military forces are usually incompetent. Critics counter that under U.S. subversion-tactics experts, much of the army that guerrillas will face has been built up into special elites (and, as such, exhibits remarkable* esprit de corps). *What's more, there are many local military men who see their role as that of the genuine reformer (the Peruvian ruling junta, for example). They nationalize flagrant foreign exploiters' property, launch agrarian reforms, etc. Whether they can succeed to change the social relations of their people or not remains to be seen (they never have yet). But they certainly do think of themselves as moral and the fighting army may catch their zeal. Furthermore, the belief (crucial to the "many Vietnams" theory) that the local professional armies will fail against guerrillas and that the United States will then have to intervene has not been borne out in Latin America. The United States did overkill the Dominican rebellion, but it has also trained local armies well enough to be able to stay in the background (as "advisers") or else send in mercenaries—who enjoy the manhunts. In Guatemala, Venezuela, Colombia, and Bolivia, for example, the United States has used Cuban exiles, Nicaraguans, Puerto Ricans and/or Paraguayans dressed up in local army uniforms for its search-and-destroy missions. The truth is that the United States has been preparing itself, just as Hart says, for the "inevitable" Revolution for years—and has perfected all the techniques it has available.*

Also missing from Hart's analysis is the question of nationalism which is so fundamental in the underdeveloped world. Debray himself finally realized this, and in a letter written in September 1969 and published in London's Sunday Times, *October 12, 1969, he states: "The nation is of the essence of these times and one must not believe a single word of any socialism that does not also contain nationalism. The near-silence of European Marxists on 'the question of nationalism' will one day be seen as the most costly and ruinous of all historic omissions. Such people work in a vacuum."*

Most Marxist analysts are wary of alliances between workers, peasants, and the petty bourgeoisie with the national bourgeoisie. Nevertheless, from Lenin and Mao to Ojeda and Bravo (Venezuela), the conclusion seems to be that the alliance is more of an asset than a liability. For Mao, such an alliance cost the Chinese Communists thousands of cadres (murdered in 1927), but it worked in the war against the Japanese—during stage one of the Revolution. In Indonesia, the alliance resulted in the murder of perhaps as many as a million communists in 1965. The possibility and at times desirability of the alliance is based on the analysts' overall view of the underdeveloped world as basically feudal. That is, the old landed gentry is seen as exploiting the peasants for its own personal benefit, then using the capital to control urban semi-industrial commerce in partnership with imperialist enterprises, thus freezing out the national bourgeoisie. That moneyed bourgeoisie is then supposed to want to drive the imperialists (and, by association, the oligarchy) out, so as to win control of the urban economy for itself. But Latin America (and the Third World in general) is not feudal (though peasants do live in feudal-like conditions). It is capitalist, and the development of all enterprises, including agriculture, is calculated in the light of markets, profit margins, growth, etc. The "national" bourgeoisie has long been incorporated into that growth. Through vast U.S.-controlled holding corporations, it participates in the capital formation schemes, in urban expansion, in banking and transforming industries, etc. In Venezuela and Chile, it is the national bourgeoisie which is in power—with U.S. imperialism and the native oligarchy. It will fight the Revolution as strenuously as will the Creole Corporations, the International Petroleum Companies, the International Basic Economy Corporation (IBEC)—in a word, the Rockefellers.

Of all the Latin American Marxist analysts, Armando and Che seem most capable of dealing with these variances. Hart, for one, has no illusions about where the bourgeoisie's allegiances lie. Still, in his analysis, problems remain. Nevertheless, his Informe *makes an excellent case for the Continental Revolution.*

ERNESTO CHE GUEVARA: CUBA—EXCEPTION OR VANGUARD?*

NEVER in America had an event taken place of such extraordinary character, such deep roots, and such transcendental consequences for the destiny of the continent's progressive movements as our revolutionary war. This is true to such an extent that it has been appraised by some as the decisive event to occur in America, on a scale of importance second only to the great trilogy of the Russian Revolution, the victory over Nazi Germany and the subsequent social transformations, and the victory of the Chinese Revolution.

Our Revolution, which has been heterodox in its forms and manifestations, has nevertheless followed the general lines of all the great historical events of this century characterized by anticolonial struggles and the transition toward socialism.

---

* Verde Olivo *(Havana), April 9, 1961. English version from* Venceremos: The Speeches and Writings of Ernesto Che Guevara, *ed. John Gerassi (New York: Macmillan, 1968). Translation by Fernando Alegría.*

Nevertheless, some groups, whether out of self-interest or in good faith, have claimed to see in our revolutionary war a series of exceptional qualities whose relative importance in the general social and historical context they tend to overstress to the point of making them determining factors. People point out the distinctiveness of the Cuban Revolution when they compare it with the lines of other progressive parties of America, and they affirm, as a consequence, that the forms and the paths of the Cuban Revolution are unique, and that in other American countries the historical transitions will be different.

Admittedly there were exceptions which give the Cuban Revolution its particular characteristics. It seems to be a clearly established fact that in every revolution there are specific factors, but it is not less true that all revolutions will follow certain general laws whose violation is not within the reach of a particular society's possibilities. Let us analyze, then, the factors which constitute the supposed distinctiveness of the Cuban Revolution.

The first and possibly the most important and original factor is Fidel Castro Ruz, whose name in but a few years has reached historical proportions. The future will provide the definitive appraisal of our Prime Minister's merits, but to us, his contemporaries, he is comparable to Latin America's greatest historical figures. Fidel is a man of such great personal qualities that in whatever movement he participates he takes command. In effect this is what he had done throughout his career, from his student days to the premiership of our country and to the position of spokesman for the oppressed peoples of America. He has the qualities of a great leader which, when added to his audacity, strength, courage, and untiring perseverance in discovering the will of the people, have taken him to the place of honor and personal sacrifice which he occupies today. He has other important qualities, such as a capacity to assimilate knowledge and experiences quickly, to understand the totality of a given situation without losing sight of details, an unbounded faith in the future, and a breadth of vision which allows him to see further and more accurately into the future than his comrades. With these qualities, with his capacity to unite, to oppose debilitating divisions, to lead all the actions of the people, with his love of the people, his faith in the future, and his capacity to predict it, Fidel Castro did more than anyone else in Cuba to create out of nothingness the formidable apparatus which today is the Cuban Revolution.

Nevertheless, no one would affirm that in Cuba there were special political or social conditions which differed totally from those in other Latin American countries, or that these differences accounted for the triumph of the Revolution. Neither would one affirm that in spite of these differences Fidel Castro made the Revolution. Fidel, a great and able leader, directed the Revolution in Cuba. He chose the form and the moment by interpreting the profound political undercurrents which pre-disposed and prepared the people for the great leap toward revolutionary paths. There were also certain conditions which were not unique to Cuba, but of which it will be difficult for other people to take advantage, because imperialism, unlike some progressive groups, learns from its mistakes.

The condition we might label exceptional is that North American imperialism was disoriented and failed to fathom the genuinely far-reaching aspects of the Cuban Revolution. This partly explains many of the apparent contradictions of the so-called North American "fourth power." The monopolies, as is common in these cases, began to think of a suc-cessor to Batista precisely because they knew that the people were opposed to him and were looking for a leader of revolutionary mind. What more intelligent stroke than to depose the unserviceable dictator and replace him with the new "boys" who would, in good time, serve the interests of imperialism? Imperialism repeatedly played this card from its continental deck, and lost pitifully. Before our triumph they suspected us, but they did not fear us. When imperialism was ready to react, when it realized that the group of inexperienced young men who marched in triumph through the streets of Havana had a clear view of their political duty and an unrelenting will to fulfill that duty, it was already too late. And thus, in January of 1959, the first social revolution of the Caribbean and the most profound of all the American revolutions was born.

We do not believe one can consider exceptional the fact that the bourgeoisie, or at least a good part of the bourgeoisie, favored the revo-lutionary war against the tyranny at the same time that it supported and promoted movements to find negotiated solutions which would permit them to replace the Batista government with elements disposed to put a brake on the Revolution.

Taking into account the conditions under which the revolutionary war broke out and the complexity of the political tendencies which opposed the tyranny, neither is it exceptional that some big landowning elements adopted a neutral attitude, or at least a nonbelligerent attitude, toward the forces of the insurrection.

It is understandable that the national bourgeoisie, oppressed by im-perialism and by a tyranny whose troops pillaged their holdings, should look with sympathy when the young rebels of the mountains punished the armed servants of imperialism who composed the mercenary army. Thus nonrevolutionary forces aided the coming of revolutionary power.

Analyzing further, we can add another distinctive factor, which is that in the majority of districts of Cuba the peasant had been progres-sively proletarianized by the demands of large-scale, semimechanized, capitalist farming and had entered upon a new level of organization which gave him a greater class consciousness. We should mention this. But we should also point out that in the primary territorial area of the rebel army, made up of the survivors of the destroyed column which made the *Granma* voyage, the peasantry had different social and cultural roots from those found in the areas of large-scale, semimechanized Cuban farming. The Sierra Maestra, which was the scene of the first revolutionary settlement, is a place where the peasants who had fought against the large landholders took refuge. They went there to find a new parcel of land which they snatched from the state or from some voracious landholder in the hope of making a little money. They struggled perpetually against the demands of the soldiers allied to the large landholding power, and their horizon was limited to the hope of securing a property title. The soldier who integrated our first peasant guerrilla army came from the section of this social class which is more aggressive in its love and possession of the land, that is, which is most strongly imbued with petty-bourgeois spirit. The peasant struggles because he wants land for himself, for his children; he wants to till it, to profit from it, and enrich himself through his labor.

Despite his petty-bourgeois spirit, the peasant quickly learns that he cannot satisfy his desire to possess land without first destroying the large landholding system. Radical agrarian reform, the only type which can give land to the peasants, collides directly with the interests of the imperialists, large landholders, and sugar and ranching magnates. The bourgeoisie is afraid of colliding with those interests. The proletariat is not. Thus the process of the Revolution unites the workers and the peasants. The workers support the demands made against the large landholders. The poor peasant, given control of the land, loyally supports revolutionary power and defends it against imperialist and counterrevolutionary enemies. There do not seem to be any other exceptional factors.

On the other hand, we see that there are great and inescapable common denominators in Latin America, and that we cannot say that we have been exempted from any of the related evils which result in the most terrible and permanent of them all: hunger of the people. Large landholding, as a form of primitive exploitation or as the expansion of capitalist monopoly of the land, conforms to the new conditions and becomes allied with imperialism, the form of exploitation and monopolistic capital that goes beyond national boundaries, to create economic colonialism, euphemistically called "underdevelopment," which results in low salaries, underemployment, unemployment, and hunger of the people. All this existed in Cuba.

The objective conditions for the armed struggle are created by the hunger of the people, the reaction to that hunger, the fear induced to suffocate the popular reaction, and the wave of hatred which repression originates. Absent from America are the subjective conditions of which the most important is the consciousness of the possibility of victory by violent means in the face of the imperialist powers and their internal allies. These conditions are created in the process of the armed struggle which progressively clarifies the necessity of the change (and permits one to predict it) and the defeat of the army and its final annihilation by the popular forces (as the necessary condition of any genuine revolution).

The scene of that struggle should be the countryside, with a peasant army pursuing the great objectives for which the peasantry should fight (the first of which is the equitable distribution of land). We will then move to take the cities. Based on the ideological force of the working class, the peasantry of Latin America will provide the great liberation army of the future, as it has already done in Cuba. That army created in the countryside, in which the subjective conditions for the taking of power mature, will proceed to conquer the cities from the outside, uniting itself with the working class, thus increasing its ideological wealth. It will defeat the oppressor army in skirmishes and surprise attacks at the beginning and in major battles at the end, when it has grown to the point where it can abandon its guerrilla form in order to become a large popular army of liberation. The stage for the consolidation of revolutionary power will be the liquidation of the old army.

If all these conditions present in Cuba existed in the rest of the Latin American countries, in other struggles to win power for the dispossessed classes, what would happen? Would it be feasible or not? If it is feasible, would it be easier or more difficult than in Cuba? Let us mention the difficulties which in our view will make the new revolutionary struggles of America harder. There are general difficulties for all the countries and more specific difficulties for some whose level of development or national peculiarities are different. We mentioned at the beginning of this paper that we could consider as exceptional factors the attitude of imperialism, disoriented in the face of the Cuban Revolution, and to a certain extent, the attitude of the national bourgeoisie, also disoriented, even looking sympathetically upon the action of the rebels due to the pressure of imperialism on their interests (a situation which is, indeed, common to all our countries).

This is to say that imperialism has learned well the lesson of Cuba, and that it will not allow itself to be caught by surprise in any of our twenty republics, in any of the colonies that still exist in America. This means that vast popular struggle against powerful invading armies await those who now attempt to violate the peace of the sepulchers, the Roman peace. This is important, because if the Cuban liberation war was difficult, with its two years of continuous struggle, anguish, and instability, infinitely more difficult will be the new battles which await the people in other places in Latin America.

In many countries of America there are objective conflicts between the national bourgeoisies struggling to develop and the imperialism which inundates the markets with its products in order to destroy in unequal competition the national industrialist, as well as other manifestations of struggle for value and wealth. In spite of these conflicts the national bourgeoisies are not capable, in general, of sustaining a consequential struggle against imperialism. They fear the popular revolution more than the sufferings under the oppressive and despotic domination of imperialism, which destroys nationality, affronts patriotic sentiments, and colonizes the economy. The great bourgeoisie openly opposes the revolution and does not hesitate in allying itself with imperialism and landowners to fight against the people and to cut off their access to revolution.

These are the difficulties, which one must add to the usual ones in this type of struggle, under the new conditions of Latin America since the consolidation of the Cuban Revolution. Countries that, although still unable to accomplish an effective industrialization, have developed their light and middle industry or have undergone a process of population concentration in large urban centers, find it more difficult to prepare guerrillas. Moreover, the ideological influence of dense population centers inhibits guerrilla warfare and encourages peacefully organized masses. All this gives rise to a certain "institutionalization," which in more or less "normal" periods makes conditions less harsh than the usual ones inflicted upon the people.

It might even be conceived that a possible quantitative change in the number of revolutionary elements in Congress could one day bring about a qualitative change. Given present conditions, this hope, in our view, is groundless in Latin America. While the possibility is not excluded that change in any country may be initiated through electoral means, the prevalent conditions in Latin America make that possibility remote.

Revolutionaries cannot predict all the tactical variants that may present themselves in the course of the struggle for their liberation. The real capacity of a revolutionary is measured by his being able to find adequate revolutionary tactics to meet each change in the situation—to keep all tactics at hand and to exploit them to the maximum.

ARMANDO HART: OUR HOMELAND IS THE AMERICAS*

THE men who reached our America five centuries ago to conquer the aborigines in the name of a strange religion brought with them the archaic concepts of their own feudal society. They were inspired by

---

* Unsigned position paper (*Informe de la Delegación Cubana a la Primera Conferencia de las OLAS*), prepared for the first OLAS Conference (Havana, July-August 1967) in booklet form and distributed to delegates only; actually written by Armando Hart, member of the Political Bureau and the Central Committee of the Cuban Communist Party. Translation by John Gerassi.

religious fanaticism and the most reactionary ideologies of the time. They were men of iron will, distinguished by an unbridled individualism and a merciless ambition to conquer. Blinded by the insatiable lust for gold that characterized early capitalism, they carried out their inhuman and criminal conquest of the continent.

Their empires spread through our virgin lands and within a few decades they had decimated many aboriginal peoples, had enslaved millions of human beings and had achieved one of the first bloody and cruel exploits of European capitalism which, in the words of Karl Marx, "was born oozing with blood and slime from every pore." Later they had to repopulate the lands in order to guarantee a labor supply. Men and women were brought in chains from Africa and the slave traffic became the most lucrative business of that time.

The descendants of those first Europeans to step on American soil in many cases overcame their prejudices and gave up their reactionary ideas; some of them in fact joined the Indian, Negro slaves, and mulattos as part of the dense mass of our people and suffered with them under colonial exploitation. Beginning with the liberation of Haiti in 1803 and ending for many of them with the Cuban Revolution of 1895. Some of us have not yet succeeded in liquidating the colonial regime: this is the unresolved historical duty that we must all face in the anti-imperialist liberation struggle of Latin America. This is the epic task of our generation to which we shall devote ourselves until the final chapter of victory is written.

In the struggle for liberation, slaves, peasants, progressive intellectuals, and even members of the clergy became leaders of entire peoples. Members of the privileged classes fought alongside the masses. Thousands gave their lives for the ideals they defended. Many heroes of the liberation struggle were men of great culture who had found their inspiration in the literature and philosophy of the bourgeois revolution, and who placed their culture in the service of liberty. On the other hand, the list of illiterate and ill-educated revolutionaries who fill the pages of our history with their immortal deeds is no shorter.

We could give endless examples of how today, in 1967, Latin America is virtually unknown in terms of its history, the richness and depth of its ideas, and the wealth of its potentialities resulting from one fundamental fact: that the extraordinary complexity and the unique nature of class contradictions in this part of the world are richly manifested on ideological, cultural, and political levels. The outside world knows nothing of the inhuman exploitation of our peoples, the diversity of conditions that create class contradictions, the social development of certain sectors of the population, the universal range of our outlook and aspirations, the literary and artistic works we have created. Nor is the true significance and potential of our armed struggle against colonialism recognized.

In taking a look at the fundamentals of our history, let us remember that one hundred and fifty years ago, there were in this part of the world men with continental ideas leading continental armies. They were men who, inspired by the most progressive elements of the liberal bourgeoisie, instigated America's liberation movement before the cycle of bourgeois revolutions had ended in Europe. During the first decades of the past century when many European nations were vacillating between the bourgeois revolution and feudalism, and when internationalist concepts had not assumed the character they have today, there were in Latin America figures such as Simón Bolívar who was simultaneously a military genius, a revolutionary committed to the most progressive program of his time, and a politician of unequaled vision.

The concept of internationalism was very different in those days, as were the popular preoccupations and objectives that led to the liberation of America in the nineteenth century. Nevertheless, in Latin America the struggle was already viewed in terms of the whole continent and its international significance was realized.

There is a further fact of particular importance that is frequently disregarded—that never before has there been such a numerous group of nations, with such large populations and covering such a vast area, which share such similar cultures and interests and have formulated identical anti-imperialist policies. Every single one of us feels that we are a part of our America, for this identity is part of our historic tradition. It has been inherited from our ancestors and defended by our heroes.

It is right that patriots should participate in the independence struggles of other peoples. This is what happened in the United States when Lafayette and Kosciusko, citizens of France and Poland, respectively, took part in the liberation war of the thirteen English colonies.

Today, the revolutionary solidarity among the peoples of America goes deeper than it did in its earlier manifestations because today the continental concept of a single Latin American people has been greatly strengthened. This is the result of a long historical process in which we have all shared and which has been distinguished by exploitation, deceit, oppression, and theft.

The bonds between us are indestructible and exist in the fighting spirit which unifies our peoples together against Yankee imperialism, the robber of our national resources, the intruder who subverts our economy and tramples on our rights.

There are numerous examples of Latin American solidarity.

In his letter from Jamaica (September 6, 1815), Bolívar made an admirable analysis of the American Revolution. He foresaw events that would later take place, he sketched the future of the American nations, and he specified unity as the cornerstone of our strength. Some of these ideas reappeared in the Panama Congress in 1826. An attempt was made at this Congress to examine the need to liberate Cuba and Puerto Rico. Mexico and Colombia were charged with the liberation mission, but the machinations of the United States foiled the attempt. Cuba does not see that attempt as an act of intervention but rather is grateful to the forerunners of its struggle for independence.

The policy of the United States government at the Panama Congress was, and still officially is, one of intervention only in matters concerning the peoples south of the Rio Grande.

Cubans consider Simón Bolívar to be a hero of their own independence struggle and see his actions in terms of revolutionary solidarity. The intervention, then, was by the U.S. government which exerted pressure on a small group of nascent and weak nations against the liberation attempts of an exploited colony which they wanted for themselves. The principles of independence which Bolívar defended for Cuba were not an imposition but rather an expression of solidarity, simply because the aim was to free a people whose happiness was directly bound up with the happiness of other peoples and could be achieved only through a common effort.

These are important chapters in Latin American history and of great significance in the life of the continent. Many historical events confirm our combative solidarity. Let us recall a few of them.

Francisco Miranda, forerunner of Venezuelan independence, treated Spanish America as a single unit in his concept of freedom.

Pétion (Alexander Sabés), President of Haiti, provided Bolívar in 1815 with weapons, money, men, and boats to fight for Venezuelan independence, making the sole proviso that he abolish slavery after his victory.

Antonio José de Sucre, a Venezuelan, put an end to the Spanish domination of the continent when he won the battle of Ayacucho in Peru.

General José de San Martín fought for the independence of Argentina and defeated the Spanish forces at the battle of San Lorenzo. He crossed the Andes and instigated the liberation struggle in Peru, whose independence he proclaimed in 1821.

Antonio José de Irissari, a Guatemalan who joined the struggle for the independence of Chile in the days of the "old fatherland," became supreme leader of that country.

The Chilean government formed a navy to transport San Martín's army to Peru. Chilean and Argentine sailors landed in Caracas and completed the first stage in the liberation of Peru. The second stage was carried out by soldiers from New Granada, Venezuela, and Peru, under the command of Bolívar and Sucre.

Juan Lindo, president of Honduras in 1847, reacted to the invasion of Mexico by the United States by issuing a proclamation to Central Americans in which he urged them to aid the people of Mexico. The proclamation read: "You are our brothers; we share your risks and we have a common fate; we must not remain silent but must assist in some way your honorable struggle."

In 1865 Peru was attacked and the Chincha Islands were occupied by the Spanish. An offensive and defensive alliance was signed between Peru and Chile. The Chilean government and people repudiated the aggression and entered the war against Spain. In 1866, Ecuador and Bolivia joined the Chile-Peru alliance.

In 1869, when Cuba's first War of Independence commenced, the Peruvian government expressed its sympathy with the Cubans who were fighting for their freedom: "The citizens and soldiers who are serving the cause of independence in Cuba will be considered the friends of Peru." The same year, the Peruvian government recognized Cuba's independence and the rebel Cuban government. The Peruvian sailor, Leoncio Prado, while in the service of the Cuban Revolution seized a ship of the Spanish fleet on the high seas. He renamed it *Céspedes* in honor of the Cuban hero and placed it at the disposal of Free Cuba.

Many foreigners demonstrated their solidarity with the struggle for independence by fighting with the American peoples.

General Daniel F. O'Leary, of Irish origin, rose from second lieutenant to general. He was Bolívar's first aide-de-camp and his confidant. Because of the memoirs that he wrote, he is known as "the Liberator's favorite Evangelist."

General William Miller, an Englishman who fought in Peru under the command of San Martín and Bolívar, distinguished himself by his daring in leading the Patriots' Cavalry in the battle of Ayacucho.

Lord Cochrane, a British admiral, was chief of the Chilean squadron. He transported San Martín's army and carried out deeds of extraordinary daring which contributed to the destruction of Spanish naval power in the Pacific.

The Italian Giuseppe Garibaldi fought in Uruguay from 1836 to 1846 in the service of the Montevidean government during the Great War instituted by the Argentinian dictator, Juan Manuel de Rosas, in 1843.

During America's wars of independence, some seven thousand English, French, Scottish, and German men served in the Army of Gran Colombia under Bolívar's command, making an inestimable contribution to the cause of freedom.

At the end of the last century, José Martí developed and acted upon the ideas that Bolívar had outlined eighty years before. Based on the vision of earlier heroes, he portrayed Latin America as one people united by the same historical, political, and economic interests. In the program of the Cuban Revolutionary Party, 1892, Martí stated that the aim of the Revolution "was to win the joint independence of Cuba and Puerto Rico." He saw the achievement of this aim as a chapter in the independence of America. The courage and depth of Martí's concepts are illustrated in the following instances: he utilized the Bolivarian view of Latin America as a single and great nation; he established the struggle for Cuban independence as part of the Latin American Revolution; he analyzed, as nobody had done before, a significant and fundamental factor in the history of mankind—the development of North American society and the dangers entailed in this development for North America and the world. No foreigner ever understood the United States so well or at such an early date. If there are those on other continents who doubt this fact, let them examine the works of this extraordinary man whom we call the Apostle of Cuba. Martí pointed out the dangerous contradictions engendered by imperialist development within the United States: "We love the homeland of Lincoln as much as fear the homeland of Cutting."

Through Martí's penetrating vision the Latin American peoples were warned of the inevitable results of Yankee imperialism, the danger that it presented to their sovereignty and resources, and how Pan-Americanism, created by the United States, had the sole aim of "bringing back the prey in the claws of the thieving falcon." In his articles of 1889 and 1890 which dealt with the first Pan-American Conference in Washington, D.C., he accurately predicted the nature of the association between our Latin republics and the Empire of the North. He summarized his warning in passages such as this: "Only unanimous and courageous action, for which there is still time, can free the Spanish-speaking peoples of America from the restlessness and uncertainty in which they are held *by the confessedly aggressive policies of our ambitious and powerful neighbor in the north* with the possible complicity of the weaker neighboring republics. Such uncertainty is fatal at this stage of our development. The United States has never done anything for Latin America save hinder our growth, as in Panama, or take over our territory as in Mexico, Nicaragua, Santo Domingo, Haiti, and Cuba, threaten to undermine our treaties with the outside world as in Colombia, oblige us—as it does now—to buy what it cannot sell, or join us together in a confederation created *simply to facilitate its own domination over our peoples*." Martí, as the consul from Uruguay, represented that brother people at the Monetary Conference of the American Republics held in 1891. There, in giving his opinion on the North American report concerning the "adoption of a common silver currency by all member governments," he said: "As long as the United States fails to develop a greater knowledge of and respect for Hispano-America . . . how can they invite Hispano-America into a union which will be truly useful and valuable to both parties? How would we benefit from a political and economic union with the United States?"

Martí was fighting not only for Cuba's independence but for that of other peoples as he clearly stated in a letter written the day before he died: "My aim . . . through the independence of Cuba is to halt the extension of the U.S. sphere of influence into the Antilles, before it is too late; to resist their onslaught upon our American lands. Whatever I have done until now, and whatever I shall do in the future, has been directed to that end."

During the nineteenth century, Latin America produced men of genius whose concept of freedom went far beyond the liberation of their own countries and became a historical mission of universal nature. There are few events in the history of humanity that surpass the American liberation movement in ideological depth, combative ability, military experience, or social and political content. The men who participated in this movement were not the random products of their time but accurate interpreters of the will of the people.

Revolutionary solidarity is a universal phenomenon which transcends national boundaries. Generalissimo Máximo Gómez, a Dominican by birth, fought for Cuba's independence for more than thirty years and is recognized as one of the leading figures in Cuban history.

Cubans do not consider it strange that a man born in Argentina, who made humanity his homeland, should have come to fight for Cuban national liberation. He has won a place of honor in the hearts of Cubans and the other peoples of Latin America. His name is known to all of us: Commander Ernesto Che Guevara.

Those who make a careful study of the development of our history in the nineteenth century, those who can interpret and understand what our great have written, will come to the conclusion that America indeed does have a history and that this history is yet to be discovered. One of the undeniable duties of OLAS, as inheritors of the tradition of Bolívar and Martí, is to write the history of America. To tell men and women on every continent that here, in this part of the world, there exist peoples endowed with talent, imagination, and courage that can be of crucial importance for the future of mankind. We who have a scientific concept of history know that together with the outstanding heroes there are thousands upon thousands of other men who fight and suffer; we know that this historical process is the result of social and economic conditions which have determined the existence of such men and the realization of their deeds.

What happened later? After Latin America became independent of the European colonial regime, there was virtually no industrial and technical development of the bourgeois variety and the ownership of the land remained in the hands of a tiny minority of landowners. To a great extent, Latin America inherited from its principal colonial rulers, Spain and Portugal, their forms of exploitation. The decisive force in the struggle for independence was constituted by the unredeemed masses of peasants, slaves, Indians, and manual workers who were the real rank-and-file combatants. During the independence struggle different sectors and social groups emerged in the Americas, each one of which had its own interests.

The struggle for independence was manifested in some countries of Latin America at the same time as the emergence of certain social groups who were fighting for the right to trade in the products of their land. The colonial powers opposed these demands. The landowning classes saw in independence the way to consolidate their political and economic powers. These classes, therefore, although some of their spokesmen were influenced by the most advanced ideas of the liberal bourgeoisie, had no interest in changing the system of exploitation. And they were at that time by definition the classes who owned the means of production. This was the essence of tragedy which awaited Latin America at the moment of winning independence and throughout the subsequent period. In this way, the landowning classes and agrarian bourgeoisie maintained intact the social and economic structures that served to support their interests. It could not have happened any other way.

The change that truly did take place was the liquidation of the power of the old colonial capitalists and the political institutions passed into the hands of the agrarian oligarchies. The gigantic movement against colonial power in Latin America did not represent, therefore, a change in the system of land ownership which remained in the hands of a small group of *latifundistas*. On the other hand, the thirteen colonies of North America were in a very different situation, because they were undergoing a dynamic process of bourgeois development with its corresponding technical level. The social system that predominated in England before the independence of the United States was much more advanced than that of Spain and Portugal. The bourgeois revolution of the seventeenth century and the Industrial Revolution had already taken place in Great Britain. The thirteen North American colonies were therefore founded and organized on the basis of the capitalist system of production.

The process which could have led in Latin America to a full and independent development (and therefore to the formation of a strong national bourgeoisie) was held back. The chance for unrestrained and independent capitalist development was frustrated in several ways: in the first place, by the existence of an agrarian oligarchy of landowners who were virtually the absolute masters of the basic means of production —lands and markets; in the second place, by the appearance on the continent first of English commercial capitalism and later of North American imperialism which paralyzed economic development at precisely the time when conditions favorable to the growth of a strong national bourgeoisie might have been created.

It is well known that the development of the bourgeoisie as an independent and powerful social class is intimately related to the disintegration of the landowning monopoly with the resulting growth of agricultural production and the nation's internal market. This has proved to be an impossible task for the Latin American bourgeoisie not only for the reasons mentioned above but due to something more profound—the fact that in the majority of Latin American nations the interests of the landowners and of the parasitic proimperialist bourgeoisie are extremely closely linked and interdependent. Under these conditions, it would be naïve to expect independent actions on the part of the so-called Latin American bourgeoisie.

The revolutionary ideals which inspired the struggle for independence were never realized. The monopoly on the ownership of the land remained intact in almost every single Latin American country. A slavelike form of exploitation of human labor survived, land ownership remained in the hands of an insignificant minority of large property-holders, and there was only the beginning of the formation of a nascent agrarian bourgeoisie. On the basis of such an impoverished system of social and economic organization, it was impossible to unite against the brutal assault of universal imperialist expansion.

The Latin American bourgeoisie, unable to effect changes in the system of land ownership, and unable to stand up to imperialism, joined their interests to those of the landowners and the foreign monopolies to whom they subordinated themselves both economically and politically. In this way, there arose a strong oligarchy of landholders and bourgeoisie who served as the agents of imperialism. This oligarchy controls the professional army over which large landowners and large foreign monopolies exert a decisive influence. A typical example of such a group is the Somoza family of Nicaragua.

All of this contributed to the underdevelopment of the nations of our America, which persists in our own time.

By wielding their power, North American imperialists have exploited the great natural resources of Latin America. An example of this is their almost absolute control of the minerals that constitute the principal and almost the only source of income for certain countries; their almost exclusive control of markets through their great financial consortiums; the constant pressure they exert on Latin American peoples through the system of prices of goods manufactured in the United States and sold in Latin America; and the agricultural and mineral products that they buy.

The imperialists are a constant drain on our economy because they control the channels of these imports and exports. If we add to this list the interest they receive through their control of the banking system and their loans for agricultural and industrial production, their control of the mass media, the profits accruing to the great service enterprises, the direct exploitation of great tracts of land, and their ownership of the principal industries, we will have a clear idea of the complete submission into which Latin America has sunk.

Of all the continents, our America has some of the largest deposits of natural resources. It possesses within the capitalist world 16 percent of the tin, zinc, and lead reserves; 20 percent of manganese reserves; 33 percent of copper, nickel, and iron ore; 25 percent of cobalt and graphite; 50 percent of vanadium, beryllium, and sulphur; 12 percent of the known reserves of petroleum; and much more. In spite of this, our nations have not managed to free themselves from underdevelopment, much less begin the process of independent growth which would transform them into nations with a reasonable level of industrial and agricultural production. The economic situation of Latin America shows such dramatic symptoms that the Director of the U.N. Special Fund deemed it necessary to designate the entire group of nations as "poor." The real cause of our economic backwardness lies in the penetration and exploitation of our economies by foreign capital. Among the underdeveloped regions of the world, Latin America has the dubious distinction of occupying first place for the volume of North American capital invested in its territory. For the year 1960, this region supplied more than 60 percent of all North American imports of crude oil; 100 percent of their bananas; 87 per cent of their coffee; 73 percent of their sugar; 83 percent of their molasses; 50 percent of their cocoa; 45 percent of their vegetables, etc., etc. Besides these, it provided 40 percent of all the strategic metals imported by the United States.

Imperialism's direct investments in Latin America for the period from 1956 to 1965 reached the sum of $2.898 billion, which yielded profits amounting to $7.441 billion. That is, the Yankee monopoly corporations drew from the continent in the years 1956–65 in the form of profits yielded by their direct investments riches with a net value of $4.548 billion; for every dollar invested, the United States has drawn almost three from our countries. And we must not forget that these are the official figures supplied by the U.S. Department of Commerce itself which do not include what Latin America pays in exorbitant interest for the loans they have received; nor does it include the profits earned by North American capital "associated" with national capital; nor the profits they accrue through their manipulation of invoice prices. The United States annually carries off more than $2 billion in *declared* profits.

It is not difficult to imagine what those investments and control of resources represent in terms of political power within each one of our countries.

These investments are concentrated fundamentally within the mining branches which receive 12 percent of the total investments; petroleum, 32 percent; commerce, 11 percent; manufactured goods, 29 percent.

Investments in the latter section are aimed mostly at light industry with the ultimate intention of taking over the internal markets of Latin America. All of this means that the Latin American economy is an extension of the United States economy. Those branches of national capital that could offer a certain amount of competition to North American products either stagnate or else disappear completely. National capital is basically restricted to the spheres of trade and manufacture which have been entirely subordinated to the interests of the foreign monopoly consortiums.

It must also be noted that the industries depend technically and for their spare parts on factories within the United States itself. There exists a technological control that ties the industrial production of every country to the large factories within the United States. This obliges them to get their spare parts and technical assistance from the colonialists and increases the dependence of the puppet oligarchy on foreign monopoly interests.

As a result, the ruin of our national industries which cannot function at competitive levels, the manipulation of the economy, and the chronic deficit in the balance of payments. In analyzing how this domination of the Latin American economy is achieved by foreign monopolies, we have found the following facts in some of the principal sectors.

Agriculture: Although North American investments in this sector are relatively small, hovering between 8 and 10 percent of the total, this does not imply a lesser control, since in this area, thanks to the low salaries paid out to large-scale production, very high profits are yielded without the need for large capital investments.

Mining: In 1960, the mining industry of Latin America supplied to the capitalist world 34 percent of the production of antimonyl; 40 percent of silver; 16 percent of tin; 14 percent of lead; 13 percent of mercury; 10 percent of nickel, etc. This fabulous mineral wealth is lost to us because the mining and preparation are controlled by the large North American corporations. Of the 586,600 tons of copper produced in Chile, 90 percent is controlled by three U.S. corporations.

Petroleum: Oil is the principal sphere for the investment of North American capital in Latin America. In 1965, 32.4 percent of all the direct North American investments were in this area, while almost half of the total profits collected by the monopolies in this region during the last few years have come from this industry. The great monopoly corporations control production, refining, and selling, and share the Latin American market with a great international cartel directed by the Standard Oil Company and Royal Dutch Shell which appear under different names in various countries. The daily extraction of petroleum by the enterprises affiliated with Standard Oil of Latin America is higher than in the United States itself. The level of extraction from North American deposits is kept at a low level for practical purposes, to keep them in reserve, while the oil resources of the underdeveloped countries, especially in Latin America and the Near East, are being exhausted at a rapid rate.

In Venezuela, 87 percent of the extraction and refining of oil is under the control of three foreign companies The Creole Petroleum Company [or simply the Creole Corporation], a subsidiary of the Standard Oil Company, by itself controls 40 percent of the entire extraction and refining of petroleum. Such is the voracity of these monopolies that it is calculated that at the present level of extraction, the known geological reserves of petroleum will last only another fourteen years.

Banking: Of the 132 banking branches that the United States had abroad at the beginning of 1960, 69 of them were in Latin America. Of this total, the First National City Bank of New York had 36 branches; the Chase Manhattan Bank, of the Rockefeller group, had 12; the First National Bank of Boston had 6, scattered among various countries. These North American banks, in which are concentrated a considerable and at times predominant part of all the deposits and banking credits of Latin America, practically dictate the credit and financial policies of our countries.

The political submission of the Latin American countries is so great that the Yankee corporations carry out their financial transactions with the national capital deposited in the banks in the same country where they are located.

North American imperialism's sack of our peoples is expressed in two ways, one of them clearly apparent and the other indirect. The latter arises fundamentally from *exchange*—"effects of losses due to deterioration in prices." It consists of continually increasing the prices of products bought by Latin America and steadily decreasing the prices of the goods she sells. The result is a constant reduction in the buying power of Latin American exports. That is, our nations must make steady increases in the volume of their export products in order to receive in return the same or smaller volume of imported goods. The losses due to this process amounted to $13.296 billion for the period between 1955 and 1965.

The former more apparent method stems from the payment to agents who convert the "gross internal product" into the "gross national product," whereby profits leave the country in the form of foreign investments. There are other methods: the "gold reserve" and the "foreign public debt," which between them cost Latin America $14.564 billion in the period between 1955 and 1965. The foreign debt for that period increased from $4.046 billion to $10.6 billion.

In six Latin American countries it must be noted that more than three-quarters of the urban population saw their cost of living increase by more than eighteen times in the last ten years. The constant increase in prices has been an inevitable side effect of the inflationary process which so many Latin American countries suffer. The most serious situation was in Brazil, which during the above period saw food prices multiply thirty-sevenfold in only eight years; clothing and shoes, as well as housing, more than fifteenfold. The cost of living was twenty-eight times higher in 1964 than in 1956.

In absolute terms, the wages in Latin America are incredibly low. Hourly salaries, in terms of dollars, amount to 32 cents an hour in Argentina; 28 cents in Brazil; 18 cents in Costa Rica; 17 cents in Colombia; 10 cents in Guatemala; the reduction in actual salaries is reflected in the extremely low living standards of the people, principally in their food, housing, and social security. Latin America's population, excluding Cuba, in 1966 reached the figure of 243,127,000 (32.45 percent higher than in 1956), which means that the population has increased at a cumulative annual rate of 2.9 percent; a growth rate much higher than the world average of 1.8 percent.

It is clear that the Latin American bourgeoisie constitute an extension or satellite of North American imperialism. And it is also clear that the Latin American bourgeoisie has contradictions with Yankee imperialism. But because the bourgeoisie finds itself in a completely subordinate and dependent position, it is unable to confront and challenge the imperialists. Its position is reflected in the political, juridical, and social institutions of the continent which are extremely weak.

Because of the political instability of the government and institutions since the days of independence, the professional armies have come to possess great power. The bourgeoisie through its weak position has not been able to organize—as was possible in the United States and Europe —strong civil institutions. In this way the professional armies have become the most important political weapon of the oligarchies, and sometimes the only weapon. Whereas in most developed capitalist countries, the power of the army is limited by civil institutions, on our continent the army represents a force that intervenes directly and constantly in basic political decision-making and continues to defend the most reactionary interests of the oligarchies and imperialism. This can be seen in the numerous coups d'état suffered by Latin America whenever the oligarchies and imperialism have been threatened. The progressive ideas of our liberators have never been practiced because they do not correspond to the interests of the class which owns the means of production.

The impotence of the bourgeoisie has created a feeling of frustration which influences their behavior and culture. This must be kept in mind when we review the role of the bourgeoisie in the Latin American liberation struggle which is already in progress. Our countries are said to be politically independent, but we are not; we live under a system of neo-colonialism and our independence is an illusion.

During the OAS meetings at Punta del Este in 1961 and 1962, the submission of the puppet governments could be seen quite clearly and was expressed in official form. Diplomatic relations with Cuba were broken off by the puppet governments on the order from Washington and with the approval of the so-called "Alliance for Progress."

The principles of free trade and freedom of the seas were upheld and defended by the bourgeoisie when they were a revolutionary and progressive force several centuries ago. But imperialism, monopoly capitalism, and neo-colonialism deny the very origin of the bourgeois system in their violations of such principles. Certain European countries have rejected U.S. policy in this area but essentially this is due to the fact that European capitalist countries need to seek new markets for their goods. If these countries supported the blockade, their business interests would be seriously affected. This trade with the capitalist countries of Europe allows us to acquire important means of production. That is, this is a trade in which Cuba receives machines and farm equipment to increase the development of its economy. And what Europe wants from Cuba is agricultural and food products. This kind of exchange is extraordinarily favorable to our peoples.

It is in this area that the puppet governments are revealed in their true colors, because they have no independent trade or foreign policies but simply support the imperialist line. The puppet governments are *gorila*,[1] reformist, and proimperialist, and the weaknesses of the bourgeoisie are now aggravated because internally they must confront the growing demands of the workers, the peasants, and the immense mass of the unemployed and underemployed (almost the entire population of Latin America); a situation they are incapable of solving by themselves. Confronted by the growth of the revolutionary movement in Latin America, they see in the support, alliance, and intervention by imperialism the best guarantee for their own survival and the only power able to defend their interests. Any analysis of their political position and future possibilities must be based on an awareness of these factors. The Latin American so-called bourgeoisie is incapable of assuming a position independent of the rest of the oligarchy and of imperialism. If they were to do this, they would have to join the masses of workers who represent a great potential revolutionary force and who would demand even more radical change.

As we have already mentioned, in almost every one of our countries the latifundio system of land ownership has remained unchanged. Nevertheless, it cannot be denied that there has been a real growth of a capitalist, urban, commercial, and, in certain ways, industrial nature, but one that is essentially subordinated to the interests of the foreign monopolies.

This capitalist growth in certain areas had engendered a proletariat with a class consciousness so that alongside the survival of the latifundio and the oligarchy, there has also grown up a populous working class. In the same way, large middle sectors have been developing. Sections of the middle sectors have taken a progressive and revolutionary position and they subscribe to the national and continental patriotic tradition of past centuries. It would be absurd to characterize the middle sectors with the same terms used in referring to the European petty bourgeoisie. Some sectors of the Latin American middle classes are much closer to the interests of the exploited masses than to those of the oligarchy. In short, there exists on the continent, in the first place, the oligarchy, made up of the landowners as well as the highest levels of the commercial

[1] Latin American term for military or promilitary leaders who obey Washington's dictates.—*Ed.*

and industrial bourgeoisie. In the second place, there exists the working class in the cities and the giant mass of workers in the countryside, who in many cases live under feudal conditions; to these must be added the other sectors of the rural population, the unemployed, and the under-employed. All these social groups form different classes and levels which have as a common denominator the exploitation they suffer, the misery in which they live, and the terrible backwardness of their environment.

To the sharp nature of class contradiction is added the fact of an ideological and cultural development among the proletariat and certain sectors of the middle classes in some urban centers, many of whom sub-scribe to the most radical revolutionary ideas. Large sectors of the student population and the Latin American intelligentsia subscribe to the com-munist line or at least to leftist thought in general. These great masses, although still without a clear strategy, can acquire a high level of revolu-tionary training and preparedness. In the same way in which the con-tradictions among the various oligarchic groups on the continent are transcended and a common struggle unites them against the Revolution, so the different popular classes are integrating in their fight against the oligarchies and imperialism.

In the final analysis, class contradictions are polarized, are placed at two poles: on one side the working people, the small farmers, certain sectors of the middle classes, the intelligentsia, and students; on the other, the native oligarchy—the bourgeoisie and the landowners. In this way there unfolds on the Latin American continent the complex pattern of the class struggle.

In Latin America the conditions exist for making the Revolution. It is necessary to clarify what we mean by this. Apparently, according to the Leninist definition, such conditions do not exist at present on our continent. But we are focusing on a problem different from the one confronting Lenin. What we are asserting is: *In Latin America there exists a situation that favors the advancement of the guerrilla war, as well as the organization of a popular army which would develop a war of this nature and which would provoke a disintegration of the army of the oligarchy and the puppet governments*, and would later lead to the destruction of oligarchic power and the creation of revolutionary power.

The conditions for beginning and developing that war exist because in the countryside there are large groups of unemployed and underemployed and an immense mass of people who live under a regime of semifeudal exploitation. The concentration of the ownership of the land has reached the point where about 1 percent of the landowners hold 62.5 percent of the land, under the system of private property. This is the continental average. The great latifundios continue to survive. Only a tiny portion of the land is under cultivation. In the cities, the majority of the popu-lation live in miserable conditions alongside the mansions and incredible riches of the large landowners and of a commercial and therefore parasitic bourgeoisie.

The so-called shanty towns of the poor on the outskirts of the cities hold about 40 percent of the population; their misery is surpassed only in the rural zones, which are illiterate and lack the most basic benefits of civilization. The process of urbanization of the population in Latin America is reaching extraordinary dimensions. This is not determined by the development of industry, but rather by the conditions of misery, hunger, and malnutrition that are found in the countryside. Thus the problems of the urban areas principally exist in the sphere of housing and food.

On the other hand, *capitalist development has been creating in certain areas of the continent a proletariat with a class consciousness.* Along with this, there exists an *intelligentsia* and especially *a student population with a long combative tradition,* who forcefully subscribe to the most progressive ideas. Furthermore, in the cities themselves and in the countryside, there exist large oppressed middle sectors, who are also demanding social changes. The professional armies, the landlords, and the imperialists complete the portrait of the exploitation of the classes of Latin America. The professional army has become the last bastion of the power of the reactionary classes of imperialism.

But the professional armies do not therefore possess social and political resources to confront the movement of the people. They are corrupted by *caudillismo,* ambition, and a profound moral disintegration. This moral corruption is also found among the exploitive classes in general, in the wealthy upper classes that control the state. This makes them extremely weak in confronting the assaults of the people.

The professional armies and repressive police, with no moral and ideological values, have to confront the armed movement of the peasants, workers, and students, who are fighting for an ideal and for clear and well-defined class interests. Moral strength, the spirit of sacrifice, and historical tradition are all on our side. The oligarchies and imperialism must resort to brute force, to police and military violence and repression, which all contribute to the development of a combative consciousness and make us fully understand the road to Revolution. They show the necessity of opposing reactionary violence with revolutionary violence. The triumphs of the guerrilla forces are pointing the way to victory.

The conditions in Latin America resemble the feudal latifundio and bourgeois structures that prevailed in Russia and China in the years prior to the Revolution in those countries. There was also a strong working class, with a tradition of struggle, an exploited and combative peasantry, a large political and ideological movement within the progressive intelligentsia and the proletariat. In the particular circumstances of Latin America and bearing in mind the examples of revolution in Cuba, Vietnam, Korea, China, and other underdeveloped countries, it is clear that, when one speaks of "conditions," one is speaking of the existence of conditions for developing the armed struggle and, through that, for later reaching what Lenin would call "a revolutionary situation" resulting in the people taking power. The conditions within the majority of the countries of this continent are ripe for that task to begin, led by a revolutionary vanguard forged in the mountains and firmly linked to the peasant and labor masses. A political vanguard created with a daring, revolutionary, determined, and brave leadership can and must turn itself into the center of leadership for a mass movement whose ideological, organizational, and political range will be decisive.

In this way, the armed struggle turns the guerrilla into the political vanguard of all the exploited masses who are firmly opposed to the oligarchic forces of the continent, specifically, to the professional armies.

In 1958, the gross national product increased in relation to 1957 by 4.5 percent. In 1966, it increased in relation to 1965 by 3 percent. All of which shows a collapse of the "growth of the gross national product." In 1958, the population of Latin America increased in relation to the previous year by 2.9 percent. In 1966, it increased by 2.9 percent in relation to 1965. The population of Latin America has grown from 1958 to 1966 by 60,200,000 inhabitants, and the growth of the gross national product has decreased. This means that with an additional 60,200,000 inhabitants, Latin America has a smaller growth of the gross national product than in 1957.

On the continent as a whole, 105 million receive a per-capita income of $8.76 per month, 94 million receive $31.10 per month. According to CEPAL,[2] 4 million, considered the highest salaried, receive on the average $259 per month. That is, the 4 million declared by CEPAL to be the highest salaried receive 30 times more than 100 million on the lowest rung of the scale. Therefore, if the analysis were made by employing smaller groups of people, the inequality of income would seem much greater. It is evident, for example, that in Latin America 4 million people do not receive the $259 per month to which CEPAL refers. CEPAL has not made calculations for smaller groups of people. But in any form, the inequality and injustice cannot be hidden.

The situation cannot be resolved except by a radical change in the system of land ownership, and by a rapid development of agriculture, based on the training of thousands of technicians, the use of machines, and the raising of the cultural level of the entire population. It would be impossible to emerge from this backwardness and underdevelopment without first meeting the following conditions:

Liquidation of the latifundios.

Nationalization of the holdings of foreign monopolies.

[2] In English, ECLA: Economic Commission on Latin America, a U.N. regional agency.—*Ed.*

Guaranteeing a stable, secure, and just regime.

Raising the cultural level of the masses and development of broad agricultural and industrial sectors.

Latin America is centuries behind, and it must accomplish in a few years what it could not do in 150 years of formal democracy. "Good intentions," "plans," and words do not suffice. Nobody in their right mind could believe that all of this could be accomplished through simple changes or reforms. Something else is called for: a true Revolution which would confront the latifundio owners, the native oligarchies, the puppet administrators, the bourgeoisie, *and* imperialism.

The bourgeoisie cannot lead a Revolution that promises to change completely the economic and political structures of our countries, to win back our sovereignty and, very fundamentally, to abolish the present exploitation of land. But we must consider what role the bourgeoisie will play in the realization of the Revolution. If we remember that it has remained subordinate to imperialist interests and that its own interests have become merged with those of the Latin American landowning classes, we will know that it could never be expected to lead a movement for agrarian reform, national independence, and freedom from imperialism. Its weakness and inefficacy to produce change are demonstrated, for example, in the case of the land reforms recently proposed by João Goulart's government in Brazil. The people were sympathetic to these reforms but the North American monopolies, in alliance with the land-owning oligarchies and with the support of the professional army, defeated Goulart and prevented the implementation of the reforms. In Chile, a further example is provided: the president gained office under a reformist banner but has been unable to effect any changes in the existing system because of the interdependence of the landowning and oligarchic circles of the country.

Nevertheless, sectors of the so-called Latin American bourgeoisie, which are all linked in some way with imperialism, could aid—once united—the national liberation movements. They would not play a leading role. Whatever role they would play would be determined in the last instance by national conditions, local circumstances, by the links that they have with imperialism, by the level of political and ideological development and patriotic feeling of the leadership, and by the policy that the anti-imperialist parties and organization follow within these sectors. It would be sectarian and dogmatic to say that no sector of the bourgeoisie could play a role in the Latin American struggle against imperialism, but it would also be a political error to overestimate their part, an error which would entail making concessions which would weaken the revolutionary movement considerably.

The intransigence that we must maintain in dealing with our irreconcilable class enemies must correspond to a strong determination and political talent, to a broad and antisectarian position, when we analyze the different levels and sectors of the working class and bourgeoisie, peasants, workers, students, and intellectuals who are joining the revolutionary struggle. In Latin America the bourgeois revolution has never taken place. And it will not take place—ever. But this flat statement is made in continental terms, without ignoring the fact that in particular countries certain sectors of the bourgeoisie can play a part of great historic and political importance.

The most the bourgeoisie can offer is a pseudoreformist like Frei. And when a bourgeois leader tries to do something more, there happens to him what happened to Goulart in Brazil. Even if we supposed that there were sectors of the bourgeoisie capable of playing an anti-imperialist role, we would have to call them exceptions. And therefore, one does not elaborate a revolutionary strategy on the basis of such exceptions, although it is true that in certain countries and under certain conditions these exceptions must be taken very much into consideration.

If we analyzed from a chronological and traditional point of view the most pressing task in Latin America, it would be the agrarian revolution. According to the traditional models, the bourgeoisie should take an interest in it and support it, but we are talking about the anti-imperialist agrarian revolution and the bourgeoisie cannot compromise in an anti-imperialist undertaking its most important interests as an exploitive class.

On our continent, there will only be a single revolution of oppressed people which will continue until it has become a socialist revolution.

Along with this revolutionary stance, there are *reactionary positions* which, like the two sides of a single coin, at times appear under the deceitful masks of reformism and at times without the mask as the stark reality of *gorila* regimes, oligarchies, the Pentagon, or the Department of State. The reformist position is identical to that adopted by some of the most alert and advanced sectors of imperialism.

The imperialist rulers of the United States recognize that an explosive and revolutionary situation exists in Latin America. Some of them have suggested structural reforms in the system of land ownership and large Yankee investments in Latin America to pull it out of economic stagnation. This formula, suggested by Senator Robert Kennedy and Senator Fulbright, is aimed at sidetracking or stopping the advance of the social revolution. Those who propose this thesis accept the fact that in Latin America revolution is inevitable and in response they have stated: "The only thing the United States can do is change the nature of that revolution."

The so-called "Alliance for Progress," created in 1961, was the imperialist formula for solving the revolutionary situation of the continent. In essence, its aim was to produce certain changes in the landowning system for the benefit of the members of the national bourgeoisie and to increase imperialist investments in these countries. It was a conciliatory formula, aimed at increasing imperialist investments in the Latin American countries in order to further subordinate imperialism's Latin American allies, all of which further aggravated the situation of subservience and surrender.

These investments were not meant to stimulate an independent economic development; rather they were only applied in those sectors of the economy where they would produce a greater submission to foreign monopoly interests.

The economic strengthening of the bourgeois groups would simply increase their dependence and would not bring about the smallest change in the structure of the ruling classes. Structural reforms in the system of land ownership would clash with the fact that the interests of the sell-out bourgeoisie are to a great extent linked to those of the large landowners. In many cases, the land is the property of a few and its exploitation is carried out under the system of wage labor for which there have been created large groups of agricultural laborers. The foreign monopolies themselves have economic interests that are tied to those of the national bourgeois groups. For this reason, a change in the system of land owner-ship cannot be made without the social revolution first taking place.

The single act of expropriating the landowners would constitute a social revolution. They hold tremendous power in Latin America. They will not let their holdings be taken away without putting up violent resistance. They will especially use their strong influence in the profes-sional armies. Furthermore, in order to emerge from underdevelopment in a short time, it is necessary to mobilize a great number of economic resources as only a radical revolution can do. The resources that might have come by way of loans and new imperialist investments—besides not being directed to vital areas of developments—could never be enough to assure the leap toward progress: in the first place, because the profits from such investments would end up abroad and in the hands of a few native bourgeois, and in the second place, to pull Latin America out of underdevelopment would be beyond the resources of U.S. private investors.

Twenty or thirty years ago these imperialist positions might have held back the Revolution. Today, the strengthening of the bourgeois groups and of the national oligarchies is totally ineffectual given the explosively revolutionary situation on the continent. The fact that some sectors of imperialism have suggested this formula is an indication of the strength of the Revolution. The imperialists possess a powerful class instinct; they know what they are doing and why. That class instinct has taught them that with the victory of the Cuban Revolution, a new chapter in Latin American history was opened. It was for this reason that certain im-perialist sectors began to suggest the need for social reform. It must be remembered that this attack of conscience took place after the triumph of the Cuban Revolution and with the rise of the revolutionary movement in the past several years.

The history of the anticolonialist struggle shows that with the advance of revolutionary movements there begin to emerge with the colonial regime certain currents attempting to find formulae to protect their interests by accepting selected social and political changes. This is an attempt to sidetrack the Revolution. What we revolutionaries must learn from it is to see the suggestion of such reforms in their true light and remember that we shall advance and grow strong until we liquidate imperialism completely. The conditions exist for the people's army to gain victory over the army of the oligarchies. First, the puppet governments of Latin America and the professional armies in their service are totally unable, in the majority of our countries, to confront the revolutionary actions of a popular army efficiently led and oriented with a political and revolutionary line. Second, imperialism does not have the military, economic, and political strength to resist the joint assault of the Latin American armies of liberation.

Our confidence in the victory of the peoples of Latin America is based on *the experience of the struggle against the system of colonial, neocolonial, and imperialist exploitation, which is showing us that when the people have decided to fight, and have at their head a daring, able, and firm leadership, they are already assured of victory. A whole chain of examples in Asia, Africa, and Latin America confirms this statement. The neo-colonial and imperialist system which the peoples of Latin America suffer will be defeated by the same political, economic, and social forces that defeated the colonial system, and by forces similar to those which destroyed the imperialist system itself in a whole series of underdeveloped countries.*

This may be confirmed by the historical experiences of the Cuban Revolution, and we could prove it irrefutably if we consider the situation that would arise for the puppet governments and their professional armies in Latin America when the revolutionary and popular forces gain the power that the national liberation movement in Vietnam has now.

The annual amount spent on military intervention in the United States went from $2.6 billion during 1950–54, to $20 billion during 1966. The entire budget for the United States for the fiscal year 1967–68, is $135 billion; of that budget $25 billion are earmarked for the war in Vietnam, which represents 18.5 percent of the expenses for every branch of the Washington government. Furthermore, the effects of the war in Vietnam are felt in the U.S. economy, which has gradually been transformed into a war economy marked by a sudden increase in military orders and the generation of the resultant tensions in other sectors of the nation's economy. War costs represent a third of the increase in the entire production of the United States for 1966. The war has also increased prices in the areas of supplies, transportation, and storage. Various war needs are purchased abroad, which results in the dwindling of the country's gold reserves, and the resultant inflation and reduction of the dollar's buying power. The impact on the economy is manifested in national life, as demonstrated in labor, peace, and civil rights movements, as well as in the fiscal measures aimed at controlling inflation and increasing taxes.

If a nation like South Vietnam with 170,230 square kilometers and 14,000,000 inhabitants is victoriously confronting imperialism and is resisting that brutal assault, the peoples of Latin America, who number 250,000,000, can do the same and with much more strength. The Latin American revolutionary combatants are defending their interests and the aspirations of the masses, and they are favored in their struggle by knowledge of the terrain in which they are fighting and because they speak the same language as the people of whom they form a part. The Yankees represent the negation of all these features: They are fighting against popular wishes in defense of monopoly and oligarchic interests; they are ignorant of the feelings of the people and their language also; and they lack moral aims for their fight.

The next imperialist war undertaken by the United States government, unless it is finished forever in Vietnam, will be its last criminal adventure because it will go against the interests of the North American people themselves. It will mobilize universal feeling against it. It will force its former allies to abandon it. And it will stimulate on a continental scale the war of liberation already begun by various peoples of America and the world. The elimination of imperialism's bases of support in Latin America is a decisive contribution toward its destruction and, therefore, an important step in the liberation of the still dependent peoples and the colonies of Asia and Africa. It is also linked to the struggles of the North American people who are daily becoming more aware of the repressive role of Yankee imperialism and who are protesting against the war in Vietnam. It is linked to the struggle of the black people of North America for their rights. And finally, it is linked to every man anywhere in the world who is fighting for his full human dignity.

The success of our struggle depends, in the first place, on our ability to develop the Revolution in every one of our countries: That is, every one of the national revolutionary movements must see their own struggle as part of the continental struggle. In the second place, success depends on our finding the right path and the proper combat methods. And in the third place, success depends on our ability to fight and to lead the political and military activities of the revolutionary movement.

The Cuban Revolution has emphatically defended the need and the possibility of the armed revolutionary struggle. This is our firm conviction and we have thus always lent our support and solidarity to the revolutionary movement on this continent. The imperialists try to call this Cuban intervention. We refute this and maintain that the only interventionists on the continent are the North Americans themselves. The cooperation and solidarity of the Cuban people with other peoples, and their reciprocation, constitute a decisive force against the only true intervention taking place in Latin America: that of Yankee imperialism.

The armed revolutionary struggle must have two major stages: victory over the obligarchy, and the frontal struggle against the direct intervention of imperialism. The former would be relatively easy to achieve because of the weakness, military incompetence of most of the professional armies, and the corruption and political instability of those whom they would serve. We would be facing a more complex situation if the U.S. government intervened militarily in the war of liberation. This would be a crucial moment in our history when the Revolution would acquire with full strength a continental nature which it today possesses only in embryonic form. Military intervention in any one country could achieve a more or less immediate success—experience confirms this—but if it had to be carried out simultaneously in a group of countries, it would not be successful. This is why it becomes important that the combat fronts be multiplied and extended. This is why it is essential that preparation be made for developing simultaneous struggles.

In the past, the isolated movements, independent of each other and with essentially national characteristics, have allowed imperialism to succeed by attacking them one by one. Today, we are working to create a situation in which imperialism and the oligarchies will have to confront, not isolated movements, but rather an entire armed continent.

On the Latin American continent, we all suffer from the same system, and our strategy must therefore be continental. This is also dictated by our historical, political, and cultural traditions which reveal Latin America as a single unit.

To determine our strategy we must determine our revolutionary priorities. We must decide upon the most pressing revolutionary tasks.

The conditions of economic and social development in every country have their own peculiarities, and the development of the Revolution in different countries requires a separate analysis for each of them. We cannot elaborate identical forms of struggle for every country, but what we must do now is determine precisely the most advanced form of struggle, the most developed methods, and the fronts and countries where the Revolution can be advanced with greatest force. In certain countries the development of the guerrilla struggle is firmly planted in immediate actions, and in others it appears as a support for the deeds of the people who are fighting.

Peaceful forms of struggle have no revolutionary content if they are not aimed at supporting the armed struggle that is developing in other countries, and the preparation for the inevitable revolutionary confrontation in their own. In this sense, peaceful struggle is correct and well-founded and can help accelerate the Revolution on the continent by preparing the masses for participation. If it has as its aim both revolution and the limitation of violent means in the class struggle, then it still lacks revolutionary content and becomes, on the contrary, a reformist and conciliatory practice.

The peaceful struggle is valuable only where conditions do not exist for the development of armed struggle and where it can help develop those conditions or lend support to the armed movements of other American peoples. If parliaments could be used to spread these principles, to defend people who are fighting with weapons of war, then parliaments would have a certain positive function. But that would be something truly exceptional given the present conditions on the continent.

We Latin American revolutionaries know that the sharp and complex class contradictions cannot be resolved through peaceful means and we value our historical experience. So-called peaceful transition has failed miserably in Latin America and the armed struggle is imposed by constant aggression against us and by the irreconcilable nature of the conflict between the interests of the oppressor and the oppressed. Violence is the midwife of history. There is not a single case in the long history of mankind where revolution succeeded without violence.

Should this revolutionary aspiration be concealed? If we revolutionaries do not speak frankly to the people, the people will think that we are concealing bad intentions. If we do speak clearly to them, they will realize that it is they themselves who must make the Revolution—and they will! A revolution cannot triumph by hiding its aims. The principles of a revolution must always be clearly proclaimed and serve as guidance even if they cannot be translated into immediate action. It is not proper to deceive the people, and it would be naïve to think that we could hide the truth from our class enemy.

Since we believe the revolutionary duty belongs to the present generation of Latin Americans and since we fully understand that our continental mission lies in the destruction of the military, political, and economic power of imperialism and its supporters in Latin America, we must make a careful and precise study of what we should do in terms of a global strategy for the revolutionary struggle. Then we can analyze how that strategy can be applied to the specific conditions of every country. There is a single strategy, but different situations can arise. It is necessary to establish a general strategy, to determine the forms of struggle and the basic channels of the Revolution on a continental scale, and to become aware of what that revolution means and what aims it is pursuing.

The basic scenario in which the vanguard of the revolutionary struggle may develop is not in the city but in the countryside, not in the urban areas but in the mountainous zones. The triumph of the armed revolutionary movement in the cities could only be achieved through the classic model of the European revolution, passing from a general strike or grave political crisis to armed insurrection. Under Latin American conditions, the application of this formula has provided bitter experience for revolutionaries. Apart from the fact that in the last few decades there have been developed modern weapons especially designed to combat popular uprisings, we would have to make the assumption that the oligarchy had gained no experience in this field. This is simply and obviously not true.

Recently, in the Dominican Republic, a movement of political protest became an insurrection in the city. This insurrection was immediately successful and managed to seize power. However, we all know of the events that followed.

The conditions for the revolutionary struggle in the countryside are quite different. There, the organization of the people's armed forces, arising from an embryonic form—the guerrilla—and developing the class struggle within the most dispossessed sectors, can gain all the advantages offered by the enormous stretches of land, geographic features, and the fact that it is much more difficult for the reactionary military forces to fight the guerrillas than to crush a labor strike or student demonstration. Within this strategy, we must decide what are the roles of the peasantry and of the proletariat in light of this revolutionary perspective.

In our analysis of the Latin American peasantry we are dealing with an immense mass of people, grouped into different social levels and groups, all of which are disinherited, miserable, slaves, servants, and workers in the fields. At times they make up a rural petty bourgeoisie, drained and exploited by the great monopoly consortiums. The current ideas applied in the study of the European peasantry would be inappropriate and irrelevant to Latin America where, strictly speaking, we should refer to a "rural population," or an exploited population living in the countryside.

It is sufficient to recall that 80 percent of the Cuban Rebel Army was made up of men of peasant origin: farm workers, smallholders, and unemployed. In Latin America as a whole the rural population throughout all its levels under the same system of exploitation constitutes therefore a revolutionary force of the utmost importance. But this does not mean that the direction of the struggle should not be oriented by a proletariat ideology. On the contrary, the ideas of the proletariat and their best cadres must be at the head of this struggle. *The question is one of a war in the countryside and not of a peasant war.*

As a continental strategy, we must point out that the best and most politically developed cadres of the proletariat will fulfill their revolutionary duty by joining the guerrillas, by placing themselves in the front of the people's army, and by bringing to the peasant mass and the rural dispossessed the message of social and human redemption offered by the

Revolution. Furthermore, the role of the urban workers and of large urban middle sectors is also of great importance as a means of collaborating with the guerrilla fighter, and it will assume, at decisive moments, an outstanding mission within the vanguard.

For their ideological development, for the experience they can bring to the revolutionary movement, the Latin American working class, laborers, urban middle classes, revolutionary intelligentsia, are invaluable. By offering their best cadres to the guerrilla struggle they can bring about a wide and deep mobilization, an effective agitation and propaganda campaign about the aims of the Revolution. Their role must not be analyzed on the basis of different social and political realities. This would be a grave error and if we do not make a correct analysis, we shall be preventing the working class from fulfilling its role as the vanguard.

In Latin America the problem of the role of the working class is essentially different from that treated by Marx and Engels, since, as we have already explained, the bourgeois revolution will never be made in Latin America. Instead, the proletariat and revolutionary cadres of the Left will lead an antifeudal and anti-imperialist revolution and transform it into a socialist revolution. This is how they will fulfill their role on our continent.

It has become clear during these last years that leadership ability has become an invaluable factor. That ability is not limited to the theoretical knowledge of laws that govern historical development, nor to a profound knowledge of social and historical processes. It is very important for the most advanced cadres of the revolutionary movement to broaden their studies and analyses of their problems, but when we speak of leadership ability, we are referring to something ever more essential: That is, the ability to lead the Revolution, and to lead it under the conditions imposed by the course of the people's war. This requires a great practical experience in the military sphere and a great political talent, above all in the proper guidance of the war. Given the conditions in Latin America, it is indispensable to accumulate a wide military experience. On the other hand, it must be pointed out that the liberation armies require a unified political and military leadership involving the same people. Thus in the countries where the armed struggle is developing, the leaders of the war must also be the political leaders.

Political and military leadership must be in the hands of the same people, otherwise the guerrilla fighter can fall into professional militarism and caudillismo which would render totally impossible the advance of the guerrilla war. The vice of military professionalism has a long tradition in Latin America. The vanguard must be among the guerrillas, it must be among the leaders of the war. Historical experience confirms this. Whoever does not accept this completely has failed to understand the historical experience of the Cuban Revolution and the role of the guerrillas in the class struggle. If the guerrilla is the fundamental form that the struggle takes, and if it forms the vanguard, then political leadership should coincide with the leadership of the guerrilla war.

The guerrilla is an instrument for furthering and making violently active the class struggle, not a simple means of pressuring for changes or reforms or of bringing about coups d'état or political changes of lesser importance. The guerrilla's revolutionary nature is dictated by its role as the embryonic form of the popular army and its chance for developing the armed might of the people as well as achieving their immediate political aims: liquidating the army of the oligarchy and replacing it with the armed people.

Where the guerrilla is active, it should direct the policy of carrying out the revolutionary tasks in the various countries. International duties must be subordinated to the realization of the revolutionary tasks of a national nature because only in this way can the Revolution assume an international character. Our principal task, our revolutionary duty in fact, is to make the revolution in those nations where it has not yet been made. In the continental range, the most important obligation is the expression of solidarity with the Cuban Revolution and unreserved support for the armed revolutionary movement. Solidarity with Cuba and aid to the armed revolutionary movement constitute a single idea. Because, in the final analysis, Cuba represents nothing more than the vanguard of that armed movement. Expressing solidarity with Cuba results in solidarity with the whole armed revolutionary movement. Our support is most needed precisely when the movement is in its hardest stage, its struggle against tyranny and the puppet governments.

At the present moment and with a worldwide perspective, the fundamental duty of revolutionaries is to support and assist the struggle of the Vietnamese people. Solidarity with Vietnam obliges us to fulfill our own duties in our own countries. Commander Guevara pointed out the need to create "two, three . . . many Vietnams," and at this meeting we must plan, as the highest synthesis of our revolutionary feelings, the creation of "a gigantic liberation movement in Latin America!"

The analysis of our reality, and the balance of internal and international circumstances in which our struggle is waged, indicate that the triumph of the Latin American Revolution is inevitable. It is a struggle which involves, without exception, the workers of every country, and which has a special meaning for the peoples of Africa and of Asia, whose interests are closely linked to those of America.

Our ideas and goals are not concerned with conquest, but with social and human liberation—and because the ideas that guide this struggle are inspired by the most advanced scientific, philosophical, and political concepts; and because those ideas are a response to the interests of the revolutionary proletariat of the entire world; and because the peoples of

Latin America have sufficient strength, energy, and talent to take the successful road to revolution; and because the liquidation of imperialism constitutes an extremely important and world-historical task; and because this struggle is a factor of transcendental significance in the march of humanity toward the elimination of every form of exploitation of man by man; and because the class battles that the peoples of Latin America are launching against their enemies will make possible a higher development in science, technology, and culture; and because this is the only way to achieve the total liberation of our peoples and a stable and permanent peace; and because this constitutes an undeniable right for millions of men and women who live in the most frightful misery, who are victims of ignorance, lack of culture, and exploitation; and because it contributes to the better future of all mankind—we declare that our struggle merits and will receive the respect and unreserved support of all progressive men and all the clear and revolutionary consciences of the world.

The hour of revolution has struck—the hour for Latin America's second and final independence. This time we shall decide, in the jungles, in the mountains, in the cities, and in the factories, with rifle in hand, the future of our countries, the future of Latin America. We are part of "that mass of humanity" which, as the Declaration of Havana proclaims, ". . . has said enough, and has begun to move. Marching with giant strides they will not be detained until they have conquered true independence.

"THE DUTY OF EVERY REVOLUTIONARY IS TO MAKE THE REVOLUTION."

Venezuela

The revolutionary struggle in Venezuela has long been both the most serious and the most complicated of South America, the most concerted and the most diffuse, the most successful and the least victorious. It has also been the one to attract most international scrutiny—mainly because its ideological disputes have been most public.

The revolutionary forces have certainly been varied—and still are. They include: the Communist Party (CPV), founded in 1931, relatively big (30,000 members), very tough, with a long history of militant and often armed combats, but faithful followers of Moscow; the Movement of the Revolutionary Left (MIR), originally the left wing of the Democratic Action (AD) Party that came to power with the election of Rómulo Betancourt in 1958 but now what is left after the "legalistic" elements (followers of founder Domingo Alberto Rangel) joined with other dissident groups into the Nationalist Integration Revolutionary Party (PRIN); the People's National Vanguard, also composed of dissidents from the 1958 coalition and which also split into "hard" and "soft" elements, the "soft" joining PRIN; dissidents from the Republican Democratic Union (URD) which followed Fabricio Ojeda; and finally, a group of independent students and intellectuals who had neither joined nor opposed the electoral process of 1958 but by 1962 had become unaffiliated revolutionaries. All of these forces, plus elements from AD and COPEI (the Christian Democrats) had participated in the coalition that overthrew the dictatorship of Pérez Jiménez in January 1958.

That coalition, the "Patriotic Council," was headed by Fabricio Ojeda, one of the purest revolutionaries in Venezuela's history. Born in 1929, Ojeda was a student leader at seventeen and a militant in the URD by twenty, being groomed for national prominence by the URD patriarch, Jovito Villalba. One of the main organizers of the Resistance in 1957, Ojeda was, in effect, president of Venezuela at twenty-nine, when Pérez

Jiménez was overthrown. In the subsequent general elections that year, Ojeda was elected to Parliament. But in June 1962, after massive and bloody repressions of leftists by Betancourt had led to two unsuccessful rebellions by left-wing elements in the armed forces (at Carupano and Puerto Cabello), Ojeda resigned his seat and joined the guerrillas, which had just been launched by the MIR. In fear of being left out of the Revolution (as had happened in Cuba), the CPV also joined the guerrilla movement then.

Ojeda was captured in October and condemned to eighteen years in jail. With Luben Petkoff, a long-time communist who had taken up arms, Ojeda escaped from prison in September 1963, rejoined the guerrillas, and was soon chosen president of the National Liberation Front (FLN), which was meant to encompass all guerrilla groups (and which it did when the MIR agreed to join the combined command). On June 17, 1966 (a few days after he wrote the letter read by Fidel Castro in his March 13, 1967, speech, the third article in this section), Ojeda was betrayed and captured. He was on a mission to try to reconcile the "revolutionaries" and the Communist Party, which was abandoning the armed struggle. Four days later, after extensive tortures by the Armed Forces Intelligence Service (SIFA), he was murdered in jail, so as to conceal his wounds, and declared a suicide.

Ideologically, Ojeda was no Marxist. He believed in the 1961 Constitution, free elections, free speech, and a free economy. A genuine patriot and nationalist, he was shocked at the constantly expanding dependency of Venezuela on U.S. monopolies and finally became convinced that only through armed struggle could U.S. imperialism be chased out of his country. As he fought, he radicalized, and by the time he wrote the booklet included here he was a confirmed revolutionary. Committed to people's war, Ojeda was nevertheless never dogmatic about strategy. He believed that all modes of anti-imperialist struggles were acceptable, that final victory would only come as a result of a popular front which would include all anti-imperiailsts. In effect, he hoped to see a coalition of revolutionaries behave much the way his own Patriotic Council coalition had in 1957–58—except that then the enemy was the dictatorship, now it was the oligarchy-U.S. imperialist alliance. His strategy thus ends up combining that of the CPV (prior to 1965), the Fidelistas, the Maoists, and the revolutionary democrats and nationalists. But the one thing he was absolutely certain of was that the CPV's withdrawal from armed combat was a betrayal.

That withdrawal was caused by two considerations: first, that the FALN (Armed Forces of National Liberation, the armed wing of the FLN) had suffered too many defeats between the years 1962–65 to be successful, at least within the foreseeable future; and second, that guerrilla warfare is meant to be a weapon in the political arsenal of the CPV, hence its use or nonuse is to be dictated by strictly political considerations. Thus, when the CPV Central Committee and Politbureau decided that the party could gain more—in a deal with the government for the release of CPV officials and legalization—by stopping the armed struggle, it saw no reasons not to order a "retrenchment." This is clear from the CPV documents quoted by Fidel below.

But not all communists agreed with such political considerations. Among those who did not were Douglas Bravo and Elías Manuitt Camero, members of the CPV's political bureau. Keeping many of the CPV con-batants with them, they issued the Manifesto of Iracara *(the mountain range in the province of Falcón where their FALN columns were fighting) in March 1966. That manifesto, though never mentioning the CPV Central Committee's "retrenchment" policy—in fact never referring to the CPV at all—simply called on all guerrilla fighters to join into a unified command. Bravo and Manuitt did not even condemn electoral politics, and their emphasis on a united front was very much part of CPV tactics. But they made it absolutely clear that they planned to continue fighting—and why.*

The CPV responded by throwing Bravo, Manuitt, Luben Petkoff, and other unreconstructed communist guerrillas out of the Party. It branded them adventurist, deviationist, anarchist, and denounced the FALN which they headed as "anti-Party" (for there was then still another FALN, the CPV-directed one, led by Medina Silva, a leader of the Puerto Cabello uprising). The CPV went on to criticize every revolutionary who refused to obey Party directives.

The FALN led by Bravo, meanwhile, continued to fight, both in the mountains and, through commandos, in the cities. And when the government forces captured, then murdered, two revolutionary leaders, the Bravo-Manuitt command ordered their commandos to kill in retaliation one of Venezuela's most unpopular officials, Julio Iribarren Borges, director of the hated Social Security agency and a brother of the foreign minister. From Cuba, Manuitt issued a proclamation accepting responsibility for the assassination. From Caracas, the CPV, trying to stick to its new respectable image, condemned the retaliation, all acts of terrorism, and Fidel for supporting Manuitt. That unleashed Fidel.

In his March 13, 1967, speech, one of the most important he has made, Fidel not only condemned the Communist Party of Venezuela, but also every CP which does not fight. With no attempt to create a "theory," he laid down the basis for the so-called Guevarist-Debrayist proposition that revolutionary leaders should be in the hills, not in the cities. He further condemned that CP strategy which uses guerrillas as a tactical weapon, instead of committing itself to armed struggle wholeheartedly. He also blasted Russia for giving aid to the oligarchies (specifically the Colombian) who are at war with revolutionaries. What would the world say if we traded with South Vietnam? he asked.

The Central Committee of the CPV answered Fidel in an open letter published in El Nacional *(Caracas), March 17. It asked Fidel why Cuba traded with Spain and told him, as far as Venezuela is concerned, to mind his own business. On August 10, 1967, at the end of OLAS, Fidel answered the CPV's Central Committee in turn, pointing out that trade with anybody is acceptable but not aid (long-term credits, technical assistance, etc.). He went on to blast the whole Moscowphile Latin American group of communist parties who dogmatically follow peaceful coexistence orders instead of fighting, referring to them as an "international mafia."*

Another letter did not get the attention it merited. That was the Answer to Fidel *written by communist guerrillas (the last article in this section). All of the signatories of this letter had actually fought and, at the time, considered themselves part of the genuine FALN. That they proceeded to lay down their arms and that their commander, Medina Silva, eventually turned himself in to the government should not detract from the value of their main argument. And that was that revolution is not exhibitionism; to fight or not to fight should be an empirical decision, based on a careful analysis of conditions in each country.*

Indeed, the question remains: Is Venezuela ripe for revolution? Only history can be the ultimate judge. But one fact does exist to reinforce Bravo, Manuitt, and the other MIR and communist guerrillas who joined the restructured Unified Command (CUFF) of the FLN-FALN, but then went on to fight each in their own areas. That fact is that despite the ideological disputes, denunciations, and fragmentations, despite the army's massive assault on guerrilla strongholds, despite the rain of napalm and fragmentation bombs, helicopter raids, and brutal police repressions of peasants in guerrilla areas, despite the huge influx of U.S. Ranger and Special Forces "advisers," and despite the recent break between Bravo and Fidel (on the grounds, said Bravo, that Cuba has stopped helping the guerrillas in order to focus on its own material well-being, abandoning its commitment to the "Continental Revolution"), the FLN-FALN is surviving. It even continues to attack.

FABRICIO OJEDA: TOWARD REVOLUTIONARY POWER*

RECENTLY I spoke to a close friend of mine. We discussed at length the current Venezuelan political scene. The arguments he expressed—and I have always considered him to be a revolutionary within his own social

* *Hacia el Poder Revolucionario* (Havana: Instituto del Libro, 1967). Sections were first printed in English in *Latin American Radicalism*, ed. I. L. Horowitz, Josué de Castro, and John Gerassi (New York: Random House, 1969). Translation by Morton Marks and Juan Mechón.

class, the national bourgeoisie—revealed the great need for better understanding of the broad revolutionary problems that affect our country.

I noticed how his whole thought led him, along with reformist politicians, to feelings of fatalism, impotence, and resignation. In his mind there is room only for those ideas and strategies which fall within the framework of traditional politics. For my friend, as well as for all those who think like him, Venezuela and Latin America can change their present situations only in a slow and gradual way, without a head-on collision with oppressive forces. He believes that a struggle should develop, which, through the evolution of the present state, could progressively transform social, economic, and political institutions.

His arguments for this thesis are based upon the tremendous power of imperialism and the oligarchy, whose enormous force would be used against any revolutionary insurgency, or against any government which attempted to alter the present colonial situation.

These fatalistic ideas populate the political thought of whole groups, in important sectors of the colonized, neo-colonial, and dependent world. In Venezuela, this also includes a large part of the working class who are under the influence of déclassé leaders in the service of reaction. The influence of reactionary ideas on the minds of the ruling groups is the logical result of the control that imperialism and the ruling bourgeoisie exercise on all the communications media, which they hold as a consequence of their control of political power.

In the colonized, neo-colonial, and dependent world, imperialism grasps the basic tools for molding mind and consciousness. It owns the press, radio, television, and movies. It has in its service waiters, political leaders, governors, parliaments, historians, sociologists, et al., who, through all their activities, twist events, distort realities and build an artificial world which with the help of the state's coercive apparatus, fills the eyes and ears of the entire nation.

The present colonial regime prevents the free circulation of revolutionary literature and of new ideas in much the same way that the Spanish colonial regime forbade the reading of the French encyclopedists. The closing of book stores such as Magrija and El Siglo was not done as a whim. Neither was the purge of leftist newspaper writers and workers at El Nacional, or the discrimination against scriptwriters and actors in the television and radio companies.

Venezuela's neo-colonial situation creates a state of affairs which many find incomprehensible if they refuse to accept what we really are: a dependent country. They wrack their brains without ever clearly understanding the causes of our political crises, our economic development, our social system. As long as we view our country through a cracked lens, there will be a distorted image, an unreal view whereby events appear as partial, circumstantial, and capricious. This is the case with the great majority of politicians, historians, and sociologists. It was the case with Laureano Villenilla Lanz, the old man with his pessimistic theory of the "necessary gendarme." And it is happening to many who are presently formulating their fatalistic theories concerning the revolutionary transformation of the country, the chance for its liberation, and the erasure of the causes of oppression and misery.

For a long time I shared these ideas. I honestly believed that our country, and others in similar situations in the Western Hemisphere under the domain of the United States, would remain in a situation of dependency. I also believed that, because we were of the same family—the international family—the older brother would not refuse aid to the younger. The older brother would not refuse a generous act, and would instead take the other brothers by the arm and lead them to a higher level, toward a state of full development, which would enable them to have an independent existence. This mental image of mine, which required great personal effort to correct, was molded chiefly by those people for whom, in the desperation of my intellectual and political unease, I felt the greatest admiration. When I was seventeen I joined the URD in Boronó, my hometown, where I had always lived. My joining the party followed an eloquent speech by Jovito Villalba, whom I met that day and for whom I felt deep admiration for his struggles in 1928 and 1936. In 1948, after working for a year as a schoolteacher for the Creole Petroleum Corporation and simultaneously continuing my studies, I got to know Caracas, and turned the dream of every provincial into a reality. I lived for a long time in Caracas in the Urredista National House.

In his desire to aid my political career, Jovito adopted an almost paternal attitude toward me. He recommended many books. The first was Harold Laski's *Introduction to Politics*. He spoke with me almost constantly, as did many of the prominent figures of Urredismo. Little by little they gave me greater responsibilities in public life. My thinking revolved around their advice and the books they put in my hands. For me the world was Jovito's world. I imitated his gestures and even his tone of voice. I repeated as my own, in my first speeches, many of the expressions and phrases that he had made famous.

I had gone to Caracas to continue my studies. I planned to enroll in the National Pedagogic Institute, but politics completely absorbed me. I became enmeshed in its complex theories, with Jovito firmly leading me by the arm. I listened to him discuss geopolitics and Latin America's destiny to be united into one great nation. There are things to be done, he would always say, but not to be discussed. And those things that were in the political sphere could be done only after gaining power. But if they were discussed beforehand, they could never be carried out, because they would be stopped by the powers of reaction.

The URD, he told me, apropos of a speech I had given in Cumaná, would come to power if we did not frighten the bourgeoisie and Americans with radical statements. What you are saying, he added, we will save for when we're in the government. Let's not talk about it now, because if we discuss it, we'll never be able to carry it out.

I timidly accepted the master's admonition, and only recently have I fully understood what it meant. It is the same argument that today is supported by large sectors of the country.

The personal story I have related is not an isolated case. It is the reason why the majority of speechmakers imitate Rómulo Betancourt, or they copy Caldera,[1] and it is the reason why large sections of the population develop their own fatalistic and reformist political notions. Just as my own thought was influenced by the advice and lessons of the Urredista leaders, so too the minds of a great portion of humanity were influenced by the ideologies of imperialism and their agents.

Reactionary ideologists are unceasing in their efforts to fit thought into rigid patterns, within which state violence with its coercive agencies plays a crucial role. They create an artificial world of freedom. Progressive ideas move unimpeded through proper channels. But only in this way, that is, through the proper channels, can one be a revolutionary, and that means revolutionary in a reactionary way. This type of revolutionary accepts the established rules, the imposed limits. Once those channels overflow and everyone is freed of feelings of submission and fatalism, state violence goes into action to defend "freedom."

This is a problem not limited only to Venezuela, nor even to Latin America, as when the Monroe Doctrine was in force. It is a problem for the whole colonized and dependent world. In order to progress and develop, it is necessary to be freed from the economic and political domination that imperialism exercises, as well as from the oligarchic groups that have long controlled the instruments of political power. In Venezuela, power has traditionally been in the hands of a strong and well-organized oligarchy. They are descendants of the Creole nobility that rebelled first against the monopolistic control of the Compañía Guipuzcoana and against the colonial laws of Spain. The obstacles created by Spanish domination to the expansion of the Venezuelan economy, by the need for the Creole families to increase their profits, to join the international market, developed a power-oriented mentality in the leading socioeconomic groups. Since independence was won from Spain, the social composition of the Venezuelan government has been unvaried. Sociologists, historians, and politicians have developed the thesis of military-civilian struggle, in the sense that they represent different sectors. This is in reality a constant struggle between the rising social classes and the reactionary

[1] Betancourt, head of the Democratic Action Party (AD), was president from 1959 to 1964; Rafael Caldera, leader of the Christian Democrats (COPEI), became president in 1969 (in between, AD's Raúl Leoni was president). All three represent the interests of the oligarchy and the national bourgeoisie.—*Ed.*

classes, between the developing and the already consolidated economic groups.

In the independent and developed capitalist countries, the formation of contradictions is different and establishes a different correlation of forces. The principal part of the struggle is between the proletariat and the bourgeoisie, or really, between socialism and capitalism, where the working class is directed toward the conquest of political power and the establishment of a proletariat dictatorship in a transitional stage on the road to communism. Class alliances are formulated in relation to this objective. It is the union of workers, peasants, and certain sectors of the petty bourgeoisie against bourgeois capitalist society. This is not the case in the colonial, neo-colonial, and dependent countries. There, the main struggle is of a different nature: It is that of revolution of national liberation, which greatly widens the area of alliances, the type of state, and the social makeup of the revolutionary government.

Few would dispute the need for a revolutionary transformation of the present Venezuelan situation. My good friend of the agrarian bourgeoisie wouldn't, nor would the groups controlling the political parties. Neither would leading spokesmen for the industrial bourgeoisie; much less the nonreformist leaders of the working class. There is a sort of general consensus among the majority of our people and their political, professional, cultural, and union organizations, concerning the urgency of national liberation. The government itself—Betancourt's and Leoni's—for demagogic reasons—have never stopped talking about their anti-imperialist and antifeudal leanings. It is here that the ideological terrorism of imperialism and its servant classes enters into play. The right of a country to make its own revolution and free itself is undeniable, and the course that the "revolutionary movement" must take is clear.

For a long time we have been reading documents from Venezuelan industry and the political parties. In these, there is established as an urgent need of the country the necessity for a radical transformation of the present political and economic structures, in order to move national development to a higher level. There are concrete suggestions for the radical modification of the present system of landholding and eradication of the landed estate, for enlargement of the consumer market, for the elimination of unemployment, and for the introduction of industrial planning as the primary way of utilizing industrialization as one of the fundamental tools for gaining national economic independence.

The imperialists and those classes who in our country serve them as agents are not blind to reality. The ideologists constantly study the changes that are operating. They know very well that "the sun cannot be hidden with one's finger"; that in the face of concrete and objective facts in Venezuela and Latin America, it is impossible to hide the need for revolutionary transformation.

President Kennedy, in numerous speeches, recognized this need and appealed to progressive "revolutionaries" in Latin America to put the revolution in motion and to develop higher standards of living. To do this, they could depend on the "generous help" of the North American people and government "who view with horror the state of misery in which the greater part of the people of this continent live."

It did not take long for events to catch up with the words of the Yankee president. The course of the "revolution" opened up almost immediately: the revolution of the Alliance for Progress, "which the free peoples have been successfully practicing for four years." This kind of revolution or any other which counts on the prior consent of imperialism and the classes it controls can be realized without utilizing any form of struggle other than the traditional democratic forms. It operates in a gradual manner without disturbing the status quo, without clashing head-on with oppressive forces, and without challenging their sovereignty.

An alternative to passive acceptance of the "sanctioned revolution" (which is only a revolution in the faulty theories of the imperialists) implies a substantial change in the attitude of individuals and groups. The most important thing is to understand exactly the causes of the country's problems. Then one must know the range of conflicting interests and the behavior of each social class toward the whole country. A complete analysis of the situation, combined with the detailed examination of the relationships of national and international forces, determine the characteristics and possibilities of a true revolution.

In Venezuela and other countries, the extent to which the need for revolution becomes apparent to the different national sectors, and the extent to which the people and their revolutionary vanguard throw themselves into the real struggle, is the extent to which the imperialists and other reactionary classes rush to maintain their terrorist control. This is done with threats and shows of force against groups and classes who don't dare to risk what they have gained. The recent statements by President Johnson at the beginning of the Dominican crisis, announcing that the U.S. government would not allow the appearance of "another Cuba" on the continent; the House of Representatives' resolution to support the military intervention; the proposal to create an Inter-American Military Force—all these are aimed at collective terror, and make clear to the people the immense risks, sacrifices, and difficulties that true revolutionary struggles must confront.

Just as there would be no let-up in the use of their military might, the imperialists never let up in their attempt to create an artificially easy atmosphere. This presents the wavering groups and classes with a less risky and insecure path, designed to satisfy the imperialistic interests. On the occasion of the last anniversary of the Alliance for Progress, after the military intervention in Santo Domingo crushed a democratic movement, President Johnson said, "The social democratic revolution is the alternative—the only alternative—to bloodshed, destruction, and tyranny. For the past is past. And those who struggle to save it unwittingly join the ranks of their own destroyers." But who is it that opposes democratic revolution in the Dominican Republic, Venezuela, Peru, Guatemala, Brazil, the whole world? Who but the same North American troops increase "bloodshed, destruction, and tyranny" in Vietnam? Who but the North American government struggles to preserve the past and to bloody our country and the whole American continent?

In Venezuela, as we have said, few would dispute the need for a revolutionary transformation to put an end to the present state of underdevelopment, backwardness, and misery. A problem arises when ways are considered for achieving this revolutionary transformation. It is then that doubts and discordant opinions appear. On one side are those who believe (with my friend) that there are still ways to gain national liberation through the vote or through the peaceful struggle of the masses. On the other side are those who believe (as I do) that such a conquest is possible only through popular insurrection, which would result from the proper combination of all forms of struggle, with a correct notion of the people's war.

There are then two camps into which the progressive classes and sectors of the country are divided, in the same way that the entire Venezuelan society is divided in two. At our present historical stage, in which the liberating revolution is the national alternative, this division will become more clearly defined as the consciousness of the people grows. The progressive classes and sectors, to which my friend belongs, are now reformist and opt for the "sanctioned revolution." They lack any clear consciousness of power, which means essentially the conquest of political power as an instrument of struggle between the rising, temporarily in transition, and the backward conservative classes, whose control is also transitory. Many of those who today are in the revolutionary vanguard, myself included, did at one time take a position similar to the progressive bourgeoisie. We had no idea of power in 1958.[2] For me, representative democracy was the same as it is today for my friend. Luckily, I freed myself from reformism in order to become a real revolutionary. I achieved a consciousness and, above all, a clear notion of power. This same process has been carried out by many others, some sooner, some later, as the result of objective realities, which the imperialists' intensive propaganda campaigns have not been able to hide.

The psychology of power played an important role in the conversion, since gaining power is the aim of every political movement. Yesterday's revolutionary classes, which are today's reactionaries, are what they were

[2] The year that dictator Pérez Jiménez was overthrown. Ojeda played a major role in the Revolution and was then chosen acting president, in effect, by the ruling temporary junta pending elections.—Ed.

and what they have become precisely as a result of their psychology of power. It developed to win a war (in Venezuela against Spanish colonialism), and it was maintained to try to preserve power, also through war. The revolutionaries triumphed yesterday because they were new forces brewing within society. They had at their side the invincible support of the people (mulattos, plainsmen, and mountaineers), and they represented the road to independence.

Politics are practiced only through power, whether revolutionary or reactionary, the two halves into which power is divided. In every historical period there are revolutionaries and reactionaries; a large sector in the middle, without a consciousness of its own, wavers from one side to the other. Their consciousness develops late, as a product of harsh struggle and class interests. But at the beginning of the whole revolutionary process, the middle sector, under the direct influence of the classes in power (the reactionary classes) plays into their hands, even as it tries to escape the oppression. Nevertheless, they slowly acquire consciousness and awareness of power. This has important consequences for the entire revolutionary movement.

Imperialism no longer has, in spite of its strength, the same power it had twenty years ago. Its foundations have undergone steady erosion, and it faces a changed world. Such a phenomenon in political and military affairs contributes to the tempering or the frustrating (as the case may be) of the fury of the police. The world situation grows increasingly more favorable to the peoples' progress. Alongside everyone's consciousness and determination to shake off the chains of colonialism and oppression, the moral and material support of all the peace-loving countries turns the Revolution into an invincible enterprise. The colonized, neo-colonial, and oppressed people, in exercising their sovereignty, are not alone. Their struggle is not an isolated cause waged at their own expense, with their own means and resources. There exists a worldwide reactionary camp, in which the oppressors join hands, support one another, and arrange all their forces around the preservation of their control. There is also a worldwide revolutionary camp, where the people make militant solidarity effective. This circumstance, that of the new realities in the world, eloquently explains the reason for the defeat of the imperialists in Vietnam. It explains why the 40,000 troops landed in Santo Domingo in the face of universal criticism could not restore the *gorilas* Wessin y Wessin and Imbert Barrera to office. It explains why the imperialist blockade of Cuba, one of our era's strongest sanctions, has not been able to produce the effects predicted by the Pentagon and the State Department.

No people in the process of liberation can fight an isolated struggle; no two forces or two belligerent armies, like a rabbit and a tiger, fight before the impassive gaze of the rest. To think so would be a grave error that would lead to opportunism and resignation. Today's revolutionary struggle (as we must see it) is a struggle on the part of all the progressive forces in the world. We are in a situation having great popular appeal, and in which the objective conditions of each country constitute the principal factor. Already in Latin America, as in the early 1800's, there are several countries which have begun their struggle against neo-colonialism. These include three of the Bolivarian countries (Venezuela, Colombia, and Peru), and others such as Santo Domingo, Guatemala, and Paraguay. They have taken the true path to the liberating revolution, at whose center is the principal instrument of power: the armed forces of liberation. The chances for imperialism to triumph are even further reduced to the extent that the struggle grows and liberation movements in Africa and Asia continue to develop. The entire North American army would be insufficient to function as an occupational force in the far-flung areas shaken by revolution.

Venezuela is an important factor in the worldwide revolutionary camp. Its struggle for liberation complements that of other people in similar conditions. Whether we like it or not, one is necessarily the continuation of the other. Although every country, including Venezuela, must act according to its own realities, and must realize the kind of revolution its own history allows, the integration of these revolutionary movements is possible. It is not the fault of the Venezuelan revolutionaries that their struggle against the imperialists is in its first stage. Their struggle is identical to that being waged in Vietnam, in Angola, in the Congo, or to that which freed Cuba and Algeria. The fault in this case belongs to the imperialists who have respected neither frontiers nor continents in extending their exploitation.

Venezuela struggles today against the North American yoke, as it did yesterday against Spanish colonialism; as the North Americans did against English domination; and the Brazilians did against the Portuguese Empire. There are still people who adhere to theories of geographical fatalism and view the world as it was at the time of the Monroe Doctrine, whose slogan of "America for the Americans" reflected a situation far different from today.

The geopolitics theses have been overtaken by the dynamics of history. The North American imperialists erased all continental frontiers. President Johnson recently said (as if any doubt remained) that the military forces of the United States will be present in any part of the world, in any country, where "freedom is endangered by communist aggression." This aggressive conduct on the part of the Yankee imperialists openly reveals the breakdown of schemes for intercontinental cooperation, for the North American government behaves toward Venezuela or Santo Domingo, geographically located in America, as if they were located in Indochina (an area that until recently was synonymous with unfathomable distance).

To develop a firm concept of power on the part of the popular, patriotic, and progressive classes, the first step is to be free of geographic fatalism and the thesis of the invincibility of imperialism and the forces of reaction. The second step is to be convinced, once and for all, that without seizing political power, no change in the national crisis can be effected. The implementation of an agrarian reform that would liquidate the present system of landholdings is not possible. This is shown by six years of a progressive Agrarian Reform Law. It is impossible without radically transforming the nation's economic and political system; it is impossible without changing the social makeup of the government, where, until today, the landed interests have predominated and maintained the concentration of land ownership in a few hands.

The men who have passed through the Ministry of Agriculture and Livestock in the past decade have invariably been representatives of the classes opposed to a full and real agrarian reform. But even if they did belong to the progressive classes, they would not have been able to do things differently, due to the fact that agrarian policy is not independent from the national economic complex. It forms part of a whole, a system that is entirely responsive to political control by the reactionary classes.

In the industrial development, too, no change can be operative if it is not a result of a modification of our whole system of dependency. One cannot pretend that Venezuelan industry is anything but a simple processor of imports. This pretense hinders the real study of the causes that keep industry relegated to such a position. In Venezuela imperialism has one of its most important markets in Latin America. The import bourgeoisie that derive juicy profits from its activities will never, by themselves, be able to support changes that would even remotely suggest the disappearance of such privileges.

None of the problems that affect our country and the popular and progressive classes (concentration of land ownership in a few hands; low level of industrial development; unemployment; technical and scientific backwardness; undernourishment; underdeveloped consumers' market; lack of housing, schools, health centers, and hospitals; low salaries; foreign exploitation of the chief sources of wealth; control of sovereignty; etc., etc.) can be resolved without changing the whole national structure, or without removing its basis, which amounts to the same thing.

It has been shown that Venezuela is living through a full and growing crisis whose seriousness calls for great efforts to end it. Neither the Alliance for Progress nor circumstantial reforms have been able to conjure away the tremendous ills. Nevertheless, many sectors, conscious of the need for revolution, have still not left the reformist camp, the camp of illusions, contributing by their attitude to the prolonging of the oppressive situation. They still believe, ingenuously (and this is the result of a poorly defined concept of power), that other means exist to solve the national problems, without the need to expose their lives, their freedom, or their private interests.

The Revolution must be made at any price. The process of pauperization, reabsorption of small enterprises by monopoly capital, will continue inevitably with their corresponding unemployment, backwardness, and misery. The national bourgeoisie (agrarian and industrial), the petty bourgeoisie (students, professors, small businessmen and employees), together with the peasant and working classes, whose vanguard advances along the road of armed insurrection by means of the people's war, must come together. They must move with a single will, becoming the liberation front. They are the decisive force for victory.

Our country and our people live at the moment of a revolutionary crisis, where the old political schemes suffer the jarring impact of the struggle between the worn-out that requires constant tinkering, and the new that grows with unusual vigor. This struggle between life and death dislocates everything. The proliferation of political parties that for some is the expression of stability, is nothing more than the product of this same revolutionary crisis, where each sector is involved in the search for its own truth and tries to break with the moribund past. Each one proposes to find the truth. Some align themselves without having found it, and are still vacillating. They are fundamentally ignorant of the crisis and they don't understand the true causes that feed it. Others, who become fully aware and develop a concept of power, understand what this means as a class tool. They decide to struggle and take the road of revolutionary politics.

We have already said that in Venezuela, as in the rest of the world, two forces exist: the patriotic and progressive revolutionaries, and the conservative and neo-colonial reactionaries. And in the middle, a crowded area that wavers between one side and the other, and which includes both revolutionaries and reactionaries. My friend and I—both with revolutionary ideas—were together in the middle ground. I, in spite of my youth, was slightly more reactionary than he. His advice and the books he gave me were certainly different from what Jovito Villalba had given me. And they opened up the correct path to politics. Today, the roles are inverted, and my friend remains, without having changed his revolutionary ideas, in the same place where I left him five years ago. He understands the need for our liberation. Until now he has been a fervent partisan of the social ownership of land; of independent industrial development; of full democracy and sovereignty. In stating Venezuela's problems and in outlining strategic objectives, there is little difference between us. Nor is there much difference between those of us who drive for change by means of the people's war and those who remain under the influence of reformist ideology and under the terror of national and international reaction.

The reformist thesis is that imperialism and the oligarchy maintain an immense force that will be used against any insurgency or against any government that attempts to modify the present situation. This has already happened, both on our continent and elsewhere. It happened in Cuba, and failed. It happened in Santo Domingo, but did not fully achieve its objective. It happened in Brazil and the imperialists imposed their rule. Imperialism has not rested for a moment in its aggressive conduct against Cuba. From the moment when the revolutionary government took its first step toward reclaiming its riches exploited by the North American monopolies and began a full agrarian reform to break up the landed estates, counterrevolutionary reaction was manifested. The internal military conspiracy (Díaz Lanz, Urrutia, and Hubert Matos), sabotage (burning of El Encanto, explosion of the steamship *La Coubre*, etc.), the assassination of revolutionary workers (Conrado Benítez, Azcunce Domenech, and others), the invasion of the Bay of Pigs, prepared, armed, and financed by the State Department and the CIA in the United States and Nicaragua, the expulsion of Cuba from the OAS and the multilateral breaking of diplomatic and commercial relations by U.S. pressure on Latin American countries, and the general blockade are the concrete expression of a steady repression. Such a chain of events has been produced in two stages of the Cuban revolutionary regime: first, with the democratic-bourgeois government, at the fall of the tyrant, Fulgencio Batista, on January 1, 1959; and second, with the socialist regime, proclaimed during the mercenary invasion in April of 1961.

The transition from the democratic-bourgeois government to the socialist regime was the direct result of popular radicalization in the face of imperialist aggression, and the product of the revolutionary firmness of the new leaders, headed by Fidel Castro. But in their aggressive and confusing attitude, the reactionary forces have never made any difference. And when it is said that the U.S. government will not allow the appearance of a "new Cuba" on the continent, this refers not only to the presence of socialism, but to the triumph of any national liberation movement under the democratic-bourgeois regime.

The reactionary forces, who know what power is for, permit freedom only when it does not affect their interests and privileges. In Brazil and other Latin American countries, the governments that tried to go beyond their real capacity stepped beyond what is allowed by reaction. Such governments, without a popular policy defined to avoid a clash with the interests of the ruling classes, never succeed in waking the consciousness of the people, or in placing at their sides the progressive sectors, whose support is necessary in defeating "coupism." Nonrevolutionary politicians think that everything stems from the majority vote needed to win the government. They think that if a democratic representative government is formed, and if it aims at the total enforcement of the law, no one would dare challenge the law. They haven't yet understood—and this comes out in all their statements—that in order to exercise real power, force is required; force that is able to confront and successfully defeat the reactionary classes affected by constitutional change.

In the largest nation in Latin America, which has the greatest air, sea, and land army, and seventy million inhabitants, all imperialism had to do was move a few marshals and generals to end the governments of Quadros and Goulart. In Cuba, on the contrary, imperialism called upon all its resources, except direct military aggression (and this was because popular support for the Revolution and the international grouping of force impeded it), without the slightest change in the rising tide of revolution.

This appears paradoxical, but for those who finally understand that the people's forces are not related solely to numbers of inhabitants, but also to the level of their morale, consciousness, and power psychology, what is happening in Brazil, Cuba, and Santo Domingo is the specific revelation of the need for placing political power in the hands of the people.

In terms of population, Venezuela is a small country in which the reactionary and proimperialist elements constitute an obvious minority. In the National Armed Forces, officers of bourgeois origin do not account for even 1 percent of the total and the troops are exclusively of peasant and working-class origins. Both politically and economically Venezuelans are under the absolute control of a foreign power and thus it is obviously essential that we win national independence. Although we have a democratically elected government, the evils of neo-colonialism pervade every aspect of our national life: They can be seen in politics, in our economy, business, and culture; they contaminate even the customs and traditions that make up the national heritage.

Any deep analysis of Venezuelan problems points the way to liberation. The two great movements in our contemporary history (the electoral triumphs of November 30, 1952, and January 23, 1958) never got anywhere because both lacked power psychology which in the final analysis is what leads to an understanding of the real magnitude of the popular forces. The leaders of these formidable national movements (myself among them) were criticized for their failure to bring about revolutionary change by taking advantage of the power of the masses—on the first occasion, through defending their electoral decisions, and on the second, through effecting a qualitative change in the composition of the new government. However, neither of these methods is designed to win power.

Unlike the situation of January 23, 1958, when there was nothing of a socioeconomic nature to damage the success of the broadest unity in opposing the dictator, the popular mobilization which preceded the victory of November 30, 1952, was determined by an electoral platform of a democratic and nationalist orientation whose aims coincided with those of national liberation. It was precisely that character of the program that made possible the electoral triumph which in turn excited the reaction of the defeated forces, especially those of imperialism, and led to the ignoring of the popular will.

The URD had not planned to win the election and did not go into the election fight to gain power. It was simply fulfilling a civic duty and taking advantage of one of the few democratic and patriotic processes the government had left intact. In its surprise and confusion, it did not know how to use this victory. Taking advantage of the vacillation of the popular leaders, the government recaptured the initiative and struck at the crucial moment. We are not sure what could have happened, but we do know that the Military Junta and its imperialist advisers would never have permitted elections to take place if they had been aware of the remotest possibility of their own defeat.

Imperialism is concerned only with protecting its own interests and its strategy is to strike wherever the anticolonial struggle manifests itself. The way of reactionary violence exists no matter what the road taken to replace the colonial regime. As a result, it is clearly senseless to challenge it unless the attempt is made to completely overthow it.

Our country's political life has been marked by violence and there are few periods in which it has been absent. The ruling classes have throughout our history maintained their hegemony through the use of force and have not hesitated to use all their political and military power to maintain control. The effects of Pérez Jiménez's regime are still fresh in our memory. Since 1959 there has been a lessening of the terrorist and criminal outbursts of those days but the use of force is still used to the same end today: to maintain control in the hands of the reactionary classes.

Rómulo Betancourt on the day he took office as president announced the principal aim of his policies: "to isolate and segregate from the domestic community" the revolutionary forces which he labeled "extremist." The powerful and united movement that arose to end the violence of Pérez Jiménez, and of which the most important sector of AD was a part, suffered the first assault. The "Treaty of New York" signed by Betancourt, Villalba, and Caldera, later known as the Treaty of Punto Fijo, was aimed at dividing the united front of the Patriotic Junta. The latter did not enjoy the sympathy of the imperialists because the Venezuelan Communist Party participated in it.

I remember that a North American journalist asked me at the end of January 1958 why the Venezuelan Communist Party had not been segregated from the movement against Pérez Jiménez and why we had allied ourselves with that party. My answer was very simple: the alliance with the communists, I told him, was motivated by the same factors that allied the U.S. with the USSR in their fight against fascism.

The presence of revolutionary elements within the Patriotic Junta led to a conspiracy against it. The leaders of AD who returned from exile with Rómulo Betancourt at their head were responsible for many maneuvers. Once in office, Betancourt dedicated himself to dividing the popular and democratic forces. The compromises achieved in the Treaty of New York began to be applied in our country as a fundamental formula in shaping a policy contrary to the collective will of the Venezuelans, and in realizing a program that was openly antinational and proimperialist. In the face of this, the people were determined to fight for the maintenance of their democratic gains and for the fulfillment of their economic and social demands. The base of support of the new government was lost. The split within the AD and then the breaking of the Punto Fijo Treaty by the URD were the result of the policy of capitulation which opened the breach immediately. The struggle for democratic rights and popular claims was stepped up and Betancourt launched into his reign of terror.

Five years have passed since the Resistance entered this new phase of the struggle. The revolutionaries have not retreated, as the reformists do whenever their way is blocked. The ruling classes are aware of the situation and are moving further down the road of repression and violence once again, but the historic decision to meet reactionary violence with popular violence has already been made and acted upon. The beginning of the Resistance was dealt harsh blows, among which the defeats at Carupano and Puerto Cabello[3] and the annihilation of the first guerrilla detachments were almost fatal. It has faced imprisonment, torture, and death, but the armed struggle goes on. The objective conditions of the country today, on the one hand, and the maturity of the revolutionary vanguard with their armed detachments on the other, make the current process an invincible cause that can hold out for a long time, as has been shown, against the onslaught of the reactionary forces.

The new integration for the conquest and exercise of real power has extraordinary possibilities. The strengthening of the guerrilla detachments is an obvious one, and the incorporation of the peasant masses into the revolutionary struggle is a factor of paramount importance. Venezuelan peasants once made up the most backward sector of our political movement due to feudal exploitation, illiteracy, and limited means of communications. Today the politicization of the peasantry through the efforts of the guerrillas has made this section of the community a formidable stalwart in the liberation movement.

Another important factor is that the liberation movement does not rely on a single form of struggle. It uses all means at its disposal, legal and illegal, peaceful and nonpeaceful. There has been confusion in the minds of some people on this point—they have felt that armed struggle is opposed to other forms of popular combat. Another mistaken notion which has persisted is that of a "great battle"—the confrontation of two military forces. In our situation we cannot use the methods of classical warfare; we must use multiple forms of struggle covering all fronts, political, military, social, etc., and must create an insurrectional complex

[3] Two towns where the military garrison, led by communist and other left-wing cadres, rebelled against Betancourt in 1962.—*Ed.*

that rests on small and continuous victories, of a cumulative nature, which widen the influence of the people's war.

The revolutionary struggle cannot be concluded without the full control of revolutionary theory, its methods, organization, and ethics. There is a constant need for profound ideological battles which will win the masses over to the struggle and great initiative must be used to deepen the people's revolutionary consciousness. Propaganda and continuous agitation are indispensable weapons. Our war is a politico-military affair that goes from the most elementary protest, the lightning meeting or the strike, to sabotage, the capture of weapons, the harassment or destruction of an enemy force, the taking of a military position, the overthrow of the government.

To keep the people under their permanent influence, the theorists of proimperialist reformism are always trying to present easier, less risky solutions. They portray the revolutionary struggle as the express manifestation of desperate ideas, contrary to popular sentiment. And while they continue to advocate "democratic" measures, they practice a policy of restriction against the people. Verbally they condemn the oppression of the ruling classes but in fact they serve them diligently by accepting the institutional bulwarks of reaction and giving them democratic standing. In this way they keep the people tied down and apathetic. One cannot underestimate the illusions created by their promises. Therefore it is impossible to change overnight the mentality of the classes and sectors of our society, influenced by the ideas of proimperialist reformism. To achieve it, it is necessary to realize titanic struggles, aimed at unmasking the falseness of the puppet labor leaders and politicians; to show the antipopular content of representative democracy; and the impossibility of gaining political power for the people through any way other than the revolutionary struggle. To this end, every combatant in the people's war has the responsibility of turning himself into an effective leader, into a brave and daring activist, into a cadre respected by the masses, into their organizer and leader.

Since 1811, when the founders of our nation promulgated the first Bill of Rights of the Republic, Venezuela has had many constitutions. The expression that "the Constitution is good for everything" has become a popular saying. Fortunes have been amassed in its name; crimes committed under its protection; dubious transactions have been effected in its shadow. It has been used by the majority of leaders to serve their own interests and designs. The pages of our history are spattered with blood, but at last Venezuela was granted a new alternative, thanks to the indomitable will and struggle of the people, that of representative democracy. This reappeared with the defeat of the military dictatorship in January 1958 and the elections held in December of the same year when programs of a high progressive content were offered to the people. Most

ƒ

important was the return to democratic constitutionality, the state of law. The new Congress, made up of representatives of every party and every social class, met for the study, discussion, and approval of a new Bill of Rights that would abolish the spurious Constitution of 1953. The new Democratic Constitution was issued on January 23, 1961.

On the very day of its birth, it was violated by Betancourt. The civil rights it established were suspended and its full standing was postponed indefinitely. This Constitution is democratic and progressive and the liberation movement is not opposed to it; rather, we call for its full implementation. It states that "the Republic of Venezuela shall be forever irrevocably free and independent of all foreign domination and protection," and among the provisions of its numerous articles are the abolition of the death penalty, the inviolability of personal freedom and security, the prohibition of torture, the guarantee of habeas corpus, freedom of travel, the right to express opinions through any medium without fear of censorship, the right of assembly, the protection of youth against exploitation, the maintenance of public health and education, the right to full employment and a minimum wage, the legality of trade unions and strike action, the outlawing of monopolies, the enactment of a complete land reform, political freedom, and the definition of the National Armed Forces as servants of the Republic. Every one of these articles has been violated.

The enforcement of the 1961 Constitution, many of whose articles strongly affect the reactionary bourgeoisie and the landholders who wield political power, has been blocked by those classes. Thus the very essence of the Constitution, its democratic nature, is applied in their favor and against the masses and the petty bourgeoisie who lack constitutional protection in their constant struggle for the improvement of their working and living conditions.

Venezuela has witnessed three attempts at democratic constitutionality during the last thirty years. The first was during the government headed by General Isaías Medina Angarita between 1941 and 1945 and contained important reforms and the guarantee of civil rights; in October 1945 the reactionary classes of the oligarchy and imperialism rose up against this Constitution. The second was the new Bill of Rights formulated in 1947 under President Rómulo Gallegos, who was then made the target of a military coup. The third was the 1961 Constitution.

The military governments, like those of representative democracy, have lost historical meaning in our country. The failure of both, which expresses the breakdown of formal power, is due, in the first place, to the absence of democratic freedoms for the national majorities; and in the second place, to the persistence of Venezuela as a dependent nation, oppressed by the huge problems which engender the colonial regime in the political and economic spheres.

The situation has given rise to the revolutionary crisis that is shaking the country today; the masses and the progressive sectors cannot live as before, and the reactionary and exploitative classes cannot govern as before. The dikes raised by the reactionary classes and imperialism against the democratic revolution have obliged the vanguards of the liberation struggle to carry on their activities through other means, which is the present situation of the people's war.

DOUGLAS BRAVO AND ELÍAS MANUITT CAMERO: MANIFESTO OF IRACARA*

FOUR years after taking up arms in the mountains of Falcón, we the guerrillas of the José Leonardo Chirinos Front send this message to the nation. We have had a hard struggle these four years but the revolutionary movement, particularly its guerrilla front, has been gaining in experience and ability. We have conceived a coherent strategy, clarified our perspectives, and recognized the inevitability of victory through the organized, dynamic, and direct support of the masses in rural communities and cities.

We have suffered some setbacks; many of our comrades have died. A campaign of lies has been directed against prominent leaders of the Front asserting that they wish to suspend armed combat. These tactics should deceive no one and we appeal to the revolutionary army and the Venezuelan people to stand firm against the enemy's attempts to divide and demoralize us. With four years' fighting experience behind us, we can confidently affirm that our Guerrilla Front and the entire revolutionary movement are cogent realities in the life of Venezuela today.

Within the revolutionary movement at present there exist numerous ideological differences. The intense conflict resulting from these affects all elements of the movement, both the Marxists and the "democratic" factions, both those who advocate armed combat and those who favor "legal" methods. This conflict between the various groups dedicated to liberation should be understood as a product of the maturity and autonomy of the movement and it is therefore imperative that we discuss and interpret our disagreements responsibly and creatively. In seeking to resolve our problems thus, the discussion can be only strengthening to the movement and we shall be able to articulate a positive concept of tactics and strategy. Such a concept will retain its validity for the duration of the liberation struggle. At present it is of the utmost importance that we formulate our campaign to overthrow the government whose violence and oppression are known to us all.

---

* Proclamation issued in March 1966 (mimeographed) from the command post of the Venezuelan guerrilla forces known now as the Armed Forces of National Liberation (FALN). Translation by Juan Mechón.

If we are to succeed, unity must be the basic principle of the movement: unity of all factions striving to achieve liberation, especially those civil, military, economic, and professional factions wishing to overthrow the government and replace it with another which guarantees the civil rights of all citizens, the legality of all political parties, and the release of both civil and military political prisoners. To this end, we must analyze the situation accurately, recognize and seize the opportunities which arise. The people must be taught a more sophisticated level of armed combat and must also take advantage of the opportunities presented to them, particularly in the electoral process.

It is a strategic concept of combined insurrection such as ours that armed struggle and legal maneuvering, politico-military action in the countryside and in the city, military declarations and FLN-FALN operations, should be constantly interrelated and developed. The inconsistencies of the enemy, both short-term and long-term, are becoming more obvious every day. Although there have been defeats in certain areas of the country and nonviolent protest predominates in specific stages of the struggle for liberation, *armed combat must continue* because in all revolutions offensives must be launched on both the civil *and* the military fronts. This theory must be put into practice so that through the victories of our army the enemy is weakened and its military power undermined as correspondingly the triumphs of our nonviolent protests demoralize the enemy politically and contribute to the development of the liberation forces. In our country at present there is a permanent crisis of political power manifested by the chaos in which the traditional parties find themselves, the repressive government measures, and the violation of the Constitution. Economically, the crisis has arisen through the subordination of our national economy to imperialist capital through direct inversion and the recent introduction of mixed foreign and home capital in industry and public services such as banks, savings banks, public transport, etc. The economic dependence of Venezuela wears the disguise of mixed capital which offers protection to national and foreign industries while creating unfair competition for nationalist groups. The cost of living is high, the bolivar has been devalued, direct and indirect taxes cripple the consumer while foreign capital remains unaffected. The nation is thus being prepared for a further devaluation of the bolivar and subsequent U.S. intervention through its various "development" banks, the Alliance for Progress, etc. These organizations provide the means whereby the crises of the capitalist countries are transferred to colonies and neo-colonies.

The petroleum companies are taking advantage of the government's deficit of more than 800,000,000 bolivars to obtain concessions. The government has made a great show of readjusting the taxes imposed on these companies and has justified their measures by calling them "service contracts"—merely a new name for concessions.

All classes and strata of society are affected by the social crisis. There are 600,000 unemployed, 2,000,000 peasants deprived of their land, 5,000,000 children have been abandoned in various ways, crime has reached unparalleled proportions. Newspapers daily report, without comment, new chapters in the saga of our social decline. We can read that poverty is spreading everywhere; the moral and social consequences are apparent all around us.

Imperialism has exercised political power through numerous governments in Venezuela and to overthrow imperialism we must overthrow the whole regime. We must unite into one vast front all those who oppose the regime, including those members of the government itself who have resisted its policies. We must remember also that COPEI is foremost among the enemies of our liberation movement because it constitutes the principal reserve of imperialism and the Creole oligarchies.[1] Just as we differentiate in the other reformist parties between the popular front which still exerts a strong influences and the conservative leaders who betray the interests of the masses, so must we with COPEI. It is a vital distinction. There is a risk that many people, disillusioned with the AD, URD, etc., may be temporarily deceived once more by false promises. COPEI is compactly organized and still ideologically united but it is the enemy of the people. With the other political parties in chaos, its stability may appear attractive but its policies in practice provide no advance toward the aims of liberation.

We cannot deny the skill with which COPEI is conducting its apparent opposition to the government but this opposition is in fact purely verbal. While the AD and FND identify themselves with the maintenance of the neo-colonial system in our country, COPEI presents itself as a traditional reformist party. Nonetheless, it supports the politics of repression, torture, and mass arrests. COPEI is relying on the elections to place it in power. However, it maintains contact with other reactionary organizations and with the U.S. Embassy so that if it fails to win the election, the alternative of a coup d'état will be open to it with the support of these "allies." If the people do not democratically and constitutionally give it power, it will seize power for itself as an overt dictatorship and our country will remain in the grip of imperialism and the Creole oligarchies.[2]

Mass arrests are a common occurrence today, providing a permanent means of repressing the peasants and attacking guerrilla fronts. These are the methods of the Pentagon in its fight against world liberation move-

[1] The Creole Corporation, a subsidiary of Standard Oil of New Jersey (Rockefeller), is the dominant oil corporation among the various U.S. companies in Venezuela. And since oil is the most important asset of Venezuela, Creole can be said to be the determining factor in the country's economy.—*Ed.*

[2] COPEI won the elections.—*Ed.*

ments. The aim is to isolate the guerrillas from the rest of the peasant population, to cut off all support, to break down the interdependence of the armed liberation movement and the peasants, in order to finally destroy completely guerrilla activities and the peasant revolution. Imperialism has had long experience in this sphere of operations: it knows that while communication and mutual cooperation are maintained between peasants, guerrillas, and the people in general, the liberation struggle is invincible, no matter what suppression and terror it may suffer.

In our Front we have survived five periods of intensive persecution. The result has been that we emerged stronger in organization, experience, combat techniques, territory, and popular support. We are no longer operating at subsistence level: We have developed and consolidated our forces considerably. Other Fronts have also survived the fiery baptism of antiguerrilla persecution. There are more than 10,000 soldiers in the present antiguerrilla reserve. They are a permanent force who try, in vain, to crush our guerrilla operations. There are also uniformed members of DIGEPOL who, through the AD, conduct a program of repression in the rural communities and carry out police functions within the army. These antiguerrilla forces will be increased in proportion to our growth in accordance with the antirevolutionary tactics taught by the U.S. Military Mission in Panama, Lima, and Puerto Rico. Because of the system of military service in this country, one half of the army is each year made up of recruits and this makes it difficult for a permanent, specialized antiguerrilla force to be maintained. These difficulties will no doubt be overcome by lengthening the period of military service and employing mercenaries.

The U.S. Embassy and their Military Mission have been invited by high-ranking army officials to act as "advisers" to the antiguerrilla troops of the National Armed Forces. This is an insult to the nation and the Bolivarian tradition of our army. It is no secret that this intrusion by the American Military Mission has the full approval of high-ranking army officers and the economic oligarchy, of the AD, URD, FND, and COPEI, whose aim is to stifle the public conscience so that they may justify the direct intervention of the United States at the psychological moment. This is exactly what happened in Santo Domingo. With a few exceptions, the members of the parties we have mentioned are enemies of the masses who can be identified by their extreme anticommunism and their defense of the neo-colonialist system of exploitation.

Imperialism through its military missions gives the coup d'état decisive importance in those countries where the stability of a repressive regime is threatened. Although our "representative democracy" is relatively stable, Venezuela is no exception. The government faces a social, economic, and political crisis and has shown itself incapable of crushing the revolutionary movement—on the contrary, it has encouraged its growth. As a result, the U.S. Embassy and the Military Mission have begun intensive mobilization in all parties and in all sectors of society—military, economic, religious, and professional. The ground is being prepared. Seminars, discussions, cultural events, parties, and so on, are organized by the U.S. Embassy and Military Mission in order to "talk" to their hosts. Also they place their representatives at the heart of the army, the economic groups, etc. Thus, by devious and underhand methods, imperialism digs its claws ever more deeply into every aspects of life in our country.

It is clear that we are entering an extremely complex strategic period—that of national liberation. During this period there must be a unification of all the most radical political forces that have a tradition of highly disciplined organization in the various forms of armed and unarmed combat, legal and "illegal" politics, and have achieved unity among themselves. Nonviolent political protest must be subordinated to our central strategic concept in order to guarantee the continued accumulation of forces, the creation of revolutionary conditions, and the formation of our liberation army.

In our attempts to find a solution for pacification of the nation, we have never refused to enter into discussions with any interested group. But if anyone thinks we shall make peace while the prisons are full and our basic demands are unfulfilled, he is deceiving himself. The government knows this better than anybody. The guerrillas will not lay down their arms until they have achieved the objectives for which they are fighting. We in the Guerrilla Front of José Leonardo Chirinos support the FLN and FALN in their program to achieve true peace in Venezuela. We state once again for the government, the political parties, and all individuals dedicated to peace, the program of the FLN to guarantee a government which satisfies the hopes and needs of the majority of the nation.

1. Total amnesty for civil and military prisoners.

2. Re-enlistment of all soldiers expelled from the National Armed Forces for political reasons.

3. Legalization of all political parties which function according to the national constitution.

4. Dissolution of the DIGEPOL and other repressive bodies.

5. Fulfillment of the constitution and its laws, and equality of opportunity for all Venezuelans.

6. Economic policies to benefit the people, with the emphasis on nationalism.

7. Suspension of antiguerrilla mass arrests which are in effect intimidation and persecution of the peasants. Closure of concentration camps.

As far as we are concerned, we are willing to discuss this program or any other which is acceptable to our principles. But the people and our enemies should remember at all times that if the proposals for peace collapse, our capacity to continue fighting is unlimited and we shall not cease armed combat until we gain complete victory and the liberation of our people.

FIDEL CASTRO: FIGHT OR BE SILENT*

FOR several days a tremendous campaign against our country has been carried on by the government of [Venezuela] and by the Yankee news services, following the death of an ex-functionary of the Venezuelan government. And for several months in the clandestine and semiclandestine press, even in the legal press of that country, and at different international events, the rightist leadership of the Communist Party of Venezuela has been making similar charges against our Party. The proimperialist oligarchy says that we interfere in the internal affairs of Venezuela, and the rightist Party leadership that we interfere in the internal affairs of the Party in Venezuela.

For example, according to the Associated Press, Venezuela's Minister of Interior says: "The criminal acts of political terrorism are prepared, directed, and financed in the Cuba of Fidel Castro." AP goes on: "Yesterday, in Havana, the Venezuelan leader of the so-called Armed Forces of National Liberation, Elías Manuitt Camero, said in a public communiqué that the FALN assumed full responsibility for the kidnapping and assassination of Iribarren Borges.[1] 'This reveals,' declared Interior Minister Leandro Mora today, 'that the participants are not only delinquents, but are protected as well by a delinquent government'. . . ."

Agence France-Presse, on the other hand, says: "The Communist Party of Venezuela disclaims the statement of Elías Manuitt Camero who, in the name of the so-called National Liberation Forces, credits that organization with the murder of Dr. Julio Iribarren Borges. A document of condemnation, signed by Dr. Héctor Mujica, member of the Political Bureau of the Communist Party of Venezuela, reads: 'Manuitt Camero's statements were as shocking as the abominable crime itself.' It adds that it is deplorable that *Granma*, the organ of a fraternal Party, should lend itself to the publication of such bombast. The document adds that anti-Cuban feelings never existed among the people of Venezuela and that now the enemies of the Cuban Revolution are taking advantage of the opportunity to introduce such feelings among them. The document em-

[1] The "ex-functionary" in question, former head of the Social Security tax (which is very high) and brother of Venezuela's foreign minister.—*Ed.*

* Speech delivered at the University of Havana on March 13, 1967; official Cuban translation, from the English edition of *Granma*, March 19.

phasizes an unequivocal repudiation of the crime against the brother of the Venezuelan Minister and of the ranting declarations of an ex-militant who was publicly expelled from the ranks of the Communist Party for divisionist activities and slackening of his political position. The same action was applied to Douglas Bravo, Gregorio Lunar Márquez, Freddy Carqués, Francisco Prada, and others using the name of the national movement of liberation."[2]

Of all the many happenings on this uneasy continent, there is not one that does not lead to the immediate and familiar accusation against Cuba. A few weeks ago, at the time of the Nicaraguan electoral contest, Somoza's gangs carried out a massacre of the opposition party. At once, logically—despite the fact that it was a question of a party bearing the name of "Partido Conservador"—Cuba turned out to be guilty of promoting that clash, that bloodshed. If there is a military uprising in Santo Domingo that leads to the intervention of Yankee troops, troops that even now remain stationed in that sister nation, the inevitable justification is Cuba. There is hardly anything that happens in this continent that is not blamed on Cuba. But Cuba is to be blamed for just one thing: for having made a Revolution and for being ready to carry it forward to its final, ultimate consequence!

And that is Cuba's responsibility. We assume that responsibility!

But what does that mean? How can we explain the insinuations of the oligarchies, and those of the Venezuelan oligarchy in particular, blaming Cuba for revolutionary action in their countries? And the insinuations made by the rightist leadership of the Communist Party of Venezuela? It is necessary to make a brief résumé of the history of the revolutionary struggle in Venezuela.

First: a few months prior to the triumph of the Cuban Revolution, there was a formidable popular movement in Venezuela that overthrew the Pérez Jiménez regime. Participating in this movement were ample popular forces, among them the Communist Party of Venezuela. And a young newspaper man was especially outstanding: Fabricio Ojeda, who was president of the Patriotic Council that ousted Pérez Jiménez. However, that victory of the people of Venezuela was frustrated, because from that moment the Partido Acción Democrática which at one time had played a certain revolutionary role, a certain role in the anti-imperialist struggle, that had mass support, not in the capital—because naturally the most advanced sectors had majority support in the capital—this party had particularly broad support in extensive regions of the interior of the country, and began to act as a fundamental factor in hindering the maturing and development of the Venezuelan revolutionary movement.

Betancourt won some elections, coming up with a ridiculous minority

[2] All former CP members who refused to abandon the armed struggle when the CC of the CP ordered them to do so.—*Ed.*

in the capital and getting his majority in the interior of the country—similar to what sometimes happened in our country. And from the moment it was sworn in, that government dedicated itself to developing a clear policy of conciliation, kowtowing to imperialism, and defending imperialist interests in Venezuela. Naturally, it became one of the instruments of U.S. policy.

There began to be repression of the revolutionary movement; repression of the workers, of the students, of the revolutionaries. Those repressions became more and more brutal, and the first massacres of students and the general population took place in Caracas. Betancourt felt a deep resentment toward the people of the capital; he could not pardon that lack of support, the affront he had been given by the population of Caracas.

And soon, just as soon as the repression had become intolerably brutal, supporters of the armed struggle arose. One of the first of these was the Movement of the Revolutionary Left, organized by a group of progressive leaders who had broken off from the official party, Acción Democrática. They began to prepare for armed struggle. Similarly, the Communist Party began to prepare for armed struggle. The Third Congress of the Communist Party of Venezuela approved the road of armed struggle for the Revolution in Venezuela. Other dissident forces from different parties also began preparations for armed struggle. Among these was a sector of the political party to which Fabricio Ojeda belonged. And Fabricio Ojeda, friend of Cuba, friend of our Revolution—like so many other Venezuelans —one day resigned his position as member of Parliament and went into the mountains to organize a guerrilla movement.

Several years passed. Undoubtedly the Venezuelan revolutionaries, as in all revolutions in every part of the world, made a number of errors in their conception of the struggle, a number of errors of a strategic and of a tactical nature. Different factors contributed to these errors. One of these was the fact that the revolutionary movement was very strong in the capital, and on the other hand—as has or had happened in many other countries in Latin America—and for this the communist parties are to blame—the revolutionary movement was weak in the country. Why? Because the Marxist parties concentrated their attention mainly on the city, on the workers' movement, which is, of course, quite correct. But in many cases—for naturally all these generalities have their exceptions—they greatly underestimated the importance of the peasantry as a revolutionary force.

As the official party of Venezuela was strong in the countryside and the parties of the Left were weak there, although strong in the capital, for a long time the leadership of the Venezuelan revolutionary movement overestimated the importance of the capital and the struggle in the capital and underestimated the importance of the guerrilla movement.

Venezuela was one of the countries—or the country in recent times—

where the revolutionary movement had the greatest influence in the ranks of the professional army. Many young Venezuelan army officers openly showed their sympathy for the revolutionary movement, even in its most radical form, inspired in Marxist concepts. So the force of the revolutionary movement was strongly felt in the ranks of the army. And this led to another conceptual error: to a downgrading of the guerrilla movement in favor of great hopes in a military uprising.

They accuse us of promoting subversion; they accuse the Cubans of directing the armed revolutionary movement in Venezuela. And if we Cubans had had anything to do with the leadership of that revolutionary movement, we would never have fallen, and that revolutionary movement would never have fallen, into those two major conceptual errors. Why?

Because it is the revolutionaries, they and only they who decide, who are able to determine their general strategy and their specific tactics. And the revolutionaries always do that, always! In Venezuela, in all other countries, their criteria—and these criteria may often be mistaken—are only rectified as a consequence of the process itself, of the experience of the process itself, of the blows received in the process. It is not we, the Cuban revolutionaries or leaders, who tell them what they must do; it is their own experience. And the best teachers of revolutionaries in every country of Latin America—as it was in Cuba—the best teachers, the great teachers, were the setbacks.

And naturally the Venezuelan revolutionary movement suffered many setbacks, as revolutionary movements in all parts of the world have always suffered setbacks, and Latin America's movement logically had to go through a long apprenticeship. Today it can be affirmed that that movement has learned a great deal, not from Cuba, but from its own experience, from the blows it has received. And therefore that more experienced revolutionary movement is growing and consolidating itself, and the rulers are showing themselves unable to crush it. They are impotent to crush it in Guatemala, unable to crush it in Venezuela.

But reverses always take a toll; they frequently take a toll in desertions from the revolutionary ranks by the weakest, the least tenacious, the least persevering, in a word the least revolutionary.

Apart from erroneous strategic conceptions in themselves, these erroneous conceptions in turn gave rise to serious errors of a practical nature: the guerrillas found themselves abandoned and deprived of the most elementary resources. The revolutionary leadership of the Party was trying to direct the guerrillas from the city, from the capital. What ought to have been done, was not done—what a daring and truly revolutionary leadership would have done, what the leadership of the great and historic contemporary movements that have triumphed have done—that is, go up to the mountains with the guerrillas to lead the war from the battlefield, to lead the war from the mountains.

It is absurd and almost criminal—we don't call it a hundred percent criminal because it is a question of ignorance more than of willful fraud— to try to direct guerrillas from the city. The two experiences are so different, so utterly distinct, the two settings so completely dissimilar, that the greatest insanity—a painfully bloody insanity—that can be committed is to try to direct guerrillas from the city. And the guerrillas were not really seen as a force that could be developed to take revolutionary power in countries such as ours, but rather as an instrument of agitation, a tool for political maneuvering, for negotiation. Underestimation of the guerrillas led to the errors committed subsequently.

And in Venezuela the guerrillas were constantly being ordered to cease fire, and that is madness! A guerrilla contingent that agrees to a truce in fighting is one condemned to defeat.

A guerrilla contingent can agree to a truce of one or two days as we did on some sectors of our front to return prisoners to the Red Cross. As a matter of principle, a guerrilla contingent must never agree to a truce of any other kind. The men get used to the quietude of the camp, a weakening and demoralization of forces sets in. But the commanders of the city-led guerrillas constantly received orders to make truces, more and more truces. That was happening in Venezuela.

And naturally, as a result of an inept leadership, blows and setbacks followed in succession. Nevertheless, in spite of the conceptual errors, the government could not eliminate the guerrillas. Yet what the repressive and proimperialist forces of Betancourt and Leoni could not achieve was very nearly achieved thanks to the ineptness of the revolutionary leadership.

The leaders of the Communist Party of Venezuela began to speak of a democratic peace.

"What is this about democratic peace?" many people asked. "What is this about democratic peace?" we, the leaders of the Cuban Revolution, asked ourselves. We did not understand. We did not understand but, nevertheless, we wanted to understand. "What does this mean?" we asked some Venezuelan leaders. As a reply we received the same old worn-out elaborate theory of a tactic, a maneuver—by no means an abandonment of the war. No! No! It was only a maneuver to broaden the base, to destroy the regime, to weaken and undermine it.

And, of course, we by no means considered this a correct point of view. Nevertheless, we had hope and confidence, in spite of the fact that a democratic peace seemed absurd, ridiculous. For only a revolutionary movement that is winning the war can speak of peace, because then it can begin to mobilize national opinion in favor of a peace that can only be won by winning the Revolution. Then one can mobilize people's spirits, public opinion, the people and their desire for peace on the only possible foundation: the defeat of tyranny and of exploitation. But to speak of peace when the war is being lost is precisely to concede peace by defeat.

In reality, behind their explanation lay deceit. They told us that their democratic peace was a maneuver, but that the struggle would be stepped up, guerrilla warfare would be stepped up. Nevertheless, they were lying. In reality, the intention was to abandon the armed struggle and they were simply preparing the way.

I have mentioned Fabricio Ojeda's name, his clean record, his participation in the overthrow of Pérez Jiménez, the rarely seen phenomenon of his resignation from office when he gave up his parliamentary privileges to go into the mountains. A rare case in a politician in our America. Fabricio was ignominiously assassinated on June 21, 1966. Sixteen days earlier, on June 4, 1966, Fabricio wrote a letter, the letter was addressed to me and was probably one of the last things he ever wrote. And that letter, which I have kept without knowing that I would need to reveal its contents one day, goes as follows:

"My dear friend:

"Here, all of the time, as always, attempting to overcome the burden of temporary difficulties in order to wage the struggle on a more serious and precise basis; we have made some advances toward this end. The fundamental step has been that of going directly to the solution of the problems of leadership, the structuring of our national organizations, such as the FLN Executive Committee and the Executive Command of the FALN; starting points for a general reorganization of the movement's entire structure. To this end we are working intensely. We intend to hold a national FLN-FALN conference as soon as possible which, as a constituent power, will devote itself to a study and analysis of the situation, to establishing strategy and tactics, political and military lines, and to defining the effective constitution of our directing organism at all levels. In this way the liberation movement will break out of its present state of stagnation, overcome differences, and clarify its historic potential, in addition to consolidating the factor indispensable to further progress, revolutionary unity of the revolutionary forces.

"Our project of restructuring the struggle on new bases has forced us to define certain important questions. The first of these is the provisional restructuring of the present directing organism of the national FLN-FALN. In this regard, we have decided to increase the number of nuclei in the existing leadership, which has produced a critical situation within the Communist Party of Venezuela. This includes the sanctioning of Comrade Douglas Bravo by the majority of the Political Bureau of the Party, who have removed him from this organism, accusing him of an attitude of anti-Party factionalism.

"The second question of importance is the decision to confront any circumstance whatsoever in order to bring all revolutionary forces together with the purpose of incrementing the war of national liberation as the only means of advancing toward the conquest of power and the achievement of national independence, taking into account the objective conditions prevailing in the country and the peculiarities of the Venezuelan process.

"In both areas we have made advances. Steps are being taken to set up a unified FLN-FALN command. This will be led by myself as President in charge of the FLN, together with the First Commander of the FALN, Douglas Bravo. A leader from the MIR will join us this week as Secretary-General.[3]

"The General Command of the FALN now includes the commanding officers of the guerrilla fronts. This new form was arrived at after an analysis of the present situation of these organisms, since it was considered that a nucleus of three members of the FALN General Command who were still active was insufficient for general military leadership, since the other members of the Command have either been taken prisoner or are abroad. In relation to the unification of the revolutionary forces for the purposes of advancing the war of national liberation, a unified commission will be designated to study and draw up the theoretical material on strategy, tactics, and the political and military line of the movement to be presented for discussion in the coming FLN-FALN national conference.

"The incorporation of the MIR into the directing organism and the preparatory work for the conference are steps of great significance, since in this way a period of internal discussion on present differences will begin replacing polemic diatribe in our talks, and opening up truly democratic roads for the ideological and political unity of the revolutionary movement.

"Nonetheless, a new breach has been opened in our ranks by the disciplinary measures taken by the majority of the Political Bureau of the Communist Party of Venezuela.

"In respect to this new problem, I have been informed that the intermediate and basic sectors, including those in the Central Committee itself, have been reacting against the sanction imposed on Comrade Bravo.

"Already certain documents have been circulated which expressly state this reaction. In my opinion, the disciplinary measures taken by the majority of the Political Bureau correspond to problems of a truly ideological and political nature, to profound questions, which they have attempted to cover up by talking of methods or supposed errors on the part of Comrade Douglas and other comrades whose ideas on strategy and tactics of our revolutionary process coincide with his. The fact is

[3] Américo Martín, leader of the MIR (Movement of the Revolutionary Left), which split off from the ruling Democratic Action (AD) Party, did in fact become Secretary-General. He was captured while attempting to reach Cuba as a delegate to OLAS, then apparently renounced the armed struggle.—Ed.

that within the Communist Party of Venezuela two important currents are being debated.

"One of these is held by a minority in the base of the Party but is very prevalent among the members of the Political Bureau and the Central Committee. Its essence is as follows: Present developments permit the revolutionary movement to take the initiative on the political front. Nonetheless, the FALN must order the guerrillas and the UTC (Tactical Combat Units) to fall back. It does not mean simply another truce but rather something more profound; it means diverting the form of struggle. That is, a new tactical period begins, which in place of combining all forms of struggle, would suspend guerrilla and UTC operations. The guerrillas and the UTC should make an orderly retreat and the revolutionary movement introduce a change in tactics. Several conditions are indispensable, to maintain unity and internal cohesion, to maintain iron discipline, and to support and aid the directing nucleus. To achieve these ends the Party and the Young Communists must act in two ways. First, employ persuasion, using every kind of reasoning and political arguments in support of the new tactical changes, discussing matters calmly with all who must be convinced. Second, carry on an active campaign against adventurist tendencies and provocations. (This is a synthesis of two documents presented to this organization by prominent members of the Political Bureau.)

"The other, held by a majority of the Party, but with little support among members of the leadership of higher organizations, is headed up by Comrade Douglas Bravo, who not only opposes the alteration of plans and the changes in tactics, but who presents strong criticisms of the way that the revolutionary struggle has been carried out.

"It is quite obvious that the crux of these differences is the question of armed struggle, which a group of leaders within the Communist Party of Venezuela have opposed since the very beginning.

"There is no doubt that the sanctioning of Comrade Douglas is the beginning of these alterations, and that these are designed to eliminate, by means of disciplinary actions, any who oppose a new tactical period which rather than combining all forms of struggle would choose to suspend all action by the guerrillas and the Tactical Units.

"In a situation like this, the decision to enlarge the integral organizations of leadership by incorporating the most responsible and firm cadres, is a step forward of great magnitude.

"The majority of the Political Bureau has opposed this measure and has proceeded to repudiate us publicly, denying the validity and legitimate nature of the groups already formed.

"We have, however, remained firm and we have been pleased to note that a great body of opinion has formed in support of our cause, in the guerrilla fronts and in the intermediate organizations, as well as at the base of the Communist Party of Venezuela. In addition, some members of the Central Committee, parties within the FLN, and urban units of the FALN have lent their support.

"A period of clarification of ideology and definition of the revolutionary road has begun. There is one unfavorable transitory factor involved in this situation and which places us in a rather difficult spot. That is the problem of economic resources, since it has been the Political Bureau which has exercised control over this sector.

"Until now all funds for the revolutionary movement have been centralized in that organization and used to further their policies—that is, snuff out guerrilla centers by economic means."

The letter ends as follows:

"Our guerrilla fighters have maintained a high state of morale and there is gigantic resolution in our movement. We are conscious that the present picture is full of difficulties but we are sure that these will be overcome within a short time. Truth will be borne in on the skeptics and then a bright future will appear on our horizon. Not one step backward, not even to gain speed!

"The bearer can give more details and better explain some things.

"We go forward, toward victory. To fight until victory. A warm embrace from your friend, Fabricio Ojeda."

In addition, some documents which came to our hands verified what Fabricio had said, one hundred percent; documents which were distributed among the militants of the Communist Party of Venezuela for discussion; documents which, without any doubt, indicate and at the same time explain the policy followed in recent times by the government of Venezuela.

One of the documents is written by Pompeyo Márquez, Teodoro Petkoff, and Freddy Muñoz,[4] and in essence says the following in its main lines:

"First. Some changes have taken place which force the revolutionary movement to revise certain aspects of its tactics in a fundamental way regarding the armed struggle.

"In broad outline the situation is the following: The armed struggle has suffered several blows and has weakened. The revolutionary movement at present is not in a condition to continue the frontal and open attacks on its enemies. The armed apparatus of the Party has been severely damaged; a bloody and brutal repression is affecting the ability of the revolutionary movement to organize, unify, and mobilize the broad masses and give an adequate riposte to government policy.

"Due to the continual reverses and blows suffered, to its own weakness

[4] Members of the CC of the Venezuelan CP (Luben and Teodoro Petkoff are brothers). Fidel's version of the CC document coincides with the photostat version in my possession.—*Ed.*

which impede successful actions, the armed struggle, by not taking appropriate measures to safeguard its instruments, could lose the role it has played in the recent past, in which it offered a perspective of revolutionary transformation to the masses. In reality, it is not playing this role at present and its future depends on the measures we take today.

"The weak armed operations which do nothing but repeat similar former operations, without attaining progress of true significance, are:

"a. making political action difficult and impeding the regrouping of forces against the Betancourt *gorilas*;

"b. letting the Betancourt *gorila* clique maintain its alliances;

"c. acting as a brake and preventing the rapid decomposition of its broad base;

"d. wiping out convictions, faith in the correct general strategy of the revolutionary movement, whose basis was set down in the Third Congress of the CPV and was later strengthened in the successive plenaries of the CC.

"Second. Consequently, the Party must undertake a retrenchment on the military front and recommend the suspension of armed actions in favor of proceeding to a regrouping of its forces and their preparation for a new revolutionary stage which must be qualitatively superior to those existing up to now.

"Until recovery has been attained in a fundamental sense, and until some advance is achieved in the promotion of new forces and the regrouping of nationalist sectors, all operations of the FALN must cease.

"This military retrenchment must be accompanied by a political offensive which will permit us to cover the retrenchment, alleviate the pressures of repression, and recover the political initiative.

"In short, it is not a new truce, but something deeper"—textually what Fabricio explained—"it is a temporary about-face in the forms of struggle, that is, suspending the actions of the guerrillas and the UTC, and giving political initiative priority."

At the same time, other leaders sent a similar document to the Party, this time signed by Guillermo García Ponce and other leaders. It is, in essence, the same with some slight variations. They themselves explain these differences in the introduction.

It reads: "Document enclosed. As you will note, the resolutions and conclusions are the same: retrenchment of the guerrillas and of the UTC, as well as a change of tactics toward an emphasis on political acts. There are, therefore, no differences on fundamental decisions; there is full unity on the essence of the problems. The motivations, the reasons for the change in forms of struggle for a specific period are also the same. Nevertheless, there is one shade of difference: our document places prime importance on political motivations and secondary importance on setbacks conceived as a reason for change.

"For the other comrades this order is reversed. First: the blows received constitute a very important factor, but we should not change our tactics for this reason. Setbacks help us to become aware of the changes that we ought to introduce, but they form part of a concrete and principally political reality which has forced us to make a certain change in course. The truth of the matter is that we should have retrenched before receiving the blows."

In other words, and in essence, Pompeyo, Teodoro, and Freddy Muñoz speak of retrenchment because of receiving blows. And they say: Yes, yes, very well, we're in agreement. There is only one fundamental difference: we should have retrenched before receiving the blows.

"Second, upon giving prime importance to political elements, we emphasize one of the peculiarities of the present situation; namely, while the guerrillas and the UTC are in retrenchment, the revolutionary movement can take the offensive on the political front, where all militants, organizations, etc., of the Party and the UTC can place the weight of their activity in a high combative spirit, free of all passivity and terrorist attempts."

Further on, the document reads:

"The need for retrenchment of the FALN. The events transpiring permit the revolutionary movement to take the initiative on the political front; nevertheless, it will be necessary for the FALN to order a retrenchment of the guerrillas and the UTC. This will not be a new truce, but something deeper: an attempt to change the forms of struggle, that is, to open a new tactical period in which, instead of combining all forms of struggle, guerrilla and UTC actions will be suspended. Prime importance will be taken by political events; a grouping of the leftist organization; promotion of new forces of struggle against 'Betancourtism'; unity, organization, and mobilization of the popular masses; alliance with nationalist sectors of the Armed Forces; action by the workers on behalf of their demands; struggle against repression, etc."

The only thing they didn't put in was the colloquy, the electoral struggle, which they obviously did not insert here because they intended to insert it later on.

The Communist Party was not the only one constituting the FALN; at least two or three other organizations were also members. One of them was the Movement of the Revolutionary Left (MIR), which was one of the first organizations to initiate the struggle. The FALN also included the URD forces represented by Fabricio Ojeda as well as the Communist Party and several organizations of fighting men.

Notice how these allies are not mentioned in the two documents; rather they are mentioned, but only to accuse them of adventurism. Not one word is said about the sector represented by Fabricio Ojeda. No! They do not recognize the right of other organizations to participate in the formulation of policy; they launch the policy, and publish it as an order. Not only do they violate the agreements taken in a Party Congress, which should be inviolate, but they also refuse to recognize the forces that in all loyalty had been fighting side by side with the Party.

And what happened? The principal guerrilla chief—among them the most respected one, who from within the Communist Party from the very beginning, since 1959, was in charge of the military section, organizing cadres for armed struggle, who remained in the mountains for years and fought many victorious battles, not great ones, but hard-fought ones, to the extent of his own forces and this while harassed by continuous orders of truce and more truce—and along with him a large number of guerrilla commanders—reacted against that line. We can see how Fabricio and his followers rejected that conception.

The MIR, and with them the fighters of El Bachiller front, also rejected that defeatist conception. And the Party's best men, the most courageous, the most experienced men, those who had carried the heaviest load in the struggle, refused to accept such a defeatist conception. Out of three organizations, two remained in the struggle. Some of the first leaders of the MIR deserted, but the majority, represented by Sáez Mérida, who upon being taken prisoner was replaced by Américo Martín—who now heads the MIR fighters at El Bachiller—maintained their position in favor of armed struggle and continued their ideological line until he died. And Douglas[5] and the most respected guerrilla commanders maintained theirs.

On what basis can we be accused of fomenting divisionism within the Venezuelan Party? What can be used as a base to blame Cuba for problems resulting only and exclusively from an inefficient political leadership?

It is not incumbent upon us to decide the problems of strategy or tactics in the Venezuelan revolutionary movement. Nobody has ever asked us to make any decisions on such problems nor have we ever attempted to do so. But we do have an inalienable right, and that is the right to think, the right to have an opinion, the right to express our sympathy and solidarity with the fighters.

And it was not possible that we, revolutionaries—have to choose between capitulators, between defeatists, and men determined to convert to reality the watchword of "make our country free or die for Venezuela," men who were not a group of theorizing charlatans, but a group of combatants—it was impossible for us, as an elemental question of revolutionary principle and morality, to do other than express our solidarity with those combatants.

How can we consider Douglas Bravo a common divisionist, a common adventurer, a commonly ambitious person, if Douglas Bravo has made

[5] Douglas Bravo, a former member of the CC and Politbureau of the CP, became commander-in-chief of the FALN.—*Ed.*

within the sector of the revolutionary movement deriving from the Party
a kind of protest against the peace which a defeatist leadership wanted to
impose on the Party?

For this reason he has our support and solidarity. And we have the
inalienable right to express with all honesty what we think and what we
feel. He did not side with the capitulators; he sided with the combatants.
Acceptance of the capitulationist theory would have meant that we, as
well, would have had to deny our solidarity to Américo Martín and the
combatants of the MIR who are fighting in the mountains of El Bachiller;
it would have meant denying our solidarity to Fabricio Ojeda and his
comrades.

Proof that the capitulators were wrong and proof that their theory
amounted to handing the revolutionary struggle of Venezuela to the proimperialist government of Leoni on a silver platter is that in spite of
this virtual treason, the proimperialist government of Leoni, aided by
Yankee officials, supported by and supplied with Yankee weapons, has not
been able to crush the heroic and unvanquished guerrillas that fight in the
western mountains of Venezuela and in the mountains of El Bachiller.

Anyone can give himself the name of "eagle" without having a single
feather on his back. In the same way, there are people who call themselves
communists without having a communist hair on their head. The international communist movement, to our way of thinking, is not a church,
it is not a religious sect or a Masonic Lodge that obliges us to hallow
any weakness, any deviation, that obliges us to follow the policy of a
mutual admiration society with all kinds of reformists and pseudorevolutionaries.

And if in any country those who call themselves communists do not
know how to fulfill their duty, we shall support those who, without calling
themselves communists, conduct themselves like real communists in action and in struggle. For every true revolutionary, who bears within
him the revolutionary spirit, revolutionary vocation, will always come
to Marxism! It is impossible for a man, traveling the road of revolution,
not to arrive at Marxism! And every revolutionary on the continent who
is deserving of the name will arrive at the Marxist conception of society!
What is important are the revolutionaries, those who are capable of
making revolutions and developing themselves in revolutionary theory.
To exclude, to deny, to reject a priori all those who from the beginning
did not call themselves communists is an act of dogmatism and un-
qualified sectarianism. Whoever denies that it is the road of revolution
which leads the people to Marxism is no Marxist, although he may call
himself a communist.

This will be our line of conduct. It is the line that has guided our
conduct in relations with the revolutionary movements.

At the Tricontinental Conference in Havana representatives of revolutionary organizations of the three continents met. Some called themselves communists and others did not. What defines a communist is his attitude toward the oligarchies, his attitude toward exploitation, his attitude toward imperialism; and on this continent, his attitude toward the armed revolutionary movement. What will define the communists of this continent is their attitude toward the guerrilla movement, toward the guerrilla movement in Guatemala, in Colombia, and in Venezuela. No one who claims to call himself communist will support the rightist official leadership opposing Douglas Bravo. Communist parties must differentiate between the guerrillas who are fighting in Venezuela and the defeatists who wish to renounce the struggle, who in practice wish to give up the guerrilla movement.

And this will be a dividing line, for we are arriving at the time of definitions, not by anyone's whims, but by the force of the process itself, of historical events themselves. Those who condemn the guerrillas for the simple reason of sect or dogma, in the spirit of freemasonry, cannot consider themselves revolutionaries.

One must ask the revolutionary guerrillas in Guatemala, Colombia, or any other country, who in their opinion are the revolutionaries; who in their opinion are those who show them solidarity, who are their real supporters: the Venezuelan guerrillas or the defeatists? For those who fight in Venezuela, those who force the imperialists to use up part of their resources against them, who bear their share of imperialist bombs, aid those who are fighting in Guatemala or Colombia. Those who fight in the mountains of Venezuela are the only real and possible allies of those who are fighting in the mountains of Colombia and in the mountains of Guatemala.

It is perfectly legitimate for a revolutionary to disagree with a deed, a method, a concrete aspect. What is immoral, what is unrevolutionary, is to make use of a given deed in order to join the hysterical chorus of the reactionaries and imperialists to condemn the revolutionaries. If revolutionaries are responsible for this deed, we may give our opinion, but we may never join the hysterical chorus of the hangmen who govern in Venezuela, in order to condemn the revolutionaries.

What has the official leadership of the Communist Party of Venezuela done in this instance? What have they said officially? Just what we read here:

"The Communist Party of Venezuela disowns Elías Manuitt, who, in the name of the so-called Armed Forces of National Liberation, claimed his organization had assassinated Dr. Julio Iribarren Borges. . . . Elías Manuitt is an ex-militant who was publicly expelled from the ranks of the Communist Party for divisionist activities and slackening of his political position. The same action was applied to Douglas Bravo, Gregorio Lunar Márquez, Freddy Carqués, and others using the name of the national movement of liberation."

Our policy is clear. We recognize only revolutionaries as representatives of the peoples. We do not consider any of those oligarchic and traitorous governments that broke with Cuba, following orders from the Yankee embassy, as representatives of their peoples. We will not re-establish diplomatic relations with any of those governments that obeyed imperialist orders; we have no interest in doing so; we have no desire to do so. We will only establish diplomatic relations with revolutionary governments, with governments that show they are independent. We will not give financial aid to any oligarchy to put down the revolutionary movement with blood. And whoever, no matter who,[6] aids those oligarchies where guerrillas are fighting will be helping to suppress the Revolution, for repressive wars are carried on not only with weapons but also with the millions of dollars used for purchasing the weapons and for paying the mercenary armies.

An unmistakable proof of the lack of independence of those governments is to be found in the recent case of Colombia, where at 6 A.M. a few days ago, because of a guerrilla attack against a train, they arrested the General Secretary of the Communist Party of Colombia and all the leaders of that Party who were found in their customary places. They did not hesitate a bit because at that very moment a delegation of high Soviet officials were present for the signing of a commercial, cultural, and financial agreement with the Lleras Restrepo government; that same day, it was said there was to be an interview between Restrepo and the high Soviet officials. And that same day not only did they arrest the Communist leadership but they also attacked, according to the wire service dispatches, the offices of the news agency TASS. What a friendly spirit those puppets have! There is reciprocity for you! That is a proof of the lack of independence, of the hypocrisy of the international policy of those puppet governments.

What would the Vietnamese revolutionaries think if we were to send delegations to South Vietnam to deal with the Saigon puppet government? What would those who are fighting in the mountains of America think were we to seek close relations with the puppets of imperialism on this side of the continent, with the puppets of the future Yankee aggressions and interventions in this continent?

And all of them, imperialists and puppets, join in a conspiracy against our revolutionary, socialist nation, which is as it is, not because we have imported revolution from any other country, but rather because we have generated it on our own soil and under our own skies.

There are some who speak of supposed cases of fatalism, but there is no fatalism that can hold back this Revolution, not the ninety-mile fatalism, or any other kind of fatalism! This Revolution that sprang from

---

[6] The reference is to Soviet Russia and other East European countries which offered long-term credits and technical aid to Colombia.—*Ed.*

nothing at all, this Revolution that sprang from a tiny group of men who for whole years lived in conditions of encirclement by the enemy, where nothing could get through, is a Revolution which has its own particular right to exist. It is a Revolution—understand this well, all puppets, oligarchs, and shilly-shalliers and pseudorevolutionaries of all stripes—it is a Revolution which no one or nothing will be able to crush or halt!

And this Revolution will maintain its position of absolute independence, that kind of independence to which all people capable of fighting for it are entitled, that kind of independence all honorable people are entitled to have.

We proclaim it to the world: This Revolution will hold true to its path, this Revolution will follow its own line, this Revolution will never be anybody's satellite or yes-man. It will never ask anybody's permission to maintain its own position either in matters of ideology, or on domestic or foreign affairs; proudly and courageously our people are ready to face the future, whatever that future may hold.

COMMUNIST GUERRILLAS: ANSWER TO FIDEL*

WE were angered and grieved by the unjust and unworthy attack made against our Party, the Communist Party of Venezuela, by Fidel Castro. It grieved us that a revolutionary of such outstanding merit as Fidel should get involved in the absurd business of attacking a Party which suffers enough persecution through its position in the front line of battle against imperialism.

We Venezuelan communist guerrillas who are offering armed resistance to Betancourtism and the *gorilas*, claim for ourselves the titles of waverers, traitors, renegades, bunglers, right-wingers, and opportunists which Fidel has bestowed upon our Party. These names we can add to those of "bandits" and "highwaymen" which we have been called by the *gorilas*.

Perhaps Fidel was referring to the leadership and not to the guerrillas, but we remain faithful to the Party, we have not abandoned arms and the Party has not betrayed us, as Fidel affirms. Is not Fidel repeating, somewhat tardily, the lies which the fractionalists invented? The fractionalists have taught Fidel an unhappy role: to repeat lies and calumnies that don't fool anyone in our country. We can only interpret Fidel's

---

* Declaration dated March 1967, published in *Tribuna Popular*, clandestine organ of the Central Committee of the Venezuelan Communist Party, April 3, 1967, and signed by Tirso Pinto and Ramón Paris "for the Simón Bolívar Guerrilla Front, Eastern Mountains, Venezuela," and by Juan Vicente Cabezas, Rafael Ramos, Capitán Blanco, Alfredo Maneiro, Lucas Matheus (Horacio) "for the José A. Páez Guerrilla Front." Translation by Jenny James.

attack against the CPV as a desperate effort directed toward boosting those adventurist, anti-Party groups which, while calling themselves supporters of armed struggle, are leading it to disaster. To cry down the prestige of the CPV in front of the people won't harm its reputation in the slightest, for it has proven itself in a thousand battles, but it will harm Fidel Castro himself.

In his contradictory speech, Fidel says that no one can accuse him of interfering in the internal affairs of our Party and movement. Yet further on he declares that the commander of the FALN is Douglas Bravo whom he (Fidel) supports. Isn't that interference?

Since when was Fidel Castro granted the right of choosing the leader of the FALN? What is more, according to what Fidel says, we aren't even Venezuelan fighters, because "for some time now" the majority of Venezuelan guerrillas, and we among them, have recognized Pedro Medina Silva as legitimate commander of the FALN.[1] We reject the attempts of Fidel Castro to appoint and dismiss FALN commanders and to decide according to his own criteria who are the true revolutionaries in Venezuela. We also reject as unworthy and ungenerous the insults made about our political commissars of the FALN. Fidel accused them of being cowards because they weren't in a guerrilla encampment. According to this peculiar method of reasoning, in order to merit the title of "brave," you have to have been in a guerrilla camp (we don't know if Fidel would by virtue of this narrow criterion disqualify that hero and martyr of the Cuban Revolution, Frank País, symbol of the underground battle against Batista, and José A. Echevarría, who died precisely on 13th March, the day Fidel decided to deny the title of fighter to all those who run a thousand risks in the underground armed battle of the cities).

We guerrillas reject this concept. We reject it because it sows discord among the guerrilla fighters and insults the underground fighters who are as much heroes as any guerrilla. As far as we are concerned, fighters who risk their lives in a battle with the army and those who risk it daily in the struggle against repressive authorities are equally brave. And how can you accuse a man of cowardliness who has taken part in the Puerto Cabello uprising, the most important battle that has been waged recently in our country, and men who fled with Pedro Medina Silva from the Island of Tacarigua and, after staying abroad, returned secretly to the country to face their revolutionary duties, risking their lives at every turn?

And why the attack by Fidel on the general commander and political commissar of the FALN? Perhaps because these comrades, having regard for the reputation of the FALN, deposed Manuitt Camero? This

[1] One of the leaders of the abortive Puerto Cabello military insurrection of May 1962, who was given a thirty-year jail sentence, Medina Silva escaped and became commander-in-chief of the FALN. He stopped fighting in 1965 and surrendered in 1969.—*Ed.*

could doubtless be a reason. With this attack on our comrades, a sort of smoke screen, Fidel could be trying to save the face of Manuitt who in a most irresponsible manner, from Havana, encumbered the FALN with responsibility for some obscure murder, basing his opinions on the versions of the [non-CP] FALN.[2] Nobody in Venezuela was convinced, nor are they yet, that this distasteful crime could have been committed by revolutionaries. The Venezuelan people have a high opinion of the revolutionaries. But Manuitt hastened to blame the FALN for this death, thus saying exactly the same thing as the Venezuelan *gorilas*. Was it not right that at that time the true representatives of the FALN should reject and condemn such a declaration and denounce it as a provocation to our enemies and those of the Cuban Revolution? Was it not right to point out to the people the difference between revolutionary methods of fighting and nonrevolutionary ones to give the masses an opportunity to distinguish between those who are guided by revolutionary ideas and those who are of an adventurist and anarcho-terrorist mentality? All this was right and good and was what the FALN command, led by Medina Silva, decided to do. And then, as Silva had also censured terrorist activities, when Fidel's pupil put his foot in it, he tried to save him from the mire by throwing insults when everyone in Venezuela knew that it was Manuitt's stupid statements that had opened the floodgate of reactionary oppression.

And another reason for the attack was that Fidel hoped to destroy Medina Silva and to prop up Douglas Bravo and Manuitt. And all this after having declared that nobody could accuse him of interfering in our affairs.

Fidel further accused the leadership of our Party of wanting to direct the war from the cities and he remarks that this is a grave mistake as the leadership should be on the scene of the action, which is in the mountains. We ask in return: Isn't it a worse mistake to try to direct it from abroad, as seems to be Fidel Castro's intention? The Venezuelan revolutionary movement, under the leadership—be it good or bad—of the CPV has come through five years of armed struggle. Exactly twice as long as the armed struggle of Fidel lasted in the mountains of Cuba. And if it is true, as it certainly is, that we have not triumphed, it is also true that we have not been defeated and liquidated, precisely because the CPV took the struggle into its hands. In spite of all the mistakes we may have made, this is the truth. If it hadn't been like that, if the struggle in our country had been under the direction of adventurist groups, the armed resistance would have been wiped out long ago, and whoever

[2] The confusion here arises from the fact that in 1967 there were still two FALN's —the one commanded by Douglas Bravo and Manuitt Camero, and the old CP guerrilla units from which the former emerged and which was in the process of being disbanded on order of the Central Committee of the CPV.—*Ed.*

doubts that can ask the antiguerrilla Pentagon bosses. In these five years we have suffered heavy setbacks but we have learned a lot and accumulated experience. And the main lesson we have learned is that in Venezuela there can be no victory in the armed struggle without the CP or in opposition to the CP. From our position we know the characteristics of the armed struggle in our country and what role it must play and the exact position of guerrilla warfare in our revolutionary development. We do not ignore the experiences of other countries, but we do disregard advice we haven't asked for.

Fidel's opinions on the guerrilla struggle and its role in Venezuela are disputable—for these opinions derive from memories of his own experience in the Cuban context. Our opinions are born of the experience of five years of fighting in Venezuela, they arise from our own Venezuelan reality. Fidel is mistaken, and will continue to be so, in his grasp of the situation because he is using a stereotype; the CP of Venezuela is right and will continue to be right because it is dealing with concrete reality. Fidel is forgetting the individual characteristics of the Cuban revolutionary process, the quality of flexibility he imprinted upon it from the first moments, free from all dogmatism and sectarianism. And now he is attempting to deny us the right to think for ourselves and to carry our Revolution forward based in our own reality. No one except the Venezuelan revolutionaries, no one except the CPV, is in a position to determine day by day the right direction for our struggle.

We communist guerrillas completely support the policy outlined by the Central Committee of our Party. Our country, tired of violence, wants a democratic, peaceful government. But such a government will only be attained when we are able to dislodge from power the *gorila*-Betancourt gang and their rule of violence. Our Party has never said that a democratic government which will assure peace to all can be obtained without first dislodging from power the *gorila*-Betancourt gang. Much less have we said that this kind of government can be attained by means of compromises with the country's criminals. It is only those interested in falsifying the policy of the CPV for their own twisted ends that have put out this lie and gone around repeating it. And it is these same anti-CPV circles that have sold this anticommunist merchandise to Fidel and have got him to repeat the same false accusations against the CPV. However, from this distance, following the public attacks on our political line, we don't really know who's speaking for whom. We don't know whether the anti-CPV groups are repeating Fidel's opinions or whether Fidel is repeating those of the anti-CPV groups. In any case, anyone, whether inside or outside the country, who thinks that the CPV will change its mind through flattery or intimidation has made a big mistake, which goes as well for those who think we're longing for legality or comfort. How little those that think like this know the CPV! The Venezuelan communists, and the only communists in Venezuela, are those who for a long time now, fearing no one, and in the face of the whole world, have always called themselves communists and have been militant and continue to be militant in the CPV. Nothing in the world would make us give up fulfillment of the historical task belonging to us or prevent us facing the long, hard struggle toward national liberation and socialism.

We communists who have taken up arms to resist the aggression of the *gorila*-Betancourt gang will not allow ourselves to be confused or discouraged by threats from reactionary quarters or by the blackmail of anti-Marxist groups who have not interpreted correctly the situation in our country. We stand by our Central Committee, and will continue to do so, for it is they who decide, *collectively*, the policy our Party is to follow in Venezuela. Faithful till death to the CPV, the instrument of the Venezuelan Revolution, *we will continue our fight in the way the Party decides*.

We do not deny a role to other revolutionary groups or movements, nor do we consider that we have a monopoly over the Revolution, but we have a duty to defend our Party and to safeguard the instrument which our people, the Venezuelan working class, have been building up for their liberation in a glorious process which has lasted thirty-five years. If there are some who are mistaken about the role of our Party, at least imperialism has made no mistakes. Thus to defend the CPV is the most sacred thing for all revolutionaries and anyone who attacks the CPV, no matter from where he comes, is playing the same game as the imperialists and the other enemies of our country.

We would also say that Fidel's attacks on our Party and on the leaders of the FALN do not lessen our active and militant solidarity with the Cuban Revolution. Moreover, these unfortunate attacks against us by Fidel trouble us not only because they create difficulties for our revolutionary development but also because they reduce his stature and prejudice the prestige of the Cuban Revolution in Venezuela. We shall continue to be soldiers who are ready to defend the first socialist country in America.

Fidel's attacks create fresh difficulties for us. Our guerrillas are having to prepare themselves for the greatest hardships and to be able to surmount the greatest difficulties. If it becomes necessary to march barefoot and naked, we will do it; but we will never succumb to any kind of blackmail. The moment the enemy attacks or an assault comes from the friendly camp, we communist guerrillas raise our guns and proclaim before our people and the world: NO ONE CAN DESTROY THE CPV! LONG LIVE THE CPV!

Guatemala

The most successful guerrilla war
waged in Latin America during the 1960's was the Guatemalan. Not because the guerrillas won battles against the government forces and not
because they established liberated areas—though they did both in modest
fashion for a while. But because they successfully set up the structure,
the support, and the organization for a protracted people's war. And this,
despite formidable defeats in the late sixties. Relentlessly pursued by
U.S.-trained Guatemalan counterinsurgency troops, U.S. Rangers, and
Green Beret Special Forces "advisers," continuously harassed by right-
wing military terrorists and assassins coordinated outside "legality" by
army and police officials, and often plagued by internal disputes, defec-
tions, and betrayals, Guatemala's Rebel Armed Forces (FAR) nevertheless managed not only to survive—quite a feat in itself—but also to
spread and pick up some local peasant support. By the end of the decade,
however, the FAR was seemingly irrevocably split.

The armed struggle of Guatemala was begun by a group of young army
officers who, at first, hoped for quick insurrectional success. Few, if any,
of these officers, headed by Marco Antonio Yon Sosa, then belonged to
revolutionary or regular political parties. In fact, most of them had been
trained in counterinsurgency by the United States (either in Panama, Fort
Benning, Fort Bragg, or Fort Leavenworth). Had they succeeded in 1960,
they would most probably have set up a military-nationalist regime and
proceeded to try to launch a "revolution" from above—without the
people's support or participation and, even more probably, without a
chance of survival against U.S.–Cuban-exile armed intervention. Yet,
unlike the popularly elected radical reformist government of Jacobo
Arbenz (1951–54), which was overthrown by a CIA-planned and -financed
armed intervention, these young military officers were predisposed to fight
intervention and, if necessary, the United States. More important, they

467

were ready to trust the people—that is, arm them. They were very much aware that Arbenz, though extremely popular with the Guatemalan masses for his agrarian, labor, and educational reforms, was basically just a reformist. When the chips were down, it did not occur to him to fight. Furthermore, these officers knew their history—and that of the United States: Never had an elected or golpista (brought to power via a coup) government tried to carry out genuine reforms in Latin America without having been overthrown by the United States, directly or indirectly. Still, these officers, too, would have probably failed had they taken power, for the only way that the people would have fought with them against a U.S. or mercenary invasion would have been if the officers had fought with the people in the first place.

The military insurrection of 1960 failed, however, and the surviving officers had only two choices: go into exile or wage a guerrilla war. Most chose the latter—and they have been fighting ever since. But their real troubles began with that choice: how to get along with the Guatemalan Labor Party (PGT), that is, the basically Moscow-oriented Communist Party. Yon Sosa, whose guerrillas were known as the MR-13 (Revolutionary Movement of the 13th of November, the date of the unsuccessful insurrection), was willing to cooperate with the PGT. In 1962, joining forces with another smaller guerrilla unit, the M-12, and the PGT, he established the FAR. But relations were strained. The PGT wanted to use the guerrillas as a blackmail weapon in its legalistic struggle; it considered Yon Sosa "ultra-leftist" and "adventuristic." It is then that agents of the Posadist wing of international Trotskyism began to infiltrate the FAR. A former Argentine soccer player who believes that the best hope for international socialism is a U.S.-Russian atomic war, Posadas considered the Guatemalan guerrillas subservient to the worldwide anti-U.S. movement and hence "expendable" if continental strategy demanded it.

In 1965, Luis Turcios Lima, who had been the FAR's second-in-command, left Yon Sosa, set up the "Edgar Ibarra" front and accepted PGT direction. Yon Sosa then renamed his guerrillas the MR-13, Turcios took on the FAR label and the PGT sent César Montes, a member of the Party's Political Bureau, to be Turcios' next-in-command. It was the FAR and not the MR-13 which was represented at Havana's Tricontinental meeting, and it was then, in January 1966, that Fidel Castro denounced Yon Sosa as an "agent of Trotskyism and imperialism."

While accusations continued to fly both ways, Yon Sosa decided to investigate the implications of Fidel's charges. He found that, indeed, some of his lieutenants were Posadist agents and did filter large sums of money obtained from kidnappings and assaults in Guatemala, to Posadas' Mexican operations. Yon Sosa immediately purged these agents, and Turcios responded by offering to reunite both guerrilla armies. Yon Sosa, however, would not agree on one fundamental point: He refused to accept any alliances with national bourgeois elements. Since the FAR was politically directed by the PGT, which like all traditional communist parties insists on such alliances, a union was theoretically impossible. But Turcios Lima, who had always agreed with Yon on the sell-out character of the national bourgeoisie, rejected both the government's amnesty offers and CP advice, and announced the merger of FAR and MR-13. A few weeks later, he was killed in a car crash—sabotaged, some say, by the PGT. César Montes, a communist official, then assumed command of the FAR and it was expected that the merger would be called off.

But it was not. Instead, Montes denounced the Communist Party as opportunistic and the two guerrilla armies were totally combined into one again, called the FAR. By the end of 1968, it was headed by Yon Sosa and seconded by Montes. Its explicitly stated position included protracted people's war until the end, no compromises with governments, militarists, or the bourgeoisie. The FAR, considering itself part of a continental army, was willing to coordinate its activities with other liberation movements (Yon Sosa was one of the most fervent advocates of both the Tricontinental and OLAS, despite his exclusion). The FAR was openly committed to the so-called Guevarist "many Vietnams" theory, but remained nationalist as well. It advocated people's participation, workers' control, and collectivization. It was preparing itself for a long long war, "perhaps twenty-five years, or more," once said Yon Sosa, "most probably longer than my lifetime." In 1969, however, the FAR split once again, Yon Sosa's forces retiring deeper into the countryside while Montes' men focused mainly on urban guerrilla activity (based partly on the experience of Uruguay's Tupamaros). In the summer of 1970, Yon Sosa was killed by Mexican "border guards," directed by CIA operatives; apparently, he was trying to cross the border to abandon the struggle.

In the two articles below, the chronological order of publication has been reversed. The first one, by "Cardona Fratti" (who is probably César Montes himself), explains the internal struggle between revolutionary communists and the Communist Party. If not Montes, the author has nevertheless undergone Montes' trajectory: from membership in the PGT to inclusion in its hierarchy to joining the guerrillas to denouncing the PGT as undermining the Revolution. It was written before FAR and MR-13 merged in 1968. The second article, the manifesto issued in 1964 by Yon Sosa, Turcios Lima, and other MR-13 leaders, spells out the principles that MR-13 then and the various groups of the FAR today uphold—and explains the guerrillas' program for the future.

ARNOLDO CARDONA FRATTI (CÉSAR MONTES?):
DOGMA AND REVOLUTION*

THE triumph of the Cuban Revolution on January 1, 1959, and the rapid succession of events that followed upon that victory had the effect of a "ray of lightning from a calm sky"—to put it in Marx's words—upon the political prospects of the American continent.

The political forces of Latin America underwent a new polarization under the influence of these events and the new revolutionary attitude of the young Cuban leaders. It is well known that this shakeup also reached the continent's communist movement, because the dynamic and vital reality of the Cuban Revolution in fact invalidated the traditional revolutionary concepts that had been upheld for forty years by the Latin American communist parties without their being able to bring about substantial changes favorable to the people in the correlation of forces confronting each other on the continent. The general line, the scheme of the decisive moving forces, the methods of struggle, and the structures created and in operation for decades that have emerged from the Latin American communist movement are all inadequate or ineffective for achieving the objective that gives the movement its reason for being: the taking of power and the triumph of Revolution.

This commotion did not lead, as it had been hoped it would, to the honest and self-critical revision of the ample experience obtained in the long life of the Latin American communist movement. On the contrary, the eagerness to keep Marxism deprived of its skeleton, the theory and practice of revolutionary violence, led to the adulteration of theory and a search for explanations that had nothing Marxist or scientific about them. Those of us who have come from the communist ranks know that, instead of analyzing positive lessons of the Cuban Revolution, those that might be deemed negative were sought; there was a great deal of discussion on the "exceptionalism" of the Cuban case, an exceptionalism which curiously converged on the most essential aspects: on the life of the Revolution—that is, the armed struggle—and on the vanguard that led that struggle—that is, the fact that it was not a Communist Party which had done so.

Where the revolutionary tension of the people is sharpest, as in the case of Guatemala, the thesis of the road of armed struggle as an exception could not be defended. The same thing occurred in Venezuela and Colombia, with their natural differences. The apparently ideal formula, acceptable

---

* Written in the jungles of Guatemala early in 1968 and published in *Tricontinental*, No. 8 (September–October 1968).

in principle by all revolutionaries, then arose: armed revolutionary struggle led by the Communist Party. In Guatemala, Colombia, and Venezuela, there were conditions for the practical application of this formula. The facts, however, have shown that the acceptance of this formula by the leading bodies of the communist parties was simply a tactical turn on their part. Full acceptance was not possible, because it would lead them inevitably into an essential contradiction with the theoretical and structural platform that makes their base and which is constructed of partial Marxist elements lacking their inner dialectics. This platform has shown its effectiveness in carrying out a political game of election-aimed alliances, but it is not designed to take power from the hands of the ruling classes or openly assume the leadership of the Revolution.

The following account is a personal, direct, eyewitness account of the antecedents of our revolutionary war, many of which have been deliberately withheld. These antecedents are useful to provide us with insight and a basis for our present renovating revolutionary action; they are also useful to comrades from other countries who will surely be called upon to face similar situations.

In Guatemala the development of the democratic-bourgeois revolution, with its partial popular demands, was interrupted in 1954 by reactionary violence on the part of imperialism and its agents among the native oligarchy. Counterrevolutionary violence[1] was used as blackmail to cause the capitulation of the national bourgeoisie which led the revolutionary process. No-holds-barred violence was unleashed against the people, the worker, and peasant masses, to crush resistance. Neither the leading political nucleus as a whole—composed, at the time, of the Party of the Guatemalan Revolution (PRG, which most thoroughly embodied the interests of the national bourgeoisie), the Revolutionary Action Party (PAR, democratic petty-bourgeois), the National Renewal Party (PRN, petty-bourgeois intellectual), and the Guatemalan Labor Party (PGT, communist)—nor any single one of these parties alone succeeded in opposing popular violence to the imperialist, reactionary aggression. Underestimating the fighting capacity of the people and feeling themselves overwhelmed by the apparent might of the military machinery mobilized by imperialism, plus that of the army—which they considered their own force but which betrayed them and answered the call of the counterrevolutionary camp—these parties and President Arbenz gave up the battle as lost and succumbed without firing a single shot.

Nevertheless, at no time in our past history has there existed in the people a greater mass readiness to fight than in those moments when, in

---

[1] The invasion forces—trained, armed, financed and air-supported by the CIA—came from Honduras and Nicaragua, and were headed by Colonel Armas, who followed his victory with wholesale repressions and executions of the previously elected officials. —Ed.

the face of the mercenary invasion and domestic conspiracy, the peasants, armed only with machetes, spontaneously kept watch on the highways, stood guard on the bridges, and captured enemy spies and agents. The workers and students organized themselves in volunteer brigades and, quartered in union offices, courtrooms, and youth organizations, waited in vain to be given the weapons needed to defend their country and their Revolution. The political leaders of that Revolution never knew—because they were not in close enough contact with the masses—of their will to fight, the combativity, and the optimism that inspired the "people's brigades" that marched unarmed through the streets in order to grow accustomed to military orders and that felt instinctively, in spite of government or Party directives, that the army pompously called the army "of the revolution" would guarantee neither national sovereignty nor the continuity of the Revolution and that both would be secure only in the armed hands of workers, peasants, and students.

The fall of the Arbenz government dragged the people along with it. The political parties of the national bourgeoisie and the petty bourgeoisie disbanded completely; their leaders filled the embassies. Only isolated groups of middle-level or local cadres survived. The mass organizations were beheaded, and their bases, which had not played any real role in leadership and had been formed not in a revolutionary spirit of class consciousness but rather in a trade union and "economist" direction, were paralyzed by the unexpected flight of their leaders and the repressive action of the army in which they had previously been urged to trust.

Only in the country were there spontaneous outbreaks of desperate resistance—which were, of course, brutally drowned in blood. Among the poor peasants, who in some regions caught a glimpse of the return of the land, there remained engraved the certainty that only through violence would they one day be able to recover the little that they had been given —which was snatched away from them by the violence of their oppressors —and, even more, their definitive liberation and all that it implies.

The only branch of the state apparatus that showed firmness and clarity was the police, whose chief was more loyal to the Revolution than to Arbenz and gave evidence up to the last moment of his willingness to play his last card. He proposed to the president that repressive action be taken against the military brass, whose treason was perfectly evident days before the final collapse.

The only party that survived as a political body was the Guatemalan Labor Party (PGT), founded at the end of Arévalo's presidential term[2] under the name Communist Party of Guatemala. As the principal standard bearer for the Arbenz government's democratic program, the PGT won considerable support in the southern part of the country and sympathy

[2] Juan José Arévalo, liberal democratic politician, elected president of the first "revolutionary government" (1945–51).—Ed.

among the popular sectors in other geographic zones. It was thanks to such backing and the consistent attitude of two or three members of the leadership and a handful of middle-level cadres that, although it could not issue a line of struggle for the new phase that the country was going through, it was able to continue acting, taking up again on an underground basis part of its work in the capital. This meant that the PGT, unlike the other components of the Arbenz front, was not completely dissolved: From the culminating moments of the invasion and the coup d'état, all the parties mentioned, forgetting the masses and their need to organize themselves to continue the struggle under different conditions, devoted their efforts to seeking refuge or making deals with the sector of the army that seemed least involved in the betrayal.

Placed in the front line of counterrevolutionary persecution, the PGT leaders who remained in the country also realized, from the underground, that in order to modify the situation it was necessary to have recourse to violence. But their mentality was formed by a dependence on the national bourgeoisie, which constituted the traditional line, leaving them unable to assume the historical role corresponding to them in virtue of taking upon themselves the leadership of a Communist Party, the vanguard of the proletariat and the people; thus, they did not succeed in finding the revolutionary, popular form of violence, armed struggle. They became involved, along with some political and military figures left over from the Arbenz period, in barracks-room plotting. To reach this point, no Marxist analysis or conception of the Revolution as a popular process was needed. It was simply a military plot, with the political counseling of *Arbencista* cadres, because the PGT leaders were viewed more in that light than as leaders of the proletariat.

Isolated from the masses, imprisoned by their dependence on the bourgeoisie and the theoretical schemes in universal use among the communist parties, the PGT leaders did not turn to the countryside, where with little effort but great decisiveness it would have been possible to organize armed resistance and prepare a fighting revolutionary line.

The institutionalizing tendencies encouraged by the State Department to quiet the international scandal caused by the "glorious victory" took effect, and the country slowly returned to the reactionary "normalcy" required by its oppressors in order to exploit it with ease. Although it was a constant participant in the successive, unsuccessful military plots—such as that of 1957, when Francisco Méndez Montenegro (brother of the present Yankee puppet governing Guatemala) and Carlos Sarti were murdered—the PGT also entered a sort of "clandestine normalcy." Its main efforts were aimed at the constitution or strengthening of legal bodies: the Association of University Students (AEU), the Autonomous Union Federation of Guatemala (FASGUA), the newspaper *El Estudiante*, the Committee for the Return of the Exiles, etc. The rebuilding of the Party was envisioned within this framework of action. Important battles were waged in these spheres, and they, too, took their toll of martyrs. But their undefined prospects could not lead to anything more than the democratization and liberalization of the regime that imperialism and reaction imposed by violence on the Guatemalan people; those costly battles did not weaken even the bases of that regime or spend its forces.

In 1957, in the wake of the enigmatic murder of Castillo Armas by his own followers and the logical struggle for power that it caused among the different factions of the oligarchy, the old Ydígoras, representative of the most ultra-right of them, took full advantage of the hate inspired by Castillo Armas and his clique in the people and the urban middle masses and mobilized them in a catch-all opposition to the regime of what was badly misnamed the "liberation"[3]—a mobilization that concretely favored his own personal designs and those of his class faction.

At that time the policy of the PGT also leaned in the direction that the game of the reactionary factions imposed on the political process in our country. It divested itself of the revolutionary class spirit which must be essentially subversive, against the oppressors, to such an extent that, when Ydígoras astutely and demagogically proclaimed a "clean slate" and committed himself to permit the return of the 1954 exiles, the PGT, in a meeting of its Central Committee, adopted the line known as "national conciliation," basing it on the supposed need to take advantage of the comparatively liberal policy with which the sly Ydígoras inaugurated his term.

A few months later, the Guatemalan masses were instinctively shaken by the Cuban events, and the revolutionary ferment latent in them, sharpened by the economic and political crises in the country, found new prospects and began to manifest themselves in massive popular demonstrations that took on a virulence dangerous for the regime.

The PGT leadership, once again complete with the return of its members who had gone into exile in 1954, held its Third Party Congress in June 1960—the only one in the past fourteen years—in the midst of growing discontent and pressure from the base. To prepare the line and the other resolutions that emanated from this Congress, the leadership group found itself faced with the need to consider simultaneously the following objectively active factors: (1) a diametrical change in the national political situation, characterized by the counterrevolutionary victory and the institutionalization of the regime that arose from it; (2) the

---

[3] The counterrevolutionary movement headed by Castillo Armas, tool of the State Department in the invasion of Guatemala and the overthrow of the Arbenz government in 1954, took the name of National Liberation Movement because, according to its propaganda, its purpose was to "liberate" Guatemala from communism. This is why in Guatemala the terms "liberation" and "liberationist" have a reactionary meaning in the political lexicon.—A.C.F.

uncontainable mass influence exerted by the nearby example of the Cuban Revolution and its method of struggle—the people's guerrilla war—as a revolutionary road which could not be left without channeling; (3) the discontent at the base of the Party, which originated in 1954 and was revived by the political failures that crowned the "national conciliation" policy; (2) the resentment of the Party's middle cadres who had remained in the country after the fall of Arbenz and who, although they played the principal role in the underground reconstruction of the PGT, were in fact replaced upon the arrival of the leaders who had been in exile; and (5) the mistaken obligation of keeping within theoretical schemes that, elevated to dogma and elaborated in other countries with different conditions, have constituted the line, the strategy, and the tactics of the Latin American communist parties.

Formed with the idea of Marxism as a rigid series of postulates, isolated from the masses, eager to maintain the hegemony of their sect, the PGT leading group, unable to size up events with independent criteria and lacking doctrinal audacity, underestimated and sacrificed to a great extent the first four factors, precisely those that are real and changing, the living sources of Marxism, and took refuge in the abovementioned theoretical schemes, the magic formulas that are so comfortable for mentalities that have little practice in dialectical thought.

As a consequence, the Congress did not adopt a new program, but rather approved "programmatic points" of only passing validity organized into a "political platform." This notable exercise in subtlety was aimed at covering up the fact that the PGT did not ratify the program passed by its Second Congress, held in full legality during the time of the Arbenz government, *nor did it prepare a new one.* Evidently the basis of this problem was to be found in the fact that, trusting in the national bourgeoisie, the PGT leadership maintained its hopes that the Arbenz case would be repeated, and it did not wish to run the risk that a program with a more marked class character would interfere with its tactical freedom in the game of alliances. In reality, the programmatic points approved by the Third Congress are no more than clarifications and specifications of the program of the Second Congress, a current that inspired the program of the Arbenz government. It even ignored the fundamental experience of the 1954 defeat by doing no more than posing a "reform" of the army. These programmatic points did not take up the problem of the road to Revolution—that is, the method by which the people should take power. Instead of this, the already classic preparation for "all forms of struggle" was posed. The statutes were reformed only in some points of a technical character in regard to the frequency of congresses, attributes of the higher bodies, etc. A paragraph was inserted in the general introduction stating that the Party did not propose the establishment of socialism at that time. Despite numerous challenges, the old Central Committee was maintained without modifications except for the filling of vacancies due to desertion or death. With the adoption of this line, the PGT characterized itself and put the seal on its historical prospects: It placed itself at the rear of the revolutionary process, leaving the vanguard vacant. A month after the debut of the new Party line a group of young people (including some communists) led by Lieutenant Lavagnino unsuccessfully attempted to assault the Cobán Military Garrison. Their aim was to capture weapons and go up into the mountains (Sierra de las Minas) to begin armed struggle against the Ydígoras government. Although the leadership of the Party was informed of the plan, it refrained from giving any guidelines and simply waited to see what would happen.

Conspiracies multiplied within the army, and different tendencies flourished. The promoters were no longer just the colonels left over from the Arbenz period: new currents were emerging among the young officers who were stifled by the swollen old officer caste. They rebelled against the corruption that Ydígoras encouraged as the main incentive for his followers, against the stain left by the 1954 betrayal, and very concretely against the use of Guatemalan soil by Cuban counterrevolutionaries training at various localities in the country. The efforts made by former *Arbencista* military chiefs to direct and control the discontent among the young officers were in vain, and they thus drew apart from the rebel ferment.

This ferment led, on November 13, 1960, to an unsuccessful uprising of young officers, sergeants, and military police in Guatemala City. When they did not receive the support of other military zones of the country involved in the rebellion, they left the city and dug themselves in at the Zacapa Military Garrison, which had already been taken from within by some officers headed by Lieutenant Luis Trejo Esquivel (later to become one of the leaders of the MR-13 and still later an outstanding guerrilla in the Rebel Armed Forces, until his death in combat in July 1967). Although, as we know, this rebellion was put down after several days without any important clashes taking place—put down with the help of bombings carried out by Cuban mercenary pilots—these events left a deep mark on the people's state of mind and on the thinking of several officers. When the most patriotic officers (Alejandro de León, Marco Antonio Yon Sosa, Luis Turcios, Luis Trejo, Augusto Loarca, Emilio Zaldívar, Rodolfo Chacón, and Julio Bolaños San Juan) had taken the Zacapa Military Garrison, they saw for themselves the willingness to fight of the people, who went on their own accord to ask for arms to fight beside the young officers. The aim of this attack did not go beyond the limits of the army, but the gesture of the Zacapa peasants and the attitude that peasants from other departments and even from neighboring countries were to show made a deep impression and brought about a qualitative change in the thinking of the military men involved.

A group of officers and soldiers who took refuge in Honduras and El Salvador decided to continue the struggle against the Ydígoras government and, leaning on political groups from the right-wing opposition, returned secretly to the country. They named their organization the 13th of November Revolutionary Movement (MR-13) and began to seek new contacts with army chiefs and officers on active service as well as political support to undertake a new military coup. Governmental repression was aimed at them, but, for the first time since 1954, those political fugitives met their pursuers with fire-power, invariably escaping capture. This fighting attitude—which contrasted sharply with the heroic but passive stoicism with which the revolutionaries had, until then, accepted capture—immediately won popular sympathy and enthusiasm.

These facts forced the PGT leadership to look with greater seriousness at the prospect of armed struggle, but without sufficient determination and understanding of its importance. The leaders wallowed in hesitations at a time when the adoption of a clear combat line and its organized application would have truly placed the organization at the vanguard of the Revolution. Although in April 1961 the Central Committee passed a resolution leaping from the vagaries of the Third Congress line to the definition of armed struggle as the principal form of struggle that the Revolution would adopt in Guatemala, to the formation of a military commission and an organizational outline for the first armed groups, this line never reached the base, nor was it even known to the middle-level cadres. Meanwhile, the Party's best efforts were aimed at strengthening the base of the Revolutionary Unity Party (PUR), an organization intended to group diverse sectors of *Arbencismo* for electoral purposes, a legal entity in which the PGT hoped to be able to express its political influence.

The preparation of the first military group at that time was rather a precautionary measure with an eye to being prepared for participating in any attempt at seizing power on the part of the progressive groups that were constantly considering a military coup. Other measures adopted by the military commission were of a preventive nature, and none of them led in reality to putting the adopted line into practice. They were adopted due to pressure on the Party from the base in view of the continuing outbreaks of armed struggle.

While this was taking place, the 13th of November rebels were changing their view of the struggle and radicalizing their thought. Like all military careerists in our country, they had felt the scorn and hatred of the people when they were in the army, and they were thus that much better able to appreciate the affection and admiration of which they were the object in their new role of rebels. Convinced by their past experience that they could only obtain success with the backing of the people, they began to search for a political organization that could guarantee this support. They made contact with practically all the country's political opposition groups, from extreme right to extreme left. The party with which the MR-13 found greatest identification was the PGT, and relations were established that were to bring about mutual influences—and mutual reserves. The PGT's influence on the MR-13's principal cadres was ideological. In turn, Party middle cadres and activists were influenced toward a more radical determination to struggle and the livening-up of their work methods. On the other hand, the reserves that the PGT leadership maintained regarding the MR-13 chiefs consisted mainly in the latter's accentuated inclination toward immediate armed action and their indiscriminate search for military contacts in their eagerness to bring about conditions favorable to a military coup. For their part, the military men resented the hesitation they saw among the communist leaders and the exaggerated slowness to be noted in their carrying out of practical measures. At first impressed by the theoretical appeal of the ideology introduced to them by the PGT, the young rebel officers were not long in becoming aware of the lack of decisiveness which was becoming evident in the performance of the PGT leaders, and the lack of precision in the prospects they indicated. Nevertheless, they maintained fraternal esteem and respect for the Party.

Waiting for a coup d'état or a military coup to jell, the MR-13 rebels began to suffer unfortunate losses. Alejandro de León, who was emerging as the MR-13's main political cadre, was murdered while he tried to get away from his captors after a spectacular confrontation in the heart of the capital. Convinced of the need to act and of the impossibility of pulling the PGT leadership out of its static state, Yon and his comrades turned to the countryside, established ties with the peasants of the Izabal banana-growing region, and, with their backing, planned a series of actions which were communicated to the Party in a gesture of trust and identification. These actions began in January 1962 with the execution of the chief of the Secret Police, who had assassinated Alejandro de León. They continued with the taking of the Bananero and Mariscos detachments and the Morales Police Station. They captured weapons and a sizable amount of money from the United Fruit Company offices, and then they made off in three columns. Although the fundamental nucleus of these columns was made up of officers and soldiers, a good number of them from the attacked garrison, one of the objectives of the actions consisted in the massive recruitment and arming of peasants. However, the planning of the actions virtually went no further. The three columns, after covering a certain amount of territory, were to meet at a given point and then decide upon their future line, which almost surely would be that of attacking and taking the Zacapa military base with the aid of sympathizers within the garrison. Although it began successfully, the plan failed as a whole. One of the columns lost its commanding officers in its first encounter with the enemy, when Lieutenant Zenón Reina and Sergeant

Antonio López were killed in combat and Lieutenant Julio Bolaños San Juan was captured with serious wounds. The second column, commanded by Luis Trejo and Rodolfo Chacón, was dispersed, and the third, led by Yon and Turcios, after staying for two weeks in the Sierra de las Minas, where it made important contact with the peasants of the zone, fell back again to the city, where it formed the Marco Antonio Gutiérrez urban guerrilla unit (named after a student martyr murdered at that time), which with new and daring actions sharpened the March and April crisis and contributed to give it the character of a popular rebellion.

In the face of such circumstances the Party lacked—in spite of having been previously informed—a clear guideline and a minimum of organizational preparation. Wavering before the bourgeoisie and unsure in the face of the responsibility it ought to assume, the PGT leadership did not fight for its right—and obligation—to lead the movement by deepening the crisis through promoting and guiding the masses' spontaneous violence to the point of no return. Thus, by tacit agreement, the leadership of the entire movement fell into the hands of the AEU, an organization that was acceptable precisely because it guaranteed the *lack of hegemony of any particular group* and allowed all, according to their calculations—including the Party—to "influence" the movement and, in a word, not be excluded entirely. With the people in the streets, no party tried to take over the leadership of the movement among the masses. Everyone sought behind-the-scenes negotiations. The result was that the massive actions of the people, backed by armed actions in the city carried out by the MR-13 and groups from the communist youth organization and the Party acting on their own initiative, in reality lacked guidance. Once again, a "coup d'état mentality" dominated the directives of all the groups involved in the struggle. With the idea of a coup from within and the constitution of a possible junta of representatives, the PGT and the leadership of the PUR organized and carried out the unsuccessful guerrilla attempt of the October 20 Detachment. The true but unproclaimed aim of this tragic attempt was to form an armed detachment, which, installed in the mountains, would constitute a decisive argument for discussing the right of Colonel Paz Tejada, head of the Detachment, and a coalition of democratic forces to participate in a government junta. The majority of the members of this group lacked sufficient military training. The geographical area selected met just one requirement: it was sufficiently close to Guatemala City for them to exert pressure on the political and military groups disputing the succession of Ydígoras and for the people in rebellion to feel them sufficiently close to warrant giving them all possible mass support in the streets.

The defeat and then the massacre in which the October 20 Detachment ended, just two days after its departure from the city, marked the crucial point of the March and April crisis. All further action, although at times it grew in intensity, was characterized by a certain bewilderment and confusion among the leading revolutionary circles, which saw their trump card lost. Lacking leadership, pursuing limited immediate objectives, the masses in the streets and even their improvised cadres lost perspective; the working class, lacking clarity, did not decide to declare a revolutionary strike; the high tide ebbed through exhaustion; and the broad and spontaneous front forged by the base, without leadership or responsibility, could not hold up against the government maneuver of a cabinet that placated the middle-class and bourgeois opposition sectors, which at the time played a considerable role in sustaining popular unrest.

The conclusions obtained from the March and April actions formed two distinct currents of opinion that manifested themselves within all the revolutionary groupings, the PGT included. The most radical, advanced, and resolute elements reaffirmed their willingness to fight, based on the fact that the violent actions had created conditions for a wave of massive rebellion that not only had made the government totter dangerously but had also caused true lack of control and fear in the repressive apparatus. This position was expressed mainly by the members of the MR-13; the survivors of the guerrilla detachments organized at the urging of the PGT; groups of workers and artisans from the capital, especially those belonging to small firms; strong sectors of the university students; almost all the secondary students; the Communist Youth en bloc; the Party organizations in the departments of Escuintla, Zacapa, and Izabal; and the leadership cadres assigned to incipient military tasks. The other current emphasized the negative experiences, and in its conclusions there were differences ranging from the exclusion of violence to the formal acceptance of the same—as long as it be studied and organized with sufficient time and care—and, once it was prepared, to wait for "an adequate political situation," an expression that possesses the virtue of adapting itself to many varying concepts. This position was expressed by the petty-bourgeois leadership of the PUR; union leaders; small and middle business sectors; pro-Arévalo political groups, who were very interested in maintaining constitutionality so that their leader could once again participate in the presidential elections (which they were sure he would win); and the majority of the Communist Party leadership, fearful of two things fundamentally: "Prematurely committing" the Party to a bloody struggle and clashing head-on with the groundswell of *Arevalismo*, which could eventually "isolate" the Party from the masses.

Of the improvised organization adopted by the masses during March and April there remained worker and student groups, and, in some places near the capital, peasant groups, which maintained their combative spirit. For weeks the normal functioning of the state administration and vigilance in one or two Guatemala City neighborhoods which had been declared "free territories" during the popular rebellion could not be restored. The groups of university students not only maintained that rudimentary organization but also tried to consolidate it and turn it into a permanent entity under the name of the 12th of April Revolutionary Movement. A large number of these students were members of the Communist Party or its youth organization; there were also quite a large number of workers and craftsmen, some of them also communists or former members of the Party. This confirmed the need felt by many Communist Party members to act within a more lively and combative organization than their own— which, given the situation through which the country was passing, was becoming a brake on the initiative to struggle.

The internal ideological conflict among the communists became more tense and difficult because wavering and rightist concepts seemed at that time to be confirmed by reality, and any refutation gave the impression of being abstract and hypothetical. However, when the balance of the disastrous fate met by the October 20 Detachment was drawn up, the vestiges of the major mistakes in its line began to appear and were so notorious that, in order to justify them, absurd arguments were brandished, such as that the peasants were a "reserve force of reaction" due to their "backwardness." But, nevertheless, the error in line had to be recognized in its basic features.

The MR-13 comrades immediately set up new contacts with high-up military brass to sound out once again the possibilities for a partial rebellion of the armed forces that would allow the arming of popular sectors; the PGT and the PUR also made similar moves, all of which made the conspiratorial atmosphere remain alive long after the March and April events were ended. These circumstances allowed the carrying out of work of limited military preparation among the worker and student groups that kept themselves spontaneously organized. Many of those who were later to become outstanding guerrillas or resistance fighters received their initiation in these groups, which, repeating a situation which has been a constant in our movements, appeared as a hurried device in the face of events which had already taken place or were inevitable, but not as conscious planning and preparation to direct events with a given orientation.

The relations between the PGT and the MR-13 were kept up on the basis of mutual information and negotiations in the following two ways: joint and complementary participation in the event of a coup taking place and the establishment of an alliance to organize and begin armed struggle in the countryside. As to the second, there was a polemical point on which there was never any agreement and which was finally solved by revolutionary practice: when actions were to begin. The MR-13 maintained that this should be effected at once, as soon as basic preparations were finished. The PGT maintained that, in addition to preparations, it was necessary to wait for the "politically opportune moment." What seems a secondary issue was in reality a basic problem that essentially affected the concept of armed struggle as a whole. It is not to be wondered that no agreement was reached. When the comrades posed the "immediate" launching of the war, they did so without elaborating it consciously, in answer to a strategic view of the war in the revolutionary process for the beginning of which there already existed the essential conditions. When the PGT proposed to wait for the "politically opportune moment," it was once again reflecting the same tactical vision that it had (and still has) of armed struggle. In that concrete case, the "politically opportune moment" was that of the presidential elections in which Arévalo seemed to be a sure winner. If he were prevented from taking office, "*then* we will take to the mountains to launch guerrilla warfare." This was, concretely, the thinking of the PGT leadership on the beginning of popular guerrilla warfare. It was clear, though at the time we did not realize it, that this tactical conception of armed struggle could only be the reflection of a subordination in reality to the liberal bourgeoisie, of which Arévalo was the main political exponent. The worker and peasant masses, the power behind armed struggle, would take up arms *to claim the power won at the ballot box* by the *Arevalista* bourgeoisie and petty bourgeoisie. With the pretext of "broadening"—as the PGT ideologists argued—the front of armed struggle among these sectors, in reality we were leading the workers and peasants to wage a bloody clash for the interests of a bourgeoisie which, even in power, did not have the spirit to take up arms to defend that power from imperialism and reaction. We know that the bourgeoisie has historically used the popular masses to remove from power its competitors from other ruling classes, but that the same kind of operation be prompted by a Communist Party simply reveals its complicity with a sector of the exploiters. When the MR-13 leaders argued for the "immediate" start of armed struggle they expressed not only the willingness of their members, mostly of rural petty-bourgeois origin, but also that of the poor peasants and farm workers of the Zacapa and Izabal departments, whose friendship they had set out to win after they had received their spontaneous aid, as Yon Sosa says, in the moments of danger.

Apart from the points described above, there were no other topics that caused discussions between the PGT leadership and the MR-13. Neither of the two proposed a military strategy or a concrete political line. Both prospects were left to the unfolding of events, on the part of the MR-13 possibility, because it did not at the time have a clear awareness of their necessity, and, on the part of the PGT, because it had a political line that excluded the need for military strategy. Other political and military topics which were later to become central polemical points—such as program, content of the Revolution, and military tactics—were taken up at that time. The relations between the PGT and the MR-13, more or less tense at one time or another, were maintained for months at a certain positive level of trust.

It was in December 1962 that the wait without definitions became untenable and Yon Sosa, Turcios, and Trejo, the three principal leaders of the MR-13, took the initiative and proposed a very concrete action plan to be carried out jointly. The proposal left no room for a possible refusal, and it consisted in the following: an alliance on an equal footing of the two organizations to prepare and undertake armed struggle on three fronts, each commanded by one of the MR-13 leaders but in general commanded by a joint command. Aside from their respective human and material support, the PGT was to assume the responsibility of the political leadership. The MR-13 was to put into the project all its men, resources, and weapons, and it was to take on the military leadership of the alliance. The general command was to be composed of two members of the MR-13 and one of the PGT (a year later, when differences had already begun to arise, the command was increased to four members, including a representative of the MR-April 12).

The PGT representatives who discussed this proposal accepted without great resistance and at once, only making two stipulations, which were also accepted at once: the inclusion of the 12th of April Revolutionary Movement, to take part on all levels of the new alliance except the National Command, and the making public of the PGT's participation, under the name of the October 20 Detachment, explaining that the purpose was to avoid making the new organization seem sectarian in the public eye. The explanation and proposal were accepted, although not without certain suspicions on the part of some MR-13 representatives. Later, this fact, without apparent importance, was perfectly in consonance with the PGT leadership's vision of armed struggle and therefore of its participation—a partial participation, a new work front like that of women's or labor organizations.

The new alliance was named the Rebel Armed Forces (FAR), and three work commissions were formed: military operations, political program, and supplies and communications. The fronts were established as follows: Yon Sosa with the rank of major at the head of Zone 1, Izabal; Trejo was named to Zone 2, between the departments of Zacapa and Chiquimula; and Turcios, also with the rank of major, was named head of Zone 3, in the Sierra de las Minas.

In spite of almost two years of periodic contacts with the MR-13 leaders, of keeping informed of almost all their plans and the unfolding of their way of thinking, these concrete proposals took the PGT leadership by surprise.

Despite all the previous factors, the leadership had not seriously envisioned such an alliance, nor had it come up with any practical proposal of its own. Thus, the initiative at that time was completely in the hands of the three MR-13 leaders.

Of course, the PGT Central Committee was not consulted on the alliance prior to its agreement, not only due to the slight practical role it had always played but also because no important implications for the Party's line were attributed to the establishment of this revolutionary coalition.

Turcios relied more than the others on the PGT military commission to organize his detachment and choose its zone of operations. When we refer here to the military commission, we are speaking in reality of its activists and not of the leadership of the body, largely composed of comrades who lacked, and continue to lack, military preparation, theoretical or practical. The fact that Turcios sought this support was possibly due to three reasons:

1. From the beginning of his revolutionary life he manifested sympathy with and later adhesion to the principles of Marxism-Leninism. He related, for instance, how, finding himself on duty as a military instructor at the Poptún Base, he met the Nicaraguan Marxist revolutionary Carlos Fonseca Amador, who was a prisoner there. Turcios, as he himself related, enjoyed visiting Fonseca and provoking political discussions because communist ideas had held an irresistible attraction for him since his first ideological contact.

2. It was with some cadres of the PGT military commission who were already beginning to take issue with the leadership's contradictory and erratic line that he found greater understanding in the military and political spheres, an understanding which was to become friendship. Some of these cadres were studying and trying to assimilate the principles of guerrilla warfare, which Turcios picked up quickly and incorporated into his own thinking, freeing himself fairly easily from the weight of military careerism.

3. He was concerned about how defenseless his comrade and chief appeared in the political sphere, and, feeling himself also to be unsure in this sense, he sought in the ranks of the Party (he was already aware of its wavering and deficiencies as a vanguard organization) the possibility of finding the basis for a correct and firm orientation either through the personal participation of communist cadres dissatisfied with the passivity of the PGT leadership or through his gathering together, through discussions and contacts, the elements to formulate such an orientation on his own.

If the Party had had a different policy, a clear revolutionary line—if its leadership had had confidence in the revolutionary strength emanating from the people and security in the historical vigor of the theory it claimed to profess—it would have been able to form through developing and complementing the abilities of this group of young and restless officers—each of whom, following a different, tortuous, and difficult road, arrived through his own efforts at Marxism and Revolution—an unbeatable team for leading our people's revolutionary war.

The preparations of Zone 3 moved at a slower pace. Yon Sosa and

Trejo had selected zones with which they were familiar for one reason or another.

On the other hand, the geographic sector for the Turcios detachment was selected hurriedly and under police pursuit. Preparations had been undertaken for the readying of an area in the Sierra de las Minas that Turcios had visited in March and April, placing supplies and weapons caches and superficially organizing the peasants of the zone, but a police raid investigation of some of the movement's houses in the capital where materials and documents were kept allowed the repressive bodies not only to locate the caches but also to submit the inhabitants of the projected area of operations to such systematic persecution that practically all the preparatory work was undone.

While the FAR was preparing these conditions for guerrilla warfare, within the Party intense discussions were taking place which had as their aim the submission of the cadres of the military commission and the rural rank-and-file cadres to disciplinary measures in order to put a brake on armed actions and thus, also, contain the impetus of the MR-13. When the detachments of Yon Sosa and Trejo were already acting, the PGT leadership insisted on waiting for the politically opportune moment and employed its best efforts in seeking a way out of the situation that the election campaign in favor of Dr. Arévalo was creating. In the first months of 1963, in the midst of this situation, the PGT leadership held a meeting of its Central Committee to discuss the tactics to be adopted by the Party in regard to the elections. This fact made patent once again the thinking of the leadership on armed struggle and the election campaign. Neither the alliance with the MR-13 nor the founding of the FAR was discussed by the Central Committee. The Central Committee, in fact, held no meetings to consider and come to conclusions on this step, which had every reason to be considered important. On the other hand, almost *one year before* the possible holding of the elections, a Central Committee meeting was called to discuss the tactics to be followed. We see on the one hand that the concept of armed struggle, the real importance that it received from the Party, did not lead it to undertake any significant practical measures but rather led it to accept the clear, concrete, and immediate initiative of the MR-13, although it was taken by surprise. Forming an alliance with the MR-13 to carry on the war had so little importance attached to it that it did not even merit a Central Committee meeting. But electoral maneuvers did require the attention of the Central Committee and the carrying out of its directives to the base eight months ahead of time in order for there to be profound and well-thought-out preparatory work. The war fell within the administrative functions of the Secretariat; the elections were a task for the Party as a whole.

The discussion at the Central Committee meeting was very intense.

Called to study the electoral situation, of necessity it took up problems of armed struggle, in fact leaving the question of electoral tactics as a tangential issue. But the resolutions did not reflect this. When the time came to vote, a well-oiled apparatus gave victory to the thesis of "waiting for the politically opportune moment" to launch the Party into the war. The central leadership nucleus created the belief that this moment coincided with the general insurrection mentioned by Lenin in 1917, basing itself on quotes from him. As was to be expected, no very clear resolution on the electoral tactics emerged. The taking of a stand on Arévalo's candidacy was left hanging. According to the PGT leadership, defining a position could lead only to one of two situations: complete submission to Arévalo or "isolation" from the masses. What a choice! As will be recalled, Peralta Azurdia, who defeated the decrepit Ydígoras, took charge of facilitating the definition of the hesitant. He abrogated the Constitution, kicked Arévalo out of the country, and established a regime of military despotism.

In the midst of the repression that followed, Turcois and his comrades organized the detachment and carried out a minimum of preparations in Zone 3 for the establishment of the guerrilla force which took the name Edgar Ibarra Guerrilla Front (FGEI).

The composition of this detachment differed from that of the other two. Except for Turcios, none of its members had belonged to the MR-13. The large majority were members of the PGT or its youth organization, including a few middle-level cadres. In addition to Turcios himself, a veteran of almost all the MR-13's actions, there were also veterans of the attempt to take the Cobán Garrison and peasants of high quality, some of them former army soldiers.

But, before some of the PGT cadres left, they found themselves obliged to open a serious discussion within the Party's political commission because of an alarming orientation given by it. Before this, some youth cadres had been sent to Zone 1 to strengthen Yon Sosa. One of them who was killed in combat was Edgar Ibarra. These comrades, resolute and firm but lacking clear orientation, committed some errors, and they were unable to fulfill the main purpose of their presence in the zone.

These circumstances, in the wake of the attitude of studied caution that the Kennedy Administration publicly adopted regarding the military coups carried out against the legally constituted governments in Honduras and Guatemala, plus a conspiracy that the chief of one of the capital's garrisons (Colonel Callejas, who later became one of the heads of the rightist terrorist band MANO) was trying to organize, caused the appearance within the PGT leadership of a current that posed the following: The prevailing influence within the U.S. government was aimed at supporting governments of "representative democracy" and, *therefore*, at turning its back on the guerrillas. It is predictable, therefore, that by supporting some military men of a "democratic mentality"—Callejas was identified as one of them because, in the process of seeking a situation favorable to a coup, he had established contacts with PUR leaders—a coup could take place that would restore constitutionality and form a democratic government. Just how democratic would be determined by the amount of political pressure that the revolutionary forces were able to exert. In view of the fact that Major Yon Sosa had not allowed any member of the PGT to be in command of troops in his detachment, the need for the formation of a separate guerrilla force with a communist commander, to be a trump card when the time came to negotiate, was recognized. The Turcios detachment did not meet the requirements of this plan. Therefore, the reopening of the sector of operations that had been under Chacón's jurisdiction and which, because of its proximity to Puerto Barrios, facilitated a rapid and public upsurge of the guerrilla force, was proposed. The tactic to be followed was the cutting of the route to the Atlantic.

The discussion that took place in the enlarged political commission was fraught with tension. For those who saw armed struggle as a revolutionary line and not a tactical maneuver, it was evident that this proposal was a repetition of the scheme that underlay the October 20 Detachment, which had been massacred in Concuá, and, therefore, a fresh disaster was foreseeable. Although at the end of the meeting it was promised that this directive would be reviewed, plans went ahead for the project. Command—with the immediate prospect of the rank of major—was offered to several Party activists, but neither the basic proposal nor the concrete conditions were very convincing. The comrade who finally accepted and took charge of the project was evidently deceived; when he saw objectively how senseless the plan was, he came down from the mountains with his handful of troops. He was taken prisoner, and the others managed to return to Guatemala City.

The spreading confusion also made Yon Sosa come down from the mountains, a victim of the same ill. Trotskyite cadres from the Mexican Revolutionary Workers Party—a member of the self-styled Latin American Bureau of the Fourth International, headed by Argentine adventurer and former football player J. Posadas—that, disguised as practical collaborators, had infiltrated the MR-13, made an appearance, criticizing the errors and weaknesses of the PGT. This attitude, apparently sincere and, above all, based on an undeniable reality, strengthened the confidence Yon Sosa already had in them and at first confused some members of the PGT and the youth, dissatisfied with the way things were going and convinced that the pressure that could be exerted by the communists attached to the armed struggle and by the MR-13 people on the Party leadership would lead these last to a more consistent position, a defined and clear orientation, and a determined course of action.

The PGT leadership did not detect the Trotskyite infiltration. These leaders identified it with the comrades maintaining radical positions on armed struggle within the Party itself, labeling one and all as "extremists." All alike were considered adversaries of their "correct Marxist-Leninist position." They took so little notice of the ideological content of these essentially different positions that, in order to appease the opposition to the Trotskyites in the FAR Command and thus "weaken" the divergences arising in the ranks of the Party itself, the former were given the responsibility of attending to the guerrilla fronts and handling the FAR's finances in exchange for the PGT leadership's keeping the post of spokesman in the negotiations with other political sectors to set up the United Resistance Front (FUR), an imitation of the Venezuelan National Liberation Front—which was organized by the Communist Party of that country as a political body of national unity to lead the armed struggle (the FUR was supposedly to include, in addition to the FAR member organizations, the PUR and possibly some sectors of the now dispersed *Arevalismo*).

The Trotskyites ably made use of these concessions by the PGT to make their influence felt on the two existing guerrilla detachments in two ways: by carrying out supply line activities that the Party had not succeeded in when this task was in the hands of its apparatus and by introducing a veritable avalanche of theoretical materials, mainly national and international news. Their energy contrasted sharply with the PGT's inactivity in this sphere. Later on it became evident that the news and commentaries on national and international events were being deliberately twisted and blown up out of all proportion to suit the convenience of Posadas's Bureau and, in many cases, were even written by him.

The group of Trotskyite cadres that virtually took over the MR-13 leadership felt in mid-1964 that the time was coming to take over the leadership of the entire guerrilla movement. They published the first issue of the MR-13's official publication, *Revolución Socialista*, and in its pages proposed their own program in the face of the absolute lack of a joint program for the FAR. This clearly Trotskyite program centered on the definition of the nature of the Revolution and on a sketch of a classic Trotskyite policy which led precisely to the distortion and denial of revolutionary armed struggle! In addition to other aberrations, it posed inopportune and dangerous tactical slogans. Criticisms of the PGT were openly divisionist and ceased to be doctrinary.

The appearance of the first issue of *Revolución Socialista* in fact posed the dissolution of the FAR and broke the alliance with the PGT. The unilateral program, the divisionist manifestations, and the elements contributed by a woman comrade made the need for a careful analysis of the situation and a discussion of some problems relating to programmatic questions evident in the FGEI. These took place after the brilliantly executed attack on and capture of the Río Hondo Garrison fully defined the military and combative features of the FGEI.

The position of the FGEI regarding the internal problems of the revolutionary movement was clear and defined. It took shape in the document known as the "Letter from the FGEI to the PGT and the MR-13." It defined the contradictions inherent in the revolutionary camp, stated they should be solved through seeking a new basis for unity, and, to do so, proposed a sketch for a structure, a strategical aim, and an outline of military strategy.

It analyzed the PGT and MR-13 programs, pointing out their errors, and, in particular, denounced the infiltrated Trotskyism and pointed out its harmfulness. It proposed the seeking of a unity platform excluding the Trotskyites, but it contemplated—in the event that the contradictions should not be solved at once and, instead, became sharper—the selection of its own road by the FGEI under the banners of proletarian ideology.

The Trotskyite influence never reached the point of affecting the guerrilla force. Some points that had a basis in reality caused some confusion and discussions on the leadership level, but they never reached the ranks of the fighters. Therefore, the FGEI's position, in which many wished to see the shadow of one or another ideological influence, constituted in reality an objective tendency which arose and developed in the very heart of the Marxist revolutionary movement, and it fed on its most alive experiences. It constituted the résumé of its own military and political experiences and those of others which took place at the outbreak of armed struggle in Guatemala.

With its first successful actions, the FGEI broke the isolation that it had maintained for many months. A rapid grouping of popular masses took place around it. Then both the PGT leadership and the Trotskyites were very interested in discussing and paying attention to the opinions of the FGEI, to the surprise of the guerrillas. An objective and undeniable fact had arisen. The contact with the realities of the struggle and the country itself, about which many speculations had been made but very little had been experienced in practice; the experiences which, though few and localized, were sufficiently vital and typical to constitute the bases for a relative generalization; daily life and the political and social integration which took place in the guerrilla force in the light of these conditions; and the loosening of ties with the deforming and blind routine of the Party's bureaucratized apparatus forged in the detachment a personality of its own and gave it a point of view independent of both the official Party position and that of the Trotskyite faction. Its military and political activity, although limited and deficient in absolute terms, was more serious and profound than what was being done in the rest of the country and gave it growing authority. It became evident that the sudden attention from both sides was aimed at winning the adhesion of the embryo political and military strength contained in the FGEI.

On the basis of the points contained in the letter from the FGEI, discussions were held with the PGT and the MR-13. The Trotskyite faction, which had the help of able elements such as Adolfo Gilly,[4] was able to keep its influence in the MR-13 and dodge the FGEI's arguments. As a consequence, Major Turcios publicly resigned from membership in that organization, thus consolidating the independent character of the FGEI. These events caused two reactions among the young communists who were discontented with the Party's line and leadership. For some, it opened up new perspectives; for others, it meant a starting point and a point of support for exerting pressure on the Party leadership to institute necessary changes.

This situation placed the PGT in a very difficult and complex position. Although the communists of the FGEI did not give up Party membership, in fact they did have a position different from the Party line and discipline. The inner decomposition that had taken place in the PGT had led to this; it did not allow the leadership to act as it formally was supposed to in the leading of a class body, one more proof of its inability to face qualitatively different situations and the lack of correspondence that appears when an organization tries to act according to a mechanical and theoretical scheme in the face of an ebullient, living, and explosive reality.

The PGT leadership, faced with this situation, acted with an equal measure of flexibility and revolutionary inconsistency. It did not act in the revolutionary way corresponding to the historical role it had assumed, as it did not make a frank and honest review of its line, concepts, and methods of work and struggle in the face of the qualitative change which the revolutionary process had undergone in our country with the appearance and initial consolidation of the people's war. The change was clearly perceptible because of the transformations that the incipient war imposed on the ideas and structures, methods, and procedures of the people and its enemies. On the other hand, the PGT leadership did discuss the FGEI's points; it accepted the criticisms of the Party line and programmatic points that were made in the letter of the FGEI, claiming only that they were "relative, and not absolute, errors"; and it attended the unification conference called by Major Turcios to form a Provisional Center of Revolutionary Leadership consisting of the FGEI, the PGT, the Patriotic Labor Youth (the Communist Party youth movement), and some resistance zones that were acting autonomously. This body was intended to give the revolutionary movement in arms a single, centralized command and a revolutionary line for war. The PGT leadership approved the constitution of this body, signed the communiqué announcing its establishment, and incorporated some of the concepts proposed by the FGEI on the character of the Revolution and the forces active in it—*all of this without offering any explanations to its rank and file, without discussing things seriously with its Central Committee, and,*

[4] Argentine journalist and Posadist militant, jailed in Mexico in 1967 without charges and still in jail.—*Ed.*

finally without modifying its essential orientation or its procedures. Neither the PGT rank and file nor its Central Committee knew the details behind all these events or even the factors that caused this situation and its mechanism. The resolution of the Central Committee, along with the statement of the founding of the Provisional Center of Revolutionary Leadership—which appeared at this time—was, as many people know, prepared on the basis of the agreements signed previously by the Party leadership group with the FGEI, the youth organization, and the resistance zones, and approved when the Center was already functioning. The PGT leadership was not consequent with the Revolution, nor was it with its own line, which it did not defend openly; with its statutes, which it did not dare apply; with its Central Committee, which it did not inform and whose opinion was not asked; and especially with the local organizations, which were fed only formal, twisted versions making everything seem like a normal process, with the Party bodies operating not only with efficiency but with correctness and foresightedness. If the Party leadership was sure of the correctness of its line, why didn't it defend it to its own rank and file and Central Committee? If the Party leadership was convinced of the effectiveness of its statutes, why did it not dare to apply them to those who were called factionalists behind their backs— Party members who openly upheld a different line or, with their practical attitude, rejected as unserviceable the official Party line? If it was sure of acting honestly and frankly, why didn't it have the Central Committee function as it should have, according to the classical scheme of discussing, judging, and preparing the resolutions on such essential problems? Why was its entire performance a maneuver tending to gain time and new positions, to once again be in a position to impose its classic line through pressure or demagogy, to once again be in a position to make its concepts prevail, although neither one nor the other corresponded to reality or to the revolutionary need of the people, just because—and it was their only virtue—they fit the hallowed scheme?

The phase that followed[5] after what we have just dealt with here no longer corresponds to the outbreak of armed struggle. It corresponds to the difficult development that followed upon the conflictive birth of that struggle, with its painful amount of errors, losses, and reverses—but also heartening experiences and confirmations in the revolutionary line of armed struggle. And one of the most important things for us at this time is that the structures and the concepts in the class struggle cannot be revolutionary if they do not reflect a reality of struggle and if they are not useful to solve the problems that are posed by that reality and that struggle.

[5] Yon Sosa expelled the Posadists from the MR-13; Turcios was killed and replaced by César Montes; the MR-13 and the FAR united into the new FAR headed by Yon Sosa, seconded by Montes. The FAR broke with the PGT.—*Ed.*

YON SOSA, TURCIOS LIMA, *et al.*:
FIRST DECLARATION OF SIERRA DE LAS MINAS*

THE Revolutionary Movement of November 13, which organizes and commands the guerrilla forces, has reached the decision that we must develop and expand the armed struggle against imperialism and capitalism. Our determination to fight is due not only to this decision but also to the fact that we believe the Guatemalan Revolution lives in the heart of the peasant masses throughout the entire country. The proletariat, the students, petty bourgeoisie in the cities, are today caught in the current of revolutionary ferment which, although it lacks apparent cohesion, is nonetheless clearly manifested in their support and solidarity with the guerrilla struggle. This support was demonstrated on the barricades in March and April 1962. Soon it will be expressed in the violent and organized operations which will be launched in the cities against the military, capitalist, and proimperialist dictatorship.

Our revolutionary struggle, in which the masses are the decisive factor, is part of the worldwide Revolution and the movement toward socialism which is taking place in South Vietnam, the Congo, Egypt, Algeria, Zanzibar, Indonesia, Argentina, Bolivia, Venezuela, Colombia, Panama, and many other countries. Within the workers' states themselves, the Revolution continues, as can be seen in the Sino-Soviet conflict and the struggle of the Soviet masses against the privileged caste in the USSR. This was doubtless a factor in the fall of Khrushchev, who was the most prominent spokesman of the policy of "peaceful coexistence" and of collaboration with imperialism.

Although we have not yet set up a coherent central organization, the force of our movement is already weakening Peralta Azurdia's capitalist dictatorship. Every bourgeois and petty-bourgeois political party is in crisis, lacks an effective social base, and fails to present any real opposition to the regime. Nevertheless, in spite of the fact that there is no "legal" opposition, the dictatorship, because of its own internal weakness, is forced into maneuvering and concessions, such as the promise of elections, etc. If it were not so reliant on imperialist support, there would be no need for the staging of such farces.

So long as the capitalist system continues, no real improvements or reforms are possible because any such democratic measures would

---

* Dated December 12, 1964, and distributed in mimeographed pamphlet form in December 1964 and early 1965, signed by Marco Antonio Yon Sosa, Luis Augusto Turcios Lima, Augusto Vicente Loarca Argueta, Francisco Amado Granados, and J. Evaristo Aldana. Translated by Juan Mechón.

threaten the whole basis of capitalism. Therefore, if capitalism is to survive as it intends to do, it must derive its support from the dictatorship which, while giving this support, is incapable of making any concessions to the people. The bourgeois or petty-bourgeois opposition parties simply play ball with the dictatorship and attempt to foster legalistic and electoral illusions in the masses who are only temporarily deceived. They are in no position to capitalize on the popular hostility to the military government, nor do they in any way represent the proletariat. In fact, an alliance exists between the government and the official opposition to maintain the status quo and prevent the growth of the revolutionary movement, particularly its armed forces.

Guerrilla activity offers the only true alternative to the electoral and "democratic" processes which have been so subverted and abused by our enemies. The guerrilla is only the vanguard of an immense struggle involving a great number of peasants without whose assistance, protection, and sustenance he could not survive. Hence the inability of the capitalist army to crush the revolutionary armed struggle despite all their "mopping-up" operations. They are met by a silent and hostile people who carry out acts of sabotage and combative resistance.

The guerrilla front has organized village and farm committees, elected by the peasants themselves. These function clandestinely and give aid to the guerrilla army as well as resolving problems raised within their own communities. In some areas these committees have created their own militia, made up of peasants who continue their daily work on the land but also participate in specific guerrilla actions although they are not part of the regular forces. In the face of capitalist domination, the power of peasants and workers is growing. Many wealthy landowners have been forced to withdraw repressive measures and to abolish the payment of rent on some estates. Other landowners have fled and military agents have been brought to justice.

The guerrilla army has been consolidated in the peasant zones; it has its own organizations and bases of support. It can no longer be flushed out or suppressed, and new zones are getting ready to join the struggle. The activities of the propaganda wing of guerrilla patrols are also being extended.

It is impossible for the capitalist dictatorship to absorb the process of peasant insurrections by electoral means. To begin with it lacks the economic means to make even token concessions, as well as the necessary social base. Secondly, the leadership of our guerrilla front has shown unequivocally that it does not believe in "peaceful coexistence" between exploiters and exploited, landowners and peasants, capitalism and labor. To hold such a belief is simply to collude with exploitation and suppression. In no Latin American country, least of all in Guatemala, can the masses gain power through the electoral process or any other peaceful means. The enemy must be overthrown in the only way possible, through armed struggle.

The MR-13 has also put forward a revolutionary socialist program which directs that struggle and which rejects completely all compromises and deals with the capitalist regime and the military dictatorship that represents it. Nor is it willing to negotiate any truce in the armed struggle in exchange either for promises of reforms, elections, or amnesties of any kind.

The masses have not been coerced into the armed struggle. They have willingly chosen to participate on the basis of their collective experience of the previous stage of the revolution (1944–45) and the fall of the Arbenz government [1954]. The people who are joining or collaborating with the guerrilla front today are the direct descendants of those who in 1954 demanded arms to defend the Revolution and to put down the invasion of foreign mercenaries led by Castillo Armas. The masses were aware even then that the electoral or constitutional road was in fact a blind alley and that they must resort to armed struggle to defend their freedom and their progress. The experience has never been forgotten and it is the basis of the present revolutionary stage in this country.

The idea that we can advance peacefully toward socialism by maintaining the capitalist regime with the participation of the bourgeois in the government, was attempted by Arbenz. A Revolution on the Cuban model is now necessary—with the destruction of the present machinery of state, redistribution of land by armed peasants themselves and expropriation of property now in the hands of the bourgeoisie. The Cuban struggle and the experience of the Chinese Communist Party are of immense value to us in the achievement of our aims.

The MR-13, which has been terrorized more than any other political group by the government, already acts as a magnet for workers, peasants, and students throughout the entire country who see in our movement the way to true liberation. Our struggle has been affirmed by three crucial actions: the launching, organization, and consolidation of the guerrilla war; the proclamation of our program with our mobilization; and organization of great masses of peasants, workers, and students in their committees, unions, and combat units.

However, the people still lack sufficient decision-making agencies of their own. But they clearly express their aims through their solidarity and identification with the guerrillas. All the petty-bourgeois parties are torn between the two opposing forces in the nation today, the military dictatorship and the MR-13. Many of them will come to fight with us under the socialist revolutionary banner.

To implement the line of the Guatemalan socialist revolution, the MR-13 has taken up arms against the capitalist dictatorship and at the same time has waged a political battle against the wavering, reformist groups, who, with their false perspective, advocate the "democratic-national revolution." Foremost among such groups is the leadership of the PGT (Communist Party of Guatemala).

Smears, gossip, demoralization tactics, all have been used in a vain attempt to dispel the discontent of many real communists—militant communists—with the PGT leadership. The purpose of such maneuvers within the PGT is to avoid discussion of the ideological content of the revolutionary process, in Guatemala, Latin America, and the world. MR-13, on the other hand, has attempted to publicly engage the masses in such discussion so that they may see our struggle as a step on the way to socialist revolution—a revolution which consists of wresting power through the participation of the proletariat, the destruction of the capitalist state, and the setting up of a workers' and peasants' government. Because it lacks political arguments to contest the line and program of MR-13, the PGT has resorted to a campaign of lies and slander in a desperate endeavor to control its members and neutralize their criticisms of the Party line and leadership.

It should be made clear that there is no such thing as "democratic-national revolution." If we were to do as the PGT suggests, it would involve the guerrillas in working for bourgeois objectives, converting their armed movement into a kind of pressure group to win a coalition government which would include members of the bourgeoisie. This would obviously be quite absurd and is naturally unacceptable to the peasants and workers who want their own government and the expropriation of their exploiters' wealth. To this end, the Guatemalan socialist revolution intends to strike a mortal blow at the PGT's advocacy of coexistence with imperialism.

Guatemala is ripe for socialist revolution. This does not mean an immediate transformation to socialism but rather, as in China and Cuba, the establishment of workers' control and the dictatorship of the proletariat that creates socialism. This will entail the destruction of the bourgeois structure of the state and its tools of repression—the army, the police, and the law courts—and the setting up of the workers' and peasants' government with distribution of the land among the peasants. It will entail also arming the entire population and expropriating the possessions of the imperialists and national bourgeoisie, organizing workers' and peasants' committees in every factory, village, business, and city, supporting and extending the Revolution in Central and Latin America.

The guerrilla movement has flourished under this program in Izabal, in Upper and Lower Verapaz, and in Zacapa. The peasants have a perfect understanding of our concept and policy which so closely reflects their own aspirations. The socialist revolution has won the support of the masses, and conditions are right for the extension of the guerrilla war into new areas of the country, the subsequent establishment of new guerrilla foci and fronts, and the organization of peasant unions supported by the armed action of the guerrillas.

In the cities, various sectors of workers are entering new labor struggles and the MR-13 program is winning respect and support from the working class. At a meeting of electricians in November a reading of our manifesto was called for and other sectors are expressing their solidarity with us in one form or another. The repressive measures of the dictatorship have hindered but not halted the activities of the working class: despite the obstacles set up by labor leaders, workers are gathering in their homes or in meeting halls to collectively discuss their problems. The documents of the MR-13 are introduced into such discussions and our program is now widely known and supported.

One of the main problems is that the working class lacks the means to make known its support since it has no independent or democratic role to play in the unions, and in fact, in many areas, union organization is suppressed by the bosses or the police, or else is rendered ineffective by a union leadership in alliance with the bosses, the government, and the forces of imperialism. Nevertheless, pressure is mounting and there is a growing desire among the workers for meaningful action. Thus an urgent need exists for the formation of a Workers' Central to unite all union organizations on an independent and democratic basis.

Groups committed to the MR-13 program must be organized, including among their demands a mobile wage scale, a minimum wage, equal salaries for equal work, security of employment, general increases in wages, independent and democratic unions, the removal of government agents, police, and bosses from the unions, full rights of union organization, as well as freedom of speech and assembly, union autonomy, joint labor and peasant centrals, and workers' control of production. Conditions must be prepared from below for the revolutionary reorganization of the whole union movement and for the formation of the joint worker and peasant central with a militant leadership and socialist program to unite the labor struggle with the peasant and labor movement.

In each farm and factory committee there must be armed groups and detachments to combat political repression and defend our comrades. These armed groups will be the basis of the workers' militia and their activities will be determined by the course of the whole revolutionary struggle.

Without an alignment with the guerrilla forces and others who have taken up arms, it would be impossible to make any real improvement in the workers' conditions. The formation of efficient and cohesive groups in every farm, factory, and office is a prerequisite in our fight to overthrow the capitalist dictatorship and we call upon workers everywhere to join the common front that we propose.

Among the student population revolutionary discontent and agitation are most immediately expressed. The problem once again, as demonstrated by the events of March and April 1962, is the lack of a central and a concrete objective. Even without these, the students displayed enormous revolutionary potential and gained the support of the Guatemalan people as a whole. Their activities and identification with the guerrilla struggle were an indication of the general support among the population for the MR-13.

The students have a task of tremendous importance to perform. They must involve themselves in the revolutionary movement at all levels and in alliance with all labor and peasant groups. In fact, they must place themselves in the vanguard of the people's war against imperialism, capitalism, and the military dictatorship.

The solidarity of the Association of University Students (AEU) is of great importance in our struggle. The AEU is potentially a spokesman and defender of the guerrilla movement and can best fill this role by extending its demonstrations, distributing pamphlets, holding meetings—even painting slogans on the city walls until the metropolis echoes with our message.

It is necessary to combine these activities with the demands of the guerrillas themselves: for better conditions in the universities and schools; for the right of student representation on the board of governors; against the interference of the military regime and imperialism in the educational programs. The MR-13 advocates a secular and free education, available to the poor as well as the rich.

Universities and schools should be transformed into liberated territories just as the Sierra de las Minas has been transformed by the guerrilla occupation. We therefore repeat our call to all students and student organizations to play their essential role in the vanguard of the revolutionary movement.

Our purpose is to defeat capitalism and its allies not only by armed struggle but by all means available to us. The guerrilla movement constitutes the center of action and the stimulus for organization of the masses in all areas of our national life. Occupations, invasions of the land, student strikes, and the takeover of the universities, demonstrations—all these are part of our struggle. And this struggle, whether it be manifested in armed combat or simply in pamphleteering, has a politico-military objective geared to broadening the social struggle of the exploited classes against capitalism and toward a people's government.

The next stage must be one in which the guerrilla war is extended by the proliferation of the various groups and committees we have already mentioned, by the unification and incorporation of these organizations in our movement. The decision to take up arms must be made by the student and labor groups so that they can give support to every branch of revolutionary endeavor. They must be mobilized against the repression of the peasantry by the National Armed Forces and in support of the MR-13, in accordance with our slogan: "Workers, Peasants, Students, Arm Yourselves."

We have already made clear the importance of unifying all forces hostile to the capitalist dictatorship and imperialist intervention. We plan to carry out a program of expropriation without compensation with regard to the property and business enterprises of imperialism on Guatemalan soil. This will include the expropriation of the United Fruit Company and its subsidiaries, land reform and land distribution among the peasants, expulsion of the U.S. missions, annulment of all military and political treaties with imperialist nations, solidarity with the Cuban socialist revolution, freedom to organize, freedom of press, speech, and assembly for workers, peasants, students, and soldiers, general increase in salaries, a mobile wage scale, worker control of production, arming of the masses, and an end to police and military repression.

We denounce the Congress set up by the dictatorship and declare its resolutions null and void. We denounce the electoral farce as a crude attempt to alleviate the crisis of the dictatorship. We denounce as accomplices of capitalism and imperialism all those who participate or seek to participate in the elections. And once again we call upon workers, peasants, and students, teachers and professors, craftsmen and merchants, soldiers and officers, the population at large, to organize, mobilize, to join us in our fight that they may truly share in our final resounding victory.

Our call to the citizens of the nation is not only to fight for the restitution of land to their communities but also for the right of equality in employment, in social and political participation. The discrimination practiced against the Indians of Guatemala is a violation of human rights and we invite the full cooperation of the Indians in our revolutionary guerrilla struggle.

The MR-13 calls upon the people of Central America to organize a single front to expel imperialism and defeat capitalism, in the hope that this front will become the vanguard movement of the Federation of Socialist Republics of Central America.

The revolutionary struggle reverberates throughout Latin America and the way is being prepared for important new advances in every country. In Colombia and Venezuela the guerrilla movements continue fighting. New guerrilla forces are springing up in other countries on the continent and it is essential that we plan the immediate unification of all combatants in the Latin American Revolution. During his trip to Algeria, Commander Ernesto Che Guevara called for the formation of such an anti-imperialist front on our continent. The MR-13 supports wholeheartedly this proposal. We ourselves propose the organization of an Anti-Imperialist Conference,[1] which would include all the revolutionary movements of Latin America, to coordinate the fight against imperialism, to give militant support to socialist Cuba, and to enter into alliance with workers' states and liberation struggles throughout Asia and Africa.

The MR-13 calls especially on the guerrillas, militia, and comrades in Venezuela, Colombia, and the Republic of Marquetalia, to organize collectively a guerrilla conference in which would participate representatives of the armed struggle in these countries. The aim of the conference[2] would be to pool experiences, combat techniques, and tactics, and to organize the collective struggle, mutual aid, and the extension of the guerrilla and revolutionary war into new countries of Central and South America. The MR-13 proposes that this conference be held in any of the three countries, in free territory controlled by the guerrillas, under the protection of our own armed forces and the masses who support us. We suggest that this conference be held in 1965.

The only way to advance the revolutionary process in Guatemala and Latin America is to correlate the overthrow of imperialism with the duties of the socialist revolution. Guatemala, with its twenty years of fighting, has demonstrated this. The bourgeois and petty-bourgeois leadership were unable to implement measures of agrarian reform and maintain the democratic gains of the masses. The guerrillas have been fighting now for very nearly three years and rather than having been liquidated, they are daily acquiring greater political authority. The MR-13 has developed its own line and program and the Guatemalan people will no longer be deceived by bourgeois or petty-bourgeois policies which set out to develop the country while maintaining the capitalist regime.

In Guatemala, in Latin America as a whole, and throughout the entire world, we raise our battlecry: Workers, students, peasants, arm yourselves!

[1] What later became the Tricontinental (OSPAAAL).—*Ed.*
[2] What later became OLAS.—*Ed.*

Colombia

The only country in Latin America where communists loyal to Moscow are actually fighting—with arms—is Colombia. These armed units, known as the Colombian Revolutionary Armed Forces (FARC), are not waging revolutionary warfare, however. They are fighting "self-defense" battles against government attempts to occupy the land controlled by communist-organized peasants.

Colombia's communist peasants, located in the south, have long considered themselves independent—in fact, their main area is known as the Republic of Marquetalia—and they have repeatedly and courageously fought to preserve their independence against U.S.-made napalm and fragmentation bombs, U.S.-piloted helicopter raids, and invasion by 16,000 Colombian troops "guided" by U.S. Special Forces "advisers." But they have never tried to spread their base or launch counterattacks into enemy strongholds. The reasons are that the Colombian Communist Party does not believe that the country is "ripe" for revolution, that it still considers the legal or parliamentary road to power as crucial, that it is convinced that the national bourgeoisie and the "center" can and should play an important role in the "anti-imperialist" front. Thus, the FARC's commander-in-chief, Manuel Marulanda Vélez, better known as Tiro Fijo ("Sure Shot"), who is a member of the CCP's Central Committee, does not advocate a revolutionary agrarian policy but rather a "democratic" one, where rich peasants, so long as they till their own land, can retain their wealth (see the first article below). And at its Tenth Congress, held clandestinely in January and February 1966, the Party itself, though praising guerrilla warfare as "one of the higher forms of mass struggle," insisted that it was valid only when it had a "mass character" (second article). The CP also condemned all other forms of guerrilla movements as "idealistic undertakings." Furthermore, it has refused to discuss possible coordination with these movements (third article).

500

The most important of the "idealistic" movements is the Army of National Liberation (ELN), which has been fighting since 1964. Headed by Fabio Vásquez Castaño, its purpose is to build up its peasant base until it can transform itself into the base for a people's war. Guevarist in ideology, the ELN opposes all guerrilla movements which are headed by a city-based Party bureaucracy (as is the FARC), though it is willing to co-ordinate its actions with anyone who fights the government. The ELN is convinced that the only way to build its base is by example; thus Fabio Vásquez insists (third article below) that all revolutionary leaders should be on the battlefield and not behind a desk. Since such a policy vastly increases the risks of losing top cadre, the ELN, like all Guevarist (or Debrayist) movements, does not establish a hierarchy before launching operations. Commanders, for example, are picked by the men. The result is that participatory democracy is built into the guerrilla army from the beginning.

The ELN does award rank posthumously, however, and it has awarded the rank of comandante (major, top echelon in contemporary Latin American revolutionary armies) to one of its fallen heroes—Camilo Torres Restrepo. An oligarch by birth (1929), of the same Restrepo family which has long produced Colombian patriarchal leaders (the president of Colombia in 1969 was a Restrepo), Camilo was only nine years old when he founded a newspaper which he wrote, printed, and sold himself at school. In it, each month, he denounced the abuses of his teachers. A brilliant student, he soon went to the university to study law, then switched to religion, entered a seminary, and at twenty-five, at the request of the Cardinal, offered his first mass in the cathedral of Bogotá. For the next four years he studied abroad—one year at the University of Minnesota, three at Louvain, Belgium—and upon his return was appointed to the Board of Directors of the National University. He created a sociology department, taught there, and acted as the school chaplain. He was doing both when, in April 1965, the United States invaded the Dominican Republic and the Colombian army struck at the independent republics. A few days later, he resigned as chaplain and praised the guerrillas, specifically the Army of National Liberation. "The people know that the electoral ways have been exhausted," Camilo said. "The people know that there is no other way but that of armed struggle." In a country where every election is rigged by the oligarchy, he insisted that "every Catholic who is not a revolutionary, and is not on the side of the revolutionaries, lives in mortal sin." Finally, in October 1965, he took off his religious garb (he was never defrocked). "I took off my cassock to be more truly a priest," he explained. On November 8, he disappeared. Three days later, he was incorporated into the ELN. "We must keep active," he wrote from the hills, "the struggle of the people must become a national struggle." On

February 15, 1966, in the area known as Cement Patio of Santander Department, he was killed in combat, gun in hand.

His influence has been enormous. In Argentina today, there are armed "Camilo Torres Commandos." In Brazil, Bishop Jorge Marcos de Oliveira of Santo André publicly supported Camilo and an armed revolution for his own country. In Chile and Uruguay, "Camilo Torres Fronts" are openly working for revolution. In revolutionary Cuba, he is viewed as a Latin American hero equal to Che Guevara. In the fourth article below, he explains why he joined the guerrillas, why he once said: "The duty of every Christian is to be a revolutionary. The duty of every revolutionary is to make the revolution."

MANUEL MARULANDA VÉLEZ:
THE REPUBLIC OF MARQUETALIA*

COMRADES, peasants, workers, students, handicraftsmen, revolutionary intellectuals, men and women of Colombia!

We are the core of a revolutionary movement which began in 1948. Since then we, the revolutionary peasants of southern Tolima, Huila, Cauca, and Valle situated in the heart of the Central Cordillera, have been faced with the violence of the big latifundists and cattle ranchers, the big merchants and the servants of official policy. We are the victims of the policy of fire and sword proclaimed and carried out by the oligarchic usurpers of power.

Four wars have been waged against us in fifteen years, the first beginning in 1948, the second in 1954, the third in 1962, and the fourth since May 18, 1964, when the military command officially announced the beginning of Operation Marquetalia.

We were the first victims of latifundist violence because this part of Colombia is dominated by the interests of the big landowners, the most reactionary clerical elements, the darkest reaction in the country. We have experienced all the brutality of a corrupt regime resting on latifundist monopoly of land ownership and monoculture production and export, a regime dominated by the United States.

Precisely because of this, U.S. troops, aircraft, military leaders, and specialists are taking part in the war against us. Because of this, 16,000 troops armed with the latest weapons have been sent against us. Because of this, economic blockade, encirclement with the object of destroying us by attack by air and by land, and germ warfare are used against us. Because of this, the government and U.S. imperialism are spending thou-

---

* Manifesto issued July 20, 1964, by the Armed Revolutionary Forces of Colombia (FARC), which is the armed wing of the Colombian Communist Party. English version from *Colombia: An Embattled Land*, pamphlet published in Prague, 1966.

sands of millions of pesos and dollars on arms, military supplies, and spies and informers. Because of this, the government corrupts the minds of people, kills, hounds, and imprisons Colombians who have risen to the struggle in solidarity with us, the victims of a savage, inhuman war of annihilation.

We are revolutionaries fighting to change the existing system. But we wanted to fight and did fight for these changes in the most painless way for our people—by the peaceful, democratic, and legal means indicated in the Colombian Constitution. The use of force, however, closed this road to us. And since we are revolutionaries who will perform their historical role in one or another way, these circumstances compelled us to choose another way—that of armed revolutionary struggle to win power.

From today, July 20, 1964, our guerrilla movement is fighting for the following program:

1. To the fake agrarian reform of the bourgeoisie we counterpose an effective revolutionary agrarian reform which will radically change the social structure of the Colombian countryside by transferring the land to the peasants who till it, or wish to till it, through confiscation of the latifundio in the interests of all working people.

The revolutionary agrarian reform would transfer to the peasants the instruments of labor, draught animals, machines, and farm buildings for proper use in the conduct of the economy. Such an agrarian reform is an indispensable precondition of a sharp improvement of the material and cultural level of the entire peasantry, its liberation from unemployment, hunger, and illiteracy, abolition of the fetters of latifundism, and the development of agricultural and industrial production in the country. The agrarian reform would provide for the confiscation of all land held by the U.S. imperialists regardless of the pretext on which these lands are held or the use to which they are put.

2. Settlers, squatters, tenant farmers, sharecroppers, and others working on the land belonging to the latifundists or the state shall be issued title deeds to the land they till. All other forms of land tenure, sharecropping, and rents in kind or cash paid by small peasants will be abolished. Depending on the fertility and the locality of the land allotments, the minimum size of the plots shall be set at thirty hectares [hectare=2.47 acres] in flat country, and elsewhere depending on the fertility of the soil and the communications. All peasant indebtedness to usurers, profiteers, and official and semiofficial credit institutions shall be canceled.

3. The property rights of well-to-do peasants who farm their own land shall be respected. Industrial farming methods will be preserved. For social and economic reasons the big agricultural estates will remain and will serve as a base for the planned development of national production in the interests of the entire nation.

4. The revolutionary government will introduce a widely ramified system of easily obtainable credit, it will supply seed, technical aid, im-

plements, cattle, machinery, etc., both to individual peasants and to producers' cooperatives which may appear as a result of agrarian reform. An irrigation system and a network of state agricultural experimental stations will be set up in accordance with plan. Medical service to the rural population adequate to the health needs of the countryside will be organized. Attention will be given to the problem of education for the peasants, the complete elimination of illiteracy, and a system of scholarships introduced to enable tillers of the soil to acquire a higher education in technical and other fields. An extensive plan of housing construction for peasants as well as the building of roads connecting the villages with the marketing centers will be carried out.

5. Fair prices for stable agricultural products will be guaranteed.

6. Protection will be extended to the Indian communities; they will be given land allotments sufficient to ensure their development, land seized from them by the latifundists will be returned to them, and their farming methods will be modernized. The Indian communities will enjoy all the benefits of the revolutionary agrarian reform. At the same time the autonomous organization of the communities will be firmly established, and their life, customs, culture, language, and internal organization will be respected.

Realization of this revolutionary agrarian program will depend on the worker-peasant alliance and a united front of all Colombians in the struggle to change the regime, for this is the only way to destroy the old and obsolete latifundist structure. This program will have the support of the broadest peasant masses who are vitally interested in putting an end to latifundism. We therefore call upon all peasants, all workers, all office employees, all students, all artisans, all small proprietors, the national bourgeoisie who are ready to fight imperialism, all the revolutionary and democratically minded intellectuals, all political parties of the Left and Center which yearn for progressive change, to join in the great revolutionary patriotic struggle for a Colombia for the Colombians, for the triumph of the Revolution, for democratic government and national liberation.

COMMUNIST PARTY OF COLOMBIA:
THESES ON THE GUERRILLA MOVEMENT*

THE new stage in the guerrilla movement in Colombia ushered in particularly by the splendid resistance put up by the peasants of Marquetalia, has demonstrated the following:

---

* From the "Main Report" endorsed by the Tenth Congress of the Communist Party of Colombia, January 1966, printed in the pamphlet *Colombia: An Embattled Land* (Prague, 1966).

1. The armed resistance to the aggression in Marquetalia, El Pato, Guayabero, Riochiquito, southern Tolima, and elsewhere shows that a guerrilla movement which springs from the masses, which expresses their demands and which is guided by Marxism-Leninism is invincible, however strong the forces of the enemy and even when the conditions in the country are not yet ripe for armed action to become everywhere the main form of struggle.

2. Armed struggle in Colombia began and is developing as guerrilla warfare at a time when a revolutionary situation does not yet exist throughout the country. It would be disastrous for the Colombian revolutionary movement passively to allow the peasant organizations to be destroyed on the plea that it is necessary to wait until the revolutionary situation has fully matured before taking armed action. To the armed aggression of the enemy it is necessary to counterpose in the villages guerrilla resistance and armed struggle, and when the conditions are ripe for it, the question of armed struggle must be posed also in the towns and working-class centers.

3. There is no contradiction between mass struggle and armed guerrilla struggle. Guerrilla warfare is one of the higher forms of mass struggle, and it can make headway only when it assumes a *mass character*, when it originates from the midst of the people, and when it is a faithful expression of their immediate and historical interests. The experience of revolutionaries who have sought in recent years to spark off armed struggle without enjoying the support of the peasant masses, without the backing of their resolve and activity, shows that such idealistic undertakings only spell easy victory for the army, police, or hired bandits in the service of the authorities and the latifundists.

4. The policy of mass self-defense proclaimed by our Party was and remains basically correct. But it was not carried out consistently in some areas and in others it was frustrated by more ingenious methods of repression and political and military forms of struggle employed by the enemy.

The transformation of mass self-defense into a powerful guerrilla movement in the face of a systematic wide-scale offensive waged by the army against the peasant areas represents the logical development of the entire concept of revolutionary struggle in the specific conditions of Colombia. At the same time combination of all methods of struggle and emphasis on the particular method which accords with the concrete situation in each given locality is not only a correct interpretation of the Marxist-Leninist teaching but also its correct application to the social process in our country.

5. In the areas subjected to attack in fulfillment of the plans of the U.S. military mission, guerrilla action has become the principal form of mass struggle. In these areas all other forms of struggle become auxiliary to the main form, armed struggle, on which all other forms of mass action and the defense of the people's organizations should hinge. On

the other hand, the concentration of government forces in the areas subjected to attack creates favorable conditions for taking the initiative.

6. The guerrilla movement is being consolidated and expanded in a number of peasant areas even though the vast majority of the Colombian people are continuing ever broader resolute mass actions of other types as the main forms of struggle. These mass actions include militant students' strikes, hard-fought workers' strikes, enlistment of government employees in the strike movement, and other major strike actions. Our people engage also in forms of struggle which cannot be called "peaceful," but which nevertheless are not yet armed struggle. Of these forms special mention should be made of the seizure of vacant lots in urban centers by homeless city people for the purpose of building homes in defiance of the authorities and police repressions. Such mass actions, although they nearly always are of an economic nature, are bound increasingly to raise the level of the slogans advanced by the masses and the methods they employ to a higher plane as the guerrilla struggle of the peasants is increasingly combined with the mass struggles of the workers, students, and other urban sections.

7. Although in the course of this process the peasants' guerrilla struggle is not yet the main form of struggle, it acquires growing importance as the most effective reply by the people to the policy of terror pursued by the regime subordinated to U.S. imperialism and develops into a new revolutionary factor which has a tremendous appeal to the masses. Having begun with peasant guerrilla actions, armed struggle has become inevitable in Colombia owing to the resumption on a wide scale of a policy of violence against the people on the part of the oligarchic government.

8. The growing guerrilla movement of today is of a more definitive and more advanced nature than the guerrilla struggle which developed at the preceding stages not only because this movement has accumulated rich experience but also, and mainly, because it has a clearly defined revolutionary anti-imperialist content and because its chief aim is to win power for the people. This new Colombian guerrilla movement is a patriotic reply to the growing military intervention of U.S. imperialism against our people with the object of implementing the principles of the so-called "preventive" war. The U.S. imperialist intervention is expressed also in the growing interference of the U.S. military mission in the armed forces, in the direct financing by the U.S. government of military operations against the peasant areas, and in the "loaning" of all kinds of arms, planes, and squadrons of helicopters to be used to wage war against the working people of Colombia. In this way, to the old causes of terroristic violence in Colombia, chief of which was and remains the greed of the latifundists, there is added as a decisive factor the U.S. imperialist policy of intervention.

FABIO VÁSQUEZ CASTAÑO: NOT ONE STEP BACKWARD*

Question: What is the National Liberation Army? What are its political and military objectives?

Answer: The National Liberation Army is a politico-military organization born of the need of the peasants to solve their problems. It was launched in a peasant hut in the Department of Santander, at the house of our unforgettable Captain Parmenio. Several peasants who understood the necessity of rebelling against the system of exploitation met there. The area, like the great majority of the regions of our country, concentrated to excess on the conditions for the start of the insurrectional struggle. The peasants are tired of promises, glutted with lies. By hoping peacefully that elections would solve their problems—each time more difficult— their grandparents and their parents died slaves. And if they continue thus, a no less uncertain future awaits their children. It was absolutely necessary to establish a guerrilla force. "We have no arms," one of them said. "The enemy has them," we replied. We surveyed this initial zone, gathering together those most reliable—a total of eighteen peasants. Deeply convinced of the justice of our cause, we began the difficult guerrilla life. That was on July 4, 1964.

The first stage of our guerrilla activity can be summed up in the following points: first, a permanent underground life; second, a reconaissance of the terrain; third, the politico-military training of the guerrilla personnel; fourth, the creation of a revolutionary support base among the peasants; and fifth, the establishment of nuclei of information and chains of communication. What means were at our disposal for this? Logically we had previously made a careful analysis of the real situation in our country which showed the path on which we started, unswerving and decidedly, as the only right way.

Besides the objectively analyzed conditions, we could count on the support of our peasants, who get us the supplies and our first shotguns with which we made our entrance into the Simacota area. That entry ended the first clandestine period and publicly announced our rebellion against the bourgeois and proimperialist laws that govern our people; we told the people that there was an armed vanguard fighting for their interests and, above all—the essence of the capture of Simacota—we showed the people a direction to follow: revolutionary armed struggle.

It is hard to acknowledge the armed way as the only solution to the

---

* Interview conducted by the Mexican reporter Mario Menéndez on March 21, 1967, somewhere in the Andes range of Colombia, and published in Cuba in pamphlet form. Translation by Tom Raworth.

national problem, because this is predictably difficult and painful for our people of Latin America. But to deny this fact would be dishonest; it would unquestionably be equal to treason. Our generation, our Latin American youth, must acknowledge this fact and prepare itself for revolutionary war. It must prepare itself for the days—long and difficult for sure—that are about to come. Therefore the preparation of guerrilla fighters is indispensable for the formation of a National Liberation Army which, disputing the right of the oligarchy and North American imperialism to power, will wrest it from them and form a revolutionary and democratic government that will institute a program favorable to the people in our Colombia. This program is shown in our plan: true agrarian reform that deals with the elimination of latifundios, minifundios, and *monocultivos*; that gives a just and technical distribution of the land to the peasants who work it; that gives credit, farm implements, fertilizers, seeds, and work tools to the agricultural workers; and that pushes forward the mechanization and technicalization of agriculture. A plan that creates adequate distribution systems that will eliminate intermediaries, speculators, and monopolists; that assures medical and educational assistance to the peasants, as well as the improvement of the irrigation system, of electrification, of housing, and of adequate means of communication. The latifundios that are the property of North American imperialists and great landowners will be confiscated. But properties which positively benefit the national economy will be respected. The creation of state farms planning farm production, the diversification of crops, and the development of stockraising will be promoted, as will the founding of cooperatives for production, distribution, and consumption.

We plan industrial economic progress, housing and urban reform schemes, the creation of a popular credit system, the organization of a national health plan, the development of the road network, educational reform, the inclusion of the native population in the economy and culture, freedom of thought and religion, an independent foreign policy, the formation of a permanent people's army—technically equipped and disciplined—that will guarantee the people's gains, will defend national sovereignty, and will be the firm support of the people. This people's army will be formed initially from detachments of the National Liberation Army, and will maintain a strong and constant link with the people, from whose bosom its groups of combatants sprang.

Question: I have noticed that the National Liberation Army is an army of peasants. In your opinion, must the direction of the struggle for National Liberation be from the countryside to the city, or vice-versa?

Answer: Yes, the National Liberation Army is a peasant army. Its composition is thus: a very high percentage of peasants and, playing an important role, workers, students, and professional people who have swelled our ranks. This composition is due to various factors: first, the basic area of struggle in Latin America, and certainly in Colombia, is the countryside. This fact must be kept in mind, as in the majority of Latin American countries the highest percentage of the population is peasant. Second, because the worker sector has not reached the maturity needed to take the reins of the true revolutionary struggle. However, it is under the obligation to prepare itself not fundamentally for the economic struggle, but for the struggle for national liberation. Third, because as the means of enemy repression are situated mainly in the cities they are able, with less difficulty and without spreading out their forces, to put down whatever outbreak should be attempted against their interests. Fourth, because the growing revolutionary force must take its first clandestine steps in places where the enemy finds its destruction most difficult, where the enemy fails in all efforts to crush it, and where the maximum guarantees of survival during its development exist. From these objective considerations it may be deduced, logically, that the revolutionary movement must be started in the mountains. And it is thus, for tactical reasons such as knowledge of the terrain and being used to the hard life in the mountains, that the peasants come to occupy the vanguard in this struggle. In the mountains they must pass their first tests, they must be polished, they must be purified until they reach solidarity as a revolutionary force. This must continue until other sectors of the masses can join; the workers, the students, the professional people, and intellectuals who agree with the reality of our position, in order to organize them, to show them their mistakes, to place them in the struggle, to give them aims that are not outside the true scope of their forces, to bring about the third stage in the revolutionary struggle—the correlation of their strength with that of the enemy, and the preparation for the taking of power. That is to say, the struggle for national liberation must be directed from the countryside to the city.

Question: For you, what is a guerrilla leader, and what should he be? What are his responsibilities?

Answer: A guerrilla leader must, above all, be a man fully convinced of the justice of the cause he is fighting for. He should not be irresolute; dragged into his position by interests different from those of the men he commands and who nominated him. For these reasons, not anyone can simply be declared a guerrilla chief. He is formed in the heat of battle. His faith in, and deep love for, the people; his wisdom; his astuteness; his bravery; his honesty; his tactical and strategic skill in the people's war—these are the merits looked for by the men who will faithfully follow him into any battle. A guerrilla chief should be a man with sufficient political awareness of the seriousness and responsibility of his mission before the people. A guerrilla chief should be responsible for his acts to his superior organizations which, if they exist, should obviously be in the mountains or on the battlefield, because a guerrilla chief must not permit, and should not even conceive of receiving, orders from the city. And, what is most important, he should be responsible to the people. His principal mission is the directing of the struggle in more advanced stages each time—consolidating and developing the guerrilla force. A guerrilla chief is not permitted to abandon his combat position. If he descends to the city it will only be acceptable if he does it by forcibly taking the enemy positions, totally controlling the situation.

In our organization ranks do not exist. The only ones awarded have been posthumous. We consider that ranks should not be a preoccupying problem for revolutionaries who believe in the necessity of developing the organized work of the struggle with the maximum of seriousness as fundamental. We allocate responsibilities, we maintain good discipline and good revolutiontionary military training in our ranks. And up to this moment we have not needed to award ranks to our combatants, our guerrilla leaders, or our comrades of the General Staff.

I am not a follower of the idea that a given group of men who set themselves the job of developing the organization of work should take as their principal task the solving of the problem of ranks. Already we have seen many who have wasted several years deciding who should be commanders, and who should be commander-in-chief. And we have seen others who, finally agreeing, have all become commanders, with the obvious result that the true work has been lost from view. The rank of guerrilla commander should be awarded because of organizational needs, and not as a personal satisfaction, or a prize for some small merits.

Our first rank was awarded to the beloved and unforgettable Captain Parmenio, that exemplary fighter and brilliant man, most pure and at one with the countryside, who sealed with his blood the triumph which at Simacota was shown on the horizon to our people. One year later we awarded our second rank to a man no less exemplary who also showed clearly by his death the road that must be followed by the exploited and oppressed peoples of the world—to the glorious hero of our continent, to our great Comandante Camilo Torres Restrepo.

The leadership of the National Liberation Army is made up in the following manner: a leader directly responsible, below him a second-in-command, and a General Staff. Further, every guerrilla front has a comrade directly responsible, and a second-in-command, as does every guerrilla group and every guerrilla band. As the organization develops, the leadership will be adjusted to suit the circumstances.

Question: There has been much speculation about the participation of the rebel priest, Camilo Torres Restrepo, in the revolutionary movement in Colombia, and his death has led to many different rumors. Could you explain his involvement?

Answer: The significance of the death of the priest Camilo Torres Restrepo —gun in hand, wearing a guerrilla uniform, in an offensive operation for the national liberation of his country—is something many have tried to misrepresent, but that no one could succeed in doing, because history is written by the people, the martyrs, the men like Camilo Torres Restrepo. The clarity of his example has been engraved in the memory and in the hearts of those thousands of rebel slaves who will dig the final grave of imperialist capitalism. Camilo, abandoning the sinecure offered him as a Catholic priest by bourgeois society, abandoning the diversions and comforts of the city, resolved to deprive himself of these things—even the most elementary—and link himself to the difficult country life. He succeeded in blending his thought, his practical life, with that of the peasants to a surprising degree. He had a great capacity for adapting himself, rejecting any privilege that might be offered him in his role as priest. He felt a profound love for the people—an indispensable condition for being able to put up with the hard guerrilla life. He taught peasants to read, he shared his bed with them, he shared his bitter, poor meal. He identified himself more and more with their needs until he arrived at the maximum expression of this—giving his life for the freedom of his people. Camilo said that it was necessary to raise oneself up to the height of the peasants, to learn from them, to shape oneself in the revolutionary process of the fight, to temper oneself in the noise and heat of combat. That was why he did not permit himself the right to give up participating personally in the military operations. On February 15, 1966, at a place called Patio de Cemento in the Department of Santander, in an ambush prepared against antiguerrilla forces, he fell at my side pierced by two enemy bullets at the moment he was advancing, firing his gun, to retrieve an M-1 carbine.

Question: To what do we owe the fact that the National Liberation Army and the Armed Revolutionary Forces of Colombia, both being guerrilla movements, each fight on their own account? Is there no intention of unifying the Colombian Revolution?

Answer: At the time when our first guerrilla band—the embryo of our organization—was going through its first secret stage, the reactionaries were preparing the invasion of Marquetalia. As a result, the peasants who lived in these zones were ready to enter a stage of guerrilla life. The government offensive was just beginning when we made our public appearance in Simacota, showing the way to the guerrilla offensive, the insurrectional way to gain power for the people. In the south, the government spread out part of their repressive forces to throw their first offensive at our organization together with the Fifth Brigade. In fact our nearest fighting companions were the comrades of the South Block guerrillas. For this reason we asked for an interview with a member of the central leadership of the Communist Party of Colombia. On May 15, 1965, we were visited by a member of the Executive Central Committee of the Communist Party. At this opportunity we understood with greater clarity the necessity of establishing relations, the necessity of interchanging experiences, and we expressed our need to have talks with comrades who were directly engaged in the armed struggle. The comrade delegate of the Communist Party was in agreement with our appreciation of the situation, and it was decided that, in order to establish relations, a comrade from the South Block would visit us in one month's time. With his direct knowledge, acquired in the practical terrain of the fight, he would be able to pass on to us valuable information in guerrilla tactics. We raised the question of the need for fraternal relations in the search for coordination and tactical-strategic unity of the politico-military focalization of the people's war. Many days passed without this desired offer becoming a fact. Later we took the initiative several times, after having managed to establish fraternal and direct relations with the guerrillas of the South Block. On the occasion of the Tenth Congress of the Communist Party we sent a message of solidarity to Comrade Manuel Marulanda and the fighters of that guerrilla group. Later we learned that at that Congress he took the initiative, on the part of the guerrillas, of strengthening unity with the National Liberation Army and of searching for a way to organize a national guerrilla conference without participation. We replied immediately, asking if it would be permitted for us to send a delegation to speak with Comrade Marulanda about the study of the politico-military experiences of both movements. To all these efforts of ours we received the same reply—they would see if it could be arranged in a month's time. The Second Guerrilla Conference of the South Block took place. In conclusion it stated—on constituting the FARC—that a new stage of struggle and unity with all the revolutionaries in our country had been initiated. But in spite of this, and our repeated attempts, we have received no reply, in any sense, from the comrade guerrillas of the FARC.

In August 1966, at the end of fifteen months of failure in our attempts to establish contacts or relations with Marulanda and the guerrillas in the south, we sent a letter to the Central Committee of the Communist Party. In it was analyzed and detailed all our attempts at unity with the FARC, and stressed the need to establish relations. In it was said: "Bearing in mind that the National Liberation Army is a totally illegal organization and is in open conflict with the instruments of oppression, exploitation, and repression of the Colombian oligarchy, linked to North

American imperialism, we understand that the basis of revolutionary solidarity is for us the combat activity—which in the case of the comrades of the South Block, politically oriented through the Communist Party of Colombia, is carried out by the heroic guerrillas of Comrade Marulanda—and it is therefore necessary to facilitate collaboration, knowledge, coordination, and unity with other guerrilla forces which, although young, are playing a great part in the fight for national liberation."

To this letter, undeniably revolutionary and pro-unity—as were all our other attempts, never violating regular channels—we received the incredible, the laconic reply from the Central Committee of the Communist Party which said: "Comrade Marulanda has been informed by the Party of your activities. Activities which have not been pleasing to the Party. The Party, the General Staff, and Comandante Marulanda Vélez himself consider that such relations cannot be possible until you have an understanding of the politics of the Communist Party."

Certainly we have continued to insist and to hope that the comrade guerrillas in the south, who fight with guns in their hands, who see every day the growing necessity of coordination, interchange of experiences, and combat unity, who feel in their own flesh the repressive cruelty of the ultra-reactionary and proimperialist regime, will understand clearly the purity of our revolutionary position. We can never accept conditions for solidarity. We can never accept imposed political concessions. The most just, revolutionary, and correct attitude of the people of Latin America in the face of possible U.S. counterrevolutionary invasion, and also in the most unswerving and decided solidarity with Vietnam, with Cuba, and with the other countries and continents which are in open fight with our common enemy, is to develop the people's war with all the honesty, seriousness, and revolutionary responsibility, demanded by the historic moment in which we live. We swear to our people on oath of fidelity to our motto: "Not one step backward! Liberty or death!"

CAMILO TORRES RESTREPO:
THREE REVOLUTIONARY MESSAGES*

MESSAGE TO CHRISTIANS

THE convulsions caused by the political, religious, and social events of recent times may have sown a great deal of confusion among Colombian

---

* The first two, *Message to Christians* and *Message to the Communists*, were published in *Frente Unido*, Camilo's own newspaper in Bogotá, on August 26 and September 2, 1965, respectively. The third, his last, *Message to the Colombian People*, was written in the mountains and published in *El Vespertino*, Bogotá, in the January 1966 issue which actually appeared after his death. Translations by *Tricontinental* and Juan Mechón.

Christians. At this decisive moment in our history, we Christians must take a firm stand concerning the essential bases of our religion.

In Catholicism the main thing is love for one's fellow man. "He who loves his fellow man fulfills the law" (Romans 13:8). For this love to be genuine, it must seek to be effective. If beneficence, alms, the few tuition-free schools, the few housing projects—in general, what is known as "charity"—do not succeed in feeding the hungry majority, clothing the naked, or teaching the unschooled masses, we must seek effective means to achieve the well-being of these majorities. These means will not be sought by the privileged minorities who hold power, because such effective means generally force the minorities to sacrifice their privileges. For example, employment could be increased by investing the capital now leaving Colombia in dollars in the creation of new job opportunities here in the country. But, due to the virtually daily devaluation of the Colombian peso, those with money and power are never going to prohibit currency exportation, because it frees them from devaluation.

Thus, power must be taken from the privileged minorities and given to the poor majorities. If this is done rapidly, it constitutes the essential characteristic of a Revolution. The Revolution can be a peaceful one if the minorities refrain from violent resistance. Revolution is, therefore, the way to obtain a government that will feed the hungry, clothe the naked, teach the unschooled; that carries out works of charity, of love for one's fellows—not in a haphazard and transitory fashion for only a few, but for the majority of our fellow men. This is why the Revolution is not only permissible but obligatory for those Christians who see it as the only effective and far-reaching way to make love for all a reality. It is true that "There is no authority but God" (Romans 13:1). But St. Thomas teaches that it is the people who concretely have the right to authority.

When the existing authority is against the people, it is not legitimate, and we call it a tyranny. We Christians can and must fight against tyranny. The present government is tyrannical because it receives the support of only 20 percent of the voters and because its decisions emanate from the privileged minorities.

I have given up the duties and privileges of the clergy, but I have not ceased to be a priest. I believe that I have given myself to the Revolution out of love for my fellow man. I have ceased to say mass in order to practice that love for my fellow man in the temporal, economic, and social terrain. When my fellow man has nothing against me, when he has carried out the Revolution, then I will once again offer mass if God allows me to. I believe that in this way I am following the mandate of Christ. "If you bring your offering to the altar, and there remember that your brother has something against you, go first and become reconciled with your brother, then come and make your offering" (Matthew 5:23–24).

After the Revolution we Christians will know that we have established a system which is guided by love of our fellow man.

The struggle is a long one; let us begin it now.

MESSAGE TO THE COMMUNISTS

The relations that have traditionally existed between Christians and Marxists, between the Church and the Communist Party, may give rise to doubts and misunderstandings with regard to the relations taking shape within the United Front between Christians and Marxists and between a priest and the Communist Party.

I therefore consider it necessary to make my relations with the Communist Party and its position in the United Front perfectly clear to the Colombian people.

I have said that as a Colombian, as a sociologist, as a Christian, and as a priest I am a revolutionary. I believe that the Communist Party consists of truly revolutionary elements, and hence I cannot be an anticommunist as either a Colombian, or a sociologist, a Christian, or a priest.

As a Colombian I am not an anticommunist because anticommunism hounds nonconformists among my compatriots regardless of whether they are communists or not. Most of them are simply poor people.

As a sociologist I am not an anticommunist because the communist theses concerning the fight against poverty, hunger, illiteracy, the lack of shelter, and absence of public services offer effective scientific solutions to these problems.

As a Christian I am not anticommunist because I believe that anticommunism implies condemnation of everything that communists stand for.

As a priest I am not an anticommunist because among communists themselves, whether they know it or not, there may be many true Christians. If they be of good faith they are entitled to receive Holy Communion. And if they receive Holy Communion and if they love their neighbor they will be saved. My duty as a priest, although I no longer practice the rites of the Church, is to bring people nearer to God, and the best way to do this is strive that people should serve their neighbor according to the dictates of their conscience. I do not seek to proselytize my communist brethren and induce them to accept the dogma and the rites of the Church. What I strive for is that people should act according to their conscience, that they should sincerely search for the truth and truly love their fellow men.

I am prepared to fight together with the communists for our common goals: against the oligarchy and United States domination, for the winning of power by the people.

I do not want to be identified with the communists alone and hence I have always sought to work together not only with them but with all independent revolutionaries and revolutionaries of other trends.

That the big press persists in saying that I am a communist is of no importance. I prefer to follow the voice of my own conscience and not to submit to pressures from the oligarchy. I prefer to live according to the standards of the apostles of the Church and not the standards of the apostles of our ruling class.

MESSAGE TO THE COLOMBIAN PEOPLE

For many years now the poor of our land have been waiting for the call to arms to throw themselves into the final struggle against the oligarchy.

On the occasions when it seemed that the people's desperation had reached the critical point, the ruling class always found the means to deceive the people, to distract them, appeasing them with new formulas that always added up to the same thing: suffering for the people and well-being for the privileged caste.

When the people demanded a leader, and found one in Jorge Eliecer Gaitán, the oligarchy murdered him. When the people demanded peace, the oligarchy sowed violence throughout the country. When the people could no longer withstand violence and organized the guerrillas to seize power, the oligarchy pulled the military coup out of its hat so that the guerrillas, who were tricked, would surrender. When the people demanded democracy, they were tricked once again, this time with a plebiscite and a National Front imposed upon them by the dictatorship of the oligarchy.

But the people will no longer believe, ever again. The people do not believe in elections. The people know that the legal means have been exhausted. The people know that armed struggle is the only remaining course. The people are desperate, and they are determined to risk their lives so that the next generation of Colombians will not be one of slaves. So that the children of those who now are willing to give their lives will have an education, a roof over their heads, food, clothing—and, above all, DIGNITY. And so that the Colombians of the future will have their own homeland, independent of U.S. might.

All sincere revolutionaries must realize that armed struggle is the only remaining way open. However, the people wait for their leaders to set an example and issue the call to arms by their presence in the struggle. I want to tell the Colombian people that the time is now and that I have not betrayed them. That I have gone from village to village and from city to city, speaking in the public plazas in favor of the unity and organization of the popular classes to take power.

The oligarchy means to organize another force at election time, with candidates who deny their candidacy only to be finally "drafted"; with two-party committees; pretending a new beginning with ideas and people that not only are old, but have betrayed the people. What are we waiting for, Colombians?

I have joined the armed struggle.

From the Colombian mountains I mean to continue the struggle, arms in hand, until power has been won by the people. I have joined the National Liberation Army because I have found in it the same ideals of the United Front. I found the desire and the attainment of unity at the base, a peasant base, without traditional religious or party differences, and without any interest in combating the revolutionary elements of any sector, movement, or party. And without *caudillismo*. A movement that seeks to free the people from the exploitation of the oligarchies and imperialism and that will not lay down its arms as long as power is not entirely in the hands of the people. And which, in its goals, accepts the platform of the United Front.

All we Colombian patriots must ready ourselves for war. Little by little, we will emerge ready for war. Little by little, experienced guerrilla leaders will appear in all parts of the country. Meanwhile, we must be alert.

We must gather weapons and ammunition, seek guerrilla training, talk with those who are closest to us. We must collect clothing, medical supplies, and provisions in preparation for a protracted struggle.

We must carry out small-scale attacks against the enemy where we can be sure of victory. We must put those who claim to be revolutionaries to the test. We must not refrain from acting, but neither must we grow impatient. In a long, drawn-out war everyone must go into action at some point. What matters is that the Revolution find them ready and on their guard. We must divide up the work. The activists of the United Front must be in the vanguard as far as action and initiative are concerned. We must have patience while we wait and confidence in final victory.

The people's struggle must become a national one. We have already begun, and we have a long day's work ahead of us.

Colombians: Let us not fail to answer the call of the people and the Revolution.

Not One Step Back. Liberation or Death!

Puerto Rico

The line known somewhat incorrectly as Guevarism or Debrayism insists that armed struggle is the only way of achieving revolution. The General Declaration of OLAS specifically concludes that the revolutionaries' objective of seizing power and destroying the state apparatus of feudalism-imperialism "can be achieved only through armed struggle." But neither the signers of the declaration, nor Fidel, nor Che, nor Debray ever meant to imply that peasant guerrilla warfare as people's war is the only prerequisite for the seizure of revolutionary power in each and every country. In Revolution in the Revolution? *Debray regarded Uruguay, for example, as "an exception" (though some Uruguayans disagree; see below). What Fidel, Che, and Debray did mean was that every revolutionary must be prepared to fight; that in most underdeveloped colonized countries the peasants and not the urban masses are the revolutionary force; that revolutionary example is the best way of politicizing the masses; that the ruling elites will always fight to keep their power; and that genuine structural changes in which the oppressed classes destroy the state apparatus of the oppressing classes can only come about through revolutionary violence—because the oppressors will always fight to defend their power.*

In the case of Puerto Rico, the immediate oppressors are the U.S. military-industrial elites. Naturally, they will use force to maintain the island's colonial status. And since so much of the whole island is an armed U.S. military base, there is no chance of defeating the United States in open combat. But the U.S. elites involved in Puerto Rico are so directly visible as the colonizers that it would be impossible for them to hide behind the façade of neo-colonial forces—should a serious "crisis" occur. And such a crisis would necessarily occur if the Puerto Rican masses demanded independence so vociferously as to focus world attention on U.S. colonialism. Hence, the MPI (the Pro-Independence Movement of Puerto Rico) is convinced that revolution on the island is indeed one of two stages: first, through mass, basically nonviolent organizational and confrontation activities, create the crisis; then, use revolutionary violence to destroy the oppressive bourgeois apparatus.

Because of U.S. involvement all over the world and because of its official anticolonial policy, the "crisis" would force the United States to grant Puerto Rico its independence, leaving behind a neo-colonial apparatus similar to those existing in every country of Central America. That apparatus can then be destroyed, says Juan Mari-Brás, the MPI's secretary-general, by armed revolutionary struggle, especially since the masses, having gained the political awareness to create the "crisis" in the first place, could no longer be contained by the half-measures offered by neo-colonial elites. Thus Mari-Brás, whose immediate goal is to keep MPI legal (even if it is directly involved in such individual nonlegal activities as draft resistance), cannot and does not advocate armed action. He considers himself a Guevarist and the MPI is part of the OLAS revolutionary structure. But its struggle is in the open. In effect, then, though the MPI rejects Russia's peaceful coexistence line and sides with the Fidelistas in their condemnation of city-based legalistic communist parties whose "revolutionary" activity is almost totally limited to the creation of electoral united fronts, the MPI seeks to establish precisely such a nationalistic (though nonelectoral) front to gain Stage One.

Some form of armed struggle, however, would certainly be beneficial both to the MPI's mass-consciousness line and in generating the "crisis." That is the task of the Armed Commandos of Liberation (CAL), as they see themselves. Alfonso Beal, leader of the Commandos, explains in an interview (below) just what their role is, as a catalyst to the independence movement. Since the interview, the CAL have been extremely active—bombing hotels and U.S.-owned stores in San Juan's tourist Condado area, setting fire to U.S. enterprises, destroying oil pipe lines, etc. For the very obvious reason that knowledge of such activity would seriously undermine the tourist trade, Puerto Rican officials have successfully kept most of these incidents out of both the local and the U.S. press. But judging by accounts in Le Monde, for example, CAL's urban warfare is now making itself felt across the whole island.

ALFONSO BEAL: ARMED COMMANDOS OF LIBERATION*

THE Liberation Armed Commandos have been in the process of formation during the past few years, but we started operations in September

---

* Interview by Gaspar Cuneo Elizondo for *Tricontinental* (Havana) reproduced by Liberation News Service, No. 117, November 9, 1968. The interview, writes Cuneo, "took place in the cocktail lounge of one of Condado's modern hotels on the outskirts of San Juan, Puerto Rico. The fact that this bar is patronized by the bourgeoisie and U.S. agents made it an ideal spot to meet secretly."

1967 by simultaneously burning down Bargain Town, Carolina, and three other stores owned by Yankees in the Santa Rosa, Bayamón, shopping center. Our actions are aimed at undermining the colonial stability and peace of the imperialist invaders; we are in the first stage of operations, and in this phase we intend to cause 100 million dollars' worth of damages to U.S. concerns. Our idea is to inflict such heavy losses on these enterprises that the insurance companies will have to pay out more money in indemnity than they have received in payments, thus upsetting the economy.

Question: Have you achieved any practical results?

Answer: Let me explain. When the losses amounted to 14 million dollars the first crisis of the insurance companies was precipitated; they started to cancel policies taken out on fire losses by U.S. enterprises. Furthermore, the attitude of the insurance companies forced the colonial legislature to enact a special law whereby the government of Puerto Rico subsidizes insurance companies. It was necessary to set up a special fund for policies on liabilities that are financially burdensome to the companies. By escalating this action, as we propose to do, the time will come when the government will be unable to continue to subsidize these companies. So far, it has only tried to patch up the situation.

Question: What is the basis of your actions against U.S. interests?

Answer: In our actions we have kept in mind the experiences of the revolutionary struggles in other countries—for instance, the Algerian experience—regarding this stage of urban struggle, but we apply this experience to the Puerto Rican reality, which has its own special—though not exceptional—characteristics; we apply in Puerto Rico whatever we can from the struggles all over the world. Puerto Rico is a U.S. military and economic bulwark in the Caribbean; in this appraisal we coincide with other Puerto Rican fighters for independence; it's just that they wage their struggle on a political plane, while we are waging an armed struggle. We are not the armed branch of any particular organization; we are the armed branch of the struggle for the independence of Puerto Rico, although that doesn't mean that there is any formal agreement between us and the various independence organizations. In the Commandos, we have some people who don't belong to any organization other than ours.

Question: What method do you use for getting in touch with the people and spreading armed struggle?

Answer: We begin by linking our actions with the specific problems of the working class and the people in general, affected by the presence of imperialism here. For instance, when the telephone workers' strike broke out last April we got ready to sabotage the telephone company, which is a branch of the IT&T monopoly, in solidarity with the workers on strike. Our actions against the telephone company prompted its running full-page ads in the local newspapers offering a substantial reward for any information leading to our arrest. In our first bulletin we showed the people how to take an active part in the war against the telephone company.

Question: What were CAL's fundamental tasks during its first year of struggle?

Answer: First, to organize, discipline, and train the members of our organization. We have worked not only in the formation of cadres, the organization of cells, and the training of Commandos but also in getting the necessary resources to carry on our revolutionary struggle. We took up, organized, and disciplined a spontaneous armed struggle that has been going on in Puerto Rico for the past ten years. Naturally this year we began to put into practice our plans for armed struggle, consisting of sabotaging the imperialist enterprises that have gradually taken over the economic life of our country. As part of our armed struggle, we have carried out—and will continue to carry out—operations against this Condado zone, the lair of the U.S. gangsters and mafia and Cuban counter-revolutionaries who control the casinos of the big hotels in this area and who have outdone—as far as prostitution and drug peddling are concerned—the Havana of prerevolutionary days. All these night clubs practice discrimination against Puerto Rican artists. We have declared Condado a war zone and have warned Puerto Ricans not to go through it, especially at night. Moreover, we are preparing to engage in more important operations.

Question: What about the arrests that have been made?

Answer: That's because the pressure brought to bear by U.S. investors and the reactionary press forced them to produce scapegoats; they look for these scapegoats among the more active independence organizations. That explains the arrest of members and even leaders of the Pro-Independence Movement (MPI). The government offers big rewards and twenty-four-hour-a-day police protection to all those who will testify as witnesses against these scapegoats. They also want to hit the MPI because it is the organization that gets the most people out in the streets in the struggle for the independence of Puerto Rico and especially because the MPI has refused to condemn the actions of CAL.

Question: Have you been able to ascertain the effects of your actions on investors?

Answer: We know that our actions are beginning to be felt, as we have seen their effects in various sectors that support big investment. *Time*

magazine, *U.S. News & World Report*, and the *Wall Street Journal* have
expressed their concern. In addition to this, we know that the head of
the Puerto Rico Industrial Development Office in the United States,
Danilo Ondina, resigned his post after failing to attract a number of companies that had already made tentative contacts with the government to
set up business in Puerto Rico.

*Question: The divergences in the socialist camp have had a negative effect
on the revolutionary forces of the world. Was there any such effect in
Puerto Rico?*

Answer: These divergences have not affected us, because we are quite
clear on the specific objectives of our struggle here. Such futile discussion is limited to debating circles in our country. One of the healthy effects
of the creation of CAL has been the unmasking of pseudorevolutionary
idle talk. Now, anyone who is not engaged in a task in the mass organization or is not a member of CAL is simply running off at the mouth.
We are aware that there is room for other kinds of work; let no one
think that we attack those who participate in demonstrations, picketing,
and denunciations or who struggle against the draft imposed on our youth
by the U.S. imperialists. We know that it is all part of the struggle.

*Question: I don't want to hold you here any longer, but I would like to
ask you one last question. What moved you to create CAL?*

Answer: On September 23, 1963, on the occasion of the commemoration
of the Cry of Lares,[1] all the patriotic forces signed the so-called Declaration of Lares; in it they pledged themselves to do their best to attain our
independence before the Centennial—which is this year. Perhaps that was
the biggest stimulus that led us to organize the Liberation Armed Commandos last year, since we considered it our duty to try to make good
the Lares pledge, so that the year of the Centennial would find us already
engaged in armed struggle for independence under CAL's slogan: Independence or Death!

[1] On September 23, 1868, in Lares, Puerto Rico was proclaimed an independent
republic by the leaders of all anti-Spain nationalists.—*Ed.*

Uruguay

The capitalist press has long liked to describe tiny Uruguay as the Switzerland of the Americas. Created by British imperialism as a buffer between the continent's giants, Argentina and Brazil, it has almost no national resources, except fertile pampas on which it raises cattle and sheep. Thus, except for some sugar in the north, its economy should have been limited to meat and wool. Indeed, Uruguay has always been totally dependent upon these for its foreign currency. But by controlling and varying its complicated system of exchange rates, subsidizing specific industries, developing state monopolies and various other economic juggles, the successive governments have created a synthetic industry in Montevideo and a huge civil servant bourgeoisie (one-third of the labor force). As long as it could continue to sell wool and meat at high prices and for dollars, the country seemed economically sound. Montevideo became a large, elegant metropolis with 46 percent of the country's 2,500,000 inhabitants. And though acute poverty existed, not only throughout the countryside ruled by absentee latifundists, but also in the cantegriles (shanty towns) of every urban center, Uruguay gave foreigners the impression of being a happy middle-class nation. It had more doctors and hospitals per inhabitant than the United States, solidly organized militant unions, a weak army, no censorship, and an inefficient, corrupt, but quite democratic electoral system that harmed few.

But the whole structure was illogical. So, when wool and meat prices began to collapse after the Korean War, hard times fell upon Uruguayans and gradually their precious liberties were eroded one by one. Inevitably the ruling bourgeoisie called on the United States for help, and besides having to open the country's doors to U.S. capitalists, the price paid was an austerity program dictated by the International Monetary Fund. Discontent spread and, hence, so did repressions—of students, workers, peasant unions. Opposition newspapers were shut down and in 1967, "emergency measures" made it a felony to belong to socialist, Fidelista (not the CP), and anarchist parties or groups. The Switzerland of the Americas became another neo-colonialized dictatorship. And the Left began to talk of revolution seriously for the first time.

But how can Uruguay have a revolution—except through a general insurrection? And for that, long preparations were needed, preparations brought about by years of militant strikes leading to a general political strike. Revolutionary consciousness was only just beginning. Besides, the government controlled the radio and television and most of the press, and it jailed many of the mass party leaders. As for guerrilla warfare, that seemed absurd in Uruguay, which is mostly flat and open. Even Debray, in Revolution in the Revolution?, *said that Uruguay was an exception. It seemed the best that the Left could come up with was a call to join the movements of other lands, which was stated by Ariel Collazo, a one-time reactionary deputy radicalized by his 1961 visit to Cuba, who now headed the Uruguayan Revolutionary Movement (MRO). "Uruguay does not have the terrain to support a guerrilla* foco. *It has neither mountains nor jungles. An armed insurrection in Montevideo, were conditions to exist for one, would quickly be squashed by Argentine or Brazilian and eventually Yankee paratroopers. What then are we to do?" he asked in a pamphlet entitled* We Are No Exception *(May 1967). Collazo's answer: "We must join the revolutionary columns of the continent, must help liberate our brother peoples of Brazil and Argentina, without whose victories the Liberation of Uruguay is impossible. From those peoples' armies, one day, the Uruguayan columns will then return. . . ."*

But there were other Uruguayan revolutionaries, not so romantic, who were quietly working out a strategy for revolutionary action at home. Until 1968, they made no declaration, issued no pamphlets, formulated no sweeping or grandiose theories. These were the Tupamaros. When they were ready, they struck—and the whole country suddenly listened. Named for the famed Inca revolutionary Tupac Amaru, the Tupamaros began as a militant sugarworkers' union group organized by Raúl Sendic, a Socialist Party official. After various unfruitful legal protest marches and demonstrations for better working conditions, one section of the group went underground and Sendic disappeared. Then, in July 1963, "some unknown group" raided a rifle club. Shortly thereafter armed men began to hold up banks, raid the coffers of U.S. enterprises, and kidnap unpopular government or police officials. By the end of 1967, the Tupamaros, attacking in swift military-style operations, were well known. Then, in 1968, they changed their name to National Liberation Movement, and explained their strategy (in a secret interview, below). By the end of 1969, their acts—sabotage of U.S. firms, kidnappings, bank holdups and, most spectacularly, robbing the Punta del Este casino of $250,000 despite its *formidable security precautions—had elicited the greatest police, military, CIA, and FBI ("advisers") manhunt in Uruguayan history. The Tupamaros had yet to harm a single citizen not directly involved in repression (e.g., policemen). Their casualties were low—three killed in combat, a dozen wounded and captured. These were tortured, but the police had yet to locate the Tupamaros' bases (though it has found arms caches).*

The Tupamaros hope to politicize the masses by calling attention to the enemy, by Robin Hood tactics, by discrediting the repressive forces. They want to set an example for other revolutionaries to follow—in their way, so long as armed struggle is involved. They do not accept Debray's "exception" theory, but also reject Collazo's continentalism as a tactic for Uruguayan revolutionary parties. Like Debray, they believe that the unity of the Left can be forged only in combat, but they consider the city as the main battlefield and the organized proletariat as the revolutionary force. In sum, they see themselves as "the little motor that starts the big motor of the Revolution."

THE TUPAMAROS: THIRTY ANSWERS TO THIRTY QUESTIONS*

1. What has been the fundamental principle on which you have based the activity of your organization up to the present?

The principle of revolutionary action itself: the acts of arming, training, planning, and committing acts which violate bourgeois legality and generate consciousness, organization, and revolutionary conditions.

2. What is the fundamental difference between your organization and other organizations of the Left?

The majority of these organizations seem to place more trust in manifestos, in issuing theoretical statements about revolution in order to prepare the militants and revolutionary conditions without understanding that fundamentally it is revolutionary actions which lead to revolutionary situations.

3. Can you give me any historical example which illustrates the principle of revolutionary action generating consciousness, organizations, and revolutionary conditions?

Cuba is an example. Instead of the long process of forming a party of the masses a guerrilla *foco* of a dozen men was installed, and this action

---

* Clandestine interviews carried out somewhere in Montevideo during early 1968 and distributed in mimeograph form. Translation by Tom Raworth.

generated consciousness, organization, and revolutionary conditions that culminated in a true Revolution. In the face of the accomplished revolutionary act, all true revolutionaries saw themselves obliged to follow.

4. Do you mean that once the revolutionary act has begun, the much-talked-about unity of the Left can realize itself within the struggle?

Yes. Those forces which call themselves revolutionary will see themselves obliged to choose between supporting or disappearing. In Cuba, the People's Socialist Party chose to support a struggle they had neither initiated, nor led—and survived. But Prío Socarras, who called himself the leader of the opposition to Batista, gave no support, and disappeared.

5. This is in regard to the Left. But what of the people in general?

For the people—who truly disagree with the injustices of the regime—the choice is much easier. They want change, and they must choose between the improbable and remote change which some offer them by way of proclamations, manifestos, or parliamentary action, and the direct road embodied in the armed group and their revolutionary action.

6. Do you mean that the armed struggle, at the same time as it is destroying bourgeois power, can create the mass movement necessary for an insurrectionist organization to make the Revolution?

Yes. Without considering as lost that force used in creating a party, or mass movement, before beginning the armed struggle, it must be remembered that armed struggle hastens and precipitates the mass movement. And Cuba is not the only example; in China too the mass party was created in the course of armed struggle. I mean that the rigid formula of certain theorists, "first create the Party, then begin the Revolution," historically admits of more exceptions than applications. At this point in history no one can argue that an armed group—however small—has more possibility of successes in turning itself into a large popular army, than a group that limits itself to the issuing of revolutionary "positions."

7. Nevertheless, a revolutionary movement needs a platform, documents, etc.?

Of course, but we must not be deceived. It is not only by polishing platforms and programs that the Revolution is made. The basic principles of a socialist revolution have been given and experienced in countries like Cuba—there's no argument about that. All that is needed is to adhere to these principles, and to show with acts the insurrectional way, in order to apply them.

8. Do you consider that a revolutionary movement should prepare for armed struggle at some stage, even when the conditions for armed struggle don't exist?

Yes, for at least two reasons. Because an armed movement of the Left can be attacked by repression at any point in its development, and should be prepared to defend its existence—remember what happened in Brazil and Argentina. And because if each militant is not inculcated from the beginning with the mentality of a combatant we are creating something else—a mere support movement for a revolution others will make, for example—but not a revolutionary movement itself.

9. This could be interpreted as a neglect of all other activities save that of preparing for combat?

No. Work among the masses, which brings the people to a revolutionary position, is also important. What the militant—including the ones in the mass movement—must bear in mind is that on the day when the armed struggle begins he is not going to stay in his house waiting for the result. And consequently he should prepare himself, though his actual militancy be on other fronts. This, besides, will lend authority, authenticity, sincerity, and seriousness to his real revolutionary preaching.

10. What are the concrete tasks of a militant, belonging to your ranks, in the mass movement?

If we are dealing with a militant in a union, or mass movement, he should try to create a cell, a group within a union, or all the unions, where support can be organized for the actions of the armed band and people prepared to enter it. Theoretical and practical training, and recruiting, will be the principal concrete tasks within that cell, as well as propaganda for the armed struggle. And, where possible, they should lead the union to more radical struggles and to more definite stages of the class struggle.

11. What are, in general, the fundamental objectives of the movement at this stage?

To have an armed group, as well-trained and -equipped as possible, proved in action. To have good relations with all the popular movements that support this type of struggle. To create propaganda organs aimed at radicalizing the struggle and creating consciousness. To have an efficient organization to absorb militants with the possibility of theoretical training, and to have groups inside the mass movement who will fulfill the functions already mentioned.

12. Does the importance given by the movement to the preparation for armed struggle imply the belief that a combatant cannot improvise?

The armed struggle is a technical act that needs, therefore, technical knowledge, training, practice, materials, and fighting spirit. Improvisation in this area will be paid for heavily in lives and failure. The spontaneity proposed by those who speak vaguely of "the Revolution the people will make" or "the masses," will either delay, or else leave to improvisation, that which is the precise culminating stage of the class war. Every vanguard movement, to preserve that character in the final moment of the struggle, should intervene in it and know how to technically guide the popular violence against oppression in such a way that it succeeds in its object with the least possible sacrifice.

13. Do you consider that the parties of the Left can comply with this preparation for the armed struggle by maintaining a small shock or self-defense group?

No party fulfills the revolutionary principles it gives out if it does not aim at this preparation at every level of the party. Any other way it will not reach the maximum efficiency possible to confront reaction at every stage. If they are not thought out specifically to fulfill their purpose, the small armed partisan groups can become a suitable ground, sadly, for political maneuvers.

14. What do you think the militants in the armed groups require from their respective leaders?

That their action be directed solely against the class enemy, against the bourgeois apparatus and its agents. No armed group can fulfill its specific aim if its leadership does not at least agree with these minimum requirements. That it be consistent, and demonstrate with actions its constant adherence to the principle of armed struggle, giving it the importance and the necessary means for its preparation. That it offer the necessary conditions of security and discretion for the militants who carry out illegal tasks. That by virtue of its size, and correct line, it have the chance—as quickly as possible—of constituting the leadership of the working masses.

15. Do you not think that an armed band should be dependent upon a political party?

I believe that all armed bands should form part of a political apparatus of the masses at a certain point in the revolutionary process—and, in the event of such an apparatus not existing, should contribute to its creation. This does not mean that in the present context of the Left it should be obliged to subscribe to one of the existing political groups, or should start a new one. This only means perpetuating, or joining, the mosaic. It is necessary to fight the current paltry idea of a party, identified by a headquarters, meetings, a newspaper, and positions on everything that surrounds it. It is necessary to fight against the conformism of hoping that the other parties of the Left will dissolve before your verbal broadsides, and that their bases, and the people in general, will one day come over to you. This is what has been happening in Uruguay for sixty years, and the results can be seen. One must begin from real facts. We must realize that there are true revolutionaries in all the parties of the Left, and many more who are not organized. To take these elements and groups where they are, and unite them, is a task for the Left in general. But while this is not happening, the Revolution cannot wait. For every revolutionary, for every revolutionary group, only one duty remains—to prepare to make the Revolution.

16. Can you specify the strategy for the taking of power in Uruguay?

No, I cannot give you a specific strategy. Instead, I can give you some general strategic lines, and even these are subject to modifications as circumstances change. That is to say, general strategic lines valid for the day, month, and year on which they are issued.

17. Why can you not give me a specific and definite strategy?

Because a strategy is founded on real, basic acts, and reality changes independently of our will. It should be understood that a strategy based on the fact of a strong and organized union movement is not the same as one based on the fact of that movement having been smashed—to take an illustrative example.

18. Upon which real basic facts does your organization base its general strategic lines at this moment?

The conviction that the crisis, far from being overcome, gets worse day by day. The country is bankrupt, and a capitalist plan for development by increasing the production of exportable articles—in the event of this being applicable—will bring a very miserable remedy, and only after several years. I mean that we have several years ahead of us during which the people will have to keep on tightening their belts. And with $500 million of foreign debt, it is not foreseeable that we will get enough credit from abroad to return a normal standard of living to those sectors of the population that have lost it. This is a basic concrete fact: We will have economic penury and popular discontent in the next few years.

A second basic fact for a strategy is the high level of unionization of the

Uruguayan workers. Even if all the unions do not have a high level of militancy—perhaps due to their membership, perhaps to their leaders—the mere fact that practically all the essential services of the state—banking, industry, and commerce—are organized, constitutes a highly important fact, without parallel in Latin America. The possibility of paralyzing the services of the state has created, and can create, very interesting opportunities from the point of view of the insurrection because—to take an example—it is not the same to attack a state in full strength as to attack one semiparalyzed by strikes.

Another strategic factor to take into account—this time negative—is the geographic one. We do not have impregnable areas in our territory in which to install a guerrilla *foco* that can last, although we have places in the countryside where access is difficult. In compensation, we have a great city with more than 300 square kilometers of buildings which permits the development of an urban struggle. This means that we cannot copy the strategy of those countries that, by reason of their geographic conditions, can install a guerrilla *foco* in the mountains, hills, or jungle. On the contrary, we must develop our own strategy, suitable for a different reality from that which exists in the majority of Latin American countries. We must also take into account the forces of repression. Our armed forces, consisting of some 12,000 men, precariously armed and trained, constitute one of the weakest repressive apparatuses in Latin America.

Another important strategic factor is made up of our powerful neighbors and the United States, always potentially disposed to intervene in any revolution on the continent.

And, to finish, a basic strategic factor is the level of preparation of the armed revolutionary group.

19. In what way do the factors of crisis and popular discontent enter your strategy?

In the objective and subjective conditions for the Revolution. It is fundamental that the majority of the population, while not throwing itself into the fight, at least will not kill for a regime that oppresses it. This, among other things, reduces the strategic calculations in respect to the enemies' forces, practically, to its organized armed forces, and makes a favorable climate possible for the first measures of a revolutionary government.

20. And with regard to the repressive forces?

They must be evaluated, taking into account their level of preparation for the struggle, their resources, and their distribution in the country. In the interior there is a military unit (200 men) for approximately every

10,000 square kilometers, and a police post approximately every 1,000 square kilometers. The armed forces must cover all the objectives that a revolutionary movement could attack with 12,000 men of the armed forces, and 22,000 police, of whom half the former and 6,000 of the latter are concentrated in the capital. Within the police, only about a thousand have been trained and equipped for a proper military battle.

21. Can the possibility of foreign intervention be a reason for postponing all armed struggle in Uruguay?

If this were so, Cuba could not have made its Revolution ninety miles from the United States; nor would there be guerrillas in Bolivia, a country bordered, like ourselves, by Brazil and Argentina. Foreign intervention can constitute an immediate military reverse, but also a political advantage which will, with time, change into a military advantage. Imagine the city of Montevideo occupied by foreign troops, with the consequent offense to national feeling, molested by the population and faced with a revolutionary armed group with good bases in the city. That should give you some accurate idea of what, politically and militarily, such a feared foreign intervention would mean. But in any case, our strategy is contained within the continental strategy of "creating many Vietnams," and the interventionists would have much work on many widespread fronts.

22. How does the high level of unionization weigh in a revolutionary strategy?

The unions, even within their obvious limitations, have involved, and can involve, the majority of the working population in a frontal fight with the government, which has resulted many times in the government's calling out the armed forces. With the existence of an armed revolutionary group, capable of raising the class struggle to higher levels, we can fight under better conditions—with a great part of the population behind us, and with the basic services of the state weakened.

23. Is our geography completely against the struggle in the countryside?

We do not have impregnable areas, as other countries; but certain natural accidents of geography exist which permit an armed group brief refuge. The latifundio is a great ally. In the latifundio areas—that is to say, on two-thirds of the surface of the country—the population is less than 0.6 inhabitants per square kilometer. That makes the secret movement of an armed contingent easy. At the same time the cattle latifundio solves the difficult logistic problem of food, which in other parts necessitates a supply chain with the complicity of the population. Also, the fearful living conditions of the rural wage earner—some already organized in unions—have created a spontaneously rebel sector which can be very useful in the rural struggle. If our countryside cannot serve to install a permanent *foco*, it can at least serve to spread out the repressive forces.

24. Are there conditions for an urban struggle?

Montevideo is a city sufficiently large and split by social struggles to give shelter to a large active commando contingent. It constitutes a far better framework than other revolutionaries have in the urban struggle. Of course, every organization that professes to be able to survive for a long time in the urban struggle should patiently build its material bases and the vast movement of shelter and support which an armed contingent needs to operate or exist in the city.

25. How does the fact of the existence of an armed prepared group weigh in a strategic plan?

If there is not a moderately prepared group then, simply, revolutionary opportunities will not be taken. Things like *bogotazo*[1] will happen. The armed group gives efficiency and cohesion to the struggle, and leads it to its destiny. Besides, the armed group can help to create the revolutionary opportunity or, in the words of Raúl Castro, can be the little motor that starts the big motor of the Revolution. The armed group keeps creating, or helping to create, the subjective conditions for revolution from the very moment it starts to prepare but, above all, from the moment it begins to act.

26. What will be, therefore, the general strategic lines for the present moment?

To create an armed force with the greatest possible speed, with the capacity to take advantage of any propitious opportunities created by the crisis or other factors. To create consciousness in the population by means of actions by the armed group, or other means, in order to show that without revolution there will be no change. To strengthen the unions and to radicalize their struggles, linking them with the revolutionary movement. To set up supply bases in order to develop the urban struggle and the struggle in the countryside. To link up with other revolutionary movements in Latin America for continental action.

27. Is this a work plan exclusively for your organization?

No. It is for all authentic revolutionary organizations, and for all individuals who truly desire a revolution.

[1] *Bogotazo* is the name given to the popular insurrection that took place in Bogotá Colombia, in 1948, after the murder of the popular mass leader Gaitàn.—*Ed.*

28. Do you consider all these tasks to be equally revolutionary?

Yes. Some believe that only when we are training for combat, or when we go into action, are we doing a revolutionary job. But all tasks that help a strategic plan are equally important for the Revolution.

29. Can you give me an example to illustrate this?

Whoever runs an errand for material necessary for an operational base, whoever collects money, whoever lends his car for mobilization, whoever lends his house is running as much risk—and at times more—than the member of the action group. It should be kept in mind that the majority of revolutionaries have filled the major part of their time in doing these little practical things without which there would be no Revolution.

30. Does this mean that we can open up a strategic opportunity by our daily efforts?

Yes. A strategy for revolution depends in part on the conditions we can create by our efforts, directed by a plan to gain power, while not losing sight of real conditions.

Bolivia

To every revolutionary who disagrees
with the Guevara-Debray guerilla foco *theory, the fiasco of Che's Bolivian*
guerrilla operation is ample proof that the theory doesn't work in practice.
Soviet communists, Trotskyists, and Maoists all agree on one basic criti-
cism: that guerrilla warfare cannot be waged without years of careful poli-
tical and ideological preparation both in the proposed area of fighting
and in the country as a whole. All three groups also insist that the pro-
letariat and not the peasantry should lead the Revolution, though the
Maoists clearly see peasants as a revolutionary force. Traditional com-
munists further consider guerrilla warfare as only one form of revolutionary
action and inferior to general insurrection, which can follow best from
general political strikes. Maoists oppose the foco *theory; people's war,*
developing from peasant self-defense units, must establish liberated areas
before going on the offensive. Maoists also refuse to combine the military
and political leaderships, insisting that the army must always be con-
trolled by the Party. All traditional communists condemn the "adven-
turistic" aspects of the focos—*a few men adopting hit-and-run tactics,*
living in near isolation, waiting for the surrounding masses to join them,
hoping for local aid or at least neutrality but leaving them exposed to
the repressive forces when the guerrillas withdraw (though that was pre-
cisely the tactic used by Mao on Russian orders in the early thirties).
And all traditional communists disagree, finally, with the foco *theory's*
insistence that the revolutionary chiefs actually serve as guerrilla chiefs;
at least one disastrous consequence, they say, is that the repressive forces
can then totally cut off the guerrillas from the urban centers—unless
Party leaders remain in those centers to coordinate the "overall" struggle.
To all of these criticisms, Debrayists have ready answers, and most of
them are accurately summed up in the empirical but not theoretical state-
ment that the critics are simply finding excuses not to fight. In Latin

America, that has certainly been the case. Though not always. And some of these exceptions—revolutionaries who have fought gun in hand—also criticize the foco *theory. One such critic is a Brazilian sociologist who has been active in urban guerrilla warfare. Under the pseudonym of Cléa Silva, he has pointed out the following errors in the* foco *theory (Monthly Review, July–August 1967): (1) the subordination of the party to the guerrilla force is based on the assumption that "the revolution is formed in the struggle itself." Yet the Venezuelan communists fought with arms from 1962 to 1964. (2) It is not necessarily the struggle which makes good revolutionaries but perhaps the reverse, as with Che, Raúl Castro, Fidel, etc., who were all well tempered by years of ideological struggle before the* Granma *landing. (3) When Debray says that "it is war and its immediate objectives that unify" the revolutionary forces, he forgets the Venezuelan example where the split between the CP and the Armed Forces of National Liberation (FALN) headed by Douglas Bravo came about precisely while the war was in full swing. (4) The fact that Cuba had no revolutionary party is not proof that the Revolution can always be won without such a party, any more than the fact that Russia and China did have one is proof that the Revolution can be won only with a revolutionary party. (5) A* foco *may work well in small countries such as Cuba but not necessarily in continent-size Brazil where one* foco *could be easily isolated from everyone and many* focos *kept from coordinating their action. (6) No revolution, in Latin America at least, will ever fool its enemies again—as Cuba's did—so the two-stage operation may well never work again. The "national" bourgeoisie will ally itself with imperialism, not the Revolution, hence "there will be a direct and definitive confrontation of classes, and the party will therefore be more indispensable than before." (7) To insist that the leadership go to the countryside is to ignore local conditions. Leaders should go where "the fundamental form of struggle is developing," in the capitals in Argentina and Uruguay, in the hills in Colombia and Venezuela, in both in Guatemala.*

To these and other criticisms, Debray pleaded guilty. Writing, but without notes, books, or the above-cited critical articles themselves, from his prison cell in Bolivia, he said (Monthly Review, February 1969): "The so-called foco *theory in its simplest, most skeletal form of an isolated military detonator organized by itself, independent of any national organization or urban political work, is certainly a utopian notion. It is not a coherent revolutionary line capable of assuming the complex tasks of political leadership and organization in a concrete situation. It is one thing (and an easy one) to demolish this supposed theory and quite another to use this as a pretext to reject people's war—that complex and inescapable reality—of which guerrilla struggle is the pivot and the outcome." And indeed when all is said and done, when every detail is plucked out of the writings of Che and Debray and hacked to pieces, one*

fact remains unchallenged: Not a single social revolution has ever suc-
ceeded without violence (or occupying armies, that is, superior military
strength). Furthermore, to believe that one could lead a few thousand
men and families 3,000 miles across China by foot, start again, and win;
to believe that one could launch a guerrilla war from atop a crest in the
Sierra Maestra with twelve men against all the formidable might of a
long-trained and well-armed military machine and win; to believe that
one could get the unhesitating commitment of illiterate peasants to fight
against the most devastating weapons ever invented by mankind plus half a
million troops from the richest, strongest, most technologically advanced
nation on earth and win—one has to be either mad—or romantic and
utopian. And one fundamental characteristic of that romanticism is to
be convinced that the Revolution will continue no matter how many de-
feats it suffers, no matter how many of its leaders are killed.

Fidel was such a romantic. Che was just such a romantic. Inti Peredo,
who succeeded him as head of Bolivia's Army of National Liberation, was
equally romantic. Like Che and Debray, he believed that "the struggle it-
self will bring forth its leaders." In fact it brought him forth. A long-
time communist organizer and member of his Party's Central Committee,
he joined Che despite CP orders not to. At the beginning, according to
Che's Bolivian Diary, Inti wasn't much good as a soldier or as a leader.
But he learned fast and, Che wrote, was rapidly forged into a solid guer-
rilla chief. When Che was murdered, Inti took over command of the
ELN. He reorganized it and revitalized it. Then, on September 9, 1969,
he too was killed in battle. Before he died, however, he wrote his own
answer to the critics of the Bolivian guerrilla movement—and, inevitably,
the answer of his successor as well.

INTI PEREDO: ONLY THE BEGINNING*

AS long as there is a single honest man in Latin America, guerrilla warfare will not die. Armed struggle will surge ahead vigorously until all of
the people awake and rise up in arms against the common enemy, U.S.
imperialism. Guerrilla warfare in Bolivia is not dead; it has just begun.

Both enemies and friends of the Revolution have analyzed, more or
less profoundly and from a great variety of viewpoints, the complex
phenomenon of the guerrilla activity which went on in our country. Guided
by petty reasons, they all reach the narrow and biased conclusion that
guerrilla warfare is not the correct method for the seizing of power in

---

* Written somewhere in Bolivia in July 1968 and published in English, French, and
Spanish as a pamphlet by OSPAAL.

Bolivia. But one thing has not been accomplished: the dulling of the faith and determination of our country's revolutionary forces. The clearest and most unconditional proof of this is the fact that our National Liberation Army (ELN) has remained and still remains staunchly faithful and firm in the struggle, despite the temporary setbacks we have experienced.

For us, guerrilla warfare is a form of struggle utilized by the people to seize power, it being understood that one essential characteristic of this form of struggle is its more or less protracted nature.

The first phase of any guerrilla struggle consists in the guerrillas' being able to survive until they have taken deep roots among the people, mainly among the peasants. The guerrilla nucleus will thus be in a position to renew its forces indefinitely until a stage of development is reached that will render it invincible. From that moment on, the guerrilla forces deal the regular army repeated blows, causing it to become demoralized and progressively weaker until it is finally overcome and destroyed completely, along with the regime it supports.

In our own case, the newly established guerrillas were not able to surmount the first phase, but other guerrilla groups will appear and will attain full development and eventually crush the enemy.

Based on this circumstance, our critics have come to the conclusion that our method is wrong. They fail to mention and avoid analyzing the causes of our partial and temporary defeat. The reason they do not do so is that, in so doing, they would have to judge themselves.

They observed our struggle from afar. What is more, they isolated, refused to cooperate with, and carried on antiguerrilla propaganda against our struggle within the ranks of their own organizations. Later, in order to keep up their "anti-imperialist" pretense, each one of their organizations issued a declaration of "solidarity" with the guerrilla struggle. But, in fact, that "solidarity" was mere lip service in the guise of moral support which they could not avoid giving to a small group of "romantic dreamers."

The Bolivian CP leadership speaks of the Party's preparations for seizing power by "all methods." But they want the guerrilla method to be scrapped after the first attempt results in failure, and they insist on the feasibility of the "democratic" or reformist approach in spite of the permanent failure of the latter method.

How many peaceful demonstrations have been held in which thousands of workers and ordinary people have been violently suppressed—with casualties running into the hundreds—by the government's repressive apparatus? Still fresh in our minds are the events of May and September 1965 during which factory workers and miners were brutally murdered, almost without offering any resistance. We could never forget the bloody 24th of June, 1967, when humble and defenseless miners were murdered in cold blood even as our guerrilla force, made up of scarcely forty men, dealt the murderous army hard blows, inflicting considerable casualties.

We are not against the people's struggle for the sake of obtaining reforms and other gains. But we feel sure these struggles will be much more fruitful and effective when they are waged against a government frightened and weakened by the actions of a guerrilla center.

It is this guerrilla center that will prove to the people—with facts— that it is possible to face the power of imperialism and its puppets, and that it is not only possible to face that power, but also that it is possible to win victory over it.

The people—and especially the peasants—will not support something they do not consider as being real. To expect the peasants' support for the armed struggle when this struggle has not yet come into being is to play at insurrection. The peasants will only give concrete support to a guerrilla center when the latter can show that it is strong.

That is why, in the first phase, the aim is for the guerrilla force to grow in strength, to survive on the field of operations. During this phase it is essential for the guerrilla force to be given aid from the cities. Our guerrilla center was denied this aid by political forces that knew of the existence of our movement.

How can these parties pay homage to fallen guerrillas when they attacked them as the guerrillas were preparing to fight? How can the fact be explained that Monje sounded the warning among the ranks of his Party against a "factionist group" deviating from the Party "line" and that Zamora had Comrade Moisés Guevara—who led a group of followers to join the guerrillas—expelled, for the same reason, from the pro-Chinese CPC.

We do not intend to blame the CP for our temporary failure. We do not blame anybody for the outcome of this first phase. Our object is to establish the historic responsibility of the parties which in our country claim to be anti-imperialist fighters.

Some people think that we are a force in the process of dispersal. They are wrong. We are at the point of reorganizing our armed command cadres, and we will again take up the struggle in the mountains because we firmly believe that this is the only road that will lead us to the liberation of our people and of Latin America from the clutches of Yankee imperialism.

We are not seeking the formation of a political party. We shall succeed in the structuring of an armed force capable of facing and defeating the army, the main prop of the present regime in our country. But we are not going to be the "fighting arm" of any political party. In the heat of the struggle the different forces that have set themselves the goal of liberating their country will unite, and our National Liberation Army

(ELN) will be joined by militants from the various parties. Then the true alliance of anti-imperialist forces will be a reality.

The liberation of our people can never be the work of one single group or one single political party. In that we agree with the parties of the Left. We need a broad anti-imperialist front. The question is how to achieve this.

Our short experience has shown us that much more was accomplished in a few months of armed struggle than in many years of sitting around tables. Actually, all the parties that expressed their sympathy were uniting around the guerrilla center, whether or not they want to admit it. We would have to ask ourselves how these parties would have acted had the guerrilla struggle continued and become stronger. Positions would have been clearly defined, since in an atmosphere of armed struggle, which demands a clear-cut attitude, there isn't much room for demagogy and deceit.

The title of vanguard of the people or of the working class is not self-bestowed. It is won. It will be the people, and only the people, who will bestow the title of vanguard upon those who lead them to their liberation.

The struggle itself will bring forth its leaders. The true leaders of the people will be forged in the struggle, and no one who considers himself a true revolutionary should insist on leading or fear that his position will be taken from him.

The struggle will be a cruel and bloody one, and it will be waged throughout the country—even in the most humble huts and isolated regions.

In the face of the constant violence of the Yankee imperialists, we— and the people with us—have chosen the way of revolutionary violence, a violence that punishes the oppressors and that, once it has crushed them, gives way to socialist humanism. In short, we do not preach violence for its own sake, but rather advocate the people's organized retaliation against organized oppression, in order to achieve full freedom.

The national liberation movements all over the world are dealing hard blows to the common enemy, imperialism. The criminal war in Vietnam, despite the fact that it balances the U.S. economy by converting it into a war economy and thus staving off a crisis, is creating serious problems for the imperialists. All the military power of the Yankees has already been proved ineffective in holding back that glorious people in arms.

The Yankee imperialists cannot withstand another Vietnam. And it is up to us and our people to create this second Vietnam, faithful to the legacy left us by our heroic Major Ernesto Che Guevara. The idea of creating several Vietnams is no mere whim or the figment of a warmonger mentality, as our enemies and the pseudorevolutionaries would have others believe; it is an idea in keeping with reality. The Yankee imperialists will not surrender their positions willingly—and on our continent—through their Ministry of Colonies, the OAS—they will order their lackeys in the various countries to join forces to crush any people that may rise up in arms. Our guerrillas were attacked by soldiers of the Bolivian Army advised by Yankee "instructors" (veterans of the war in Vietnam) and equipped with weapons and rations supplied by the armies of Argentina and Brazil.

The revolutionary war will extend to those countries, bringing about the same feeling of insecurity and powerlessness among their respective armies. At this point the Pentagon will be forced to change its policy of "advising" to one of "direct" ever growing participation by its troops, as is happening in Vietnam. Some pseudorevolutionaries tremble at such a prospect. They wish to spare the people this "tragedy." They do not realize that, by acting as they do, they are not avoiding anything. On the contrary, their attitude only serves to keep the people under the scourge of poverty, hunger, and death, sacrificing them on the sacrosanct altar of conformism.

This is no "tragedy," weighed against what the people would have to suffer if they were kept under their present yoke forever, their only prospect being that it would weigh heavier and heavier upon them. This is no "tragedy," weighed against the miserable lives that our people are forced to lead.

Mining towns are nothing but concentration camps, where the inhabitants don't have any rights—not even the right to amuse themselves, and even less, of course, the right to protest. The massacres that have been systematically perpetrated are the tyranny's answer to the just demands of those who bear on their shoulders the weight of the economy of the country and the luxury of the military castes.

That is why the creation of a new Vietnam does not constitute a "tragedy." It is an honor and a duty we will never refuse.

We have lost a battle, a battle in which the maximum leader of the oppressed people, Major Ernesto Che Guevara, gave his life.

But our war continues, and we will never stop. Che's blood and that of other fighters, spilled on the soil of Bolivia, will give life to the seed of liberation and will turn our continent into a volcano spewing forth fire and destruction on imperialism. We will be the triumphant Vietnam that Che, the romantic and heroic visionary, dreamed of and loved, because we understand that, as Che said:

"Wherever death may surprise us, it will be welcome, provided that this, our battle cry, reach some receptive ear, that another hand be extended to take up our weapons, and that other men come forward to intone our funeral dirge with the staccato of machine guns and new cries of battle and victory."

Our banners bear crepe, but will never be lowered. The ELN considers itself the heir to the teachings and example of Che, the new Bolívar of Latin America. Those who cravenly murdered him will never kill his thought and his example. Let the imperialists and their lackeys withhold their songs of victory, because the war has not ended; it has just begun.

Quebec

Late in 1965, a young French-Cana-
dian journalist named Pierre Vallières, who was on the staff of Montreal's
traditional daily La Presse, and edited, on the side, the theoretical socialist
journal, Révolution Québécoise, wrote an article entitled "Nationalism
and Revolution in the Imperialist Heartland." It was a fairly academic
article, which summarized the history of Quebec Province (long dominated
by the Catholic hierarchy "preaching submission to God and submission
to the English conquerors, since all authority came from God"). Vallières
then explained how most of the Province's labor movement had been captured by the U.S. "international" unions, how the Quebecois working
class was the poorest of all Canada, partly because 90 percent of Quebec's
economy was controlled by U.S. capital and partly because Ottawa reinvested most of the taxes taken out of Quebec in Ontario and other English-
speaking sections of the country. The article expressed sympathy for the
Quebecois bourgeoisie. Vallières even thought that "the working class can
freely support the middle classes of Quebec in the struggle against economic and political discrimination practiced by the Anglo-Saxon bourgeoisie, because that struggle, as Lenin would have said, has a general
democratic content directed against oppression." In short, a socialist but
not very revolutionary analysis.

By the time the article appeared (Monthly Review, February 1966), however, Quebec was in turmoil. During 1965, bombs had exploded throughout
Montreal; 100,000 farmers had marched on the Quebec parliament demanding better living conditions; even the U.S.-oriented and very moderate
unions had staged a series of protests. The Prime Minister of Quebec at
the time, Jean Lesage, warned Ottawa to give the province some form of
autonomy or the situation "might take a serious turn." Left-wing movements were mushrooming. The RIN (Rassemblement pour l'Indépendence
Nationale) was demanding outright independence, and growing. The MLP

(Mouvement de Libération Populaire) joined forces with the group known as Parti Pris, *the name of its monthly magazine, and they jointly issued a manifesto calling for the organization of a revolutionary party—and for a revolution. In that manifesto they did not exclude armed struggle, pointing out that some Quebecois were proving that such means were not impossible in Quebec.*

The reference was to the FLQ, or Quebec Liberation Front, which was then two years old. And it was its armed wing, the ALQ or Quebec Liberation Army, that was responsible for most of the bombings and acts of terrorism (disruption of federal services) that were taking place. Its militants were young, daring, efficient. And its analysis saw Quebec as a neo-colonized, underdeveloped country within the territorial domain of North American imperialism. Then, in 1967, there appeared in the underground a long typewritten manuscript called the "Manifesto of the Quebec Liberation Front." Its author was a certain Mathieu Hébert. Shortly thereafter, Canada's Royal Mounted Police (a euphemism for the country's political police or FBI) arrested an ALQ cell—or so it claimed—and charged its members with the murder of a woman who had died from a bomb explosion in 1966. The leader was convicted and sentenced to life imprisonment. He was none other than Pierre Vallières, who also turned out to be the FLQ's chief idéologist—and, it was generally believed, "Mathieu Hébert." The following article (the "What Is to Be Done" part of the manifesto) shows the FLQ to be a revolutionary Marxist movement, closely akin ideologically to OLAS and fighting communists all over the world, but solidly conscious of the need to bring the masses not only into the struggle but also into the decision-making process of the new society.

MATHIEU HÉBERT (PIERRE VALLIÈRES?): WHAT IS TO BE DONE IN THE IMPERIALIST HEARTLAND?*

NOT since the early days of "la Nouvelle France" have the workers of Quebec had any means whatsoever of influencing and controlling the "affairs of state." How can they then not merely overthrow the established regime but also deliver the state, now become *their* state, from its present dependence upon the foreign economic interests which have been exploiting our country for the past three centuries?

Electoralism is a dead end for the working class. In order to take power

---

* Concluding section ("What Is to Be Done") of the "Manifesto of the Quebec Liberation Front" (typed manuscript, written in 1967, in possession of the editor). Translated by Robert Weingarten.

through elections the workers would first have to conclude a treaty with the capitalists, and in some way "convert" the bourgeoisie to the Revolution and to socialism. The capitalists will never allow elections to bring about revolution, to bring about their own disappearance. All of which means that from the start the workers must practice illegal politics.

Illegality is quite simply the legality of the oppressed, worker legality as opposed to bourgeois legality, to exploiter legality. Illegality in action is worker violence opposed to the capitalists' legalized violence. Illegality is no more immoral than legality is moral. Class interests justify the means.

For the bourgeoisie the Law is always good. For the working class, generally, it is unjust. The Law justifies exploitation but condemns violent strikes. The workers easily justify their violence and condemn exploitation. The Law is always on one side only, on the side of the stronger. Which is why it is not with laws but with arms that class problems are resolved.

For the Law, too, is not neutral. Like the state. In every social order in which society is divided into antagonistic classes, the dominant class (which *makes* the laws) invariably finds itself in agreement with the content and orientation of the "law" and with the legal use of police and military violence (against strikers, demonstrators, etc.) whereas the dominated, exploited class (which *suffers* the laws) invariably tend to get around them, to get them modified, or to suppress them purely and simply until the day comes when it undertakes to suppress the bourgeoisie itself, author of these laws.

Thus every revolution is illegal, that much is clear. However, a revolution is much more than merely illegal; it is first and foremost the work of a class, not merely a handful of individuals. That is why it is important not to confuse *revolution* and *coup d'état*.

A coup d'état is nothing but a *transfer* of power "at the top" from one clique to another, without the participation of the masses: it is always carried out by a *minority* of military men and civilians who believe themselves invested with the mission of "re-establishing Order." A coup d'état invariably takes a conservative turn, even if its authors are imbued with reformist ideas, for, whether they like it or not, they who carry out a coup d'état, once in power, must lean not on a people armed and organized but on the interests of the *already existing* bureaucracy (financiers, military men, the clergy, high civil servants), all of whom will quell the newcomers' enthusiasm. Should the makers of a coup d'état refuse to be tamed, they will soon be overthrown in turn and replaced at the head of the bourgeois state by a more docile clique.

Obviously, for the FLQ, the only democratic way toward the Revolution and the taking of power involves the effective and conscious integration of the workers in the struggle and leads to a *general* uprising against oppression with them.

How could any revolutionary movement, after taking power, ask the people to make certain efforts required by any coherent policy for the sake of the public welfare if the masses themselves, sole foundation of the Revolution, are not strongly convinced by experience of the need for such efforts? The masses must participate actively in the struggle for liberation, for the Revolution, if they are later, collectively and democratically, to bring the arduous tasks of national reconstruction to a successful conclusion, i.e., to substitute a new order for the old capitalist structures, the objective of every revolution.

But how does the FLQ hope to integrate the workers, to interest and involve them in organizing the revolutionary struggle?

Understand that the FLQ does not ask this question as a bourgeois party would, wondering how to "buy" the votes of the workers, or bedazzle them. The FLQ is *already* a group of organized, armed, and disciplined workers. A group which has already engaged in a direct struggle against the exploiters. And was the first to do so.

This struggle is taking place in three complementary areas: agitation propaganda, armed struggle, and networks of people's liberation committees. And it is in the framework of these three areas that the workers are being integrated, and that, at the same time, the struggle against the exploiters is being developed. The integration of the workers is therefore inseparable for the FLQ from their involvement in the struggle in one way or another.

This involvement is possible right now since the organization's basic structures exist, the principal networks of activity are functioning, and the objectives are clearly defined.

For the FLQ *stirring up the masses* means above all organizing them so that as *insiders* in the FLQ, not as outsiders, they come to *understand* and to *make decisions* more and more. The cumulative experience of all revolutions shows that the masses understand the most complicated problems perfectly well—even those concerning the structures of a revolutionary and clandestine movement (just as they understand, after the Revolution, the problems pertaining to collective self-management, i.e., worker control of the means of production and the distribution and utilization of goods within the collectivity for the profit of one and all). What is important for the FLQ is not that one or two hundred partisans understand, make decisions, and act on them, but that the entire population understand, make decisions, and act, even if the price that must be paid calls for great efforts and twice as much time.

To integrate someone into the FLQ is to make him understand his alienation and the alienation of his class, and to make him understand how unnaturally this collective frustration makes him act.

The true politicization of the masses is inseparable from the integration of the masses into the midst of a collective action. Politicization is not solely what the bourgeoisie calls "popular education." It is integrating the masses into the struggle, integrating body and intelligence, freeing the workers' spontaneous efforts from confusion, giving them a clear direction, uniting them in a collective action. To politicize, in short, is to make one act consciously.

Every network of the FLQ exists to give the workers of Quebec the opportunity and the means to act consciously against the established order.

Every revolution depends on class consciousness.

The strategy of the weaker in a war is just naturally guerrilla warfare. Guerrilla warfare is not in fact a Cuban, Russian, or Chinese invention. It was used by the Iroquois against the French in the seventeenth century. It was also used by the Spanish against the armies of Napoleon in the nineteenth century. Most of the peoples "occupied" by Germany during the last world war practiced guerrilla warfare against the occupiers. All strikers or demonstrators who, at a given moment, resort to ruse to outwit the police or the army, dispersing in small groups so as to attack the forces of order simultaneously in several places at once, responding thus spontaneously against repression, are waging guerrilla warfare, or at least the rudiments of guerrilla warfare, whether they know it or not.

A guerrilla is a band of partisans, workers, youths, no matter, a band of citizens who are not career soldiers but are rather men who have decided to take up arms by necessity in order to overthrow an order that is unjust. Armies always are on the side of order; guerrillas are opposed to it.

A guerrilla is generally made up of no more than a hundred men in groups of ten or cells of three. These men are dispersed and kept in contact by liaison agents who arrange for the coordinated execution of plans of attack, withdrawals, etc. Several guerrillas together form a detachment.

The members of a guerrilla, of a group or a cell, can work during the day and fight at night. They can fight in the country or in the city. They do not use "conventional" arms. They may use dynamite, plastic bombs, copies of the revolutionary newspaper, tracts, threatening phone calls, hunting rifles, machine guns, gasoline, "spontaneous" demonstrations, etc. Guerrilla warfare is waged not with a quantity of high caliber weapons, tanks, and planes, but with the intelligent and planned utilization of weapons which are at the disposal of every worker.

A guerrilla warfare strategy is based on the dispersion of the members of a guerrilla into extremely mobile little groups. Little groups of snipers, agitators, propagandists whose *coordinated* action, albeit dispersed throughout the territory, aim at exhausting the adversary and inciting a general uprising of the population. Every guerrilla war, depending essentially on the people, tends, in any event, by the very way it develops, to transform itself into a general armed uprising. The general offensive always coincides with such an uprising, for the "poor" of course could never hope to launch a general offensive with bombers. The people can only throw *itself* into the fight, and it's the people's unity that makes victory certain. Any people can thus fight off its exploiters, just as the Spanish fought off Napoleon. The force of the people resides in its cohesion and its determination. A people organized into "guerrillas" is capable of everything.

What's more, a people that wants to free itself from slavery, to become master of its fate, has no choice. It *must* organize into guerrillas.

In our situation as an exploited people, accentuated by Quebec's situation as a colony, we are not free to opt for or against guerrilla warfare —if, that is, we really want to free ourselves from capitalist exploitation and at the same time deliver Quebec from its dependence on foreign— especially American—economic interests. For that matter our situation leaves us no choice as to the *type* of guerrilla warfare that must be waged, which will be best adapted to the Quebec milieu, and to the particular character that capitalism, colonialism, and imperialism have assumed in Quebec.

Which is why all the strategy of the FLQ responses on "guerrilla warfare," on the war of small harassments, on skirmishes, lightning-quick offensives, hit-and-run, surprise, ruse, well-spaced raids, assassinations, as well as long, hard marches in certain cases, etc. *For guerrilla warfare is the sole military strategy which truly corresponds to the capacities of the working class, as well as to its aspirations*, to its economic, political, and social ambitions.

This is evidently not the kind of war that is won in a day. It is begun by a small group, a "handful of madmen" who, by their actions, little by little, succeed in rallying round them an ever increasing number of workers determined to take up arms to overthrow the capitalist system. Then comes a day when the entire working class begins to rumble and stir in order to attain collective political and economic power. It is on this day that democracy truly begins to become a reality.

Guerrilla warfare in Quebec does not take on the form it had in Cuba or in China. Wars and types of wars are no more uniform than people themselves. Every war has its own physiognomy, although similar laws come to apply to all. Thus, for example, the dispersion of men in small groups is characteristic of all guerrilla wars, be they "civil wars" or "wars of national liberation." In both such wars, the objective pursued is *first of all* political. Our principal task is to make war in Quebec, i.e., in a semi-industrialized colony in which 75 percent of the population is urban and only 10 percent of the population can be considered to be agricultural.

In Quebec, where there is no "isolated" population surrounded by mountains or living solely off the land, the creation of "liberated areas," of states within the state, is out of the question. No part of Quebec can be liberated without the liberation of all Quebec. Certainly the struggle will not develop uniformly throughout the entire territory. Some regions will be more "agitated" than others. The revolutionary fever will only spread through all of Quebec progressively. But the struggle will never be able to *settle down* in one place without exposing itself to annihilation.

It is most important that this be kept in mind, especially now when the FLQ is laying the foundations of its organization. Some, joining the ranks of the FLQ, may be tempted to imagine a romantic struggle in the center of some virgin forest. On the contrary, the struggle the FLQ is engaged in is taking place in the center of the proletariat's daily activities, in the factory, on the farm, in the village, in the neighborhood, within the union, at the cooperative, etc.—in those places where the concrete problems are, where the need for change daily makes itself felt. *That* is where the FLQ operates.

Obviously, if it is to work effectively, the FLQ also needs an organization "outside" the places of work and social life. It needs hideouts, bases, full-time revolutionaries. But this "outside" organization only exists to support, direct, give military and ideological nourishment, unify, co-ordinate, and render victorious all the struggles engaged in by the workers in their factories, their unions, their cooperatives, in their neighborhood, locality, or region. The FLQ wages no war outside the daily life but, on the contrary, does so from daily realities. Only the "technical" organization of the Revolution must necessarily be *sheltered* from repression, informers, or even simple curiosity. What's more, only a minority of workers will be obliged to quit their daily jobs to work full time for the Revolution—unless, of course, the unemployment rate were to increase considerably, which would greatly accelerate the revolutionary process.

Guerrilla warfare does not therefore demand that every partisan, every "*guerrillero*" quit his job and disappear into the forest. Such a conception of the revolutionary struggle would be catastrophic in Quebec. A partisan may be a member of an armed group and yet work like any other worker. As such the Quebec worker most closely resembles the French, Belgian, or Yugoslav resistant of the Second World War. He has nothing about him of the South American partisan organizing Andean Indians miles away from "civilization." Which is why his revolutionary work is much more *dangerous*, much more exposed to informers and repression.

There are those who tend to reduce guerrilla organization and action to sniping, armed commandos, and the placing of bombs. In actual fact, the propagandists who are organized to distribute tracts and journals are also guerrillas. Like the armed partisans, they must work in extremely mobile, dispersed groups, and use many ruses and a great economy of means. Propaganda and infiltration also constitute military activities. Just as activity which is essentially military is also political, so is essentially political activity also military.

Whatever their network, the diverse guerrillas act according to one same plan of action, pursuing the same military, political, and social objective. Trained and grouped first in the limited framework of a network, a zone, or a region, the guerrillas must ultimately branch out to take in the whole territory.

By their very nature guerrillas work in *clandestinity*. The FLQ does not, however, make a fetish of this clandestinity: it is merely one means to carry out the revolutionary struggle with a maximum of security and, consequently, of efficacy. The more the workers, farmers, white-collar workers and youth join the FLQ as active partisans, dynamic agents fully aware of the need for radical social transformations, and the more the masses get into the habit of going out into the streets, the more the FLQ will come out into the open to merge with the open struggle of the people. We will then see the propagandists and saboteurs transform themselves into people's courts. The FLQ will appear for all to see on the public square. And will proceed to arm the people and invite them to organize themselves into militias to defend their interests, and to move on to the general offensive. Having taken power, these village or neighborhood militias will continue to protect what the Revolution has won (as, for example, worker control of factories).

Militias are not full-time armed groups. They are formed by relays of citizens taking turns defending their neighborhood, their land, their houses, their unions, or their factories. Their action will not be truly efficacious unless it is supported by full-time armed groups, capable not merely of confronting an enemy but also of vanquishing and annihilating it. These armed groups make up what might be called a "people's army." Like all other state services (administrative or social), the people's army is at the service of the people and is controlled by the people.

It is therefore immediately apparent that the people's army has little in common with a classical army. First of all, the people's army's objective is always a social one; it constantly aims at making possible and preserving the social transformation essential to the well-being of the population; it never aims at conquest or oppression; if it must make victims, they will be from the ranks of the exploiters opposed to the social transformations demanded by the workers, and will be made out of "legitimate defense."

The people's army has nothing of the bloodthirsty or swashbuckling about it. Made up of workers, students, youths, it is an "idealistic" army whose sole desire is the liberation of the people from exploitation. The people's army, stronger morally than the classical army of the capitalist world, with a revolutionary objective corresponding to the profound aspirations of the workers, farmers, and youths, enjoying the support of the masses, needs no napalm, no atomic bombs, to crush its enemies. For the people's army is first and foremost fighting not tanks and bombers, but a political, economic, and social *regime*.

The role of the people's army is not to become some kind of great private enterprise at the mercy of a caste of privileged military men, but to constitute the "mobile point" of the whole mass of workers moving forward to their liberation. Should it abandon this role and become a "clique," it will cease to enjoy popular support and will leave itself open to be disposed of in turn by the people.

In short, the people's army and the people's militias constitute the two forms of organization, each complementary to the other, of the people in arms. Without them the workers of Quebec cannot hope either to make the Revolution or to preserve what the Revolution will win.

Brown-Black
America

In recent years, the most dramatic development of revolutionary consciousness has been in the very heartland of counterrevolution—in the United States of America. For the first time since the Revolution of 1776, literally thousands of Americans have come to the conclusion that the United States will always remain an oppressive imperialist country until its whole socioeconomic-political structure is completely smashed. Some of the country's new revolutionaries are white: middle-class youth, appalled by the alienating values they see around them, are taught in school, must obey at home, and are forced by society's "law and order" to respect. Though repeatedly jailed, beaten, framed, fired from jobs, and even occasionally killed (during so-called "riots" in Berkeley, New York, and Chicago, and arbitrarily in the South)—these youths had not yet translated their revolutionary consciousness into revolutionary action by the end of 1969. That is to say, few of the whites convinced that the U.S. capitalist structure had to be destroyed were yet willing to risk their own lives to help destroy it (except, perhaps, for the Weathermen faction of SDS—Students for Democratic Society—which, however, had not yet resorted to armed struggle).

Among the colored populations, however, many were willing to die. And, therefore, willing to kill to achieve their vision of a just society. Yet, though they had suffered centuries of privation, discrimination, and domination, this consciousness among the colored was relatively new. And it had grown very gradually. Frantz Fanon had perhaps best explained why this was so. In his brilliant book, The Wretched of the Earth, *he had pointed out that colonization works not only because the colonizer is stronger, richer, and more brutal than the colonized, but also because the colonized tends to accept his "inferiority"—his spirit is colonized.*

The U.S.'s colored population has long been doomed to slave roles in America partly because of just such a spirit. Convinced that they could

551

*never effectively challenge the white man's superiority—for one thing,
because the colored were a minority—those of America's black, brown,
red, and yellow people who wanted to better their material existence felt
that only by using "the system" could they fight it (that is, get ahead).
Thus, the shrewd, ambitious member of a racial minority either worked
harder and longer than his white counterpart or else hustled, cheated, and
stole. In either case, he doomed himself even further, for he reinforced
the individual-initiative myth so central to the U.S. capitalist structure,
which is, of course, what dominated him in the first place. This, in turn,
reinforced U.S. capitalism's values and made it that much easier for the
white man to destroy the cultures of the minorities. As different, proud,
valuable peoples with magnificent heritages, the American Indian, the
Mexican American, the Afro-American, etc., were stripped of their self-
consciousness and dignity. As such, they became more malleable—better
fodder for the capitalist system. These peoples were so culturally colonized
that they ended up willingly fighting and dying "for America's freedom"
in World War I and II, the Korean War, even in Vietnam, while at
home they had no chance whatsoever to taste such freedom for themselves. In fact, they fought and died—and in Southeast Asia are still
doing so—for the white man, to strengthen him to repress them all the
more.*

*But then something happened. Just what that something was is hard
to pinpoint. James Forman, a founder and leader of the Student Non-
Violent Coordinating Committee (SNCC, now the Student National Coordinating Committee) thinks that it began with the Montgomery bus
boycott, crystallized with the African liberation movements, and developed
into a concept of power with the Cuban Revolution. The three Chicanos
(first article) also seem to attribute their political maturing to an awareness
that other colonized peoples were successfully fighting imperialist forces
much superior to their own. Stokely Carmichael so identifies with the Third
World that he refers to it as "us." But whatever the actual moment of
awakening, America's brown and black populations certainly hardened as
a result of the massive white repressions that hit them after they began
to agitate for their rights. One could conclude, then, that before consciousness, repression does succeed in stifling or softening protests, but
after the repressed become conscious of why they must live the way they
do, more repression makes them only more rebellious. Today, the browns
and the blacks are fundamentally revolutionary and it is only a question
of time before many of the activities advocated in the following six
articles are put into practice.*

*Meanwhile, repression in the United States is worse than ever before
and much, much harsher than the world—or most Americans, for that
matter—is aware or told. In New Mexico, for example, the Alianza led
by Reies Tijerina has been hounded relentlessly since 1966; its offices*

have been dynamited (by policemen, at that), its leaders shot, its members jailed on such flagrantly outrageous charges that few Americans would believe—even today—the strictly factual story. At the time of writing, Tijerina himself was locked up for years and his Alianza was flagging. As for the blacks, their repression is not less brutal, just more widespread. The whole primary and secondary leadership of the Black Panther Party has been jailed on obvious frame-ups. They have been beaten, tortured, and murdered. Twice, in Oakland, I saw with my own eyes policemen in official cars zoom by a group of Panthers talking peacefully on a street and open fire at them. Three times I witnessed policemen arrest Panthers, handcuff them, and then pistol-whip them. In over a dozen cases, after seeing Panthers arrested, I have gone to see them in jail and found them bloodied from having "fallen down the stairs" or from having "assaulted a policeman." And the whole world knows—for this time, it was reported in the press—that off-duty policemen riddled the Panther Oakland office with gunfire and on-duty Chicago policemen murdered Panthers Fred Hampton and Mark Clark in their sleep. By the end of 1969 not a single policeman had been brought to justice for these acts of violence. On the other hand, all of white America's law enforcement agents, including federal marshals and the FBI, have gone out of their way—and, often, out of their jurisdiction—to arrest Panthers, without having warrants. Federal marshals have even refused to honor a court order not to remove Chairman Bobby Seale from California (which, legally, made the marshals kidnappers). By 1970, twenty-eight Black Panthers had been murdered by the police, some beaten to death after arrest (Charles Cox in Chicago), some in unprovoked police assaults (seventeen-year-old Bobby Hutton in Oakland, Hampton and Clark in Chicago), most in front of scores of witnesses, who could never testify, as the policemen were never charged. It is little wonder, then, that the browns and blacks consider themselves colonized and imperialized, part of the same dominated world as Latin Americans, the Vietnamese, and the Congolese.

The Chicanos (first article) see themselves clearly exploited "for specific capitalist ends." "We are not Americans," they write, "we are Mexican Americans," and the first and foremost aspect of their program is to build up that consciousness. Thus, in effect, they too believe in two-stage revolution. James Forman, a leader of the Student Non-Violent Coordinating Committee (SNCC), which then changed "Non-Violent" to "National," once insisted that the awareness of being a people capable of acting together had given the blacks a concept of power which had turned them into revolutionaries—internationalists who identified with the African liberation movements and the Cuban Revolution. Stokely Carmichael, who no longer has any connections with either SNCC or the Panthers, told the delegates to OLAS in Havana in August 1967 that *"our world can only be the Third World; our only struggle, for the Third World; our only vision, of the Third World." The only difference, he said, was that "our people are a colony within the United States; you are colonies outside the United States." Because the blacks are a minority, he did not think that they could win a revolution. But he saw them as a disruptive force in the international struggle. Our duty is to neutralize the United States when it attacks the Third World, he said.*

Huey P. Newton, the Minister of Defense of the Black Panther Party who has been jailed for supposedly killing a policeman, also sees the black communities as part of the Third World (see below). "The police in our ghettos are the foot soldiers in Vietnam. The AID and Peace Corpsmen in Santo Domingo are the state and federal War-on-Poverty bureaucrats here." Unlike SNCC, however, the BPP does think it can win. It views itself as the vanguard of a revolutionary tide which will include white revolutionaries when repression has led them to seize guns. Emphasizing the importance of cultural identity as a revolutionary force, Huey recognizes the potential strength that lies in America's alienated young when they too find their own identity outside the world of their elders or the Establishment.

Robert Williams, the first black man to openly advocate armed self-defense (in 1957, when the Ku Klux Klan kept raiding the local Monroe, N.C., headquarters of the NAACP, which he headed), goes further than the rest. Though he concedes (below) the fact that "a minority revolution could only succeed as an integral part of the universal liberation struggle," he does believe blacks can and will bring down the white capitalist-imperialist U.S. government through armed struggle. He then carefully details how—tactic by tactic, weapon by weapon. If it terrifies the white reader it is unquestionably because Williams' prescription cannot be passed off as absurd. After seven years of exile in Cuba, China, and Africa, Williams is now back in the United States, more convinced than ever that racist, imperialist white America is doomed.

Eldridge Cleaver, the Panthers' Minister of Information, one of America's most eloquent black intellectuals (see his Soul on Ice*) and one of Establishment America's most pursued black militants (on May 1, 1970, he was in exile in Algeria), does not agree with Williams that black alliances with white radicals cannot lead to revolutionary warfare. For one thing, he recognizes the tremendous struggle that the whites have waged on the campuses, and he sees America's whole educational system as a fundamental part of the ruling class's racism, exploitation, and imperialism. For another, he challenges the whole concept of separate black and white movements since the enemy is one and the same. But, he says in the taped, off-the-cuff comments included in the last article in this section, that to be meaningful the campus struggle has to be brought to* *the communities because that's where the decisive battles have to be fought. What's going on in America is not a game, he says, it's a war—"a people's war against those who oppress the people."*

CELIA, ANTONIO, AND GUILLERMO CHICANO: TIERRA Y LIBERTAD*

WE'VE spent almost all last year working with militants of La Raza[1] in the West and Southwest, specifically in Los Angeles, Denver, and New Mexico, and have come to the following conclusions, which we would like to share with you. Obviously, as we could not go into depth everywhere, our analysis cannot be but tentative and our conclusions, dependent on that analysis, are offered only as a basis for further discussion. It is only in that spirit that we have been presumptuous enough to criticize aspects, and at times individuals, of the Chicano[2] movement, and we hope it will be taken in that spirit.

1. Consciousness of being a conquered people
   We have found that, though the vast majority of Chicanos in America are not aware of our people's history, all of us seem to carry the weight of our history on our shoulders. Somehow, we have inherited a whole sense of our history without knowing very many of its facts. Some knowledge *is* there, to be sure. We have found, for example, that almost every Chicano knows that what now comprises Arizona, California, New Mexico, and southern Colorado was seized from Mexico by U.S. force of arms, that Texas was annexed through a phony independence movement organized and financed by the U.S., and that the U.S. occupation army behaved like any occupying force. Few Mexican Americans, however, are fully aware that the viciousness of these occupiers was part of U.S. *official* policy, that President Polk said point-blank that unless the Mexicans stop their resistance in the conquered areas, "they must be destroyed" and that U.S. General Kearny stated, when he arrived in Santa

[1] La Raza literally means "the race," but it signifies the people, specifically the Mexican Americans conscious of their identity.—*Ed.*

[2] Chicano also means Mexican American but has a more political connotation, i.e., Mexican Americans who are not only conscious of their identity but want to assert it, like the connotation of the word "black" today to black Americans.—*Ed.*

---

* Internal memorandum prepared by three Mexican-American militants sometime during 1968. At the authors' request, certain sections pertaining mostly to tactics and strategy have been eliminated, and their names have been concealed. All three authors are active today in the Chicano movement, Celia and Antonio in Los Angeles, Guillermo in Colorado.

Fe with his troops: "No one in this world can successfully resist the power of him who is stronger." Our people realize perfectly that the U.S. government then protected, defended, and encouraged Anglo[3] atrocities, but relatively few understood that these atrocities were ingrained in the American Way of Life *from the very beginning*, that is, that America was founded on the profit motive, that racism was generated deliberately and consciously by those bent on exploiting our people—and of course the Indian, the blacks, and anybody else—as cheap or free labor. Nor do we all fully realize that, to succeed in that exploitation, the Anglo had to crush our spirit *completely*. He had to deny our heritage, denigrate our culture, forbid our language, scoff at our customs, etc. We were treated as less-than-human beings for very specific capitalist ends. Thus we were and are a colonized people in the same way as the Puerto Ricans, the blacks of Africa, in fact the whole underdeveloped world. We are not Americans, we are Mexican Americans or Chicanos. We have been stressing the latter, but it seems to us crucial that we stress the former, the negative if you will. It is important that we consider the American government, its institutions, and its Way of Life our direct enemy. If we are accused of racism-in-reverse by our would-be friends, too bad: We must not allow our movement to be dependent upon the understanding of Anglos. The genuine radicals will certainly understand and support us anyway, as they do the black Americans who are fostering pride in their own heritage through both nationalism and that consciousness of the American Way of Life as an enemy. It is important, therefore, that we constantly do the following:

1.1.—Create study groups, community schools, workshops, adult meetings, etc., where our language is taught, where our history is told correctly, where Anglo-America's crimes are emphasized. This type of Chicano Studies program should be carried out at all levels, for all age groups, open to everyone in the communities, pueblos, barrios, etc.

1.2.—Launch cadre formation study groups, in selected localities, to prepare the study group leaders for the task of 1.1.

1.3.—Only gradually, after our people are fully aware of our history and heritage, including our heroes—whom the Anglos call bandits—

---

[3] Anglo, in Chicano land, refers to the white American foreigners who came to exploit La Raza, grabbed the land, set up the laws and courts, controlled the governmental and repressive machineries and today run the areas once owned, worked, and cherished by Mexican Americans. The atrocities committed by the Anglos, which are not enumerated in this article, date back to the earliest influx of whites in 1848. "In a little over a decade," writes Daniel T. Valdes in *Political History of New Mexico* (Norman, Okla.: University of Oklahoma Press), the Anglos "made Mexican a dirty word. The Anglo made it clear he considered the Hispano an inferior, a person fit only to follow behind as a 'greaser' for the wagon wheels. Capital punishment and lynchings were unknown in New Mexico prior to the coming of the Anglo-Americans. . . ."—*Ed.*

should we relate the U.S.'s history, its capitalist structure, its imperialist policies to our suffering *directly*. That is, only after our now-unaware population begins to take pride in being La Raza should the data, analysis, and inevitability of the eventual confrontation between our people and the American Way of Life be made explicit. To try to turn our now-unaware people into anti-imperialists right from the start, without first having rekindled in them the burning desire to *want* to be Chicanos, to *want* to be brown, to *want* to read our great literature (and be able to) would be a political (i.e., tactical) mistake, as most of our people, suffering as they are from the laws of the Anglos, have not yet equated the injustice of those laws, courts, electoral systems, etc., with the Anglo's deliberate attempt to destroy our culture, language, etc.

1.3.1.—However, that does not mean that, *simultaneously*, with these local-level study groups, other means of politicizing our people should not be carried out. On the contrary, every such attempt should be given full support. One of the best ways, of course, is by creating our own underground press. To a certain extent, we are well along in this, with such newspapers as *El Grito del Norte*, *El Papel*, *La Raza*, *El Gallo*, etc. We need more of them, one in every barrio, relating to one another, *nationalizing* our struggle. By nationalizing, we mean, *our* nation, our people: *to make us all aware that our fight in Texas or in Tierra Amarilla or in Los Angeles or in Delano is the fight of all of us*. Such an underground press, which should be quickly organized in a Chicano UPS system,[4] should focus on local issues but always relate those issues to the overall struggle. Also, we should use every form of propaganda possible. Theater, especially street or truck theater, pays off most, even if audiences are limited to a handful. We need more revolutionary theater, like Luis Valdes' Teatro Campesino. The ideal aim here, of course, would be to control a radio which could beam programs to the whole Southwest.

1.3.2.—Our cadre schools, of course, should focus on the fact that we will never be free unless and until Imperial America is defeated. In such schools, we should emphasize that we are part of a world army of dispossessed fighting the same enemy, and that we can only gain from the defeat of Imperial America in Vietnam, Dominican Republic, the Congo, etc. Also, it should be strongly stressed that the fight of blacks, Indians, Puerto Ricans, etc., is also part of the same struggle. We should thus form alliances with the other liberation movements in America wherever and whenever possible *and* advantageous. But, it seems to us, it is a mistake to fuse our struggle directly with the others, because that tends to dissipate the ethnic-cultural consciousness generated by a strictly Chicano movement in the rest of the Mexican American population. For example, where we are few, like in San Francisco State College in 1967,

[4] UPS, Underground Press System, is the free and reciprocal exchange system organized by and for the regular underground press.—*Ed.*

it made sense to fuse our forces into a sort of popular front of minorities, the Third World Liberation Front. But where we are many, such as in some southern California colleges, it does not make sense; there, we should maintain a Chicano Liberation Front, in alliance with the other struggling minorities, but not in confusion with them.

1.4.—Pride in ourselves, in La Raza, should have very specific meaning in terms of whom we are fighting. Thus, our value system should emphasize at all levels that to be a white man's soldier is disgraceful, to be a soldier against the Anglo is honorable. To focus exclusively on the percentages of the Vietnam War death toll as a way of combating Chicano participation in that war is, in our opinion, a bad mistake. It is true that in Colorado, for example, our people make up only about 10 percent of the state but 50 percent of that state's casualties and thus it was correct for Corky González to condemn the war as the machinations of "ruthless financial lords of Wall Street for green dollars of profit that do not show the red stains of blood."[5] But there is a very specific reason why so many of our men join the U.S. armed forces— for many *do* volunteer—and that is that, deprived of a sense of manhood at home, they feel they can gain it in the army. Discriminated, unemployed or underemployed, uneducated at home, they hope to find equality, some respect, even education, and of course full employment—at the risk of death in Vietnam. Again, if we can help them become conscious of their belonging to a conquered people, and arouse their sense of vengeance and justice, then they will surely fight at home.

2. Consciousness of being a discriminated people

Every one of us, naturally, is aware we are discriminated upon in America. But too few realize to what extent this affects our livelihood. For example, in Texas, an adult male with ten years of school averages $4,768 if his name is Anglo, $3,200 if his name is Spanish (by official 1967 figures; God knows what the true figures are). Usually, our pay scale is about half theirs. More than 30 percent of our people can only get jobs as "operatives" (delivery men, peddlers, laundry workers, packagers, etc.). There are almost 1,000 major national companies in the Southwest, employing almost three-quarters of a million people, which hire no Mexican Americans at all. We all feel this discrimination, but few realize its purpose. On the one hand, there is the deliberately fostered racism of the ruling elites which know that if we gain economic power of any kind we will immediately demand political power. For example, there are six counties in Texas and six in New Mexico where La Raza

[5] The overall statistics are that the Mexican American population in the United States is about 5 percent while the number of deaths in Vietnam of Mexican Americans is about 13 percent. In New Mexico, Mexican Americans make up 60 percent of the *draftees* but only 30 percent of the state's population.—*Ed.*

is over 50 percent of the population. If we had economic power in those countries, we would—even by playing the ruling classes' electoral game by their own rules—inevitably control those counties and turn them into liberated areas. In Webb County, Texas, which is as big as most U.S. states, we are 80 percent of the population. In Rio Arriba, New Mexico, we are 75 percent. There can be no doubt that the racism that keeps us "in our place" is meant to keep them in theirs—on top. On the other hand, there is the nondeliberate racism that permeates all white America, the racism that makes America feel superior to every other people in the world, that justifies its imperialism on "moral" grounds. That kind of racism, generated by the former for economic profit, is now so ingrained in the American Way of Life that it won't end until the exploited peoples of the world defeat the U.S. empire, literally crush it, break it up, smash it. Meanwhile, that racism says that we Mexican Americans are good for menial jobs, as domestics, farm laborers. The only way to combat it in our people, to combat our acceptance of it, is to use it. That means:

2.1.—To launch our own "Brown Is Beautiful" campaign, much like the blacks have done.

2.2.—To propagate our art and music, our way of dress, our customs, our ideas. Our poets should praise our ways (much like Corky has done in his memorable poems). Our philosophers should reject America's pragmatism, which is so alien to our culture, and develop our own philosophies. We should work for the creation of our own university, our own colleges, our own book publications. Obviously, we won't be able to accomplish any of this on a meaningful basis until the Anglos are defeated, but we should agitate for it all the time. The Brown Berets (see below for a politico-military evaluation) should develop the cultural aspects of our struggle.

3. Consciousness of being an exploited people

Obvious enough! Most of our people work on farms, either as migrant workers or as farm hands living in or out of the farms. We are moving to the cities in greater and greater number, but we still work on the farms as hired hands. In 1965, according to their own statistics, those of us who worked on the farms averaged $805 a year. As for land, the Alianza[6] has certainly made it clear to all of us how we have been robbed, beaten, and killed by the U.S.—again not only by individual Anglos

---

[6] The Alianza Federal de los Pueblos Libres (The Federal Alliance of Free Peoples), organized and headed by Reies López Tijerina in northern New Mexico, has been struggling for a few years to regain their pueblos' inherited land. In return, the Alianza has been bombed, and members have been repeatedly arrested and jailed on all sorts of conspiracy charges; Tijerina himself has been in and out of jail almost since the beginning, and in the summer of 1969 was again in jail.—*Ed.*

but officially, through the armed force of the U.S. Forest Rangers. Reies Tijerina's attempt to rally our people in New Mexico on the land issue has been enlightening, though not very successful. A great deal of effort has been wasted trying to get our land back through the law courts, on the *legal* grounds that the Treaty of Guadalupe Hidalgo, signed by the U.S., recognized the land grants to our pueblos.[7] Naturally, Tijerina didn't get very far in the Anglo courts. Still, his attempt was very important in at least one respect: it spread that consciousness that we are an exploited people. Not just each of us individually, but all of us collectively. The U.S. forced us to register our lands individually so it could drive us off or else it just plumb stole it, as when the Sheriff of Hidalgo County, Texas, confiscated 3,027 land-grant acres and sold them to an Anglo for $15, or as when the U.S. Forest Service seized for "conservation" 95 percent of the 600,000 acres of San Joaquín. We must fight back by:

3.1.—Organizing boycotts. It is not enough to boycott California grapes, nor is such a boycott very effective since it relies on a nationwide campaign. Instead, or rather in addition, we should select stores, merchants, services in every area where La Raza predominates heavily and systematically drive them out of business completely. The purpose should not be just to get them to buy such-and-such a product or not buy one, but to force the businesses to fold.

3.2.—Organizing cooperatives to handle the business of the Anglo firm boycotted. The new Tierra Amarilla co-op, which is about to be formed (so we understand), is great: it will have 200 acres to farm cooperatively, giving our people in the area new jobs. But it is not enough. We must set up cooperative stores, cooperative services, and we must drive the Anglo competition out through a concentrated political campaign, making political points, with political results: power! The politics involved in such cases is simply to give La Raza collective economic strength so we can have the financial tools to fight for our cultural and political rights. In other words, we must stress the cooperative, and better yet where possible the collective aspect, of our fight through cooperative and collective economic struggle.

3.3.—Organizing militant workers' groups (not unions because the Anglos will then apply their antidiscriminatory laws, which they never apply to themselves, to brand our unions discriminatory), with the object of bringing about strikes and gaining economic power (of sorts). We must, however, be careful of not overplaying the legal aspect of the struggle. César Chávez' grape pickers' strike has overplayed the nonviolent,

[7] The most important aspect of the land grants recognized by the Guadalupe Hidalgo Treaty of 1848, which the U.S. signed, was that the land in question belonged *communally* to the people of the pueblo in question. It was that provision which U.S. free enterprise violated first.—*Ed.*

legal aspects: though it has, *therefore*, gained liberal support across the country, it has given too many people hope in the eventual justice of the American Way, especially after all the political demagoguery by the Kennedys and their "moral" support.

4. Consciousness of being a politically subjugated people

We all know that we have very little chance of gaining even mild reforms through political action, but it is not unimportant to try to exhaust all forms of political action, so as to broaden La Raza's awareness that we can never be free or regain our land through the ruling elite's electoral games. Thus, though it was tactically badly thought out, we think that Reies' campaign for the governorship of New Mexico was useful. One characteristic of his campaign was primordial and should, in our view, be rigid: not to run, and Reies did not, on any traditional party slot, neither in the primaries nor in general elections. For here, even if we lose, and we will, the act of running on the Democratic or Republican Party ticket reinforces the view that those are the only parties and, therefore, by unconscious implication, that we accept those parties' view of democracy. Running for elective posts must always be a tool of political education, and one of the primary tasks of that education must be to discredit the electoral system, the American Way of "democracy," the myth that there is political freedom in this country, etc. Thus, we feel that our political activity should focus on:

4.1.—Creating local political parties to run local candidates. It does not matter too much if such candidates are qualified by the Anglos' rules, though it might help convert more people if they are and then are still barred from the election on some obviously trumped-up legalism.

4.2.—Then creating and launching a national La Raza party for the same educational purpose. We realize, of course, that most states make it so hard as to be nearly impossible to register a new party, either locally or nationally. Still, the effort of the recent Peace and Freedom Party has proved worthwhile—not in gaining any offices, obviously, but in establishing the Black Panther Party throughout the black communities, for behind the PFP there was always the BPP and its candidate, Eldridge Cleaver.

5. Consciousness of being a conquered people

We thus return to point 1 of this memorandum. For all the above reasons, and almost a century and a half of more reasons, we must put our consciousness of being a conquered people into the front lines. We are colonized, neo-colonized, imperialized. As such we must rebel. Victory will take a long time, many lives will fall, more will suffer. But it is the only way we can ever hope to have Tierra y Libertad. And so we come to that touchy, uncomfortable subject: armed struggle. That it is necessary, few will deny. That it will come, fewer will contest. That we must talk about it now, fewer still will agree. And indeed, since we are barely at the beginning of the meaningful phase of our struggle, it is not the time to bandy about the phrase "armed struggle" irresponsibly, adventuristically, openly. Nor is it the time to create an Armed Liberation Front. For one thing, if eight of us decided to organize an armed commando, chances are that three of us would be too scared to go ahead with it, that two more would find an ideological, strategic, or tactical reason to denounce the group before its first action, and that at least one of us would be a paid police informer or agent. Nevertheless, counterviolence or revolutionary violence *is* necessary to (1) counter the official violence from which we suffer every day and to (2) establish the principle of revolutionary violence as a politically viable alternative constantly present. Because of the dangers involved, we recommend that:

5.1.—Public organizations which are prepared to fight back Anglo violence do so on a very carefully limited self-defense basis. As we can see by the vast extent of the official repression against the Black Panthers, every time a Chicano will resort to self-defense against the unjust violence of the Anglos, they will hit open Brown Power groups with frame-ups, gundowns, illegal arrests, etc., to an extent much worse than is now the routine, as heavy as that is already. Thus the Brown Berets, for example, so long as they wear uniforms and are clearly identifiable in public, should limit their activity to legal, political, and cultural consciousness-building.

5.2.—Small groups, of preferably no more than three, should organize to carry out revolutionary justice. For the foreseeable future that should be limited to destruction of property of collaborationists, accommodationists, and agents. Only when the activity of the collaborationists leads directly to the death of La Raza people should retaliatory execution be programmed.

5.3.—Such small groups should also begin to envision terrorist activity of a strictly political value, that is, blowing up or damaging specific institutional edifices that clearly stand for the repressive nature of the American Way.

5.4.—Such small groups should also begin to envision armed robbery of banks or national firms that are particularly odious to our people and then use the money to help finance the movement, pay for legal defenses, etc.

Once some of these activities are unleashed, La Raza's imagination and political acumen will both prevail and open up new avenues of increased activity. The object, always, must be to broaden our struggle and make us all more and more aware that we are at war. Since the American Way of Life will not allow us to enjoy La Raza Way of Life, we must liberate ourselves from American domination.

HUEY P. NEWTON: WE ARE NATIONALISTS
AND INTERNATIONALISTS*

TO understand the suffering and the developing consciousness of black Americans, you must first be aware of our cultural, economic, and political heritage. And that means, first of all, that you must remember that the blacks of Africa south of the Sahara before the slave trade began were highly organized politically, with a complex system of kings, ministers, a university (at Timbuctu), and a culture which reflected their history, religion, aspirations, and values. The slavery that did exist then in no way can be compared with what was to follow: A conquered people became the servants of the conquerors, but once the "slaves" accepted and adopted the customs and religion of the victor, they were freed. In fact, they gained complete equal status and often rose to prominence in their new environment. In any case, families were never broken up, human dignity was never violated, and they were never treated as chattels. At the beginning of the slave trade, around the 1500's or so, Africans did understand the notion of slavery as it affected those blacks who were being taken by Europeans, and sold to them, but they expected to be treated in the same way as they were in Africa when they were vanquished by other Africans.

By August 1619, however, when the first black slaves landed in Jamestown, U.S.A., the slave-trade aspect of European-American imperialism-capitalism had become ingrained in the black's experience. I say "imperialism" because that trade affected a whole slew of other countries and other cultures, and "capitalism" because the prime interest of the Europeans in the slave trade was profit. The slave trader made profit

---

* Article written for this volume at the editor's request, on tape, recorded in the visitor's cell in the Alameda County (Oakland) jail, September 1968. Born of poor, partly employed, working-class parents from the U.S. South, Huey Newton was raised in various ghettos, including Watts (Los Angeles), where he participated in the 1965 black rebellion, before ending up in Oakland. With Bobby Seale, Newton then founded and organized the Black Panther Party for Self-Defense and became its Minister of Defense. As late as March 1968, after he had been arrested for the "murder" of an Oakland policeman and the wounding of another, Newton was still emphasizing self-defense. Sample: "A panther will not attack anyone, but will back up first. But if the assailant is persistent, then the black panther will strike out, and wipe out his aggressor, thoroughly, wholly, and absolutely, and completely." Since then, however, the Black Panther Party has dropped the "Self-Defense," has moved into the forefront of the black liberation movement as its militant vanguard, has openly advocated and entered into alliances with white revolutionary groups. Meanwhile, Huey Newton has been condemned to two to fifteen years for "voluntary manslaughter," but remains the BPP's unquestioned leader and symbol—from jail.

from selling slaves, and the slave buyer made profit by using the slaves as free labor. Not only was this profit system then incorporated into our own cultural history, but so was the white man's human value system, for our background inevitably includes the fact that some 50 million blacks perished in the process of the slave system—died fighting capture, trying to escape, in rebellions before and then during the long voyage across the Middle Passage, or simply by jumping overboard en route. This capitalism in the raw, then, not only dominated African countries economically (dependence on the slave trade system by the rapidly developed entrepreneur-collaborationist class), not only set up the economic basis for the new country (the U.S.), not only dominated, partly at least, the economic development of the European countries involved in the slave trade through its entrepreneur middlemen agents, but also totally dominated the cultural values of all those countries by establishing a value system in which individual man, his family, his heritage, his tribe or group, his nation are meant to be subservient or, more, meaningless in face of the value of the profit motive. Thus it can be correctly stated that not only were the slave-trading states of Africa colonized, but so were the thousands and then millions of black Africans imported into America. We are a colonized people inside the homeland of the colonizer.

And, of course, we were treated as a colonized people. Our culture, religion, and language were forbidden. But this process of "acculturation" to the American colonizer's ways brought no benefits—nor was it meant to. It did not gain us freedom or return to us our sense of dignity. It was forced upon us only in order to make us more efficient as a labor tool, as a means of accumulating profits for the colonizers—exactly what is happening to the colonized and neo-colonized world today. There, big business controls not only the economy and the political institutions of the victim country but attempts to degrade the colonized population and inflict Western culture on it so as to spread Western values, which in turn will guarantee big business its imperialistic hold on that victim. American imperialism, quite obviously, works not only through the economy and the political institutions, but also through the arts, radio, television, press, book publishing, advertisements, product packaging, etc. The aim is equally obvious: to control the total culture so as to perpetuate the system which brings the profits home.

Well, we were imperialized in the same way for the same goals. Slaves were not allowed to congregate in threes or more without the presence of a white; they were forced to use English so as to communicate with the bosses and so that they could not maintain their culture; and though they were given no responsibility—which might reawaken their sense of dignity—they were rendered more efficient, while at the same time constantly reminded of their "native" stupidity, and naturally, their inferiority. Meanwhile, they made the South wealthy and the country wealthy.

As they did, the capital accumulation inevitably brought about an expanded industrialization. This in turn led to the slaves' Northern movement, going to the factories which were springing up everywhere and which needed a continuous inflow of cheap labor. It is interesting to note that, at the time, we had full employment. But this was not because of some fair employment act; rather because it was against the law for a slave not to work. Thus, the slogan of full employment does not impress us today; it does not guarantee any human rights unless and until it is the people themselves who control the wealth they are producing.

Anyway, in 1865, we got our so-called emancipation. The fundamental reason why we did was simply because we were needed in the North for that industrialization. The South and North were, of course, rivaling each other for economic control of the U.S., and the industrialized North was more powerful. However, the promise of industrialization in what it would mean for the blacks was illusory. For one thing, emancipation made us citizens—as defined by the ruling class, i.e., without any privileges —which meant that we were no longer required by law to be employed. And the labor demand never became large enough to guarantee us jobs, much less give us power in the labor market. The result was that many blacks stayed on in the South, waiting for the land promised by emancipation—which, of course, never materialized, for that promise, as all promises made by the U.S., was never kept. And so our lives failed to change. We remained slaves, in a country that could now boast it had no slavery.

For America's second industrialization thrust, after World War I, the entrepreneur North chose to use immigrants rather than blacks. The huge immigration of Europeans, especially the Italian and Irish, fitted well into the factories' needs. Because these immigrants were white they could also fit well into the U.S.'s cultural value system: All they had to do was work hard, adopt the North's culture, respect the ruling class's laws and traditions, and they would be given a chance, eventually, to integrate into the system as a whole. That the Italians and Irish and the other white immigrants chose to so adapt is understandable enough: It was a choice dictated by economic necessity. Though they were discriminated against and though their early life was rough, the white immigrants could dream of total integration. Eventually, they accumulated enough affluence, by playing the game as established by the ruling class, to escape their ghettos, at least in sufficient numbers to encourage all the immigrants to seek such integration. That, too, was exactly what the ruling class wanted, for it turned the immigrants into hard-working semi-slaves striving for the promised dream of integration.

But the blacks did not profit from this new industrialization. In the first place, the dream of integration could not be relevant to them. In the second place, America's racism, deeply rooted into its way of life ever since 1619, could no longer be channeled into strictly delineated economic avenues. The black man was inferior, he was stupid, he was dirty, he

was a member of the fallen race—so how could a white man pretend
to want to offer him integration? Besides, the black man served a very
much needed economic function then: As an unskilled laborer, he was
white society's servant. Indeed, if he escaped from the plantation at all,
it was to pick up a domestic job.

During the Second World War, the black man finally did enter the
factory—to replace the whites who had become soldiers. It was the blacks,
by and large, and not the women of the white man's myth, who kept
the factories going. In the process, the blacks gained new skills in considerable proportions. But when the war ended and the white soldier
returned, the blacks were fired. The whites called this fairness: The
soldier should have been guaranteed his job back for having been willing
to die for his country. And under that pretext, the blacks were deprived
of a livelihood; not only were the whites rehired for their old jobs, but
new jobs created by the spurt of production in the postwar boom also
went to whites, not blacks. We became unemployed. We have been unemployed ever since.

At the same time, we were still being officially treated as Americans.
That is, though we came from similar original backgrounds and though
our whole experience was identical—the slave experience—white America
refused to recognize our cultural identity. In fact, we were a national
minority with a very specific world outlook, with our own art and
music. But white America refused to consider it as different. While the
Irish became Irish-American, the Italians Italian-American, we were
simply American, as if we had learned everything in America, from
America, and through American-valued eyes. We were discriminated
against, exploited, dominated, treated as foreigners in every way except
in terms of respect for our identity; there, suddenly, we were genuine
Americans. This was meant to deprive us of our ethnic reality, of our
culture. And that gave the white man the justification he wanted to exploit
our talents for his profit. The white man took our raw materials—our
theater, our art, and especially our music—and refined them in his factories for his profit. We had no control over our finished product: The
records, the compositions, the cloth, the handicrafts, the ideas, the words
of black America were used to make fortunes for white America.

It is clear, then, that if you are not in control, politically and economically, of your existential entity, there is no way in which you can
exhibit or institutionalize your culture, because you need institutions, and
to have institutions you need political power, and to have political power
you need economic power, that is, the economic freedom to express yourself according to your own image. Thus, the people who are colonized
across the world are experiencing not something similar to what we,
black Americans, are, but the very same thing. It seems easy to come
to such a conclusion internationally—that the Congolese and the Dominicans are experiencing the same deprivation of their humanity—but I think

that if you carefully analyze imperialism and neo-colonialism, as we have done in the Black Panther Party, in general and in particular in America, you will come to the same conclusion: that we are just as colonialized as the people of Latin America, of Africa, of Saigon. In fact, we are even imperialized with the same tools. The police in our ghettos are the foot soldiers in Vietnam. The AID and Peace Corps men in Santo Domingo are the state and federal War-on-Poverty bureaucrats here. Our source of news, our amusement, our education are directed by the same business agents. Our livelihood is controlled by the same functionary.

And like the docile neo-colonized peoples of the world, we are—or were until we rebelled—in a state of ambivalence. We knew we had a culture of our own; yet how could we say we did when we did not have the institutions or the outlets to allow us to express it? We walked around with a unique view of the world, quite different from any other American. Yet we were not even conscious of it because we had no way to verbalize that view, even to each other. We knew we were a people. Yet we did not and could not behave like one. We were totally imperialized, in the full sense of the word—and are today.

So we must rebel. Our first task is to weld ourselves into a viable people. That means a firm political line whose aim is to gain economic strength, as a people. That's why we recommend a cooperative government in the black community, with cooperative businesses. We are not under the illusion that this will solve our problems. We know that we can only be free when capitalism is completely destroyed in America, and this will of course free all the colonies of the world. Still, our first task is to organize our ghettos, politically and economically, which in turn will give us some cultural strength as well. Eventually, of course, the whole industrial complex has to be nationalized by the peoples who produce its wealth, and by peoples I mean culturally defined. Hence, the Indians will have their culture because they will control their economy through which they will wield political power; so will the Chinese, the Mexican Americans, the Irish perhaps, the Italians probably. They must each run their communities on a cooperative basis, controlled from the bottom up, instead of from the top down. When this happens, there will be no industrial-military complex. It will be broken up among each of the communities that now exploitedly labor for it. Once broken down, each people will be able to express their culture, since culture is the expression of behavior, and the behavior of economically free and co-operative people is the expression of genuine identity. In relation to each other, such people can then unite as free men—for the only way a man is free is when he expresses his own identity—into a world community of free men, a world dictatorship of the proletariat.

But to achieve such freedom, we must all start at the bottom. We must fight as brothers, each in our own community or ghetto, but against the common enemy that deprives us of our identity, that is, that exploits us economically, politically, culturally. We are then both nationalists and internationalists. We fight for our freedom in our own terrain, but in alliance with everyone who fights our enemy, not just because we need each other tactically but because we are brothers. As internationalists, then, it is our duty to create, as Che said, many Vietnams. For us, black Americans, fighting our exploiters at home is also a necessity: As an imperialized, deculturalized, racially subjugated, economically deprived, slave-experienced people denied our basic peoplehood for four hundred years, it is the only way we can possibly feel whole men again.

ROBERT F. WILLIAMS: MINORITY REVOLUTION*

I (1964)

The fact is that the racist oppressors of the Afro-American realize the insecurity and vulnerability of the most powerful military complex in the

---

* Three articles, all bearing the same title, published in *The Crusader*, "a personal journal" (monthly), by the author in English. The first article is dated May–June 1964 (printed in Havana); the second is from August 1965 (also Havana); Part III, dated September–October 1967, was printed in Peking. The author, who was born in Monroe, N.C., and served various stints in the U.S. Marine Corps, returned to Monroe in 1953, joined the local NAACP chapter and soon became its president. In 1957, after various armed attacks by the Ku Klux Klan on NAACP headquarters and leaders' homes, Williams organized an armed self-defense unit which fired back on the KKK the next time they attacked. That gunfight, in which no one was hurt, was the first time the police intervened—against the blacks. It was also the first time that black men organized themselves into self-defense units in modern America, an event which went on to impress and influence black militants across the country. From then on, however, Williams was constantly harassed and hounded by the police, the FBI, and white vigilante groups. He was shot at, run off the road, bushwhacked and finally, in 1961, was framed by the local police and the FBI for kidnapping. He escaped and the FBI immediately issued a warrant for his arrest on the charge of interstate flight. In the subsequent "Wanted" poster, signed by J. Edgar Hoover, he was not only described as a dangerous criminal but as a "schizophrenic" as well (making one envy the FBI's secret psychiatric resources which can make diagnosis without ever analyzing or talking to patients). Williams went into exile in Cuba, where he broadcast Radio Free Dixie programs to the United States, then fell out with the Cuban Revolution over its "petty-bourgeois" mentality—i.e., he was unsatisfied with the Revolution's slowness at educating and giving positions of responsibility to Negroes. He went to China, and in 1968 to Dar es Salaam. Meanwhile, in America, the black nationalist militants who formed the Republic of New Africa elected him its president, proof that his influence, spread through his first book, *Negroes with Guns* (New York: Marzani & Munsell, 1962) as well as through his newsletter *The Crusader*, had retained its power. He returned to the United States in 1969, partly to take over leadership of the black movement at a time when most Black Panther cadres were in jail (Williams disagrees with the BBP's policy of alliances with white radicals).

world to a violent internal struggle, wherein its horrible and sophisticated weapons of war will be ineffective. The internal defense of the U.S. is a possibility that money cannot buy. Only a change in the moral and social structure of the system offers security against an enraged oppressed citizenry. The U.S.A. is either unwilling or morally incapable of bearing the cost of this type of internal security. The race question is her Achilles' heel, her Maginot Line.

But our people's freedom spirit has been ossified by the continuous harangue of "we cannot possibly win a violent struggle of liberation." It is impossible for a people to rise above their aspirations. If we think we cannot win, we most certainly cannot. Our greatest enemy is our defeatist attitude. Our oppressor's greatest weapon of repression is his psychological apparatus by which he impregnates our people with a defeatist complex. Are we to concede the fact that racial oppression and tyranny prevail invincible and unshakable? Are we to concede to the unchallenged almighty power of our dehumanizer, that he is the supreme benefactor of our freedom? Are we destined to forever kneel beggingly at his feet seeking the alms of liberty and justice?

The sweetest fruits of liberty are plucked by those who readily display boldness and daring. The cringing and the reluctant constitute the hindmost part of a civilization in constant transition. The defeatist voice of cynicism is the inevitable scum that litters the shore before all daring world-shaking exploits of embarcation. What would civilization resemble if all revolutionaries, inventors, adventurers, and scientists had heeded the inevitable voices of the doubting Thomases, who perennially admonish that every novel and daring exploit is predestined to fail? Ironically, the survival of the cynic and the conservative is assured by the dogged iconoclast.

Is it possible for a minority revolution to succeed in powerful America? The cynics, prophets of doom, and agents of the oppressive establishment maintain that to even raise such a question is insane. They energetically, with a clairvoyant air, assure us that violent self-defense or violent resistance to brutal racial oppression can lead only to suicide. How do they know? What is the basis of their logic? Are they any wiser than those cynics who brazenly stated that "man will never fly," that "it is impossible to cross the oceans," that "man can never reach the speed of a mile a minute and survive," and that "the American Revolution can never succeed against the military might of the Crown"?

Yes, a minority revolution has as much, or more, chance of succeeding in the racist U.S.A. as any place else in the world. At the very outset, all revolutions are minority revolutions. Is it because the oppressor is white and the oppressed is black that most of the world accepts the premise that our struggle must be white-led and supported by the majority race or that it is insignificant and doomed to failure?

The fact of the matter is that the Afro-American wants and has been seeking brotherhood with the white masses since his enslavement in the New World. A people as brutally oppressed as American Negroes cannot wait forever for the support of mythological and theoretical allies. Most white workers in the U.S.A. today have a vested interest in the status quo. The present system grants them special privileges in a jungle society. The cow of production may be lean and diseased but the Negro is the only herdsman limited to the cutlets of feet and tail. The vast majority of the whites have also been mentally poisoned with racism. It is asinine to expect them to recover from their race psychosis without a severe shock treatment.

The American society is a highly industrialized complex. A highly industrialized and mechanized system is also a very sensitive one. The more machinery required to serve a community, the greater the incidence of mechanical breakdown. The more dependent a community is on mechanization, the more important it is for the wheels of industry to perpetually turn smoothly. Social systems, like biological systems, tend to adjust to environmental conditions and requirements. The American society, over a long period of time, has adjusted itself to a high rate of productivity directly bearing on the relativity of consumption.

The physical conditioning of a society also manifests certain relative psychological traits. The American mind has been conditioned to think of great calamities, wars, and revolutionary upheavals as taking place on distant soil. Because of the vast upper and middle classes in the U.S.A. that have grown accustomed to comfortable living, the nation is not psychologically prepared for massive violence and a sudden disruption of the essential agencies of the affluent society. The soft society is highly susceptible to panic.

Afro-Americans have long sought a peaceful solution to the race question. It is more than obvious that a people who have manifested an unshakable faith in the vain hope that the government would eventually grant citizenship and justice, prefer a peaceful solution. Our people have dreamed and prayed for a peaceful transition from slavery to first-class citizenship and human dignity. Peaceful evolution, through the mediums of legislation, law, and negotiations, is the method that has been pursued for almost two hundred years under the present government. The results are bitter and frustrating indeed. The orderly social process has been stymied by savage violence and brute force.

Instead of the majority race extending brotherhood and justice, it has resorted to a campaign of a massive drive aimed at extermination. The fascist elements are arming, not to liberate our brutally oppressed people but to liquidate us. It is becoming next to impossible for Negroes to conduct a "peaceful" demonstration in America. A Civil Rights Bill will have no more effect than the U.S. Constitution. What is integration when the law says yes, but the police and howling mobs say no? Our only logical and successful answer is to meet organized and massive violence with massive and organized violence. Our people must prepare to wage an urban guerrilla war of self-defense. Self-defense develops the stage wherein the source of evil and terror must be eliminated.

In Monroe, North Carolina (the first instance wherein highly organized self-defense units supplemented nonviolent tactics and reduced the incidence of resulting terror), our force of defense was adequate in staving off local attacks. We had enough force and arms to reduce the entire city to ashes. The fault, however, lay in the fact that we had an isolated force without extensive outside forces to pin down, ambush, and destroy the state reinforcements moving in to overpower us. Our self-defense forces had to remain purely static and defensive. The Monroe explosion came prematurely because of our shift in emphasis from self-defense to publicly overemphasizing nonviolence. The racists seized this time of weakness and confusion to launch an attack to annihilate our forces. A six-year effective self-defense campaign terminated in an ill-fated, untimely experiment with nonviolence. The organization of external forces was just being conceived. A decision was made to spare the city, thus avoiding an all-out confrontation prematurely. The town would have been destroyed but our defense forces would have been crushed by external power, and the state and white supremacists would have used the example to intimidate other advocates of self-defense. The racist news media would have portrayed the entire operation as one conducted by psychotic extremists.

The lesson of Monroe teaches that effective self-defense, on the part of our brutally oppressed and terrorized people, requires massive organization with central coordination. External oppressive forces must not be allowed to relieve the besieged racist terrorists. The forces of the state must be kept under pressure in many places simultaneously. The white supremacy masses must be forced to retreat to their homes in order to give security to their individual families.

The weapons of defense employed by Afro-American freedom fighters must consist of a poor man's arsenal. Gasoline fire bombs (Molotov cocktails), lye or acid bombs (made by injecting lye or acid in the metal end of light bulbs) can be used extensively. During the night hours such weapons, thrown from roof tops, will make the streets impossible for racist cops to patrol. Hand grenades, bazookas, light mortars, rocket launchers, machine guns, and ammunition can be bought clandestinely from servicemen, anxious to make a fast dollar. Freedom fighters in military camps can be contacted to give instructions on usage.

Extensive sabotage is possible. Gas tanks on public vehicles can be choked up with sand. Sugar is also highly effective in gasoline lines. Long nails driven through boards and tacks with large heads are effective to slow the movement of traffic on congested roads at night. This can cause havoc on turnpikes. Derailing of trains causes panic. Explosive booby traps on police telephone boxes can be employed. High-powered sniper rifles are readily available. Armor-piercing bullets will penetrate oil storage tanks from a distance. Phosphorus matches (kitchen matches) placed in air-conditioning systems will cause delay explosions which will destroy expensive buildings. Flamethrowers can be manufactured at home. Combat-experienced ex-servicemen can easily solve that problem.

Techniques mentioned here are generalized and require a closer study; however, let the cynics take note that the mighty U.S.A. is not as snug and secure as it once was. Yes, a minority war of self-defense can succeed. The Afro-American can win. We need not submit passively to racist extermination and brutality. The race question is America's Achilles' heel.

America's great abundance is what makes America America, without it she would be a wretched land of chaos. Her economy is already under stress and her military might is spread out too thinly throughout the world.

The bourgeoisie has very little stomach for massive blood and violence. They love their property, the source of their power and wealth. They are highly susceptible to panic. The majority white supermacists do not command the loyalty of the entire race. There are a few John Brown-type students and militants.

Afro-Americans must remember that such a campaign of massive self-defense should not be based upon a lust for sadistical gratification. It cannot be a campaign of vengeance, however sweet and deserving vengeance may be. Such a campaign of self-defense and survival must be based on the righteous cause of justice. It must not be antiwhite but antioppression and -injustice. Uncle Toms should be as much a target as racist whites.

Like it or not, we cannot escape the trend of history. The hour is fast approaching when our people must make a decision to meekly submit to fascist forces of terror and extermination or surge forth to the battle to liberate ourselves, save America, and liquidate its domestic enemies. If we truly seek freedom and human dignity we must be willing to pay for it in the fashion of the Algerians. Great multitudes of our people must be willing to fight and die in America's true cause and commitment to her Constitution, democratic principles, and the rights of man, and for a victory that will not ". . . turn to ashes in our mouths," but to eternal freedom and happiness in our hearts. Such a victory would truly make the world safe for democracy. It would secure the world from extermination by hydrogen war. Not only is America's peace and security involved but also the peace and security of the whole world.

The oppressor's heart is hard. The experience of history teaches that he only relents under violent pressure and force. There is very little hope that he will see the handwriting on the wall before it is too late. This year, 1964, is going to be a violent one. The storm will reach hur-

ricane proportions by 1965 and the eye of the hurricane will hover over
America by 1966. America is a house on fire—FREEDOM NOW!—or
let it burn, let it burn. Praise the Lord and pass the ammunition!!!

II (1965)

Millions of dollars are being dumped into Afro-American communities
to convert our people to pacifism. Our people are ill-housed, ill-fed,
ill-educated, and the victims of wanton police brutality and kangaroo-
court injustice; yet these millions are not earmarked to improve the lot
of our suffering, dehumanized masses, but for nonviolent workshops and
race relations designed to maintain a more subtle form of white supremacy, under the deception of possible integration based on moral persuasion.
In regards to militancy and self-defense the power structure and their
apologists are endeavoring to keep the collective mentality of our people
in a shameful state of narcosis. Our people are constantly reminded that
to resort to defensive violence would precipitate inevitable extermination
of the race. We are constantly intimidated by the threat of extermination.
We are led to believe that we are helpless and that our deliverance must
come through the benevolence of our racist oppressors. We are made
to feel inferior and insecure. We are led to believe that our first objective
should be the prolongation of our miserable and dehumanized lives, even
at the cost of total and abject submission to tyranny.

I do not advocate violence for the sake of violence. I advocate freedom
through brotherhood and peace, but the brutal nature of our enemy
oppressor responds only to naked force. Our oppressor keeps himself
on the throne of power by unmitigated violence. Our only alternative is
to dethrone him by violence. The power structure of the nation is internally weak. Its imperialist commitments are too widespread in the
world. Racist American society is degenerate and soft. Its internal security
is based on machinery and massive production. It relies on terrifying
weapons of massive destruction to maintain its dominant position in the
world. The heart and essential organs of this oppressor and common
enemy of the oppressed peoples of the world are easily vulnerable to any
potential fire storm that may be sparked from massive social discontent.
The Afro-American is a part of his means of production and profit. Though
disinherited, the Afro-American is a portion of the oppressor's population.
He cannot wholly and instantly destroy the Afro-American without destroying himself. If he turns inward to destroy a great portion of himself he will lose his international equilibrium. He is in a great dilemma.
His power is so extended that his greatest weapon of survival is deception fed on the opium of hope, devoid of sustenance. Through deceit and
machinations he must strive to keep body and soul together by containing
the flames of rebellion to a minimum of sectors to enable him to con-

centrate terrifying forces in a deceptive façade of invincibility. His tactic is to bribe one sector into submission while crushing the other.

The racist whites of America are the haves, and they can never truly sympathize and identify with the black have-nots until they feel what it is to be poor, destitute, and oppressed. Too much prosperity dulls the sensibilities of the haves in their understanding and dealings with the have-nots. The slave labor and the starvation wages of the masses of the Afro-Americans were major contributing factors in the construction of the affluent society. If the Afro-Amercian so elects he can make the so-called affluent society poor again. He can bring it to its knees, not because of his military power, but because of world conditions and his favorable location in racist America's essential regions. If the Afro-American ever divests himself of the fantasy of hope, based on the deceptive and empty promises of the white supremacy power structure, and if the attitude of "freedom or death" continues to spread and permeate the masses, the present racist and imperialist power structure is doomed.

Could a minority revolution succeed in racist America? It most certainly could! Theoretically, how could a minority segment win if it collectively decided to embark on such a serious course? Total unity would be required among the youth and a strong revolutionary nationalist spirit would have to prevail throughout the land. The segregationists, the hypocritical politicians, and the terrorists have already paved the way for the latter. The spirit of self-sacrifice, selfless dedication to the triumph of a cause greater than any single individual, a feeling of self-confidence in ultimate victory, unshakable courage, and identification with the struggling oppressed peoples of the world would be the necessary attributes for the success of a minority revolution.

Organization would require many facets. Groups dedicated to militant demonstrations would have to apply constant pressure to the power structure, create chaos and confusion and force the oppressor to unmask his ugly face before the world by reaching even more brutally and indiscriminately against constitutional forces. This would expose the true nature of the power structure and inspire greater resistance to it.

Armed defense guards would have to be formed throughout the land. These groups would be organized within the confines of the law and when possible become sporting rifle clubs affiliated with the National Rifle Association. They would function only as defense units to safeguard life, limb, and property in the ghetto communities. Some form of central direction would be necessary. A tightly organized and well-disciplined underground guerrilla force would also have to be formed to perform a more aggressive mission. It would have to be clandestinely organized and well versed in explosives. Its mission would be retaliation and a force used to pin down and disperse concentrated fascist power. It would prevent the power structure from rushing reinforcements to encircle and crush other defense groups engaged in battle against terrorist forces by ambushing, sniping, bombing bridges, booby-trapping and sabotaging highways. A welfare corps would have to be organized to build morale, raise funds, promote legal defense and take charge of the general welfare of the fighting forces and their families. Many of the members of the welfare-organization front would not understand its total function. They would be recruited on a humanitarian basis.

The most aggressive and irrepressible arm of the overall organization would be the fire teams. They would work in complete secrecy and would be totally divorced in the organizational sense from the main bodies of defense and other forces. They would enjoy complete autonomy. The group's only tangible loyalty to them would be in times of distress. Their legal aid in court defense would be rendered by Afro-Americans giving legal aid to victims of kangaroo-court systems, as is commonly known, where black people stand no chance of obtaining justice. This would be similar to, but more vigorous and militant than, the NAACP's role. The fire teams' mission would be sabotage. Thousands of these groups would be organized throughout racist America. These teams would consist of from three to four persons. They would only know the members of their immediate team. They would not identify with the civil rights movement. They would appear to be apathetic and even Uncle Toms. They would sometimes masquerade as super-patriots, and be more than willing, in a deceptive way, to cooperate with the police. They would even infiltrate the police force and armed forces when possible, and work in the homes of officials as domestics. There would be no official meetings and discussions, only emergency calls and sudden missions.

The mission of these thousands of active fire teams would be setting strategic fires. They could render America's cities and countryside impotent. They could travel from city to city placing lighted candles covered by large paper bags in America's forests, and have time to be far removed from the scene by the time the lighted candle burned to the dried leaves. While unsparingly setting torch to everything that would burn in the cities, and while concentrating on urban guerrilla warfare, the rural countryside would not be neglected. Aside from the devastating damage that could be visited upon the countryside, such a mission could serve a twofold purpose. It would also divert enemy forces from the urban centers. State forces would be forced to spread their ranks and would not be able to sustain massive troop concentrations in a single community. The heat and smoke generated from the fires would render some of the highways impassable to repressive troop reinforcements. The rural countryside covers vast areas and would require exhaustive manpower, equipment, and security forces. America cannot afford to allow its rich timber resources and crops to go up in smoke. The fire teams roving in automobiles would find unguarded rural objectives even more accessible.

A few teams could start miles and miles of fires from one city to the other. The psychological impact would be tremendous. By day the billowing smoke would be seen for miles. By night the entire sky would reflect reddish flames that would elicit panic and a feeling of impending doom. Operating in teams of twos or threes, one freedom fighter could pour gasoline or lighter fluid from a small flask into public waste paper baskets, another could later enter and toss a lighted cigarette in the same container. Near closing time kitchen matches could be placed in the air-conditioning systems of industrial and public buildings. The property of racists would be designated as priority objectives. Through this method, the racist oppressors could be reduced to poverty in a short span of time.

These fire teams could also go on predawn missions just before the morning rush for work. Their objective would be to spread tacks fitted with wire bases to ensure their upright position when thrown from a moving automobile in heavily traveled tunnels and freeways. Pure havoc would ensue. Sugar or sand in gas tanks could be used to knock out the engines of public vehicles. During police invasions of the ghetto, lye and acid bombs could be thrown from roof tops. Many forms of booby traps could be utilized.

With or without a common cause with the Afro-American the universal freedom forces are going to triumph over U.S. racist imperialism. The question is simply whether or not the black American is going to perish with racist imperialist America as a party to her savage crimes against oppressed and progressive humanity or whether he is going to contribute to the great victory of revolutionary humanity destined to fulfill its historical role.

Each year rioting, as a result of police brutality and oppression, becomes more extensive and ferocious. We can neither pray nor hope our way out of this difficult situation. We must defend ourselves. We must fight to win. We must also consider the immediate necessity of effective self-defense and resistance to racist terror. During times of massive rioting too many of our people are forced to fight armed cops and troops with bare hands and stones. Cops and troops must be disarmed and their weapons turned against other cops to obtain weapons of defense. Tanks and armored cars must be knocked out with Molotov cocktails and captured when possible. Bazookas and mortars must be taken from troops and national guard armories to prevent heavy concentration of troops and invasion by overwhelming force. The Minutemen, Confederate Underground, and other terrorists groups are arming and training with U.S. Army gear such as bazookas, mortars, hand grenades, machine guns, and gas masks. Submachine guns are even being manufactured in small shops controlled by these fascist groups. These private arsenals must be located and raided for weapons and ammunition. These weapons can also be used to do intensive damage. Oil storage tanks and natural gas lines could be fired through delayed methods. The oppressor must be forced to pay heavily economically for his police brutality, pogroms, racist court frame-ups, and white supremacy terror.

The racist imperialist is an unmerciful bully when he can control a situation with his sophisticated weapons of death and destruction. On the international scene, he will not hesitate to embark on the world's greatest campaign of slaughter in a desperate effort to save himself. The Afro-American liberation force is the only force in the world secure from fascist America's devastating nuclear force. He cannot use nuclear weapons against his own population, property, and cities. In such a minority revolution, racist America's very essence of strength and power would become the Achilles' heel of her security and struggle for world domination.

The advanced technology of the affluent society has made it soft, nervous, and hypersensitive. It is a society fearful of the cold realities of life. A society devoid of soul and humanism. A jungle society of dog eat dog, a society of frightful automation that is addicted to tranquilizers. Racist Americans are not psychologically prepared for fire storms, power, communications and transportation failures, and long periods without public utilities. The Afro-American has been under siege since the very beginning as a captive person in the so-called New World. Terror is a way of life for the great masses of Afro-Americans. Our people have practically become immune to the fear that flows from violence and brutality.

But such a minority revolution could only succeed as an integral part of the universal liberation struggle.

III (1967)

In 1964 when I first advanced the idea of the potential of a minority revolution in the U.S.A., among other things I was called a "species of maniac out of touch with reality." Again in 1965 when I extended my discourse on the potential of a minority revolution there was very little change in attitude and response from certain "sane" quarters. Now in 1967 again I endeavor to provoke serious consideration of this highly emotional and controversial question. This time I write with certain knowledge and facts derived from Watts, Chicago, Newark, Detroit, Milwaukee, and more than a hundred other places. This is not meant to be a blueprint for revolution, but is meant to inject sobering thought into the minds of those jingoists who so arrogantly extol the myth of American invincibility.

Once again, I raise the question, Could a minority revolution succeed in racist America? It most certainly could! Theoretically, how could a minority segment win if it collectively decided to embark on such a serious course? Total revolutionary unity would be required among the youth and a strong revolutionary nationalist spirit would have to prevail throughout the land. The spirit of self-sacrifice, selfless dedication to the triumph of a cause greater than any single individual, a feeling of confidence in ultimate victory, unshakable courage, and indentification with the struggling oppressed peoples of the world would be some of the salient attributes for the success of a minority revolution. In keeping with the principles of people's war, wherein the great masses of exploited peoples of the world represent the rural masses surrounding the cities (the exploiting industrial countries) the Afro-American revolutionaries represent a mighty urban underground within the city.

A high quality leadership would have to be developed. It must be wholly committed and devoted, selfless, devoid of ego, mentally alert, imaginative, fearless servants of the people acting as an instrument responding to the desires, necessities, and aspirations of the revolutionary masses. All positions of leadership should be provisional on the basis of tried and proven performance in action. Selection on the basis of prestige is a form of accommodation that is inimical to effective struggle.

What would the black man in America have to do in order to overturn tyranny? America's strength and weakness should be carefully analyzed. The key to America's strength is its almost unlimited industrial capacity. Its staggering production is its life blood. From a military point of view it is also its greatest weakness. The American society is the most automated society in the world. It has become addicted to machinery. It has become enslaved by it. Without it it would soon wither and die like a green melon whose vine is severed from its roots.

Without consideration of the social and political ramifications of the evil systems of Hitler's Germany and Tojo's Japan, and strictly from a military point of view, we should study the causes of racist America's advantage during the Second World War. Aside from the effectiveness of dauntless allies, one very salient point is the fact that U.S. and allied air power was able to pulverize enemy production, communications, and to greatly disrupt the normal scheme of life. While the enemy was made to suffer this disadvantage, American industrial power was allowed to intensely mobilize its abundant human and natural resources, rapidly expand and fiercely feed the war effort unhampered. The American scheme of life was never violently disrupted and, relatively speaking, the civilian population was merely inconvenienced as a result of the war. In the past American production has been fortunate enough, because of technical limitations and geography, to escape the devastation of war. The fear of such devastation is the very reason the power structure is so hysterical about the proliferation of H-bombs and intercontinental rockets. Massive devastation of America's industrial centers would reduce it to a primitive nation.

The Afro-American is in range of the American giant's Achilles' heel. American production, communications, and the normal function of the affluent society are exposed to the Afro-American's natural revolutionary reaction to tyranny and oppression. A united, well-organized, armed, and trained black America is a potential force to be reckoned with in its own right. The American case is a unique case. Any Afro-American revolt would consequently constitute a unique form of urban guerrilla warfare.

As the power structure applies ever more brutal repressive measures in response to the black man's just petition for social justice, a precision-type urban guerrilla warfare is the prerequisite for the black man's survival and liberation in racist America. Such a campaign must be well organized and coordinated. There must be a vast network of communications and central planning. No matter how primitive, black freedom fighters must establish their own coded and clandestine communications system. There must be central planning and a national supreme command. Afro-American revolutionary forces must create a top-notch security agency. This agency must be responsible for the establishment of an efficient and extensive intelligence network. It must infiltrate the armed forces, the National Guard, the police, the FBI, the CIA, public utility services, and all political groups, right, center, and left. The power structure's facilities must be utilized to advance the cause of Afro-American liberation.

Such a revolutionary organization would require many facets. Armed defense guards would have to be formed throughout the land. These groups would be organized within the confines of the law. They would function only as defense units to safeguard life, limb, and property in the ghetto communities. A tightly organized and highly mobile underground guerrilla force would have to be clandestinely organized. This well-disciplined force would play a more aggressive role. It would be well versed in handling explosives and deadly accurate when deployed as snipers. Its mission would be retaliation, to visit attrition upon the enemy and to pin down and bring about a dispersal of his concentrated forces. This guerrilla force must operate in small bands and know every inch of that part of the city where it is to operate. It must control its fire and use its ammunition sparingly. It must be highly mobile and constantly shift its position when sniping to avoid detection, death, or capture. It must have a perfect understanding of its mission at all times. When operating in full view of great throngs of people, its members should cover or mask their faces to prevent revealing identity. It should handle its weapons with gloves, especially the captured ones, so as not to leave incriminating fingerprints on weapons that may later fall into the hands of repressive authority. These groups, while sniping and performing other missions of sabotage, should be extremely careful in avoiding death and injury to the friendly black population. Friendly property should be diligently protected and safeguarded. The guerrilla forces must be so organized, coordinated, and equipped as to prevent the power structure from rushing reinforcements to encircle and crush other defense groups engaged in battle with repressive forces by ambushing, sniping, bombing, and sabotaging roads. These people's warfare tactics must be executed in a fashion that will wreak frustration and exhaustion on the oppressive enemy forces.

There is a great need for the black revolutionary to become proficient in ambushing and seizing arms and equipment from the enemy oppressor. This includes even the capture and use of tanks and armored cars. Special effort should be made to locate and seize Minutemen and rightist fascist groups' arms caches. When U.S. government surplus military and sporting goods stores are peoplized (looted), first aid packets, gas masks, and helmets should not be overlooked. When stocked, the heavier type of model airplane equipped for remote control can play a big role in urban guerrilla warfare. These model planes can be used to deliver hand grenades to targets. Firing pins or mechanisms can be so constructed that the impact of a direct head-on collision will set off an explosion. Dynamite and other explosives and deadly chemicals can be utilized from these heavy model planes. These model aircraft can also be used to reach fenced-in and inaccessible targets like oil storage tanks, industrial chemical tanks, high-tension power installations, armored cars, and troop-carriers. They can also be used against inaccessible buildings and other targets that may require special attention.

The black revolutionary must become creative, must use his imagination, talent, and training in the sacred cause of liberation. He must become consciously constructive in devising ways and means of harassing, bankrupting, exhausting, demoralizing, injuring, and destroying the enemy. He must not expend himself, his forces, and supplies foolishly. While soberly respecting and analyzing the strength of the enemy, he must never fear him. He must seek the advantage of battle and be as certain as the realm of possibility will allow that skillfully planned and executed actions will heap great injury upon the enemy. Revolutionary forces must save themselves while destroying the enemy. Revolutionaries must make a strong bid for dramatic victories that will inspire the people, encourage them to want to participate in a war of dignity, retribution, and liberation. At the same time the urban guerrilla must strike terror into the hearts of the enemy forces. He must be well disciplined, of high morale, devoid of ego, and be able to work and think collectively. He must at all times project a double image. To the masses of the community he must project an image of a race-conscious, politically mature brother whose unshakable mission is to defend the human dignity of our downtrodden masses. His image should be that of a liberator rather than one of a thug rioter engaged in an orgy of pointless plunder. He should be seen as a black patriot and savior who is convinced that it is more honorable to fight and die in battle against oppression and tyranny directed against the black people of the ghettos than to die in white men's wars of imperialism and the repression of freedom-loving colored peoples abroad. He should equate his revolutionary actions not to "looting" and "rioting," but to the spirit of the Boston Tea Party, the battles of Concord, Lexington, and Valley Forge. He must feel and understand the nobility of his historical role; a role that affords him the opportunity of forging his own destiny and of bringing new direction to the world.

The fact that the power structure has called for an integrated National Guard that will be especially trained and equipped for counteracting urban guerrilla warfare will provide black revolutionaries with a never-before-available opportunity to infiltrate the first line of the power structure's repressive army and acquire the latest professional skills in military science and tactics and the handling of weapons. This is a golden opportunity that should be seized upon to the fullest extent. When security is tight and every individual concerned has been checked and double-checked as a security risk, newly acquired tactical knowledge must be discussed and disseminated among small secret groups. Marksmanship and the handling and manipulation of weapons can be taught through the use of air rifles and pellet guns. Dummy rifles can also be used to improve marksmanship, but cutting slots in cardboard boxes that will hold a rifle snugly in position. The box can be mounted on a chair or table facing a small target tacked to a wall. The trainee sights the rifle in on the bullseye of the target and leaves it in the position he thinks to be accurate. The experienced shooter or instructor looks down the gun sights of the weapon just as it was placed by the trainee and can ascertain to a certain degree the marksmanship of the trainee. This exercise is repeated until accurate sighting comes naturally to the pupil. This exercise must be supplemented by a series of exercises in the practice of trigger-squeezing. The trainee can be taught the proper method of trigger control by slowly squeezing triggers on empty rifles until he perfects a method of sniping that requires an ability to squeeze the trigger with the minimum of jerk. The shooter should not anticipate when the rifle is going to fire. The shot should come as a surprise to him. A jerk or impatient pull of the trigger throws the rifle off target and makes for poor marksmanship.

Molotov cocktails are very effective weapons in urban guerrilla warfare; however, a jumbo size is even more effective. The jumbo size or the Black Power Bomb can be most effectively used against tanks and armored troop-carriers where streets are narrow and buildings are three or four stories high. The jumbo size of the gasoline bomb can be made by using an empty syrup bottle of one gallon capacity. These gallon-sized glass jugs are usually available around confectioneries, drug stores, restaurants, and warehouses. Each is equipped with a screw-on cap and is fitted with a finger grip or a built-in ring by which to handle the bottle or jug with a single finger. This type of jug can be filled with almost three-fourths gasoline, about one-fourth extra heavy motor oil with lubrication grease added. The screw-on cap should be tightened, after which a tampax, well soaked in gasoline, should be securely taped or wired to the jug. The soaked tampax or well-soaked rag is lit when the individual is ready to heave the Black Power Bomb. The glass jug or container breaks on impact, thus igniting the gasoline, oil, and grease, resulting in a napalm-like effect. This is highly effective when heaved from a roof top into personnel (troop) carriers. It can also be thrown as a satchel charge against tanks and other armored vehicles. Satchel charges can deal deadly blows to armored vehicles.

During the time of all-out conflict fires must be set over a wide area. This spreads the enemy forces thin and makes the situation more difficult for him to control. During the height of the fire offensive, car patrols should roam widely separated sectors of the city with heavy-duty adjustable wrenches. All fire hydrants in safe, isolated, or deserted places should have their caps removed and valves completely opened. This will hamper and sometimes completely negate the power structure's fire-fighting capacity. Fire is the black man in racist America's most effective weapon. It can be just as devastating as a hydrogen bomb. America is the black man's battleground and he cannot afford to hesitate to use whatever means necessary to remove the bitter and tragic consequences of almost four hundred years of unmitigated white supremacy tyranny.

After initial incidents that trigger conflict with brutal police forces, Afro-Americans must more and more avoid massive congregation for confrontation. Fighters must quickly disperse and keep out of range of chemical sprays used to immobilize and identify freedom fighters. Some sprays can render an individual unconscious. Some types may result in permanent injury and may be used by the power structure unsparingly in a surreptitious campaign of genocide against the restive black masses. Snipers must always be conscious of the fact that even during night hours the sniper-scope, consisting of infrared telescopes, can be used by enemy forces to zero in on their positions. The only defense against this is to fire and shift positions, and keep shifting positions, and to keep shifting positions and firing only at worthwhile targets. The urban guerrilla fighter must rely on the elements of mobility, speed, surprise, terror, a friendly environment, knowledge of the community, concealment, and cover when possible. He must consciously concentrate on the enemy's weakness, attack him at his weakest point, and avoid becoming a target of his massive power.

Possibly, if the brothers should want to devise an effective defense against the thug cops' chemical warfare, club attacks, and vicious close-range shooting, it may be necessary to send special representatives to Africa for specialized training in the manufacture and use of the poisonous dart. This simple, silent, but deadly technique was highly successful when used by the Congolese revolutionaries against Tshombe's butchers. This could become a highly effective secret weapon in the arsenal of the Black

Revolution in racist America. It could be most potent at night during confrontations with killer cops. This type of warfare must be waged under top-secret conditions.

The "honky" cops and the racist power structure are deadly serious in their war against black people. Afro-Americans can expect no humane considerations from such insensate savages. They are cold-blooded killers and they have no qualms whatsoever about massacring our helpless and defenseless people. We must respond in kind. During all confrontations with racist thug cops and their loyal black running dogs, black freedom fighters must realize that it is a do-or-die situation and must fiercely act in the most violent and desperately daring fashion as a matter of survival. The thug cops are devoid of all mercy. When they have the upper hand they will not hesitate to viciously butcher black people. Revolutionaries must remember that there is no second chance or appeal from death. In situations of such savage confrontations what is to be done must be carried out instantly before the beast squeezes the trigger. It is better to die in action and to take at least one of the enemy along, than to die as butchered swine by an unscathed sadistical beast who lives to kill again and again.

No method of terror or destruction against the oppressor should be overlooked in urban guerrilla warfare. Freedom fighters should always try to invent and develop new methods of sabotage that can be carried out against targets of opportunity in particular areas. Students of electronics, chemistry, and science should be organized and mobilized in a way that they can contribute greatly to the arsenal of the urban guerrilla fighter. Fighters should also be able to obtain an almost unlimited supply of plastic bombs. When hardware stores are raided, compact sets of acetylene torches should rate high on the list of most desired weapons of struggle. These small portable sets can be ignited, set for slow cutting with the intense flame fixed to remain directed against gas mains, oil pipe lines, gas and oil storage tanks to effect explosions. If this is done at night the flame should be covered, leaving a small space at the bottom of the cover for air while the flame is concealed to prevent detection. This set-up must be completed swiftly and the fighters must get as far away from the scene as fast as possible in order to avoid being caught in the explosion.

Revolution is not a festival and it must be approached with the utmost seriousness. Freedom is not a welfare commodity to be doled out as charity. It must be seized and taken with the ferocity of a wounded tiger. Nobody is going to give the black man freedom. Nobody is going to give him justice. He must take it.

More and more the most thinking element of white America is beginning to concede the fact that the Afro-American is capable of a potential that could very well lead to the destruction of racist, imperialist America.

However, the question is invariably asked: "How can such a small minority expect to control and reconstruct a vast nation wherein the oppressors constitute such a great majority?" The fact of the matter is that the tyrannical conspirator has already offered a solution to this problem through negative example. The plundering white headhunter first appeared in the Indian's America as a very small minority. Once he broke the resistance of the courageous Indian, he solved the imbalance of red-white population by massive immigration. He encouraged everything with a white face to settle on the land that he had just robbed from the Indian. This same method of solving the racial imbalance was successful in Australia and New Zealand, and Zionist conquerors appear to have the same thing in mind in the Middle East today. For the first time in history, why can't America be opened to unlimited colored immigration? Why can it not logically pass from colored back to colored? It is a foregone conclusion that even if whites were welcomed with open arms in such a just society, the overwhelming majority would resent living in an environment justly guided by colored power.

The insensate power structure realizes the potential consequences of a Black Revolution. The very thought of such a possibility throws it into panic and hysteria. No oppressive system wittingly and willingly goes to its doom passively. It fights desperately and brutally for its existence. It does not hesitate to unleash frantic pogroms and campaigns of genocide. It has no compunction about resorting to extreme measures of fascist repression. The alternatives ahead for black America are bloody and violent revolution or meek submission to tyranny and Nazi-like extermination. Revolution is a serious and costly endeavor. In America it would claim untold numbers of human lives. Property damage would be immeasurable, but in the final analysis submission to tyranny would be an even more expensive proposition for the black population. The power structure has an alternative to the approaching holocaust. Its only hope is an intense crash program of total justice and equality and possibly a geographical separation. It is not the nature of tyrants to honor the petitions of their victims. The tyrant's response to such just demands is always unmitigated force. Tyrants always entertain the illusion that brute force is a panacea for social ills. They inevitably make the fatal mistake of thinking that violence is an invincible pillar of state hegemony.

Newark and Detroit were merely skirmishes of protest. Complete alienation is imminent. The black man is in for some rough days ahead. He will experience some jolting setbacks, but he will learn the hard way. Through negative examples he will learn the art of warfare. He will become steeled in his determination to overcome, and the conditions of battle will transform him into a fierce fighter. Great loss of life will not serve as a deterrent, but as a propellant. More and more the masses will come to realize that their greatest chance of survival lies in collective and fearless struggle. Anger will descend on the collective masses like a great torrent that flows from a crumbled dam. Such a force will be invincible. It will be powerfully driven by the fact that it has nothing to lose and a whole new world to gain. The great masses of black Americans have nothing to lose, the power structure has everything that a ruling class can ever lose.

The cynics, the Uncle Toms, the capitulationists, the timid, and those socialists who disguise their white supremacy precepts behind a façade of pseudo-Marxism are more than blunt in reminding black Americans that a minority revolution of black people cannot succeed in racist America. From a faulty dialectical point of view they have all of the stereotyped answers as to why such a noble undertaking is bound to fail. This prejudiced point of view is in the same vein as proclaiming that the black African cannot run Africa without the white man. It is like saying that a youth is not mature enough to manage a responsible position.

Seven million Cubans can take a stand against the powerful U.S.A. and the whole world cheers and inspires them to resist. Fourteen million people in South Vietnam stand up to U.S. aggression and become the "Little David" against Goliath among the nations of the world. Two million Jews unleash aggression against one hundred million Arabs and the whole reactionary world cheers the success of their imperialist-inspired aggression. More than twenty-two million black Americans, who are massed in racist America's most sensitive regions, speak of massive resistance to genocide and tyranny and we are greeted with only the demoralizing words that "you can't win because you don't have a majority. You must have the good white folks on your side." And when we ask where are the good white folks, and inasmuch as there is no possibility of their joining us, our cause is lost. In other words, we should do nothing other than to passively protest and make love to our oppressors and wait for them to fall in love with us on some vague and mythological date in the future.

In a minority Black Revolution in racist and imperialist America, the best our people can hope for, as far as the white working class is concerned, is the strategic neutralization of a great portion of these unreliable racist masses. The black man cannot leave such an accomplishment to chance either. This is why any all-out minority revolution must create a state of crisis wherein almost all of the white male population would be forced to remain in their homes to protect their property and families. A great factor in favor of the Afro-American is the fact that the middle class is very large. It is not accustomed to deprivation and terror. Because of its affluence, it has waxed soft. It has no stomach for massive fire, blood, and violence. The motive force behind its life drive is its endless pursuit of prestige, conspicuous consumption, and sensual pleasures.

A few years of violent, sporadic, and highly destructive uprisings will set the stage for the grand finale. After the stage is properly set, through protracted struggle, big bad racist and imperialist America could be brought to her knees in ninety days of highly organized fierce fighting, sabotage, and a massive fire storm. This would be a unique type of urban guerrilla warfare that is only applicable to a highly industrialized and urbanized country like racist America. Such a campaign could only be mounted by a desperate and frantic people struggling for survival. This type of warfare must be based on the expediency of the last resort. This is the final hope of the brutally oppressed wherein intolerable misery has closed the hopeful gap between life and death.

The day of such a confrontation draws near. Time is running out. The power structure prepares to respond to just and prayerful petitioning with more brute force, armor, and steel. It has not learned its lesson in Vietnam. It has no understanding of the relativity of resistant violence to applied violence. Relative to revolutions and rebellions it is like a child who does not yet understand where babies come from; for it does not yet seem to know where rebellion comes from. Rebellion is born of oppression. Tyrants are the progenitors of revolution. Conditions of tyranny constitute the womb of revolution. Revolution is a Caesarean operation to facilitate the deliverance of the child of peace. It is the surgery needed to master the complications developed by a malfunctionary parliamentary delivery system.

Yes, a minority revolution could succeed in racist and imperialist America. Its chances of success today are better than at any previous time in history. America is an imperialist power with its tentacles spread around the world. Its greed makes it want to dominate the world. It has arrogantly proclaimed its hypocritical self savior of the entire world. The fact of the matter is that it cannot even save itself. The American black man holds the balance of power in the world today. He holds the fate of America in his hands.

ELDRIDGE CLEAVER: EDUCATION AND REVOLUTION*

THE repression against the movement is not a sign of strength on the part of the ruling class, but rather the sign of weakness, and a sign of the strength and effectiveness of the movement. All of the lies, the subterfuges, the hypocrisy of the ruling class has been exposed. They can no longer hope to control or manipulate the movement by words alone, they have to resort to the brutal, repressive forces of the police department. The movement itself has drawn several lessons from this reaction of repres-

---

* Message, taped in Algiers, published in the *Black Panther* newspaper, June 28, 1969.

sion by the ruling class; in the first instance, the clear-cut nature of power in the United States is being revealed. So are the racist policies of the ruling class. On the one hand the rebellion of black students and black people thoroughly exposes the racist policies of the administration of the various colleges and high schools, and on the other hand the repression that the allies of blacks are receiving shows its fears. (It is really incorrect to speak of the white section of the movement as being the allies of blacks, because in reality there is no such thing as a black movement and a white movement in the United States. These are merely categories of thought that only have reality in terms of the lines that the ruling class itself has drawn and is implementing amongst the people. The United States is controlled by one ruling class. It's one single structure, and the whole drama of the black liberation struggle and the revolutionary struggle in the white community is being played out on one stage. Because of the division that the ruling class has historically implanted amongst the people, because of the different experiences of black people from white people, the division is more apparent than real, because at the top there's not a ruling class for blacks and a ruling class for whites. There's one single ruling class that rules all, that controls all, and that manipulates all that has a different set of tactics for each group, depending upon the tactics used by the groups, in the struggle for liberation.)

One of the great weaknesses in the movement at this particular time is in the campus focus of the attack upon the ruling class and the power of the ruling class. And this has to do with the compartmentalized thinking of the traditional American society in which the college community and the college campus are viewed as something separate and distinct from the rest of the community. The college is not really looked upon as a part of the community; people who are not going to college or who have no children in college feel that what's going on on the campus is none of their business. Nothing could be farther from the truth, because in reality, your colleges are institutions that have been set aside to perpetuate the human heritage, and to pass on human wisdom, the knowledge, and technical skills for the further development of society and civilization. And every single individual living in a given society has a stake in what goes on. They have a stake in seeing to it that what happens on the campus is proper, and that the best interest of all the community is being served. On the other hand, the attacks focused on the college campuses serve to expose the nature of power in the United States, because when we look at the composition of the board of regents and administrations and councils that control the colleges, we find them replete with military men, retired generals, foundation personnel, and big businessmen. So that we could say that the boards that administer the universities are a good barometer, or a clear barometer, of the stratification of power in the society as a whole. We don't see poor people represented on the boards or administrations of the institutions of learning. This is because poor people do not exercise or possess any power. But those who control the economy, those who control the various sources and levels of power in the community and around it, are able to have their lackeys and their flunkies appointed to administer these institutions of learning. This needs to be brought out much more clearly and brought home to the community. A connection needs to be made between the college campus and the community so that the repression and the tactics of the ruling class can be defeated, by the total community being involved. As long as the pigs are able to vamp on the college campuses, commit mass arrests, and brutalize the students, and there is no solid and massive community support, then they will be able to get away with this. Slowly but surely they will be able to grind the movement to a halt by cutting off wave after wave of leadership, by expelling the leadership, and hounding the leadership out of existence. It's a mistake to think that the ruling class cannot be successful if a proper response is not made from the movement. This is a mistake that's been made time and time again in the various revolutionary struggles around the world. There have been cases of the revolutionary movement being very highly advanced, very well organized, much more organized than we are in the United States, with a higher theoretical understanding, and with very good party machinery, etc., and they have been crushed because the power structure would resort to unlimited means of brutality. They would kill, they would imprison, and they had the mass media in their control, and they could use the mass media to justify all this, and to brainwash other people who were not organized to do anything about it.

In the U.S. now, the power structure, by overreacting, seeks to buy time for itself. The pressure that the movement puts on the power structure determines the amount of time that is left. Because if things develop and progress at such a pace that allows the ruling class to devise means of coping with the movement, then all is lost and the movement itself is doomed to failure. So that a broadening of those involved, or those concerned, and those whose support is now latent is what is required.

Poor black people and poor white people and other middle-class people, who are not themselves directly involved in the college situation, need to be made to understand that something of their own precious liberty, which either they never had or which they thought they had, is being decisively determined in the struggles that are going down on the campuses today. Every black mother, every black father, every Mexican mother, every Mexican father, every father and every mother in every group, white, Puerto Rican, Indian, Eskimo, Arab, Jew, Chinese, the Japanese—they must be made to understand that if they have no child or teenager involved in the educational process today because they were not able to afford to send them to college or something of that nature, this in itself is a criticism of the structure of education in the United States. Because it is the duty of any society to see to it that every individual in that society is invested with the human heritage and provided with the technology, the skills, and the knowledge that will enable him to cope with his environment, to survive, and to live a good life. Just as it is the duty of the society to provide the highest level of medical assistance, housing, and also employment, every benefit that exists in society; it's the duty of the government to provide all that. And as long as the government is not providing that, it is not worthy of existing, and under our form of government which is called representative democracy, it is not possible for it to provide this, it is not possible for a capitalistic economy to provide a universal education for the people. What it has been providing is universal brainwashing that masquerades as universal education. The quality of the education is contemptible. It's inhumane, and it's only geared to provide a level of intelligence or a level of competence that will enable the product of the educational system to become war material, to be exploited by the capitalistic economic entities within the United States.

So what we're into today is not only sitting back and criticizing, but actively reaching out and challenging the authority of those who control the various institutions in society, not simply challenging this authority, but by actively moving to disrupt the functioning of these facilities and in fact to take control of these facilities, so that the people will have the power to administer these facilities in the best interests of the community as a whole and no longer in the interests of the crosswork monopolies that are being administered by racists and by pigs who only want to exploit people and sentence people to be cogs in a wheel. In the final analysis, the struggle that is now going on on the college campuses cannot be settled on the college campuses, it has to be settled in the community, because those that sit on the boards of administration of the colleges do not derive their power from the fact that they're sitting on the board but rather, they sit on the board because they have power in the community. Their power is based in the economic institutions of society and other institutions that are part of the power structure, and because of their relation to these sources of power, they're able to be appointed to these positions of administration. So that we have to destroy their power in the community, and we're not reformists, we're not in the movement to reform the curriculum of a given university or a given college or to have a Black Students' Union recognized at a given high school. We are revolutionaries, and as revolutionaries, our goal is the transformation of the American social order.

In order to transform the American social order, we have to destroy the present structure of power in the United States, we have to overthrow the government. For too long we've been intimidated into not speaking out clearly what our task is: our task is the overthrow of the government, it has to be understood as being nothing but the instrument of the ruling class. The courts, the congress, the legislature and the executive branches of the state and federal government are nothing but instruments in the hands of the ruling class, to see after the affairs of the ruling class, and to conduct the life of society in the interests of the ruling class. So we're out to destroy this, to smash this machinery and to erect new machinery, but new machinery cannot be erected until the present machinery is destroyed. It is not the task of revolutionaries to keep their heads up in the sky, wondering about what they would do, when they're in power; what they have to do at the present time is to have their mind centered on destruction; we're out to destroy the present machinery of the ruling class; that is our task and that's what we must be about. And we say that we will do this by any means necessary. We must do this by the only means possible, because the only means possible is the violent overthrow of the machinery of the oppressive ruling class. That means the we will not allow the ruling class to use brutality and force upon us, without using the same force and brutality upon them. We must destroy their institutions from which they derive their power. A given college president may have his power as a result of being involved in a corporation. We must attack him on the campus but we must also pursue him off campus and attack him in his lair, the lair of his power, in his corporations; this could be through boycotts of the products of that corporation, or through the physical destruction of the property of that corporation, or the physical alienation of him as an individual.

We must not get into a bag of thinking that we're involved in a game, a revolution is not a game, it is a war. We're involved in a war—a people's war against those who oppress the people.

Conclusion

The first Conference of the Organization of Solidarity of the Peoples of Africa, Asia, and Latin America (OSPAAAL) took place in Havana from January 3 to 15, 1966. It was attended by 512 delegates representing 82 countries. Most of the delegates had long personal histories of participation in revolutionary struggles, and most were committed to continuing such struggles. In fact, many of the delegates had literally been fighting guerrilla battles up to the moment they put on their disguises and filtered out of their battlefronts through clandestine roads to attend the Conference. All of these guerrillas and delegates were united by one common bond: their determination to smash imperialism, set up politically and economically free "people's governments" in their countries, and establish some form of working solidarity and mutual assistance program among them. The need for such solidarity was based on the fact that imperialists, especially the United States, which is the main exploiting country in the world today, never respects frontiers. Having just escalated the war in Vietnam and having just sent 42,000 troops to crush a popular pro-Constitution rebellion in the Dominican Republic (led by no more than 4,000 poorly armed men), the United States was deemed an international force to be defeated by international-minded revolutionaries.

Immediately, in nonrevolutionary "left-wing" circles, the cry went up that OSPAAAL, or the Tricontinental as it became known, was simply a new Comintern. In fact, it was and is nothing of the kind. Whereas the old Russian-sponsored Comintern was an agency controlled and directed by the Central Committee of the Communist Party of Soviet Russia, the Tricon is an organization in which all delegates are equal. Whereas the old Comintern was meant to propagate Soviet policy, the Tricon sets mutual policy. Whereas Comintern delegates were appointed by itself (i.e., by the CC of the CP-USSR), Tricon members are selected by the guerrilla

591

forces and mass parties of each member nation. The main purpose of the Tricon is to stimulate, aid, and coordinate the various liberation movements so that each may be more successful in its own land. It is thus an international weapon of nationalist revolutionaries. That all the delegates make the kind of analysis which the U.S. considers communist is beside the point; the fact is that the Tricon includes various species of noncommunist revolutionaries as well as all types of communists. They all do consider the United States the world's number one villain, and they all do assume that until its imperialist force is conclusively defeated, no small country—no nation in the Third World, in the Tri Continents— can be safe. Thus they must reject Soviet Russia's definition of peaceful coexistence with the United States. Russia is almost as strong as the U.S. and it has overkill atomic potential—that is why it can feel safe. But not the small nations of the world. The following is the Tricon version of peaceful coexistence, passed unanimously on January 15, 1966, in Havana:

> Peaceful coexistence refers exclusively to the relations among states of different social and political regimes.
>
> It can not refer to coexistence among the exploited social classes and their exploiters within a country; it can neither refer to the struggle of the peoples victimized by imperialism against their oppressors.
>
> Consequently, the arguments of peaceful coexistence can not be wielded the way imperialism and its followers have pretended, to limit the rights of the peoples to make their social revolution.
>
> Peaceful coexistence assumes the unrestricted respect for the principle of self-determination of the nations and sovereignty of all states, big and small.
>
> The defense of the principle of peaceful coexistence conveys the repulse of imperialistic aggression, of the criminal use of force against the people, and the decisive repulse of foreign intervention in the internal affairs of other states, all of which represents the violation of the principle of peaceful coexistence. It entitles the progressive and democratic states of the world to repel the aggressor and help the victims with all their means. When all the democratic and progressive states offer their most decisive help to the victimized peoples, they are keeping alive the principle of peaceful coexistence.

That resolution is in keeping with both the nationalist and internationalist characteristics of the Tricon. It is the basis on which the new international is in the making. Since 1966, the Tricon has suffered huge reverses—especially in Latin America and Africa. But no revolution is ever accomplished quickly. It goes through years and decades of "ebbs and flows," as Mao would say. The Russian Revolution was not limited to the years 1917–1921, nor did it start in 1905, but in 1881. The Chinese Revolution was equally long. And the Cuban, which really began when

José Martí and Antonio Maceo first started to realize that the island's struggle for independence must be not just from Spain but from the United States as well, stretched out for more than half a century. The new revolutions may be just as long. But they are certainly coming.

Ben Barka, Frantz Fanon, Che Guevara, Patrice Lumumba, Camilo Torres, Fabricio Ojeda, Osendé Afana, Luis de la Puente, Eduardo Mondlane, Inti Peredo, Carlos Marighella, and hundreds and thousands more contemporary revolutionaries are dead—killed in battle in the "ebbs" of the rise of the new international. But the international itself is not dead, just as the 1927 massacre of thousands of communists did not kill the Chinese Revolution. In the long run, what counts are the ideas, the ideology, and the revolutionary consciousness that these "ebbs" spark. The Tricon spirit, the increasing consciousness by the people of the Third World that they must win their liberation by fighting together against their common enemy, will certainly survive the defeats, the deaths of leaders, and the errors of tactics. There will be reappraisals and retrenchments, retreats and regroupments. But what began with a few speeches and books in the late fifties and became a budding organization in the sixties will surely become a formidable force in the seventies and eighties. The New International is just beginning.

At the beginning of this book, I said that confrontation is developing into a way of life. When such is the case, events follow events with increasing speed, and the result is that, as crisis follows crisis, men change, develop and radicalize, battle lines become sharper still, and revolutionary consciousness grows faster than even its proselytizers had imagined. Since May 1970, literally hundreds of white American youths have resorted to bombings to fight their capitalist rulers, black revolutionaries have shot their way into and out of U.S. courts, Chicanos have confronted the police of Los Angeles en masse for the first time in their history, Palestinian guerrillas have battled the tanks of Arab reaction in their own sanctuary, and international solidarity has deepened to such an extent that, for example, Huey P. Newton, temporarily out of jail, could view the struggle of the Vietnamese as an integral *part of the coming Revolution in America. It is therefore appropriate that this book on* The Coming of the New International *end with Huey's statement to the Vietnamese NLF and Provisional Government, a statement issued in August 1970 which best illustrates this internationalist revolutionary solidarity.*

HUEY P. NEWTON: MESSAGE TO THE VIETNAMESE

IN the spirit of international revolutionary solidarity the Black Panther Party hereby offers to the National Liberation Front and Provisional Revolutionary Government of South Vietnam an undetermined number of troops to assist you in your fight against American imperialism. It is appropriate for the Black Panther Party to take this action at this time in recognition of the fact that your struggle is also our struggle, for we recognize that our common enemy is the American imperialist who is the leader of international bourgeois domination. There is not one fascist or reactionary government in the world today that could stand without the support of United States imperialism. Therefore our problem is international, and we offer these troops in recognition of the necessity for international alliances to deal with this problem.

Such alliances will advance the struggle toward the final act of dealing with American imperialism. The Black Panther Party views the United States as the "city" of the world, while we view the nations of Africa, Asia, and Latin America as the "countryside" of the world. The developing countries are like the Sierra Maestra in Cuba and the United States is like Havana. We note that in Cuba the people's army set up bases in the Sierra Maestra and choked off Havana because it was dependent upon the raw materials of the countryside. After they won all the battles in the countryside the last and final act was for the people to march upon Havana.

The Black Panther Party believes that the revolutionary process will operate in a similar fashion on an international level. A small ruling circle of 76 major companies controls the American economy. This elite not only exploits and oppresses black people within the United States; they are exploiting and oppressing everyone in the world because of the overdeveloped nature of capitalism. Having expanded industry within the United States until it can grow no more, and depleting the raw materials of this nation, they have run amuck abroad in their attempts to extend their economic domination. To end this oppression we must liberate the developing nations—the countryside of the world—and then our final act will be the strike against the "City." As one nation is liberated elsewhere it gives us a better chance to be free here.

The Black Panther Party recognizes that we have certain national problems confined to the continental United States, but we are also aware that while our oppressor has domestic problems these do not stop him from oppressing people all over the world. Therefore we will keep fighting and resisting within the "city" so as to cause as much turmoil as possible and aid our brothers by dividing the troops of the ruling circle.

The Black Panther Party offers these troops because we are the vanguard party revolutionary internationalists who give up all claim to nationalism. We take this position because the United States has acted in a very chauvinistic manner and lost its claim to nationalism. The United States is an empire which has raped the world to build its wealth here. Therefore the United States is not a nation. It is a government of international capitalists and inasmuch as they have exploited the world to accumulate wealth this country belongs to the world. The Black Panther Party contends that the United States lost its right to claim nationhood when it used its nationalism as a chauvinistic base to become an empire.

On the other hand, the developing countries have every right to claim nationhood, because they have not exploited anyone. The nationalism of which they speak is simply their rightful claim to autonomy, self-determination, and a liberated base from which to fight the international bourgeoisie.

The Black Panther Party supports the claim to nationhood of the developing countries and we embrace their struggle from our position as revolutionary internationalists. We cannot be nationalists when our country is not a nation but an empire. We contend that it is time to open the gates of this country and share the technological knowledge and wealth with the peoples of the world.

History has bestowed upon the Black Panther Party the obligation to take these steps and thereby advance Marxism-Leninism to an even higher level along the path to a socialist state, and then a non-state. This obligation springs both from the dialectical forces in operation at this time and our history as an oppressed black colony. The fact that our ancestors were kidnapped and forced to come to the United States has destroyed our feeling of nationhood. Because our long cultural heritage was broken we have come to rely less on our history for guidance, and seek our guidance from the future. Everything we do is based upon functionalism and pragmatism, and because we look to the future for salvation we are in a position to become the most progressive and dynamic people on the earth, constantly in motion and progressing, rather than becoming stagnated by the bonds of the past.

Taking these things under consideration, it is no accident that the vanguard party—without chauvinism or a sense of nationhood—should be the Black Panther Party. Our struggle for liberation is based upon justice and equality for all men. Thus we are interested in the people of any territory where the crack of the oppressor's whip may be heard. We have the historical obligation to take the concept of internationalism to its final conclusion—the destruction of statehood itself. This will lead us into the era where the withering away of the state will occur and men will extend their hand in friendship throughout the world.

This is the world view of the Black Panther Party and in the spirit of revolutionary internationalism, solidarity and friendship we offer these troops to the National Liberation Front and Provisional Revolutionary Government of South Vietnam, and to the people of the world.

Huey P. Newton
Minister of Defense
Black Panther Party

Index

About the Editor

John Gerassi first became interested in nationalist and revolutionary movements when he covered Latin America as an editor of *Time* and *Newsweek* and as a correspondent for *The New York Times*. That interest led to his first book, *The Great Fear in Latin America*, then to various trips to Cuba, where his personal acquaintance with Che Guevara made him well suited to edit *Venceremos: The Speeches and Writings of Che Guevara*.

In 1965, Gerassi left "straight journalism," as he says. He traveled throughout North Vietnam as an investigator for the International War Crimes Tribunal (and published his findings in *North Vietnam: A Documentary*), returned to Cuba to cover (for *Ramparts* magazine) the various meetings of Third World revolutionaries, and taught—first at New York University and at the Free University of New York, then at San Francisco State College.

While in the Bay area, Gerassi worked closely with the Black Panthers, became a close friend of the party's founders, Huey Newton and Bobby Seale, and was identified as a leader of the anti-war, anti-racist movement at the college. He was accused of being one of the main spark plugs of the college's first rebellion, was fired and arrested (and defended by the Black Panthers' formidable lawyer, Charles Garry).

Gerassi, who has also co-edited *Latin American Radicalism* and put together *Revolutionary Priest: The Complete Writings and Messages of Camilo Torres* (the Colombian priest who died fighting with the guerrillas), originally studied and taught philosophy. He has had a long association with Jean-Paul Sartre, and is currently at work on the French philosopher's authorized biography.

BOOKS BY JOHN GERASSI

The Great Fear in Latin America

The Boys of Boise

Venceremos! The Speeches and Writings of Che Guevara (Editor)

North Vietnam: A Documentary

Latin American Radicalism (Co-editor)

Revolutionary Priest: The Complete Writings and Messages of Camilo Torres (Editor)

The Coming of the New International (Editor)